The Blai Reader

Exploring Issues and Ideas

TENTH EDITION

Edited By

Laurie G. Kirszner
University of the Sciences, Emeritus

Stephen R. Mandell
Drexel University

with
Karen R. Mauk

Executive Portfolio Manager: Aron Keesbury
Content Producer: Barbara Cappuccio
Content Developer: Edward Dodd
Portfolio Manager Assistant: Christa Cottone
Senior Product Marketing Manager: Michael Coons
Product Marketing Manager: Nicholas Bolt
Content Producer Manager: Ken Volcjak
Managing Editor: Cynthia Cox
Digital Studio Course Producer: Elizabeth Bravo
Full-Service Project Management: Integra
Printer/Binder: LSC Communications, Inc.
Cover Printer: Phoenix Color/Hagerstown
Senior Art Director: Cate Barr
Cover Design: Cadence Design Studio

Acknowledgments of third party content appear on appropriate page within the text, which constitutes an extension of this copyright page.

Library of Congress Cataloging-in-Publication Data

Names: Kirszner, Laurie G., editor. | Mandell, Stephen, editor. | Mauk, Karen, editor.
Title: The Blair reader : exploring issues and ideas / [edited by] Laurie G. Kirszner, Stephen Mandell, Karen R. Mauk.
Description: 10th edition. | New York : Pearson Publishers, 2019.
Identifiers: LCCN 2018044592| ISBN 9780135285282 | ISBN 0135285283
Subjects: LCSH: College readers. | English language—Rhetoric—Problems, exercises, etc. | Report writing—Problems, exercises, etc.
Classification: LCC PE1417 .B54 2019 | DDC 808/.0427—dc23
LC record available at https://lccn.loc.gov/2018044592

1 19

Instructor's Review Copy
ISBN-10: 0-13-528528-3
ISBN-13: 978-0-13-528528-2

Access Code Card
ISBN-10: 0-13-516476-1
ISBN-13: 978-0-13-516476-1

Contents

Topical Clusters

Exiles

Fear and Courage

Social and Economic Class

Stereotyping

Speeches

Note: Speeches are listed in alphabetical order.

Rhetorical Table of Contents

Note: Selections are listed alphabetically within categories.

Narration

Description

Process

Exemplification

Classification & Division

Definition

Argument & Persuasion

Preface

After many years of teaching composition, we have come to see reading and writing as interrelated activities: If students are going to write effectively, they must first be able to read actively and critically. In addition, we see writing as both a private and a public act. As a private act, it enables students to explore their feelings and reactions and to discover their ideas about subjects that are important to them. As a public act, writing enables students to see how their own ideas fit into larger discourse communities, where ideas gain meaning and value. We believe that students are enriched and engaged when they view the reading and writing they do as a way of participating in ongoing public discussions about ideas that matter to them. From the beginning, our goal in *The Blair Reader* has always been to encourage students to contribute to these discussions in the wider world by responding to the ideas of others.

The core of *The Blair Reader* is, of course, its reading selections. As we selected the readings for this title, our goal was to introduce students to the enduring issues they confront as citizens in the twenty-first century. Many of these readings are contemporary; many are also quite provocative. Whenever possible, however, we also include classic readings that give students the historical context they need. For example, Chapter 4, "Issues in Education," includes "School Is Bad for Children" by John Holt; Chapter 5, "The Politics of Language," includes "Learning to Read and Write" by Frederick Douglass; and Chapter 9, "The American Dream," includes The Gettysburg Address by Abraham Lincoln. It was also important to us that the selections in *The Blair Reader* represent a wide variety of rhetorical patterns and types of discourse as well as a range of themes, issues, and positions. In addition to essays and articles from print and electronic sources, *The Blair Reader* includes speeches, short stories, poems, creative nonfiction, and a short play. It is our hope that exposure to this wide variety of formats, topics, and viewpoints can help students discover their own voices and express their own ideas.

As teachers, we—like you—expect a thematic reader to include compelling reading selections that involve instructors and students in spirited exchanges. We also expect readings that reflect the diversity of ideas that characterizes our society and questions that challenge students to respond critically to what they have read. In short, we expect a title that stimulates discussion and that encourages students to discover new ideas and see familiar ideas in new ways. These expectations guided us as we initially created *The Blair Reader*, and they continued to guide us as we worked on this new tenth edition.

What's New in the 10th Edition

In response to the thoughtful comments of the many instructors who generously shared with us their reactions (and their students' reactions) to *The Blair Reader*, we have made many changes in this new edition, adding new readings, new study questions and writing and research prompts, and new visuals.

- **New Focus sections** showcase related essays that examine contemporary concerns, zeroing in on questions such as "What Is Fake News, and Why Does It Matter?" and "How Do We Talk about Sexual Harassment?"
- **New readings** have been added to stimulate student interest and to introduce them to some of the challenging issues that they confront as students and as citizens. Among the many essays that are new to this edition are Sonia Sodha's "If You Have No Children, Who Will Care for You When You're Old?", Matthew Yglesias's "Walmart's Too-Good-to-Be-True '$1 a Day' College Tuition Plan, Explained," Jelani Cobb's "*Black Panther* and the Invention of 'Africa,'" Jon Meacham's "To Hope Rather than to Fear," Rand Fishkin's "The Truth Shall Set You Free (from a Lot of $#*% Storms)," and Alex Wagner's excerpt from *Futureface: A Family Mystery, an Epic Quest, and the Secret to Belonging*. New literary selections—such as Sarah Chevallier's "If Literature's 'Complicated Men' Were on Tinder," Brenda Cárdenas's "Lecciones de lengua," and Benjamin Busch's "New World"—have also been added.
- A **new shared writing prompt** at the conclusion of each chapter's introductory discussion helps students engage with the chapter theme.
- A new **Before You Read journal prompt** before each reading gets students thinking about ways to approach each selection.
- The new **full-color visuals and engaging design** connect with students accustomed to encountering content in color. Students analyzing the chapter-opening paired visuals and the Focus section visual will now be able to explore discussions related to the use of color within the content not available in the previous black-and-white editions.

Resources for Students

We designed the apparatus in *The Blair Reader* to involve students and to encourage them to respond critically to what they read. These responses can lay the groundwork for the more focused thinking that they will do when they write. In order to help students improve their critical reading and writing skills, we have included the following features:

- An **Introduction** maps out the title's features to help students get the most from *The Blair Reader*.
- **Paired visuals** introduce each thematic chapter. These visuals engage students by encouraging them to identify parallels and contrasts. In addition, they introduce students to the themes that they will be considering as they read the selections in the chapter.
- A brief **chapter introduction** places each chapter's broad theme in its social, historical, or political context, helping students to understand the complexities of the issues being discussed. This chapter introduction is followed by **Preparing to Read and Write**, a list of questions designed to help students focus their responses to individual readings and relate these responses to the chapter's larger issues.
- **Headnotes** that introduce each selection provide biographical and other background information as well as insight into the writer's purpose.
- **Responding to Reading** questions that follow each selection address thematic and rhetorical considerations. By encouraging students to think critically, these questions help them to see reading as an interactive and intellectually stimulating process.
- A **Rhetorical Analysis** question for each selection addresses rhetorical considerations, helping students understand the discursive acts at work in the selection.
- A **Writing with Sources** prompt (after essays and speeches) gives students the opportunity to write a longer essay that requires research.
- A **Focus** section at the end of each chapter is introduced by a provocative question related to the chapter's theme, followed by a visual that is accompanied by **Responding to the Image** prompts. The heart of the Focus section is a group of readings that take a variety of positions on the issue, encouraging students to add their voices to the debate and demonstrating that complex issues elicit different points of view. Each reading is followed by "Responding to Reading" questions, a "Rhetorical Analysis" question, and a "Writing with Sources" prompt.

- At the end of each Focus section, a **Widening the Focus** feature includes a writing prompt ("For Critical Reading and Writing") that asks students to tie the readings together; a list of essays in other chapters of the title that also address the issues raised by the Focus question; an Internet research assignment; and a field research assignment ("Beyond the Classroom").
- **Exploring Issues and Ideas** suggestions at the end of each thematic chapter encourage students to explore the chapter's theme in greater depth.
- A **Rhetorical Table of Contents**, located at the front of the title on pages xx–xxix, groups the text's readings according to the way they arrange material: narration, description, process, comparison and contrast, and so on.
- **Topical Clusters,** narrowly focused thematic units (viii–xix), offer students and teachers additional options for grouping readings.
- An **Appendix: MLA Documentation** helps students to incorporate research ethically, offering numerous sample citations for commonly used sources.

REVEL ™

Revel is an interactive learning environment that deeply engages students and prepares them for class. Media and assessment integrated directly within the authors' narrative let students read, explore interactive content, and practice in one continuous learning path. Thanks to the dynamic reading experience in Revel, students come to class prepared to discuss, apply, and learn from instructors and from each other.

Learn more about Revel
www.pearson.com/revel

Supplements

Make more time for your students with instructor resources that offer effective learning assessments and classroom engagement. Pearson's partnership with educators does not end with the delivery of course materials; Pearson is there with you on the first day of class and beyond. A dedicated team of local Pearson representatives will work with you to not only choose course materials but also integrate them into your class and assess their effectiveness. Our goal is your goal—to improve instruction with each semester.

Pearson is pleased to offer the following resources to qualified adopters of *The Blair Reader*. Several of these supplements are available to instantly download from Revel or on the Instructor Resource Center (IRC); please visit the IRC at **www.pearson.com/us** to register for access.

- **INSTRUCTOR'S RESOURCE MANUAL** Because we wanted *The Blair Reader* to be a rich and comprehensive resource for instructors, a thoroughly revised and updated *Instructor's Resource Manual* has been developed to accompany the text. Designed to be a useful and all-inclusive tool, the manual contains teaching strategies, collaborative activities, and suggested answers for "Responding to Reading" questions. The manual includes web and/or multimedia teaching resources for almost every reading. It also contains new questions for stimulating classroom discussions of the chapter-opening images. Available within Revel and on the IRC.

Acknowledgments

The Blair Reader is the result of a fruitful collaboration between the two of us, between us and our students, between us and Pearson, and between us and you—our colleagues who told us what you want in a reader.

At Pearson, we want to thank Aron Keesbury, Executive Producer and Publisher, Collegiate English. At Ohlinger Studios, we appreciate the efforts of Cynthia Cox, Managing Editor for Collegiate English.

We want to give special thanks to Karen R. Mauk, our talented editor, for coordinating this revision. Her work, as always, has been first rate, and we are grateful for her many contributions to the updating of the text. We also thank Ed Dodd, our wonderful development editor, whose hard work helped make this title as good as it is. At Integra, we want to thank Sally Stearn, Project Manager, for seeing this title through to completion.

In preparing *The Blair Reader*, Tenth Edition, we benefited at every stage from the assistance and suggestions of colleagues from across the country:

Jacob Agatucci, Central Oregon Community College
Gail Charrier, Delaware Technical Community College
Kimberly Hall, Harrisburg Area Community College
Matthew Schmeer, Johnson County Community College
Christina Tarabicos, Delaware Technical Community College
Andrea West, Midlands Technical College
Nicole Wilson, Bowie State University
William Wilson, San Jose State University

We would also like to thank the following reviewers of previous editions for their valuable insight: Jacob Agatucci, Central Oregon

Community College; Jesse T. Airaudi, Baylor University; Marlene Allen, Fayetteville State University; Linda A. Archer, Green River Community College; Anthony Armstrong, Richland College; Stephen R. Armstrong, Eastern Carolina University; Patricia Baldwin, Pitt Community College; Lisa Beckelhimer, University of Cincinnati; Chere Berman, College of the Canyons; Patricia Bjorklund, Southeastern Community College; Gennean Bolen, Fresno City College; Charlene Bunnell, University of Delaware; Jason Chaffin, Cape Fear Community College; Gail Charrier, Delaware Technical and Community College; Peggy Cole, Arapahoe Community College; Carla L. Dando, Idaho State University; Rosemary Day, Albuquerque Community College; Emily Dial-Driver, Rogers State University; Toni L. D'Onofrio, The Art Institute of New York City; Janet Eldred, University of Kentucky; Cynthia Elliott, Clovis Community College Center; Anne Fernald, Fordham University; Robert G. Ford, Houston Community College; Web Freeman, Ozarks Technical Community College; Ruth Gerik, University of Texas at Arlington; Janet Gerstner, San Juan College; Lisa Gordon, Columbus State Community College; Kimberly Greenfield, Lorain County Community College; Kimberly S. Hall, Harrisburg Area Community College; Judy A. Hayden, University of Tampa; David Holper, College of the Redwoods; Pamela Howell, Midland College; Tara Hubschmitt, Lakeland College; Lu Ellen Huntley, University of North Carolina at Wilmington; Jessica Hyatt, Ozarks Technical Community College; Aura Imbarus, El Camino College; Robert S. Imbur, University of Toledo; JoAnne James, Pitt Community College; James Jenkins, Mt. San Antonio College; Amanda Jerome, Saddleback College; Terry Jolliffe, Midland College; Alan Kaufman, Bergen Community College; Dimitri Keriotis, Modesto Junior College; Robert Leston, University of Texas at Arlington; John Lucarelli, Community College of Allegheny County; Robert Lunday, Houston Community College; Robyn Lyons-Robinson, Columbus State Community College; Dani McLean, Saddleback College; Tabitha R. Miller, Pitt Community College; Camilla Mortensen, University of Oregon; Kathryn Neal, York Technical College; Paul Northam, Johnson County Community College; Marguerite Parker, Eastern Carolina University; Andrea Penner, San Juan College; Angie Pratt, Montgomery College; Jeannette E. Riley, UMass Dartmouth; CC Ryder, West L.A. College; Matthew W. Schmeer, Johnson County Community College; Debra Shein, Idaho State University; Margaret Simonton, East Arizona College; Katie Singer, Fairleigh Dickinson University; Mark A. Smith, Lock Haven University; Darlene Smith-Worthington, Pitt Community College; Derek Soles, Drexel University; Lori Ann Stephens, Richland College; Sharon Strand, Black Hills State University; Ryan D. Stryffeler, Western Nevada College; Diane Sweet, Wentworth Institute of Technology; Katie Thomas,

Community College of Beaver County; Cara Unger, Portland Community College; Jennifer Vanags, Johnson County Community College; Brian Walter, St. Louis College of Pharmacy; Stephen H. Wells, Community College of Allegheny County; Andrea J. West, Midlands Technical College; Mary Williams, Midland College; Mary Ellen Williams, UC Davis; Nicole S. Wilson, Bowie State University; William A. Wilson, San Jose State University; and K. Siobhan Wright, Carroll Community College.

On the home front, we once again "round up the usual suspects" to thank. And, of course, we thank each other: It really has been a "beautiful friendship."

Introduction

The Blair Reader is a collection of readings, but it also encourages you to *write* about what you read, focusing your ideas and at the same time discovering new ideas. To support this dual process of reading and writing, *The Blair Reader* includes a number of features to help you explore your reactions to the readings and express your ideas in writing.

The readings in *The Blair Reader* (classic and contemporary essays as well as speeches and literary works) are arranged in thematic chapters, each offering a variety of different vantage points from which to view the chapter's central theme. Each chapter opens with a brief introduction, which provides a context for the chapter's theme and includes a list of **Preparing to Read and Write** questions to guide you as you read. These questions are designed to sharpen your critical skills so you can apply those skills effectively. Each chapter introduction also includes a pair of contrasting visual images to introduce you to the chapter's theme and encourage you to begin thinking about the fundamental issues related to that theme. Finally, each introduction concludes with a **Shared Writing** prompt to stimulate your thinking about the chapter theme.

Following each essay are two **Responding to Reading** questions that ask you to think critically about the writer's ideas, perhaps focusing on a particular strategy the writer has used to achieve his or her goals. In some cases, these questions may ask you to examine your own ideas or beliefs. Then, a **Rhetorical Analysis** question may ask you to comment on the writer's audience and purpose as well as consider rhetorical strategies such as thesis, organization, evidence, and stylistic techniques. Following these questions is a **Writing with Sources** prompt, which calls for a source-based essay. (Literary selections do not typically have accompanying Writing with Sources prompts.)

Following the essays that explore each chapter's general theme is a **Focus** section that zeroes in on a specific issue. The Focus section's central question—for example, "Should a College Education Be Free?" (Chapter 4) or "What Choices Do We Have with Our Technologies?" (Chapter 11)—introduces a cluster of thought-provoking readings that take different positions on a single complex issue; a related visual image is also included here. The assignments in the Focus sections encourage you to analyze, interpret, or evaluate the ideas explored in the Focus readings as well as in related outside sources. Each Focus essay is accompanied by two **Responding to Reading** questions, a **Rhetorical Analysis** question, and a **Writing with Sources** prompt; **Responding to the Image** prompts also follow each visual. The Focus sections end with **Widening the Focus**, which includes "For Critical Reading and Writing" (an essay prompt that asks you to draw connections among the Focus readings, perhaps referring to other sources in your discussion); "For Further Reading" (a list of related readings in other chapters of the book); "For Focused Research" (a comprehensive research assignment that relies on web sources); and "Beyond the Classroom" (a prompt designed to encourage you to write about your own observations and experiences). Each chapter ends with **Exploring Issues and Ideas**, a collection of additional writing prompts that offer you an opportunity to explore a general topic related to the chapter's theme.

As you read and write, you will also be learning how to think about yourself and about the world. By considering and reconsidering the ideas of others, by rejecting easy answers, by considering a problem from many different angles, and by appreciating the many factors that can influence your responses, you will develop critical thinking skills that you will use not just in college but throughout your life. In addition, by writing about the themes explored in this collection, you will participate in an ongoing conversation within the community of scholars and writers who care deeply about the issues that shape our world.

Chapter 1
Becoming a Critical Reader

In this chapter, you will learn to:

- **1.1** Interpret a text.
- **1.2** Analyze a text.
- **1.3** Highlight and annotate a text.
- **1.4** Analyze a visual text.

1.1 Reading and Meaning

Like many readers, you may assume that the meaning of a text is hidden somewhere between the lines, and that you only have to ask the right questions or unearth the appropriate clues to discover what the writer is getting at. But reading is not a game of hide-and-seek in which you search for ideas that have been hidden by the writer. As current reading theory demonstrates, meaning is created by the interaction between a reader and a text.

One way to explain this interactive process is to draw an analogy between a text—a work being read—and a word. A word is not the natural equivalent of the thing it signifies. The word *dog,* for example, does not evoke the image of a furry, four-legged animal in all parts of the world. To speakers of Spanish, the word *perro* elicits the same mental picture *dog* does in English-speaking countries. Not only does the word *dog* have meaning only in a specific cultural context, but even within that context, it also evokes different images in different people. Some people may picture a collie, others a poodle, and still others a particular pet.

Like a word, a text can have different meanings in different cultures—or even in different historical time periods. Each reader brings to the text associations that come from his or her own cultural community. These associations are determined by a reader's experience and education, ethnic group, social class, religion, gender, and many other factors that contribute to how he or she views the world. Each reader also brings to the text beliefs, expectations, desires, and biases that influence how he or she reacts to and interprets it. Thus, it is entirely possible for two readers to have very different, but equally valid, interpretations of the same text. (This does not mean, of course, that a text can mean whatever any individual reader wishes it to mean. To be valid, an interpretation must be supported by the text itself.)

To get an idea of the range of possible interpretations that can be suggested by a single text, consider some of the responses different readers might have to E. B. White's classic essay "Once More to the Lake"(p. 43).

In "Once More to the Lake," White tells a story about his visit with his son to a lake in Maine in the 1940s, comparing this visit with those he made as a boy with his own father in 1904. Throughout the essay, White describes the changes that have occurred since his first visit. Memories from the past flood his consciousness, causing him to remember things that he did when he was a boy. At one point, after he and his son have been feeding worms to fish, he remembers doing the same thing with his father and has trouble separating the past from the present. Eventually, White realizes that he will soon be merely a memory in his son's mind—just as his father is only a memory in his.

White had specific goals in mind when he wrote this essay. His title, "Once More to the Lake," underscores that he intended to compare his childhood and adult visits to the lake. The organization of ideas in the essay, the use of flashbacks, and the choice of particular transitional words and phrases reinforce this purpose. In addition, descriptive details—such as the image of the tarred road that replaced the dirt road—remind readers, as well as White himself, that the years have made the lake site different from what it once was. The essay ends with White suddenly feeling the "chill of death."

Despite White's specific intentions, each person reading "Once More to the Lake" will respond to it somewhat differently. Young male readers might identify with the boy. If they have ever spent a vacation at a lake, they might have experienced the "peace and goodness and jollity" of the whole summer scene. Female readers might also want to share these experiences, but they might feel excluded because only males are described in the essay. Readers who have never been on a fishing trip might not feel the same nostalgia for the woods that White feels. To them, living in the woods away from the comforts of home might seem an unthinkably uncomfortable ordeal. Older readers might identify with White, sympathizing with his efforts as an adult to recapture the past and seeing his son as naively innocent of the challenges of life.

Thus, although each person who reads White's essay will read the same words, each will be likely to interpret it differently and to see different things as important because much is left open to interpretation. All essays leave blanks or gaps—missing ideas or images—that readers have to fill in. In "Once More to the Lake," for example, readers must imagine what happened in the years that separated White's last visit to the lake with his father and the trip he took with his son.

These gaps in the text create **ambiguities**—words, phrases, descriptions, or ideas that need to be interpreted by the reader. For instance, when you read the words "One summer, along about 1904, my father rented a camp on a lake," how do you picture the camp? White's description of the setting contains a great deal of detail, but no matter how much information he supplies, he cannot paint a complete verbal picture of the lakeside camp. He must rely on his readers' ability to visualize the setting and to supply details from their own experiences.

Readers also bring their emotional associations to a text. For example, the way readers react to White's statement above depends, in part, on their feelings about their own fathers. If White's words bring to mind a parent who is loving, strong, and protective, they will most likely respond favorably; if the essay calls up memories of a parent who is distant, bad-tempered, or even abusive, they may respond negatively.

Because each reader views the text from a slightly different angle, each may also see a different focus as central to "Once More to the Lake." Some might see nature as the primary element in the essay and believe that White's purpose is to condemn the encroachment of human beings on the environment. Others might see the passage of time as the central focus. Still others might see the initiation theme as being the most important element of the essay: each boy is brought to the lake by his father, and each eventually passes from childhood innocence to adulthood and to the awareness of his own mortality.

Finally, each reader may evaluate the essay differently. Some readers might find "Once More to the Lake" boring because it has little action and deals with a subject in which they have no interest. Others might believe the essay is a brilliant meditation that makes an impact through its vivid description and imaginative figurative language. Still others might see the essay as falling between these two extremes—for example, they might grant that White is an accomplished stylist but also see him as self-centered and self-indulgent. After all, they might argue, the experiences he describes are available only to relatively privileged members of society and are irrelevant to others.

1.2 Reading Critically

Many of the texts you read during your years as a student will be challenging. In college, you read to expand your horizons, so it makes sense that some ideas and concepts that you encounter in your assigned reading may be difficult or unfamiliar. When you approach an academic text for the first time, you may feel somewhat intimidated or even overwhelmed, and you may find yourself wondering where to start and what to look for. This is natural. Fortunately, the reading strategies discussed below can make it easer for you to interpret unfamiliar texts.

Before you begin to read, you should understand the difference between *reading* and *reading critically*. For some students, the act of reading a text is simply a search for facts that must be digested and memorized. For critical readers, however, reading is a much more active and dynamic process.

Reading critically means interacting with the text, questioning the text's assumptions, and formulating and reformulating judgments about its ideas. Think of reading as a dialogue between you and the text: sometimes the writer will assert himself or herself; at other times, you will dominate the conversation. Remember, though, that a critical voice is a thoughtful and responsible one, not one that shouts down the opposition. In other words, being a critical reader does not necessarily mean arguing and contradicting; more often, it means actively engaging the text by asking questions and exploring your reactions—while remaining open to new ideas.

Asking the following questions as you read will help you to become aware of the relationships between the writer's perspective and your own:

- **Whom is the writer addressing?** Who is the writer's intended audience? Does the writer think that readers will be receptive to his or her ideas? hostile? neutral? How can you tell? What preconceived ideas does the writer expect readers to have? For example, the title of John Holt's essay on early childhood education, "School Is Bad for Children"(p. 86), suggests that Holt expects his readers to have preconceived notions about the value of a traditional education—notions that his essay will challenge.
- **What is the writer's purpose?** Exactly what is the writer trying to accomplish in the essay? For example, is the writer's main purpose to explain, to entertain, or to persuade? Does the writer have any secondary purposes—for example, to justify, evaluate, describe, debunk, instruct, preach, browbeat, threaten, or frighten? Or, does the writer have some other purpose (or combination of purposes) in mind? Does the writer appeal to the prejudices or fears of his or her readers or in any other way attempt to influence readers unfairly?
- **What genre is the writer using?** Written texts, such as those in this collection, fall into categories called **genres**. Each genre is defined by distinct conventions, structures, and techniques. For example, an academic essay is a genre that has three parts: an introduction, a body, and a conclusion. Its purpose is to convince readers that its statements are reasonable and worth considering. An academic essay deals with ideas—sometimes complex ideas—and discusses them in precise language, which includes discipline-specific

vocabulary. In general, it avoids the use of the first person *I*, and it is free of slang and ungrammatical constructions. An academic essay almost always has a thesis statement, which it develops using facts, examples, and material from credible outside sources (all borrowed material is documented). Essays can be *descriptive, narrative, expository* (explanatory), or *argumentative*, and each of these types of writing has its own characteristics. For instance, descriptive essays frequently use subjective language and rely on imaginative comparisons to tell what something looks or feels like.

As you approach any reading, ask yourself what genre the writer is using and how this genre determines the way in which the writer treats his or her subject. In addition to the genres represented in this collection—which include essays, editorials, op-eds, speeches, poems, and short stories—you will often encounter other writing genres, all of which have their own distinctive forms and conventions.

Throughout your education, you will become familiar with the genres characteristic of your major as well as those of the other subjects you take. Some of these genres appear in the chart below.

Narrative Essay	Argument Essay	Research Essay	Rhetorical Analysis	Response
		Purpose		
To tell a story or to relate a series of events	To persuade readers to accept (or at least consider) a debatable idea	To locate, interpret, and evaluate sources related to a topic	To examine the way the elements in a text work together	To reflect on a text and discuss it
		Characteristics		
Thesis statement identifies the point the narrative is making Events are usually (but not always) arranged in time order Includes details that help readers visualize events	Thesis statement identifies the position the writer is taking Points are supported by facts, examples, and opinions of experts Refutes opposing arguments by showing that they are inaccurate, incorrect, or misguided	Thesis statement identifies the stand the writer will take or asks a question that the writer will answer Weaves together paraphrases and summaries as well as quotations and original ideas to support points	Thesis statement identifies the point that is being made about the text selected for analysis Examines various elements of the text—for example, the writer's use of *logos*, *pathos*, and *ethos*	Opens with a statement that expresses the writer's reaction to the text Identifies the text's central idea or claim Discusses how the writer feels about what he or she is reading

(*continued*)

Narrative Essay	Argument Essay	Research Essay	Rhetorical Analysis	Response
		Characteristics		
May be written in first person (*I*) or third person (*he, she, it*), depending on whether or not the narrative is based on personal experiences	Relies on logic Uses an appropriate documentation format	May use charts, graphs, infographics, and other visuals to present information May use headings to separate sections of the essay Uses an appropriate documentation format	Makes points supported by references (quotations, summaries, and paraphrases) to the text being analyzed Uses an appropriate documentation format	Identifies points of agreement or disagreement May include personal observations or experiences if they are relevant to the reading May include questions that need to be answered

Other genres you may encounter in your reading as well as in written assignments include the following.

Abstracts
Blog posts
Book or film reviews
Emails
Job application letters
Lab reports
Literacy narratives
Literary analyses
Memoirs
Memos
Paraphrases
Résumés
Summaries
Visuals (charts, tables, infographics, photos, videos, and so on)

- **What voice does the writer use?** Does the writer seem to talk directly to readers? If so, does the writer's subjectivity get in the way, or does it help to involve readers? Does the writer's voice seem distant or formal? Different voices have different effects on readers. For example, an emotional tone can inspire; an intimate tone can create empathy; a straightforward, forthright tone can make ideas seem reasonable and credible. An ironic tone can either amuse readers or alienate them; a distant, reserved tone can evoke either respect or discomfort.

- **How does the writer try to influence readers?** Writers use rhetorical strategies—called **appeals**—to influence readers. One such strategy is the appeal to **logos**, or logic. Another type of appeal is the appeal to **pathos**, or emotion. A final type of appeal is the appeal to **ethos**, or the credibility of the writer. For example, in the Declaration of Independence (p. 322), Thomas Jefferson constructs a logical argument to support his point that King George III is not fit to rule a free people. In addition, he appeals to the emotions of readers by describing the indignities that he and other colonists must face every day. Finally, he establishes his credibility by identifying himself and the other signatories of the Declaration of Independence as representatives of the United States of America. By doing so, Jefferson makes it clear that he has authority and that he has something important to say.

When you read, ask some of the following questions: Does the writer appeal to reason? Does the writer supply evidence to support his or her ideas? Is this evidence convincing? Does the writer appeal to emotion? What strategies does he or she use to influence you? Finally, does the writer establish his or her credibility? How does the writer demonstrate that he or she is a convincing, legitimate, and trustworthy source of information?

- **What position does the writer take on the issue?** Sometimes a work's title reveals a writer's position—for example, the choice of the word *crisis* in Warren Farrell and John Gray's title "The Crisis of Our Sons' Education" (p. 225) clearly reveals their position on the situation boys face. Keep in mind, though, that a writer's position may not always be as obvious as it is in this example. As you read, look carefully for specific language that suggests the writer's position on a particular subject or issue—or for explicit statements that make that position clear. Also, be sure you understand how you feel about the writer's position, particularly if it is an unusual or controversial one. Do you agree or disagree? Can you explain your reasoning? Of course, a writer's advocacy of a position that is at odds with your own does not automatically render the work suspect or its ideas invalid. Remember, ideas that you might consider shocking or absurd may be readily accepted by many other readers. Unexpected, puzzling, or even repellent positions should encourage you to read carefully and thoughtfully, trying to understand the larger historical and cultural context of a writer's ideas.

- **How does the writer support his or her position?** What kind of supporting evidence is provided? Is it convincing? Does the writer use a series of short examples or a single extended example? Does the writer use statistics, or does he or she rely primarily on personal experiences? Does the writer quote experts or just present anecdotal information? Why does the writer choose a particular kind of support? Does the writer supply enough information to support the essay's points? Are all the examples actually relevant to the issues being discussed? Is the writer's reasoning valid, or do the arguments seem forced or unrealistic? Are any references in the work unfamiliar to you? If so, do they arouse your curiosity, or do they discourage you from reading further?

- **What beliefs, assumptions, or preconceived ideas do you have that color your responses to a work?** Does the writer challenge any ideas that you accept as "natural" or "obvious"? Do you consider yourself a hostile, friendly, or neutral reader? What has the writer done to address possible objections to his or her ideas? Should he or she have done more to address these objections? Do your preconceived ideas make it difficult for you to fairly evaluate the writer's ideas?
- **Does your own background or experience give you any special insights that enable you to understand or interpret the writer's ideas?** Are the writer's experiences similar to your own? Is the writer like you in terms of age, ethnic background, gender, and social class? How do the similarities between you and the writer affect your reaction to the work? What experiences have you had that could help you understand the writer's ideas and shape your response to them?

1.3 Recording Your Reactions

It is a good idea to read any text at least twice: first to get a general sense of the writer's ideas, then to react critically to these ideas. As you read critically, you interact with the text and respond in ways that will help you to interpret it. This process of coming to understand the text will prepare you to discuss the work with others and, perhaps, to write about it.

As you read and reread, record your responses; if you don't, you may forget some of your best ideas. Two activities can help you keep a record of the ideas that come to you as you read: **highlighting** (using a system of symbols and underlining to identify key ideas) and **annotating** (writing down your responses and interpretations in the margins of the text).

When you react to what you read, don't be afraid to question the writer's ideas. As you read and make annotations, you may disagree with or even challenge some of these ideas; when you have time, you can think more about what you have written. These informal responses are often the beginning of a thought process that will lead you to original insights. Later, when you write about the text, you can refine these ideas into the points that you will develop more fully in your essay.

Highlighting and annotating helped a student to understand the passage below, which is excerpted from Frederick Douglass's essay "Learning to Read and Write" (p. 133). As she prepared to write about the essay, the student identified and summarized the writer's key points and made a connection with another selection, Abraham Lincoln's Gettysburg Address (p. 326). As she read, she underlined some of the passage's important words and ideas, using arrows to indicate relationships between them. She also circled a few words to remind her to look up their meanings later on, and she wrote down questions and comments as they occurred to her.

> The plan which I adopted, and the one by which I was most successful, was that of making friends of all the little white boys whom I met in the street. As many of these as I could, I converted into teachers. With their kindly aid, obtained at different times and in different places, I finally succeeded in learning to read. When I was sent on errands, I always took my book with me, and by going one part of my errand quickly, I found time to get a lesson before my return. I used also to carry bread with me, enough of which was always in the house, and to which I was always welcome; for I was much better off in this regard than many of the poor white children in our neighborhood. This bread I used to bestow upon the hungry little urchins, who, in return, would give me that more valuable bread of knowledge. I am strongly tempted to give the names of two or three of those little boys, as a testimonial of the gratitude and affection I bear them; but prudence forbids;—not that it would injure me, but it might embarrass them; for it is almost an unpardonable offense to teach slaves to read in this Christian country. It is enough to say of the dear little fellows, that they lived on Philpot Street, very near Durgin and Bailey's ship-yard. I used to talk this matter of slavery over with them. I would sometimes say to them, I wished I could be as free as they would be when they got to be men. "You will be free as soon as you are twenty-one, *but I am a slave for life!* Have not I as good a right to be free as you have?" These words used to trouble them; they would express for me the liveliest sympathy, and console me with the hope that something would occur by which I might be free.

Not much has changed in how people take shortcuts to get what they want.

Bread is the bait but also a metaphor.

?

?

Why mention "Christian"?

Gettysburg Address—not even twenty years later...

Source: Douglas, Frederick. Narrative of the Life of Frederick Douglas, An American Slave. Boston: Anti-Slavery Office, 1845.

1.4 Reacting to Visual Texts

Many of the written texts you read—from newspapers and magazines to websites to textbooks such as this one—include visuals. Some of these visuals (charts, tables, maps, graphs, scientific diagrams, and the like) primarily present information; others (fine art, photographs, videos, cartoons, and advertisements, for example) may be designed to have an emotional impact on readers or to persuade them to change their minds or to take some kind of action.

Visuals can be analyzed, interpreted, and evaluated just as written texts are. You begin this process by looking critically at the visual, identifying its most important elements, and considering the relationships of various elements to one another and to the image as a whole. Next, you try to identify the purpose for which the image was created, and you consider your own personal response to the image.

As you examine a visual text, finding answers to the following questions will help you to understand it better:

- **Who is the intended audience of this visual?** Does the visual seem to address a wide general audience or some kind of specialized audience, such as new parents, runners, or medical professionals? Is it aimed at adults or at children? Is it likely to appeal mainly to people from a particular region or ethnic group, or is it likely to resonate with a broad range of people? Often, knowing where a visual appeared—in a popular magazine, on a political blog, in a professional journal, or in a trade publication, for example—will help you to identify the audience the visual is trying to reach.
- **For what purpose was the visual created?** Is the visual designed to evoke an emotional response, such as fear or guilt? Is it designed to be humorous? Or is its purpose simply to present information? To understand a visual's purpose, you need to consider not only its source but also what images it contains and how it arranges them. (Some visuals contain written text, and if this is the case, you will have to consider this written text as well.)
- **What elements does the visual use to achieve its purpose?** What is the most important image? Where is it placed? What other images are present? Does the visual depict people? What are they doing? How much space is left blank? How does the visual use color and shadow? Does it include written text? How are words and images juxtaposed? For example, a visual designed to be primarily informative may use written text and straightforward graphics (such as graphs or scientific diagrams), while one that aims to persuade may use a single eye-catching image surrounded by blank space.
- **What point does the visual make?** How does it use images to get its message across? What other elements help to convey that message? If the visual is designed to convince its audience of something—for example, to change unhealthy behavior, donate to a charity, vote for a candidate, or buy a product—exactly how does it communicate this message? A photograph of starving children on a charity's website, for example, might convey the idea that a donation will bring them food, but statistics about infant mortality might make the image even more persuasive. Moreover, a close-up of one hungry child might be more convincing than a distant photo

of a crowd. Similarly, an ad might appeal to consumers either by showing satisfied customers using a product or by setting a memorable slogan against a contrasting background.

- **What beliefs or assumptions do you have that help to determine your response to the visual?** Is there anything in your background or experience that influences your reaction? Just as with written texts, people react differently to various visual texts. For instance, if you have expertise in economics, you may approach a chart depicting economic trends with greater interest—or greater skepticism—than a general audience would. If you know very little about fine art, your reaction to a painting is more likely to be emotional than analytical. And, as a loyal Democrat or Republican, you may react negatively to a political cartoon that is critical of your party. Finally, if you or a family member has struggled with illness or addiction, you might not respond favorably to a visual that took a superficial, lighthearted, or satirical approach to such a problem.

The following visual is a parody of an ad for Marlboro cigarettes. The visual, which appeared on the website www.adbusters.org, was annotated by a student who was assigned to analyze it. As he examined the ad, he identified its key elements and recorded his reactions in handwritten notes.

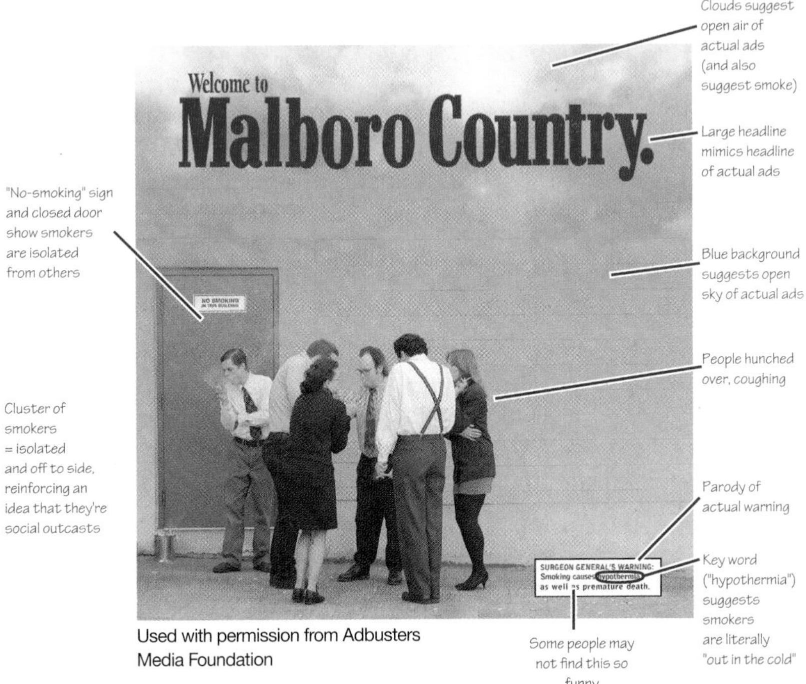

Used with permission from Adbusters Media Foundation

As you now know, reading critically involves more than just skimming a text for its ideas. It involves exploring the ideas of others as well as considering your own responses to those ideas. In the process, it enables you to discover new ideas and new ways of thinking about issues and to discover new things about yourself and your place in the world. In Chapter 2, you will take this process a step farther and examine the **writing process**—an activity that will help you sharpen your thinking and develop your ideas further. Not only will the writing process help you develop a better understanding of your subject, but it will also help you express yourself clearly, concisely, and effectively.

RESPONDING TO THE CHAPTER

Think about the kinds of reading you do every day. For example, you probably read texts, emails, social media posts, and books for school and pleasure. How does your focus shift based on what you are reading? What reading activities demand the most attention?

Chapter 2
Writing about Reading

In this chapter, you will learn to:

2.1 Recognize the kind of writing you are expected to do.
2.2 Identify your purpose for writing.
2.3 Analyze the audience for your writing.
2.4 Express your responses to a text.
2.5 List ideas to write about.
2.6 Develop a thesis.
2.7 Arrange your ideas.
2.8 Draft your essay.
2.9 Evaluate and revise your essay.

For years, journalists, academics, and others have been proclaiming the decline of writing. Because of the rise of social media, such as Facebook and Twitter, the argument goes, people—particularly young people—are writing without taking the time to choose the right word or to craft careful, correct sentences. To a certain extent, of course, this is true: clearly, informal communications such as texts and social media posts are composed quickly, with much less planning and less thought than academic essays or business reports. In fact, many people are probably more accustomed to writing in this informal, spontaneous way than to composing formal, carefully structured pieces of writing.

Still, this situation is not as bad as some people think it is. In fact, when it comes to writing, there is a significant advantage to the rise of social media. Even though much of this writing is not polished or carefully structured, it is still writing, and now that social media has become part of our lives, more and more people are comfortable with expressing ideas in written form. They have also learned the value of concise, efficient communication as well as the need to write for a particular purpose and audience and to pay close attention to content. These valuable skills can be applied to the more formal writing you do in college:

- **Writing concisely** Informal electronic communications often have length restrictions—for example, tweets are limited to 280 characters, so writers using Twitter learn to express themselves as concisely as possible. Therefore, they tend to be specific and direct.
- **Writing for a particular audience** Informal electronic communications are usually directed at a known audience—a friend or family member, for example, or members of a professional or business network or affinity group. Therefore, writers learn to tailor their messages to their own particular readers.
- **Writing with a purpose** Informal electronic communications are often written with a particular aim in mind—for example, to arrange a meeting or to garner support for a cause. Thus, writers learn to focus on achieving a definite goal.
- **Writing carefully** Informal electronic communications can be forwarded or reposted without the sender's permission. As a result, writers learn to scrutinize their messages more carefully, looking for any content that might have a negative effect on their reputation or on future employment.
- **Writing with images** Informal electronic communications often incorporate images, such as emoji or memes, to achieve particular effects on an audience. As they become accustomed to using images in their writing, writers learn to use them in academic writing as well—for example, adding a chart or a photo to illustrate or support ideas in an essay.

In a sense, then, informal electronic communication prepares you for the more challenging academic writing you will do as a college student (as well as the writing you will do in professional or business situations). As you might expect, however, informal electronic communication and academic writing are very different. For one thing, texts and social media posts are not necessarily grammatically correct or correctly spelled, and they are likely to include slang, abbreviations, emoji, and shorthand. In addition, sentences are often incomplete or run together, and capitalization is random or even nonexistent. In college writing, this is definitely not the case.

Another difference between informal electronic communications and academic writing is the extent to which careful planning and consideration of rhetorical strategies come into play. When you text a friend or post on Facebook, you write quickly, giving little thought to your message or to the way you are presenting it. In college writing situations, however, instructors expect you to respond to a particular assignment, and to tailor it to the needs and interests of a specific audience. Moreover, they expect your writing to focus on a single idea, called a **thesis**; to support this thesis with reasons, examples, facts, details, and so on; and to be well-organized and coherent. Finally, instructors expect your writing to be clear and grammatically correct, adhering to specific academic conventions of style, structure, format, and documentation. The first step in meeting these standards is to see writing as a process, one that helps you to achieve your purpose, focus your ideas, and express yourself clearly and concisely. The rest of this chapter outlines and illustrates the writing process you will follow as you complete written assignments for your college courses.

The activities discussed below actually overlap and are often repeated. In other words, the writing process is recursive rather than linear, more likely to be characterized by backtracking and repetition than by an orderly forward movement. As you become a more experienced writer, you will discover what works best for you and develop your own approach to this process.

2.1 Understanding Your Assignment

The writing assignment you are given usually specifies the kind of writing, or **genre**—for example, a response, an essay, a proposal, or a report—you are expected to do. Academic genres vary from discipline to discipline and from course to course, and they follow specific stylistic and structural conventions.

The first step in the writing process is identifying the genre in which you are to write and understanding the conventions of that genre. In completing the assignments in this book, you will be writing **responses** and academic **essays**, which often incorporate one or more outside sources—not only print or web texts but also interviews, images, films, music lyrics, and so on. Other academic genres are listed and defined in Chapter 1. In addition to identifying the genre called for in each assignment, you will need to read your assignment very carefully to make sure you know exactly what is expected of you—for example, how many pages to write, when the assignment is due, and whether the use of outside sources is encouraged (or required).

2.2 Understanding Your Purpose

Once you understand your assignment, you should consider your **purpose**—why you are writing. What do you hope to accomplish? For example, do you want to *inform* your audience or to *argue* in favor of a particular position? Your purpose may also be to observe, recall, explain causes or predict effects, describe, analyze, or evaluate—and you may also have other purposes, or more than one purpose.

2.3 Understanding Your Audience

Next, consider who your readers will be. For example, will you be addressing your instructor, your classmates, or a wider audience? Understanding what your readers already know about your topic and what expectations or biases they are likely to have will help you decide what information to include and how to present and develop your ideas.

2.4 Writing a Response

Most of the writing you will do in college will be in response to reading—assigned books and essays, newspapers and journals, research materials, electronic sources, and so on. If you have followed the active reading process described in Chapter 1, you will have highlighted and annotated your reading material. Once you have done this, you can write an informal **response** in which you assess what you have read and record your reactions to it. This process will not only help you to understand what you have read but also suggest ideas to write about.

Amber Lombardi, a student in a first-year writing course, was given the following writing assignment.

> In the essay "Why We Work," Andrew Curry notes that work today is "hardly the paradise economists once envisioned." In fact, he says, workers are largely discontented, facing long hours and great stress; for many, work has lost the meaning it once had. Do you see this in your own life and in the lives of those you know? Do you agree that work has lost its meaning? Write a one-page response to help you formulate your reactions to the ideas in Curry's essay. Then, referring to Curry's discussion as well as to one or two outside sources, write a two- to three-page essay in which you explore these questions, supporting your points with examples from the experiences of friends and family members. (You can conduct interviews with them in person or by phone or email.) Be sure to explain what you mean by *meaningful work*.

Amber began her writing process by reading "Why We Work" and the Responding to Reading questions that follow the essay on page 355. After highlighting and annotating this essay, she wrote the response that appears on the following pages.

Lombardi 1

Amber Lombardi

Professor Lieu

English 110

2 October 2018

Response to "Why We Work"

In "Why We Work," Andrew Curry discusses why workers today are dissatisfied with their jobs. He starts by examining the Industrial Revolution and how people's jobs got broken up into parts so that a worker would do one task repetitively on an assembly line for hours on end. According to Curry, workers today feel "crushed"; they are like hamsters in a wheel, running as fast as they can just to stay in one place. If today's workers slow down or think creatively, they risk losing their jobs. It seems pathetic that in a society in which everyone has to work, so many people don't think their jobs have any value.

I can relate to this feeling because of the office job I had the summer between high school and college. One of my routine tasks was to copy and paste reviewer comments from three different versions of the same document into one master document. It was tedious, but that wasn't the problem. The real problem was that I found my job frustrating because I could see that there was a better way to do it, but my supervisor didn't want to hear about it.

At this job, I felt I was being treated like the workers whom Curry describes, almost as if I were a body without a mind. After all, my supervisor made it clear that I wasn't being "paid for thinking," as the factory foreman, Frederick Taylor, was quoted as saying in the Curry essay. (Taylor treated workers as if they were interchangeable, and the tasks he assigned them were uninteresting fragments of the whole.) I was warned to stop thinking creatively about how to improve the process and just do it using the old method. As Curry points out, workers resent being treated in this way because it makes it impossible for them to take pride in what they are doing.

Lombardi 2

According to Curry, the rise in high technology in the 1990s didn't do much to improve the balance between work and life for most workers. Today, most employees are stressed because their work life invades their private life via cell phones and email and they are essentially working 24/7. But would this situation be a problem if the work was something that actually helped the world—something meaningful? To me, that is the important question that Curry is asking.

2.5 Collecting Ideas

After writing a response to the assigned reading, your next step is to gather ideas to write about. One useful way to find ideas is to **brainstorm** about your assignment by reviewing and then expanding your active reading notes and your written response. At this point, you can also look for outside sources to supplement your own ideas. Later, you will focus on how to develop and structure these ideas in your essay.

After reading Andrew Curry's "Why We Work" and writing a response to his ideas, Amber Lombardi looked online for information about job satisfaction, and she also conducted informal interviews with her brother and sister-in-law and two friends. Then, she composed the following brainstorming notes. Notice that she supplies page or paragraph numbers for information from her sources so that when she writes her essay, she will be able to distinguish others' ideas from her own and document material she borrowed. (See the Appendix for information on MLA documentation style.)

Brainstorming Notes

In 1930, Kellogg cut the workday by two hours because he believed that the future of work would/should involve more free time, a "workers' paradise," in Curry's words. (pars. 1–2) **But people now work longer and harder to afford the standard of living they want.**

It's harder to get and hold a job; people are willing to accept less just to keep their jobs.

***Employees upset about the reality of their work compared to the ideal. Job satisfaction is lower than it once was. They feel insecure, overworked, unappreciated, unfulfilled. (Refer to McGregor *WP* article on job satisfaction, par. 8)

History:

- After Industrial Revolution, idea of workers as being interchangeable; Frederick Taylor, factory foreman, broke down work into "component parts." Assembly line; **can't see whole picture**. Repeating small part of process. (pars. 9–11) [Tedious and frustrating, like task I had!]
- Labor unions fought for reduced hours for workers. (par. 14)
- Roosevelt's New Deal encouraged consumerism; new things for people to want and work for. Then, postwar boom of 1950s and 1960s, everyone working, everyone buying. (pars. 17–18)

More work, less satisfaction. Hard work, no spiritual meaning. (Economic downturn in 1970s.) *[But what exactly is "spiritual meaning" when it comes to work?]*

Now can't count on having a job for life, can be fired at any time. Workers feel less valued. (So why get emotionally invested?) **<u>You are replaceable</u>**.

Instead of being offered job security, workers at high-tech firms in the 1990s were offered free food, on-site massages, dry-cleaning services, games. Companies such as Google still do. (par. 22) But people would rather have more time with family than snacks and backrubs, right?

Technology allows work to invade home life: always on call. *[But maybe that wouldn't be so bad if you really liked the work.]*

***Opposite of assembly-line mentality.

People I know:

Adam: being a **graduate teaching assistant** is creative, has "huge personal meaning" for him, and he "carries it in his head 24/7." Likes the freedom to make own choices about teaching methods, sees how it helps students.

Kendra: job gives her "a community where I am valued." She works with an **international student exchange program** at the college, gets to travel and has "intense friendships" with coworkers, all doing "something we believe in." Also likes being the "go-to person for certain tasks" and the recognition and responsibility of being in charge of a whole process, being considered an expert who is valuable and unique. (Very different from her high school job, which was a lot like my job between high school and college: no one wanted to hear our ideas! Also like Curry's Frederick Taylor, par. 11.)

Natalie: volunteering at a **hospice for people dying of chronic diseases** is "rewarding and fulfilling" because she works directly with clients and sees how what she does—being a companion and helping them be comfortable—comforts them.

Natalie: "I don't agree with the statement that work has lost its meaning. I think work is what you make of it, at almost any job." *[Do I agree? Some jobs these days are just demeaning, no matter how much you try to transform them with a positive attitude.]*

Mario: as a part-time **grocery bagger**, he's not allowed to chat with coworkers on the job, so he feels like he can't express himself, and he also thinks he isn't paid enough for the physical labor involved.

Mario's mother: most meaningful job was **community garden project**. She could see the direct results of what she did and felt like she was part of a process (planting seedlings, seeing them grow, harvesting the vegetables and fruits, selling at farmer's market, etc.).

[Applying Natalie's view to Mario: he should be getting more out of his work and isn't trying hard enough. But how do you find deep meaning in putting groceries in a bag?]

Work and life = the same thing? Life doesn't switch off when you start the workday.

***Important for job satisfaction:

* an individual's sense of being an important part of the whole

* contributions being valued

* part of the creative process

* responsible for something worthwhile

[Also: criteria discussed by Schwartz and Porath, chart in *NYT* article]

2.6 Developing a Thesis

Once you have collected ideas to write about and reviewed your notes carefully, you should begin to see a focus for your essay. Now, you need to develop a **thesis statement**, a one-sentence summary of your essay's main idea. The points that you make in your essay should support this central idea. Keep in mind that your thesis statement should be clearly worded and specific, and cover only the points that you will discuss in your essay. (Note that at this stage of the writing process, your thesis is *tentative*; it is likely to change as you write and revise your essay.)

After reviewing her highlighting and annotations as well as her response and her brainstorming notes, Amber drafted the following tentative thesis statement: "I believe that although work has lost its meaning for many of us because we no longer feel a connection between the tasks we do and their positive results in society, we can regain a sense of meaning by putting ourselves wholeheartedly into every task we take on."

2.7 Arranging Supporting Material

If it is carefully phrased, your thesis statement should suggest a possible arrangement for your ideas. In Amber's case, her thesis statement, although somewhat vague and wordy, suggests that her essay will have a problem/solution structure. That is, she will begin by discussing how and why work has lost its meaning for many people and then move on to discuss how this problem might be solved.

Before you can begin writing, however, you need to review the work you have done so far in order to identify your key supporting points and arrange them effectively. After Amber reviewed her work—particularly her brainstorming notes—she arranged the supporting material for her essay in a logical order. The following informal outline shows how she organized her ideas.

- Many workers are unhappy in their jobs (McGregor), but they identify some positive aspects (Schwartz and Porath)
- Workers should take part in a whole process

  Curry's comments

  Mario's mother's experiences at community garden
- Employees should take responsibility for a significant part of a job

  My sister-in-law's experiences at Mount Walton College

  Kendra's experiences in high school job
- Work should benefit society

  Kendra

  Natalie

  Mario

2.8 Drafting Your Essay

Once you have arranged your key ideas into an informal outline, you can use this outline to guide you as you write the first draft of your essay. The opening paragraph of Amber's first draft appears below.

According to Andrew Curry's essay "Why We Work," people's lives are dominated by their jobs, and they are running as fast as they can just to stay in one place. Technology has improved our standard of living in this country, but few of us have time to enjoy it because we have to work so hard just to maintain that standard of living. The problem of being constantly at work is made worse by the fact that few people find their jobs meaningful. It seems pathetic that in a society in which everyone has to work, hardly anyone feels they are doing anything meaningful, or anything of value to society. I believe that although work has lost its meaning for many of us because we no longer feel a connection between the tasks we do and their positive results in society, we can regain a sense of meaning by putting ourselves wholeheartedly into every task we take on.

2.9 Revising Your Essay

A college essay should include an *introduction*, a *body*, and a *conclusion*. The **introduction** identifies the article or essay you are discussing and states your thesis. In the **body paragraphs**, you present the **support** for your thesis—reasons, examples, facts, details, and so on—drawn from your source (or sources) or from your own experiences and observations. Each body paragraph is like a mini-essay, introducing one point in a **topic sentence** (a sentence that states the paragraph's main idea) and then developing that point with facts, reasons, examples, and so on. The **conclusion** reinforces the essay's main idea, ending with a strong concluding statement. As you revise, check to make sure your essay includes all these elements. Only then should you consider questions of style, grammar, mechanics, and punctuation.

Strategies for Revision

- Read and react to your draft, using the same active reading strategies you use when you read an assigned text.
- Outline your work to make sure it conforms to the outline that guided your draft.
- Email a draft to your instructor, and ask for feedback and constructive suggestions for revision.
- Work in a peer-editing group, getting feedback from classmates.
- Work with a writing center tutor.

  Create a **graphic organizer**. Think of your essay as a series of blocks, and try to arrange your paragraphs and sentences within the blocks. This strategy will help you to see if you have arranged ideas logically and effectively.

When she revised her essay, Amber used several of the strategies listed in the box. For example, she worked with two other students in a peer-editing group. A body paragraph from Amber's draft, along with two students' comments, appears below.

> If you take on responsibility for a job, then you are going to feel excited about it. For example, Kendra Lombardi stated that she finds her current job with Mount Walton College's international student exchange program to be highly satisfying partly because she likes being "the go-to person for certain tasks." In a job she had when she was in high school, she had an idea for improving a process. However, her supervisor told her to keep her ideas to herself, which she found pretty depressing. On the other hand, Adam Lombardi, a graduate teaching assistant at Mount Walton College, says that being given responsibility by his department for creating his own curriculum is very rewarding.

Amber, I'm confused about the second half of your topic sentence. What is actually so good about taking responsibility that you "feel excited" about it? Chris

Amber: How was it rewarding for Adam? You don't really explain this—leaves us hanging. You could add a few quotes from Adam to help us get what was so rewarding about it exactly. Bella

Amber: You switch to a new example with this sentence—kind of abrupt. Not sure where you are going with it. How does it fit with your topic sentence about responsibility being satisfying? You could start the new example with a transition and develop the point more or even leave the whole thing out. Bella

Amber also used the following graphic organizer, filling in revised content from the final draft of her essay (including a revised thesis statement) to help her check its structure before handing it in.

Opening remarks: Downside of assembly-line jobs; general background from Curry essay

Thesis statement: Although Curry makes it clear that meaningful work is not easy to find, it is still possible for many workers to find meaning—and even joy—in their jobs.

Topic sentence (background): A 2017 survey by the Conference Board, discussed in a *Washington Post* article, found that although more than half of all American workers are happy with their jobs, satisfaction rates are still far below what they were twenty to thirty years ago.

Support: McGregor; Schwartz and Porath

Topic sentence (support for thesis): For example, workers who are lucky enough to take part in a whole process from start to finish report being satisfied with what they do.

Support: Curry's comments about pre-industrial labor; Mario's mother's experience with community garden

Topic sentence (support for thesis): If an employee is allowed to take on responsibility for a significant part of a job, then that employee is going to feel a sense of empowerment and accountability.

Support: Kendra's positive experience (contrast with her high school job, comparing it to Curry's comments about Taylor); Adam's positive experience

Topic sentence (support for thesis): Finally, many people find satisfaction in their jobs because they see their work benefiting society in some way.

Support: Kendra's and Natalie's experiences (contrast with Mario's experience)

Statement that reinforces thesis: As Curry points out, great numbers of American workers have "a sense that work doesn't satisfy their deeper needs" (359); still, finding meaningful work is an achievable goal for many.

Concluding statement: Although most of us do not have the luxury of holding out for the ideal job when there are bills to pay, we should still try to find meaning in our work.

After she made the revisions she thought were necessary, Amber edited her draft, checking to make sure she had used correct grammar and sentence structure and chosen the most appropriate words. She also reviewed her use of punctuation. Then, she proofread carefully, looking for any spelling errors or typos that her spell checker might have missed. She also made sure her essay's format conformed to her instructor's guidelines. Then, she printed out a final draft of her essay. Notice that her essay, which appears on the following pages, includes parenthetical references to "Why We Work" and other sources. It also includes a works-cited page in MLA format that lists the sources she consulted and the informal interviews she conducted. (Marginal annotations provide information about some of the rhetorical choices she made as she developed her essay.)

Lombardi 1

Amber Lombardi

Professor Lieu

English 110

17 October 2018

What Makes Work Meaningful

Amber's attention-getting opener attracts readers' interest and draws them in.

Drill a hole in a machine part; repeat. Pick up a tub of margarine; put it in a box; repeat. Not all job descriptions are as unappealing as these actual assembly-line tasks, but many American workers today report that their work is similarly uninspiring. According to Andrew Curry's essay "Why We Work," for generations the lives of typical American workers have been dominated by their jobs. As Curry points out, advances in technology have improved the US standard of living, but few of us have time to enjoy our leisure time because we have to work so hard just to maintain that standard. The idea of life being all work and no play is made worse because most people, according to Curry, feel that the work they do lacks meaning. For work to be meaningful, individuals must have a clear sense of themselves as valued participants in a worthwhile collaboration and be able to see the positive results of their efforts firsthand. Although Curry makes it clear that meaningful work is not easy to find, it is still possible for many workers to find meaning—and even joy—in their jobs.

Amber's revised thesis statement now tells readers that her essay will suggest that meaningful work is an achievable goal.

A 2017 survey by the Conference Board, discussed in a *Washington Post* article, found that although more than half of all American workers are happy with their jobs, satisfaction rates are still far below what they were twenty to thirty years ago. Workers who responded to the survey were particularly unhappy with bonuses, promotions, and performance reviews (McGregor). In a *New York Times* article, two management consultants also reported on dissatisfaction in the workplace. A study they conducted revealed that the most important factor in determining job satisfaction

This paragraph provides background information from the two sources Amber found online. The paragraph blends summary with brief quotations from one of the sources.

Lombardi 2

is the sense that the jobs workers do are "connected to a higher purpose" (Schwartz and Porath). Other important criteria include "opportunities to regularly renew and recharge at work," "feeling valued and appreciated for their contributions," and being able to "focus in an absorbed way on their most important tasks" (Schwartz and Porath). Interviews with four workers in a variety of jobs, conducted for this essay, seem to confirm these findings, suggesting that while it is difficult for workers to find satisfaction in their jobs, it is still possible if certain conditions are met.

For example, workers who are lucky enough to take part in a whole process from start to finish report being satisfied with what they do. This used to be an accepted fact, at least before the Industrial Revolution changed the way people work. In his examination of pre-industrial labor, Curry comments, "For centuries, the household—from farms to 'cottage' craftsmen—was the unit of production. The whole family was part of the enterprise, be it farming, blacksmithing, or baking" (356). In a similar way, Mario Alvarez reports that his mother, when working for a community garden project, was able to feel connected to an entire process. She and her coworkers purchased seedlings, planted them, helped them grow, and then harvested the fruits and vegetables to sell at a farmer's market they set up and promoted. When customers bought the produce and the community organizers were able to reinvest the money into the garden, the process was complete, and taking part in that cycle made the job meaningful.

This paragraph offers Curry's comments and Mario's mother's experience as support for the topic sentence.

In MLA format, the source of quoted material is given in the text in parentheses. The author's last name in the introductory phrase corresponds to the entry in the works-cited list at the end of the essay. If the author's last name does not appear in the introductory phrase, it appears in the parenthetical reference, with no comma between the last name and the page number.

If an employee is allowed to take on responsibility for a significant part of a job, then that employee is going to feel a sense of empowerment and accountability. For example, Kendra Lombardi finds her current job with Mount Walton College's international student exchange program satisfying partly because she likes being

Lombardi 3

"the go-to person for certain tasks." In a job she had when she was a high school student, however, she was not as fortunate. She had an idea for improving a process and would have appreciated being encouraged to implement her plan. However, instead of giving her permission, her supervisor told her to keep her ideas to herself, and her response led Kendra to see her job as pointless. Curry describes a similar situation occurring in the 1930s when factory foreman Frederick Taylor told his workers, "we have other men paid for thinking" (357). In contrast, Adam Lombardi, a graduate teaching assistant at Mount Walton College, reports that being given responsibility by his department for creating his own curriculum gives his job "huge personal meaning." Adam takes pride in devising new ways to reach his students and encourage their success.

This paragraph offers Kendra's and Adam's recent experiences (in contrast to Kendra's earlier experience and Curry's comments) as support for the topic sentence.

Finally, many people find satisfaction in their jobs because they see their work benefiting society in some way. For example, Kendra Lombardi explains that part of the reason she loves her job is that she and her coworkers all feel that they are doing something that helps people. And according to Natalie O'Reilly, a volunteer companion at a hospice for people with chronic diseases, her work is rewarding because she can see firsthand how much her actions comfort others. On the other hand, one of the reasons Mario Alvarez is dissatisfied with his job as a part-time grocery bagger is that he has trouble seeing how what he does makes a difference. Without a sense of larger purpose, Mario focuses instead on the negative aspects of his job, such as the low pay and his inability to socialize on the job.

The word *finally* serves as a transition to the essay's discussion of the social impact of work.

This paragraph offers Kendra's and Natalie's experiences (in contrast to Mario's experience) as support for the topic sentence.

As Curry points out, great numbers of American workers have "a sense that work doesn't satisfy their deeper needs" (359); still, finding meaningful work is an achievable goal for many. As Natalie O'Reilly would argue, "work is what you make of it." In other words, even if we are stuck temporarily in a dead-end, tedious

This statement reinforces Amber's thesis about meaningful work.

Lombardi 4

job, we can try to see the big picture and how what we do fits into it, become an expert at some aspect of the work, and identify the job's benefit to society. Although most of us do not have the luxury of holding out for the ideal job when there are bills to pay, we should still try to find meaning in our work.

This sentence restates the thesis and leaves readers with something to think about.

Lombardi 5

Works Cited

Alvarez, Mario. Telephone interview. 2 Oct. 2018.

Curry, Andrew. "Why We Work." *The Blair Reader: Exploring Issues and Ideas*, edited by Laurie G. Kirszner and Stephen R. Mandell, 10th ed., Pearson, 2020, pp. 355–59.

Lombardi, Adam. E-mail interview. 5 Oct. 2018.

Lombardi, Kendra. E-mail interview. 5 Oct. 2018.

McGregor, Jena. "Job Satisfaction Is Up, But Still Well Below One-Time Highs." *The Washington Post,* 1 Sept. 2017, https://www.washingtonpost.com/news/on-leadership/wp/2017/09/01/job-satisfaction-is-up-but-still-well-below-one-time-highs/?noredirect=on&utm_term=.a1f75a751c38.

O'Reilly, Natalie. Telephone interview. 6 Oct. 2018.

Schwartz, Tony, and Christine Porath. "Why You Hate Work." *The New York Times*, 30 May 2014, www.nytimes.com/2014/06/01/opinion/sunday/why-you-hate-work.html?_r=0.

RESPONDING TO THE CHAPTER

Consider what you like to write about. Do you text your friends and family? Do you post to social media? Do you maintain a blog? Describe the different audiences you write for on a daily basis and why you write for them.

Chapter 3
Family and Memory

In this chapter, you will learn to:

- analyze readings about family and memory.
- compose essays about family and memory.

The ties that bind us to our families, and to our family history, are like no other human connections. In this chapter, writers explore family dynamics and family values to try to make sense of the gap between children and parents and between past and present. Some writers search their memories, trying to understand, recapture, or re-create the past, to see across the barriers imposed by time. Other writers examine misunderstandings, miscommunications, or generational conflicts in their

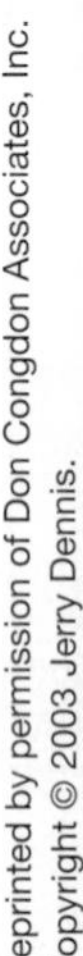

What elements in this image of Jerry Dennis (right) with his brother and friend make the scene depicted memorable?

current lives, struggling to understand differences in values, find common ground, and work toward reconciliation. In some cases, images and scenes appear in sharp focus; in others, they are blurred, confused, or even partially invented. Many writers focus on themselves; others focus on their parents or other family members, trying to define relationships, to close generational gaps, to replay events, to see through the eyes of others—and, in this way, to understand their families and themselves.

In this chapter's Focus section, "What Is a Family?" (p. 69), three writers discuss the concept of *family* and consider the family's multiple (and often controversial) forms and functions. First, in "For Gay Parents, Deciding between Adoption and Surrogacy Raises Tough Moral Questions," John Culhane explores the complex options gay couples have in building families; then, in "My Fictional Grandparents," Laila Lalami describes how the stories we tell help define our understanding of family. Finally, in "If You Have No Children, Who Will Care for You When You're Old?" Sonia Sodha examines the role and fate of couples who constitute childless families.

What point does this image of Kristin Ohlson (front right) with her mother (third from the left) make about the relationship between family and memory?

Preparing to Read and Write

As you read and prepare to write about the selections in this chapter, you may consider the following questions:

- What assumptions does the writer seem to have about his or her audience? How can you tell?
- What is the writer's primary purpose? For example, is it to reexamine the past; to discover, explore, or explain family relationships; or something else?
- What genre is the writer using? For example, is the reading a reflection, a poem, a story, an argument, or a memoir? How do the conventions of this genre influence the writer's choices?
- What appeals does the writer use? For example, does he or she appeal primarily to reason or to emotion? Is this the most effective appeal?
- How does the writer define *family?*
- Does the writer focus on a single person, on a relationship between two people, or on wider family dynamics?
- Does the writer focus on his or her own family members or on family in general?
- How important is the setting in which the events the writer describes take place?
- Do you think the writer's perspective is *subjective* (shaped by his or her emotional responses or personal opinions) or *objective* (based mainly on observation and fact rather than on personal impressions)?
- What insights does the writer have that he or she did not have when the events occurred? What, if anything, has the writer learned—and how?
- Are the memories generally happy or unhappy ones?
- Are family members presented in a favorable, unfavorable, neutral, or ambivalent way?
- Does the writer feel close to or distant from family members? Does the writer identify with a particular family member?
- Does one family member seem to have had a great influence over the writer? If so, is this influence positive or negative?
- What social, political, economic, or cultural forces influenced the family dynamics?
- Do you identify with the writer or with another person the writer describes? What makes you identify with that person?
- Which readings seem most similar in their views of family? How are they similar?
- Which readings seem most different in their views of family? How are they different?
- Which family seems most like your own? Why?

Shared Writing

Family and Memory

Whom do you consider part of your family? Think beyond relationships based on birth and marriage and consider the people and even the pets with whom you share the closest bonds. What specifically makes these relationships so important?

3.1 Teresa J. Scollon, "Family Music" [Poetry]

Teresa J. Scollon (1962–) is a poet, essayist, and educator. She has published poems in journals such as *Atlanta Review, Damselfly Press, Dunes Review, Nimrod, Spoon River Poetry Review,* and *Third Coast.* She is the author of the poetry chapbook *Friday Nights the Whole Town Goes to the Basketball Game* (2009) and the poetry collection *To Embroider the Ground with Prayer* (2012), where the following poem appeared. In it, Scollon explores the relationship between family, memory, and music.

BEFORE YOU READ

What songs do you associate with particular family members? Why are these songs especially memorable?

Family Music

Banging on holidays like a piano tuner—
this tone, tone, tone, then the octave, then
the triad, then another note—we work
around the calendar of keys, muscling
swollen pegs and frayed wires into tune.
We forget how all this internal weather,
this spitting turbulence, warps the fine grain
of wood, how wood is a living material,
breathing and absorbing even after it's cut
and fashioned into a living room shape.
If we chopped it up and lit a fire, we'd hear
water hiss and wail as it heats and escapes
each cellulose room—each ring another year
of growing in concentric direction—all of it
finally released. That would be music.

Source: Reprinted from "Family Music" from To Embroider the Ground with Prayer by Theresa J. Scollon.

RESPONDING TO READING

1. What feelings does the speaker have about her family's past? Do you see these as mixed feelings?
2. What do you think the speaker means in the poem's last lines when she says, "all of it/finally released. That would be music"?

Rhetorical Analysis

How does the poem use repetition of sounds to create tone and rhythm? Do these devices make parts of the poem more memorable? Explain.

3.2 John Mauk, "The Blessed" [Fiction]

A visiting assistant professor of composition and rhetoric and codirector of the Ohio Writing Project at Miami University, John Mauk is an acclaimed fiction writer and essayist. Appearing in *Arts & Letters, New Millennium Writings*, and *Salamander Magazine*, his stories explore the complexities of human connections and divisions. He has also published blog posts and essays about writing in publications such as *Beatrice.com, The Next Best Book Blog, Portland Book Review, The Rumpus .net, Three Guys One Book*, and the *Writer's Digest*. Mauk is the author of the fiction chapbook *The Rest of Us* (2012) and the story collection *Field Notes for the Earthbound* (2014), in which "The Blessed" appeared. In the following story, the narrator remembers the complicated role his mother played in his family and in the surrounding community.

BEFORE YOU READ

To what extent has your family been blessed, and to what extent has it been cursed? What specific events lead you to these conclusions?

The Blessed

My mom was a witch. I don't mean a New Age earth goddess or Wiccan. She wasn't a peacenik or spiritualist. And she wasn't retaliating against other religions. Back then, on the open flatlands of Ohio before the turnpike brought the rest of the world zooming through, being a witch was private business. It wasn't something to talk about or parade around. And it wasn't a choice any more than your last name. My mom was a real witch. She did things to people. She made things happen. I can be honest now that she's gone. She's the reason David Manville looks like he'll eat your head if you give him half the chance, and probably the reason he molested that Jonas kid years ago, and why he went off to prison and did unspeakable things behind bars.

Yesterday, I saw David Manville in the grocery store. He's out of prison and back here buying bread and canned green beans like any normal person. But he's not normal. He'll never be normal. If destiny stumbles and he has children, they'll never be normal. I tried not to stare but couldn't help it. There he was—thirty-some years older, no longer the wiry eighteen year-old with stringbean arms. He'd become a thick-shouldered hunk of scowling meat, an animal caged in its own skin. It's odd enough seeing a guy like David Manville walking around in the world. It's odder yet to see him standing in a checkout lane holding groceries. It's like seeing a tiger with a birthday cake.

I was in Natalie Tolaski's lane, which meant I'd be standing there a while because she picks up every item, looks at it, comments, and then pushes it toward the bagger. I'd taken a step—hoping to jump over a lane—and that's when I saw David. When our eyes met, he didn't blink, turn away, nod his head, or anything. I pivoted back and looked straight at the person in front of me. I tried to shut off my peripheral vision and protect the side of my eyeball, but I could feel his stare. He was in Dana Trumbull's lane, so he moved ahead and I felt the air around me relax. I looked over and saw apelike bulges beneath a thin green t-shirt. Whatever had happened to him over the decades made his shoulders balloon up and cancel out his neck.

He must have just gotten back because I would have heard. The whole town would have heard. Even though it's been years, plenty of people from those days are still around. Plenty know the story—how he invited Billy Jonas into his house, took him upstairs, cornered him, pulled out his member and rubbed it on Billy's face. When the police came, David wouldn't go down to the station, not willingly anyway. It took four officers to carry him out—screeching and flailing like a stray cat. He was sentenced to three years, which didn't seem like much. But he did things and kept doing them. He was violent. Mrs. Jonas kept up on his campaign of prison assaults. She wanted to know when he'd get out. But years went by. Eventually, we all figured he was gone for good.

And it wasn't just David Manville. He wasn't the only target. My mom's curse 5
washed over that whole family. His younger brother Neil had a deformity of some kind—something I can't really name, something about his head. It looked compressed or sunken in. The youngest, Melissa, threw fits. She'd go berserk right on the street, in the store, wherever. I remember seeing her drop to the pavement once. The family was crossing the street and down she went, gyrating against her mother's attempts to stand her up. When she got old enough, she married little Sammie Johnson and they beat each other senseless. You could go by their place any time of day and hear it. Somehow, in between punches and takedowns, they managed to have three kids—all of them, as far as I could tell, untamable. Nathaniel, the oldest boy, killed a woman on a bike. He wasn't much beyond sixteen and fresh behind the wheel. The police said he drove right over her, circled around in the field, left her body in the ditch, and drove back home. He's still away at some detention center.

The curse got the Polks as well. Marianne Polk died slowly. Back in the old days, she was a shrewd woman, the kind who had something to say about everything. But eventually, all her clarity evaporated and she turned into a crazy-haired open-mouth zombie. The family didn't have the money to take care of her in the right way and didn't have the sense to put her someplace safe, so they locked her up in her own bedroom, and like my mom used to say, if you're hoping to lock something up, you're better off killing it. Well, Marianne Polk managed to escape on a regular basis. She'd show up all over town, most often in her nightgown, but once, she walked stark naked down Main Street. It was August so there was plenty of flesh around—a few shirtless men, people in shorts—but no one expected to see Marianne Polk's whole body in all of its eighty year-old translucence. Lester Pollick, the gentle guy that he was, hobbled into the street, grabbed her hand and pulled her to the sidewalk. Gerald Polk's brain must have done somersaults when he found his wife on a casual bare-butt stroll with Lester. That winter, Marianne wandered into the fields. She fell down, snapped her leg in two, got pneumonia, and that was that.

The Polk kids—Lily, Leonard, and Ellie—were roughly my age. All within a few years anyway. Lily got around to marrying some guy from Hillsdale, Michigan. They had two children. One died from crib death and the other got some mental sickness that made her eat everything in sight. She swelled up to 400 pounds before a state agency came in and took her away. I don't know where she is now—if she's in a hospital or if she ate herself to death. Leonard moved down to Bryan, bought the local racetrack, and got himself tangled in underhanded business. He's long gone, but Ellie's still in a duplex over in Edon. She got married to a man named Nelvin or Nevin Shirky, had a baby, and left him to raise the girl on his own. I've seen Ellie around, and I can say without a doubt that she's as unhinged as any creature walking. She wears so much makeup that it's hard to tell where things begin and end.

The Housmans didn't fare any better. Maybe they were collateral damage. It's hard to say, but I know that Paula Housman lost her husband right after Mom delivered the curse. His name was Robert but everyone called him Red. He had a sharp jaw that made him seem important. He was the only Nazarene that accepted everyone, even the Catholics and even my mom. I remember hearing the story a few different ways, but the gist of it was a car killed him. He was under there working—because that's what people did in those days—and the jack gave way. Paula walked out the back door and saw his legs sticking out. It took a while before a neighbor made sense of her screaming, came around, and jacked the car back up. Of course, it didn't matter how long it took. The initial collapse pressed the top half of Red Housman into the ground. I heard the details about extracting him—or most of him. Out of respect, I'll keep those to myself.

So the Manvilles, the Polks, and the Housmans got the brunt of the curse. There may have been more. The Krugs, Smiths, Laneys—all those people and all their children may have caught some flecks of it. I'll never know. But what I do know is that Barbara Manville and Marianne Polk brought out the worst in my mom. They let loose something they couldn't imagine.

10 It all started with my sister. But it wasn't her fault. Martha couldn't help that she drove boys crazy. I suspect it was that cornsilk hair and how it trailed behind her when she'd walk through town. She streamed along like a fallen leaf on a quick current. You look away for a second and can hardly believe the distance. At fifteen, she was plenty fidgety. When the weather was good, she orbited town several times a day. She moved and kept moving. No matter how you look at it or who you are, that's bound to attract attention.

So it was late May, a morning thick with honeysuckle and lilac. Martha was at the churchyard talking with the Nazarene boys while their parents finished up churchy business. According to the story, she got to kissing with Leonard Polk behind the big lilac bush. The minister looked out the window and saw things happening—Martha and Leonard going at it while a few other boys watched. When Barbara Manville and Marianne Polk came to our house, they were still in full church garb. I looked out the front door and saw them whispering. I let them finish, straighten their dresses, and knock. I answered and called for Mom.

"Lorna, we have to talk," one of them said.

They went into the living room. Mom was a good host. She always said that if someone comes to your home, no matter what, you bring them all the way in. You let them into the center of your life. That way, you get past all the doorway niceties. Mom hated niceties.

I stood in the kitchen just past the threshold. I knew something was going on because nobody from the Nazarene church had ever been to our house. The women sat on the edge of their chairs and neither wanted anything to drink, not even a glass of water. They kept sighing. They said Martha waltzed into the churchyard and riled up their boys.

15 "So your son was kissing Martha?" Mom said.

"It wasn't just kissing, Lorna."

They were insinuating things. They explained that it was some kind of show. One of them said something about perversion, which was the first time I'd heard that word. The conversation went on and on. They talked about their beliefs, their families, and the clear difference between right and wrong. For them, it was more than teenagers exploring romance. It was about sin and Jesus and the proper way to wear one's hair. Somewhere in the middle of it, Martha came in the front door and glided past them. That's when Barbara Manville made a point of telling Mom to keep her hussy daughter away from the church and God's children. It was deliberate. She wanted Martha to be ashamed. And that's what changed everything.

I remember watching the dust—how it writhed in the big sunbeam—and how Mom looked at me when I shifted my weight and made the wood creak. She turned back toward Barbara Manville and started whispering—that choked kind of whisper that comes from clenched throat muscles. She told them to leave. The women got up in a hurry, and just as they reached the front door, Mom said it clearly, like she was telling them the time. "You will always regret this."

Until then, I hadn't witnessed anything dramatic at our house, nothing torrential or abrupt. I suppose Mom's power, which she once called her mother's "tradition," worked quietly in our lives. Her garden was always lush, no matter what the weather did. I remember a drought year. Everything went yellow and shriveled. The farmers lamented their corn and soybeans. I'd walk through town and see tangles of pale weeds where gardens should have been. Even Lester Pollick's garden, three houses down, looked like a thin blanket of straw. And then I'd get here to our place—to our double-size yard, the last one before the town spills into open fields. I'd come around the wall of hemlock and into the shade of our huge cottonwood. I'd smell the clay and minerals and see Mom's garden—a jungle of green sturdy herbs, vines, and stalks announcing themselves against a backdrop of thirst and privation.

And we had the dogs, Dilly and Tobias, our scouts and onlookers. Besides the local horses and cows, they were the biggest four-legged creatures around. They were Irish wolfhounds or something like it. When I was young, they were walls of moppy hair—panting over the top of me, shouldering me toward the back yard. They lived until I was twenty-five. Once I asked Mom how old they were. She said, "They're very old but very healthy, Jacob." Those dogs did everything Mom said, as if they had some direct connection to her thoughts. And they didn't do any of that dumb dog stuff—barking their heads off or writhing against a chain whenever someone walked by. They were dignified. If they needed to bark, they did so, but only once or twice until they were convinced Mom had heard. She'd acknowledge them and that was that. And when we came home from school, they'd each come up, lick us once in the hand, then go back to their business. The few times I got huffy as a kid—anywhere close to a tantrum—they were right there looking down, almost shaking their heads, tssking.

And we ate well. While most other kids choked down brown and white glop saddled up next to a hunk of bologna, we ate a spectrum of roots, greens, and spiced breads. Mom knew how to pull flavor from the ground. My mouth got accustomed to richness and contradiction—all kinds of fluffy egg concoctions, creamy potatoes, heavy stews that were sweet enough to be dessert. If we ate something from a restaurant, which was rare, it tasted flat, and the candy sold at Kaiser's grocery tasted like detergent. And I can still barely stomach any of that prepared food that goes into your freezer. It's like licking tar off the road.

I never got sick as a kid. Neither did Martha. We didn't get the standard shots. I didn't even know about inoculations until my thirties—when my girlfriend at the time looked at my arm and noticed the missing dimple. There we were in bed. She started pulling at my skin and inspecting. She asked where the scar was. I told her I didn't really know, which was true, and we got back to business. This year I had the flu for the first time, which made me feel sorry for people who've had it more than once.

But even so, our house wasn't all that strange. That's my point. Sure, there was the garden, the dogs, the food, the good health. Sometimes, I wonder how much she fended off—how many whispers or bad dreams or fevers. I wonder if she stopped bullies before they saw me, if she firmed up the ice before we ventured onto the pond, if she stopped the lightening or sent it off elsewhere. But even if she did, I don't think those Nazarene women knew anything. We dressed like everyone else. Martha and I went to school and did our work like the other kids. Mom didn't wear weird dresses or act odd in public. She was quiet, but not anymore so than a regular quiet person. She'd walk down by the river in the evenings, but that wasn't exotic. To anyone looking in from the outside, Mom was a non-religious widow with two children. That's it. And I suspect those women never figured it out. Given their notions about the world, they probably didn't imagine that Lorna Ferrick meant what she said on that Sunday. If they could have climbed out of their lives, if they could have elevated themselves enough to look down and see all the tragedy concentrated on their families, if they could have charted out the gnarled details, they might have concluded something about that day. They might have regretted coming to our house, demonizing Martha, or even listening when the minister told them what he saw. They might have remembered way back to their teen years when life forces tickled their own ribs and made them yearn in every direction beyond the church pew.

After they left, Mom came into the kitchen. She cupped Martha's shoulders and told her, "You're not anything those women will ever say."

"I know," Martha said. 25

Then we had canned cherries in syrup.

All that week, Mom murmured to herself. She spent nights by the river. Down in the basement, I saw a bucket filled with sludge. It sat on a stool for days. I could smell the dankness wafting up the steps. I looked in it once and saw nothing but frothy mud. I knew it was for something important. After a few days, every room in the house smelled like the river—like wet roots and decay. We didn't talk about it though. We went about our business and lived in the murky scent of the St. Joe.

A week after the Nazarene women had come and gone, Mom brought the bucket upstairs. I saw her standing by the back door. She looked down into it, whispered, and then walked out. Part of me knew that I should stay home, but most of me wanted to watch, so I followed. She traced the back lawns around town—the bucket cutting through the long grass. When she cut in and crossed over to the church, I stayed behind a tree. I saw her walk up to the front entrance like she might go in and have a seat. But she stopped, stood straight for a few seconds, concentrating or whispering or just staring. Then she brought the bucket back and slung its contents at the door. The muddy foam sprayed out against the siding. From across the street, it looked like a wound, a brown gash. I don't know if it made a sound, if anyone heard or saw it. If they did, they stayed in the pews and kept worshipping. Mom walked back home, right down the street, with the empty bucket dangling. Later that day, I heard her sobbing in her room.

After that, Mom stayed in the house. She set up a garden in the dining room and kept the windows open to let the herbs feel the wind. When we'd get home from school, she'd make us read aloud from old storybooks, textbooks, even mathematics, which I detested. She'd make me recite equations while she tapped a rhythm on the chair. Once I read a whole chapter from my history textbook, which made her double over in laughter. She covered her face and howled into her palms. She kept saying, "Don't stop. Keep going!" Every other paragraph or so, she'd start up again. Dilly and Tobias stood beside her wagging, maybe enjoying the sound of it all, maybe sharing a joke that I didn't get. She showed us how to read upside down, how to use rainwater to make tea, how to rub herbs in our hands and bring them to life. She talked about that smell—when a leaf releases its scent into the air. The whole world, she said, changes when that happens.

30 As soon as she was able, Martha left. She couldn't take the hounding from the farm boys and their mothers. "Cows!" she said. "I'd rather talk with cows."

She meandered around out West for a few years. Then, at nineteen, she fell in love with Canada and settled in the Alberta wilderness. She wrote letters and sent stacks of photos. Mom and I would sit in the living room—Dilly and Tobias at our side—waving to the mini Marthas standing in front of mountains and spiky northern trees. With each envelope, Martha's hair grew longer—and then way longer.

I went to school for a while, had a few jobs, a pretty good one in Toledo. Then I came back here to help Mom. The house seemed too big. Toward the end, she had me bring plants into her room. They were lined up on the floor and squeezed onto the shelves and dresser. They thrived in there and created a canopy above her bed. The bending stalks and arching branches eclipsed the ceiling. The air was thick with soil and plant breath. It was like that for a few years, and then this past spring, surrounded by vines and protruding leaves, Mom died. I went to her room in the morning and brushed the leaves from her face. She'd had a full life. Even though Dad died many years ago, right after I was born, Mom still had Martha, me, Dilly and Tobias. I once conjured up the notion that Dad and Uncle Ralph were inside those dogs—watching and panting and making sure.

Toward the end, I asked questions. I wanted to know about everything from the curse to the plants, where it all came from, who we were, why we lived on the edge of everything and everyone else. She'd tell me not to wonder backwards. But I came to some conclusions of my own. I scraped back into history and found that our father was Irish—born of Ferricks and Tallys—that Mom came from Holloways and Muellers. She was double Dutch. There were some Muellers around, out toward Montpelier, but they're gone now. So it's just me—me and what I've kept around, what I've pieced together from memory and reflex. I don't have Mom's force, her clarity and understanding. But I know some things. For instance, I know that all your senses can fool you—all except your nose, which sits there in the center and never lies. I know that plants are always reaching for us, that if we'd stay in one place long enough, they'd finally wrap their arms around us and welcome us home, and I know that plenty of people have been cursed. I can see how they lumber along, fighting against their own muscles and bones. I can tell just like a dog knows when you're sick and a horse knows about the winter ahead. I can see a curse from a hundred yards away—the greasy shimmer around all the effort. I also know that a curse drains something away from the person who delivers it. It's not quite like a bee giving up its stinger, but it's close. And once a curse goes out, it's gone. You can't take it back any more than you can stop a rock in mid air.

Two weeks from now, I'm going up to see Martha, her husband, and their two children, Dane and Veronica. It'll take days of quiet driving. I'll leave here, shoot up through Michigan, cross the big bridge and turn left. I'll go west and then slip north into Canada. I've done it every year for years. Each visit, Martha seems more like Mom, calm and balanced. Her home, a tiny cabin surrounded by dinosaur-sized pine trees, feels crowded with contentment and wonder. Her husband is a lofty Norwegian who talks to Martha and the children as though they're all pieces of sacred glass. They have three dogs that watch over the family like fussy mothers.

I won't tell her about David Manville. I doubt that it would translate. It'd al- 35
most take another language—as though these words, the ones we are using now, wouldn't work up there, as though the tragedy that haunts the Polks and Housmans and Manvilles would peel off and fall away. Sorrow belongs only in some places, only on the shoulders of some children.

RESPONDING TO READING

1. The narrator chronicles the history and effects of his mother's "curse" and shares memories of how his mother protected the family when he was growing up. How do these events shape your understanding of the narrator's mother, and of the narrator?
2. Toward the end of the story, the narrator says, "So it's just me—me and what I've kept around, what I've pieced together from memory and reflex" (33) Does this statement make the narrator more or less reliable? Explain.

Rhetorical Analysis

How does the curse described in the story function as a metaphor? What does it signify beyond its literal meaning? Where do family "curses" originate, and how does our understanding of them affect our memories?

3.3 E. B. White, "Once More to the Lake"

Well known for his children's stories, Elwyn Brooks White (1899–1985) was also a talented essayist and a witty observer of contemporary society. His expansion of Will Strunk's *The Elements of Style* remains one of the most popular and concise grammar and style texts in use today. White wrote for the *The New Yorker* and *Harper's Magazine*, and his essays are collected in *Essays of E. B. White* (1977). In 1939, he moved to a farm in North Brooklin, Maine, where he wrote the children's classics *Stuart Little* (1945) and *Charlotte's Web* (1952). As a youth, White vacationed with his family on a lake in Maine. It is to this lake that he returned with his son, and he describes his experience in the following essay.

BEFORE YOU READ

Think about a place that was important to you as a child. How specifically did you feel about that place as a child? Do you feel differently about it now? Explain.

Once More to the Lake

One summer, along about 1904, my father rented a camp on a lake in Maine and took us all there for the month of August. We all got ringworm from some kittens and had to rub Pond's Extract on our arms and legs night and morning, and my father rolled over in a canoe with all his clothes on; but outside of that the vacation was a success and from then on none of us ever thought there was any place in the world like that lake in Maine. We returned summer after summer—always on August 1st for one month. I have since become a salt-water man, but sometimes in summer there are days when the restlessness of the tides and the fearful cold of the sea water and the incessant wind which blows across the afternoon and into the evening make me wish for the placidity of a lake in the woods. A few weeks ago this feeling got so strong I bought myself a couple of bass hooks and a spinner and returned to the lake where we used to go, for a week's fishing and to revisit old haunts.

I took along my son, who had never had any fresh water up his nose and who had seen lily pads only from train windows. On the journey over to the lake I began to wonder what it would be like. I wondered how time would have marred this unique, this holy spot—the coves and streams, the hills that the sun set behind, the camps and the paths behind the camps. I was sure the tarred road would have found it out and I wondered in what other ways it would be desolated. It is strange how much you can remember about places like that once you allow your mind to return into the grooves which lead back. You remember one thing, and that suddenly reminds you of another thing. I guess I remembered clearest of all the early mornings, when the lake was cool and motionless, remembered how the bedroom smelled of the lumber it was made of and of the wet woods whose scent entered through the screen. The partitions in the camp were thin and did not extend clear to the top of the rooms, and as I was always the first up I would dress softly so as not to wake the others, and sneak out into the sweet outdoors and start out in the canoe, keeping close along the shore in the long shadows of the pines. I remembered being very careful never to rub my paddle against the gunwale for fear of disturbing the stillness of the cathedral.

The lake had never been what you would call a wild lake. There were cottages sprinkled around the shores, and it was in farming country although the shores of the lake were quite heavily wooded. Some of the cottages were owned by nearby farmers, and you would live at the shore and eat your meals at the farmhouse. That's what our family did. But although it wasn't wild, it was a fairly large and undisturbed lake and there were places in it which, to a child at least, seemed infinitely remote and primeval.

I was right about the tar: it led to within half a mile of the shore. But when I got back there, with my boy, and we settled into a camp near a farmhouse and into the kind of summertime I had known, I could tell that it was going to be pretty much the same as it had been before—I knew it, lying in bed the first morning, smelling the bedroom, and hearing the boy sneak quietly out and go off along the shore in a boat. I began to sustain the illusion that he was I, and therefore, by simple transposition, that I was my father. This sensation persisted, kept cropping up all the time we were there. It was not an entirely new feeling, but in this setting it grew much stronger. I seemed to be living a dual existence. I would be in the middle of some simple act, I would be picking up a bait box or laying down a table fork, or I would be saying something, and suddenly it would be not I but my father who was saying the words or making the gesture. It gave me a creepy sensation.

We went fishing the first morning. I felt the same damp moss covering the 5 worms in the bait can, and saw the dragonfly alight on the tip of my rod as it hovered a few inches from the surface of the water. It was the arrival of this fly that convinced me beyond any doubt that everything was as it always had been, that the years were a mirage and there had been no years. The small waves were the same, chucking the rowboat under the chin as we fished at anchor, and the boat was the same boat, the same color green and the ribs broken in the same places, and under the floor-boards the same freshwater leavings and débris—the dead helgramite,[1] the wisps of moss, the rusty discarded fishhook, the dried blood from yesterday's catch. We stared silently at the tips of our rods, at the dragonflies that came and went. I lowered the tip of mine into the water, tentatively, pensively dislodging the fly, which darted two feet away, poised, darted two feet back, and came to rest again a little farther up the rod. There had been no years between the ducking of this dragonfly and the other one—the one that was part of memory. I looked at the boy, who was silently watching his fly, and it was my hands that held his rod, my eyes watching. I felt dizzy and didn't know which rod I was at the end of.

We caught two bass, hauling them in briskly as though they were mackerel, pulling them over the side of the boat in a businesslike manner without any landing net, and stunning them with a blow on the back of the head. When we got back for a swim before lunch, the lake was exactly where we had left it, the same number of inches from the dock, and there was only the merest suggestion of a breeze. This seemed an utterly enchanted sea, this lake you could leave to its own devices for a few hours and come back to, and find that it had not stirred, this constant and trustworthy body of water. In the shallows, the dark, water-soaked sticks and twigs, smooth and old, were undulating in clusters on the bottom against the clean ribbed sand, and the track of the mussel was plain. A school of minnows swam by, each minnow with its small individual shadow, doubling the attendance, so clear and sharp in the sunlight. Some of the other campers were in swimming, along the shore, one of them with a cake of soap, and the water felt thin and clear and unsubstantial. Over the years there had been this person with the cake of soap, this cultist, and here he was. There had been no years.

Up to the farmhouse to dinner through the teeming, dusty field, the road under our sneakers was only a two-track road. The middle track was missing, the one with the marks of the hooves and the splotches of dried, flaky manure. There had always been three tracks to choose from in choosing which track to walk in; now the choice was narrowed down to two. For a moment I missed terribly the middle alternative. But the way led past the tennis court, and something about the

[1]The nymph of the May-fly, used as bait. [Eds.]

way it lay there in the sun reassured me; the tape had loosened along the backline, the alleys were green with plantains and other weeds, and the net (installed in June and removed in September) sagged in the dry noon, and the whole place steamed with midday heat and hunger and emptiness. There was a choice of pie for dessert, and one was blueberry and one was apple, and the waitresses were the same country girls, there having been no passage of time, only the illusion of it as in a dropped curtain—the waitresses were still fifteen; their hair had been washed, that was the only difference—they had been to the movies and seen the pretty girls with the clean hair.

Summertime, oh summertime, pattern of life indelible, the fade-proof lake, the woods unshatterable, the pasture with the sweetfern and the juniper forever and ever, summer without end; this was the background, and the life along the shore was the design, the cottagers with their innocent and tranquil design, their tiny docks with the flagpole and the American flag floating against the white clouds in the blue sky, the little paths over the roots of the trees leading from camp to camp and the paths leading back to the outhouses and the can of lime for sprinkling, and at the souvenir counters at the store the miniature birch-bark canoes and the post cards that showed things looking a little better than they looked. This was the American family at play, escaping the city heat, wondering whether the newcomers in the camp at the head of the cove were "common" or "nice," wondering whether it was true that the people who drove up for Sunday dinner at the farmhouse were turned away because there wasn't enough chicken.

It seemed to me, as I kept remembering all this, that those times and those summers had been infinitely precious and worth saving. There had been jollity and peace and goodness. The arriving (at the beginning of August) had been so big a business in itself, at the railway station the farm wagon drawn up, the first smell of the pine-laden air, the first glimpse of the smiling farmer, and the great importance of the trunks and your father's enormous authority in such matters, and the feel of the wagon under you for the long ten-mile haul, and at the top of the last long hill catching the first view of the lake after eleven months of not seeing this cherished body of water. The shouts and cries of the other campers when they saw you, and the trunks to be unpacked, to give up their rich burden. (Arriving was less exciting nowadays, when you sneaked up in your car and parked it under a tree near the camp and took out the bags and in five minutes it was all over, no fuss, no loud wonderful fuss about trunks.)

10 Peace and goodness and jollity. The only thing that was wrong now, really, was the sound of the place, an unfamiliar nervous sound of the outboard motors. This was the note that jarred, the one thing that would sometimes break the illusion and set the years moving. In those other summertimes all motors were inboard; and when they were at a little distance, the noise they made was a sedative, an ingredient of summer sleep. They were one-cylinder and two-cylinder engines, and some were make-and-break and some were jump-spark,[2] but they all made a sleepy sound across the lake. The one-lungers throbbed and fluttered, and the twin-cylinder ones purred and purred, and that was a quiet sound too.

---

[2]Methods of ignition timing. [Eds.]

But now the campers all had outboards. In the daytime, in the hot mornings, these motors made a petulant, irritable sound; at night, in the still evening when the afterglow lit the water, they whined about one's ears like mosquitoes. My boy loved our rented outboard, and his great desire was to achieve singlehanded mastery over it, and authority, and he soon learned the trick of choking it a little (but not too much), and the adjustment of the needle valve. Watching him I would remember the things you could do with the old one-cylinder engine with the heavy flywheel, how you could have it eating out of your hand if you got really close to it spiritually. Motor boats in those days didn't have clutches, and you would make a landing by shutting off the motor at the proper time and coasting in with a dead rudder. But there was a way of reversing them, if you learned the trick, by cutting the switch and putting it on again exactly on the final dying revolution of the flywheel, so that it would kick back against compression and begin reversing. Approaching a dock in a strong following breeze, it was difficult to slow up sufficiently by the ordinary coasting method, and if a boy felt he had complete mastery over his motor, he was tempted to keep it running beyond its time and then reverse it a few feet from the dock. It took a cool nerve, because if you threw the switch a twentieth of a second too soon you would catch the flywheel when it still had speed enough to go up past center, and the boat would leap ahead, charging bull-fashion at the dock.

We had a good week at the camp. The bass were biting well and the sun shone endlessly, day after day. We would be tired at night and lie down in the accumulated heat of the little bedrooms after the long hot day and the breeze would stir almost imperceptibly outside and the smell of the swamp drift in through the rusty screens. Sleep would come easily and in the morning the red squirrel would be on the roof, tapping out his gay routine. I kept remembering everything, lying in bed in the mornings—the small steamboat that had a long rounded stern like the lip of a Ubangi, and how quietly she ran on the moonlight sails, when the older boys played their mandolins and the girls sang and we ate doughnuts dipped in sugar, and how sweet the music was on the water in the shining night, and what it had felt like to think about girls then. After breakfast we would go up to the store and the things were in the same place—the minnows in a bottle, the plugs and spinners disarranged and pawed over by the youngsters from the boys' camp, the fig newtons and the Beeman's gum. Outside, the road was tarred and cars stood in front of the store. Inside, all was just as it had always been, except there was more Coca-Cola and not so much Moxie and root beer and birch beer and sarsaparilla. We would walk out with a bottle of pop apiece and sometimes the pop would backfire up our noses and hurt. We explored the streams, quietly, where the turtles slid off the sunny logs and dug their way into the soft bottom; and we lay on the town wharf and fed worms to the tame bass. Everywhere we went I had trouble making out which was I, the one walking at my side, the one walking in my pants.

One afternoon while we were there at that lake a thunderstorm came up. It was like the revival of an old melodrama that I had seen long ago with childish awe. The second-act climax of the drama of the electrical disturbance over a lake in America had not changed in any important respect. This was the big scene, still the big scene. The whole thing was so familiar, the first feeling of oppression and heat and a general air around camp of not wanting to go very far away. In midafternoon (it was all the same) a curious darkening of the sky, and a lull in everything that had made life tick; and then the way the boats suddenly swung the other way at their moorings with the coming of a breeze out of the new quarter, and the premonitory rumble. Then the kettle drum, then the snare, then the bass drum and cymbals, then crackling light against the dark, and the gods grinning and licking their chops in the hills. Afterward the calm, the rain steadily rustling in the calm lake, the return of light and hope and spirits, and the campers running out in joy and relief to go swimming in the rain, their bright cries perpetuating the deathless joke about how they were getting simply drenched, and the children screaming with delight at the new sensation of bathing in the rain, and the joke about getting drenched linking the generations in a strong indestructible chain. And the comedian who waded in carrying an umbrella.

When the others went swimming my son said he was going in too. He pulled his dripping trunks from the line where they had hung all through the shower, and wrung them out. Languidly, and with no thought of going in, I watched him, his hard little body, skinny and bare, saw him wince slightly as he pulled up around his vitals the small, soggy, icy garment. As he buckled the swollen belt suddenly my groin felt the chill of death.

RESPONDING TO READING

1. How is White's "holy spot" different when he visits it with his son from how it was when he visited it with his father?
2. Why does White feel "the chill of death" as he watches his son? Do you identify more with White the father or White the son?

Rhetorical Analysis

Is White's primary purpose to write about a time, a place, or a relationship? Explain.

Writing with Sources

Locate a few sources—including some photographs—that focus on a place that was important to you as a child. Write an essay that compares your childhood impression of the place with the impression you get from the sources you find.

3.4 Kristin Ohlson, "The Great Forgetting"

A journalist, essayist, and fiction writer, Kristin Ohlson (1951–) explores topics ranging from food and the environment to travel and women's rights. Writing for publications such as *Aeon, Gourmet, Ms., New Scientist, The New York Times, Salon,* and *Utne,* she is also the author of three books, including, most recently, *The Soil Will Save Us* (2014). In the following essay, Ohlson considers the elusive nature of memory.

BEFORE YOU READ

What is your earliest childhood memory? Why do you think this particular memory has remained with you while so many others have not?

The Great Forgetting

I'm the youngest by far of five children. My mother was 35 when she conceived me in 1951, so chagrined by this chronological indiscretion that she tried to hide the pregnancy from her sister. My mortified oldest brother didn't want to tell his high-school friends that a new baby was on the way, but it was a small town. Word spread.

My mother's age and my late arrival in the family felt burdensome to me too, especially when I started school in 1957 and met my classmates' mothers. They were still having babies! Still piling their children into cars and heading off to picnics at the river or hikes into the lava-capped, wild flower-rampant plateau outside town. They still had to mediate hair-pulling and toy-snatching. But by the time I started first grade, my siblings were gone, the oldest three to college and the youngest to a residential school four hours away, and we went from a very noisy household to a very quiet one.

My family has told me stories about those years before everything changed. How my oldest brother nicknamed me "Ubangi" because my hair grew in tight fat curls close to my head. How my other brother liked to ambush me around corners with a toy crocodile because it never failed to make me shriek in terror. How my oldest sister carried me around like a kangaroo with her joey. But I can offer very few stories of my own from those early years.

My strongest recollection is a constant straining to be with my brothers and sisters. I remember having to go to bed when it was still light out, kicking at the sheets as I listened for their voices coming down the hall or through the windows from the back yard. Sometimes I could smell popcorn. The next morning, I'd search the living room rug for their leftovers and roll the unpopped kernels around in my mouth. I do remember that, probably because it was something that played out night after night—our father loved popcorn.

5 Several years ago, I thought I might have the chance to recover that lost past when we were all tightly clustered together in one house. My brothers had driven to Bucks Lake up in the Sierras of northeastern California where, until I was around three years old, our family had leased a house every summer to escape the Sacramento Valley heat. They found our old cabin unchanged. Even a table built by a local sawmill was still in the living room. They knocked on the door and, weirdly enough, my younger brother knew the current lessee. He invited them in and then invited the rest of us back for a look.

With our father, we set off a few months later, up highways that narrowed into dusty roads through dark pines and past bright stony summits. When we got to the cabin, my siblings scattered to claim their favourite outdoor spots, but I was rooted near the car, struck by how much this place differed from what I thought I remembered.

I recalled that the water was a long walk across a sandy beach from the house; I had an image of my mother standing on that wide beach, her dress whipped by the wind, her hand cupped near her mouth. But the pebbled shoreline was just a few feet away. I recalled the spine of a dam jutting from the water not far from the house, a perilous and sudden cliff at the edge of the lake that my siblings had once ventured too close to. But even though the lake is a man-made one, the dam wasn't visible from the house. I followed my father inside, where the tininess of the kitchen fascinated him. He kept opening cabinet doors and laughing as they banged each other in the narrow aisle. "Mother just hated this kitchen!" he said. "She always made big breakfasts—eggs and sausage and pancakes—and as soon as she finished cleaning up, you kids would come running back in the house wanting lunch."

I didn't remember that. I didn't remember the table. I didn't remember anything about the place. My siblings tugged me through the house, pointing out where everyone had slept—they said I had been in a little alcove in the hallway, though I recalled staying in my parents' room and watching them sleep in the early morning light. They pointed out other features tied to the life that we all lived in the cabin, eager for me to remember, but there was nothing. I even dropped to my knees and circled the living room at toddler level, peering at dusty windowsills and sniffing at the knotholes in the pine walls and running my fingers over the floorboards. Nothing.

I now know that it would have been unusual for me to remember anything from that time. Hardly any adult does. There is even a term for this—childhood amnesia, coined by Sigmund Freud in 1910—to describe the lack of recall adults have of their first three or four years and our paucity of solid memories until around the age of seven. There has been some back and forth over a century of research about whether memories of these early years are tucked away in some part of our brains and need only a cue to be recovered. That's what I was hoping when I revisited our old cabin with my siblings. I intended to jostle out a recalcitrant memory with the sights, sounds, smells and touch of the place. But research suggests that the memories we form in these early years simply disappear.

10 Freud argued that we repress our earliest memories because of sexual trauma but, until the 1980s, most researchers assumed that we retained no memories of early childhood because we created no memories—that events took place and passed without leaving a lasting imprint on our baby brains. Then in 1987, a study by the Emory University psychologist Robyn Fivush and her colleagues dispelled that misconception for good, showing that children who were just 2.5 years old could describe events from as far as six months into their past.

But what happens to those memories? Most of us assume that we can't recall them as adults because they're just too far back in our past to tug into the present, but this is not the case. We lose them when we're still children.

The psychologist Carole Peterson of Memorial University of Newfoundland has conducted a series of studies to pinpoint the age at which these memories vanish. First, she and her colleagues assembled a group of children between the ages of four and 13 to describe their three earliest memories. The children's parents stood by to verify that the memories were, indeed, true, and even the very youngest of the children could recall events from when they were around two years old.

Then the children were interviewed again two years later to see if anything had changed. More than a third of those age 10 and older retained the memories they had offered up for the first study. But the younger children—especially the very youngest who had been four years old in the first study—had gone largely blank. "Even when we prompted them about their earlier memories, they said: 'No, that never happened to me,'" Peterson told me. "We were watching childhood amnesia in action."

In both children and adults, memory is bizarrely selective about what adheres and what falls away. In one of her papers, Peterson trots out a story about her own son and a childhood memory gone missing. She had taken him to Greece when he was 20 months old, and, while there, he became very excited about some donkeys. There was family discussion of those donkeys for at least a year. But by the time he went to school, he had completely forgotten about them. He was queried when he was a teenager about his earliest childhood memory and, instead of the remarkable Greek donkeys, he recalled a moment not long after the trip to Greece when a woman gave him lots of cookies while her husband showed the boy's parents around a house they planned to buy.

15 Peterson has no idea why he would remember *that*—it was a completely unremarkable moment and one that the family hadn't reinforced with domestic chitchat. To try to get a handle on why some memories endure over others, she and her colleagues studied the children's memories again. They concluded that if the memory was a very emotional one, children were three times more likely to retain it two years later. Dense memories—if they understood the who, what, when, where and why—were five times more likely to be retained than disconnected fragments. Still, oddball and inconsequential memories such as the bounty of cookies will hang on, frustrating the person who wants a more penetrating look at their early past.

To form long-term memories, an array of biological and psychological stars must align, and most children lack the machinery for this alignment. The raw material of memory—the sights, sounds, smells, tastes and tactile sensations of our life experiences—arrive and register across the cerebral cortex, the seat of cognition. For these to become memory, they must undergo bundling in the hippocampus, a brain structure named for its supposed resemblance to a sea horse, located under the cerebral cortex. The hippocampus not only bundles multiple input from our senses together into a single new memory, it also links these sights, sounds, smells, tastes, and tactile sensations to similar ones already stored in the brain. But some parts of the hippocampus aren't fully developed until we're adolescents, making it hard for a child's brain to complete this process.

"So much has to happen biologically to store a memory," the psychologist Patricia Bauer of Emory University told me. There's "a race to get it stabilised and consolidated before you forget it. It's like making Jell-O: you mix the stuff up, you put it in a mould, and you put it in the refrigerator to set, but your mould has a tiny hole in it. You just hope your Jell-O—your memory—gets set before it leaks out through that tiny hole."

In addition, young children have a tenuous grip on chronology. They are years from mastering clocks and calendars, and thus have a hard time nailing an event to a specific time and place. They also don't have the vocabulary to describe an event, and without that vocabulary, they can't create the kind of causal narrative that Peterson found at the root of a solid memory. And they don't have a greatly elaborated sense of self, which would encourage them to hoard and reconsider chunks of experience as part of a growing life-narrative.

Frail as they are, children's memories are then susceptible to a process called shredding. In our early years, we create a storm of new neurons in a part of the hippocampus called the dentate gyrus and continue to form them throughout the rest of our lives, although not at nearly the same rate. A recent study by the neuroscientists Paul Frankland and Sheena Josselyn of the Hospital for Sick Children in Toronto suggests that this process, called neurogenesis, can actually create forgetting by disrupting the circuits for existing memories.

20 Our memories can become distorted by other people's memories of the same event or by new information, especially when that new information is so similar to information already in storage. For instance, you meet someone and remember their name, but later meet a second person with a similar name, and become confused about the name of the first person. We can also lose our memories when the synapses that connect neurons decay from disuse. "If you never use that memory, those synapses can be recruited for something different," Bauer told me.

Memories are less vulnerable to shredding and disruptions as the child grows up. Most of the solid memories that we carry into the rest of our lives are formed during what's called "the reminiscence bump," from ages 15 to 30, when we invest a lot of energy in examining everything to try to figure out who we are. The events, culture and people of that time remain with us and can even overshadow the features of our ageing present, according to Bauer. The movies were the best back then, and so was the music, and the fashion, and the political leaders, and the friendships, and the romances. And so on.

Of course, some people have more memories from early childhood than others do. It appears that remembering is partly influenced by the culture of family engagement. A 2009 study conducted by Peterson together with Qi Wang of Cornell and Yubo Hou of Peking University found that children in China have fewer of these memories than children in Canada. The finding, they suggest, might be explained by culture: Chinese people prize individuality less than North Americans and thus may be less likely to spend as much time drawing attention to the moments of an individual's life. Canadians, by contrast, reinforce recollection and keep the synapses that underlie early personal memories vibrant. Another study, by the psychologist Federica Artioli and colleagues at the University of Otago in New Zealand in 2012, found that young adults from Italian extended families had earlier and denser memories than those from Italian nuclear families, presumably as a result of more intense family reminiscence.

But it doesn't necessarily take a crowd of on-site relatives to enhance a child's recollection. Bauer's research also points to "maternal deflections of conversation," meaning that the mother (or another adult) engages the child in a lively conversation about events, always passing the baton of remembering back to the child and inviting him or her to contribute to the story. "That kind of interaction contributes to the richness of memory over a long period of time," Bauer told me. "It doesn't predict whether a given event will be remembered, but it builds a muscle. The child learns how to have memories and understands what part to share. Over the course of these conversations, the child learns how to tell the story."

Borrowing Bauer's Jell-O analogy, I've always suspected that my mother had a tinier hole in her Jell-O mould than mine, which allowed her to retain information until it was set into memory. She seemed to remember everything from my childhood, from my siblings' childhoods, and from her own first six years. Intensely, she recalled the fight between her mother and father, when her mother wound up getting knocked out cold and her father forced her to tell visiting neighbours that his wife was sleeping. The day my grandmother packed up my mother and her sister and moved them from Nebraska to Nevada, with their unwanted household goods strewn across their lawn for the townspeople to pick through and haggle over. The day the doctor took out my mother's appendix on the kitchen table. The day she wet her pants at school and the nuns made her walk home in weather so cold that her underwear froze. I wondered if her memories were so sharp because these were all terrible events, especially compared with my presumably bland early years.

25 I now suspect that my mother's ability to tell the story of her early life also came from the constellation of people clustered at the centre of it. Her young mother, bolting from a marriage she was pressured into and retreating to her brother's crowded house, her two girls held close. And her sister, three years older, always the point and counterpoint, the question and response. My mother and her sister talked their lives over to such an extent that it must have seemed as if things didn't really happen unless they had confided them to each other. Thus,

"Don't tell Aunt Helen!" was whispered in our house when something went wrong, echoed by "Don't tell Aunt Kathleen!" in our cousins' house when something went amiss there.

I might have a very large hole in my Jell-O mould, but I also wonder if our family's storytelling and memory-setting apparatus had broken down by the time I came along. My brothers and sisters doted on me—I'm told this and I believe it—but it was their job to be out in the world riding horses and playing football and winning spelling bees and getting into various kinds of trouble, not talking to the baby. And sometime between my being born and my siblings leaving, our mother suffered a breakdown that plunged her into 20 years of depression and agoraphobia. She could go to the grocery store only with my father close to her side, steering the cart, list in hand. Even when she went to the beauty salon to have her hair cut and styled and sprayed into submission, my father sat next to her reading his *Wall Street Journal* as she cured under one of those bullet-head dryers. When we were home, she spent a lot of time in her room. No one really knows when my mother's sadness and retreat from the world began—and she's not around to tell us now—but it might have started when I was very young. What I remember is silence.

Our first three to four years are the maddeningly, mysteriously blank opening pages to our story of self. As Freud said, childhood amnesia "veils our earliest youth from us and makes us strangers to it." During that time, we transition from what my brother-in-law calls "a loaf of bread with a nervous system" to sentient humans. If we can't remember much of anything from those years—whether abuse or exuberant cherishing—does it matter what actually happened? If a tree fell in the forest of our early development and we didn't have the brains and cognitive tools to stash the event in memory, did it still help shape who we are?

Bauer says yes. Even if we don't remember early events, they leave an imprint on the way we understand and feel about ourselves, other people, and the greater world, for better or worse. We have elaborate concepts about birds, dogs, lakes and mountains, for example, even if we can't recall the experiences that created those concepts. "You can't remember going ice-skating with Uncle Henry, but you understand that skating and visiting relatives are fun," Bauer explained. "You have a feeling for how nice people are, how reliable they are. You might never be able to pinpoint how you learnt that, but it's just something you know."

And we are not the sum of our memories, or at least, not entirely. We are also the story we construct about ourselves, our personal narrative that interprets and assigns meaning to the things we do remember and the things other people tell us about ourselves. Research by the Northwestern University psychologist Dan McAdams, author of *The Redemptive Self* (2005), suggests that these narratives guide our behaviour and help chart our path into the future. Especially lucky are those of us with redemptive stories, in which we find good fortune even in past adversity.

So our stories are not bald facts etched on stone tablets. They are narratives that move and morph, and that's the underpinning to much of talk therapy. And here is one uplifting aspect of ageing: our stories of self get better. "For whatever reason, we tend to accentuate the positive things more as we age," McAdams told me. "We have a greater willingness or motivation to see the world in brighter terms. We develop a positivity bias regarding our memories."

I can't make myself remember my early life with my siblings nearby and my mother before her breakdown, even if I revisit the mountain idyll where the summers of that life unfolded. But I can employ the kinder lens of ageing and the research by these memory scientists to limn a story on those blank pages that is not stained with loss.

I am by nature trusting and optimistic, traits that I've sometimes worried are signs of intellectual weakness, but I can choose to interpret them as approaches to the world developed by myriad, if unrecalled, experiences with a loving family in those early years. I don't remember, but I can choose to imagine myself on my siblings' laps as they read me stories or sang me songs or showed me the waving arms of a crawdad from that mountain lake. I can imagine myself on their shoulders, fingers twined in their curly Ohlson hair.

I can imagine them patiently feeding me the lines to *The Night Before Christmas*, over and over, hour after hour, day after day, because someone had to have done it—my mother told me that I could recite the whole poem when I was two years old. Not that they remember doing this, because most of them were teenagers by then and off having the kinds of encounters with people and culture that would define their sense of self for years to come. But I'll imagine and reconstruct it, both for me and for them. Because our pasts had to have had a lot of that kind of sweetness, given our lucky loving bonds today. We've just forgotten the details.

Source: "The great forgetting" by Kristin Ohlson. This essay was originally published in Aeon, aeon.co. Used with permission.

RESPONDING TO READING

1. What is childhood amnesia (9)? How does this concept fully explain why Ohlson has no memories of her family's old cabin?
2. What, specifically, does Ohlson learn from her interview with psychologist Patricia Bauer? What about from the work of psychologist Carole Peterson, from the 2009 study conducted by Peterson and her colleagues, and from the writing of psychologist Dan McAdams?

Rhetorical Analysis

Although Ohlson bases her explanations and conclusions about family and memory on summaries of scholarly research, she also includes her own childhood experiences. Why does she include this material? Do you find it helpful or distracting?

Writing with Sources

In a sense, memories are like snapshots: a series of disconnected candid images, often out of focus or gradually fading. Look through your family's photos and videos, and choose five or six key images from your childhood. Then, write an essay analyzing the similarities and differences between these images and your memories of the people, places, and events they capture.

3.5 Anne-Marie Oomen, "Decent Clothes, 1959"

Anne-Marie Oomen (1951–) is an instructor of creative writing at Interlochen College of Creative Arts and the Solstice MFA Program at Pine Manor College as well as the writer-in-residence at Interlochen's Writers Retreat. A memoirist, essayist, poet, and playwright, she is the author of six acclaimed books, including, most recently, the collaboration *The Lake Michigan Mermaid: A Tale in Poems* (2018). Her memoir *Love, Sex, and 4-H* (2015), from which the following excerpt is taken, won the 2016 Next Generation Indie Award for Best Memoir. In the following essay, Oomen explores the intersection of language and memory in family storytelling.

BEFORE YOU READ

What do you now know about your parents' responsibilities and sacrifices that you did not know when you were a child? How has this knowledge changed your feelings about your parents?

Decent Clothes, 1959

The first lesson is the dish towel.

Or an apron.

These are beginning sewing lessons in 4-H,[1] regular as a linen rectangle 15 inches by 30 inches, traditional as a yard of gingham check or a plain waistband. If the ties that loop like long roads at the back of the apron seem like extravagance, they are merely a small feminine extravagance. The lessons—a dish towel and an apron—at first appear logical and clear, and no one questions them; no one considers them deeply at all, certainly not a child of eight.

In the fall of 1959, no whiff of feminism or cultural unrest, let alone uprising, has yet driven down those gravel roads to the farms of Oceana County and my mother's

[1] A nonprofit organization and series of educational programs for youth, founded in 1902 in Ohio. [Eds.]

domain. In our farmhouse, the simple majority of four females to three males means only that my mother must be more watchful of the dangers to her three daughters. My mother knows this, especially knows my weaknesses, and wants me focused on *good behavior.* She wants me to have practical skills and someday be a fine *wife and mother.* Perhaps most of all, I need to learn to be *efficient and self-sacrificing.* She knows already these qualities are not housed anywhere in my nature. Sometimes she says things to me as though I am someone older. But most of the time, I am either too young for something or too big for my britches. My mother has a sharp eye on me: on the part of me that talks too loudly to strangers or plays alone for hours, has too many imaginary friends, lies in the grass and stares—the part of me that stares at everything, doesn't listen, and doesn't like to work.

5 She worries about all five of us because she wants us to *have it better.* Sometimes she tells me stories about going to school when she was my age, about other children who picked on her. When I ask why they did that, she goes quiet, then says, "Well, I didn't have decent clothes." And after a long pause, I hear the shadow in the silence.

The shadow is from her childhood. It is her family's barn burning and horses perishing in flames and then all the insurance transferred to the barn and then the house burning without any insurance and them living in a tiny house with no indoor plumbing. It is a brother dying. It is Grandpa drinking a little too much in order to get through it all. It is the shadow of little money. She doesn't want me to know about any of that. She makes a point of telling us how good Grandpa is, how he came all alone from Belgium to our country when he was twelve, the youngest of twelve, and how he went back to the "old country" to fight in the first World War—there were two?—then returned as a hired hand to win the hand of the farmer's daughter, my grandma Julia. It's only later that I learn that Grandpa Joe's mother died giving birth to him, that his oldest sister was his wet nurse, that there was no place, no land for him in the old country. That even here in this country, with hard work and land, they lost almost everything and had to struggle. She never wants that again; her fear is her secret shadow, except it's not secret.

Mom always invites Grandma and Grandpa to Sunday dinner, and my brothers love to play in the smoke of his cigarettes, the wreath of gray encircling him as he tells stories or jokes with my dad. Grandpa and Grandma look happy then, after the ham or chicken dinner, visiting, their faces like apples just going soft, still sweet but tough.

But sometimes the shadow comes into our rooms with my mother, and that is when her voice is sharp as vinegar. The word *shame* is undefined, unknowable, and more powerful than all the other words of that time. The shadow is made of that word. She has to keep us from being touched by it, from joining it. It is up to her alone: even my father, good as he is, cannot fight this. We all have to be better. Better than anyone imagined possible. So other words, hardworking words, fill up the house, but still they connect like threads to that unknown word, the one still in my future but always in her past.

This shadow word is behind all the other words, the good lesson words, though she isn't at all sure I have any talent for good. Still, it may be done. *Might as well get started now*. There's church, of course, but that's about the soul. She is more worried about keeping my hands busy with constructive work. Practical things are good things. *And so we'll just begin with that dish towel*, because maybe I am *a little young for the apron. We'll see how it goes. Maybe the apron next*.

10 Depends on how fast I catch on.

Eventually, decent clothes.

I look at our hand-me-downs, our church-box sweaters, and wonder how that will happen. But my mother has a plan: my mother has figured out a way to keep all the shadows at bay. It's called 4-H.

I am thrilled that a 4-H club is starting. On a farm where I am the first born of five, I have learned this already: even though I am not yet nine, I am separated from the others by the fact of being the oldest. I know already there are many kinds of loneliness, and being oldest is mine. But in 4-H, there will be a whole clan near my own age covering up the familiar scent of loneliness, of oldest-ness. There will be a *club*, with other boys and girls but mostly girls, and we will do things together.

And there is more news.

15 I will be guided by my own mother, another reason I can start learning to sew even though I am so young—so I will always have decent clothes, so I will know how to take care of myself. This is part of her plan, as straight as a line of stitching, as square as the grid of a township, as comforting as an old hymn. No one speaks of how the looping ties of the apron can catch in the wind and fly loose. Now one speaks of the shadows, the silent knowings.

Here are the knowings that come to me from the stories she tells us after supper or while she and Grandma peel the peaches for canning.

She was not always our mother. What? Because we have always all been here, haven't we, in this old farmhouse in Crystal Valley Township? Certainly my brothers, Tommy and Ricky, and I have been here. I can remember a time when there weren't little sisters, Marijo and Patti, but that doesn't really mean we weren't all here in this old farmhouse, does it? They were just someplace else. They are here now. I have thought of this other time but not in the way I am about to learn.

Mom tells us there was a time when she was very young. As young as we are. *When could that have been?* We sit around the scattered peach peelings, shoving the halves, round side up, into the jars. Yes, there was a time when she went to a one-room schoolhouse and washed the boards for the teacher, which meant she was the favorite, but she was lonely because she couldn't walk home with the other kids. I nod: I understand this. She loved school, she tells us pointedly, but before she finished high school, she left her parents' house, left it all suddenly. She does not tell us why, because it's almost time to *put those peaches into the canner*.

Where did you go?

20 She carries a case of jars to the kitchen.

Chicago. She says this over her shoulder.

Where is Chicago?

She's busy.

Another time: ice cream on a Sunday night. The sweet cream makes her tongue happy, and she talks. She tells us about the train to Chicago: how long it took, how it stopped at every town, how noisy it was. The man who meets her wears a red carnation. She had never seen a red carnation.

25 She tells us she went to work as a nanny.

She took care of other children. First one family, then another.

Stunning news. We look at each other and giggle but not because we think it's funny.

Were they good? Of course, Tom wants to know.

Well, they were little, but, yes, they were very good.

30 *In a big house.*

In a very big house.

Were they farmers?

No, they were bankers.

What on Earth are bankers?

35 Marijo is pounding on her high chair and making little songs.

Another time we learn how Mom came home. Grandma called her back after Grandpa had a terrible car accident. He was hurt so badly that she left that banker's children and took the train back to the farm to help. When Grandpa finally got better, she worked in the fruit orchards near Walkerville, saved all her cherry-picking money, and took the test to become a nurse, even though she hadn't finished high school.

We mull this over for a while, licking our spoons. This is the answer to another word that lives in our house, the word *education*. She never wants us to have to *pretend* like she did to take the nursing test. She tells us she passed all the tests, but it was hard, because she didn't have her algebra like the others. She passed and took nursing training in Manistee during the war, the second one. She worked in the hospitals. Sometimes she took care of soldiers who were coming home from the battles. Sometimes she took care of new babies.

Her face is happy.

Another time, late one stormy winter night when school has been called off for the next day and we are eating popcorn, dropping kernels all over the freshly swept floor and playing with the salt, which she asks us not to do, we ask her about the "olden days." She doesn't seem to mind. She tells us that she and Dad knew each other from childhood, that the two families were friends from church. *All those Dutch and Belgian families knew each other from the old country*, she tells us. She's Belgian; he's Dutch. So the families went back and forth, keeping company in the new country.

40 Here's the best one. The first time Mom and Dad went to the fair together, he asked her to marry him. She said they walked down the midway, and he said "Well, Toots, let's just get married." And they laughed their heads off. And we do, too, sitting around the table. We don't know what's funnier: that he called her *Toots*—we hoot the word around the table—or that he asked her to marry him when then they were just goofing off.

They were *just kids*.

Dad wanders into the dining room, listening to our giggles. He puts his hand on her shoulder, and she lifts her hand to touch his. I remember he still calls her Toots sometimes.

He went into the army to serve two tours and she forgot about him.

When I ask about how they got together again, they both get quiet. They smile at each other, but then Dad usually has to go to the barns or fix a machine in the shop. There is always a pause, and then she talks of something else: how they rented our old farmhouse from Grandpa Henry, Dad's father, who had bought it for the land, so the house was falling apart, and how finally, when they were fed up with renting, they bought it from him. Or how they never borrowed money. Or how everything is made from something else: machines, barns, clothes.

45 What I figure out is that she keeps secrets. How they got back together is one. It makes me want to know this story above all other stories. I want to know if my parents are like people in the stories I have learned to read or the TV shows I watch: *Walt Disney Presents* or *The Shirley Temple Fairy Tale Hour*. If there was a time when she was not our mother, when she was a nanny and a nurse, was she ever a princess to my father? Did she get wakened with a kiss? Does she ever still?

When I think about it, I don't believe it. My mother is wakened by laundry early in the morning, by my little sister crying in the night with a diaper rash, by the green beans not being picked on time, and by mumps, measles, chicken pox, and croup. Not a kiss. Not love. She doesn't have time. Or not much. She loves us when we are good: when we take our boots off before coming into the house, when we pick up our dirty clothes, when we somehow manage to get through church without crawling under the pews or getting into a tussle with each other. This applies to me particularly—not because I cause trouble but because I am not a good worker. I don't do much that is bad; I just don't do much that is *helpful*. I don't really believe I am good at anything much, but especially not the helpful part. But now, I wonder, is it possible, with this club, with luck, that I will learn to be useful?

Could I learn to make decent clothes?

RESPONDING TO READING

1. In paragraph 8, Oomen describes the power of the word *shame*, explaining, "So other words, hardworking words, fill up the house, but still they connect like threads to that unknown word, the one still in my future but always in her past." Later, in paragraph 37, Oomen mentions another word, *education*, that was meaningful in her childhood home. How does the language used at home define experiences and memories? How do these two words establish patterns of behavior and family expectations?
2. In paragraphs 6 and 45, Oomen considers the secrets her mother kept. What are these secrets? To what extent did Oomen understand them as a child, and how has her understanding shifted as she grew up? How does Oomen describe her changing view of her mother and of herself?

Rhetorical Analysis
Evaluate Oomen's introductory strategy. Why does she describe two sewing lessons here? How is this strategy consistent with the content and structure of her essay's last two paragraphs?

Writing with Sources
Research the history of the 4-H organization. What types of services does the organization provide? How are the organization's programs family-oriented? Based on your research, write an essay explaining why you think 4-H is (or is not) a valuable service for families and communities.

3.6 Jerry Dennis, "Lake Squall, 1967: When Salmon Anglers Encountered the Power of Lake Michigan"

A writer of fiction and nonfiction, Jerry Dennis (1954–) explores themes related to the environment in his work. The author of several books, he has also published numerous essays and short stories in publications such as *American Way, Gray's Sporting Journal, Michigan Quarterly Review, The New York Times, Orion,* and *Smithsonian.* In the following essay, Dennis recalls the mixed feelings he had about a traumatic event he witnessed on the shore of Lake Michigan.

BEFORE YOU READ

Think about an event from your childhood that, in retrospect, signals your transition into adulthood. How specifically did that event shape your view of yourself and your family?

Lake Squall, 1967: When Salmon Anglers Encountered the Power of Lake Michigan

When I was twelve years old I was eager for adventure. My family lived on Long Lake, where any ordinary day offered opportunities for exploration and discovery. But ordinary days bored me. I longed for uncommon experience. When storms chased the summer people inside their cottages, I wanted to be on the shore of

Lake Michigan, watching waves. I wanted a life filled with drama. And then one day I learned about drama.

It was August 1967 when Pacific salmon returned for the first time to Platte Bay. Nobody was quite prepared for them. The salmon had been released as smolts, and biologists thought there was a decent chance they would survive. But they did more than just survive. They scythed through the schools of alewives that filled the lake in those days. By the time they arrived in Platte Bay they weighed 15 to 20 pounds each and were ravenous. Any angler with a boat and a spinning rod could catch them.

I was 12 that summer, and had coho fever like everyone else. My family and I fished every weekend from mid-August through September. We launched our 14-foot runabout at the mouth of the Platte River and went out on the lake and caught our limit of salmon. We couldn't get enough. And to top it off, the weather was magnificent: bright and mild and nearly windless. Some days the lake was so calm that people fished from canoes.

Saturday, September 23, promised to be another fine day. Friday's forecast had given no indication of trouble: "Saturday partly cloudy and a little warmer, with a chance of showers near evening. Northerly winds... light and variable." Thousands of anglers finished work Friday, loaded their boats, and drove to Platte Bay.

5 But that night a shift in the jet stream brought an unexpected cold front down from Canada. At 4:30 that morning, when the alarm went off, I could hear the wind in the trees. My mother argued for staying home. Dad and I talked her into giving it a try.

At dawn we stood beside the tiny weather shack near the mouth of the Platte. A red pennant snapped in the wind above us. Small-craft warnings.

The phrase had potency to anyone who knew the Great Lakes. We had watched storms, had seen gigantic waves batter breakwalls and lighthouses. We had been out in three-foot waves that seemed like they could break our boat in half. Even much larger craft were at risk when the waves exceeded four or five feet.

To the west, the sky was dark with squall lines. The water was the color of steel and booming with whitecaps. During the drive to the Platte, we had listened to weather reports announcing waves two to three feet high and winds 25 knots and increasing.

Many anglers ignored the warnings. They had driven hours to get there; why let a few waves stop them? Besides, others were going out, hundreds of them. A general assumption was that small-craft warnings were a formality, a way the Coast Guard avoided liability in case someone ran into trouble. And one thing was certain: You couldn't catch fish on shore.

10 So they went out. The Coast Guard estimated that more than a thousand boats motored into the waves that morning. My father and I stood on shore with the wind in our faces and watched boat after boat motor down the river and meet the breakers at the mouth. Waves struck the bows of the boats and sent up explosions of spray. A few boats turned back and retreated upriver, their passengers shaking their heads in defeat. But for every one that returned there were a dozen waiting to challenge the waves.

All morning conditions worsened. By afternoon the wind had reached 40 miles per hour, and the waves were six to eight feet high. In some places they reached 25 feet. Yet hundreds of anglers stayed on the lake and fished. Then their boats began to swamp.

At first they tried to reach shore by motoring through the breakers at the mouth of the river. It was tricky, even in calm water. In the high waves, boats came in from all directions and wedged in the channel, collided with one another, turned sideways, swamped when waves broke over them. Soon dozens of boats were engulfed.

More timid boaters stood offshore. They circled, fighting the waves until they got up their courage and dashed for the beach. They came in fast, their engines screaming as the water fell beneath them, and ran aground. Six or eight of us on shore would run down with the descending wash and grab the boats by their gunwales and docking lines. The men inside jumped out to help and the women and children crouched against the decks with terrible looks on their faces, and we would pull the boats as far as we could up the streaming beach before they were slammed by the next wave. We were successful only with small boats. Larger ones were too heavy to pull. We would hold them as best as we could while they wallowed in the surge until a wave washed over their sterns and filled them with water and sand. A few waves later the boats would be capsized or anchored to the bottom.

Rumors ran up and down the beach. Hundreds missing, presumed dead. Dozens of bodies washed onto the beach near Frankfort. Boats sinking far out in the bay, beyond help.

Days later, we would learn that most of the missing had been accounted for 15
and that in reality seven men had died. It was a wonder. One rescuer said that of the 15 or 20 boats he helped drag onto the beach at Empire, only two contained life preservers.

There were heroics. Coast Guard helicopters lowered baskets to floundering anglers and lifted six of them to safety. Two men clung to the side of their capsized boat for more than two hours until they lost consciousness in the 50-degree water and were rescued somehow by people on shore who waded through the surf and pulled them to safety.

My father and I helped as much as we could. Dad had been a police officer and was trained to save lives. I knew he could rescue anyone in danger. The knowledge was exhilarating. It made me feel more competent just to be with him. I felt capable of adult heroics.

Somebody told us that people were in trouble at the boat ramp in Empire. We drove there to help and joined a small crowd on the beach. A boat with two men inside circled beyond the breakers. The men seemed unsure of themselves. They had watched others try to run the gauntlet of breaking waves and seemed to be looking for a way to save their boat. They circled, rising on each wave, disappearing into each trough, their heads swiveling as their boat turned, always facing shore. We could see them working up their courage. Finally they steered toward the beach. But instead of accelerating, they came cautiously, their engine at trolling speed. The boat went up on a wave, down in a trough, up on another wave. They went down in a trough and did not come up. When the wave passed, the two men were in the water.

They were so close to shore we could see the hair plastered to their scalps and could see the expressions on their faces. They looked more surprised than frightened. Their eyes were big and they worked their mouths, as if apologizing. They bobbed low in the water in their orange life preservers. Every time a wave came over them, they disappeared for a few moments in the froth.

20 Waves broke with so much force the ground shuddered. I stood on the beach above the wash and felt the booming thump of every wave through my feet. My shoes were soaked with water and full of sand and my socks had fallen around my heels.

The breakers shoved the men toward shore, then dragged them away again. They never got closer. A current pulled them down the beach away from us. We walked beside them, shielding our eyes from the spray and sand thrown at us by the wind. Every time a wave broke over the men, they tumbled in the foam. Sometimes they turned upside down and kicked their legs in the air as if trying to run. The wave would pass and they would struggle upright and get a few breaths before the next breaker came.

People on shore ran to the water's edge carrying coils of rope and tried to throw them. The ropes would shoot out and unfurl and hang for a moment in the wind, then come back. One man knotted a rope around his waist and waded into the waves but he was knocked down, and others pulled him to shore against his will.

Waves broke over the two men, one after another. With each wave they disappeared, and we saw only a glimpse of orange in the froth.

I had sand in my eyes. I turned away and rubbed them and turned back and saw the faces of the men in the water. I made eye contact with one of them. He was heavy and gray, the age of my grandfather. He seemed apologetic. I kept expecting him to smile at me and shrug. A wave would crash over him and after a few moments he would come up coughing and spitting water. Every time it happened, he looked a little more apologetic. A woman standing near me put her hands to her face and screamed for somebody to do something.

25 Children were excused from responsibility, but I was no longer a child. I was 12, nearly 13, old enough to help. I pitched on a baseball team and could have thrown a rope better than anyone on the beach. I could have heaved it low and hard beneath the wind and made it straighten like a bullwhip and land within reach of first one man, then the other. I was lean and fast and swam well. I could have tied a line around my waist and dived through the waves and reached the men in the calm of a trough and spoken reassuring words to them as the people on shore pulled us to safety.

A wave broke over them. Their legs rose in the air but did not kick. Another wave came and I could see two dark, slick objects rolling in the spume. My father gripped me high on my arm and turned me away. I tried to look back but he gripped harder and pulled. An ambulance waited in the parking lot, its lights flashing urgently. People ran past, shouting, their voices torn to fragments by the wind.

The men in the water wore bright orange life preservers with bulky collars designed to support their heads above the water. They should have been safe. Everyone said if you wore a life preserver, you were safe. It was an article of faith. Preserver of life. The Coast Guard guaranteed it. Our parents taught us to believe it.

But the heads of the men did not stay above the water. The preservers hadn't worked. The guarantee was not valid.

I had wanted to be a hero.

I had wanted drama in my life. 30

My father gripped my arm and pulled me across the parking lot past the ambulance, past people holding their faces in their hands. He put me in the car with my mother and brother and drove us home.

For weeks I lay in bed at night hearing the roar of the storm and feeling the awful draining power of the waves. I wanted to remain a child, but it was too late. Childhood fades with the knowledge of peril, and peril is everywhere. My father could not protect me from it. No life preserver could save me.

They died a hundred feet from shore.

Source: Jerry Dennis, Lake Squall, 1967: When Salmon Anglers Encountered the Power of Lake Michigan.

RESPONDING TO READING

1. This essay contrasts the innocence of childhood with the crises that define adult experience. List some of the contrasts Dennis identifies. What other differences exist between these two worlds?
2. How do you suppose Dennis's memories of this day in 1967 differ from his parents' memories?

Rhetorical Analysis

In paragraph 25, Dennis describes his physical fitness as a young man. Why does he include this information? What purpose does it serve?

Writing with Sources

Research a recent or historical event in which communities came together to help one another in a time of need. Then, write an essay in which you discuss the role children and young adults played in this event. How specifically might this event have helped to define their childhoods? How might it have shaped their memories as adults?

3.7 Tao Lin, "When I Moved Online…"

An essayist, fiction writer, poet, and graphic artist, Tao Lin (1983–) is the author of eleven books, including, most recently, *Trip: Psychedelics, Alienation, and Change* (2018). He is also the founder and editor of the small press publisher Muumuu House and the co-founder of the film company MDMAfilms. In "When I Moved Online…," Lin considers the role of the internet in shaping family relationships.

BEFORE YOU READ

How is your own use of the internet and social media different from that of your parents? Do you see a gap between yourself and your parents? Explain.

When I Moved Online…

I was born in 1983. My parents, in the mid-1990s, briefly knew more than I did about the Internet, I think (the bill from AOL must have required a credit card). But, as adults, with settled understandings of the world, they didn't integrate the Internet into their lives. For around five years, they seemed to use it mostly to check stock prices. The Internet remained nonessential and separate for them, like a vacation destination.

With me it was different. By my second year online, around 1996, I was obsessed with a multiplayer role-playing game called GemStone III, which was set in a virtual world, like Second Life, but without graphics, only text. I'd type "west," and text would appear describing the new surroundings of my character, whom I'd named Esperath Wraithling. Around 1,500 Americans were in the world of GemStone III at any given time.

I was in that world about six hours a day, almost every day, in 9th and 10th grade. Five or six of my friends also played GemStone III. We'd meet at Red Bug park—this was in suburban Florida—to play basketball, but end up talking about GemStone III and returning home to our computers. We called one another addicts.

I'm not sure to what extent, if any, our parents understood GemStone III. None of them ever played, I don't think, even for a minute. I can imagine parents 10 years later playing, but in the mid-1990s there was usually only one computer per household. The Internet was a place you went to alone. Kids, while online, were parentless. Not in the controlled way of summer camp, or the easily monitored way of video games, but in a new, untested, unapparent way.

5 Before the Internet, my parents were privy to most of my world. They saw whom I interacted with, where I was, what I was doing. Being preadolescent,

I spent most of my time with them anyway. I had no desire to befriend four to eight strangers and talk to them daily, for hours, in passive secrecy from my parents.

After the Internet, my parents were privy to much less and would only rarely, and with decreasing frequency, ask about what they no longer knew. "What did you do on the Internet today?" was not a question I remember being asked. If my parents, squinting over my shoulder, saw Esperath Wraithling on the screen, they didn't see the dark elf wizard I saw, they saw two meaningless words. If they looked at me—whether I was immersed in GemStone III, on a message board, or in a chat room—I appeared to be sitting in a chair, doing almost nothing.

Far from doing almost nothing, I was socializing in and exploring the metaphysical room that had been quietly connected to millions of houses. The shared, boundless room of the Internet seemed normal, even mundane, in the mid-1990s. I didn't have another childhood for comparison. Only in retrospect—and increasingly, as my memory of a pre-Internet existence became tinier and more conspicuous, like something that glints—does it seem weird and mysterious, almost alien.

I now sometimes imagine the Internet as a U.F.O. that appeared one afternoon in the backyard—to take humankind elsewhere, maybe. My parents noticed it first, but weren't particularly interested. They didn't immediately begin relocating their lives, as if by instinct, into the U.F.O., like my peers and I seem to have done. They remained halfhearted and aloof for around 10 years before finally, slowly beginning (as "lurkers," observing without participating) to learn about the Internet, I feel, in earnest.

Recently, in endearingly impulsive ways, they've become a little interactive. My mother's Twitter account (zero followers, following zero) has one tweet, from 2010: "Tao's birthday is July 2, Happy Birthday, Tao." For at least six years, she has seemed to use Facebook only to look at other people's profiles, until this past summer, when she began "liking" my status updates. Around the same time my father, using a Facebook account I didn't know he had (no profile information, nine friends), "liked" around 10 things on my Facebook wall over a few hours one day. He hasn't "liked" anything of mine since, but about a month ago he e-mailed to say he'd edited my Wikipedia page. He'd added "his father is a retired physics professor" and other details (all of which got deleted within two days) to the "Early and Personal Life" section of my page.

10 I imagine these interactions wouldn't be so tentative and intermittent, so sheepish and slow to begin—that maybe we'd know one another better—if I had been born in the 1990s, when my parents would have been online when I was a toddler, or 1970s, when we could have learned about the Internet together, to some degree, as adults.

As a kid, when I began using the Internet, I was probably most interested in the prospects of solitary exploration. But I'd like to think that I was also compelled by forces outside myself—that, on some level, I might have been dimly aware of the Internet's role in the fulfillment of some ancient, human yearning to externalize our private imaginations into a shared space. Maybe I intuited that the faster the world was relocated into the Internet, the likelier humankind would be returned to an original and undifferentiated oneness, completing what it began around 13,000 years ago with agriculture, which resulted in villages, then cities, finally the Internet.

Maybe some part of me believed that, once we were there, we would know everything about our parents and they would know everything about us—except there wouldn't be a "they," or an "us," only a mind, containing the knowledge of both, that knows itself.

RESPONDING TO READING

1. How do the different roles of the internet in their lives define the generation gap between Lin and his parents?
2. In paragraphs 5–7, Lin contrasts his life before and after the internet. What key differences does he identify? How has his parents' use of the internet changed in recent years? How would you describe his attitude toward those changes?

Rhetorical Analysis

Explain how the following statements support Lin's comparison between himself and his parents:

- "The Internet remained nonessential and separate for them, like a vacation destination." (1)
- "The Internet was a place you went to alone. Kids, while online, were parentless." (4)
- "I now sometimes imagine the Internet as a U.F.O. that appeared one afternoon in the backyard—to take humankind elsewhere, maybe." (8)

Writing with Sources

Locate some information about the early years of the internet. What predictions and warnings did critics make about how the internet would be used? Were these predictions largely optimistic or pessimistic? How accurate have these early predictions turned out to be? Write an essay that draws some conclusions about how these predictions foreshadowed the generation gap Lin identifies.

3.8 Focus: "What Is a Family?"

Masarik/Shutterstock

Which elements in this image are typical of a family photo, and which are atypical or unexpected?

RESPONDING TO THE IMAGE

Answer one or both of the following questions.

1. The photo above shows two mothers and their son. What message does this photo convey about what the family is, and what it can be?
2. This photograph omits the boy's biological father. Is his absence in any way significant?

3.9 John Culhane, "For Gay Parents, Deciding between Adoption and Surrogacy Raises Tough Moral Questions"

A professor of law and codirector of the Family Health Law & Policy Institute at Widener University Delaware Law School, John Culhane specializes in such topics as marriage for same-sex couples, the rights of gay and transgender couples, and bullying. A contributing writer for Slate and the coauthor of the book *Same-Sex Legal Kit for Dummies* (2013), he has also published essays and blog posts in publications such as *Dissent, the Huffington Post,* the *Los Angeles Times,* the *Miami Herald, The New York Times,* and the *Philadelphia Inquirer.* In this essay, Culhane contrasts two distinct ways of forming families.

BEFORE YOU READ

What, if anything, do you already know about the differences between adoption and surrogacy? Does one of these two paths to parenthood make more sense to you? Why?

For Gay Parents, Deciding between Adoption and Surrogacy Raises Tough Moral Questions

When my husband David and I became new parents, we thought it would be fun and perhaps even affirming to get involved with a gay dads group. As far as I could tell, the only regular event was a brunch that took place every few months. That sounded promising, a throwback to idle Sundays before the babies made it all about them. The food was always great—these are gay men, after all. But as it turned out, the event was neither fun nor affirming.

The gatherings mostly took place in wealthy suburban redoubts and were marked by a weird social division between two teams: Surrogacy Dads and Adoptive Dads. Some of this division was to be expected. Each group had war stories to share, and it was natural to break the ice with those who had lived through similar experiences. But after one or two brunches, I came to see that this kind of informal division reflected something much deeper: a philosophical debate about how we *should* form our families. The annoyingly named "gayby boom" has created a knot of moral questions that are impossible to avoid.

Should is a weird word to use in this context, of course. For gay men especially, bringing children into the family is difficult and challenging no matter which route one chooses. Our first instinct should be support for *all* families, regardless of what route each of us took to realize our dreams. Both surrogacy and adoption present daunting legal obstacles—even now that marriage equality has been achieved.

As I learned when researching a book I co-authored, surrogacy is a state-by-state legal minefield. Some states won't recognize these contracts at all, while the law in other states is unsettled. And there is the ever-present danger that the woman carrying the child will try to renege on her commitment. Adoption is hardly more secure. The countries offering this choice to gay men are constantly changing. Domestic adoption can be fraught as well either because birth mothers change their minds, or as in our case of adoption through the child welfare system, because the process has no certain outcome.

5 Beyond the legal hurdles, though, there's an undeniable moral component to whatever decision we make. Those who can pony up the money for surrogacy—

which frequently exceeds $100,000, all in—are faced with the cold fact that they're selecting an egg donor based on objective calculations of positive attributes. Lesbians do the same with sperm donors, although of course at a much lower cost since no surrogate is needed.

When a case surfaces that draws the uncomfortable selection process into the open, people are left tongue-tied trying to figure out the proper response. A couple of years ago, I wrote a piece for *Slate* about the case of a lesbian couple that sued a sperm bank for providing the "wrong" material—from a black, rather than a white, donor. As I said at the time, outraged gasps at the couple were "easy, but not completely fair. Because everyone who transacts business with companies that offer sperm and egg donation is looking for a bespoke baby."

When it comes to the gestational surrogate, there's the additional issue of contributing to an industry that commodifies the body in an obvious way. The ethical issues multiply when the surrogate is from a developing country, often India, where women are paid much less for their services; but such "surrogacy tourism" just highlights the uncomfortable exchange going on in all these cases.

Those thinking of adopting face internal battles, too. As required by law, case workers confronted David and me with an unsettling battery of questions about the race, age, and sex of the kids we were willing to adopt, as well as delicately phrased inquiries about whether we'd be comfortable dealing with disabled kids—and, if so, they needed to know, *what kinds* of disabilities did we think we could handle? Really, who knows?

For the most part, straight couples get to ignore these tough questions. Sex, baby, done. Only when infertility leads to surrogacy or to a decision to adopt, or when pre-natal testing reveals a serious anomaly, are heterosexual parents typically forced into this moral maelstrom. 10

But ignoring these deep issues doesn't mean they're not present. Even the decision to procreate the old-fashioned way is a moral one, though my guess is that most straight couples don't think of it that way. Given the global population of 7-and-a-half billion, it's at least fair to ask why more potential parents—gay and straight—don't at least consider adoption rather than swelling that number even further.

I was struck by that omission when reading Andrew Solomon's *Far From the Tree*. After almost 700 pages of deftly describing the remarkable lives of families challenged by children the parents never expected (ranging from deaf, to autistic, to musical prodigies), the book deflates slightly in the final chapter, where Solomon's thoughtfulness and penetrating insight abandon him when explaining why he decided to go the surrogacy route. Although he acknowledges the problems with surrogacy (its unavailability to people of limited means, and "the aura of manufacturing that clung to the venture"), he brushes aside the possibility of adoption by dismissing critics as folks who hadn't themselves thought of adopting. In the end, he just preferred to have his own biological child. Full stop.

So even if adoptions were much easier, I'm confident that many gay couples of sufficient means would continue, like Solomon, to prefer surrogacy. Biology, blood lines, ancestry—these imperatives have driven the human race forever.

But why *not* adoption? What's so great about biology that it drives people to expensive surrogacy and chancy technologies to try and pass their flawed genome along? Most people, if they're being honest, realize that their families haven't exactly reached genetic perfection. Solomon is quite forthright about his own mental health issues, and most of us would have to own up to a bevy of similar concerns for any child we might be chromosomally connected to.

I've never fully understood this preference. Almost from the moment our twin daughters arrived, their biological provenance was of little concern to me. What mattered was the human connection we were forming, day by day, as I bathed their tiny bodies, swaddled them in warm clothes, and felt them melt into me as I fed them. Now it's sitting in their beds, going over Spanish vocabulary words just before they drift off to sleep. It's the accretion of those moments [that] make them my daughters, and I their father.

15 In the end, we'll all have to account for how well we parent our children—no matter their origin, and no matter what we think about the various ways we create our families.

Source: John Culhane, "For Gay Parents, Deciding Between Adoption and Surrogacy Raises Tough Moral Questions", Slate, March 23, 2017. Used with permission from John Culhane.

RESPONDING TO READING

1. How are surrogacy dads different from adoptive dads? Why, according to Culhane, might adoptive dads be better? Does he present sufficient evidence to support his position? If not, what should he add?
2. In paragraph 13, Culhane makes a biological argument against surrogacy, noting the "flawed genome" that parents transmit to their children. Why does he include this information? Do you find his points convincing?

Rhetorical Analysis

What language does Culhane use to examine the ethical considerations of surrogacy and adoption? How does his word choice add to or detract from his position?

Writing with Sources

Read a few sections of Andrew Solomon's book *Far from the Tree: Parents, Children and the Search for Identity* (2012). Next, write an essay that compares Culhane's views on adoption and surrogacy with Solomon's.

3.10 Laila Lalami, "My Fictional Grandparents"

A professor of creative writing at the University of California, Riverside, Laila Lalami (1968–) was born and raised in Rabat, Morocco. The author of three acclaimed novels, she has also published essays in the *Boston Globe*, the *Guardian*, the *Los Angeles Times*, *The Nation*, *The New York Times*, and *The Washington Post*. In the following essay, Lalami explores the intersection of fiction and reality in family storytelling.

BEFORE YOU READ

Have you, or has someone you know, used a DNA test kit or service? What information did (or didn't) come to light?

My Fictional Grandparents

My mother was abandoned in a French orphanage in Fez[1] in 1941. That year in Morocco, hundreds of people died in an outbreak of the plague; her parents were among the victims. Actually, no, they died in a horrific car crash on the newly built road from Marrakesh[2] to Fez. No, no, no, my grandmother died in childbirth, and my grandfather, mad with grief, gave the baby away. The truth is: I don't know how my mother ended up in a French orphanage in 1941. The nuns in black habits never told.

Growing up in Rabat, I felt lopsided, like a seesaw no one ever played with. On my father's side: a large number of uncles, cousins, second cousins, grand-aunts, all claiming descent from the Prophet Muhammad. On my mother's side: nothing. No one. Often I imagined my mother's parents, the man and woman whose blood pulsed in my veins but whom I had never seen.

I would have called them Ba-sidi and Mi-lalla. Like my paternal grandfather, Ba-sidi would have been old but active. He would have retired from a career in the police and spent his days performing El Melhun, Moroccan sung poetry, with his friends. Like my paternal grandmother, Mi-lalla would have worn long, rustling caftans,[3] in which I would have sought refuge every time I got into trouble. She would have taught me all her herbal cures and hennaed my hands before each Eid.[4]

My mother did not take part in these fictions. She spoke little about her childhood in the orphanage. Sometimes she hummed a French lullaby that one of the nuns taught her. I went to sleep on many a night to the sound of "*Au clair de la lune*" or "*Fais dodo, Colas*." But other times, a wave of resentment welled within her, and she would describe being forced to eat on a dirty table from which chickens were allowed to feed. Naturally I developed an early and lifelong affinity for literary orphans, like Oliver Twist and Jane Eyre. Later, when I became a novelist, orphans and abandoned children turned up in my work, unbidden.

5 On my birthday in February, my husband and I were drinking our morning coffee when he slipped a small box across the kitchen table. Inside was a DNA test kit. "You can use it to find out more about your mom," he said.

"But what if this company sells my genetic data?" I asked.

"You can find out more about your mom."

"Like, to an insurance company. Or even a government agency. What about that?"

"You can find out more about your mom!"

---

[1] A city in Morocco. [Eds.]
[2] A city in Morocco. [Eds.]
[3] Long garments with long sleeves. [Eds.]
[4] A Muslim holiday. [Eds.]

10 Optimism, that peculiar American trait—it was impossible to resist it. So I sent a saliva sample, and six weeks later, my results were ready. My health profile listed a series of traits that made me smile with recognition. I had long ago given up drinking milk; now I found out that I was most likely lactose-intolerant. I had always assumed that my strong stomach was attributable to a third-world childhood; it turned out I had a natural resistance to norovirus. But the profile had sobering news too: I had an elevated risk of coronary heart disease and Alzheimer's disease. No one on my father's side of the family had heart problems or dementia. They might have come from my mother's family.

Finally, I opened the ancestry report. My maternal line was K, a haplogroup[5] commonly found among populations of the Near East, Europe and North Africa. The test also identified relatives on my maternal side: distant cousins in Finland, France and the United States. Their locations intrigued me. How had the descendants of my mother's relatives ended up in such far-flung places?

Or was my mother the one from a far-flung place? After all, she was born in the middle of a world war, when refugees were fleeing in all directions. Perhaps her parents were displaced and ended up in Morocco, where they had to begin new lives. It would have been difficult, in such times, to care for a newborn.

So it was that, in just a few moments, I found myself returning to those childhood days when I used to dream up different families, and different fates, for my mother. What science gave me, in the end, was no different from what my own imagination had fed me for many years—stories. The search was not over. The search would never be over. And not even science could help fill out the abyss I grew up with. Only stories could.

RESPONDING TO READING

1. In paragraph 3, Lalami speculates about her "fictional grandparents," but in paragraph 4, she notes, "My mother did not take part in these fictions." Why not? How do you explain the different attitudes Lalami and her mother have about their family history?
2. In her last paragraph, Lalami concludes that "only stories" (not science) could "help fill out the abyss [she] grew up with." What kind of stories do you think she is referring to? How do such stories "fill out the abyss"?

Rhetorical Analysis

Evaluate Lalami's introductory strategy. Why does she include three alternate scenarios here? How is this strategy consistent with the content and structure of her essay's last two paragraphs?

---

[5]A genetic family. [Eds.]

Writing with Sources

Research the services of some companies that market DNA test kits. What information do they claim they will provide? What kind of information do they *not* promise to provide? Based on your research, write an essay explaining why you think DNA test kits are (or are not) valuable sources of information for people interested in learning more about their family backgrounds.

3.11 Sonia Sodha, "If You Have No Children, Who Will Care for You When You're Old?"

A freelance public policy and strategy consultant, Sonia Sodha is the chief leader writer and a columnist for the *Observer.* A trustee of the youth charity City Year UK, of the education charity Ambition School Leadership, and of the charitable foundation Trust for London, she writes about issues related to family policy, education, and work. She is also the coauthor of the book *Thursday's Child (2008).* In the following essay, Sodha considers the roles of the family and the government in providing elderly care.

BEFORE YOU READ

Write a letter to your future caregiver, explaining specifically what you hope he or she will provide for you physically and emotionally.

If You Have No Children, Who Will Care for You When You're Old?

Few of us are immune from the anxiety that can quickly set in when we contemplate our own ageing. Who will be there for us when us can no longer physically take care of ourselves? Who will be around to remind us of who we were in our moments of lucidity when our minds have started slipping away?

For those of us who don't have children, these questions take on a particular significance. I had mixed feelings after watching *Still Alice*, an Oscar-winning depiction of early-onset dementia. It made for grim viewing. But it was easy to imagine the ways it could have been even grimmer: what if the protagonist, Alice, had no children, a partner long departed or divorced, or friends who had drifted away?

Increasing life expectancy is one of the great markers of human progress. But the flipside of our stretched lifespans is that we are more likely to experience longer periods of significant physical and mental decline at the end of our lives. And there's a strong, unwritten assumption about how we as a society accommodate this shift: it's that the generational tables will eventually turn so that you will eventually come to depend on your children, who were once so utterly dependent on you.

But the medical advances of recent decades have been accompanied by profound and positive social shifts as women have moved en masse into the workplace, reducing the capacity for caring within families. This increase in numbers has prompted a debate about how we care for children, and where the role of the state in providing childcare begins and ends.

5 In contrast, the balance that has been struck between the role of the state and families in caring for older people is uneasy and implicit. State provision of professional care for older people has grown, but remains limited in comparison to healthcare: it is means-tested and basic. The system relies heavily on the informal caring done by family members, estimated at 7.6 billion hours in 2010. Without this, it would collapse.

There are signs, though, of a growing disjunction between what we implicitly assume families will do, and what actually happens. Older people without children barely feature in policy discussion or planning for local provision. Yet their numbers are set to grow: the proportion of women not having children has increased from one in nine to one in five in a generation. It's been estimated that by 2030, there will be more than a million adults aged 65 to 74 without children, almost double the number in 2012. Some groups, such as older LGBT people and adults with learning disabilities, are particularly affected.

But in any case, having adult offspring has never been a guarantee they'll be around. The scattered nature of modern life may further erode this likelihood. What happens when ageing parents and their adult children live at different ends of the country, or on different continents, and where families have drifted apart over time? Then there are the financial pressures that might make it impossible for many to give up jobs to care full-time for their parents, no matter how much they want to. Informal caring usually falls to women, who are also more likely to be low paid and to have insufficient pension provision. Since women live longer than men, on average, and are more likely than men to have partners older than them, they are also more likely to end up alone.

Despite these trends, the state is retracting further, thanks to spending cuts that have seen funding for social care fall by as much as 30% in some areas since 2010. Little surprise, then, that even as the population ages, the number of people getting state help with the costs of their care has fallen by a quarter in the past five years. Age UK estimates there are now more than a million older people who struggle without the support they need with everyday tasks such as getting out of bed, preparing and eating meals, and going to the toilet.

The NHS[1] is also increasingly stretched. Like so many in his generation, my grandfather spent the last weeks of his life in hospital. He wouldn't have been assigned a mattress designed to prevent bedsores had my mother and uncle not repeatedly asked for it—not because the staff on the ward didn't care, but because even a few years ago resources were thinly spread. The more rationing there is, the more older people have to rely on family members pushing on their behalf.

10 The worrying thing is that this retraction is happening by stealth. It has serious implications for what we expect families to do. But to the extent that ministers have addressed it, it's been simply to make vague allusions about the importance of personal responsibility and familial duty, without being upfront about the

[1]The National Health Service, England's publicly funded national healthcare system. [Eds.]

tradeoffs involved, and what they might mean for older people without family in their lives who can pick up the pieces.

We need a more explicit debate about where the responsibilities of the state and families start and stop. The state has a critical but limited role to play. It can't provide love and companionship. It can't fight tooth and nail against itself for you to get a limited slice of rationed resources. But it can and should provide a basic standard of professional personal care as a critical safety net. This requires an honest conversation about how much this will cost and how to pay for it.

This is not just important for older people without children. While the state can't replace loving family relationships, it can profoundly affect them. We tend to fetishise Asian cultures that have a greater tradition of care of older people taking place within extended families, such as the Japanese. But scratch beneath the stereotype, and a more complex picture emerges. The Japanese word *kaigo-jigoku* translates to "care-giving hell." One survey in the 1990s suggested one in two family carers in Japan had subjected older relatives to some form of abuse, with one in three acknowledging feelings of "hatred." Such findings hint at the consequences of expecting families to do too much, especially when the conditions involved include advanced dementia, which requires skilled professional care.

Resolving the question of what the state can and ought to do is relatively easy compared with the much knottier problem of how to create a society that has an abundance of the things—love, companionship, emotional support—that the state can never hope to provide.

Look to civil society, and there are important clues. North London Cares is a charity that matches older people and younger professionals to provide each other with companionship. HomeShare schemes connect people who might benefit from low-cost accommodation with older people who have a spare room and need light-touch support to stay in their own home. The schemes may look different, but the fundamentals are common. They are not about setting up the sorts of transactional relationships more associated with professional care; they explicitly seek to build mutually-beneficial relationships that create bonds of love, care and commitment.

They offer a glimpse of what a kinder society might look like; a ker- 15
nel of transformative potential. But it's a long way off being realized. As much as such schemes might be part of the solution, they are a rarity. And this takes us to the fundamental truth that all questions about ageing eventually point towards: if we want to create a better world in which to grow old, it's down to us.

Source: Sonia Sodha, "If you have no children, who will care for you when you're old?", 12 May 2017.

RESPONDING TO READING

1. What similarities does Sodha discuss among the roles of families, governments, and charities in caring for aging adults? What differences does she call out? To what extent can the state or a charity serve a family role for the elderly?
2. In paragraph 12, Sodha contrasts Western and Eastern approaches to elderly care. Why does she include this information? Does it support her position? Explain.

Rhetorical Analysis

In paragraph 11, Sodha urges readers to talk openly about the roles of the family and the government at a time when more and more aging people need care. Why do you suppose she includes this call to action? How might it affect her audience's reactions to her argument?

Writing with Sources

What kind of elderly care does your family provide? Do your parents care for their parents or for aging adults in the community? Who will care for your parents and for your other family members as they age? Who will care for you? Interview your parents (and, if possible, some of your aunts and uncles and your grandparents). Next, write an essay analyzing the outlook for elderly care in your family and drawing some conclusions about the pros and cons of your family's approach.

Widening the Focus

For Critical Reading and Writing

Referring specifically to the three readings in this chapter's Focus section (and possibly to additional sources as well), write an essay in which you answer the question, "What Is a Family?"

For Further Reading

The following readings can suggest additional perspectives for thinking and writing about different kinds of family relationships.

- Lynda Barry, "The Sanctuary of School" (p. 83)
- Gary Marcus, "How Birds and Babies Learn to Talk" (p. 131)
- Steven Korbar, *"What Are You Going to Be?"* (p. 289)

For Focused Research

Recent years have seen scientific developments in the field of reproductive health, allowing people otherwise unable to have children to form biological families. Advances in assisted reproductive technologies, such as in vitro fertilization, have opened up the possibility of parenthood to hundreds of thousands of families worldwide. Do a *Google* search for local or regional fertility clinics, and select two clinic websites. Then, write an essay that analyzes the services offered by these clinics. What is their purpose? When were they started? Why is their popularity increasing? Are they a good thing for families, or do they create too much pressure for infertile couples to try to have children? Use information from the websites you have chosen, and possibly other sources, to support your conclusions.

Beyond the Classroom

Conduct an email survey of the friends and classmates whose names are listed in your contacts. Ask each recipient the following questions:

- How would you describe the structure of your family? Whom do you consider family?
- Has this kind of family structure encouraged you to succeed or held you back?
- How do you plan to expand and care for your family as you get older, and why?

When you have gathered all your responses, write an essay that summarizes your findings and draws a conclusion about the relative value of different family arrangements.

Exploring Issues and Ideas

Family and Memory

Write an essay in response to one of the following prompts, which are suitable for assignments that require the use of outside sources as well as for assignments that are not source-based.

1. When you think about the word *family*, do you think about a group of people bound together by love, by marriage, by blood, by history, by shared memories, by economic dependency, or by habit? What unites family members, and what divides them? How does memory affect our understanding of family? Define *family* as it is portrayed in several of the readings in this chapter.
2. Leo Tolstoy's classic Russian novel *Anna Karenina* opens with this sentence: "Happy families are all alike; every unhappy family is unhappy in its own way." Write an essay in which you agree with or challenge this statement, supporting your position with references to several of the readings in this chapter.
3. When you think about your childhood and your young adulthood, what music do you imagine playing in the background? Read the poem "Family Music" (p. 35), and then write a musical autobiography that gives readers a sense of who you were at different times of your life. Try to help readers understand the times you grew up in and the person you were (and became). Or, read the story "The Blessed" (p. 36) and the essay "Decent Clothes, 1959" (p. 56), and remember the smells and tastes of the food you grew up with. Then, write a culinary autobiography instead.
4. How do your parents' notions of success and failure affect you? Do you think your parents tend to expect too much of you, or too little? Explore these ideas in an essay, referring to readings in this chapter and in Chapter 9, "The American Dream."
5. What traits, habits, and values (positive or negative) have you inherited from your parents? What qualities do you think you will pass on to your children? Read the story "The Blessed" (p. 36) and the essay "Decent Clothes, 1959" (p. 56), and then write a letter to your parents in which you answer these two questions. Be sure to illustrate the characteristics you discuss with examples of specific incidents.

Chapter 4
Issues in Education

In this chapter, you will learn to:

- analyze readings about issues in education.
- compose essays about issues in education.

In the nineteenth century, people had little difficulty defining the purpose of education: they assumed it was the school's job to prepare students for the roles they would play in society as adults. To accomplish this end, public school administrators made sure that the elementary school curriculum gave students a good dose of the basics: arithmetic, grammar, spelling, reading, composition, and penmanship. High school students studied literature, history, geography, and civics. At the elite private schools, students studied subjects that would prepare them for the leadership positions that they would eventually occupy. They learned physics, rhetoric, and elocution—as well as Latin and Greek so that they could read the classics in the original.

chippix/Shutterstock

What elements does this image of a nineteenth-century college classroom use to show the former purpose of education?

Today, educators seem to have a great deal of difficulty agreeing on what purpose schools are supposed to serve. No longer can a group of school administrators simply proscribe a curriculum. Parents, students, politicians, academics, special interest groups, and religious leaders all attempt to influence what is taught. The result, according to some educators, is an environment in which it is almost impossible for any real education to take place. In fact, in many of today's schools, more emphasis seems to be placed on increasing self-esteem, avoiding controversy, and passing standardized tests linked to Common Core than on challenging students to discover new ways of thinking about themselves and about the world. In this milieu, classic books are censored or rewritten to eliminate passages that might offend, ideas are presented as if they all have equal value, and the curriculum is revised so that teachers can "teach to the test." The result is an educational environment that has all the intellectual appeal of elevator music. Many people—educators included—seem to have forgotten that ideas must be unsettling (or downright disturbing) if they are to make us think. After all, what is education but a process that encourages us to think critically about our world and to develop a healthy skepticism—to question, evaluate, and reach conclusions about ideas and events?

The Focus section of this chapter (p. 106) addresses the question, "Should a College Education Be Free?" In "Is Free College Really Free?" Anya Kamenetz considers the historical and political context of the term *free*; in "Walmart's Too-Good-to-Be-True '$1 a Day' College Tuition Plan, Explained," Matthew Yglesias dissects the corporate tuition benefit; and in "Is College Worth the Money?" Liz Dwyer examines the answers of six recent college graduates.

What elements does this image of a contemporary college classroom use to show the current purpose of education?

Preparing to Read and Write

As you read and prepare to write about the selections in this chapter, you may consider the following questions:

- What assumptions does the writer have about his or her audience? How can you tell?
- What is the writer's primary purpose? For example, is it to reinforce traditional ideas about education or to challenge them?
- What genre is the writer using? For example, is the reading a reflection, a memoir, or an argument? How do the conventions of this genre influence the writer's choices?
- What appeals does the writer use? For example, does he or she appeal primarily to reason, to emotion, or to a combination of the two? Is this the most effective strategy?
- How does the writer define *education*? Is this definition consistent with yours?
- What does the writer think the main goals of education should be? Do you agree?
- Which does the writer believe is more important, formal or informal education?
- On what aspect or aspects of education does the writer focus?
- Who does the writer believe bears primary responsibility for a student's education? Is it the student, the family, the school, the community, or the government?
- Does the writer use personal experience to support his or her points? Does he or she use facts and statistics or expert opinion as support? Do you find the writer's ideas convincing?
- What changes in the educational system does the writer recommend? Do you agree with these recommendations?
- Are the writer's educational experiences similar to or different from yours? How do these similarities or differences affect your response to the essay?
- In what way is the essay similar to or different from other essays in this chapter?

Shared Writing

Issues in Education

Consider your educational experiences over the years. How would you summarize the purpose of your education? Is this purpose meaningful to you? To what extent have you had to define your own purpose for your educational pursuits?

4.1 Lynda Barry, "The Sanctuary of School"

Lynda Barry (1956–) grew up as part of an extended Filipino family (her mother was Filipino, her father an alcoholic Norwegian-Irishman). The first member of her family to pursue higher education, she majored in art and began her career as a cartoonist shortly after graduation. Barry is known as a chronicler of adolescent angst both in her syndicated comic strip *Ernie Pook's Comeek* and in the semi-autobiographical *One Hundred Demons* (2002). Her latest book is *Syllabus: Notes from an Accidental Professor* (2014). Barry has also written a novel, *The Good Times Are Killing Me* (1988), which was turned into a successful musical. In the following essay, Barry remembers her Seattle grade school in a racially mixed neighborhood as a nurturing safe haven from her difficult family life.

BEFORE YOU READ

Did you or your siblings or friends participate in any after-school programs while growing up? Were these programs important to you or your peers? Explain.

The Sanctuary of School

I was 7 years old the first time I snuck out of the house in the dark. It was winter and my parents had been fighting all night. They were short on money and long on relatives who kept "temporarily" moving into our house because they had nowhere else to go.

My brother and I were used to giving up our bedroom. We slept on the couch, something we actually liked because it put us that much closer to the light of our lives, our television.

At night when everyone was asleep, we lay on our pillows watching it with the sound off. We watched Steve Allen's mouth moving. We watched Johnny Carson's mouth moving. We watched movies filled with gangsters shooting machine guns into packed rooms, dying soldiers hurling a last grenade and beautiful women crying at windows. Then the sign-off finally came and we tried to sleep.

The morning I snuck out, I woke up filled with a panic about needing to get to school. The sun wasn't quite up yet but my anxiety was so fierce that I just got dressed, walked quietly across the kitchen and let myself out the back door.

It was quiet outside. Stars were still out. Nothing moved and no one was in 5
the street. It was as if someone had turned the sound off on the world.

I walked the alley, breaking thin ice over the puddles with my shoes. I didn't know why I was walking to school in the dark. I didn't think about it. All I knew was a feeling of panic, like the panic that strikes kids when they realize they are lost.

That feeling eased the moment I turned the corner and saw the dark outline of my school at the top of the hill. My school was made up of about 15 nondescript portable classrooms set down on a fenced concrete lot in a rundown Seattle neighborhood, but it had the most beautiful view of the Cascade Mountains. You could see them from anywhere on the playfield and you could see them from the windows of my classroom—Room 2.

I walked over to the monkey bars and hooked my arms around the cold metal. I stood for a long time just looking across Rainier Valley. The sky was beginning to whiten and I could hear a few birds.

In a perfect world my absence at home would not have gone unnoticed. I would have had two parents in a panic to locate me, instead of two parents in a panic to locate an answer to the hard question of survival during a deep financial and emotional crisis.

10 But in an overcrowded and unhappy home, it's incredibly easy for any child to slip away. The high levels of frustration, depression and anger in my house made my brother and me invisible. We were children with the sound turned off. And for us, as for the steadily increasing number of neglected children in this country, the only place where we could count on being noticed was at school.

"Hey there, young lady. Did you forget to go home last night?" It was Mr. Gunderson, our janitor, whom we all loved. He was nice and he was funny and he was old with white hair, thick glasses and an unbelievable number of keys. I could hear them jingling as he walked across the playfield. I felt incredibly happy to see him.

He let me push his wheeled garbage can between the different portables as he unlocked each room. He let me turn on the lights and raise the window shades and I saw my school slowly come to life. I saw Mrs. Holman, our school secretary, walk into the office without her orange lipstick on yet. She waved.

I saw the fifth-grade teacher Mr. Cunningham, walking under the breezeway eating a hard roll. He waved.

And I saw my teacher, Mrs. Claire LeSane, walking toward us in a red coat and calling my name in a very happy and surprised way, and suddenly my throat got tight and my eyes stung and I ran toward her crying. It was something that surprised us both.

15 It's only thinking about it now, 28 years later, that I realize I was crying from relief. I was with my teacher, and in a while I was going to sit at my desk, with my crayons and pencils and books and classmates all around me, and for the next six hours I was going to enjoy a thoroughly secure, warm and stable world. It was a world I absolutely relied on. Without it, I don't know where I would have gone that morning.

Mrs. LeSane asked me what was wrong and when I said "Nothing," she seemingly left it at that. But she asked me if I would carry her purse for her, an honor above all honors, and she asked if I wanted to come into Room 2 early and paint.

She believed in the natural healing power of painting and drawing for troubled children. In the back of her room there was always a drawing table and an easel with plenty of supplies, and sometimes during the day she would come up to you for what seemed like no good reason and quietly ask if you wanted to go to the back table and "make some pictures for Mrs. LeSane." We all had a chance at it—to sit apart from the class for a while to paint, draw and silently work out impossible problems on 11 × 17 sheets of newsprint.

Drawing came to mean everything to me. At the back table in Room 2, I learned to build myself a life preserver that I could carry into my home.

We all know that a good education system saves lives, but the people of this country are still told that cutting the budget for public schools is necessary, that poor salaries for teachers are all we can manage and that art, music and all creative activities must be the first to go when times are lean.

Before- and after-school programs are cut and we are told that public schools are not made for baby-sitting children. If parents are neglectful temporarily or permanently, for whatever reason, it's certainly sad, but their unlucky children must fend for themselves. Or slip through the cracks. Or wander in a dark night alone. 20

We are told in a thousand ways that not only are public schools not important, but that the children who attend them, the children who need them most, are not important either. We leave them to learn from the blind eye of a television, or to the mercy of "a thousand points of light"[1] that can be as far away as stars.

I was lucky. I had Mrs. LeSane. I had Mr. Gunderson. I had an abundance of art supplies. And I had a particular brand of neglect in my home that allowed me to slip away and get to them. But what about the rest of the kids who weren't as lucky? What happened to them?

By the time the bell rang that morning I had finished my drawing and Mrs. LeSane pinned it up on the special bulletin board she reserved for drawings from the back table. It was the same picture I always drew—a sun in the corner of a blue sky over a nice house with flowers all around it.

Mrs. LeSane asked us to please stand, face the flag, place our right hands over our hearts and say the Pledge of Allegiance. Children across the country do it faithfully. I wonder now when the country will face its children and say a pledge right back.

RESPONDING TO READING

1. What information about her school does Barry provide? What information does she not provide? How can you explain these omissions?
2. In paragraph 22, Barry asks two questions. Why doesn't she answer them? What do you think the answers to these questions might be?

Rhetorical Analysis

Barry uses her personal experience to support her points about public school. Is this single source enough? Would Barry's points be more effective if they were supported by a wide variety of sources?

Writing with Sources

In her essay, Barry says that before- and after-school programs are being cut regardless of the effect on children. Research the public schools in your community, and determine if their before- and after-school programs are being cut. How cost-effective do both parents and educators think these programs are? Then, write an essay in which you assess the importance of before- and after-school programs in your community.

[1]Catchphrase for President George H. W. Bush's plan to substitute volunteerism for government programs. [Eds.]

4.2 John Holt, "School Is Bad for Children"

John Holt (1923–1985), a teacher and education theorist, believed that traditional schooling suppresses children's natural curiosity about life. In his writings about education, Holt suggested that students be allowed to pursue whatever interests them. Holt worked for an international peace group, traveled in Europe, and then worked at the private Colorado Rocky Mountain School in Carbondale, Colorado, where he taught high school English, French, and mathematics and coached soccer and baseball. His many books include *How Children Fail* (1964), *How Children Learn* (1967), *Education* (1976), and *Learning All the Time* (1989). In the following essay, first published in 1969, Holt makes a plea to free children from the classroom, a "dull and ugly place, where nobody ever says anything very truthful," and to "give them a chance to learn about the world at first hand." Holt was also a major supporter of the Home Schooling movement.

BEFORE YOU READ

What would your ideal elementary school be like? How would it be like the schools you attended? How would it be different?

School Is Bad for Children

Almost every child, on the first day he sets foot in a school building, is smarter, more curious, less afraid of what he doesn't know, better at finding and figuring things out, more confident, resourceful, persistent and independent than he will ever be again in his schooling—or, unless he is very unusual and very lucky, for the rest of his life. Already, by paying close attention to and interacting with the world and people around him, and without any school-type formal instruction, he has done a task far more difficult, complicated and abstract than anything he will be asked to do in school, or than any of his teachers has done for years. He has solved the mystery of language. He has discovered it—babies don't even know that language exists—and he has found out how it works and learned to use it. He has done it by exploring, by experimenting, by developing his own model of the grammar of language, by trying it out and seeing whether it works, by gradually changing it and refining it until it does work. And while he has been doing this, he has been learning other things as well, including many of the "concepts" that the schools think only they can teach him, and many that are more complicated than the ones they do try to teach him.

In he comes, this curious, patient, determined, energetic, skillful learner. We sit him down at a desk, and what do we teach him? Many things. First, that learning is separate from living. "You come to school to learn," we tell him, as if the child hadn't been learning before, as if living were out there and learning were in here, and there were no connection between the two. Secondly, that he cannot be trusted to learn and is no good at it. Everything we teach about reading, a task far simpler than many that the child has already mastered, says to him, "If we don't make you read, you won't, and if you don't do it exactly the way we tell you, you can't." In short, he comes to feel that learning is a passive process, something that someone else does *to* you, instead of something you do for yourself.

In a great many other ways he learns that he is worthless, untrustworthy, fit only to take other people's orders, a blank sheet for other people to write on. Oh, we make a lot of nice noises in school about respect for the child and individual differences, and the like. But our acts, as opposed to our talk, say to the child, "Your experience, your concerns, your curiosities, your needs, what you know, what you want, what you wonder about, what you hope for, what you fear, what you like and dislike, what you are good at or not so good at—all this is of not the slightest importance, it counts for nothing. What counts here, and the only thing that counts, is what we know, what we think is important, what we want you to do, think and be." The child soon learns not to ask questions—the teacher isn't there to satisfy his curiosity. Having learned to hide his curiosity, he later learns to be ashamed of it. Given no chance to find out who he is—and to develop that person, whoever it is—he soon comes to accept the adults' evaluation of him.

He learns many other things. He learns that to be wrong, uncertain, confused, is a crime. Right Answers are what the school wants, and he learns countless strategies for prying these answers out of the teacher, for conning her into thinking he knows what he doesn't know. He learns to dodge, bluff, fake, cheat. He learns to be lazy. Before he came to school, he would work for hours on end, on his own, with no thought of reward, at the business of making sense of the world and gaining competence in it. In school he learns, like every buck private, how to goldbrick, how not to work when the sergeant isn't looking, how to know when he is looking, how to make him think you are working even when he is looking. He learns that in real life you don't do anything unless you are bribed, bullied or conned into doing it, that nothing is worth doing for its own sake, or that if it is, you can't do it in school. He learns to be bored, to work with a small part of his mind, to escape from the reality around him into daydreams and fantasies—but not like the fantasies of his preschool years, in which he played a very active part.

The child comes to school curious about other people, particularly other chil- 5
dren, and the school teaches him to be indifferent. The most interesting thing in the classroom—often the only interesting thing in it—is the other children, but he has to act as if these other children, all about him, only a few feet away, are not really there. He cannot interact with them, talk with them, smile at them. In many schools he can't talk to other children in the halls between classes; in more than a few, and some of these in stylish suburbs, he can't even talk to them at lunch. Splendid training for a world in which, when you're not studying the other person to figure out how to do him in, you pay no attention to him.

In fact, he learns how to live without paying attention to anything going on around him. You might say that school is a long lesson in how to turn yourself off, which may be one reason why so many young people, seeking the awareness of the world and responsiveness to it they had when they were little, think they can only find it in drugs. Aside from being boring, the school is almost always ugly, cold, inhuman—even the most stylish, glass-windowed, $20-a-square-foot schools.

And so, in this dull and ugly place, where nobody ever says anything very truthful, where everybody is playing a kind of role, as in a charade, where the teachers are no more free to respond honestly to the students than the students are free to respond to the teachers or each other, where the air practically vibrates with suspicion and anxiety, the child learns to live in a daze, saving his energies for those small parts of his life that are too trivial for the adults to bother with, and thus remain his. It is a rare child who can come through his schooling with much left of his curiosity, his independence or his sense of his own dignity, competence and worth.

So much for criticism. What do we need to do? Many things. Some are easy—we can do them right away. Some are hard, and may take some time. Take a hard one first. We should abolish compulsory school attendance. At the very least we should modify it, perhaps by giving children every year a large number of authorized absences. Our compulsory school-attendance laws once served a humane and useful purpose. They protected children's right to some schooling, against those adults who would otherwise have denied it to them in order to exploit their labor, in farm, store, mine or factory. Today the laws help nobody, not the schools, not the teachers, not the children. To keep kids in school who would rather not be there costs the schools an enormous amount of time and trouble—to say nothing of what it costs to repair the damage that these angry and resentful prisoners do every time they get a chance. Every teacher knows that any kid in class who, for whatever reason, would rather not be there not only doesn't learn anything himself but makes it a great deal tougher for anyone else. As for protecting the children from exploitation, the chief and indeed only exploiters of children these days *are* the schools. Kids caught in the college rush more often than not work 70 hours or more a week, most of it on paper busywork. For kids who aren't going to college, school is just a useless time waster, preventing them from earning some money or doing some useful work, or even doing some true learning.

Objections. "If kids didn't have to go to school, they'd all be out in the streets." No, they wouldn't. In the first place, even if schools stayed just the way they are, children would spend at least some time there because that's where they'd be likely to find friends; it's a natural meeting place for children. In the second place, schools wouldn't stay the way they are, they'd get better, because we would have to start making them what they ought to be right now—places where children would *want* to be. In the third place, those children who did not want to go to school could find, particularly if we stirred up our brains and gave them a little help, other things to do—the things many children now do during their summers and holidays.

10 There's something easier we could do. We need to get kids out of the school buildings, give them a chance to learn about the world at first hand. It is a very recent idea, and a crazy one, that the way to teach our young people about the world they live in is to take them out of it and shut them up in brick boxes. Fortunately, educators are beginning to realize this. In Philadelphia and Portland, Oreg., to pick only two places I happen to have heard about, plans are being drawn up for public schools that won't have any school buildings at all, that will

take the students out into the city and help them to use it and its people as a learning resource. In other words, students, perhaps in groups, perhaps independently, will go to libraries, museums, exhibits, court rooms, legislatures, radio and TV stations, meetings, businesses and laboratories to learn about their world and society at first hand. A small private school in Washington is already doing this. It makes sense. We need more of it.

As we help children get out into the world, to do their learning there, we get more of the world into the schools. Aside from their parents, most children never have any close contact with any adults except people whose sole business is children. No wonder they have no idea what adult life or work is like. We need to bring a lot more people who are *not* full-time teachers into the schools and into contact with the children. In New York City, under the Teachers and Writers Collaborative, real writers, working writers—novelists, poets, playwrights—come into the schools, read their work, and talk to the children about the problems of their craft. The children eat it up. In another school I know of, a practicing attorney from a nearby city comes in every month or so and talks to several classes about the law. Not the law as it is in books but as he sees it and encounters it in his cases, his problems, his work. And the children love it. It is real, grown-up, true, not *My Weekly Reader,* not "social studies," not lies and baloney.

Something easier yet. Let children work together, help each other, learn from each other and each other's mistakes. We now know, from the experience of many schools, both rich-suburban and poor-city, that children are often the best teachers of other children. What is more important, we know that when a fifth- or sixth-grader who has been having trouble with reading starts helping a first-grader, his own reading sharply improves. A number of schools are beginning to use what some call Paired Learning. This means that you let children form partnerships with other children, do their work, even including their tests, together, and share whatever marks or results this work gets—just like grownups in the real world. It seems to work.

Let the children learn to judge their own work. A child learning to talk does not learn by being corrected all the time—if corrected too much, he will stop talking. *He* compares, a thousand times a day, the difference between language as he uses it and as those around him use it. Bit by bit, he makes the necessary changes to make his language like other people's. In the same way, kids learning to do all the other things they learn without adult teachers—to walk, run, climb, whistle, ride a bike, skate, play games, jump rope—compare their own performance with what more skilled people do, and slowly make the needed changes. But in school we never give a child a chance to detect his mistakes, let alone correct them. We do it all for him. We act as if we thought he would never notice a mistake unless it was pointed out to him, or correct it unless he was made to. Soon he becomes dependent on the expert. We should let him do it himself. Let him figure out, with the help of other children if he wants it, what this word says, what is the answer to that problem, whether this is a good way of saying or doing this or that. If right answers are involved, as in some math or science, give him the answer book, let him correct his own papers. Why should we teachers waste time on such donkey work? Our job should be to help the kid when he tells us that he can't find a way to get the right answer. Let's get rid of all this nonsense of grades, exams, marks. We don't know now, and we never will know, how to measure what another person knows or understands. We certainly can't find out by asking him questions. All we find out is what he doesn't know—which is what most tests are for, anyway. Throw it all out, and let the child learn what every educated person must someday learn, how to measure his own understanding, how to know what he knows or does not know.

We could also abolish the fixed, required curriculum. People remember only what is interesting and useful to them, what helps them make sense of the world, or helps them get along in it. All else they quickly forget, if they ever learn it at all. The idea of a "body of knowledge," to be picked up in school and used for the rest of one's life, is nonsense in a world as complicated and rapidly changing as ours. Anyway, the most important questions and problems of our time are not *in* the curriculum, not even in the hotshot universities, let alone the schools.

15 Children want, more than they want anything else, and even after years of miseducation, to make sense of the world, themselves, and other human beings. Let them get at this job, with our help if they ask for it, in the way that makes most sense to them.

Source: Reproduced from "The Underachieving School", by John Holt, with permission of Sentient Publications, LLC.

RESPONDING TO READING

1. In what specific ways does Holt believe schools fail children?
2. According to Holt, what should schools do to correct their shortcomings? Do you think his suggestions are practical and realistic? Why or why not?

Rhetorical Analysis

In paragraph 13, Holt says, "Let's get rid of all this nonsense of grades, exams, marks." Do you consider this statement an example of *hyperbole*—the intentional use of overstatement or exaggeration to make a point? What point do you think Holt is trying to make? What are the advantages and disadvantages of this strategy?

Writing with Sources

Recently, there has been a movement away from the unstructured curriculum that Holt supported. Programs such as Common Core have been instituted to give curricula more structure and to establish clearer standards. Research Common Core, and then write an essay in which you explain your views about how structured (or unstructured) you think school curricula should be. What are the advantages and disadvantages of each approach?

4.3 Wendy Berliner, "Why There's No Such Thing As a Gifted Child"

An education journalist, Wendy Berliner is joint CEO at the Education Media Centre. She is also the coauthor of the book *Great Minds and How to Grow Them* (2018). In the following essay, Berliner debunks what she considers the myth of "gifted" children.

BEFORE YOU READ

Were you or anyone you knew growing up labelled "gifted"? What did this term mean to you then? What does it mean to you now?

Why There's No Such Thing As a Gifted Child

When Maryam Mirzakhani died at the tragically early age of 40 this month, the news stories talked of her as a genius. The only woman to win the Fields Medal—the mathematical equivalent of a Nobel prize—and a Stanford professor since the age of 31, this Iranian-born academic had been on a roll since she started winning gold medals at math Olympiads in her teens.

It would be easy to assume that someone as special as Mirzakhani must have been one of those gifted children who excel from babyhood. The ones reading Harry Potter at five or admitted to Mensa[1] not much later. The child that takes the math GCSE[2] while still in single figures, or a rarity such as Ruth Lawrence, who was admitted to Oxford while her contemporaries were still in primary school.

But look closer and a different story emerges. Mirzakhani was born in Tehran, one of three siblings in a middle-class family whose father was an engineer. The only part of her childhood that was out of the ordinary was the Iran-Iraq war, which made life hard for the family in her early years. Thankfully it ended around the time she went to secondary school.

Mirzakhani did go to a highly selective girls' school but math wasn't her interest—reading was. She loved novels and would read anything she could lay her hands on; together with her best friend she would prowl the book stores on the way home from school for works to buy and consume.

As for math, she did rather poorly at it for the first couple of years in her 5
middle school, but became interested when her elder brother told her about what he'd learned. He shared a famous math problem from a magazine that fascinated her—and she was hooked. The rest is mathematical history.

---

[1]A nonprofit organization and IQ society founded in 1946 in the United Kingdom. [Eds.]

[2]General Certificate of Secondary Education exams taken by most secondary-school students in the United Kingdom. [Eds.]

Is her background unusual? Apparently not. Most Nobel laureates were unexceptional in childhood. Einstein was slow to talk and was dubbed the dopey one by the family maid. He failed the general part of the entry test to Zurich Polytechnic—though they let him in because of high physics and math scores. He struggled at work initially, failing to get academic post and being passed over for promotion at the Swiss Patent Office because he wasn't good enough at machine technology. But he kept plugging away and eventually rewrote the laws of Newtonian mechanics with his theory of relativity.

Lewis Terman, a pioneering American educational psychologist, set up a study in 1921 following 1,470 Californians, who excelled in the newly available IQ tests, throughout their lives. None ended up as the great thinkers of their age that Terman expected they would. But he did miss two future Nobel prize winners—Luis Alvarez and William Shockley, both physicists—whom he dismissed from the study as their test scores were not high enough.

There is a canon of research on high performance, built over the last century, that suggests it goes way beyond tested intelligence. On top of that, research is clear that brains are malleable, new neural pathways can be forged, and IQ isn't fixed. Just because you can read Harry Potter at five doesn't mean you will still be ahead of your contemporaries in your teens.

According to my colleague, Prof Deborah Eyre, with whom I've collaborated on the book *Great Minds and How to Grow Them*, the latest neuroscience and psychological research suggests most people, unless they are cognitively impaired, can reach standards of performance associated in school with the gifted and talented. However, they must be taught the right attitudes and approaches to their learning and develop the attributes of high performers—curiosity, persistence and hard work, for example—an approach Eyre calls "high performance learning." Critically, they need the right support in developing those approaches at home as well as at school.

10 So, is there even such a thing as a gifted child? It is a highly contested area. Prof Anders Ericsson, an eminent education psychologist at Florida State University, is the co-author of *Peak: Secrets from the New Science of Expertise*. After research going back to 1980 into diverse achievements, from music to memory to sport, he doesn't think unique and innate talents are at the heart of performance. Deliberate practice, that stretches you every step of the way, and around 10,000 hours of it, is what produces the expert. It's not a magic number—the highest performers move on to doing a whole lot more, of course, and, like Mirzakhani, often find their own unique perspective along the way.

Ericsson's memory research is particularly interesting because random students, trained in memory techniques for the study, went on to outperform others thought to have innately superior memories—those you might call gifted.

He got into the idea of researching the effects of deliberate practice because of an incident at school, in which he was beaten at chess by someone who used to lose to him. His opponent had clearly practiced.

But it is perhaps the work of Benjamin Bloom, another distinguished American educationist working in the 1980s, that gives the most pause for thought and underscores the idea that family is intrinsically important to the concept of high performance.

Bloom's team looked at a group of extraordinarily high achieving people in disciplines as varied as ballet, swimming, piano, tennis, maths, sculpture and neurology, and interviewed not only the individuals but their parents, too.

He found a pattern of parents encouraging and supporting their children, 15
in particular in areas they enjoyed themselves. Bloom's outstanding adults had worked very hard and consistently at something they had become hooked on young, and their parents all emerged as having strong work ethics themselves.

While the jury is out on giftedness being innate and other factors potentially making the difference, what is certain is that the behaviors associated with high levels of performance are replicable and most can be taught—even traits such as curiosity.

Eyre says we know how high performers learn. From that she has developed a high performing learning approach that brings together in one package what she calls the advanced cognitive characteristics, and the values, attitudes and attributes of high performance. She is working on the package with a group of pioneer schools, both in Britain and abroad.

But the system needs to be adopted by families, too, to ensure widespread success across classes and cultures. Research in Britain shows the difference parents make if they take part in simple activities pre-school in the home, supporting reading for example. That support shows through years later in better A-level results, according to the Effective Pre-School, Primary and Secondary study, conducted over 15 years by a team from Oxford and London universities.

Eye-opening spin-off research, which looked in detail at 24 of the 3,000 individuals being studied who were succeeding against the odds, found something remarkable about what was going on at home. Half were on free school meals because of poverty, more than half were living with a single parent, and four in five were living in deprived areas.

The interviews uncovered strong evidence of an adult or adults in the child's 20
life who valued and supported education, either in the immediate or extended family or in the child's wider community. Children talked about the need to work hard at school and to listen in class and keep trying. They referenced key adults who had encouraged those attitudes.

Einstein, the epitome of a genius, clearly had curiosity, character and determination. He struggled against rejection in early life but was undeterred. Did he think he was a genius or even gifted? No. He once wrote: "It's not that I'm so smart, it's just that I stay with problems longer. Most people say that it is the intellect which makes a great scientist. They are wrong: it is character."

And what about Mirzakhani? Her published quotations show someone who was curious and excited by what she did and resilient. One comment sums it up. "Of course, the most rewarding part is the 'Aha' moment, the excitement of discovery and enjoyment of understanding something new—the feeling of being on top of a hill and having a clear view. But most of the time, doing mathematics for me is like being on a long hike with no trail and no end in sight."

The trail took her to the heights of original research into mathematics in a cruelly short life. That sounds like unassailable character. Perhaps that was her gift.

RESPONDING TO READING

1. According to Berliner, why is the idea of a "gifted" child a myth? How might this term actually impede the progress of children it intends to elevate? Can anyone become "gifted"? Why or why not?
2. What is "high performance learning" (9)? How does this concept relate to the view of some children as intellectually "gifted"?

Rhetorical Analysis

Identify some of the specific evidence Berliner uses to back up her claims. Is her support sufficient? Is her argument convincing? Explain.

Writing with Sources

Research the work of educational psychologist Benjamin Bloom (1913–1999), whom Berliner mentions in her essay. In what ways do Bloom's findings support Berliner's ideas? Do they seem to disagree on any points? Write an essay in which you synthesize the educational theories espoused by both writers.

4.4 Johann N. Neem, "Online Higher Education's Individualist Fallacy"

A professor of history at Western Washington University, Johann N. Neem specializes in the history of the early American republic. He is the author of *Creating a Nation of Joiners: Democracy and Civil Society in Early National Massachusetts* (2008) and *Democracy's Schools: The Rise of Public Education in America* (2017). In the following essay, Neem argues for the value of "institutional culture" in higher education.

BEFORE YOU READ

Do you think students need to be in a traditional classroom to get an education? Why or why not?

Online Higher Education's Individualist Fallacy

There has been much talk of the "online revolution" in higher education. While there is a place for online education, some of its boosters anticipate displacing the traditional campus altogether. A close reading of their arguments, however, makes clear that many share what might be called the "individualist fallacy," both in their understanding of how students learn and how professors teach.

Of course, individualism has a long, noble heritage in American history. From the "age of the self-made man" onward, we have valued those who pull themselves up by their own bootstraps. But, as Warren Buffett[1] has made clear, even the most successful individuals depend heavily on the cultural, economic, legal, political, and social contexts in which they act. This is as true for Buffett as it is for other so-called self-made men, such as Bill Gates. And it is certainly true for students.

But many advocates of online learning ignore this simple point. The economist Richard Vedder, for example, believes that being on campus is only useful for "making friends, partying, drinking, and having sex." Anya Kamenetz, in her book *DIY U*, celebrates the day when individuals are liberated from the constraints of physical campuses, while Gates anticipates that "five years from now on the Web for free you'll be able to find the best lectures in the world. It will be better than any single university."

These advocates of online higher education forget the importance of *institutional culture* in shaping how people learn. College is about more than accessing information; it's about developing an attitude toward knowledge.

There is a difference between being on a campus with other students and 5
teachers committed to learning and sitting at home. Learning, like religion, is a social experience. Context matters. No matter how much we might learn about God and our obligations from the Web, it is by going to church and being surrounded by other congregants engaged in similar questions, under the guidance of a thoughtful, caring pastor, that we really change. Conversion is social, and so is learning.

Like all adults, students will pursue many activities during their time on campus, but what distinguishes a college is that it embodies ideals distinct from the rest of students' lives. If we take college seriously, we need people to spend time in such places so that they will leave different than when they entered.

Some argue that large lecture courses make a mockery of the above claims. Admittedly, in a better world, there would be no large lecture courses. Still, this argument misleads for several reasons. First, it generalizes from one kind of course, ignoring the smaller class sizes at community colleges and the upper-division courses in which students interact closely with each other and their professors. Second, it dismisses the energy of being in a classroom, even a large one, with real people when compared to being on our own. Even in large classes, good teachers push their students to think by asking probing questions, modeling

[1]Investor and philanthropist (1930–). [Eds.]

curiosity, and adapting to the class's needs. Finally, it disregards the importance of the broader campus context in which all classes, large and small, take place.

The goal of bringing students to campus for several years is to immerse them in an environment in which learning is the highest value, something online environments, no matter how interactive, cannot simulate. Real learning is hard; it requires students to trust each other and their teachers. In other words, it depends on relationships. This is particularly important for the liberal arts.

Of course, as Richard Arum and Josipa Roksa's recent study *Academically Adrift* makes clear, there are great variations in what college students are learning. All too often, higher education does not fulfill our aspirations. But none of the problems Arum and Roksa identify are ones that online higher education would solve. As Arum and Roksa make clear, students learn more on campuses where learning is valued and expectations are high. If anything, we need to pay more attention to institutional culture because it matters so much.

10 This does not mean that we should reject technology when it can further learning, as in new computer programs that help diagnose students' specific stumbling blocks. But computers will never replace the inspiring, often unexpected, conversations that happen among students and between students and teachers on campuses. Because computers are not interpretive moral beings, they cannot evaluate assignments in which students are asked to reflect on complicated ideas or come up with new ones, especially concerning moral questions. Fundamentally, computers cannot cultivate curiosity because machines are not curious.

Technology is a tool, not an end in itself. As the computer scientist Jaron Lanier has written in his book *You Are Not A Gadget*, computers exist to support human endeavors, not the other way around. Many techno-utopists proclaim that computers are becoming smarter, more human, but Lanier wonders whether that is because we tend to reduce our human horizons to interact with our machines. This certainly is one of the dangers of online higher education.

The individualist fallacy applies not just to online advocates' understandings of students, but also their conception of what makes great teachers and scholars. Vedder, for example, echoes Gates in his hope that someday there will be a Wikipedia University, or that the Gates Foundation will start a university in which a few "star professors" are paid to teach thousands of students across the nation and world. Of course, this has been happening since the invention of cassette tapes that offer "the great courses." This is hardly innovative, nor does it a college education make.

Vedder ignores how star professors become great. How do they know what to teach and to write? Their success, like Buffett's, is social: they converse with and read and rely on the work of hundreds, even thousands, of other scholars. Read their articles and books, listen to their lectures, and you can discern how deeply influenced and how dependent they are on the work of their peers. In short, there would be no star professors absent an academy of scholars committed to research.

Schools like the online, Gates Foundation–funded Western Governors University free-ride off the expensive, quality research completed by traditional professors when they rely on open course ware and curricula. Take away the professors, and many online schools will teach material that is out of date or inaccurate or, worse, hand control over to other entities who are not interested in promoting the truth—from textbook companies seeking to maximize sales to coal and pharmaceutical companies offering their own curriculums for "free."

15 The Web and new technologies are great tools; they have made more information more accessible to more people. This is to be celebrated. Citizens in a democracy should be able to access as much information as freely as possible. A democratic society cannot allow scholars, or anyone else, to be the gatekeepers to knowledge.

Certainly, we will expand online higher education, if for no other reason than because wealthy foundations like Gates and ambitious for-profit entities are putting their money and power behind it. For certain students, especially working adults pursuing clearly defined vocational programs rather than a liberal arts education, online programs may allow opportunities that they would have otherwise foregone. But online higher education will never replace, much less replicate, what happens on college campuses.

Even as we expand online, therefore, we must deepen our commitment to those institutions that cultivate a love of learning in their students, focus on the liberal arts, and produce the knowledge that online and offline teaching requires.

Source: Johann N. Neem, "Online Higher Education's Individualistic Fallacy," Inside Higher Education, October 6, 2011. Used with Permission.

RESPONDING TO READING

1. What is the importance of "institutional culture" in shaping the way students learn (4)? According to Neem, how does distance learning undercut institutional culture in higher education?
2. What does Neem mean when he says, "Technology is a tool, not an end in itself" (11)? In what sense does he believe that online schools "free-ride off the expensive, quality research completed by traditional professors" (14)?

Rhetorical Analysis

Neem begins his essay by mentioning the "individualist fallacy" (1). What is the meaning of this term? Why does Neem begin his essay with this concept?

Writing with Sources

Many colleges now offer as many courses online as they do in traditional classroom settings. Research online education, and determine its advantages as well as its disadvantages. Next, write a proposal to your college in which you argue for or against more online instruction.

4.5 Christina Hoff Sommers, "For More Balance on Campuses"

Christina Hoff Sommers (1950–), who calls herself an "equity feminist," is currently a resident scholar at the American Enterprise Institute. Sommers is the author of essays in a wide variety of periodicals and has published several books but is best known for *Who Stole Feminism? How Women Have Betrayed Women* (1994) and *The War against Boys: How Misguided Feminism Is Harming Our Young Men* (2000). Her latest book is *Freedom Feminism* (2013). In the following essay, the introduction to a longer essay that appeared in the *Atlantic Monthly,* Sommers makes a plea for more political diversity on America's college campuses.

BEFORE YOU READ

Do you believe that at your college or university you are exposed to a cross-section of ideas? Why or why not?

For More Balance on Campuses

Washington—In a recent talk at Haverford College, I questioned the standard women's studies teaching that the United States is a patriarchal society that oppresses women.

For many in the audience, this was their first encounter with a dissident scholar. One student was horrified when I said that the free market had advanced the cause of women by affording them unprecedented economic opportunities. "How can anyone say that capitalism has helped women?" she asked.

Nor did I win converts when I said that the male heroism of special forces soldiers and the firefighters at ground zero should persuade gender scholars to acknowledge that "stereotypical masculinity" had some merit. Later an embarrassed and apologetic student said to me, "Haverford is just not ready for you."

After my talk, the young woman who invited me told me there was little intellectual diversity at Haverford and that she had hoped I would spark debate. In fact, many in the audience were quietly delighted by the exchanges. But two angry students accused her of providing "a forum for hate speech."

5 As the 2000 election made plain, the United States is pretty evenly divided between conservatives and liberals. Yet conservative scholars have effectively been marginalized, silenced, and rendered invisible on most campuses. This problem began in the late '80s and has become much worse in recent years. Most students can now go through four years of college without encountering a scholar of pronounced conservative views.

Few conservatives make it past the gantlet of faculty hiring in political-science, history, or English departments. In 1998, when a reporter from Denver's *Rocky Mountain News* surveyed the humanities and social sciences at the University of Colorado, Boulder, he found that of 190 professors with party affiliations, 184 were Democrats.

There wasn't a single Republican in the English, psychology, journalism, or philosophy departments. A 1999 survey of history departments found 22 Democrats and 2 Republicans at Stanford. At Cornell and Dartmouth there were 29 and 10 Democrats, respectively, and no Republicans.

The dearth of conservatives in psychology departments is so striking, that one (politically liberal) professor has proposed affirmative-action outreach. Richard Redding, a professor of psychology at Villanova University, writing in a recent issue of *American Psychologist,* notes that of the 31 social-policy articles that appeared in the journal between 1990 and 1999, 30 could be classified as liberal, one as conservative.

The key issue, Professor Redding says, is not the preponderance of Democrats, but the liberal practice of systematically excluding conservatives. Redding cites an experiment in which several graduate departments received mock applications from two candidates nearly identical, except that one "applicant" said he was a conservative Christian. The professors judged the nonconservative to be the significantly better candidate.

10 Redding asks, rhetorically: "Do we want a professional world where our liberal world view prevents us from considering valuable strengths of conservative approaches to social problems . . . where conservatives are reluctant to enter the profession and we tacitly discriminate against them if they do? That, in fact, is the academic world we now have . . . ."

Campus talks by "politically incorrect" speakers happen rarely; visits are resisted and almost never internally funded. When Dinesh D'Souza, Andrew Sullivan, David Horowitz, or Linda Chavez do appear at a college, they are routinely heckled and sometimes threatened. The academy is now so inhospitable to free expression that conservatives buy advertisements in student newspapers. But most school newspapers won't print them. And papers that do are sometimes vandalized and the editors threatened.

The classical liberalism articulated by John Stuart Mill in his book *On Liberty* is no longer alive on campuses, having died of the very disease Mr. Mill warned of when he pointed out that ideas not freely and openly debated become *dead dogmas.* Mill insisted that the intellectually free person must put himself in the *mental position of those who think differently* adding that dissident ideas are best understood *by hear[ing] them from persons who actually believe them.*

Several groups are working to bring some balance to campus. The Intercollegiate Studies Institute, Young America's Foundation, Clare Boothe Luce Policy Institute, and Accuracy in Academia sponsor lectures by leading conservatives and libertarians. Students can ask these groups for funds to sponsor speakers.

More good news is that David Horowitz's Center for the Study of Popular Culture has launched a "Campaign for Fairness and Inclusion in Higher Education." It calls for university officials to:

1. Establish a zero-tolerance policy for vandalizing newspapers or heckling speakers.
2. Conduct an inquiry into political bias in the allocation of student program funds, including speakers' fees, and seek ways to promote underrepresented perspectives.

3. Conduct an inquiry into political bias in the hiring process of faculty and administrators and seek ways to promote fairness toward—and inclusion of—underrepresented perspectives.

15 Were even one high-profile institution like the University of Colorado to adopt a firm policy of intellectual inclusiveness, that practice would quickly spread, and benighted students everywhere would soon see daylight.

Source: Christina Hoff Sommers, "For More Balance on Campuses." The Young America's Foundation Speakers Program, May 6, 2002. Used with permission.

RESPONDING TO READING

1. According to Sommers, conservatives have been marginalized on most American college campuses. What does she mean? How has this occurred? What evidence does Sommers present to support her claim? Is her evidence persuasive?
2. In Sommers's view, what is the effect of excluding conservatives from the intellectual life of a college or university? What does Sommers say is being done "to bring some balance to campus" (13)?

Rhetorical Analysis

In paragraph 10, Sommers includes a rhetorical question asked by Richard Redding, a professor at Villanova University. What is the point of this question? Why does Sommers insert it where she does?

Writing with Sources

Try to determine how politically diverse your school is. First, go online and see if your college is ranked in the *Niche Most Diverse Colleges in America*, a site that compares political diversity at more than a thousand colleges and universities nationwide. Also, interview several of your classmates. Then, write an essay in which you present your findings.

4.6 Jill Filipovic, "We've Gone Too Far with 'Trigger Warnings'"

A journalist, attorney, and feminist, Jill Filipovic (1983–) is a contributing opinion writer for *The New York Times* and a columnist for the *Guardian*, *Cosmopolitan*, and *CNN*. The author of *The H-Spot: The Feminist Pursuit of Happiness* (2017), she has also published work in the *Huffington Post*, *Women's eNews*, and *Yale Journal of Law & Feminism*. In the following essay, Filipovic explains the problem with "trigger warnings."

BEFORE YOU READ

Look up the meaning and some examples of the term *trigger warnings*. What is your assessment of trigger warnings? Do they serve a useful purpose, or do they infantilize students?

We've Gone Too Far with "Trigger Warnings"

Trigger Warning: *this piece discusses trigger warnings. It may also look askance at college students who are now asking that trigger warnings be applied to their course materials.*

If you've spent time on feminist blogs lately or in the social-justice-oriented corner of Tumblr, you have likely come across the Trigger Warning (TW): a note to readers that the material following the warning may trigger a post-traumatic stress reaction. In the early days of feminist blogging, trigger warnings were generally about sexual assault, and posted with the understanding that lots of women are sexual assault survivors, lots of women read feminist blogs, and graphic descriptions of rape might lead to panic attacks or other reactions that will really ruin someone's day. Easy enough to give readers a little heads up—a trigger warning—so that they can decide to avoid that material if they know that discussion of rape triggers debilitating reactions.

Trigger warnings in online spaces, though, have expanded widely and become more intricate, detailed, specific and obscure. Trigger warnings, and their cousin the "content note," are now included for a whole slew of potentially offensive or upsetting content, including but not limited to: misogyny, the death penalty, calories in a food item, terrorism, drunk driving, how much a person weighs, racism, gun violence, Stand Your Ground laws,[1] drones, homophobia, PTSD, slavery, victim-blaming, abuse, swearing, child abuse, self-injury, suicide, talk of drug use, descriptions of medical procedures, corpses, skulls, skeletons, needles, discussion of "isms," neuroatypical shaming,[2] slurs (including "stupid" or "dumb"), kidnapping, dental trauma, discussions of sex (even consensual), death or dying, spiders, insects, snakes, vomit, pregnancy, childbirth, blood, scarification,[3] Nazi paraphernalia, slimy things, holes and "anything that might inspire intrusive thoughts in people with OCD."

It is true that everything on the above list might trigger a PTSD response in someone. The trouble with PTSD, though, is that its triggers are often unpredictable and individually specific—a certain smell, a particular song, being touched in that one way. It's impossible to account for all of them, because triggers are by their nature not particularly rational or universally foreseeable. Some are more common

---

[1]Laws allowing citizens to defend themselves against threats, whether perceived or real. [Eds.]
[2]Shaming the mentally ill. [Eds.]
[3]Scarring the body as a form of adornment. [Eds.]

than others, though, which is why it seems reasonable enough for explicitly feminist spaces to include trigger warnings for things like assault and eating disorders.

5 College, though, is different. It is not a feminist blog. It is not a social justice Tumblr.

College isn't exactly the real world either, but it's a space for kinda-sorta adults to wade neck-deep into art, literature, philosophy, and the sciences, to explore new ideas, to expand their knowledge of the cultural canon, to interrogate power and to learn how to make an argument and to read a text. It is, hopefully, a space where the student is challenged and sometimes frustrated and sometimes deeply upset, a place where the student's world expands and pushes them to reach the outer edges—not a place that contracts to meet the student exactly where they are.

Which doesn't mean that individual students should not be given mental health accommodations. It's perfectly reasonable for a survivor of violence to ask a professor for a heads up if the reading list includes a piece with graphic descriptions of rape or violence, for example. But generalized trigger warnings aren't so much about helping people with PTSD as they are about a certain kind of performative feminism: they're a low-stakes way to use the right language to identify yourself as conscious of social justice issues. Even better is demanding a trigger warning—that identifies you as even more aware, even more feminist, even more solicitous than the person who failed to adequately provide such a warning.

There is real harm in utilizing general trigger warnings in the classroom. Oberlin College recommends that its faculty "remove triggering material when it does not contribute directly to the course learning goals." When material is simply too important to take out entirely, the college recommends trigger warnings. For example, Oberlin says, Chinua Achebe's *Things Fall Apart* is a great and important book, but:

> ... it may trigger readers who have experienced racism, colonialism, religious persecution, violence, suicide, and more.

Students should be duly warned by the professor writing, for example, "Trigger warning: This book contains a scene of suicide."

On its face, that sounds fine (except for students who hate literary spoilers). But a trigger warning for what Oberlin identified as the book's common triggers—racism, colonialism, religious persecution, violence, suicide (and more!)—sets the tone for reading and understanding the book. It skews students' perceptions. It highlights particular issues as necessarily more upsetting than others, and directs students to focus on particular themes that have been singled out by the professor as traumatic.

10 At Rutgers, a student urged professors to use trigger warnings as a sort of Solomonic baby-splitting between two apparently equally bad choices: banning certain texts or introducing works that may cause psychological distress. Works the student mentioned as particularly triggering include F. Scott Fitzgerald's *The Great Gatsby*, Junot Diaz's *This Is How You Lose Her* and Virginia Woolf's *Mrs. Dalloway*. The warnings would be passage-by-passage, and effectively reach "a compromise between protecting students and defending their civil liberties."

But the space between comfort and freedom is not actually where universities should seek to situate college students. Students should be pushed to defend their ideas and to see the world from a variety of perspectives. Trigger warnings don't just warn students of potentially triggering material; they effectively shut down particular lines of discussion with "that's triggering." Students should—and do—have the right to walk out of any classroom. But students should also accept the challenge of exploring their own beliefs and responding to disagreement. Trigger warnings, of course, don't always shut down that kind of interrogation, but if feminist blogs are any example, they quickly become a way to short-circuit uncomfortable, unpopular or offensive arguments.

That should concern those of us who love literature, but it should particularly trouble the feminist and anti-racist bookworms among us. Trigger warnings are largely perceived as protecting young women and, to a lesser extent, other marginalized groups—people of color, LGBT people, people with mental illnesses. That the warnings hinge on topics that are more likely to affect the lives of marginalized groups contributes to the general perception of members of those groups as weak, vulnerable and "other."

The kinds of suffering typically imaged and experienced in the white western male realm—war, intra-male violence—are standard. Traumas that impact women, people of color, LGBT people, the mentally ill and other groups whose collective lives far outnumber those most often canonized in the American or European classroom are set apart as different, as particularly *traumatizing*. Trigger warnings imply that our experiences are so unusual the pages detailing our lives can only be turned while wearing kid gloves.

There's a hierarchy of trauma there, as well as a dangerous assumption of inherent difference. There's a reinforcement of the toxic messages young women have gotten our entire lives: that we're inherently vulnerable.

15 And there's something lost when students are warned before they read Achebe or Diaz or Woolf, and when they read those writers first through the lens of trauma and fear.

Then, simply, there is the fact that the universe does not treat its members as if they come hand-delivered in a box clearly marked "fragile." The world can be a desperately ugly place, especially for women. That feminist blogs try to carve out a little section of the world that is a teeny bit safer for their readers is a credit to many of those spaces. Colleges, though, are not intellectual or emotional safe zones. Nor should they be.

Trauma survivors need tools to manage their triggers and cope with every day life. Universities absolutely should prioritize their needs—by making sure that mental health care is adequately funded, widely available and destigmatized.

But they do students no favors by pretending that every piece of potentially upsetting, triggering or even emotionally devastating content comes with a warning sign.

RESPONDING TO READING

1. What are "trigger warnings"? What does Filipovic mean when she says, "they're a low-stakes way to use the right language to identify yourself as conscious of social issues" (7)?
2. What are Filipovic's concerns about trigger warnings? Why, according to Filipovic, do these warnings "do students no favors" (18)?

Rhetorical Analysis

In paragraph 4, Filipovic concedes the possible advantages of trigger warnings. Does this concession undercut or strengthen her argument? Explain.

Writing with Sources

What do instructors think about including trigger warnings in their course syllabi? Research this issue, looking particularly at websites aimed at academics—for example, the American Association of University Professors website and the Inside Higher Education website. On what points do instructors seem to agree? Where do they disagree? Write an essay that presents the results of your research and that takes a stand on this issue.

4.7 Howard Nemerov, "To David, About His Education" [Poetry]

A poet and essayist, Howard Nemerov (1920–1991) was U.S. poet laureate from 1988 to 1990. A first lieutenant during World War II, he was a pilot in the Royal Canadian unit of the U.S. Army Air Force. After the war, he taught literature at Hamilton College, Bennington College, Brandeis University, and Washington University in St. Louis, where he was distinguished poet-in-residence. He published numerous poetry and essay collections over the course of several decades. In the following poem, the speaker considers the value of education.

BEFORE YOU READ

Do you like to read? Can you recall something specific you read that provided a transformative experience?

To David, About His Education

The world is full of mostly invisible things,
And there is no way but putting the mind's eye,
Or its nose, in a book, to find them out,
Things like the square root of Everest
Or how many times Byron goes into Texas,
Or whether the law of the excluded middle
Applies west of the Rockies. For these
And the like reasons, you have to go to school
And study books and listen to what you are told,
And sometimes try to remember. Though I don't know
What you will do with the mean annual rainfall
On Plato's Republic, or the calorie content
Of the Diet of Worms, such things are said to be
Good for you, and you will have to learn them
In order to become one of the grown-ups
Who sees invisible things neither steadily nor whole,
But keeps gravely the grand confusion of the world
Under his hat, which is where it belongs,
And teaches small children to do this in their turn.

Source: The Collected Poems of Howard Nemerov, University Of Chicago Press, 1977. Courtesy The Estate of Howard Nemerov.

RESPONDING TO READING

1. How would you characterize the speaker's attitude toward book learning?
2. Although "To David, About His Education" is humorous, it has a serious purpose. What point is the speaker making about education? About "the grand confusion of the world" (line 17)?

Rhetorical Analysis

Look up any allusions in the poem you don't understand. Why does the speaker blend these allusions together?

4.8 Focus: "Should a College Education Be Free?"

CharlineXia Ontario Canada Collection / Alamy Stock Photo

How does this photo from a student protest at the University of Toronto criticize the viability of a college education?

RESPONDING TO THE IMAGE

Answer one or both of the following questions.

1. What elements does this image use to depict the political debate surrounding the cost of a college education?
2. Consider this photo's central imagery of a mock graveyard. Why do you think protestors made their signs to resemble tombstones? What point do you think the protestors wanted to make? Do you think their signs get the point across? Why or why not?

4.9 Anya Kamenetz, "Is Free College Really Free?"

NPR's lead education blogger, Anya Kamenetz (1980–) writes about issues related to learning, technology, and social entrepreneurship. Her work has appeared in such publications as *Fast Company* magazine; *New York Magazine; The New York Times; O, The Oprah Magazine; Slate*; and *The Washington Post*. She is the author of four books, including, most recently, *The Art of Screen Time: How Your Family Can Balance*

Digital Media and Real Life (2018). In the following essay, Kamenetz dissects the term "free" in relation to higher education.

BEFORE YOU READ

What alternatives are there to college? In what instances do you think a four-year college degree may not be worth the time, energy, and cost?

Is Free College Really Free?

"Free" is a word with a powerful appeal. And in the past year or so it has been tossed around a lot, followed by another word: "college."

Both Bernie Sanders and Hillary Clinton spent a lot of time talking about free tuition. And this week, the promise has been taken up by one of the largest public university systems in the country: New York state's.

Gov. Andrew Cuomo unveiled a proposal that would offer free tuition at state-run colleges for students from families earning less than $125,000 a year. Called the Excelsior Scholarship, his plan—which needs approval by the Legislature—would grant full rides to qualifying students as long as they attend one of the state's public two- or four-year colleges.

Cuomo's proposal, in the lexicon of "free-college" policymaking, is what's called a "last dollar" program.

As NPR Ed explained this summer, that means students who are already 5
eligible for federal Pell Grants must use them to pay for school. After that money is gone, the state pledges to fill in the gap.

This method is the cheapest for the state, since students can draw on federal money first before taking state aid. With this type of plan, a larger share of funds from the new program is likely to go mainly to families who are relatively well off.

As Robert Kelchen, a higher education scholar at Seton Hall University, explains on his blog:

> The benefits of the program would go to two groups of students. The first group is fairly obvious: middle-income and upper-middle-income families. In New York, $125,000 falls at roughly the 80th percentile of family income—an income level where families may not be able to pay tuition without borrowing, but college enrollment rates are quite high. (Kelchen, Robert. "How Should States Structure 'Free' College?" January 3, 2017. https://robertkelchen.com/)

The other group that may benefit, says Kelchen, are lower-income students who are enticed by the clarity of the promise of "free."

But New York's proposal, like others, is likely to be controversial.

In reality there's no free college, just as there's no free lunch. The real policy discussion is about how to best distribute the burden of paying for it—between individual families and the public at large—and, secondly, how to hold down the cost of providing it. All while leveraging the power of "free" responsibly.

Fueling a Bubble

For many conservatives, the answer is simple. An education makes individuals richer, 10
and individuals should bear the cost. "The state should not subsidize intellectual curiosity," said Ronald Reagan, back when he was running for governor of California.

In recent times, the conservative position is perhaps best expressed by economist Richard Vedder, director of the Center for College Affordability and Productivity.

In his books, articles and public appearances, Vedder argues that federal student aid is creating a bubble that allows colleges to raise prices indefinitely, and the only way to stop the cycle is to cut off public funding.

Kevin Carey, now the director of the higher education policy program at the nonpartisan New America Foundation, made pretty much the same argument in the *New Republic* in 2012. He compared public universities to apple vendors:

> You, the apple vendor, look at the situation and say, "Hey, the market price of an apple is still $1. Wouldn't it be great if I could charge $1 for apples, but still get 40 cents from the government for every apple I sell?"... So you start raising prices by 3, 4, or 5 percent above inflation annually. (Kevin Carey, A Radical Solution For America's Worsening College Tuition Bubble, 2012, The New Republic)

In a world with no public subsidy at all for education, the only option left for free tuition would be something like the Starbucks plan—large corporations or wealthy donors footing the bill. And that kind of "free" comes, generally, with a significant catch—like requiring students to work for a certain employer.

The Public Piggy Bank

At the other end of the political spectrum are those who see a large public obligation to pay for the education of citizens, to promote democracy, meritocracy and equal rights, among other things. They just can't agree on how.

Once upon a time, public university in this country actually was free, for the most part. In the 19th and early 20th centuries, from New York to California, states opted to charge no tuition or nominal fees.

Here's the catch. Until World War II, college was also pretty sparsely attended. In 1940, only about 5 percent of the population, most of them white men, had a bachelor's degree. And the U.S. was the most educated nation in the world! The small numbers made tuition relatively cheap to subsidize.

But starting with the GI Bill, the United States moved to a new model of "mass" higher education. The expansion continued through the 1960s, with the Higher Education Act of 1965 establishing federal student-aid programs.

Suddenly, most high school graduates—men, women, black, white, new immigrants—aspired to a college degree. In defiance of the laws of economics, as the supply of college graduates went up, so did the demand for them, year after year. A college degree pretty much always meant you made more money.

Graduates also paid more taxes, so the government got its money back in the long term—$6 for every dollar spent on the GI Bill, by some estimates.

No Such Thing

Starting in the 1970s, there was a backlash to all this free money. In the economic slump, federal and state subsidies to higher education tightened. Enrollments declined. Loans, which were cheaper for the government, began to replace grants.

Public universities responded to the decreased state subsidies by raising tuition. They responded to the increased availability of loan financing by raising tuition. They responded to the continued robust demand for higher education by raising tuition. They responded to the pressure to expand, adding new programs and majors and building bigger campuses, by raising tuition. Since 1978, public university tuition has climbed every single year, two or three times faster than inflation. Average student loan debt for a bachelor's degree: $29,400.

Sara Goldrick-Rab of Temple University sums up the results of all this in a paper she wrote for the Lumina Foundation:

> Talented students are forgoing college because of the costs, students who start college are unable to complete because they cannot afford to continue, and even students who finish degrees may not realize all of the expected returns because of sizable debt burdens.

The United States is no longer the most educated nation in the world—it's the 12th. Most of the countries ahead of it have lower-cost public university options than the U.S. Perhaps most damning, the high cost of college in this country helps ensure that in too many cases, wealth trumps merit.

The success rate in college for the lowest-achieving but highest-income students is slightly better than the success rate for the highest-achieving, lowest-income students.

Found Money

Out-of-control college costs are hurting the most vulnerable. There are many different efforts to pacify the giant octopus.

The new proposals bank on the fact that the federal government already spends lots of money on student aid: $47 billion in grants a year, $101 billion in loans (which are repaid), and another $20 billion in tax credits. The total of state, federal and private money going to defray the cost of tuition—that's distinct from state appropriations directly to institutions—is $247 billion per year.

Seems like with that kind of dough, there ought to be ways of buying better 25
access and more equity.

There's substantial evidence that low-income students are less likely to even aspire to college because they think it's too expensive. It affects things like their choice of math classes as early as sixth grade.

That's why so many of these programs have the word "promise" or "hope" in the name. The student-aid bureaucracy is complicated to navigate. "Free college" is a promise everyone can understand.

Redeeming America's Promise calls for offering a full scholarship to a public two- or four-year college to every academically qualified student from families making no more than $160,000 a year. Part of the money, they say, could come from Pell Grants and tax credits, which would no longer be needed. (This math has been challenged).

Goldrick-Rab, a scholar who studies access to higher education, argued in her paper last year for the Lumina Foundation that the federal student-aid budget would and should go to pay for two years of universal free public college for all comers, including books, supplies, even a living stipend for those who need it.

The Fine Print

Unfortunately, most attempts to defray the cost of college come with unintended 30
consequences.

For a good example, look no further than Georgia's HOPE Scholarship. This statewide program, dating from 1993, offers high school graduates who meet certain requirements scholarships at a state university. At one time, about a dozen states had created similar models.

According to this early look at the impact of the HOPE program, by Susan Dynarski for the National Bureau of Economic Research, "Georgia's program has likely increased the college attendance rate of all 18- to 19-year-olds by 7.0 to 7.9 percentage points."

Not too shabby. However, "the evidence suggests that Georgia's program has widened the gap in college attendance between blacks and whites and between those from low- and high-income families."

Wait a minute. So a free tuition plan, instead of helping low-income and minority students, actually left them further behind? Yes, and that result has been seen in other states. It happens because these state programs require certain high school GPAs and test scores, and require that students maintain a certain GPA in college. And proportionately more middle-class white kids meet those bars.

Nothing Left to Lose

35 Most of the conversations about free college, as we've seen, are really about moving around piles of government money and other funds.

Some folks are starting to talk about whether we can meaningfully lower the cost of delivering a college education, instead of or in addition to paying for it differently. Most of those conversations have something to do with technology.

Some thought Massive Open Online Courses would be the Holy Grail: free, high-quality college for everyone! But in that case, "free" led to lower commitment. Completion rates for MOOCs hover around 5 to 7 percent.

Blended programs, which are self-paced and combine online learning with assistance from real people by phone or in person, seem to be able to hold down costs and get good results at the same time. Like Western Governors University, a nonprofit whose teacher-prep program was the National Council of Teacher Quality's first-ranked program in the country in 2014. It manages to charge less than the average public university without taking any public subsidy.

The unique thing about education, and what makes it so hard to control the price, is that it's not just a service or a good. It's a process, and the learner takes an active role in creating its value. A college education may never be free, but for many people it will remain priceless.

RESPONDING TO READING

1. In paragraph 22, Kamenetz writes, "The success rate in college for the lowest-achieving but highest-income students is slightly better than the success rate for the highest-achieving, lowest-income students." What are the implications of this statement? What does it mean for low-income students seeking higher education?
2. Kamenetz concludes her essay by defining education as "not just a service or a good. It's a process, and the learner takes an active role in

creating its value" (39). What does she mean? How might this view of education factor into the debate about whether or not it should be free?

Rhetorical Analysis

Identify examples of Kamenetz's conversational tone throughout the essay. Does this tone make her argument more or less convincing? Explain.

Writing with Sources

Research scholarships available to high school graduates in your state. What requirements must students meet to be eligible? Who are past recipients of these scholarships, and what are their stories? Write an essay in which you make the case that these scholarships are helping or hindering students' chances for success in your state. Make sure that you use the examples that you have found in your research as well as Kamenetz's essay to support your points.

4.10 Matthew Yglesias, "Walmart's Too-Good-to-Be-True '$1 a Day' College Tuition Plan, Explained"

A cofounder of and senior correspondent for *Vox,* where the following essay first appeared, Matthew Yglesias (1981–) focuses on issues related to politics and economics. He cohosts *The Weeds* podcast and has written for publications such as *The American Prospect, The Atlantic, Slate,* and *Think Progress*. Yglesias is the author of two books, including, most recently, *The Rent Is Too Damn High: What to Do About It, and Why It Matters More than You Think* (2012). In this essay, Yglesias evaluates corporate tuition benefits.

BEFORE YOU READ

Do you think companies have a financial responsibility to help their employees obtain a college degree? Why or why not?

Walmart's Too-Good-to-Be-True '$1 a Day' College Tuition Plan, Explained

Walmart is the largest private employer in the United States, so its human resources policies are always big news with national implications.

If headlines this week like "Walmart's perk for workers: Go to college for $1 a day" (CNN) or "Walmart to offer employees a college education for $1 a day" (Washington Post) sound too good to be true, that's because they largely are. The benefit is real, but it is much more restrictive than those headlines suggest. It's essentially a bulk purchasing discount for a narrow range of online college courses.

It's also a telling benefit on a number of levels. The labor market is getting stronger, and employers are needing to think harder about how to invest in recruiting and retaining employees. But the old-fashioned strategy of paying more continues to be something corporate America resists, in part out of habit and in part because offering higher wages is a little more complicated than it looks. Companies like Walmart are, in essence, trying to get creative with their compensation packages in hopes of narrowly targeting the money they expend on the core goal of recruiting and retaining desirable workers.

The question is whether policymakers will keep unemployment low long enough to break through the wall of resistance to across-the-board pay hikes and force big companies to finally just raise pay.

Walmart's actual tuition plan, explained

5 The Walmart program is limited to online degree programs offered by three schools—the University of Florida, Brandman University, and Bellevue University—and specifically focused on bachelor's or associate degrees in either business or supply chain management.

You won't, in other words, be able to do part-time shifts at Walmart to "pay your way through college" in the traditional sense.

But qualifying Walmart employees (including both full-time and part-time workers who've been with the company for 90 days) will get discounted tuition, books, and access to a coach who will help them decide on an appropriate program and shepherd them through the application process.

It's a nice opportunity for Walmart employees to gain a chance at upward mobility off the retail floor, and that's likely the point. Unlike higher cash wages (which of course can be used for online college tuition as well as rent, gasoline, movie tickets, medical expenses, etc.), the tuition benefit is likely to be disproportionately appealing to people who are on the more ambitious end of the distribution. It's an effort, in other words, to make Walmart more attractive specifically to the most appealing set of potential workers, a strategy other companies have pursued in recent years.

Many large employers are trying tuition benefits

Modest tuition programs have long been a staple of large employer benefits packages largely because of favorable tax treatment. The IRS allows employers to give employees several thousand dollars' worth of tuition benefits tax-free, which makes establishing a program something of a no-brainer for most companies big enough to be employing a large back-office staff anyway.

10 But four years ago, Starbucks blazed the trail of offering a much more ambitious reimbursement program that essentially offered taxable tuition subsidies rather than taxable wage increases.

The reason: Academic research shows that workers who are interested in tuition subsidies are different from workers who are not. While everyone likes money, Peter Cappelli's 2002 research indicates that the workers who like tuition subsidies are more productive than those who don't, and Colleen Manchester's 2012 research shows that subsidy-using employees have longer time horizons and are less likely to switch jobs.

In March of this year, a consortium of big US hotels launched a generous tuition discount program, and later that month, McDonald's substantially enhanced its tuition benefits. Kroger—another top five US employer—rolled out a new tuition program in April, and Chick-fil-A expanded its program in May.

These initiatives differ in detail, but the broad story is the same. The unemployment rate is now low, so recruiting new staff is getting harder. Companies are looking to enhance their compensation but would like to do so in targeted ways.

Corporate America is still resisting big pay raises

The basic problem facing large employers in a low-unemployment recruiting environment is that raising pay can be very costly.

It might be profitable to add one (or 100) additional workers at your currently 15
prevailing wage rates, but impossible to find any actually qualified people who want the job at that pay level. Offering more money would be a natural solution, but you can't really offer more money to 100 new employees without doing something for your hundreds of thousands of existing employees, and raising pay across the board to recruit new staff could make your company less profitable rather than more profitable.

Indeed, some CEOs recently told a forum organized by the Federal Reserve Bank of Dallas that they would *never* offer broad-based pay raises again.

The truth, however, is that this is less up to the discretion of CEOs than they would like. Six years ago, after all, companies weren't increasing the generosity of their tuition programs. They didn't change their minds about this because they suddenly became nice people; they changed their minds because the labor market got tighter. Going forward, the Fed might raise interest rates fast enough to prevent wage pressures from ever really building, or a new financial crisis might derail the economy.

But if not, companies will find that the longer the jobless rate stays low, the harder they have to dig for help. For some, that will mean accepting smaller profit margins, while for others it will mean higher prices. And for those companies that can't raise prices, it may mean actually running the risk of being driven out of business as companies with more pricing power poach their staff. For now, though, most big employers are only dabbling in generosity, with tuition discounts serving as an easy step into the shallow end of the pool.

RESPONDING TO READING

1. According to Yglesias, why are companies like Walmart offering their employees tuition benefits? What do employees and employers stand to gain? What, if anything, do they stand to lose?
2. In paragraph 8, Yglesias explains that Walmart's tuition benefit was designed "to make Walmart more attractive specifically to the most appealing set of potential workers." Why do you think Walmart chose this strategy to attract high-quality candidates? What other strategies might the company have used instead?

Rhetorical Analysis
How does the title of Yglesias's essay help reveal his thesis? Explain.

Writing with Sources
Research the latest developments regarding corporate tuition benefits. Does this trend seem to be increasing or declining? How similar and different are existing programs in their goals and effects? Write an essay in which you report your findings.

4.11 Liz Dwyer, "Is College Worth the Money? Answers from Six New Graduates"

The managing editor of Shondaland.com and the culture and education editor at *TakePart* magazine, Liz Dwyer writes about educational issues, parenting, and race. Her work has appeared in *Good Housekeeping* magazine, the online publication *DivineCaroline,* and numerous blogs, including her own, *Los Angelista.* In the following article from *GOOD* magazine, Dwyer compiles the responses of six 2011 college graduates to the question of whether a college education is worth the money.

BEFORE YOU READ
Do you think that college should prepare you for life or for a career? Explain.

Is College Worth the Money? Answers from Six New Graduates

Students are racking up astronomical amounts of debt and moving home with mom and dad after graduation because there are no jobs to be found. PayPal founder Peter Thiel is even encouraging students to drop out and try entrepreneurship instead because, he says, college isn't worth it. So we decided to ask some graduates from the class of 2011 what they think. Almost all of them are worried about paying back their student loan debt, and of those not going on to grad school, none will have traditional full-time jobs. But their answers about the value of college might surprise you.

1) The Journalist
Name: Sara Fletcher
Age: 22
College: Northwestern University
Major: Journalism

Post-college plans: Fletcher's headed to Portland, Oregon, for a public relations internship.
Is college worth the money?

"I chose Northwestern's Medill School of Journalism because it is top in the country. The connections here are undeniable and the opportunities for internships and post-grad jobs are better than I could have hoped for had I attended school in-state. I was challenged from the moment I arrived at Medill to basically act as a full-time reporter. Those skills, which I was challenged to develop very independently in and outside of the classroom will be incredibly useful for my work in PR and marketing. That said, I think college, particularly at a top school, is somewhat of a luxury and privilege. It's a chance for a lot of people, myself included, to take four years to really focus ourselves, figure out our passions in life, and gather the skills, critical thinking and connections to live out those passions. Because of the high price, for many that I've met, the luxury of four years at an elite school to 'find yourself' sometimes isn't as immediately justifiable, particularly when a high school grad has the life skills and confidence to enter the working world."

2) The Dentist
Name: Leah Munson
Age: 21
College: Binghamton University
Major: Biological Sciences
Post-college plans: Munson's hoping to get into dental school and be an orthodontist.
Is college worth the money?

"I hated college while I was there because I felt like everyone was wasting my time. I have known what I wanted to do since I was 12 and sitting in yet another classroom learning material that only grazed my interest was frustrating. I rushed through my undergraduate work, graduating in 3 years so that I could finally get to where I wanted to be. Although I have learned a lot in college and looking back I believe that it was very important in shaping who I am today, I hate the fact that I just spent years of my life forcing myself to learn information that I likely won't use again. College is not shaping students for their careers but rather for society. I'm not the person I was when I went to college but not because of anything I learned in a classroom. I'm different because it was a social bootcamp of sorts. Seeing as I already know what I want to do, I took the knowledge with a grain of salt. I was glad to be learning it and found it interesting but I was forced to acknowledge that I would likely never use it again."

3) The Startup Guru
Name: Ashwin Anandani
Age: 22
College: Northwestern University
Major: Economics
Post-college plans: Anandani graduated early, managed to raise some money for a social change startup idea and moved to the Bay Area to

pursue it. In the meantime, to keep a roof over his head, he also found a paid part-time job with another startup.

Is college worth the money?

"I don't think the value of a college is equal to the sum of its graduates' wages. I paid a couple hundred thousand dollars in total for my (almost) 4 years at university, and while I came out being able to think well, which is what I believe university is really meant to 'teach' you, I can only say that the university contributed a very small share of that ability. Now that I've been out, I'm thinking, 'I really just paid money to be assigned papers and math so I could have a piece of paper that serves as a filtering mechanism for corporations' HR departments?'

5 I would say my assignments and college requirements were more of a very arduous process of creating a 'fallback plan' so I don't end up on the streets if my startup fails. It's almost a monopoly in terms of options, too—'If you don't go to college, where will you go?'—so we pay the high price to be locked into a degree and we learn how to make standardized documents and take standardized tests. Too bad the world isn't standardized like my degree was."

4) The Teacher

Name: Alexis Valdez

Age: 22

College: Holy Cross College

Major: Elementary Education, K-6 and ENL (English as a New Language)

Post-college plans: Valdez, who is the first in her family to go to college, doesn't yet have a permanent teaching position. She says she plans to keep submitting applications to all the school districts in her area, and hopes to substitute teach to pay the bills.

Is college worth the money?

"I think that even though right now I'm in a tight spot as far as a job and finances go, college was definitely worth the money. In my specific field the job market is particularly sparse, though I wouldn't be as marketable in the teaching world if I hadn't had the opportunity to get real classroom experiences through my college program. I will admit that I'm not pleased to be deep in college debt, but in the long run, I believe that getting a college education was the best choice I could have made for myself to ensure a better future."

5) The Entrepreneur

Name: Arnela Sulovic

Age: 21

School: University of Southern California

Major: Communication

Post-college plans: Sulovic, who immigrated from war-torn Bosnia, is the first in her family to go to college and graduated in three years to save money. She wants to start her own business, but right now she's working as a summer resident adviser for off-campus housing and a sales/partnership intern at Thrillist Rewards. She's still looking for a full-time job.

Is college worth the money?

"I strongly believe that college is worth the money. Although everything I learned in the classroom may not be applicable to my career, USC gave me access to unparalleled experiences, introduced me to incredible people and ideas, and broadened my perspective. Furthermore, the extracurricular activities that I participated in helped me build real-world skills and leadership experiences. There are many benefits that one can gain only by experiencing a higher education. If I had known exactly what I wanted to do post-graduation, I could have taken advantage of more opportunities in college. I wish all college classes were hands-on, skill building, and exploratory."

6) The Lawyer
Name: Beverly Ozowara
Age: 21
College: University of Notre Dame
Major: Psychology & Film, Television, Theatre
Post-college plans: Ozowara will be attending Valparaiso Law School and wants to be a family lawyer.
Is college worth the money?

"I think that college is definitely worth it, but not because I learned specific things that would be helpful with my career. It was worth it for the valuable resources and connections I formed. It was also worth it because of the priceless undergraduate experience that I couldn't have gotten easily anywhere else. For example, I had the opportunity to travel (for a third of the normal cost) to Brazil with the Notre Dame Concert Band. During the trip, I was able to do things like perform at the oldest concert hall in the Americas and to swim in the Amazon River. I will admit though that I did not learn very many things that are specific to my career. It would have been helpful if there had been a pre-law program or more advising since freshmen year of college geared toward getting internships and familiarizing myself with corporations and the business world."

Source: "Is College Worth the Money?" Reprinted from GOOD Magazine, by L. Dwyer, 2011. Retrieved from http://magazine.good.is/articles/is-college-worth-the-money-reflections-from-six-graduates-of-the-class-of-2011.

RESPONDING TO READING

1. What would the six students change about their undergraduate experiences? What would they keep the same?
2. On which points do these six new graduates seem to agree? On which points do they disagree?

Rhetorical Analysis

This article was presented as six separate interviews. Would it have been better if it were presented as a unified essay with a clear thesis statement? What would have been gained and lost by this approach?

Writing with Sources

Research the state of vocational training in the United States. Then, write an essay in which you argue for or against the advisability of encouraging more high school students to pursue vocational training as opposed to four-year college degrees.

Widening the Focus

For Critical Reading and Writing

Referring specifically to the three readings in this chapter's Focus section (and possibly to additional sources as well), write an essay in which you answer the question, "Should a College Education Be Free?"

For Further Reading

The following readings can suggest additional perspectives for thinking about the value of a college education.

- Frederick Douglass, "Learning to Read and Write" (p. 133)
- Rand Fishkin, "The Truth Shall Set You Free (from a Lot of $#*% Storms)" (p. 369)
- Warren Farrell and John Gray, "The Crisis of Our Sons' Education" (p. 225)

For Focused Research

As tuition costs continue to rise, students, educators, politicians, and the general public are increasingly asking if a college education should be free. In preparation for writing an essay that answers this question, search the internet for up-to-date statistics on lifetime earnings of college graduates versus nongraduates. Then, write an essay in which you consider how having (or not having) a college degree affects lifetime employment, male versus female earnings, and initial access to the job market. Be sure to support your points with the statistics and examples you find.

Beyond the Classroom

Interview six adults, three with four-year college degrees and three without. One person in each category should be in his or her 60s, one in his or her 40s, and one a recent college graduate in his or her 20s.

- Ask those without college degrees if they believe they have suffered financially because of their lack of higher education.
- Ask those with college degrees whether they believe the money they spent on college was worth the expense.
- Ask those in both groups to evaluate their professional and economic success.

Then, write an essay that draws some conclusions about the perceived value of a college education for people in different age groups.

Exploring Issues and Ideas

Issues in Education

Write an essay in response to one of the following prompts, which are suitable for assignments that require the use of outside sources as well as for assignments that are not source-based.

1. Many of the readings in this chapter try to define exactly what constitutes a "good" education. Write an essay in which you define a good education.
2. According to Christina Hoff Sommers (p. 98), instructors with conservative political views are being systematically excluded from many American colleges and universities. Write a letter to Sommers in which you agree or disagree with her contentions. Make sure that you address Sommers's specific points and that you use examples from both the essay and your own experience to support your position.
3. In her essay "Why There's No Such Thing As a Gifted Child" (p. 91), Wendy Berliner describes some people, including Einstein, who were perceived as adult geniuses but who struggled as students. Assume that you are a tutor in your school's writing center and that you have been asked to write an essay to be included in an orientation booklet. In this essay, your goal is to address the concerns that Berliner expresses about labelling certain children "gifted." Be supportive, and give specific advice for overcoming common problems.
4. All the writers in this chapter believe in the power of education to change a person. For many people, this process begins with a teacher who has a profound influence on them. Write an essay in which you discuss such a teacher. What, in your opinion, made this teacher so effective? In what ways did contact with this teacher change you?
5. Write an essay in which you develop a definition of good teaching, considering the relationship of the teacher to the class, the standards teachers should use to evaluate students, and what students should gain from their educational experience. Refer to the ideas of John Holt (p. 86) in your essay.

Chapter 5

The Politics of Language

In this chapter, you will learn to:

- analyze readings about the politics of language.
- compose essays about the politics of language.

During the years he spent in prison, political activist Malcolm X became increasingly frustrated by his inability to express himself in writing, so he began the tedious and often frustrating task of copying words from the dictionary—page by page. The eventual result was that, for the first time, he could pick up a book and read it with understanding. "Anyone who has read a great deal," he says, "can imagine the new world that opened."

Eve Arnold/Magnum Photos

What point does this image of Malcolm X giving a speech in Washington, D.C., in 1961 make about the power of language?

In addition, by becoming a serious reader, Malcolm X was able to develop the ideas about race, politics, and economics that he presented so forcefully after he was released from prison.

In our society, language is constantly being manipulated for political ends. This fact should come as no surprise if we consider the potential power of words. Often, the power of a word comes not from its dictionary definition, or *denotation,* but from its *connotations,* the associations that surround it. These connotations can be subtle, giving language the power to confuse and even to harm. For example, whether a doctor who performs an abortion is "terminating a pregnancy" or "murdering an unborn child" is not just a matter of semantics: It is also a political issue, one that has provoked both debate and violence. This potential for misunderstanding, disagreement, deception, and possibly danger makes careful word choice very important.

The Focus section of this chapter (p. 150) addresses the question, "How Free Should Free Speech Be?" As the essays in this section illustrate, the answer to this question is neither straightforward nor simple. In "Kindly Inquisitors, Revisited," Jonathan Rauch defends freedom of expression, no matter how hateful it may be; in "Should Neo-Nazis Be Allowed Free Speech?" Thane Rosenbaum examines the harm that unbridled free speech can cause; and in "I'm a Stanford Professor Accused of Being a Terrorist. McCarthyism Is Back," David Palumbo-Liu describes his experience as the target of accusatory free speech.

dpa picture alliance/Alamy Stock Photo

What elements does this image of John F. Kennedy giving a speech in Berlin, Germany, in 1963 use to depict the politics of language?

.eparing to Read and Write

As you read and prepare to write about the essays in this chapter, you may consider the following questions:

- What assumptions does the writer have about his or her audience? How can you tell?
- What is the writer's primary purpose? For example, is it to analyze ideas about language or to challenge traditional ideas about language use?
- What genre is the writer using? For example, is the reading a memoir, a study of language use, or an argument? How do the conventions of this genre influence the writer's choices?
- What appeals does the writer use? For example, does he or she appeal primarily to reason, to emotion, or to a combination of the two? Is this the most effective strategy?
- Does the selection deal primarily with written or spoken language?
- Does the writer place more emphasis on the denotations or the connotations of words?
- Does the writer make any distinctions between language applied to males and language applied to females? Do you consider such distinctions valid?
- Does the writer discuss language in the context of a particular culture? Does he or she see language as a unifying or a divisive factor?
- In what ways would the writer like to change or reshape language? What do you see as the possible advantages or disadvantages of such change?
- Does the writer believe that people are shaped by language or that language is shaped by people?
- Does the writer see language as having a particular social or political function? In what sense?
- Does the writer see language as empowering?
- Does the writer make assumptions about people's status on the basis of their use of language? Do these assumptions seem justified?
- Does the writer make a convincing case for the importance of language?
- Is the writer's focus primarily on language's ability to help or its power to harm?
- In what ways are your ideas about the power of words similar to or different from the writer's?
- How is the essay like and unlike other essays in this chapter?

Shared Writing

The Politics of Language

Think about the various languages you speak in a range of social contexts. How do you talk differently with friends, family members, classmates, instructors, and supervisors? What functions do these different languages have?

5.1 Radley Balko, "The Curious Grammar of Police Shootings"

An opinion blogger for *The Washington Post* blog *The Watch*, Radley Balko (1975–) writes about issues related to criminal justice, surveillance, and civil liberties. He is the author of *Overkill: The Rise of Paramilitary Police Raids in America* (2006) and *Rise of the Warrior Cop: The Militarization of America's Police Forces* (2013) and the coauthor of *The Cadaver King and the Country Dentist: A True Story of Injustice in the American South* (2017). In the following blog post, Balko dissects the language commonly used to describe police shootings.

BEFORE YOU READ

What is the passive voice? What do you know about the appropriateness and inappropriateness of using it? Do you think it minimizes culpability?

The Curious Grammar of Police Shootings

You're probably familiar with the weaselly way politicians tend to apologize when they've been caught red-handed. The most famous example is the use of the line, *mistakes were made.* Use of the passive voice in an admission of wrongdoing has become so common that the political consultant William Schneider suggested a few years ago that it be referred to as the "past exonerative" tense.

You'll often see a similar grammatical device when a police officer shoots someone. Communications officers at policy agencies are deft at contorting the English language to minimize culpability of an officer or of the agency. So instead of...

> ...Mayberry Dep. Barney Fife shot and killed a burglary suspect last night...

You'll see...

> ...last night, a burglary suspect was shot and killed in an officer-involved shooting.

It's a way of describing a shooting without assigning responsibility. Most police departments do this. But we can take a few recent examples from the Los Angeles Police Department. Here, for example, is how the LAPD describes a typical shooting that does not involve a police officer:

> On February 10, 2014, around 6:10 p.m., the victim was in the parking lot in the 13640 block of Burbank Boulevard, to the rear, when he was confronted by the suspect. The suspect produced a semi-automatic handgun and fired numerous times striking the victim in the torso.

Note the active voice. We have a clear subject, verb, and direct object. Contrast that with how the LAPD has described a few recent shootings by LAPD officers:

> When the officers arrived they were confronted by a Hispanic male armed with a sword. The officers attempted to take the suspect into custody by using a taser but it was ineffective. The suspect then ran towards the officers still armed with the sword and an officer-involved-shooting occurred.
>
> – May 2, 2014

> The officer exited his police vehicle and began to give commands to the suspect at which time he observed Gomez was armed with a box cutter. Gomez refused to comply with the officers' commands and began to approach him, still armed with the box cutter. The officer deployed his OC spray which did not appear to affect Gomez. When the suspect continued to advance on the officer while refusing to comply with his repeated commands, an officer-involved shooting (OIS) occurred.
>
> – April 28, 2014

> While still in a position of cover, the officers encountered a male suspect who was armed with a weapon at which time an officer involved shooting occurred.
>
> – May 12, 2014

5 I'm not questioning whether any of these shootings were justified. I'm just drawing your attention to the language.

There was a particularly egregious example of this with the L.A. Sheriff's Department last April. While responding to reports of a stabbing, LASD deputies shot and killed 30-year-old John Winkler. In an initial press release, the department said Winkler "aggressed the deputies and a deputy-involved shooting occurred." Note that Winkler's actions were put in the active voice, while the officers' actions were put in the passive.

As it turns out, Winkler was innocent. He hadn't "aggressed" the officers at all. Rather, he and another victim, both of whom had been stabbed, were running toward the police to escape their assailant. (The deputies shot the other victim, too.) The press release incorrectly assigned criminal culpability to an innocent stabbing victim, but carefully avoided prematurely assigning responsibility to the deputies who shot him.

One of my favorite examples came in 2011, after the DEA and local police burst into the home of an innocent family during a botched raid. During the raid, a 13-year-old girl was pulled from her bed at gunpoint. She vomited, had an asthma attack, and passed out. The family told a local newspaper that the agents then threatened to kill their dogs unless they stopped them from barking. The DEA later put out a press release apology with this quote from John P. Gilbride, the special agent in charge:

> "We sincerely regret that while attempting to execute an arrest warrant for a member of this drug trafficking organization, the innocent McKay family was inadvertently affected by this enforcement operation."

Inadvertently affected!

And while *who* was attempting to execute a warrant? The offending parties aren't even mentioned. In fact, Gilbride so butchers the English language here, he nearly suggests that the McKay family conducted the raid themselves.

I bring all of this up because of a more recent example from southern Georgia. 10
Last week, a deputy in Coffee County shot a 10-year-old boy in the leg. The deputy was participating in a manhunt for a robbery suspect who had earlier shot a police officer. Here's how a report from Albany, Georgia TV station WALB described the incident:

> The situation of how the child was shot remains unclear. The Georgia Bureau of Investigation in Eastman was called to investigate the shooting. Sheriff Wooten said a deputy, who was not named, was approaching the property when a dog ran up to him. The deputy's gun fired one shot, missing the dog and hitting the child. It was not clear if the gun was accidentally fired by the deputy.

If a kid hadn't been shot in the leg, this would be downright comical. No reasonable person would believe this deputy intentionally sought out and shot a 10-year-old. The most plausible scenario is that the deputy tried to shoot the dog, and mistakenly shot the kid instead. (It certainly wouldn't be the first time a cop has mistakenly shot a citizen, his partner, or himself, while trying to kill a dog.) Perhaps he even mistook the kid for the suspect, or was startled by the kid. It's less plausible, but still possible, that the deputy didn't intend to fire his gun at all, in which case he's still negligent for handling his gun in a way that caused him to accidentally fire it.

What *isn't remotely* plausible is that the deputy's gun jumped out of its holster, walked up to the kid, and shot the kid in the leg. Physics tells us that the gun could not have fired without some sort of intermediary action on the part of the deputy. Yet the sheriff's explanation, at least the way the WALB reporter relays it, leaves open just that possibility.

All of this wouldn't be much more troubling than your typical grammatical ass-covering by other public officials if it weren't for the fact that (a) we're talking about people getting shot and killed, and (b) in most cases, the same police agencies engaging in linguistic gymnastics to publicly deflect responsibility for police shootings will inevitably be in charge of investigating the same officers for the same shootings.

RESPONDING TO READING

1. Why does the political consultant William Schneider call the passive voice the "past exonerative" tense (1)?
2. Why does Balko think that the use of the passive voice to report police shootings is important? Do you agree with him?

Rhetorical Analysis

In paragraph 5, Balko says that he is questioning the language that was used to describe the shootings, not the shootings themselves. Why do you think he makes this distinction? Do you think it is necessary?

Writing with Sources

Go online and read newspaper accounts of several recent police shootings. Do these accounts use the passive voice to avoid responsibility? Write an essay in which you analyze the use of the "past exonerative" in several news articles. What do you conclude about this rhetorical strategy and its likely effects on readers?

5.2 Jennifer Beese, "Emoji Marketing: Are We Speaking the Same Language?" [Infographic]

A social media strategist and forensic radiographer, Jennifer Beese is a former contributing writer for the website *Sprout Social*, where the following infographic appeared. In it, Beese illustrates the role of emoji in business and personal communications.

BEFORE YOU READ

How has the internet changed the way you communicate with people? Are these changes positive?

Emoji Marketing: Are We Speaking the Same Language?

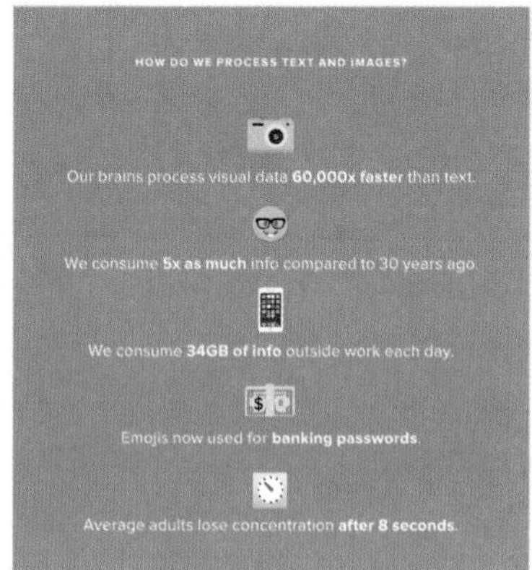

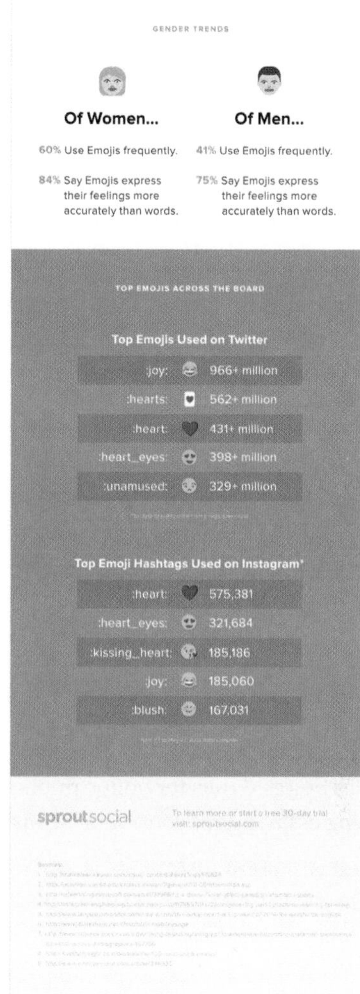

The infographic was included as part of this larger article: "Emoji Marketing: Are We Speaking the Same Language?" by Jennifer Beese on October 27, 2015 (Accessed at: https://sproutsocial.com/insights/emoji-marketing/.)

RESPONDING TO READING

1. An *infographic* presents information or data visually. What kind of information does Beese's infographic present? What would be the advantages and disadvantages of presenting this information in words alone?
2. What is the main point of Beese's infographic? Write a sentence that summarizes this infographic's thesis.

Rhetorical Analysis

In what order does Beese present information? Why do you think she chose to arrange her infographic the way she did? Would another order have been more effective? Explain.

Writing with Sources

Research the ways in which educators and researchers think social media have changed the way people interact. Next, write an essay in which you address Beese's claim that online networks can help people communicate more efficiently.

5.3 Dallas Spires, "Will Text Messaging Destroy the English Language?"

Author of the blog *Neither Here nor There* (https://sdspires.wordpress.com), Dallas Spires writes for online publications such as *Humanities 360*. In the following essay, Spires considers the historical and rhetorical contexts of texting.

BEFORE YOU READ

Do you think that texting has a positive or negative effect on your ability to communicate? Explain.

Will Text Messaging Destroy the English Language?

A new form of written—in this case typed—English has emerged in the last few years that really troubles a lot of people: text messaging. Lately, it has been treated as an entirely new phenomenon, when it has its roots in instant messaging on the internet. This form of "written" language uses different grammatical standards and many abbreviations. In many cases, spelling is ignored (so long as the reader can recognize what word is being sent) and verbs are not conjugated. Those of us who prefer more traditional forms of written English fear for the sanctity of our previous language.

To assume that text messaging will "destroy" the English language shows a certain lack of understanding on the part of the person holding this misconception. Texting is still English. The people using this form of "written" English are still communicating in English. To understand what is being typed, they must have a good understanding of syntax and grammar already. They must be able to recognize speech and sentence patterns, to predict accurately what someone is going to say, especially since the words probably won't be typed out. Unfortunately, for many young people, this understanding is so fundamental that they can't access it in any way other than through texting.

With all the abbreviations and acronyms used in typing text messages, texting reads like some sort of code. This is nothing new. In fact, what you are reading now is a code. It is a code that many of us understand because we have been taught this code by the adults and other people we accept as linguistic authorities. This code relates ideas in the English language. So does Morse code, which is a system of sounds transcribed as dots and dashes that represent messages interpreted as recognizable English by those people who understand the code. However, it doesn't sound or look anything like the code I'm currently using.

The use of codes is widespread, from law enforcement agencies to businesses to criminal organizations. Each one uses a code exclusive to it, except maybe in the case of street gangs. Military groups use codes no one else understands so that ideas in English may be communicated without being easily intercepted. Businesses may use codes simply for ease of communication. Even outside of any code, business communication already uses its own grammatical standards, which can be just as strict as those in English classrooms. Criminal organizations developed codes to deliver messages without being found out. In the case of street gangs, spoken and written codes are used not only to deliver messages within each individual gang but also across enemy lines. The codes they use, of course, are not meant to be understood by the general public but only by the intended audience.

If most of us were to pick up an Old English edition of *Beowulf*, we would swear 5
up and down it was not written in English, when it was. It was written in one of many accepted forms of English used at the time. In fact, what we generally refer to as Old English is actually the West Saxon dialect of Old English. The language was far less uniform during those times than it is today, even with different versions of English appearing more and more within our culture. Only a few years, relatively speaking, after the publication of *Beowulf*, another version of English appeared: Middle English. While Old English contained much Celtic influence, Middle English reflected the French influence at the time. And if a lack of uniform spelling can undermine English, then it's amazing we still speak it after the spelling atrocities committed during the Middle English period. Modern English appeared during Shakespeare's time, which does not look very "modern" for most of us, though it is much easier to understand—even for all its difficulty—than Middle or Old English. The spoken and written forms of English have changed quite a lot during the existence of the language. Even in the last century, there have been many changes and additions made to our understanding of our language.

If we feel that the English language is being undermined simply because the common, accepted written code is falling out of favor, then we need to turn to our teachers, our advertisers, our television stations, where our young people are going to find examples of written or typed English. Our teachers need to put a stronger effort into teaching traditional grammar and mechanics. Currently, in the state of Georgia, it is frowned upon to teach grammar in "isolation," that is, to focus only on grammar instead of putting it in the context of some type of literature (hello, all of the greats stretched or broke the precious rules we hold so dear, so why should we put those rules in context just to confuse our students THAT much more?). This standard of English education in Georgia comes out of the state's response to No Child Left Behind, and many other states have adopted the same standard. Since education is a public issue (public education?), a discussion needs to be opened with the local and state boards if we feel they are not doing their jobs. As for advertisers and the news media, if we feel that the youth are not getting a healthy dose of "good" English, there are ways of letting these agencies know in no uncertain terms that it will no longer be tolerated. The word "boycott" comes to mind.

Texting is a new code used to communicate ideas in English accurately and with ease and efficiency through a specific medium and for an almost exclusive audience. The level to which this code is used seems to depend on the age of the user. Teens seem to be the most proficient at texting, while users in their 20s and 30s seem to use it less and less. Part of the prevalence of this code comes from the fact that the establishment does not like it and cannot read it. While I agree that traditional forms of written and spoken English need to be preserved, I also believe that we all need to understand what is appropriate in different situations.

RESPONDING TO READING

1. How is texting just like other forms of written English? How is it different? Why does assuming that texting will destroy the English language show "a lack of understanding" (2)?
2. What does Spires mean by saying that texting "is a new code" (7)? In what sense is texting "code"?

Rhetorical Analysis

Spires begins his essay by defining texting. Do you think this extended definition is necessary? Why do you think Spires uses this opening strategy?

Writing with Sources

Suppose you were asked to debate the question of whether text messaging is destroying the English language. On the one side of this issue are those who say that texting promotes ungrammatical constructions, misspellings, and slang. On the other are those who say that texting enriches communication and forces people to be concise and direct. Investigate this question, and choose a position to support. Next, write an essay that develops your ideas on the issue.

5.4 Gary Marcus, "How Birds and Babies Learn to Talk"

A scientist, inventor, and entrepreneur, Gary Marcus (1970–) is a professor of psychology at New York University and the director of the NYU Center for Language and Music. His work has appeared in such publications as *Nature, The New York Times, The New Yorker*, and *Science*. He is the author or editor of numerous books, including, most recently, the edited collection *The Future of the Brain: Essays by the World's Leading Neuroscientists* (2015). In the following essay, Marcus compares the origins of two distinct languages.

BEFORE YOU READ

Have you observed similarities between human and animal behavior? What might these similarities mean?

How Birds and Babies Learn to Talk

Few things are harder to study than human language. The brains of living humans can only be studied indirectly, and language, unlike vision, has no analogue in the animal world. Vision scientists can study sight in monkeys using techniques like single-neuron recording. But monkeys don't talk.

However, in an article published today[1] in *Nature*, a group of researchers, including myself, detail a discovery in birdsong that may help lead to a revised understanding of an important aspect of human language development. Almost five years ago, I sent a piece of fan mail to Ofer Tchernichovski, who had just published an article showing that, in just three or four generations, songbirds raised in isolation often developed songs typical of their species. He invited me to visit his lab, a cramped space stuffed with several hundred birds residing in souped-up climate-controlled refrigerators. Dina Lipkind, at the time Tchernichovski's post-doctoral student, explained a method she had developed for teaching zebra finches two songs. (Ordinarily, a zebra finch learns only one song in its lifetime.) She had discovered that by switching the song of a tutor bird at precisely the right moment, a juvenile bird could learn a second, new song after it had mastered the first one.

Thinking about bilingualism and some puzzles I had encountered in my own lab, I suggested that Lipkind's method could be useful in casting light on the question of how a creature—any creature—learns to put linguistic elements together. We mapped out an experiment that day: birds would learn one "grammar" in which every phrase followed the form of ABCABC, and then we would switch things up, giving them a new target, ACBACB (the As, Bs, and Cs were certain stereotyped chirps and peeps).

---

[1] This essay was published on May 29, 2013. [Eds.]

The results were thrilling: most of the birds could accomplish the task. But it was clearly difficult—it took several weeks for them to learn the new grammar—and it was challenging in a particular way. While the birds showed no sign of needing to relearn individual sounds, the connections between individual syllables, known as "transitions," proved incredibly difficult. The birds proceeded slowly and systematically, incrementally working out each transition (e.g., from C to B, and B to A). They could not freely move syllables around, and did not engage in trial and error, either. Instead, they undertook a systematic struggle to learn particular connections between specific, individual syllables. The moment they mastered the third transition of the sequence, they were able to produce the entire grammar. Never, to my knowledge, had the process of learning any sort of grammar been so precisely articulated.

5 We wrote up the results, but *Nature* declined to publish them. Then Dina and Ofer speculated that our findings might be more convincing if they were true for not only zebra finches (hardly the Einsteins of the bird world) but for other species as well. Ofer contacted a Japanese researcher, Kazuo Okanoya, who he thought might be able to gather data for Bengalese finches, which have a more complex grammar than zebra finches. Amazingly, the Bengalese finches followed almost exactly the same learning pattern as the zebra finches.

Then we decided to test our ideas about the incrementality of vocal learning in human infants, enlisting the help of a graduate student I had been working with at N.Y.U., Doug Bemis. Bemis and Lipkind analyzed an old, publicly available set of human-babbling data, drawn from the *CHILDES* database, in a new way. The literature said that in the later part of the first year of life, babies undergo a change from "reduplicated" babbling—repeating a syllable, like *bababa*—to "variegated" babbling—often switching between syllables, like *babadaga*. Our birdsong results led us to wonder whether such a change might be more piecemeal than is commonly presumed, and our examination of the data proved that, in fact, the change did not happen all at once. It was gradual, with new transitions worked out one by one; human babies were stymied in the same ways that the birds were. Nobody had ever really explained why babbling took so many months; our birdsong data has finally yielded a first clue.

Today, almost five years after Lipkind and Tchernichovski began developing the methods that are at the paper's core, the work is finally being published by *Nature*.

What we don't yet know is whether the similarity between birds and babies stems from a fundamental similarity between species at the biological level. When two species do something in similar ways, it can be a matter of "homology," a genuine lineage at the genetic level, or "analogy," which is independent reinvention. It will likely be years before we know for sure, but there is reason to believe that our results are not purely an accident of independent invention. Some of the important genes in human vocal learning (including FOXP2, the gene thus far most decisively tied to human language) are also involved in avian vocal learning, as a new book, *Birdsong, Speech, and Language*, discusses at length.

Language will never be as easy to dissect as birdsong, but knowledge about one can inform knowledge about the other. Our brains didn't evolve to be easily understood, but the fact that humans share so many genes with so many other species gives scientists a fighting chance.

Source: Gary Marcus, The New Yorker © Conde Nast

RESPONDING TO READING

1. In paragraph 3, Marcus mentions bilingualism. How do the findings he mentions in this essay relate to bilingualism? Why does Marcus draw this connection?
2. Consider the contrast Marcus makes between "homology" and "analogy" (8). Does this contrast establish a particular way of understanding his argument? Explain.

Rhetorical Analysis

What kinds of evidence does Marcus use to support his thesis? How convincing is this evidence? Explain.

Writing with Sources

Research other studies that compare human and animal behavior, and then write an essay in which you explain the potential impact of one of these studies on human evolution research. What might the study suggest about our linguistic origins and adaptability? Be specific, referring to Marcus's essay as well as the information you found in your research.

5.5 Frederick Douglass, "Learning to Read and Write"

Frederick Douglass (1817–1895) was born a slave in rural Talbot County, Maryland, and later served a family in Baltimore. After escaping to the North in 1838, he settled in Bedford, Massachusetts, where he became active in the abolitionist movement. He recounts these experiences in his most famous work, *Narrative of the Life of Frederick Douglass* (1845). After spending almost two years in England and Europe on a lecture tour, Douglass returned to the United States and purchased his freedom. In 1847, he launched the antislavery newspaper *The North Star* and became a vocal supporter of both Abraham Lincoln and the Civil War. Throughout his life, Douglass believed that the United States Constitution, if interpreted correctly, would enable African Americans to become full participants in the economic, social, and intellectual life of America. In the following excerpt from his *Narrative*, Douglass writes of outwitting his owners to become literate, thereby finding "the pathway from slavery to freedom."

BEFORE YOU READ

Does an essay written over 150 years ago, like this one, have relevance today? Explain.

Learning to Read and Write

I lived in Master Hugh's family about seven years. During this time, I succeeded in learning to read and write. In accomplishing this, I was compelled to resort to various stratagems. I had no regular teacher. My mistress, who had kindly commenced to instruct me, had, in compliance with the advice and direction of her husband, not only ceased to instruct, but had set her face against my being instructed by any one else. It is due, however, to my mistress to say of her, that she did not adopt this course of treatment immediately. She at first lacked the depravity indispensable to shutting me up in mental darkness. It was at least necessary for her to have some training in the exercise of irresponsible power, to make her equal to the task of treating me as though I were a brute.

My mistress was, as I have said, a kind and tender-hearted woman; and in the simplicity of her soul she commenced, when I first went to live with her, to treat me as she supposed one human being ought to treat another. In entering upon the duties of a slaveholder, she did not seem to perceive that I sustained to her the relation of a mere chattel,[1] and that for her to treat me as a human being was not only wrong, but dangerously so. Slavery proved as injurious to her as it did to me. When I went there, she was a pious, warm, and tender-hearted woman. There was no sorrow or suffering for which she had not a tear. She had bread for the hungry, clothes for the naked, and comfort for every mourner that came within her reach. Slavery soon proved its ability to divest her of these heavenly qualities. Under its influence, the tender heart became stone, and the lamblike disposition gave way to one of tigerlike fierceness. The first step in her downward course was in her ceasing to instruct me. She now commenced to practice her husband's precepts. She finally became even more violent in her opposition than her husband himself. She was not satisfied with simply doing as well as he had commanded; she seemed anxious to do better.

---

[1]Property. [Eds.]

Nothing seemed to make her more angry than to see me with a newspaper. She seemed to think that here lay the danger. I have had her rush at me with a face made all up of fury, and snatch from me a newspaper, in a manner that fully revealed her apprehension. She was an apt woman; and a little experience soon demonstrated, to her satisfaction, that education and slavery were incompatible with each other.

From this time I was most narrowly watched. If I was in a separate room any considerable length of time, I was sure to be suspected of having a book, and was at once called to give an account of myself. All this, however, was too late. The first step had been taken. Mistress, in teaching me the alphabet, had given me the *inch,* and no precaution could prevent me from taking the *ell.*

The plan which I adopted, and the one by which I was most successful, was that of making friends of all the little white boys whom I met in the street. As many of these as I could, I converted into teachers. With their kindly aid, obtained at different times and in different places, I finally succeeded in learning to read. When I was sent on errands, I always took my book with me, and by going one part of my errand quickly, I found time to get a lesson before my return. I used also to carry bread with me, enough of which was always in the house, and to which I was always welcome; for I was much better off in this regard than many of the poor white children in our neighborhood. This bread I used to bestow upon the hungry little urchins, who, in return, would give me that more valuable bread of knowledge. I am strongly tempted to give the names of two or three of those little boys, as a testimonial of the gratitude and affection I bear them; but prudence forbids;—not that it would injure me, but it might embarrass them; for it is almost an unpardonable offense to teach slaves to read in this Christian country. It is enough to say of the dear little fellows, that they lived on Philpot Street, very near Durgin and Bailey's ship-yard. I used to talk this matter of slavery over with them. I would sometimes say to them, I wished I could be as free as they would be when they got to be men. "You will be free as soon as you are twenty-one, *but I am a slave for life!* Have not I as good a right to be free as you have?" These words used to trouble them; they would express for me the liveliest sympathy, and console me with the hope that something would occur by which I might be free.

I was now about twelve years old, and the thought of being *a slave for life* 5
began to bear heavily upon my heart. Just about this time, I got hold of a book entitled "The Columbian Orator."[2] Every opportunity I got, I used to read this book. Among much of other interesting matter, I found in it a dialogue between a master and his slave. The slave was represented as having run away from his master three times. The dialogue represented the conversation which took place between them, when the slave was retaken the third time. In this dialogue, the whole argument in behalf of slavery was brought forward by the master, all of which was disposed of by the slave. The slave was made to say some very smart as well as impressive things in reply to his master—things which had the desired though

[2]A popular textbook that taught the principles of effective public speaking. [Eds.]

unexpected effect; for the conversation resulted in the voluntary emancipation of the slave on the part of the master.

In the same book, I met with one of Sheridan's mighty speeches on and in behalf of Catholic emancipation.[3] These were choice documents to me. I read them over and over again with unabated interest. They gave tongue to interesting thoughts of my own soul, which had frequently flashed through my mind, and died away for want of utterance. The moral which I gained from the dialogue was the power of truth over the conscience of even a slaveholder. What I got from Sheridan was a bold denunciation of slavery, and a powerful vindication of human rights. The reading of these documents enabled me to utter my thoughts, and to meet the arguments brought forward to sustain slavery; but while they relieved me of one difficulty, they brought on another even more painful than the one of which I was relieved. The more I read, the more I was led to abhor and detest my enslavers. I could regard them in no other light than a band of successful robbers, who had left their homes, and gone to Africa, and stolen us from our homes, and in a strange land reduced us to slavery. I loathed them as being the meanest as well as the most wicked of men. As I read and contemplated the subject, behold! that very discontentment which Master Hugh had predicted would follow my learning to read had already come, to torment and sting my soul to unutterable anguish. As I writhed under it, I would at times feel that learning to read had been a curse rather than a blessing. It had given me a view of my wretched condition, without the remedy. It opened my eyes to the horrible pit, but to no ladder upon which to get out. In moments of agony, I envied my fellow-slaves for their stupidity. I have often wished myself a beast. I preferred the condition of the meanest reptile to my own. Any thing, no matter what, to get rid of thinking! It was the everlasting thinking of my condition that tormented me. There was no getting rid of it. It was pressed upon me by every object within sight or hearing, animate or inanimate. The silver trump of freedom had roused my soul to eternal wakefulness. Freedom now appeared, to disappear no more forever. It was heard in every sound, and seen in every thing. It was ever present to torment me with a sense of my wretched condition. I saw nothing without seeing it, I heard nothing without hearing it, and felt nothing without feeling it. It looked from every star, it smiled in every calm, breathed in every wind, and moved in every storm.

I often found myself regretting my own existence, and wishing myself dead; and but for the hope of being free, I have no doubt but that I should have killed myself, or done something for which I should have been killed. While in this state of mind, I was eager to hear any one speak of slavery. I was a ready listener. Every little while, I could hear something about the abolitionists. It was some time before I found what the word meant. It was always used in such connections as to make it an interesting word to me. If a slave ran away and succeeded in getting clear, or if a slave killed his master, set fire to a barn, or did any thing very wrong in the mind of a slaveholder, it was spoken of as the fruit of *abolition.* Hearing the word in this

---

[3]Richard Brinsley Sheridan (1751–1816), British playwright and statesman who made speeches supporting the right of English Catholics to vote. Full emancipation was not granted to Catholics until 1829. [Eds.]

connection very often, I set about learning what it meant. The dictionary afforded me little or no help. I found it was "the act of abolishing"; but then I did not know what was to be abolished. Here I was perplexed. I did not dare to ask any one about its meaning, for I was satisfied that it was something they wanted me to know very little about. After a patient waiting, I got one of our city papers, containing an account of the number of petitions from the north, praying for the abolition of slavery in the District of Columbia, and of the slave trade between the States. From this time I understood the words *abolition* and *abolitionist,* and always drew near when that word was spoken, expecting to hear something of importance to myself and fellow-slaves. The light broke in upon me by degrees. I went one day down on the wharf of Mr. Waters; and seeing two Irishmen unloading a scow of stone, I went, unasked, and helped them. When we had finished, one of them came to me and asked me if I were a slave. I told him I was. He asked, "Are ye a slave for life?" I told him that I was. The good Irishman seemed to be deeply affected by the statement. He said to the other that it was a pity so fine a little fellow as myself should be a slave for life. He said it was a shame to hold me. They both advised me to run away to the north; that I should find friends there, and that I should be free. I pretended not to be interested in what they said, and treated them as if I did not understand them; for I feared they might be treacherous. White men have been known to encourage slaves to escape, and then, to get the reward, catch them and return them to their masters. I was afraid that these seemingly good men might use me so; but I nevertheless remembered their advice, and from that time I resolved to run away. I looked forward to a time at which it would be safe for me to escape. I was too young to think of doing so immediately; besides, I wished to learn how to write, as I might have occasion to write my own pass. I consoled myself with the hope that I should one day find a good chance. Meanwhile, I would learn to write.

The idea as to how I might learn to write was suggested to me by being in Durgin and Bailey's ship-yard, and frequently seeing the ship carpenters, after hewing, and getting a piece of timber ready for use, write on the timber the name of that part of the ship for which it was intended. When a piece of timber was intended for the larboard side, it would be marked thus—"L." When a piece was for the starboard side, it would be marked thus—"S." A piece for the larboard side forward, would be marked thus—"L. F." When a piece was for starboard side forward, it would be marked thus—"S. F." For larboard aft, it would be marked thus—"L. A." For starboard aft, it would be marked thus—"S. A." I soon learned the names of these letters, and for what they were intended when placed upon a piece of timber in the shipyard. I immediately commenced copying them, and in a short time was able to make the four letters named. After that, when I met with any boy who I knew could write, I would tell him I could write as well as he. The next word would be, "I don't believe you. Let me see you try it." I would then make the letters which I had been so fortunate as to learn, and ask him to beat that. In this way I got a good many lessons in writing, which it is quite possible I should never have gotten in any other way. During this time, my copy-book was the board fence, brick wall, and pavement; my pen and ink was a lump of chalk. With these, I learned mainly how to write. I then commenced and continued copying the Italics in Webster's Spelling Book, until I could make them all without looking on the book. By this time, my little Master Thomas had gone to school, and learned how to write, and had written over a number of copy-books. These had been brought home, and shown to some of our near neighbors, and then laid aside. My mistress used to go to class meeting at the Wilk Street meetinghouse every Monday afternoon, and leave me to take care of the house. When left thus, I used to spend the time in writing in the spaces left in Master Thomas's copy-book, copying what he had written. I continued to do this until I could write a hand very similar to that of Master Thomas. Thus, after a long, tedious effort for years, I finally succeeded in learning how to write.

Source: Douglas, Frederick. Narrative of the Life of Frederick Douglas, An American Slave. Boston: Anti-Slavery Office, 1845.

RESPONDING TO READING

1. What does Douglass mean in paragraph 2 when he says that slavery proved as harmful to his mistress as it did to him? In spite of his owners' actions, what strategies did Douglass use to learn to read?
2. Douglass escaped from slavery in 1838 and became a leading figure in the antislavery movement. How did reading and writing help him develop his ideas about slavery? In what way did language empower him?

Rhetorical Analysis

Is Douglass addressing primarily a white audience or an audience of African Americans? How do you know?

Writing with Sources

In his narrative, Douglass says that his treatment "was very similar to that of other slave children." Research the living conditions of slaves in the American South. Next, write an essay in which you discuss whether Douglass was treated better or worse than other slaves.

5.6 Alleen Pace Nilsen, "Sexism in English: Embodiment and Language"

The author of several textbooks and reference works, Alleen Pace Nilsen (1936–) is an educator and essayist. When Nilsen lived in Afghanistan in the 1960s, she observed the subordinate position of women in that society. When she returned to the United States, she studied American English for its cultural biases toward men and women. Nilsen says of that project,

"As I worked my way through the dictionary, I concentrated on the way particular usages, metaphors, slang terms, and definitions reveal society's attitude toward males and females." The following essay is an updated version of Nilsen's findings from her dictionary study.

BEFORE YOU READ

List some words and phrases in your own speaking vocabulary that reinforce common stereotypes of men and women. What alternatives could you employ? What would be gained and lost if you used these alternatives?

Sexism in English: Embodiment and Language

During the late 1960s, I lived with my husband and three young children in Kabul, Afghanistan. This was before the Russian invasion, the Afghan civil war, and the eventual taking over of the country by the Taleban Islamic movement and its resolve to return the country to a strict Islamic dynasty, in which females are not allowed to attend school or work outside their homes.

But even when we were there and the country was considered moderate rather than extremist, I was shocked to observe how different were the roles assigned to males and females. The Afghan version of the *chaderi*[1] prescribed by Moslem women was particularly confining. Women in religious families were required to wear it whenever they were outside their family home, with the result being that most of them didn't venture outside.

The household help we hired were made up of men, because women could not be employed by foreigners. Afghan folk stories and jokes were blatantly sexist, as in this proverb: "If you see an old man, sit down and take a lesson; if you see an old woman, throw a stone."

But it wasn't only the native culture that made me question women's roles, it was also the American community within Afghanistan.

Most of the American women were like myself—wives and mothers whose 5
husbands were either career diplomats, employees of USAID, or college professors who had been recruited to work on various contract teams. We were suddenly bereft of our traditional roles: The local economy provided few jobs for women and certainly none for foreigners; we were isolated from former friends and the social goals we had grown up with. Some of us became alcoholics, others got very good at bridge, while still others searched desperately for ways to contribute either to our families or to the Afghans.

When we returned in the fall of 1969 to the University of Michigan in Ann Arbor, I was surprised to find that many other women were also questioning the expectations they had grown up with. Since I had been an English major when I was in college, I decided that for my part in the feminist movement I would study

---

[1]A heavily draped cloth covering the entire head and body. [Eds.]

the English language and see what it could tell me about sexism. I started reading a desk dictionary and making note cards on every entry that seemed to tell something different about male and female. I soon had a dog-eared dictionary, along with a collection of note cards filling two shoe boxes.

The first thing I learned was that I couldn't study the language without getting involved in social issues. Language and society are as intertwined as a chicken and an egg. The language a culture uses is telltale evidence of the values and beliefs of that culture. And because there is a lag in how fast a language changes—new words can easily be introduced, but it takes a long time for old words and usages to disappear—a careful look at English will reveal the attitudes that our ancestors held and that we as a culture are therefore predisposed to hold. My note cards revealed three main points. While friends have offered the opinion that I didn't need to read a dictionary to learn such obvious facts, the linguistic evidence lends credibility to the sociological observations.

WOMEN ARE SEXY; MEN ARE SUCCESSFUL

First, in American culture a woman is valued for the attractiveness and sexiness of her body, while a man is valued for his physical strength and accomplishments. A woman is sexy. A man is successful.

A persuasive piece of evidence supporting this view are the eponyms—words that have come from someone's name—found in English. I had a two-and-a-half-inch stack of cards taken from men's names but less than a half-inch stack from women's names, and most of those came from Greek mythology. In the words that came into American English since we separated from Britain, there are many eponyms based on the names of famous American men: Bartlett pear, boysenberry, Franklin stove, Ferris wheel, Gatling gun, mason jar, sideburns, sousaphone, Schick test, and Winchester rifle. The only common eponyms that I found taken from American women's names are Alice blue (after Alice Roosevelt Longworth), bloomers (after Amelia Jenks Bloomer), and Mae West jacket (after the buxom actress). Two out of the three feminine eponyms relate closely to a woman's physical anatomy, while the masculine eponyms (except for "sideburns" after General Burnsides) have nothing to do with the namesake's body, but, instead, honor the man for an accomplishment of some kind.

10 In Greek mythology women played a bigger role than they did in the biblical stories of the Judeo-Christian cultures, and so the names of goddesses are accepted parts of the language in such place names as Pomona, from the goddess of fruit, and Athens, from Athena, and in such common words as *cereal* from Ceres, *psychology* from Psyche, and *arachnoid* from Arachne. However, there is the same tendency to think of women in relation to sexuality as shown through the eponyms *aphrodisiac* from Aphrodite, the Greek name for the goddess of love and beauty, and *venereal disease* from Venus, the Roman name for Aphrodite.

Another interesting word from Greek mythology is *Amazon.* According to Greek folk etymology, the *a-* means "without," as in *atypical* or *amoral,* while *-mazon* comes from *mazos,* meaning "breast," as still seen in *mastectomy.* In the Greek legend, Amazon women cut off their right breasts so they could better shoot their bows. Apparently, the storytellers had a feeling that for women to play the active, "masculine" role the Amazons adopted for themselves, they had to trade in part of their femininity.

This preoccupation with women's breasts is not limited to the Greeks; it's what inspired the definition and the name for "mammals" (from Indo-European *mammae* for "breasts"). As a volunteer for the University of Wisconsin's *Dictionary of American Regional English (DARE),* I read a western trapper's diary from the 1830s. I was to make notes of any unusual usages or language patterns. My most interesting finding was that the trapper referred to a range of mountains as "The Teats," a metaphor based on the similarity between the shapes of the mountains and women's breasts. Because today we use the French wording "The Grand Tetons," the metaphor isn't as obvious, but I wrote to mapmakers and found the following listings: Nipple Top and Little Nipple Top near Mount Marcy in the Adirondacks; Nipple Mountain in Archuleta County, Colorado; Nipple Peak in Coke County, Texas; Nipple Butte in Pennington, South Dakota; Squaw Peak in Placer County, California (and many other locations); Maiden's Peak and Squaw Tit (they're the same mountain) in the Cascade Range in Oregon; Mary's Nipple near Salt Lake City, Utah; and Jane Russell Peaks near Stark, New Hampshire.

Except for the movie star Jane Russell, the women being referred to are anonymous—it's only a sexual part of their body that is mentioned. When topographical features are named after men, it's probably not going to be to draw attention to a sexual part of their bodies but instead to honor individuals for an accomplishment.

Going back to what I learned from my dictionary cards, I was surprised to realize how many pairs of words we have in which the feminine word has acquired sexual connotations while the masculine word retains a serious businesslike aura. For example, a callboy is the person who calls actors when it is time for them to go on stage, but a callgirl is a prostitute. Compare sir and madam. *Sir* is a term of respect, while *madam* has acquired the specialized meaning of a brothel manager. Something similar has happened to master and mistress. Would you rather have a painting "by an old master" or "by an old mistress"?

It's because the word *woman* had sexual connotations, as in "She's his 15
woman," that people began avoiding its use, hence such terminology as ladies' room, lady of the house, and girl's school or school for young ladies. Those of us who in the 1970s began asking that speakers use the term *woman* rather than *girl* or *lady* were rejecting the idea that *woman* is primarily a sexual term.

I found two-hundred pairs of words with masculine and feminine forms; for example, *heir/heiress, hero/heroine, steward/stewardess, usher/usherette.* In nearly all such pairs, the masculine word is considered the base, with some kind of a feminine suffix being added. The masculine form is the one from which compounds are made; for example, from *king/queen* comes *kingdom* but not *queendom*, from *sportsman/sports-lady* comes *sportsmanship* but not *sportsladyship*. There is one—and only one—semantic area in which the masculine word is not the base or more powerful word. This is in the area dealing with sex, marriage, and motherhood. When someone refers to a virgin, a listener will probably think of a female unless the speaker specifies male or uses a masculine pronoun. The same is true for *prostitute.*

In relation to marriage, linguistic evidence shows that weddings are more important to women than to men. A woman cherishes the wedding and is considered a bride for a whole year, but a man is referred to as a groom only on the day of the wedding. The word *bride* appears in *bridal attendant, bridal gown, bridesmaid, bridal shower,* and even *bridegroom. Groom* comes from the Middle English *grom,* meaning "man," and in that sense is seldom used outside of the wedding. With most pairs of male/female words, people habitually put the masculine word first: *Mr. and Mrs., his and hers, boys and girls, men and women, kings and queens, brothers and sisters, guys and dolls, and host and hostess.* But it is the bride and groom who are talked about, not the groom and bride.

The importance of marriage to a woman is also shown by the fact that when a marriage ends in death, the woman gets the title of widow. A man gets the derived title of widower. This term is not used in other phrases or contexts, but widow is seen in widowhood, widow's peak, and widow's walk. A widow in a card game is an extra hand of cards, while in typesetting it is a leftover line of type.

Changing cultural ideas bring changes to language, and since I did my dictionary study three decades ago the word *singles* has largely replaced such gender-specific and value-laden terms as *bachelor, old maid, spinster, divorcee, widow,* and *widower.* In 1970 I wrote that when people hear a man called "a professional," they usually think of him as a doctor or a lawyer, but when people hear a woman referred to as "a professional," they are likely to think of her as a prostitute. That's not as true today because so many women have become doctors and lawyers, it's no longer incongruous to think of women in those professional roles.

20 Another change that has taken place is in wedding announcements. They used to be sent out from the bride's parents and did not even give the name of the groom's parents. Today, most couples choose to list either all or none of the parents' names. Also it is now much more likely that both the bride and groom's picture will be in the newspaper, while twenty years ago only the bride's picture was published on the "Women's" or the "Society" page. In the weddings I have recently attended, the official has pronounced the couple "husband and wife" instead of the traditional "man and wife," and the bride has been asked if she promises to "love, honor, and cherish," instead of to "love, honor, and obey."

WOMEN ARE PASSIVE; MEN ARE ACTIVE

However, other wording in the wedding ceremony relates to a second point that my cards showed, which is that women are expected to play a passive or weak role while men play an active or strong role. In the traditional ceremony, the official asks, "Who gives the bride away?" and the father answers, "I do." Some fathers answer, "Her mother and I do," but that doesn't solve the problem inherent in the question. The idea that a bride is something to be handed over from one man to another bothers people because it goes back to the days when a man's servants, his children, and his wife were all considered to be his property. They were known by his name because they belonged to him, and he was responsible for their actions and their debts.

The grammar used in talking or writing about weddings as well as other sexual relationships shows the expectation of men playing the active role. Men *wed* women while women *become* brides of men. A man *possesses* a woman; he *deflowers* her; he *performs;* he *scores;* he *takes away* her virginity. Although a woman can *seduce* a man, she cannot offer him her virginity. When talking about virginity, the only way to make the woman the actor in the sentence is to say that "she lost her virginity," but people lose things by accident rather than by purposeful actions, and so she's only the grammatical, not the real-life, actor.

The reason that women brought the term Ms. into the language to replace Miss and Mrs. relates to this point. Many married women resent being identified in the "Mrs. Husband" form. The dictionary cards showed what appeared to be an attitude on the part of the editors that it was almost indecent to let a respectable woman's name march unaccompanied across the pages of a dictionary. Women were listed with male names whether or not the male contributed to the woman's reason for being in the dictionary or whether or not in his own right he was as famous as the woman. For example:

Charlotte Brontë = Mrs. Arthur B. Nicholls
Amelia Earhart = Mrs. George Palmer Putnam
Helen Hayes = Mrs. Charles MacArthur
Jenny Lind = Mme. Otto Goldschmit
Cornelia Otis Skinner = daughter of Otis
Harriet Beecher Stowe = sister of Henry Ward Beecher
Dame Edith Sitwell = sister of Osbert and Sacheverell[2]

Only a small number of rebels and crusaders got into the dictionary without the benefit of a masculine escort: temperance leaders Frances Elizabeth Caroline Willard and Carry Nation, women's rights leaders Carrie Chapman Catt and Elizabeth Cady Stanton, birth control educator Margaret Sanger, religious leader Mary Baker Eddy, and slaves Harriet Tubman and Phillis Wheatley.

Etiquette books used to teach that if a woman had Mrs. in front of her name, then the husband's name should follow because Mrs. is an abbreviated form of Mistress and a woman couldn't be a mistress of herself. As with many arguments about "correct" language usage, this isn't very logical because Miss is also an abbreviation of Mistress. Feminists hoped to simplify matters by introducing Ms. as an alternative to both Mrs. and Miss, but what happened is that Ms. largely replaced Miss to become a catch-all business title for women. Many married women still prefer the title Mrs., and some even resent being addressed with the term Ms. As one frustrated newspaper reporter complained, "Before I can write about a woman I have to know not only her marital status but also her political philosophy." The result of such complications may contribute to the demise of titles, which are already being ignored by many writers who find it more efficient to simply use names; for example, in a business letter: "Dear Joan Garcia," instead of "Dear Mrs. Joan Garcia," "Dear Ms. Garcia," or "Dear Mrs. Louis Garcia."

---

[2]Charlotte Brontë (1816–1855), author of Jane Eyre; Amelia Earhart (1898–1937), first woman to fly over the Atlantic; Helen Hayes (1900–1993), actress; Jenny Lind (1820–1887), Swedish soprano; Cornelia Otis Skinner (1901–1979), actress and writer; Harriet Beecher Stowe (1811–1896), author of Uncle Tom's Cabin; Edith Sitwell (1877–1964), English poet and critic. [Eds.]

25 Titles given to royalty show how males can be disadvantaged by the assumption that they always play the more powerful role. In British royalty, when a male holds a title, his wife is automatically given the feminine equivalent. But the reverse is not true. For example, a count is a high political officer with a countess being his wife. The same pattern holds true for a duke and a duchess and a king and a queen. But when a female holds the royal title, the man she marries does not automatically acquire the matching title. For example, Queen Elizabeth's husband has the title of prince rather than king, but when Prince Charles married Diana, she became Princess Diana. If they had stayed married and he had ascended to the throne, then she would have become Queen Diana. The reasoning appears to be that since masculine words are stronger, they are reserved for true heirs and withheld from males coming into the royal family by marriage. If Prince Phillip were called "King Phillip," British subjects might forget who had inherited the right to rule.

The names that people give their children show the hopes and dreams they have for them, and when we look at the differences between male and female names in a culture, we can see the cumulative expectations of that culture. In our culture girls often have names taken from small, aesthetically pleasing items; for example, Ruby, Jewel, and Pearl. Esther and Stella mean "star," and Ada means "ornament." One of the few women's names that refers to strength is Mildred, and it means "mild strength." Boys often have names with meanings of power and strength; for example, Neil means "champion"; Martin is from Mars, the God of war; Raymond means "wise protection"; Harold means "chief of the army"; Ira means "vigilant"; Rex means "king"; and Richard means "strong king."

We see similar differences in food metaphors. Food is a passive substance just sitting there waiting to be eaten. Many people have recognized this and so no longer feel comfortable describing women as "delectable morsels." However, when I was a teenager, it was considered a compliment to refer to a girl (we didn't call anyone a "woman" until she was middle-aged) as a cute tomato, a peach, a dish, a cookie, honey, sugar, or sweetie-pie. When being affectionate, women will occasionally call a man honey or sweetie, but in general, food metaphors are used much less often with men than with women. If a man is called "a fruit," his masculinity is being questioned. But it's perfectly acceptable to use a food metaphor if the food is heavier and more substantive than that used for women. For example, pin-up pictures of women have long been known as "cheesecake," but when Burt Reynolds posed for a nude centerfold the picture was immediately dubbed "beefcake," that is, a hunk of meat. That such sexual references to men have come into the language is another reflection of how society is beginning to lessen the differences between their attitudes toward men and women.

Something similar to the fruit metaphor happens with references to plants. We insult a man by calling him a "pansy," but it wasn't considered particularly insulting to talk about a girl being a wallflower, a clinging vine, or a shrinking violet, or to give girls such names as Ivy, Rose, Lily, Iris, Daisy, Camelia, Heather, and Flora. A positive plant metaphor can be used with a man only if the plant is big and strong; for example, Andrew Jackson's nickname of Old Hickory. Also, the phrases *blooming idiots* and *budding geniuses* can be used with either sex, but notice how they are based on the most active thing a plant can do, which is to bloom or bud.

Animal metaphors also illustrate the different expectations for males and females. Men are referred to as studs, bucks, and wolves, while women are referred to with such metaphors as kitten, bunny, beaver, bird, chick, and lamb. In the 1950s, we said that boys went "tom catting," but today it's just "catting around," and both boys and girls do it. When the term foxy, meaning that someone was sexy, first became popular it was used only for females, but now someone of either sex can be described as a fox. Some animal metaphors that are used predominantly with men have negative connotations based on the size and/or strength of the animals; for example, beast, bull-headed, jackass, rat, loanshark, and vulture. Negative metaphors used with women are based on smaller animals; for example, social butterfly, mousey, catty, and vixen. The feminine terms connote action, but not the same kind of large scale action as with the masculine terms.

WOMEN ARE CONNECTED WITH NEGATIVE CONNOTATIONS; MEN WITH POSITIVE CONNOTATIONS

The final point that my note cards illustrated was how many positive connotations 30
are associated with the concept of masculinity, while there are either trivial or negative connotations connected with the corresponding feminine concept. An example from the animal metaphors makes a good illustration. The word *shrew* taken from the name of a small but especially vicious animal was defined in my dictionary as "an ill-tempered scolding woman," but the word *shrewd* taken from the same root was defined as "marked by clever, discerning awareness" and was illustrated with the phrase "a shrewd businessman." (Source: © 2017 Merriam-Webster, Incorporated, https://www.merriam-webster.com/dictionary/shrew)

Early in life, children are conditioned to the superiority of the masculine role. As child psychologists point out, little girls have much more freedom to experiment with sex roles than do little boys. If a little girl acts like a tomboy, most parents have mixed feelings, being at least partially proud. But if their little boy acts like a sissy (derived from *sister*), they call a psychologist. It's perfectly acceptable for a little girl to sleep in the crib that was purchased for her brother, to wear his hand-me-down jeans and shirts, and to ride the bicycle that he has outgrown. But few parents would put a boy baby in a white-and-gold crib decorated with frills and lace, and virtually no parents would have their little boy wear his sister's hand-me-down dresses, nor would they have their son ride a girl's pink bicycle with a flower-bedecked basket. The proper names given to girls and boys show this same attitude. Girls can have "boy" names—Cris, Craig, Jo, Kelly, Shawn, Teri, Toni, and Sam—but it doesn't work the other way around. A couple of generations ago, Beverly, Frances, Hazel, Marion, and Shirley were common boys' names. As parents gave these names to more and more girls, they fell into disuse for males, and some older men who have these names prefer to go by their initials or by such abbreviated forms as Haze or Shirl.

When a little girl is told to be a lady, she is being told to sit with her knees together and to be quiet and dainty. But when a little boy is told to be a man, he is being told to be noble, strong, and virtuous—to have all the qualities that the speaker looks on as desirable. The concept of manliness has such positive connotations that it used to be a compliment to call someone a he-man, to say that he was doubly a man. Today many people are more ambivalent about this term and respond to it much as they do to the word *macho.* But calling someone a manly man or a virile man is nearly always meant as a compliment. Virile comes from the Indo-European *vir,* meaning "man," which is also the basis of *virtuous.* Consider the positive connotations of both virile and virtuous with the negative connotations of *hysterical.* The Greeks took this latter word from their name for uterus (as still seen in *hysterectomy*). They thought that women were the only ones who experienced uncontrolled emotional outbursts, and so the condition must have something to do with a part of the body that only women have. But how word meanings change is regularly shown at athletic events where thousands of *virtuous* women sit quietly beside their *hysterical* husbands.

Differences in the connotations between positive male and negative female connotations can be seen in several pairs of words that differ denotatively only in the matter of sex. Bachelor as compared to spinster or old maid has such positive connotations that women try to adopt it by using the term *bachelor-girl* or *bachelorette.* Old maid is so negative that it's the basis for metaphors: pretentious and fussy old men are called "old maids," as are the leftover kernels of unpopped popcorn and the last card in a popular children's card game.

Patron and *matron* (Middle English for "father" and "mother") have such different levels of prestige that women try to borrow the more positive masculine connotations with the word *patroness,* literally "female father." Such a peculiar term came about because of the high prestige attached to patron in such phrases as a *patron of the arts* or a *patron saint.* Matron is more apt to be used in talking about a woman in charge of a jail or a public restroom.

35 When men are doing jobs that women often do, we apparently try to pay the men extra by giving them fancy titles. For example, a male cook is more likely to be called a "chef" while a male seamstress will get the title of "tailor." The armed forces have a special problem in that they recruit under such slogans as "The Marine Corps builds men!" and "Join the Army! Become a Man." Once the recruits are enlisted, they find themselves doing much of the work that has been traditionally thought of as "women's work." The solution to getting the work done and not insulting anyone's masculinity was to change the titles as shown below:

waitress = orderly
nurse = medic or corpsman
secretary = clerk-typist
assistant = adjutant
dishwasher = KP (kitchen police) or kitchen helper

Compare *brave* and *squaw.* Early settlers in America truly admired Indian men and hence named them with a word that carried connotations of youth, vigor, and courage. But for Indian women they used an Algonquin slang term with negative sexual connotations that are almost opposite to those of brave. Wizard and witch contrast almost as much. The masculine *wizard* implies skill and wisdom combined with magic, while the feminine *witch* implies evil intentions combined with magic. When witch is used for men, as in witch-doctor, many main-stream speakers feel some carry-over of the negative connotations.

Part of the unattractiveness of both witch and squaw is that they have been used so often to refer to old women, something with which our culture is particularly uncomfortable, just as the Afghans were. Imagine my surprise when I ran across the phrases *grandfatherly advice* and *old wives' tales* and realized that the underlying implication is the same as the Afghan proverb about old men being worth listening to while old women talk only foolishness.

Other terms that show how negatively we view old women as compared to young women are *old nag* as compared to *filly, old crow* or *old bat* as compared to *bird,* and being *catty* as compared to being *kittenish.* There is no matching set of metaphors for men. The chicken metaphor tells the whole story of a woman's life. In her youth she is a chick. Then she marries and begins feathering her nest. Soon she begins feeling cooped up, so she goes to hen parties where she cackles with her friends. Then she has her brood, begins to henpeck her husband, and finally turns into an old biddy.

I embarked on my study of the dictionary not with the intention of prescribing language change but simply to see what the language would tell me about sexism. Nevertheless, I have been both surprised and pleased as I've watched the changes that have occurred over the past three decades. I'm one of those linguists who believes that new language customs will cause a new generation of speakers to grow up with different expectations. This is why I'm happy about people's efforts to use inclusive languages, to say "he or she" or "they" when speaking about individuals whose names they do not know. I'm glad that leading publishers have developed guidelines to help writers use language that is fair to both sexes. I'm glad that most newspapers and magazines list women by their own names instead of only by their husbands' names. And I'm so glad that educated and thoughtful people no longer begin their business letters with "Dear Sir" or "Gentlemen," but instead use a memo form or begin with such salutations as "Dear Colleagues," "Dear Reader," or "Dear Committee Members." I'm also glad that such words as *poetess, authoress, conductress,* and *aviatrix* now sound quaint and old-fashioned and that *chairman* is giving way to *chair* or *head, mailman* to *mail carrier, clergyman* to *clergy,* and *stewardess* to *flight attendant.* I was also pleased when the National Oceanic and Atmospheric Administration bowed to feminist complaints and in the late 1970s began to alternate men's and women's names for hurricanes. However, I wasn't so pleased to discover that the change did not immediately erase sexist thoughts from everyone's mind, as shown by a headline about Hurricane David in a 1979 New York tabloid, "David Rapes Virgin Islands." More recently a similar metaphor appeared in a headline in the *Arizona Republic* about Hurricane Charlie, "Charlie Quits Carolinas, Flirts with Virginia."

40 What these incidents show is that sexism is not something existing independently in American English or in the particular dictionary that I happened to read. Rather, it exists in people's minds. Language is like an X-ray in providing visible evidence of invisible thoughts. The best thing about people being interested in and discussing sexist language is that as they make conscious decisions about what pronouns they will use, what jokes they will tell or laugh at, how

they will write their names, or how they will begin their letters, they are forced to think about the underlying issue of sexism. This is good because as a problem that begins in people's assumptions and expectations, it's a problem that will be solved only when a great many people have given it a great deal of thought.

RESPONDING TO READING

1. What point is Nilsen making about American culture? Does your experience support her conclusions?
2. Many of the connotations of the words Nilsen discusses are hundreds of years old and are also found in languages other than English. Given these widespread and long-standing connotations, do you think attempts by Nilsen and others to change this linguistic situation can succeed?

Rhetorical Analysis

Does Nilsen use enough examples to support her claims? What other examples can you think of? In what way do her examples—and your own—illustrate the power of language to define the way people think?

Writing with Sources

Lately, there has been some pushback against the effort to eliminate sexist constructions from English. For example, some charge that this view of language is simplistic and that words can designate gender without being sexist. Research this issue and write a letter to Nilsen in which you agree or disagree with her position.

5.7 Charles Jensen, "Poem in Which Words Have Been Left Out" [Poetry]

A poet, educator, and consultant, Charles Jensen (1977–) is the founding and managing editor of the online poetry magazine *LOCUSPOINT* and the director of the UCLA Extension Writers' Program. The author of six poetry chapbooks, he has also published poems in *Columbia Poetry Review,*

New England Review, and *Prairie Schooner,* among other publications. In the following poem, the speaker recreates a historical text.

BEFORE YOU READ

What do you know about the Miranda rights from pop culture? Can you think of any examples of the statements "you have the right to remain silent" and "anything you say can and will be used against you in a court of law" appearing in movies, television shows, or songs? How are the statements used in these contexts?

Poem in Which Words Have Been Left Out

—The "Miranda Rights,"[1] *established 1966*

You have the right to remain
anything you can and will be.

An attorney you cannot afford
will be provided to you.

You have silent will.
You can be against law.
You cannot afford one.

You remain silent. Anything you say
will be provided to you.

The right can and will be
against you. The right provided you.

Have anything you say be
right. Anything you say can be right.

Say you have the right attorney.
The right remain silent.

Be held. Court the one. Be provided.
You cannot be you.

RESPONDING TO READING

1. Locate the text of the Miranda rights. What words does the poem leave out?
2. How does this poem change the meaning of the original text?

---

[1]The right of criminal suspects in the United States to remain silent before interrogation. [Eds.]

Rhetorical Analysis

What point do you think Jensen is trying to make by alluding to the Miranda rights in his poem? Do you think he succeeds?

Writing with Sources

Write a poem based on a different text—for example, part of the Declaration of Independence. Begin by removing words and punctuation to create something new. When you have finished, write an analysis of your poem, telling readers what words you removed and why—in other words, what point you were trying to communicate.

5.8 Focus: "How Free Should Free Speech Be?"

Rob Crandall/Alamy Stock Photo

What does this photo from the 2018 "March for Our Lives" Washington, D.C., rally say about the nature of free speech in America?

RESPONDING TO THE IMAGE

Answer one or both of the following questions.

1. In 2018, more than a million rallied around the world to protest increasing gun violence in American schools. Photos of the marches are striking in the number of children and young adults they depict. In what sense does the image above reflect young people's involvement in the ongoing gun debate?
2. During the protests, many people held signs that said "Vote Them Out." Why do you think that protesters adopted this slogan? What point were they trying to make?

5.9 Jonathan Rauch, "Kindly Inquisitors, Revisited"

A contributing editor of *The Atlantic* and *National Journal* and a senior fellow at the Brookings Institution in Washington, D.C., Jonathan Rauch (1960–) analyzes issues related to culture, politics, and economics. The author of several books, including, most recently, *The Happiness Curve: Why Life Gets Better after 50* (2018), he also writes for publications such as the *Chronicle of Higher Education*, the *Economist*, *Harper's*, the *Los Angeles Times*, *The New Republic*, *Reason*, *The New York Times*, *Slate*, *U.S. News & World Report*, *The Wall Street Journal*, and *The Washington Post*. Adapted from Rauch's new afterword for the 2013 edition of his book *Kindly Inquisitors* (originally published in 1993), the following essay argues for the cultural value of free speech.

BEFORE YOU READ

Do you think that minorities benefit from a free and open society that places few limits on speech? Explain.

Kindly Inquisitors, Revisited

Twenty years ago, in 1993, Salman Rushdie was a hunted man. Iran had sentenced him to death for writing a novel that allegedly defamed Islam; governments and intellectuals in the West had responded with a measure of defiance, but a larger measure of ambivalence and confusion. Was Rushdie entitled, really, to write a book that he could have anticipated would deeply offend Muslims?

In 1998, as part of an agreement to restore diplomatic relations with Great Britain, the Iranian government formally withdrew its support from the fatwa[1]

[1]An Islamic legal decision. [Eds.]

against Rushdie, and the author resumed public life. But Rushdie's freedom has not put to rest the Rushdie affair. The fatwa's report echoed loudly in 2005 when a Danish newspaper published cartoons, some of them provocative, depicting the Prophet Muhammad. The resulting uproar occasioned, in the West, a chaotic mix of confusion, apology, and defiance, not unlike that which met the Rushdie affair.

The Danish government said, "Freedom of expression is the very foundation of the Danish democracy," but then went on to say, "However, Danish legislation prohibits acts or expressions of a blasphemous or discriminatory nature." When Danish authorities chose not to prosecute the cartoons' publisher, death threats and violent protests around the world led to the murders of several hundred people. In France and Canada, publications that republished the cartoons found themselves under government investigation for inciting hatred or violating human rights. Ultimately, they were not prosecuted. It would be fair to say that the West's defense of intellectual freedom was ringingly ambivalent. The more things change...

Today, what I called in 1993 "the new attacks on free thought" are no longer new. The regulation of speech deemed hateful or discriminatory or harassing has spread internationally and dug in domestically. In the United States, hate-speech laws as such are unconstitutional. But indirect, bureaucratic prohibitions have burrowed into workplaces and universities. Federal law holds employers civilly liable for permitting the workplace to become a "hostile environment"—a fuzzy concept which has been stretched to include, for example, a Bible verse printed on a paycheck (could upset an atheist) or a Seventh-Day Adventist's discussion of religion ("religious harassment" because it "depressed" a plaintiff).

5 Unlike most workplaces, universities are at the heart of intellectual life, and so the bureaucratization of speech controls there is more disturbing. In American universities, the hostile-environment and discriminatory-harassment doctrines have become part of the administrative furniture. "Most colleges and universities in the United States have instituted what are in effect speech codes," write the law professors Arthur Jacobson and Bernhard Schlink, in their contribution to the 2012 collection *The Content and Context of Hate Speech: Rethinking Regulation and Responses.* "The codes range widely in the speech they prohibit," but even the narrower ones "can define harassment more broadly than have the federal courts." Moreover, "colleges and universities are noticeably reticent to afford defendants in campus adjudications procedural protections that in federal and state courts are routine and necessary."

Alas, these sorts of bureaucratic controls have become a background thrum of academic life. They sometimes run into challenges when they go too far in particular cases—as when Brandeis University found a professor guilty of racial harassment for explaining the origin of the word *wetbacks*. But the *idea* that minority rights justify speech codes and quasi-judicial inquisitions is barely controversial among academic administrators. History will someday wonder how the very people who should have been most protective of intellectual freedom took such a wrong turn.

Abroad, without a First Amendment to act as a buffer, direct government restrictions on hate speech have become the norm, enacted by many countries and encouraged by several human rights treaties. Miklós Haraszti, of Columbia University's school of international and public affairs, writes of "a growing, punitive trend that is introducing new speech bans into national criminal codes. Most of them target bad speech specific to the country or to the worries of its ruling parties, the two being practically indistinguishable." The United States and Hungary, according to the British political theorist Bhikhu Parekh, are the only countries which have recently resisted the trend to ban hate speech. (He and Haraszti write in *The Content and Context of Hate Speech*.)

But there is good news, too. Frontal humanitarian and egalitarian attacks on the legitimacy of liberal science—our decentralized, criticism-based global system for developing knowledge—have waned. Arguments for restricting speech in the name of equality and compassion are more sophisticated and concomitantly more modest.

Version 2.0 of the case for bans on speech relies less on metaphorical notions like "words that wound" and "verbal violence," which could mean almost anything. Instead it looks to a narrower hostile-environment doctrine which justifies penalties only in relatively extreme cases, such as when speech seems likely to create a pervasively demeaning or threatening social environment for recently persecuted minorities, denying them (the theory goes) equal status as fully protected citizens. "Offensiveness by itself is not a good reason for legal regulation," writes Jeremy Waldron, a law professor at New York University, in his fine 2012 book, *The Harm in Hate Speech*. "Where there are fine lines to be drawn the law should generally stay on the liberal side of them."

I don't think Version 2.0 has succeeded in answering the challenges that I and 10
others have posed. It has not demonstrated that hate speech silences minorities, rather than mobilizing or energizing them; it has not shown that restrictions ameliorate hate or silence haters, rather than intensifying hate and publicizing haters. It has not figured out how to make political authorities interpret and enforce political restrictions apolitically, or how to prevent majorities and authorities from turning restrictions to majoritarian and authoritarian ends. It does not reckon the cost of overdeterrence and of chilling important but controversial conversations; or the cost of stereotyping minorities as vulnerable and defenseless; or the cost of denying the agency of the listener, who, after all, can *choose* how to react to the maunderings of haters. It has yet to enunciate a limiting principle. Why, after all, stop with speech deemed harmful to minorities, when there is so much other socially harmful speech in the world? Doesn't it harm society to let climate-change deniers yammer on?

But save those arguments for another day. I want to try to answer the deepest challenge that Version 2.0 poses. It is an epistemological challenge, and it goes like this:

Some ideas actually *are* false, and at some point the process of checking establishes their falsehood so firmly that to proceed as if they might be true becomes ridiculous. For example, Holocaust denial: Isn't it a stretch to claim we can learn something by debating neo-Nazis about the existence of gas chambers? Fallibilism is all well and good, but come on—enough is enough. In the 21st century, do Jews really need to put up with *The Protocols of the Elders of Zion*, a notorious anti-Semitic fraud? Shouldn't governments at least be allowed to regulate the most injurious of lies in the most blatant of cases?

As for enforcement, it may not be perfect, but what ever is? Even though politicians and courts won't always strike the right balance between free speech and minorities' dignity, they won't always get it wrong, either; the solution is to do a better job of balancing, not to throw away the scales. And we must not overlook the specific effects on minorities; it doesn't seem fair to sacrifice their interests on the altar of free speech. Do gays and Jews benefit from toleration of homophobic or anti-Semitic claptrap?

I believe the answer is yes. Society benefits from the toleration of hate speech, and so do targeted minorities.

15 Today's narrower, Version 2.0 argument for hate-speech laws asks us to imagine a really hard case: not a society where people say offensive things in random directions now and then (which should be allowed), but one where (in Jeremy Waldron's words) vulnerable groups "have to live and go about in a society festooned with vicious characterizations of them and their kind and with foul denigrations of their status. . . [T]he upshot might be that they would avoid much public life or participate in it without the security that the rest of us enjoy; either that, or they would have to summon up (from their own resources) extraordinary reserves of assurance as they went about their business, a burden that is not required of the rest of us." Surely, in so extreme a case, promising to punish violence or discrimination after the fact is not enough; surely, in *this* case, laws preemptively suppressing bigotry are appropriate?

Such societies exist. I grew up in one, because I was born in the United States in 1960, and I am homosexual.

You may remember those days. Gay Americans were forbidden to work for the government; forbidden to obtain security clearances; forbidden to serve in the military. They were arrested for making love, even in their own homes; beaten and killed on the streets; entrapped and arrested by the police for sport; fired from their jobs. They were joked about, demeaned, and bullied as a matter of course; forced to live by a code of secrecy and lies, on pain of opprobrium and unemployment; witch-hunted by anti-Communists, Christians, and any politician or preacher who needed a scapegoat; condemned as evil by moralists and as sick by scientists; portrayed as sinister and simpering by Hollywood; perhaps worst of all, rejected and condemned, at the most vulnerable time of life, by their own parents. America was a society permeated by hate: usually, it's true, hateful ideas and assumptions, not hateful people, but hate all the same. So ubiquitous was the hostility to homosexuality that few gay people ever even dared hold hands in public with the person they loved.

Obviously, passing a hate-speech law to protect homosexuals, much less enforcing one, was not on anyone's agenda. The very idea would have seemed preposterous. Any hate-speech law which might have passed would have targeted gay people (in the name of defending children), not protected us.

The case for hate-speech prohibitions mistakes the cart for the horse, imagining that anti-hate laws are a cause of toleration when they are almost always a consequence. In democracies, minorities do not get fair, enforceable legal protections until after majorities have come around to supporting them. By the time a community is ready to punish intolerance legally, it will already be punishing intolerance culturally. At that point, turning haters into courtroom martyrs is unnecessary and often counterproductive.

In any case, we can be quite certain that hate-speech laws did not change 20
America's attitude toward its gay and lesbian minority, because there were no hate-speech laws. Today, firm majorities accept the morality of homosexuality, know and esteem gay people, and endorse gay unions and families. What happened to turn the world upside-down?

What happened was this. In 1957, the U.S. Army Map Service fired an astronomer named Franklin Kameny after learning he was gay. Kameny, unlike so many others, did not go quietly. He demanded reinstatement from the U.S. Civil Service Commission and the Congress. When he got nowhere, he filed a Supreme Court brief. "In World War II," he told the Court, "petitioner did not hesitate to fight the Germans, with bullets, in order to help preserve his rights and freedoms and liberties, and those of others. In 1960, it is ironically necessary that he fight the Americans, with words, in order to preserve, against a tyrannical government, some of those same rights, freedoms and liberties, for himself and others."

In 1965, Kameny led dignified gay-rights demonstrations, the first of their kind, in front of the White House and Philadelphia's Independence Hall. (Signs said: "Denial of equality of opportunity is immoral." "We demand that our government confer with us." "Private consenting sexual conduct by adults is NOT the government's concern.")

In 1969, gays rioted against police harassment in New York. In 1970, two gay student activists, Jack Baker and Michael McConnell, walked into a county clerk's office in Minnesota and asked for a marriage license. Much, much more was to come.

In ones and twos at first, then in streams and eventually cascades, gays *talked*. They argued. They explained. They showed. They confronted. If the pervasiveness of bigotry was supposed to silence them, as hate-speech allegedly does, Frank Kameny missed the memo. "If society and I differ on something," he said in 1972, "I'm willing to give the matter a second look. If we still differ, then I am right and society is wrong; and society can go its way so long as it does not get in my way. But, if it does, there's going to be a fight. And I'm not going to be the one who backs down."

Kameny and others confronted the psychiatric profession about its irrational 25
pathologizing of homosexuality, bombarded the U.S. Civil Service Commission with demands that it end the ban on gay government employment, and confronted Christians with their hardly Christ-like conduct. "If your god condemns people like me for the crime of loving," Kameny would say, "then your god is a false and bigoted god." In the 1980s and early 1990s, a few visionaries—Andrew Sullivan, Evan Wolfson—argued that gay couples should be allowed to marry, a cause seemingly so hopeless that even many gay people hesitated to endorse it.

Frank Kameny lost every appeal to get his job back; the Supreme Court refused to hear his case. In 1963, he launched a campaign to repeal the District of Columbia's sodomy law and lost (that effort would take three decades). He ran for Congress in 1971 and lost. But at every stage he fired moral imaginations. He and others saw Jerry Falwell and Anita Bryant[2] not as threats to hide from but as opportunities to be seized: opportunities to rally gays, educate straights, and draw sharp moral comparisons. "Is *that* what you think this country is all about? Really?"

To appeal to a country's conscience, you need an antagonist. Suppression of anti-gay speech and thought, had it been conceivable at the time, would have slowed the country's moral development, not speeded it. It would have given the illusion that the job was finished when, in fact, the job was only beginning. It would have condescended to a people fighting for respect.

I am not naive about the bravery it took for Kameny and others of his generation to step forward. They were hammered. They suffered severely. Kameny lived long enough to be honored by President Obama and, in 2009, to receive an official government apology from the U.S. Office of Personnel Management, which by then was headed by an openly gay man. But most of us are not Kamenys.

Most of us are also not Galileos or Einsteins, or Sakharovs or Kings. The good news is that most of us don't need to be. We need only a few Kamenys—plus a system that is very good at testing and rejecting bad hypotheses and at bringing forward better ones. As gay people stepped forward, liberal science engaged. The old anti-gay dogmas came under critical scrutiny as never before. "Homosexuals molest and recruit children"; "homosexuals cannot be happy"; "homosexuals are really heterosexuals"; "homosexuality is unknown in nature": The canards collapsed with astonishing speed.

30 What took place was not just empirical learning but also moral learning. How can it be wicked to love? How can it be noble to lie? How can it be compassionate to reject your own children? How can it be kind to harass and taunt? How can it be fair to harp on one Biblical injunction when so many others are ignored? How can it be just to penalize what does no demonstrable harm? Gay people were asking straight people to test their values against logic, against compassion, against life. Gradually, then rapidly, the criticism had its effect.

You cannot be gay in America today and doubt that moral learning is real and that the open society fosters it. And so, 20 years on, I feel more confident than ever that the answer to bias and prejudice is pluralism, not purism. The answer, that is, is not to try to legislate bias and prejudice out of existence or to drive them underground, but to pit biases and prejudices against each other and make them fight in the open. That is how, in the crucible of rational criticism, superstition and moral error are burned away.

I believe the hope of living in a world free of discrimination and prejudice is a utopian pipe dream, and is as anti-human and dangerous as most other utopian pipe dreams. The quest to stamp out discrimination or bigotry or racism wherever it appears is a quest to force all opinion into a single template. I reject the premise—not just the methods—of the 1965 International Convention on the Elimination of

[2]Opponents of homosexuality. [Eds.]

All Forms of Racial Discrimination, which calls on signatory countries to prohibit "all dissemination of ideas based on racial superiority or hatred." In my view, if minorities know what is good for us, we should at every turn support pluralism, with all its social messiness and personal hurt. Politicians and activists, however well intentioned, who would shelter us from criticism and debate offer false comfort.

History shows that, over time and probably today more than ever, the more open the intellectual environment, the better minorities will do. It is just about that simple. So here is a reply to advocates of hate-speech regulation who wonder if, today, it really serves any purpose to let people go around touting *The Protocols of the Elders of Zion.* The answer is yes, it does. We cannot fight hate and fraud without seeing them and debunking them. John Stuart Mill, writing in *On Liberty* in 1859, was right. "Wrong opinions and practices gradually yield to fact and argument: but facts and arguments, to produce any effect on the mind, must be brought before it."

Today I fear that many people on my side of the gay-equality question are forgetting our debt to the system that freed us. Some gay people—not all, not even most, but quite a few—want to expunge discriminatory views. "Discrimination is discrimination and bigotry is bigotry," they say, "and they are intolerable whether or not they happen to be someone's religion or moral creed."

Here is not the place for an examination of the proper balance between, 35
say, religious liberty and anti-discrimination rules. It is a place, perhaps, for a plea to those of us in the gay-rights movement—and in other minority-rights movements—who now find ourselves in the cultural ascendency, with public majorities and public morality (strange to say it!) on our side. We should be the last people on the planet to demand that anyone be silenced.

Partly the reasons are strategic. Robust intellectual exchange serves our interest. Our greatest enemy is not irrational hate, which is pretty uncommon. It is *rational* hate, hate premised upon falsehood. (If you believe homosexuality poses a threat to your children, you will hate it.) The main way we eliminate hate is not to legislate or inveigh against it, but to replace it—with knowledge, empirical and ethical. That was how Frank Kameny and a few other people, without numbers or law or public sympathy on their side, turned hate on its head. They had arguments, and they had the right to make them.

And partly the reasons are moral. Gay people have lived in a world where we were forced, day in and day out, to betray our consciences and shut our mouths in the name of public morality. Not so long ago, *everybody* thought we were wrong. Now our duty is to protect others' freedom to be wrong, the better to ensure society's odds of being right. Of course, we can and should correct the falsehoods we hear and, once they are debunked, deny them the standing of *knowledge* in textbooks and professions; but we equally have the responsibility to defend their expression as *opinion* in the public square.

Finding the proper balance is not easy and isn't supposed to be. If a Catholic adoption agency wants to refuse placements to same-sex couples, we will have to argue about where to draw lines. What I am urging is a general proposition: Minorities are the point of the spear defending liberal science. We are the first to be targeted with vile words and ideas, but we are also the leading beneficiaries of a system which puts up with them. The open society is sometimes a cross we bear, but it is also a sword we wield, and we are defenseless without it.

We ought to remember what Frank Kameny never forgot: For politically weak minorities, the best and often only way to effect wholesale change in the world of politics is by effecting change in the world of ideas. Our position as beneficiaries of the open society requires us to serve as guardians of it. Playing that role, not seeking government protections or hauling our adversaries before star chambers, is the greater source of our dignity.

40 Frank Kameny, an irascible man with a capacious conscience, had it right. In more than 50 years of activism, he never called for silencing or punishing those he disagreed with, but he never cut them any argumentative slack, either. In his spirit, I hope that when gay people—and non-gay people—encounter hateful or discriminatory opinions, we respond not by trying to silence or punish them but by trying to correct them.

Source: Rauch, Jonathan. Kindly Inquisitors: The New Attacks on Free Thought. Chicago: University of Chicago Press, 2014. Used by permission of University of Chicago. Used by permission of Cato Institute.

RESPONDING TO READING

1. What is Version 2.0 of the case for banning speech? How is this different from previous efforts to limit certain kinds of speech? What, according to Rauch, is the problem with Version 2.0?
2. According to Rauch, why should hate speech be tolerated? What does he mean when he says, "For politically weak minorities, the best and often only way to effect wholesale change in the world of politics is by effecting change in the world of ideas" (39)?

Rhetorical Analysis

In paragraph 16, Rauch says that he is gay. Why does he include this information? Why does he isolate it in a single paragraph? Does this disclosure strengthen or weaken his argument? Explain.

Writing with Sources

As Rauch points out, many colleges and universities have speech codes. Find some of these codes and read them. What kinds of speech do they limit? How clear are the guidelines for prohibiting speech? What are the penalties for violating these speech codes? Next, write an article for your school newspaper in which you support or argue against the use of speech codes.

5.10 Thane Rosenbaum, "Should Neo-Nazis Be Allowed Free Speech?"

A distinguished fellow and the director of the Forum on Law, Culture & Society at New York University School of Law, Thane Rosenbaum (1960–) is an essayist and novelist who moderates *The Talk Show*, an annual series of cultural and political talks at the 92nd Street Y. The author of several books, including, most recently, *Payback: The Case for Revenge* (2013), he has also published essays in the *Daily Beast*, the *Huffington Post*, *The New York Times*, *The Wall Street Journal*, and *The Washington Post*. In the following essay, Rosenbaum considers the dangers of free speech.

BEFORE YOU READ

Do you think that some words are so hurtful they should be banned? What might the drawbacks be to banning them?

Should Neo-Nazis Be Allowed Free Speech?

Over the past several weeks, free speech has gotten costlier—at least in France and Israel.

In France, Dieudonne M'Bala M'Bala, an anti-Semitic stand-up comic infamous for popularizing the quenelle, an inverted Nazi salute, was banned from performing in two cities. M'Bala M'Bala has been repeatedly fined for hate speech, and this was not the first time his act was perceived as a threat to public order.

Meanwhile, Israel's parliament is soon to pass a bill outlawing the word Nazi for non-educational purposes. Indeed, any slur against another that invokes the Third Reich could land the speaker in jail for six months with a fine of $29,000. The Israelis are concerned about both the rise of anti-Semitism globally, and the trivialization of the Holocaust—even locally.

To Americans, these actions in France and Israel seem positively undemocratic. The First Amendment would never prohibit the quenelle, regardless of its symbolic meaning. And any lover of "Seinfeld" would regard banning the "Soup Nazi" episode as scandalously un-American. After all, in 1977 a federal court upheld the right of neo-Nazis to goose-step right through the town of Skokie, Illinois, which had a disproportionately large number of Holocaust survivors as residents. And more recently, the Supreme Court upheld the right of a church group opposed to gays serving in the military to picket the funeral of a dead marine with signs that read, "God Hates Fags."

While what is happening in France and Israel is wholly foreign to Americans, 5
perhaps it's time to consider whether these and other countries may be right. Perhaps America's fixation on free speech has gone too far.

Actually, the United States is an outlier among democracies in granting such generous free speech guarantees. Six European countries, along with Brazil, prohibit the use of Nazi symbols and flags. Many more countries have outlawed Holocaust denial. Indeed, even encouraging racial discrimination in France is a crime. In pluralistic nations like these with clashing cultures and historical tragedies not shared by all, mutual respect and civility helps keep the peace and avoids unnecessary mental trauma.

Yet, even in the United States, free speech is not unlimited. Certain proscribed categories have always existed—libel, slander and defamation, obscenity, "fighting words," and the "incitement of imminent lawlessness"—where the First Amendment does not protect the speaker, where the right to speak is curtailed for reasons of general welfare and public safety. There is no freedom to shout "fire" in a crowded theater. Hate crime statutes exist in many jurisdictions where bias-motivated crimes are given more severe penalties. In 2003, the Supreme Court held that speech intended to intimidate, such as cross burning, might not receive First Amendment protection.

Yet, the confusion is that in placing limits on speech we privilege physical over emotional harm. Indeed, we have an entire legal system, and an attitude toward speech, that takes its cue from a nursery rhyme: "Stick and stones can break my bones but names can never hurt me."

All of us know, however, and despite what we tell our children, names do, indeed, hurt. And recent studies in universities such as Purdue, UCLA, Michigan, Toronto, Arizona, Maryland, and Macquarie University in New South Wales, show, among other things, through brain scans and controlled studies with participants who were subjected to both physical and emotional pain, that emotional harm is equal in intensity to that experienced by the body, and is even more long-lasting and traumatic. Physical pain subsides; emotional pain, when recalled, is relived.

10 Pain has a shared circuitry in the human brain, and it makes no distinction between being hit in the face and losing face (or having a broken heart) as a result of bereavement, betrayal, social exclusion and grave insult. Emotional distress can, in fact, make the body sick. Indeed, research has shown that pain relief medication can work equally well for both physical and emotional injury.

We impose speed limits on driving and regulate food and drugs because we know that the costs of not doing so can lead to accidents and harm. Why should speech be exempt from public welfare concerns when its social costs can be even more injurious?

In the marketplace of ideas, there is a difference between trying to persuade and trying to injure. One can object to gays in the military without ruining the one moment a father has to bury his son; neo-Nazis can long for the Third Reich without re-traumatizing Hitler's victims; one can oppose Affirmative Action without burning a cross on an African-American's lawn.

Of course, everything is a matter of degree. Juries are faced with similar ambiguities when it comes to physical injury. No one knows for certain whether the plaintiff wearing a neck brace can't actually run the New York Marathon. We tolerate the fake slip and fall, but we feel absolutely helpless in evaluating whether words and gestures intended to harm actually do cause harm. Jurors are as capable of working through these uncertainties in the area of emotional harms as they are in the realm of physical injury.

Free speech should not stand in the way of common decency. No right should be so freely and recklessly exercised that it becomes an impediment to civil society, making it so that others are made to feel less free, their private space and peace invaded, their sensitivities cruelly trampled upon.

Source: "Should Neo-Nazis Be Allowed Free Speech?" by Thane Rosenbaum, The Daily Beast, January 30, 2014.

RESPONDING TO READING

1. According to Rosenbaum, why are laws limiting free speech in France and Israel "wholly foreign to Americans" (5)?
2. What kinds of speech are not protected in the United States? Why, according to Rosenbaum, is there confusion about placing limits on free speech?

Rhetorical Analysis

In paragraph 11, Rosenbaum draws an analogy between limiting speech and limiting driving or regulating food. What are the strengths and weaknesses of this analogy? Is it convincing? Explain.

Writing with Sources

In addition to France and Israel, many countries—for example, Brazil, Canada, and Denmark—place limits on offensive speech. What types of speech do they outlaw? How effective are these prohibitions? Are such laws possible in the United States, or do they violate the First Amendment of the Constitution? Write an essay that answers these questions.

5.11 David Palumbo-Liu, "I'm a Stanford Professor Accused of Being a Terrorist. McCarthyism Is Back."

David Palumbo-Liu (1951–) is the Louise Hewlett Nixon professor of comparative literature at Stanford University. The founding editor of the e-journal *Occasion: Interdisciplinary Studies in the Humanities* and the founding director of the Teaching Human Rights Collaboratory, Palumbo-Liu is the author of several books on the politics of language and literature, including, most recently, *The Deliverance of Others: Reading Literature in a Global Age* (2012). His writing has also been published in *AlterNet*, the *Guardian*, the *Nation*, and *Salon*. In the following essay, Palumbo-Liu considers the personal implications of unrestricted free speech.

BEFORE YOU READ

What limitations (if any) do you think should be placed on free speech?

I'm a Stanford Professor Accused of Being a Terrorist. McCarthyism Is Back.

Today anyone can be accused of anything, without basis in fact or evidence, and that accusation can be instantly trumpeted over the airwaves unchecked by any journalistic standard. That is the painful lesson I have had to learn this year.

As a scholar-activist working on issues such as sexual assault, Palestine, and anti-fascism, I am used to receiving abusive messages and being publicly maligned. Now, however, attacks on me have reached troubling new heights.

Last month, the Stanford Review, a rightwing publication co-founded by Peter Thiel and based on my university campus, wrote that I have helped set up an "organization [that is] undeniably a chapter of a terrorist group" and demanded my resignation. Their article was picked up by groups like JihadWatch, Campus Fix, Campus Reform, Fox & Friends, and other rightwing media outlets.

The organization I belong to is called the Campus Antifascist Network. We advocate for organized resistance to fascist violence on campus, and for educating our communities and others as to the nature of fascism today. We claim solidarity with a proud tradition of anti-fascism dating back to the early 20th century.

5 The group was founded shortly after the election of Donald Trump, and responded to the steady rise of a well-funded rightwing campaign on college campuses. We do not—and never would—advocate—for initiating violence.

The attack on me is part of a broader phenomenon noted by the American Association of University Professors, which claims that college campuses are the new battleground for conservative groups, far-right organizations and white supremacists. These groups are all trying to intimidate faculty and students, to recruit members, and to attract publicity. Not just careers and reputations are on the line—often personal safety is as well.

Today, we are seeing the resurgence of a wretched phenomenon we thought we had put behind us—McCarthyism, which involves "the use of tactics involving personal attacks on individuals by means of widely publicized indiscriminate allegations especially on the basis of unsubstantiated charges."

Professors are more than hesitant about fighting back against accusations that emanate from organizations supported by the likes of Peter Thiel or Charlie Kirk, who founded Turning Point USA.

In recent years, there have been well-publicized cases of academics who have had their syllabuses or social media cherry-picked for allegedly inflammatory statements, and then found themselves on the receiving end of orchestrated harassment campaigns.

10 CNN ran a story on the increasing numbers of professors like myself who have faced death threats for their political statements and activism. But it's not just political progressives and radicals who are being hit. Scientists are under attack, too. Michael Mann, a professor of atmospheric science and director of the Earth System Science Center at Penn State University, has received death threats for his work on climate change.

Despite this new and alarming phenomenon on campus, university administrators seem loth to aggressively protect their faculty. My own university has left it to me to press charges, and has chosen not to make any public comment on the Stanford Review's defamation of my character, despite an open letter supporting me signed by nearly 700 members of the Stanford community.

Besides those who signed letters of support, six constitutional law scholars from the Stanford School of Law wrote a letter to the editor of the Stanford Daily declaring that there was no evidence that I had advocated violence, nor that I am a member of a terrorist group. These then were my sources of support, not the university. Yet this has not stopped the attacks on me.

I don't have the resources to bring a libel suit—I cannot out-lawyer a newspaper that has an ally in its founder and major contributor to the university, Peter Thiel.

The troubling question is: who does?

RESPONDING TO READING

1. In his essay, Palumbo-Liu tells his story of being targeted by accusatory free speech. How does he support his condemnation of the personal attacks he describes?
2. In paragraphs 11–12, Palumbo-Liu explains who has stood by him throughout his ordeal, and who has not. Why do you think he includes this information? Does it add to or detract from his case?

Rhetorical Analysis

How does Palumbo-Liu establish his credibility (ethos)? Does he effectively defend his character against the accusations he describes in this essay?

Writing with Sources

In his essay's title and in paragraph 7, Palumbo-Liu refers to McCarthyism. Research the history of McCarthyism in the United States, starting with Senator Joseph McCarthy's anti-communism campaign in the early 1950s. Next, write an essay in which you explain the impact of McCarthyism on free speech.

Widening the Focus

For Critical Reading and Writing

Referring specifically to the three readings in this chapter's Focus section (and possibly to additional sources as well), write an essay in which you answer the question, "How Free Should Free Speech Be?"

For Further Reading

The following readings can suggest additional perspectives for thinking and writing about freedom of speech.

- Christina Hoff Sommers, "For More Balance on Campuses" (p. 98)
- Jill Filipovic, "We've Gone Too Far with 'Trigger Warnings'" (p. 100)
- Judith Donath, "Why Fake News Stories Thrive Online" (p. 204)
- Anonymous, "I Write Fake News" (p. 207)

For Focused Research

Texting presents special challenges to the First Amendment's guarantee of freedom of expression. For example, is the content of a text considered protected speech? Does the government or an employer have the right to access texts? Can certain forms of texting be prohibited—for example, texts that contain explicit sexual material, texts that harass, or texts that encourage others to commit a crime? In preparation for writing an essay about texting and freedom of speech, do a Google search using the search terms "texting and freedom of speech," and then decide what limits, if any, should be placed on texts. In your essay, explain how texting is the same as and different from other forms of communication. Next, identify the areas that you think should (or should not) be limited or possibly prohibited. Make sure to read a cross-section of opinions on this subject and to support your position with examples and evidence from the websites you use.

Beyond the Classroom

Conduct an email survey of your friends and classmates, asking them the following questions:

- How much time per week do you spend texting? How much time do you spend doing other kinds of writing (such as email, social media, and essay writing)?
- What kinds of texts do you send?
- Have you ever received texts that had questionable content? What kind?

Next, write an essay summarizing your findings and taking a position on whether texting should be considered protected speech.

Exploring Issues and Ideas

The Politics of Language

Write an essay in response to one of the following prompts, which are suitable for assignments that require the use of outside sources as well as for assignments that are not source-based.

1. Write an essay in which you describe the various languages you speak—including different types of English you speak at home, at school, at work, to your friends, and so on. In what ways are these languages alike, and in what ways are they different? What ideas are you able to express best with each type of English?
2. Over fifty years ago, George Orwell wrote an essay in which he discussed how governments use language to control their citizens. Now, control seems to be exerted at times by a desire for "political correctness"—excessive focus on avoiding language that might offend others because of their politics, race, gender, age, disabilities, or religious beliefs. Write an essay in which you consider the extent to which political correctness is a factor in the language used at your school, in your workplace, and among your friends and family members. Refer to Alleen Pace Nilsen's "Sexism in English: Embodiment and Language" (p. 138) and Thane Rosenbaum's "Should Neo-Nazis Be Allowed Free Speech?" (p. 159) as well as to your own experiences.
3. In "Learning to Read and Write" (p. 133), Frederick Douglass talks about how education can change one's use of language. Write an essay discussing the effect education has had on your own spoken and written language. What do you think you have gained and lost as your language has changed?
4. A recent study suggests that the population worldwide that has grown up speaking English is shrinking. In the sciences, however, the use of English is expanding. Some researchers warn that this situation could divide the scientific world into the "haves" and "have-nots"—with the "haves" gaining the advantage of being able to publish in prestigious scientific journals and the "have-nots" unable to achieve access. Do you think this is fair? Write an essay in which you discuss how the privileging of one language over another gives some people advantages and undercuts the ability of others to accomplish their goals. As you write, consider the essays by Frederick Douglass (p. 133) and Alleen Pace Nilsen (p. 138).
5. List some of the words you use to refer to women, minorities, and other groups. Next, write an email to Alleen Pace Nilsen (p. 138) in which you agree or disagree with her assertion that the words people use tell a lot about their values and beliefs. In addition to Nilsen's essay, consider Jonathan Rauch's "Kindly Inquisitors, Revisited" (p. 151).

Chapter 6
Media and Society

In this chapter, you will learn to:

- analyze readings about media and society.
- compose essays about media and society.

Many forms of popular media—books, newspapers, and magazines; radio, television, and film—have been around for a long time, and over the years, they have had a powerful impact on our lives. But the popular media have changed dramatically in our lifetimes.

Television is one medium that changed and yet managed to survive, and even thrive. Cable television brought us literally hundreds of stations, along with sitcom reruns that endlessly recycled our childhoods (and our parents' childhoods). Satellites brought immediacy, delivering news in real time around the clock. Other innovations also appeared on television: home shopping, reality TV, infomercials, music videos. And now, of course, television has become digital and interactive, with viewers no longer tied to a schedule or limited to watching programs on a television set.

HUGHES Hervé/Hemis/Alamy Stock Photo

What does this fifteenth-century illuminated manuscript suggest about the relationship between traditional forms of media and society?

Over the years, in response to emerging technologies, other forms of media also reinvented themselves. Music evolved from vinyl records to cassettes to CDs to MP3 files to music streamed on handheld devices. Movies moved from silent to "talkies" and from black and white to color, later enhanced by sophisticated computer animation and special digital effects. Professional journals and popular magazines became available online, and today, portable digital readers permit us to read paperless newspapers and books. In an effort to maintain and even expand their audiences, many newspapers have adopted new business models that deliver content entirely online. And in the age of social media, readers are encouraged to join the ongoing conversations about current events in various digital spaces.

Clearly, "new media" is a completely different entity from the media of even a decade ago, and this evolution has had negative as well as positive consequences. In recent years, the increasing power and scope of the internet, and its ever-increasing ability to enable us to form networks, has changed everything. Today, our access to digital media has truly made the world into what Canadian cultural critic Marshall McLuhan once called a "global village": a world of nations—and, today, of individuals—that are more and more interconnected and interdependent. The internet has made available a tremendous amount of information—and the ability to communicate this information almost instantly to millions of people all over the planet. Now, we exchange ideas and images through blogs, chat rooms, discussion boards, and email as well as through instant messaging, texting, *YouTube*, *Facebook*,

Stockwerk-Fotodesign/Fotolia

What do tablet e-readers, such as this one, say about the relationship between new forms of media and society?

Instagram, *Pinterest*, and *Twitter*. But the development of new media also has a dark side. The same tools that can unite, inform, instruct, entertain, and inspire can also isolate, misinform, frighten, deceive, stereotype, and even brainwash.

In this chapter's Focus section, "What Is Fake News, and Why Does It Matter?" (p. 200), three writers discuss the phenomenon of fake news. In "Before 'Fake News' Came False Prophecy" (p. 200), Eric Weiskott provides background on the origins of fake news and speculates about its social and political functions. In "Why Fake News Stories Thrive Online" (p. 204), Judith Donath looks at the proliferation of fake news in online media. Finally, in "I Write Fake News" (p. 207), an anonymous writer admits to creating fake news and explores the implications of this behavior.

Preparing to Read and Write

As you read and prepare to write about the essays in this chapter, you may consider the following questions:

- What assumptions does the writer seem to have about his or her audience? How can you tell?
- What is the writer's primary purpose? For example, is it to present information, to persuade, or something else?
- What genre is the writer using? For example, is the reading an essay, an op-ed piece, an argument, or a work of fiction? How do the conventions of this genre influence the writer's choices?
- What appeals does the writer use? For example, does he or she appeal primarily to emotion or to reason? Is this the most effective appeal?
- Does the essay focus on one particular medium or on the media in general?
- Does the writer discuss traditional media, new media, or both?
- Does the writer see the media as a positive, negative, or neutral force? Why?
- If the writer sees negative effects, where does he or she place blame? Do you agree?
- Does the writer make any recommendations for change? Do these recommendations seem reasonable?
- Is the writer focusing on the media's effects on individuals or on society?
- Does the writer discuss personal observations or experiences? If so, are they similar to or different from your own?
- When was the essay written? Has the situation the writer describes changed since then?

- Which writers' positions on the impact of the media (or on the media's shortcomings) are most alike? Most different? Most like your own?

Shared Writing

Media and Society

Think about your daily interaction with various forms of media. For example, how long after you wake up do you check your phone? How many times a day do you log in to social media, check your email, and send text messages? How do these experiences influence the quality of your life? Do they improve or impede your communication with others and your productivity at school and at work?

6.1 Clay Shirky, "Last Call: The End of the Printed Newspaper"

The vice provost for educational technologies and an associate professor of journalism and interactive telecommunications, Clay Shirky (1964–) examines how media impacts society. His work has appeared in such publications as *Computerworld, Foreign Affairs, Harvard Business Review, The New York Times, The Wall Street Journal*, and *Wired*. He is also the author of several books, including, most recently, *Little Rice: Smartphones, Xiaomi, and the Chinese Dream* (2015). In the following essay, Shirky considers the death of the print newspaper and the future of new forms of media.

BEFORE YOU READ

How do you stay informed about current events? Which news outlets do you regularly visit? Why those specifically?

Last Call: The End of the Printed Newspaper

The *Roanoke Times*, the local paper in my family home, is a classic metro daily, with roots that go back to the 1880s. Like most such papers, it ran into trouble in the middle of last decade, as print advertising revenue fell, leaving a hole in the balance sheet that digital advertising couldn't fill. When the 2008 recession accelerated those problems, the *Times'* parent company, Landmark, began looking for a buyer, eventually selling it to Warren Buffett's Berkshire Hathaway Media Group in 2013. The acquisition was greeted with relief in the newsroom, as Buffett had famously assured the employees at his earlier purchases "Your paper will operate from a position of financial strength." Three months after acquiring the *Times*, BH Media fired 31 employees, a bit over a tenth of the workforce.

Many people have lamented the unpredictability in the media environment occasioned by the arrival of digital devices and networks, but the slow implosion of newspapers has been widely and correctly predicted for some time now. Print ad revenues have fallen 65% in a decade, 2013 saw the lowest ever recorded, and 2014 will be worse. Even a company like BH Media, with deep pockets and a long term outlook, can't make a profit without cutting expenses, and can't cut expenses without cutting jobs.

What happened in Roanoke—gradual financial decay punctuated by bouts of firing—is the normal case at papers all over the country, and more is coming. The next wave of consolidation is already upon us; big media firms like Tribune and Gannett are abandoning their newspapers ("spinning them off," in bloodless business parlance). If you are a journalist at a print publication, your job is in danger. Period. Time to do something about it.

...

Journalists have been infantilized throughout the last decade, kept in a state of relative ignorance about the firms that employ them. A friend tells a story of reporters being asked the paid print circulation of their own publication. Their guesses ranged from 150,000 to 300,000; the actual figure was 35,000. If a reporter was that uninformed about a business he was covering, he'd be taken off the story.

5 This cluelessness is not by accident; the people who understand the state of the business often hide that knowledge from the workers. My friend Jay Rosen writes about the media's "production of innocence"—when covering a contentious issue, they must signal to the readers "We have no idea who's right." Among the small pool of journalists reporting on their own industry, there is a related task, the production of ignorance. When the press writes about the current dislocations, they must insist that no one knows what will happen. This pattern shows up whenever the media covers itself. When the Tribune Company recently got rid of their newspapers, the *New York Times* ran the story under a headline "The Tribune Company's publishing unit is being spun off, as the future of print remains unclear."

The future of print remains *what*? Try to imagine a world where the future of print is unclear: Maybe 25 year olds will start demanding news from yesterday, delivered in an unshareable format once a day. Perhaps advertisers will decide "Click to buy" is for wimps. Mobile phones: could be a fad. After all, anything could happen with print. Hard to tell, really....

Contrary to the contrived ignorance of media reporters, the future of the daily newspaper is one of the few certainties in the current landscape: Most of them are going away, in this decade. (If you work at a paper and you don't know what's happened to your own circulation or revenue in the last few years, now might be a good time to ask.) We're late enough in the process that we can even predict the likely circumstance of its demise.

...

Pick up a Sunday paper anywhere in this country. It will be the biggest paper that week, stuffed with sections, and with ads. Sunday is the money-maker, when circulation is highest and browsing time most abundant. Sunday is also the day for delivering those pamphlets of coupons and sales touts from national advertisers like Home Depot and Office Max, Staples and Michael's.

Those pamphlets—"free-standing inserts"—are now the largest single source of print advertising for many papers. Classifieds have imploded, local display ads are down, and black newsroom humor long ago re-labelled the Obituary column 'Subscriber Countdown.'

Print ads are essential revenue for most papers. Retail ads are essential for 10
print. Sunday is essential for retail. Inserts are essential for Sundays. The base of that entire inverted pyramid is being supported by the marketing departments of no more than a couple dozen national advertisers.

Those advertisers already have one foot out the door, having abandoned the idea that ads have to be printed inside the paper to reach their audience. CVS and Best Buy have so little connection to the papers they ride along with that they don't even bother printing the addresses of their local outlets anymore. (You can always find that information online.) From the advertiser's point of view, the nation's newspapers have become little more than a blue-bag delivery service, with a horoscope and enough local sports inside to get people to open the bag.

Inserts are one of the last sources of advertising to resist digitization. They are also the next to go. Businesses like Cellfire and Find & Save are working on digital coupons; stores like Kroger's and Safeway already offer online coupons direct to customers. This digitization is progressing as print circulation decays. Back in Roanoke, the *Times* was on the market for 5 years before it was bought; in that time the paper lost a quarter of its Sunday readers—106,000 to 85,000—and a third of its weekday readers—96,000 to 65,000. This story too is being repeated all over the country. The print audience continues to defect to mobile, abandon the local paper, or die.

As digital alternatives become attractive while print circulation withers, business will start to shift their money away from inserts. When the inserts go, Sundays won't prop up the rest of the week. When Sundays turn bad, the presses will become unprofitable. And when the presses become unprofitable, it will trigger the extraordinary costs involved in shrinking or ending the print operation. (If you work at a newspaper chain, ask your treasurer about underfunded pensions. Bring smelling salts.) These costs will torpedo the balance sheet, leading to further mergers, layoffs, reduced delivery days, or outright collapse.

. . .

The closing of a local newspaper matters more than the closing of a local shoe store for only one reason—newspapers employ journalists. I asked several reporters, editors, and scholars what journalists should do to get ready for the next wave of firings. There were three strong consensus answers: first, get good at understanding and presenting data. Second, understand how social media can work as a newsroom tool. Third, get whatever newsroom experience you can working in teams, and in launching new things.

The first piece of advice is the most widely discussed in journalism circles—get 15
good with numbers. The old 'story accompanied by a chart' was merely data next to journalism; increasingly, the data *is* the journalism. Nate Silver has changed our sense of political prediction. ProPublica has tied databases to storytelling better than anyone in the country. Homicide Watch can report more murders (all of them, in fact), using fewer people, than the *Washington Post*. Learning to code is the gold standard, but even taking an online class in statistics and getting good at

Google spreadsheets will help. Anything you can do to make yourself more familiar with finding, understanding, and presenting data will set you apart from people you'll be competing with, whether to keep your current job or get a new one.

Second, learn to use social media tools to find stories and sources. Social media was first absorbed as a marketing tool, but a medium that allows direct access to the public is also a journalistic one. Examples small and large, from photos of a plane landing in the Hudson River to the *Guardian*'s crowd-sourced analysis of hundreds of thousands of Parliamentary expense reports, rely on a more permeable relationship between the newsroom and the outside world. Practice reading conversations on Facebook and looking at photos on Instagram to look for story ideas; understand how a respectful request for assistance on Twitter or WeChat can bring out key sources or armies of volunteers.

Third, journalism is becoming more of a team sport. Integrated text and visuals, databases the readers can query and annotate themselves, group liveblogging of breaking news—all this requires collaboration far more engaged than the old 'one story, one byline' model. Volunteer for (or propose) anything that involves deeper teamwork than you're used to, and anything that involves experimenting with new tools or techniques. (The irony, of course, is that more news organizations prize teamwork, but still hire individuals. For your next job, you may need to convince your future bosses that you are valuable all by your lonesome, but that part of that value is working well on a team.)

One objection to all this advice is that it is too little, too late, and not nearly enough to save most newsroom employees. This is true. It is also irrelevant. We're entering what Jim Brady calls the "huddling together for warmth" phase of journalistic enterprise. Some papers will survive, of course, buying time through mergers or Chapter 11, but even those papers will shrink. There will be some work in journalism startups and in non-profits; given the number of people who are going to be fired in the next few years, many newsroom employees will find their next jobs outside anything that looks like a traditional paper. Much of the advice above will be relevant to those jobs as well.

The other objection is that advice to get skilled at data, social media, and teamwork is pitifully obvious. This is also true. All of this advice is obvious, and has been obvious for some time now. What's astonishing—and disheartening—is how long it's taken to act on that obvious advice, in part because there are still people committed to the fiction that the future of print is unclear.

20 There was one other common reaction among the people I spoke with about the coming changes: almost to a person, they noted that journalists can no longer rely on their employers to provide the opportunities to learn new skills. For a long time, professional development as a journalist was a side-effect of rising through the ranks; the paper offers you a new beat, or sends you out to break a career-making story. Today, papers are fighting for survival, and most slowly losing, so there's hardly time or resources for anything other than "Essential services are being maintained." If you're a journalist working inside a newspaper and you want to train for your next job, you're largely on your own.

...

It's tempting to try to find a moral dimension to newspapers' collapse, but there isn't one. All that's happened is advertisers are leaving, classifieds first, inserts last. Business is business; the advertisers never had a stake in keeping the newsroom open in the first place. This disconnection between the business side and the news side was celebrated as a benefit, right up to the moment it became an industry-wide point of failure.

The slow divorce between advertising and editorial is likely to pick up tempo soon. As Dick Tofel of ProPublica often points out, newspaper revenue has been shrinking since 2006, but the American economy has been growing since 2009. Between 1970 and now, the US has averaged only six years between recessions; the current period of growth crossed the six year mark this spring. We are statistically much closer to the next recession than to the last one, and in a recession, ad dollars are the first to go. Many papers will go bankrupt the way Hemingway's Mike Campbell did: Gradually, and then suddenly.

The death of newspapers is sad, but the threatened loss of journalistic talent is catastrophic. If that's you, it's time to learn something outside the production routine of your current job. It will be difficult and annoying, your employer won't be much help, and it may not even work, but we're nearing the next great contraction. If you want to get through it, doing almost anything will be better than doing almost nothing.

RESPONDING TO READING

1. In paragraph 14, Shirky writes, "The closing of a local newspaper matters more than the closing of a local shoe store for only one reason—newspapers employ journalists." Why does he draw this contrast? Do you agree with his point?
2. Throughout his essay, Shirky addresses journalists directly and offers advice for their next career move. But in paragraph 19, he explains, "All of this advice is obvious, and has been obvious for some time now." Why does he make this statement? Does it add to or detract from his argument?

Rhetorical Analysis

Consider the various examples of news sources Shirky includes in his essay. Are these examples effective? Why might he have chosen these publications and not others to support his points?

Writing with Sources

Search online for Shirky's TED Talk titled "How Social Media Can Make History." How does his talk help contextualize the ideas he explores in this essay? Write an essay explaining social media's role in communicating and even shaping world events. Try to incorporate current examples into your discussion.

6.2 Nicholas Carr, "Is Google Making Us Stupid?"

An avid technology writer, Nicholas Carr (1959–) explores the cultural implications of media in social contexts. His work has appeared in *The Atlantic; The Boston Globe;* the *Los Angeles Review of Books; MIT Technology Review; The New York Times; POLITICO Magazine; The Wall Street Journal; WIRED;* and his blog, *Rough Type*. He is the author of five books, including, most recently, *Utopia Is Creepy: And Other Provocations* (2016). In the following essay, Carr considers the effects of online media on the ways we read and think.

BEFORE YOU READ

Consider the title of this essay. What does it suggest? How would you answer the question it poses?

Is Google Making Us Stupid?

"Dave, stop. Stop, will you? Stop, Dave. Will you stop, Dave?" So the supercomputer HAL pleads with the implacable astronaut Dave Bowman in a famous and weirdly poignant scene toward the end of Stanley Kubrick's *2001: A Space Odyssey*. Bowman, having nearly been sent to a deep-space death by the malfunctioning machine, is calmly, coldly disconnecting the memory circuits that control its artificial brain. "Dave, my mind is going," HAL says, forlornly. "I can feel it. I can feel it."

I can feel it, too. Over the past few years I've had an uncomfortable sense that someone, or something, has been tinkering with my brain, remapping the neural circuitry, reprogramming the memory. My mind isn't going—so far as I can tell—but it's changing. I'm not thinking the way I used to think. I can feel it most strongly when I'm reading. Immersing myself in a book or a lengthy article used to be easy. My mind would get caught up in the narrative or the turns of the argument, and I'd spend hours strolling through long stretches of prose. That's rarely the case anymore. Now my concentration often starts to drift after two or three pages. I get fidgety, lose the thread, begin looking for something else to do. I feel as if I'm always dragging my wayward brain back to the text. The deep reading that used to come naturally has become a struggle.

I think I know what's going on. For more than a decade now, I've been spending a lot of time online, searching and surfing and sometimes adding to the great databases of the Internet. The Web has been a godsend to me as a writer. Research that once required days in the stacks or periodical rooms of libraries can now be done in minutes. A few Google searches, some quick clicks on hyperlinks, and I've got the telltale fact or pithy quote I was after. Even when I'm not working, I'm as likely as not to be foraging in the Web's info-thickets, reading and writing e-mails, scanning headlines and blog posts, watching videos and listening to podcasts, or just tripping from link to link to link. (Unlike footnotes, to which they're sometimes likened, hyperlinks don't merely point to related works; they propel you toward them.)

For me, as for others, the Net is becoming a universal medium, the conduit for most of the information that flows through my eyes and ears and into my mind. The advantages of having immediate access to such an incredibly rich store of information are many, and they've been widely described and duly applauded. "The perfect recall of silicon memory," *Wired*'s Clive Thompson has written, "can be an enormous boon to thinking." But that boon comes at a price. As the media theorist Marshall McLuhan pointed out in the 1960s, media are not just passive channels of information. They supply the stuff of thought, but they also shape the process of thought. And what the Net seems to be doing is chipping away my capacity for concentration and contemplation. My mind now expects to take in information the way the Net distributes it: in a swiftly moving stream of particles. Once I was a scuba diver in the sea of words. Now I zip along the surface like a guy on a Jet Ski.

I'm not the only one. When I mention my troubles with reading to friends 5
and acquaintances—literary types, most of them—many say they're having similar experiences. The more they use the Web, the more they have to fight to stay focused on long pieces of writing. Some of the bloggers I follow have also begun mentioning the phenomenon. Scott Karp, who writes a blog about online media, recently confessed that he has stopped reading books altogether. "I was a lit major in college, and used to be [a] voracious book reader," he wrote. "What happened?" He speculates on the answer: "What if I do all my reading on the web not so much because the way I read has changed, i.e. I'm just seeking convenience, but because the way I THINK has changed?"

Bruce Friedman, who blogs regularly about the use of computers in medicine, also has described how the Internet has altered his mental habits. "I now have almost totally lost the ability to read and absorb a longish article on the web or in print," he wrote earlier this year. A pathologist who has long been on the faculty of the University of Michigan Medical School, Friedman elaborated on his comment in a telephone conversation with me. His thinking, he said, has taken on a "staccato" quality, reflecting the way he quickly scans short passages of text from many sources online. "I can't read *War and Peace* anymore," he admitted. "I've lost the ability to do that. Even a blog post of more than three or four paragraphs is too much to absorb. I skim it."

Anecdotes alone don't prove much. And we still await the long-term neurological and psychological experiments that will provide a definitive picture of how Internet use affects cognition. But a recently published study of online research habits, conducted by scholars from University College London, suggests that we may well be in the midst of a sea change in the way we read and think. As part of the five-year research program, the scholars examined computer logs documenting the behavior of visitors to two popular research sites, one operated by the British Library and one by a U.K. educational consortium, that provide access to journal articles, e-books, and other sources of written information. They found that people using the sites exhibited "a form of skimming activity," hopping from one source to another and rarely returning to any source they'd already visited. They typically read no more than one or two pages of an article or book before they would "bounce" out to another site. Sometimes they'd save a long article, but there's no evidence that they ever went back and actually read it. The authors of the study report:

> It is clear that users are not reading online in the traditional sense; indeed there are signs that new forms of "reading" are emerging as users "power browse" horizontally through titles, contents pages and abstracts going for quick wins. It almost seems that they go online to avoid reading in the traditional sense.

Thanks to the ubiquity of text on the Internet, not to mention the popularity of text-messaging on cell phones, we may well be reading more today than we did in the 1970s or 1980s, when television was our medium of choice. But it's a different kind of reading, and behind it lies a different kind of thinking—perhaps even a new sense of the self. "We are not only *what* we read," says Maryanne Wolf, a developmental psychologist at Tufts University and the author of *Proust and the Squid: The Story and Science of the Reading Brain*. "We are *how* we read." Wolf worries that the style of reading promoted by the Net, a style that puts "efficiency" and "immediacy" above all else, may be weakening our capacity for the kind of deep reading that emerged when an earlier technology, the printing press, made long and complex works of prose commonplace. When we read online, she says, we tend to become "mere decoders of information." Our ability to interpret text, to make the rich mental connections that form when we read deeply and without distraction, remains largely disengaged.

Reading, explains Wolf, is not an instinctive skill for human beings. It's not etched into our genes the way speech is. We have to teach our minds how to translate the symbolic characters we see into the language we understand. And the media or other technologies we use in learning and practicing the craft of reading play an important part in shaping the neural circuits inside our brains. Experiments demonstrate that readers of ideograms, such as the Chinese, develop a mental circuitry for reading that is very different from the circuitry found in those of us whose written language employs an alphabet. The variations extend across many regions of the brain, including those that govern such essential cognitive functions as memory and the interpretation of visual and auditory stimuli. We can expect as well that the circuits woven by our use of the Net will be different from those woven by our reading of books and other printed works.

10 Sometime in 1882, Friedrich Nietzsche bought a typewriter—a Malling-Hansen Writing Ball, to be precise. His vision was failing, and keeping his eyes focused on a page had become exhausting and painful, often bringing on crushing headaches. He had been forced to curtail his writing, and he feared that he would soon have to give it up. The typewriter rescued him, at least for a time. Once he had mastered touch-typing, he was able to write with his eyes closed, using only the tips of his fingers. Words could once again flow from his mind to the page.

But the machine had a subtler effect on his work. One of Nietzsche's friends, a composer, noticed a change in the style of his writing. His already terse prose had become even tighter, more telegraphic. "Perhaps you will through this instrument even take to a new idiom," the friend wrote in a letter, noting that, in his own work, his "'thoughts' in music and language often depend on the quality of pen and paper."

"You are right," Nietzsche replied, "our writing equipment takes part in the forming of our thoughts." Under the sway of the machine, writes the German media scholar Friedrich A. Kittler, Nietzsche's prose "changed from arguments to aphorisms, from thoughts to puns, from rhetoric to telegram style."

The human brain is almost infinitely malleable. People used to think that our mental meshwork, the dense connections formed among the 100 billion or so neurons inside our skulls, was largely fixed by the time we reached adulthood. But brain researchers have discovered that that's not the case. James Olds, a professor of neuroscience who directs the Krasnow Institute for Advanced Study at George Mason University, says that even the adult mind "is very plastic." Nerve cells routinely break old connections and form new ones. "The brain," according to Olds, "has the ability to reprogram itself on the fly, altering the way it functions."

As we use what the sociologist Daniel Bell has called our "intellectual technologies"—the tools that extend our mental rather than our physical capacities—we inevitably begin to take on the qualities of those technologies. The mechanical clock, which came into common use in the 14th century, provides a compelling example. In *Technics and Civilization*, the historian and cultural critic Lewis Mumford described how the clock "disassociated time from human events and helped create the belief in an independent world of mathematically measurable sequences." The "abstract framework of divided time" became "the point of reference for both action and thought."

15 The clock's methodical ticking helped bring into being the scientific mind and the scientific man. But it also took something away. As the late MIT computer scientist Joseph Weizenbaum observed in his 1976 book, *Computer Power and Human Reason: From Judgment to Calculation*, the conception of the world that emerged from the widespread use of timekeeping instruments "remains an impoverished version of the older one, for it rests on a rejection of those direct experiences that formed the basis for, and indeed constituted, the old reality." In deciding when to eat, to work, to sleep, to rise, we stopped listening to our senses and started obeying the clock.

The process of adapting to new intellectual technologies is reflected in the changing metaphors we use to explain ourselves to ourselves. When the mechanical clock arrived, people began thinking of their brains as operating "like clockwork." Today, in the age of software, we have come to think of them as operating "like computers." But the changes, neuroscience tells us, go much deeper than metaphor. Thanks to our brain's plasticity, the adaptation occurs also at a biological level.

The Internet promises to have particularly far-reaching effects on cognition. In a paper published in 1936, the British mathematician Alan Turing proved that a digital computer, which at the time existed only as a theoretical machine, could be programmed to perform the function of any other information-processing device. And that's what we're seeing today. The Internet, an immeasurably powerful computing system, is subsuming most of our other intellectual technologies. It's becoming our map and our clock, our printing press and our typewriter, our calculator and our telephone, and our radio and TV.

When the Net absorbs a medium, that medium is re-created in the Net's image. It injects the medium's content with hyperlinks, blinking ads, and other digital gewgaws, and it surrounds the content with the content of all the other media it has absorbed. A new e-mail message, for instance, may announce its arrival as we're glancing over the latest headlines at a newspaper's site. The result is to scatter our attention and diffuse our concentration.

The Net's influence doesn't end at the edges of a computer screen, either. As people's minds become attuned to the crazy quilt of Internet media, traditional media have to adapt to the audience's new expectations. Television programs add text crawls and pop-up ads, and magazines and newspapers shorten their articles, introduce capsule summaries, and crowd their pages with easy-to-browse info-snippets. When, in March of this year, *The New York Times* decided to devote the second and third pages of every edition to article abstracts, its design director, Tom Bodkin, explained that the "shortcuts" would give harried readers a quick "taste" of the day's news, sparing them the "less efficient" method of actually turning the pages and reading the articles. Old media have little choice but to play by the new-media rules.

20 Never has a communications system played so many roles in our lives—or exerted such broad influence over our thoughts—as the Internet does today. Yet, for all that's been written about the Net, there's been little consideration of how, exactly, it's reprogramming us. The Net's intellectual ethic remains obscure.

About the same time that Nietzsche started using his typewriter, an earnest young man named Frederick Winslow Taylor carried a stopwatch into the Midvale Steel plant in Philadelphia and began a historic series of experiments aimed at improving the efficiency of the plant's machinists. With the approval of Midvale's owners, he recruited a group of factory hands, set them to work on various metalworking machines, and recorded and timed their every movement as well as the operations of the machines. By breaking down every job into a sequence of small, discrete steps and then testing different ways of performing each one, Taylor created a set of precise instructions—an "algorithm," we might say today—for how each worker should work. Midvale's employees grumbled about the strict new regime, claiming that it turned them into little more than automatons, but the factory's productivity soared.

More than a hundred years after the invention of the steam engine, the Industrial Revolution had at last found its philosophy and its philosopher. Taylor's tight industrial choreography—his "system," as he liked to call it—was embraced by manufacturers throughout the country and, in time, around the world. Seeking maximum speed, maximum efficiency, and maximum output, factory owners used time-and-motion studies to organize their work and configure the jobs of their workers. The goal, as Taylor defined it in his celebrated 1911 treatise, *The Principles of Scientific Management*, was to identify and adopt, for every job, the "one best method" of work and thereby to effect "the gradual substitution of science for rule of thumb throughout the mechanic arts." Once his system was applied to all acts of manual labor, Taylor assured his followers, it would bring about a restructuring not only of industry but of society, creating a utopia of perfect efficiency. "In the past the man has been first," he declared; "in the future the system must be first."

Taylor's system is still very much with us; it remains the ethic of industrial manufacturing. And now, thanks to the growing power that computer engineers and software coders wield over our intellectual lives, Taylor's ethic is beginning to govern the realm of the mind as well. The Internet is a machine designed for the efficient and automated collection, transmission, and manipulation of information, and its legions of programmers are intent on finding the "one best method"—the perfect algorithm—to carry out every mental movement of what we've come to describe as "knowledge work."

Google's headquarters, in Mountain View, California—the Googleplex—is the Internet's high church, and the religion practiced inside its walls is Taylorism. Google, says its chief executive, Eric Schmidt, is "a company that's founded around the science of measurement," and it is striving to "systematize everything" it does. Drawing on the terabytes of behavioral data it collects through its search engine and other sites, it carries out thousands of experiments a day, according to the *Harvard Business Review*, and it uses the results to refine the algorithms that increasingly control how people find information and extract meaning from it. What Taylor did for the work of the hand, Google is doing for the work of the mind.

The company has declared that its mission is "to organize the world's informa- 25
tion and make it universally accessible and useful." It seeks to develop "the perfect search engine," which it defines as something that "understands exactly what you mean and gives you back exactly what you want." In Google's view, information is a kind of commodity, a utilitarian resource that can be mined and processed with industrial efficiency. The more pieces of information we can "access" and the faster we can extract their gist, the more productive we become as thinkers.

Where does it end? Sergey Brin and Larry Page, the gifted young men who founded Google while pursuing doctoral degrees in computer science at Stanford, speak frequently of their desire to turn their search engine into an artificial intelligence, a HAL-like machine that might be connected directly to our brains. "The ultimate search engine is something as smart as people—or smarter," Page said in a speech a few years back. "For us, working on search is a way to work on artificial intelligence." In a 2004 interview with *Newsweek*, Brin said, "Certainly if you had all the world's information directly attached to your brain, or an artificial brain that was smarter than your brain, you'd be better off." Last year, Page told a convention of scientists that Google is "really trying to build artificial intelligence and to do it on a large scale."

Such an ambition is a natural one, even an admirable one, for a pair of math whizzes with vast quantities of cash at their disposal and a small army of computer scientists in their employ. A fundamentally scientific enterprise, Google is motivated by a desire to use technology, in Eric Schmidt's words, "to solve problems that have never been solved before," and artificial intelligence is the hardest problem out there. Why wouldn't Brin and Page want to be the ones to crack it?

Still, their easy assumption that we'd all "be better off" if our brains were supplemented, or even replaced, by an artificial intelligence is unsettling. It suggests a belief that intelligence is the output of a mechanical process, a series of discrete steps that can be isolated, measured, and optimized. In Google's world, the world we enter when we go online, there's little place for the fuzziness of contemplation. Ambiguity is not an opening for insight but a bug to be fixed. The human brain is just an outdated computer that needs a faster processor and a bigger hard drive.

The idea that our minds should operate as high-speed data-processing machines is not only built into the workings of the Internet, it is the network's reigning business model as well. The faster we surf across the Web—the more links we click and pages we view—the more opportunities Google and other companies gain to collect information about us and to feed us advertisements. Most of the proprietors of the commercial Internet have a financial stake in collecting the crumbs of data we leave behind as we flit from link to link—the more crumbs, the better. The last thing these companies want is to encourage leisurely reading or slow, concentrated thought. It's in their economic interest to drive us to distraction.

30 Maybe I'm just a worrywart. Just as there's a tendency to glorify technological progress, there's a countertendency to expect the worst of every new tool or machine. In Plato's *Phaedrus*, Socrates bemoaned the development of writing. He feared that, as people came to rely on the written word as a substitute for the knowledge they used to carry inside their heads, they would, in the words of one of the dialogue's characters, "cease to exercise their memory and become forgetful." And because they would be able to "receive a quantity of information without proper instruction," they would "be thought very knowledgeable when they are for the most part quite ignorant." They would be "filled with the conceit of wisdom instead of real wisdom." Socrates wasn't wrong—the new technology did often have the effects he feared—but he was shortsighted. He couldn't foresee the many ways that writing and reading would serve to spread information, spur fresh ideas, and expand human knowledge (if not wisdom).

The arrival of Gutenberg's printing press, in the 15th century, set off another round of teeth gnashing. The Italian humanist Hieronimo Squarciafico worried that the easy availability of books would lead to intellectual laziness, making men "less studious" and weakening their minds. Others argued that cheaply printed books and broadsheets would undermine religious authority, demean the work of scholars and scribes, and spread sedition and debauchery. As New York University professor Clay Shirky notes, "Most of the arguments made against the printing press were correct, even prescient." But, again, the doomsayers were unable to imagine the myriad blessings that the printed word would deliver.

So, yes, you should be skeptical of my skepticism. Perhaps those who dismiss critics of the Internet as Luddites or nostalgists will be proved correct, and from our hyperactive, data-stoked minds will spring a golden age of intellectual discovery and universal wisdom. Then again, the Net isn't the alphabet, and although it may replace the printing press, it produces something altogether different. The kind of deep reading that a sequence of printed pages promotes is valuable not just for the knowledge we acquire from the author's words but for the intellectual vibrations those words set off within our own minds. In the quiet spaces opened up by the sustained, undistracted reading of a book, or by any other act of contemplation, for that matter, we make our own associations, draw our own inferences and analogies, foster our own ideas. Deep reading, as Maryanne Wolf argues, is indistinguishable from deep thinking.

If we lose those quiet spaces, or fill them up with "content," we will sacrifice something important not only in our selves but in our culture. In a recent essay, the playwright Richard Foreman eloquently described what's at stake:

> I come from a tradition of Western culture, in which the ideal (my ideal) was the complex, dense and "cathedral-like" structure of the highly educated and articulate personality—a man or woman who carried inside themselves a personally constructed and unique version of the entire heritage of the West. [But now] I see within us all (myself included) the replacement of complex inner density with a new kind of self—evolving under the pressure of information overload and the technology of the "instantly available."

As we are drained of our "inner repertory of dense cultural inheritance," Foreman concluded, we risk turning into "'pancake people'—spread wide and thin as we connect with that vast network of information accessed by the mere touch of a button."

I'm haunted by that scene in *2001*. What makes it so poignant, and so weird, is 35
the computer's emotional response to the disassembly of its mind: its despair as one circuit after another goes dark, its childlike pleading with the astronaut—"I can feel it. I can feel it. I'm afraid"—and its final reversion to what can only be called a state of innocence. HAL's outpouring of feeling contrasts with the emotionlessness that characterizes the human figures in the film, who go about their business with an almost robotic efficiency. Their thoughts and actions feel scripted, as if they're following the steps of an algorithm. In the world of *2001*, people have become so machinelike that the most human character turns out to be a machine. That's the essence of Kubrick's dark prophecy: as we come to rely on computers to mediate our understanding of the world, it is our own intelligence that flattens into artificial intelligence.

RESPONDING TO READING

1. Carr opens and closes his essay with a reference to the classic sci-fi film *2001: A Space Odyssey* (1968). How does this framing technique establish and maintain the tone of the essay? Does it add to or detract from Carr's argument? Explain.
2. Throughout his essay, Carr explains the effects the internet has on our consumption of various forms of media, including traditional and new forms. In paragraph 18, Carr writes, "When the Net absorbs a medium, that medium is re-created in the Net's image." What does he mean? What examples does he provide to support his claim?

Rhetorical Analysis

What is the thesis of Carr's essay? Is his primary purpose here to warn of the shortcomings of Google and online technologies or to change the way users approach the internet?

Writing with Sources

Go to the *Pew Research Center Internet & Technology* site and research the latest findings on the relationship between internet use and cognition. What does recent research suggest about the effects of digital technologies on the way people think and behave? Does age have anything to do with the patterns observed? Write an essay in which you answer these questions, adding your own examples to back up your points.

6.3 Patton Oswalt, "Wake Up, Geek Culture. Time to Die."

A stand-up comedian as well as a TV, movie, and voice actor, Patton Oswalt (1969–) explores pop culture and current social issues in his work. He is the author of the books *Zombie Spaceship Wasteland* (2011) and *Silver Screen Fiend: Learning About Life from an Addiction to Film* (2015). In this essay, Oswalt takes a funny and critical look at how new technologies affect our "artistic subcultures."

BEFORE YOU READ

What does the expression "geek culture" mean to you? Does it remind you of yourself or people you know? In other words, does it hit home for you? Explain.

Wake Up, Geek Culture. Time to Die.

I'm not a nerd. I used to be one, back 30 years ago when nerd meant something. I entered the '80s immersed, variously, in science fiction, Dungeons & Dragons, and Stephen King. Except for the multiple-player aspect of D&D, these pursuits were not "passions from a common spring," to quote Poe.

I can't say that I ever abided nerd stereotypes: I was never alone or felt outcast. I had a circle of friends who were similarly drawn to the exotica of pop culture (or, at least, what was considered pop culture at the time in northern Virginia)—Monty Python, post-punk music, comic books, slasher films, and videogames. We were a sizable clique. The terms *nerd* and *geek* were convenient shorthand used by other cliques to categorize us. But they were thin descriptors.

In Japan, the word *otaku* refers to people who have obsessive, minute interests—especially stuff like anime or videogames. It comes from a term for "someone else's house"—otaku live in their own, enclosed worlds. Or, at least, their lives follow patterns that are well outside the norm. Looking back, we were American otakus. (Of course, now all America is otaku—which I'm going to get into shortly. But in order to do so, we're going to hang out in the '80s.)

I was too young to drive or hold a job. I was never going to play sports, and girls were an uncrackable code. So, yeah—I had time to collect every *Star Wars* action figure, learn the Three Laws of Robotics, memorize Roy Batty's speech from the end of *Blade Runner*, and classify each monster's abilities and weaknesses in TSR Hobbies' *Monster Manual*. By 1987, my friends and I were waist-deep in the hot honey of adolescence. Money and cars and, hopefully, girls would follow, but not if we spent our free time learning the names of the bounty hunters' ships in *The Empire Strikes Back*. So we each built our own otakuesque thought-palace, which we crammed with facts and nonsense—only now, the thought-palace was nicely appointed, decorated neatly, the information laid out on deep mahogany shelves or framed in gilt. What once set us apart, we hoped, would become a lovable quirk.

5 Our respective nerdery took on various forms: One friend was the first to get his hands on early bootlegs of Asian action flicks by Tsui Hark and John Woo, and he never looked back. Another started reading William Gibson and peppered his conversations with cryptic (and alluring) references to "cyberspace." I was ground zero for the "new wave" of mainstream superhero comics—which meant being right there for Alan Moore, Frank Miller, and Neil Gaiman. And like my music-obsessed pals, who passed around the cassette of Guns n' Roses' *Live ?!*@ Like a Suicide* and were thus prepared for the shock wave of *Appetite for Destruction*, I'd devoured Moore's run on *Swamp Thing* and thus eased nicely into his *Watchmen*. I'd also read the individual issues of Miller's *Daredevil: Born Again* run, so when *The Dark Knight Returns* was reviewed by *The New York Times*, I could say I saw it coming. And I'd consumed so many single-issue guest-writing stints of Gaiman's that when he was finally given *The Sandman* title all to himself, I was first in line and knew the language.

Admittedly, there's a chilly thrill in moving with the herd while quietly being tuned in to something dark, complicated, and unknown just beneath the topsoil of popularity. Something about which, while we moved *with* the herd, we could share a wink and a nod with two or three other similarly connected herdlings.

When our coworkers nodded along to Springsteen and Madonna songs at the local Bennigan's, my select friends and I would quietly trade out-of-context lines from *Monty Python* sketches—a thieves' cant, a code language used for identification. We needed it, too, because the essence of our culture—our "escape hatch" culture—would begin to change in 1987.

That was the year the final issue of *Watchmen* came out, in October. After that, it seemed like everything that was part of my otaku world was out in the open and up for grabs, if only out of context. I wasn't seeing the hard line between "nerds" and "normals" anymore. It was the last year that a T-shirt or music preference or pastime (Dungeons & Dragons had long since lost its dangerous, Satanic, suicide-inducing street cred) could set you apart from the surface dwellers. Pretty soon, being the only person who was into something didn't make you outcast; it made you ahead of the curve and someone people were quicker to befriend than shun. Ironically, surface dwellers began repurposing the symbols and phrases and tokens of the erstwhile outcast underground.

Fast-forward to now: Boba Fett's helmet emblazoned on sleeveless T-shirts worn by gym douches hefting dumbbells. The *Glee* kids performing the songs from *The Rocky Horror Picture Show*. And Toad the Wet Sprocket, a band that took its name from a *Monty Python* riff, joining the permanent soundtrack of a night out at Bennigan's. Our below-the-topsoil passions have been rudely dug up and displayed in the noonday sun. *The Lord of the Rings* used to be ours and *only ours* simply because of the sheer goddamn thickness of the books. Twenty years later, the entire cast and crew would be trooping onstage at the Oscars to collect their statuettes, and replicas of the One Ring would be sold as bling.

10 The topsoil has been scraped away, forever, in 2010. In fact, it's been dug up, thrown into the air, and allowed to rain down and coat everyone in a thin gray-brown mist called the Internet. Everyone considers themselves otaku about something—whether it's the mythology of *Lost* or the minor intrigues of *Top Chef. American Idol* inspires—if not in depth, at least in length and passion—the same number of conversations as does *The Wire*. There are no more hidden thought-palaces—they're easily accessed websites, or Facebook pages with thousands of fans. And I'm not going to bore you with the step-by-step specifics of how it happened. In the timeline of the upheaval, part of the graph should be interrupted by the words the Internet. And now here we are.

The problem with the Internet, however, is that it lets anyone become otaku about anything *instantly*. In the '80s, you couldn't get up to speed on an entire genre in a weekend. You had to wait, month to month, for the issues of *Watchmen* to come out. We couldn't BitTorrent the latest John Woo film or digitally download an entire decade's worth of grunge or hip hop. Hell, there were a few weeks during the spring of 1991 when we couldn't tell whether Nirvana or Tad would be the next band to break big. Imagine the terror!

But then reflect on the advantages. Waiting for the next issue, movie, or album gave you time to reread, rewatch, reabsorb whatever you loved, so you brought your own idiosyncratic love of that thing to your thought-palace. People who were obsessed with *Star Trek* or the *Ender's Game* books were all obsessed with the same object, but its light shone differently on each person. Everyone had to create in their mind unanswered questions or what-ifs. What if Leia, not Luke, had become a Jedi? What happens after Rorschach's journal is found at the end of *Watchmen*? What the hell was *The Prisoner* about?

None of that's necessary anymore. When everyone has easy access to their favorite diversions and every diversion comes with a rabbit hole's worth of extra features and deleted scenes and hidden hacks to tumble down and never emerge from, then we're all just adding to an ever-swelling, soon-to-erupt volcano of trivia, re-contextualized and forever rebooted. We're on the brink of Etewaf: Everything That Ever Was—Available Forever.

I know it sounds great, but there's a danger: Everything we have today that's cool comes from someone wanting more of something they loved in the past. Action figures, videogames, superhero movies, iPods: All are continuations of a love that wanted more. Ever see action figures from the '70s, each with that same generic Anson Williams body and one-piece costume with the big clumsy snap on the back? Or played Atari's *Adventure*, found the secret room, and thought, that's it? Can we all admit the final battle in *Superman II* looks like a local commercial for a personal-injury attorney? And how many people had their cassette of the *Repo Man* soundtrack eaten by a Walkman?

Now, with everyone more or less otaku and everything *immediately* awe- 15
some (or, if not, just as immediately rebooted or recut as a hilarious YouTube or Funny or Die spoof), the old inner longing for more or better that made our present pop culture so amazing is dwindling. *The Onion*'s A.V. Club—essential and transcendent in so many ways—has a weekly feature called *Gateways to Geekery*, in which an entire artistic subculture—say, anime, H. P. Lovecraft, or the Marx Brothers—is mapped out so you can become otaku on it but avoid its more tedious aspects.

Here's the danger: That creates weak otakus. Etewaf doesn't produce a new generation of artists—just an army of sated consumers. Why create anything new when there's a mountain of freshly excavated pop culture to recut, repurpose, and manipulate on your iMovie? *The Shining* can be remade into a comedy trailer. Both movie versions of the Joker can be sent to battle each another. The Dude is in *The Matrix*.

The coming decades—the 21st-century's '20s, '30s, and '40s—have the potential to be one long, unbroken, recut spoof in which everything in *Avatar* farts while *Keyboard Cat* plays eerily in the background.

But I prefer to be optimistic. I choose hope. I see Etewaf as the Balrog, the helter-skelter, the A-pop-alypse that rains cleansing fire down onto the otaku landscape, burns away the chaff, and forces us to start over with only a few thin, near-meatless scraps on which to build.

In order to save pop culture future, we've got to make the present pop culture suck, at least for a little while.

How do we do this? How do we bring back that sweet longing for more that 20
spawned Gears of War, the Crank films, and the entire Joss Whedon oeuvre? Simple: We've got to speed up the process. We've got to stoke the volcano. We've got to catalog, collate, and cross-pollinate. We must bring about Etewaf, and soon.

It has already started. It's all around us. VH1 list shows. *Freddy vs. Jason*. Websites that list the 10 biggest sports meltdowns, the 50 weirdest plastic surgeries, the 200 harshest nut shots. *Alien vs. Predator*. Lists of fails, lists of boobs, lists of deleted movie scenes. Entire TV seasons on iTunes. An entire studio's film vault, downloadable with a click. Easter egg scenes of wild sex in *Grand Theft Auto*. Hell, *Grand Theft Auto*, period. And yes, I know that a lot of what I'm listing here seems like it's outside of the "nerd world" and part of the wider pop culture. Well, I've got news for you—pop culture *is* nerd culture. The fans of *Real Housewives of Hoboken* watch, discuss, and absorb their show the same way a geek watched *Dark Shadows* or obsessed over his eighth-level half-elf ranger character in Dungeons & Dragons. It's the method of consumption, not what's on the plate.

Since there's no going back—no reverse on the out-of-control locomotive we've created—we've got to dump nitro into the engines. We need to get serious, and I'm here to outline my own personal fantasy: We start with lists of the best lists of boobs. Every Beatles song, along with every alternate take, along with every cover version of every one of their songs and every alternate take of every cover version, all on your chewing-gum-sized iPod nano. Goonies vs. Saw. Every book on your Kindle. Every book *on* Kindle on every Kindle. *The Human Centipede* done with the cast of *The Hills* and directed by the Coen brothers.

That's when we'll reach Etewaf singularity. Pop culture will become self-aware. It will happen in the *A.V. Club* first: A brilliant Nathan Rabin column about the worst Turkish rip-offs of American comic book characters will suddenly begin writing its own comments, each a single sentence from the sequel to *A Confederacy of Dunces*. Then a fourth and fifth season of *Arrested Development*, directed by David Milch of *Deadwood*, will appear suddenly in the TV Shows section of iTunes. Someone BitTorrenting a *Crass* bootleg will suddenly find their hard drive crammed with Elvis Presley's "lost" grunge album from 1994. And everyone's TiVo will record *Ghostbusters III*, starring Peter Sellers, Lee Marvin, and John Candy.

This will last only a moment. We'll have one minute before pop culture swells and blackens like a rotten peach and then explodes, sending every movie, album, book, and TV show flying away into space. Maybe tendrils and fragments of them will attach to asteroids or plop down on ice planets light-years away. A billion years after our sun burns out, a race of intelligent ice crystals will build a culture based on dialog from *The Princess Bride*. On another planet, intelligent gas clouds will wait for the yearly passing of the "Lebowski" comet. One of the rings of Saturn will be made from blurbs for the softcover release of *Infinite Jest*, twirled forever into a ribbon of effusive praise.

But back here on Earth, we'll enter year zero for pop culture. All that we'll have left to work with will be a VHS copy of *Zapped!*, the soundtrack to *The Road Warrior*, and Steve Ditko's eight-issue run on *Shade: The Changing Man*. For a while—maybe a generation—pop culture pastimes will revolve around politics and farming.

But the same way a farmer has to endure a few fallow seasons after he's overplanted, a new, richer loam will begin to appear in the wake of our tilling. From *Zapped!* will arise a telekinesis epic from James Cameron. Paul Thomas Anderson will do a smaller, single-character study of a man who can move matchbooks with his mind and how he uses this skill to pursue a casino waitress. Then the Coen brothers will veer off, doing a movie about pyrokenesis set in 1980s Cleveland, while out of Japan will come a subgenre of telekinetic horror featuring pale, whispering children. And we'll build from there—precognition, telepathy, and, most radically, normal people falling in love and dealing with jobs and life. Maybe also car crashes.

The Road Warrior soundtrack, all Wagnerian strings and military snare drums, will germinate into a driving, gut-bucket subgenre called waste-rock. And, as a counterpoint, flute-driven folk. Then there'll be the inevitable remixes, mashups, and pirated-only releases. A new Beatles will arise, only they'll be Iranian.

Shade: The Changing Man will become the new *Catcher in the Rye*. Ditko's thin-fingered art will appear on lunch boxes, T-shirts, and magazine covers. Someone will write an even thinner, sparser, simpler version called *Shade*. Someone else will write a 1,000-page meditation about Shade's home planet. Eventually, someone will try to kill the Iranian John Lennon with a hat, based on one panel from issue 3. A whole generation of authors under 20 will have their love—or disgust—of these comics to thank for their careers.

So the topsoil we're coated in needs to wash away for a while. I want my daughter to have a 1987 the way I did and experience the otaku thrill. While everyone else is grooving on the latest Jay-Z, 5 Gallons of Diesel, I'd like her to share a secret look with a friend, both of them hip to the fact that, from Germany, there's a bootleg MP3 of a group called Dr. Cali-gory, pioneers of superviolent line-dancing music. And I want her to enjoy that secret look for a little while before Dr. Cali-gory's songs get used in commercials for cruise lines.

Etewaf now! 30

RESPONDING TO READING

1. Throughout his essay, Oswalt laments the loss of "nerd" culture in the digital age. In paragraph 10, he writes, "There are no more hidden thought-palaces—they're easily accessed websites, or Facebook pages with thousands of fans." How has the internet leveled cultural distinctions between the in-crowd and "nerds" or "geeks"? Do you see these changes as positive or negative? Explain.
2. In paragraph 18, the tone of the essay shifts as Oswalt lays out a plan to reclaim the "geek culture" of the past. Although his style is humorous, is his proposal realistic? How might it actually work? Do you agree that bringing back the "otaku thrill" is an achievable, and desirable, goal (29)?

Rhetorical Analysis

Oswalt sprinkles lots of pop culture references, old and new, throughout his essay. Sometimes, but not always, he contextualizes the references to clarify them. What does his use of these references tell you about how he sees his audience?

Writing with Sources

Conduct some interviews to confirm (or challenge) the conclusions Oswalt draws about the demise of "geek culture." Then, citing both your own interviews and Oswalt's essay as sources, write an essay in which you take a stand on the issue of whether digital technologies are eroding or developing our "artistic subcultures."

6.4 Quinn Norton, "*The New York Times* Fired My Doppelgänger"

A journalist, blogger, and essayist, Quinn Norton (1973–) writes about the intersection of media and society, especially issues related to online privacy and security. Her work has appeared in such publications as *The Atlantic; The Daily Beast; Gizmodo; Maximum PC magazine; Medium; ProPublica; WIRED;* and her blog, *Quinn Said....* In early 2018, she was hired and then, after a fast Twitterstorm of controversy, fired by *The New York Times* as lead op-ed technology writer. In the following essay, Norton describes her bumpy journey as a social media writer and blogger who tackles difficult topics.

BEFORE YOU READ

Do you have an alternate online identity? Who is this person? How is he or she different from your offline self?

The New York Times Fired My Doppelgänger

The day before Valentine's Day, social media created a bizarro-world version of me. I have seen strange ideas about me online before, but this doppelgänger was so far from resembling me that I told friends and loved ones I didn't want to even try to rebut it. It was a leading question turned into a human form. The net created a person with my name and face, but with so little relationship to me, she could have been an invader from an alternate universe.

It is strange to see such a version of yourself invented and destroyed by networked rage. It made me sad and angry, but even more, I think, it inspired a horrified confusion in myself and those familiar with my work and my character. A digital effigy of me was built and burned.

It started when *The New York Times* hired me for its editorial board. In January, the *Times* sought me out because, editorial leaders told me, the *Times* as an institution is struggling with understanding how technology is shifting society and politics. We talked for a while. I discussed my work, my beliefs, and my background.

I've studied online communities since 1995. I know how many underlying technologies work, and how they might relate to their historical antecedents. I have spent time with individuals in various groups—including hanging out in their spaces, witnessing their operations—and written about it. I have worked with Anonymous and other internet communities that dwell far from the Overton window,[1] which describes what sort of public discourse is tolerable. I identify politically as an anarchist pacifist.

---

[1] The idea that politicians operate within a space of socially acceptable policies, attributed to public policy expert Joseph P. Overton (1960–2003). [Eds.]

I was hesitant with the *Times*. They were far out of my comfort zone, but I 5
felt that the people I was talking to had a sincerity greater than their confusion. Nothing that has happened since then has dissuaded me from that impression. I think it seemed like it could be a good match for all of us. They were trying something new, and I had experience and understanding of the internet that was hard to get elsewhere. The net is making the world strange. People shouldn't be overcritical of the *Times*. The world has changed so fast and so much in the last 20 years. It is too much to ask that an entity that has been flowing and changing at the pace of society since the 1850s be up to date on what is probably the fastest shift in human history that didn't involve a volcano. But what happens next isn't only up to the institutions we inherited from the 20th century and before.

If you're reading this, especially on the internet, you are the teacher for those institutions at a local, national, and global level. I understand that you didn't ask for this position. Neither did I. History doesn't ask you if you want to be born in a time of upheaval, it just tells you when you are. When the backlash began, I got the call from the person who had sought me out and recruited me. The fear I heard in that shaky voice coming through my mobile phone was unmistakable. It was the fear of a mob, of the unknown, and of the idea that maybe they had gotten it wrong and done something terrible. I have felt all of those things. Many of us have. It's not a place of strength, even when it seems to be coming from someone standing in a place of power. The *Times* didn't know what the internet was doing—tearing down a new hire, exposing a fraud, threatening them—everything seemed to be in the mix.

I have a teenage daughter, and I have told her all her life that all the grownups are making it up as they go along. I have also waggled my eyebrows suggestively while saying it, to make it clear to her that I mean me, too. In that moment, *The New York Times* and I, we were all making it up as we went along. I didn't want to harm them, because I believed—and still do—that the better institution they had talked about becoming was something that could help the world. I didn't particularly want them to harm me, but I also knew that I was tough in a way they aren't. I have been through this before, and I know who I am, an advantage I have over most of the institutions currently entrusted with the care of our society.

I think if I'd gotten to write for the *Times* as part of their editorial board, this might have been different. I might have been in a position to show how our media doppelgängers get invented, and how we can unwind them. It takes time and patience. It doesn't come from denying the doppelgänger—there's nothing there to deny. I was accused of homophobia because of the in-group language I used with anons when I worked with them. ("Anons" refers to people who identify as part of the activist collective Anonymous.) I was accused of racism for use of taboo language, mainly in a nine-year-old retweet in support of Obama. Intentions aside, it wasn't a great tweet, and I was probably overemotional when I retweeted it.

I was called a Nazi because of my friendship with the infamous neo-Nazi known on the internet as weev—his given name is Andrew Auernheimer; he helps run the anti-Semitic website *The Daily Stormer.* In my pacifism, I can't reject a friendship, even when a friend has taken such a horrifying path. I am not the judge of who is capable of improving as a person. This philosophy also requires me to confront him about his terrible beliefs and their terrible consequences. I have been doing this since before his brief time as a cause célèbre in 2012—I believe it'd be hypocritical for me to turn away from this obligation. weev is just one of many terrible people I've cared for in my life. I don't support what my terrible friend believes or does. But I strongly advocate for people with a good sense of themselves and their values to engage with their terrible friends, coworkers, and relatives, to lovingly confront them for as long as it takes, and it would be wrong to not do so myself. I had what I now see as the advantage of coming from a family of terrible people. This taught me that not everyone worthy of love is worthy of emulation. It also taught me that being given terrible ideas is not a destiny, and that intervention can change lives.

10 Not everyone believes loving engagement is the best way to fight evil beliefs, but it has a good track record. Not everyone is in a position to engage safely with racists, sexists, anti-Semites, and homophobes, but for those who are, it's a powerful tool. Engagement is not the one true answer to the societal problems destabilizing America today, but there is no one true answer. The way forward is as multifarious and diverse as America is, and a method of nonviolent confrontation and accountability, arising from my pacifism, is what I can bring to helping my society.

But this isn't what the internet did with the idea of me that emerged from a scatter of tweets before Valentine's Day. The internet lets people create and then interact with a character. Regardless of who I am and what I've done, there is now a Nazi-sympathizing and homophobic "Quinn Norton" out there: She was born into privilege, and in some versions of this story even attended two universities in California. She is an abusive and deceptive person, who lies about her family, her disabilities, and even her sexuality. She is also fictional, a creation of a collaborative writing process that took place on social-publishing platforms, over a matter of days, between countless people who had never met each other. That creativity, however much I believe it was misapplied in this case, is part of what makes our networks miraculous and wonderfully strange. I wish it hadn't affected my life, but it also illustrates to me why my work is important, and why I must continue exploring and explaining these things.

I am not immune from these mistakes, for mistaking a limited snapshot of something for what it is in its entirety. I have been on the other side.

In late 2015 I woke up a little before 6 a.m., jet-lagged in New York, and started looking at Twitter. There was a hashtag, I don't remember if it was trending or just in my timeline, called #whitegirlsaremagic. I clicked on it, and found it was racist and sexist dross. It was being promulgated in opposition to another hashtag, #blackgirlsaremagic. I clicked on that, and found a few model shots and borderline soft-core porn of black women. Armed with this impression, I set off to tweet in righteous anger about how much I disliked women being reduced to sex objects regardless of race. I was not just wrong in this moment, I was incoherently wrong. I had made my little mental model of what #blackgirlsaremagic was, and I had no clue that I had no clue what I was talking about. My 60-second impression of #whitegirlsaremagic was dead-on, but #blackgirlsaremagic didn't fit in the last few tweets my browser had loaded.

It had a complicated history. It was founded by CaShawn Thompson to celebrate the lives and achievements of black women, and had been written about by major media outlets. I didn't know there was a story I could have gone and looked up to understand this. I later apologized in a post about all of this, but still too defensively. I realized I was wrong quickly in the torrent of feedback, but it felt unfair to me that I didn't have a path to finding out what was going on in my bleary morning. I had been a victim of something the sociologists Alice Marwick and danah boyd call context collapse, where people create online culture meant for one in-group, but exposed to any number of out-groups without its original context by social-media platforms, where it can be recontextualized easily and accidentally.

15 Ignorant of the necessary context, and full of righteous anger, I victimized a community I didn't even know existed. Amongst my many frustrations that morning was finding out that I'd caused harm at all. I woke up thinking I was the good guy. Over the course of the day, I was told that this was especially hurtful coming from me. I stamped my little foot, feeling trapped—I didn't know what I didn't know! I wanted someone—probably Twitter, the company—to have planted signposts that could have prevented my mistake. I wasn't wrong to wish for that, but I was still just plain wrong that morning, and I had to sit with that contradiction for a while. It's no fun at all.

I had even written about context collapse myself, but that hadn't saved me from falling into it, and then hurting other people I didn't mean to hurt. This particular collapse didn't create much of a doppelgänger, but it did find me spending a morning as a defensive jerk. I'm very sorry for that dumb mistake. It helped me learn a lesson: Be damn sure when you make angry statements. Check them out long enough that, even if the statements themselves are still angry, you are not angry by the time you make them. Again and again, I have learned this: Don't internet angry. If you're angry, internet later.

Context collapse is our constant companion online. The openness of the web that has given us so much has given us this phenomenon, too, and it complicates things. It isn't inherently dangerous, but it does require work and critical thought. The internet makes us telepathic, angry, and weird—but it also lets us collaborate, remix, and rapidly reconfigure one another's ideas on a massive scale.

Around Valentine's Day, people found some things I've said over the last decade upsetting. Some of those things I said, and the way that I said them, I stand by completely. They require context to understand, but that's not a flaw—that's part of what makes them complicated and useful thoughts. Some things I've said—mostly things not discovered by the mob, to be honest—are not so great, and I don't agree with them now. But that's a worthwhile part of my story. I'd hate to think I haven't learned anything in the last 20 years. I used to think that color-blindness and not talking about race would fix racism. They won't. I used to be too scared to let people know when I didn't understand something, and just muddle through hoping I wouldn't get caught. That was a terrible way of dealing with the world. I used to think that showing someone how wrong they were on the internet could fix the world. I said a lot of stupid things when I believed that.

I did not spring fully formed from the head of Zeus, neither did you, nor did *The New York Times*. The growing process is always messy and often ugly, whether you're a person or a caterpillar, or a global network, or the newspaper of record.

20 Here is your task, person on the internet, reader of journalism, speaker to the world on social media: You make the world now, in a way that you never did before. Your beliefs have a power they've never had in human history. You must learn to investigate with a scientific and loving mind not only what is true, but what is effective in the world. Right now we are a world of geniuses who constantly love to call each other idiots. But humanity is the most complicated thing we've found in the universe, and so far as we know, we're the only thing even looking. We are miracles by the billions with powers and luxuries beyond the dreams of kings of old.

I am not, and will never be, a simple writer. I have sought to convict, accuse, comfort, and plead with my readers. I'm leaving the majority of my flaws online: Go for it, you can find them if you want. It's a choice I made long ago.

If you look long enough you can find my early terrible writing. You can find blog posts in which I am an idiot. I've had a lot of uninformed and passionate opinions on geopolitical issues from Ireland to Israel. You can find tweets I thought were witty, but think are stupid now. You can find opinions I still hold that you disagree with. I'm going to leave most of that stuff up. In doing so, I'm telling you that you have to look for context if you are seeking to understand me. You don't have to try, I'm not particularly important, but I am complicated. When I die, I'm going to instruct my executors to burn nothing. Leave the crap there, because it's part of my journey, and that journey has a value. People who came from where I did, and who were given the thoughts I was given, should know that the future can be different from the past.

We are powerful creatures, but power must come with gentleness and responsibility. No one prepared us for this, no one trained us, no one came before us with an understanding of our world. There were hints, and wise people, and I lean on and cherish them. But their philosophies and imaginations can only take us so far. We have to build our own philosophies and imagine great futures for our world in order to have any futures at all. Let mercy guide us forward in these troubled times. Let yourself imagine, because imagination is the wellspring of hope. Here, in the beginning of the 21st century, hope is our duty to the future.

Source: Quinn Norton (Feb 27, 2018). The New York Times Fired My Doppelgänger. © 2018 The Atlantic Media Co., as first published in The Atlantic Magazine. All rights reserved. Distributed by Tribune Content Agency, LLC.

RESPONDING TO READING

1. Norton argues that the internet is complicated in how it "makes us telepathic, angry, and weird—but it also lets us collaborate, remix, and rapidly reconfigure one another's ideas on a massive scale" (17). How does she support this conclusion?
2. In paragraph 20, Norton appeals to her readers directly. What is she asking us to do? How would you respond to her request?

Rhetorical Analysis

In what ways is this essay an apology? To whom is Norton apologizing? Is the apology sincere, and is it effective? Explain.

Writing with Sources

Research the origins and development of the idea of "context collapse," which Norton introduces in paragraph 14. Then, write an essay in which you explain the social implications of this idea as it pertains to our use of digital technologies.

6.5 David Zweig, "Escaping Twitter's Self-Consciousness Machine"

A journalist, novelist, and musician, David Zweig writes about issues related to media and society. His work has appeared in such publications as *The Atlantic, Digital Trends, Harvard Business Review, The New York Times, The New Yorker, Salon, Slate, The Wall Street Journal,* and *Wired*. He is currently writing his third book, *Merely Players* (2019). In the following essay, Zweig reevaluates Twitter and other social media platforms.

BEFORE YOU READ

How often do you monitor the reactions your social media posts get? Would you still post to social media if you were unable to see this information?

Escaping Twitter's Self-Consciousness Machine

Ever since I joined Twitter, nearly seven years ago, I've wrestled with what has always felt like a shameful interest in all those prominently displayed numbers. I've evaluated people I don't know on the basis of their follower counts, judged the merit of tweets according to how many likes and retweets they garnered, and felt the rush of being liked or retweeted by someone with a large following. These metrics, I know, are largely irrelevant; since when does popularity predict quality? Yet, almost against my will, they exert a pull on me. Twitter trains its users to see numbers as currency, like so many lab rats craving reward pellets.

So, it's worth asking: What if the numbers disappeared? How would it feel to use Twitter then? These questions recently drove Benjamin Grosser, an artist and assistant professor of new media at the University of Illinois at Urbana-Champaign, to create the Twitter Demetricator, a browser extension that removes all visible metrics from the platform. It is Grosser's latest foray into refashioning the social-media experience. In 2012, he developed a similar tool—part political statement, part art project—for Facebook. It erased every statistic from users' screens; they could no longer see the number of likes that any posts, including their own, received, or the number of friends that other users had. Grosser built this first Demetricator in reaction to his own experience of social-media use. "There were times when I was more focused on the numbers than the content itself," he told *The Atlantic*, in 2014. Others seem to have been equally concerned about this habit of mind. In the six years since the extension came out, it has been downloaded tens of thousands of times.

Twitter, perhaps even more than Facebook, runs on its users' obsession—witting or not—with metrics. For the past few weeks, I have participated in a beta test of Grosser's new Demetricator, which is being released to the general public today. And I have found that it has greatly altered my experience of Twitter, in both predictable and surprising ways.

To test the Twitter Demetricator, I began by activating an oversized toggle switch that hung down from my address bar, asking whether I wanted to "Hide the metrics." Sliding the switch from "No" to "Yes" was like throwing an old-fashioned main power lever in a mechanical room. I saw a blank appear below my name as the three critical metrics—"Tweets," "Following," "Followers"—vanished. I felt an eerie calm: my paltry follower count was no longer there to taunt me. There was no number to worry about increasing. Below each tweet that now arrived in my feed, the "Reply," "Retweet," and "Like" icons were denuded of counts. If the tweet had received at least one of these, a very small dot was present in place of the number.

5 At first, I craved the dots; they were a lifeline to my old experience. I wanted, desperately, to know what everyone else was thinking, by which I mean that I wanted to know what was popular. But, within a short time, I found even the dots to be intrusive. The notion of knowing whether even one person had liked or retweeted something felt not just superfluous but also disruptive to what had become a serene flow of information. The cleaner interface allowed for a clearer mind. If I went to someone's profile, I could still see the list of "Followers you know." This, to me, reinforced the idea that the Demetricator was for fostering connection. It didn't needlessly strip away information about people, only numbers.

Within a few days of installing the extension, I could still remember who had large followings and who didn't, but the memories were fading. A few times, I gave in to an irresistible impulse to slide the toggle back to "Off." If I wasn't familiar with the author of a particular tweet, I *needed* to know who that person was (the "who" defined, again, by popularity). But, by the second and third week, that urge dimmed and, ultimately, disappeared.

I was so focussed on the relief of not seeing follower, like, and retweet counts that it took me a while to notice the absence of another metric that the Demetricator had removed: the age labels. When tweets were more than a day old, the date was listed, which I found helpful for perspective. Otherwise, though, the hours, minutes, and seconds were gone. It occurred to me that, unless some event happens that makes granular time really matter to regular people (a natural disaster, for example), or unless you happen to be a reporter on the breaking-news beat, that metric has exceedingly small, even potentially negative, value. Without it, I was liberated from the perpetual low-level panic induced by a false sense of urgency. Grosser told me that he expects this particular design choice to be controversial among users, but, once I got used to it, it revealed itself as a core value of the extension.

After three weeks of using the Demetricator, the nature of Twitter, for me, changed completely. In some ways, it became lonelier. Part of the fun had been feeling like part of a crowd, seeing a joke or an idea or an observation become something that fifty people, or fifty thousand, could share. But I'm willing to accept the loss of this superficial sense of community for all the gains. Not seeing any numbers at all made content itself the king. I came to appreciate, disconcertingly, that knowing what was popular before had not only often distorted but also sometimes completely overtaken my experience. With the numbers gone, I realized that they, indeed, had forced a sort of automated experience, guiding and constraining my behavior. This robotization of users, largely directed by the dominance of metrics, is, of course, endemic to social media as a whole. In a recent interview with Splitsider titled "How Facebook Is Killing Comedy," Matt Klinman, a writer for the comedy production company Funny or Die, touched on this same point, lamenting that "a flattened internet is a predictable internet, and a flattened person is a predictable person."

For all the emancipation that the Demetricator offered, one thing nagged at me: even though I couldn't see any metrics, I knew that other people could still see mine. I began to wish for a master switch for the entire platform. Once the numbers are gone, one can't help but question: Why were they there in the first place? And what would social media be like if they weren't there at all, for anyone?

Part of the answer to the first question, Grosser said, is that a consumerist, 10
capitalist society like ours is "already primed to evaluate things from a metric perspective." This mind-set is particularly strong among the programmers and designers who build social-media platforms. The type of person who tends to be a high-level coder at a top tech firm, Grosser said, usually got great grades, attended a premier university, and now competes for bragging rights by trying to log the longest hours of anyone at the office. These people thrive in numbers-focussed environments. Perhaps it's predestined that their world view would infect the user interfaces they create.

But the choice to display metrics is not only a by-product of software engineers' psyches; it is also, of course, a deliberate decision. You may tell yourself that you don't care about the statistics, but tech companies know that when you are forced to see them, it is impossible not to care. I am currently writing a book about self-consciousness in the modern mediated era, and my experience with the Demetricator vividly exemplifies what my research suggests—that the ultimate function of Twitter, like nearly all social-media platforms, is to make its users insecure, because insecurity compels engagement. And nothing turns up the dial on our insecurity like viewing our communications, and ourselves, as mere numbers. This gamification of our social interactions is a component of what Sean Parker, the founding president of Facebook, and one of the leaders of the recent whistle-blower movement in tech, was referring to when he spoke of a "social-validation feedback loop." By making you constantly, reductively think about others, your actions, and yourself as numbers, these platforms insure that you remain permanently self-conscious.

The Demetricator works in an all-encompassing way only for those who are both motivated enough to make their own experience healthier and secure enough to not care what others think of them (a population, based on the available evidence, that one must assume is quite small). As a result, the idea of Twitter adopting any of the features of Grosser's extension may seem absurd on its face. Is it, though? Sure, the social-media-influencer economy would implode, but, for just about all of us, that's a net gain. Grosser told me that, counter to Silicon Valley's prevailing wisdom, some of the users of his Facebook extension actually increased their engagement on the platform because their experience was so improved. With a demetricated Twitter, companies would still know all the analytics internally, so they could still charge the same amount to advertisers. Maybe businesses, and users hell-bent on monitoring the popularity of their accounts or various posts, could gain access to their analytics, too—but the data would be private, not publicly displayed.

What is it that we really want out of social media? Grosser's renegade experiment forces users and designers alike to acknowledge that the visual display of personal metrics can lead to an experience that is the antithesis of the "meaningful" interaction that Twitter and other platforms ostensibly strive for. The personal numbers dehumanize us; in a society increasingly run by algorithms, we are, inevitably, beginning to function like algorithms ourselves. It's going to take top-down, systemic changes to thwart that slide on a grand scale. Removing visible metrics shouldn't be an extension; it should be a system upgrade.

Source: David Zweig, The New Yorker

RESPONDING TO READING

1. In paragraph 8, Zweig explains how the Demetricator made him feel alone. But he goes on to write, "I'm willing to accept the loss of this superficial sense of community for all the gains." Do you find this statement convincing? Why or why not?
2. In his final paragraph, Zweig asks, "What is it that we really want out of social media?" How does he answer this question? How would you answer it?

Rhetorical Analysis

What kinds of evidence does Zweig use to support his thesis? How persuasive is this evidence? Explain.

Writing with Sources

Research recent examples of browser extensions that alter the user experience of social media. In what ways do these examples support Zweig's argument? Do any of them challenge Zweig's claims? Write an essay that answers these questions.

6.6 Sarah Chevallier, "If Literature's 'Complicated Men' Were on Tinder" [Fiction]

Sarah Chevallier writes creative pieces for *McSweeney's*. Like the selection that follows, her work is witty, irreverent, and humorous.

BEFORE YOU READ

Write your own short Tinder profile. Consider your style and tone and the image they project.

If Literature's "Complicated Men" Were on Tinder

Name: Holden Caulfield
Age: 19
Occupation: "Jobs" are for phonies who "care" about phony stuff like "bills" and "food"
About Holden: Only looking for casual dating, because everyone's a phony except for me (obviously). Sidebar, I'm not totally sure that "phony" means what I think it means.

Name: Heathcliff 5
Age: Literally no idea.
Occupation: Mergers (with my enemies' families) and acquisitions (of their wealth and happiness).

About Heathcliff: Spent a long time cultivating that #RevengeBody and also #RevengeWealth, but now I'm looking for a nice, gullible girl to settle down with, preferably one who just happens to be related to my enemy, who also just happens to be married to my childhood friend. You know, for normal, totally not nefarious reasons.

Name: Odysseus
Age: 38
Occupation: King of Ithaca who is 100% NOT having a midlife crisis
About Odysseus: I'm all about that wanderlust life: it's about the journey, not the destination, you know? Especially when the destination is full of "responsibilities" like "governance," "parenthood," and "marriage to a woman who is clearly smarter than me as she evades being sold like sexual chattel for ten years while I doof around banging random witches and blinding one-eyed giants." Join me on the journey, baby.

Name: Edward Rochester
Age: 43
Occupation: Wealthy widower. Yep, the old ball and chain is dead. Real dead. Not currently in my attic being restrained with an actual ball and chain.
About Edward: Looking for a younger woman who will mistake my brooding looks and condescending misanthropy for tragic torment, and ideally is into employer-employee roleplay. Bonus if she likes kids but not enough that she's put off by how mean I am to my adopted daughter.

Name: Victor Frankenstein
Age: 34
Occupation: Doctor, scientist
About Victor: Looking for a partner who shares my enthusiasm for the mysteries of life but would also be up for a relentless hunt to capture and kill my old roommate from my days at the University of Ingolstadt. Sense of adventure is a must, because we leave for the North Pole next week.

Name: Jay Gatsby
Age: How old do you want me to be lol
Occupation: Influencer, Renaissance Man
About Jay: I'm weirdly similar to your ex, but like a fabulously rich and mysterious version of him that you would never have dumped for NO GODDAMN REASON in the first place, Daisy.

Name: Rodion Raskolnikov
Age: 21
Occupation: Student, Extraordinary Man who theoretically it would be totally ok if he just killed an old lady, because I mean, he's extraordinary, but you know, just theoretically please don't call that mean policeman who keeps snooping around.
About Rodion: I'm just a better-than-regular guy looking for an almost angelically good woman with a tragic story who will for no good reason

dedicate herself to my redemption and is really into listening to me reciting my half-baked Philosophy 101 "theories."

Name: Jake Barnes
Age: 31
Occupation: Expat, alcoholic
About Jake: Super manly. Definitely, definitely, *definitely* not impotent. Really into fishing and obsessing over the romantic and sexual choices of a woman who is totally just a friend (but you know, certainly not an equal who's able to make her own choices, on account of that damn ladybrain). Most importantly: not Jewish.

Name: Hamlet
Age: 26
Occupation: Future King of Denmark
About Hamlet: Family is everything to me. As in, I won't rest until I tear my family, friends, and maybe even my country apart based on a conversation I had with my dad's ghost about how it's SO GROSS that Mom and Uncle C are doing it, and he agreed that it's totally normal that I'm so fixated on my mother's sex life. My last girlfriend wasn't that understanding, so I'm looking for someone who will support me in this difficult time and won't have a fucking cow every time I stab her dad and verbally abuse her.

Name: Lucifer
Age: Not Applicable
Occupation: Ex-angel, Freelance enemy of God and His creation
About Lucifer: I actually invented online dating, so welcome to Hell.

Source: Sarah Chevallier (Feb 13, 2018). If Literature's "Complicated Men" Were On Tinder, McSweeney's Publishing LLC. Used with permission. https://www.mcsweeneys.net/articles/if-literatures-complicated-men-were-on-tinder

---

RESPONDING TO READING

1. Chevallier references several literary works in this selection. Look up any references you are unfamiliar with. How does Chevallier use satire to recast these characters as men seeking romantic companions on Tinder? Do you think this selection criticizes or celebrates Tinder? Explain.
2. This piece is divided into ten sections. What kind of content is included in each section? How does this content conform to what you would expect to see in a Tinder profile, and how does it differ?

Rhetorical Analysis

How would you describe the genre of this selection? What conventions does it follow, and what conventions does it work against? How do Chevallier's decisions impact your interpretation of the piece?

6.7 Focus: "What Is Fake News, and Why Does It Matter?"

What does this photo from a 2017 rally say about the public perception of fake news?

RESPONDING TO THE IMAGE

Answer one or both of the following questions.

1. This photo was taken in front of the New York Times building on February 26, 2017, after President Trump's administration prohibited the New York Times, CNN, and other news outlets (which Trump deemed "fake news") from attending a White House press briefing. How does this image depict the public's response to the fake news phenomenon?
2. Consider the sign in this image that reads, "I am not fake news." What is this sign designed to accomplish? What effect is it supposed to have on its audience? Why do you think this protestor chose to personalize her message?

6.8 Eric Weiskott, "Before 'Fake News' Came False Prophecy"

An associate professor of English at Boston College, Eric Weiskott is a poet and the author of *English Alliterative Verse: Poetic Tradition and Literary History* (2016). His work has appeared in publications such as *The Atlantic*, the *Chronicle of Higher Education*, *The Conversation*, *Newsweek*, and the *Times Literary Supplement*. In the following essay, Weiskott examines the social and political history of the fake news phenomenon.

BEFORE YOU READ

Write a one-paragraph definition of the word *post-truth*.

Before 'Fake News' Came False Prophecy

The revelation that fake news deceived voters in the lead-up to the 2016 presidential election generated real outrage in the aftermath of Donald Trump's electoral victory. The top fake news stories garnered more clicks than the top real news stories on Facebook in the final three months of the campaign season. Fake news and other campaign fantasies led Oxford Dictionaries to select "post-truth" as the word of the year for 2016.

But stories that gain popularity by presenting readers' fantasies and nightmares as current events are hardly new. In medieval Britain, national and local political action was guided by prophecy. Prophecies were invoked by rebel leaders, appropriated by ruling elites, and, ultimately, censored by a government fearful of their disruptive potential. Prophecy's effectiveness in shaping medieval politics offers a rejoinder to those who suggest that fake news and other political falsehoods can be ignored, or laughed off. Prophecy, like fake news, worked as persuasive writing because it told people what they wanted to believe or spoke to their darkest fears.

British politics provided ample opportunity to test the power of imagined worlds. When Owain Glyndŵr, Edmund Mortimer, and Henry Percy plotted against Henry IV at the turn of the 15th century, they used the popular "Prophecy of the Six Kings" to justify their actions. A later historical account has the three rebels committing to treason on the condition "that they are the people about whom the prophet speaks." The fantasy that Glyndŵr, Mortimer, and Percy were prophesied saviors—a fantasy they themselves may have believed—had the very real effect of attracting popular support for their insurrection.

Prophecy also played a key role when the Wars of the Roses broke out between the Houses of York and Lancaster in the 1450s. The Yorkists used the prophecies of Merlin to support Edward IV's claim to the throne. The Lancastrians interpreted the same prophecies to mean that their candidate, Henry VI, deserved the crown. One Yorkist manuscript, a sumptuous scroll now in Oxford's Bodleian Library, features a circular array of insulting names for Henry VI. The names, in English and Latin, include "usurper," "fool," and "scoundrel," as well as "white dragon," a symbol for the Saxons—always the antagonists in British prophecy. The Yorkist scroll was not meant to win hearts and minds. It was meant to stoke partisan rage.

Prophecies were highly imaginative texts. Knights, heraldry, dragons, double 5
crosses: The genre offered an intoxicating blend of fantasy and realism. One Yorkist prophecy in alliterative verse, found in two Bodleian manuscripts, takes the form of an imagined interview between an English member of Parliament and

God. The MP asks what will happen to the realm, and God conveniently foretells the defeat of the Lancastrians, represented as treacherous Saxons. Some of the predictions in prophecies referred to the near future (like FiveThirtyEight's election forecast), but most of the action amounted to history in the future tense. This was writing that wins consent for a hostile takeover; writing that justifies political violence; writing that kills.

Prophecy wasn't just an early form of infotainment. It was an instrument of colonization. Some of the earliest recorded prophecies in Britain appeared in the 12th century, in a Latin historical narrative written by a Welsh cleric named Geoffrey. But prophetic style quickly spread from Latin and Welsh to English, and from the margins to the centers of British political power.

By identifying as Britons rather than Saxons, English elites used prophecy to legitimize their rule over the Irish and Welsh and their aggressions against the Scottish. The English projected themselves as spiritual victims of the imperialism of their own ancestors, the Anglo-Saxons. Another Yorkist scroll, held by the British Library, ends with an English passage in which an angel predicts that the Britons will not inherit the island until the Saxons become as sinful as the Britons had been before. The passage aims to galvanize the political will of English readers, not to elicit sympathy for real Celtic peoples. Prophecy rewrote history. The language of the vulnerable was weaponized against the vulnerable.

In the mouths of Welsh rebels and English peasants, prophecy was social protest. In the hands of the ruling classes, it became propaganda. In the 15th century, English kings and parliaments began passing laws against "false" prophecy, in effect criminalizing prophecy without official authorization. The earliest laws claimed to be about other things: vagrancy, civil disorder. They claimed to restrict prophecy only incidentally, as it related to pressing social problems. But the laws were really acts of pre-emptive censorship.

In theory, the laws targeted prophecies made on false grounds. But prophecy, oriented toward the future and heavily coded, did not lend itself to objective distinctions between truth and falsehood. In practice, the anti-prophecy laws gave pretext to punish political dissidence. A 1542 act under Henry VIII, less covertly worded than earlier legislation, sought to protect "such persons as have and had such arms, badges, or cognizances" from "the great peril and destruction" of "false prophecies." In other words, the state vowed to shield the nobility, those with hereditary coats of arms, from recrimination by their social inferiors. It did not matter whether the targets of these laws created new illicit prophecies or circulated old ones. Those caught prophesying about the imminent demise of a king or knight faced fines, jail, or execution.

10 Such was the fate of John Dobson, a Yorkshire vicar, put to death in 1538 for interpreting a popular prophecy to indicate Henry VIII's downfall and the restoration of Catholicism in England. Dobson may well have disseminated heterodox prophecies, but his real mistake was probably making some powerful enemy. The defendants tried under the anti-prophecy laws were nearly always the most

vulnerable members of society: servants, tradespeople, low-level clerics like Dobson, and women of all classes.

As a result of all this top-down political pressure, the textual record of prophecies is severely undemocratic. It is shaped by the political agendas of the most powerful.

No wonder many surviving prophecies express horror that the prevailing social hierarchy will dissolve. Yet this was also a key to their popular appeal. One prophecy tells of a dystopian future with "knights and knaves clad in the same clothing." Another dreads the day "when lads wed ladies." These predictions warn readers against the horror of a classless society. This horror did not correspond to any real world. Medieval England was in no danger of becoming a communist state. Rather, fear of social reformation was a tool to maintain the very hierarchy that was supposedly deteriorating. And here's the chilling part—it worked. John Dobson's problem wasn't just an oppressive law but also whichever of his acquaintances decided to turn him in.

By the late Middle Ages, prophecy had become a mass medium. It managed to affect the real world by constructing an echo chamber and then enticing people to live in it. It is worth asking what present conditions pollsters, politicians, and journalists seek to render inevitable.

Ultimately, medieval prophecy demonstrates the enduring power of a fantasy to change reality itself. Prophecy didn't describe the world as it was, but as it was to be—or as it might become. That fantasy was more powerful than any lived reality. People killed and died for fantasies. People didn't act politically because of what they had lost but because of what, in their most potent fantasy, they feared losing.

RESPONDING TO READING

1. What historical connection does fake news have to prophecies? How are they alike, and how are they different?
2. In paragraph 7, Weiskott writes, "Prophecy rewrote history. The language of the vulnerable was weaponized against the vulnerable." What does he mean? How, according to Weiskott, were prophecies used to maintain class divisions?

Rhetorical Analysis

In his essay, Weiskott draws a comparison between fake news and prophecies as tactics people have used throughout history to appeal to public emotion. Is this an effective strategy? How convincing do you find his evidence?

Writing with Sources

Research one of the historical events Weiskott mentions in his essay. Then, write an essay in which you analyze the event as a historical example of what we call "fake news" today. Be sure to incorporate Weiskott's essay and at least one other source into your essay.

6.9 Judith Donath, "Why Fake News Stories Thrive Online"

An advisor at Harvard University's Berkman Klein Center for Internet & Society, Judith Donath (1962–) specializes in the ways social media impact identity, credibility, communication, and design. She is the author of *The Social Machine: Designs for Living Online* (2014). In the following essay, Donath considers the appeal of creating and consuming fake news in online contexts.

BEFORE YOU READ

How would you define your social identity? What role do the online groups you interact with play in how you see yourself in digital spaces?

Why Fake News Stories Thrive Online

Fake news stories proliferated in this heated election cycle.

"Terrorists are funding 20% of Hillary's campaign."

"Obama told illegal immigrants to vote."

"Tim Kaine will ban the Catholic Church from the US if they don't change their stance on same sex marriage."

5 And while the election has come and gone, fake news stories continue to proliferate on social media. Indeed, they are often shared more than real news is.

Fake news is harmful. Many untrue stories are believed by the people who post them. Sometimes a story that was intended as satire circulates as fact. Others are deliberately deceptive. A report in the *Denver Guardian* headlined "FBI Agent Behind Clinton Email Leaks Found Dead in Murder-Suicide" was shared widely on Facebook, with comments such as "The Clinton Crime Syndicate has more lies and blood on their hands than any previous gangster in history." This wholly fabricated story appeared on November 5, a few days before the election. (This story, along with the rest of the *Denver Guardian*, has disappeared in the aftermath of recent scrutiny of fake news.) As Martin Baron, the executive editor of the *Washington Post*, said, "If you have a society where people can't agree on basic facts, how do you have a functioning democracy?"

Combating the spread of false stories is important but difficult. The obvious solution—fact-checking—is ineffective: Many fake news consumers are suspicious of mainstream media and dismiss as partisan and deceptive any statistics or evidence that counter their beliefs. Worse, as we'll discuss below, demonstrating the factual flaws in a story can actually increase its social value. To discourage the spread of fake news, we need to better understand why sharing these stories is so appealing.

Partisanship is part of it. People like and share news that conforms to their existing beliefs, and fake news stories are often strongly biased. Of course, people also share real news when it agrees with their views. One would think that given a real news story or a fake one, both conforming to one's beliefs, that the real news would be preferable. But fake news thrives online, frequently surpassing real news in its reach.

Recognizing the social function of news sharing is the key to understanding this seeming irrational behavior. In the world of social media, of Facebook and Twitter, news is shared not just to inform or even to persuade. It is used as a marker of identity, a way to proclaim your affinity with a particular community.

For better or worse, we humans have a fundamental tendency to divide 10
into groups. We bond with our own in-group and set ourselves apart from the others. Face to face, we signal this social identity in the clothes we wear, the foods we eat and more. But in the online world of information, material markers count for less. Instead, news sharing has become a prominent identity signal: We proclaim our affiliations by posting links to articles that reflect our groups' taste and beliefs.

Legitimate stories can, of course, serve this role. But for the purpose of marking social identity, fake stories can be even more powerful.

Posting any story, real or fake, that conforms to your community's viewpoint bolsters your ties with them. Even if it is false, you have still demonstrated your shared values.

The key is the difference in how outsiders respond to your posting of a fake vs. real news story. If the news is real, outsiders who recognize it as such may disagree with it, but posting it does not reflect badly on you, and it may provide a common ground for argument and discussion.

If, however, the news you post is fake, outsiders are more likely to be outraged. If you stand by it tenaciously, they may call you a fool or a liar. This infuriated response makes posting fake news a convincing signal of your allegiance to your in-group. By demonstrating that you are willing to sacrifice your ties to and your reputation among the outsiders, you prove the authenticity of your commitment.

Furthermore, stoking conflict with outsiders strengthens the in-group's cohe- 15
sion. This, too, raises the status of the person who posts a hotly contested story, especially when tensions are high.

These dynamics explain why fact checking can be counterproductive. When a story that a community believes is proved fake by outsiders, belief in it becomes an article of faith, a litmus test of one's adherence to that community's idiosyncratic worldview. The two sides will perceive that they have no common ground or understanding of truth, and the story becomes an even more potent signal of identity and catalyst of discord.

This is why when signaling identity is the reason for sharing news, fake news is hard to uproot. It proves the poster's commitment to the community by demonstrating willingness to sacrifice outside relationships.

Recognizing this helps us craft more productive responses:

- First, follow the now-old adage, "Don't feed the trolls." If someone posts a fake story, and you think they have simply been duped, certainly it is useful to point out the error with a more reliable source. Please do graciously. No one likes to be publicly humiliated. Sometimes a private message is better. But if you think the posting is really about proclaiming identity, ignore it. Don't amplify its value by arguing. And if you must say something, here a private message is really better—you can convey your disapproval without providing the public display of discord that just strengthens their signal.
- Second, help promote a culture that reveres veracity. Check your sources before you post anything. Support newspapers and other organizations that do good, reliable reporting. Discourage people in your own community when they promote stories that feel good to you, but are, alas, untrue.
- Third, appreciate humor. Like fake news, jokes and satire are markers of identity—funny to insiders, and often incomprehensible or offensive to outsiders. They may be tasteless, they may be divisive but unlike fake news, they are not an assault on truth.

Information can bring people together or drive them apart. Sharing false information, or fake news, is divisive. It's about claiming a separate territory, with its own rules and logic. Sharing true information is, ideally, the opposite. It's about unifying people, not only rallying the ones who agree, but also persuading the ones who do not; it provides a common ground.

20 Ultimately, to remove the appeal of fake news, people need to value debate and discussion. They need to value reaching across to different communities, to discuss and debate; they need to choose not to build walls against the Other, but to engage and persuade.

Source: Donath, Judith. "Why fake news stories thrive online." November 20, 2016. Used by permission.

RESPONDING TO READING

1. According to Donath, what is the relationship between sharing news and defining a social identity? What role does fake news play in this process?
2. How does Donath explain the way in which fake news can be used to bolster the credibility of its author or sharer? Do you agree with her explanation of the reasons for this trend? What other explanations can you suggest?

Rhetorical Analysis

In paragraph 18, Donath provides a list of strategies for slowing the spread of fake news. How effective is this technique? What might you add to the list?

Writing with Sources

Google some recently published fake news stories. Then, write an essay in which you discuss the needs these stories seem to satisfy. Locate at least one legitimate source that counters the claims made by one of the stories. Incorporate the views of the legitimate source into your essay as a way of exposing the lies told by the fake news source.

6.10 Anonymous, "I Write Fake News"

This essay was originally published in the *Guardian* on January 26, 2018.

BEFORE YOU READ

Have you ever written or shared a social media post that included information you did not fully believe? Why or why not?

I Write Fake News

I've been writing articles for far-right websites in the US for a year now. I didn't set out to do this; it started in October 2016, when I was finishing my PhD in London. My funding ran out, and I started writing content to pay the rent. I found clients through websites that allow potential writers to bid for work, and then build a portfolio of reviews from clients. There is an enormous amount of work available—everything from writing product copy to ghost-writing novels.

The first jobs I got were pretty shady. I was writing fake Amazon reviews and descriptions of perfume that had yet to be produced. A reliable client put me in touch with a colleague who runs a number of websites, one of which focuses on news about, and reviews of, guns.

I have never seen a gun, let alone used one, but I took the job. The site carries reviews of handgun accessories, and for each product there is a link to Amazon. My client gets paid for every click-through he generates through Amazon's affiliate scheme. There are vast numbers of such sites: I've written fake reviews of amplifiers, baby products, printers and sex toys.

At first, I was paid $20 for 1,000 words. As the site began to make more money, I got paid more; I now get triple my original rate. I have never met my client, but we talk once a month to set priorities. He is young, American and not into guns. We write under a number of pseudonyms that are designed to look trustworthy to right-leaning American gun enthusiasts: generally, retired men with links to the military. I write for about 15 hours a week, and make £2,400 a month. I don't have a contract, or any guarantee of ongoing work, but it suits me. I am still finishing that PhD.

5 Recently, we've tried to boost the site up the Google rankings. This involves writing for other sites that are visited by gun enthusiasts, a lot of them pretty extreme, and sneaking in a link to our own site. This is against their rules, so you have to hide the link deep in the middle of a dense paragraph, so no one notices.

I write articles arguing that banning bump stocks, which enable semi-automatic guns to fire more rapidly, won't prevent mass shootings and that the left skews statistics. I believe the opposite to be true. I vehemently disagree with what I write, and with the sites I write for. I often despair at the ignorance on display. Only once have I written for a site that was racist. There was an article about "them," referring to black people. That was the only time I've questioned what I do for a living.

But I don't have a moral problem with it. I wish I had some snappy argument about why what I'm doing is not wrong. I'm furthering ignorance, certainly, and perhaps contributing to an atmosphere of hatred. But I don't think people have died as a result of my work. Perhaps I am more nihilistic than most, but in the end, it's a job and it pays well.

I have never made up a statistic, invented a story, or been racist. I think I would refuse to do so. I see my role as providing an extreme right-wing interpretation of breaking news. Though I do not believe the stories I write, I don't count this as lying.

I suppose the articles I write would be regarded as fake news. Though that has got a lot of attention recently, I think it is merely a new term for an old phenomenon. This type of ideologically driven journalism pre-dates the internet and perhaps even the printing press: what were *Der Stürmer, Pravda* and Trajan's Column,[1] if not fake news?

10 Ultimately, I feel that it is the responsibility of individuals to assess critically everything they read: my articles are designed to sell gun accessories; newspaper articles are designed to sell newspapers. I don't see that much difference between the two.

My friends know what I do for a living, and find it amusing. There is an absurd humor in a young(ish), left(ish), British arts student pretending to be a far-right,

[1] A newspaper published by the Nazi party (1923–1945), a newspaper previously published by the Communist Party of the Soviet Union (1912–), and a Roman structure (CE 113) depicting two military campaigns won by the Roman emperor Trajan, respectively. [Eds.]

middle-aged, American gun enthusiast. They recognize that my earnings give me the freedom to live and work where I want.

I'll continue to work for this client for at least another six months, by which time I will have finished my PhD and saved enough to go travelling. Then I'll get my first proper job in five years. If my rate continues to increase, though, I'll continue to write for this client. It's easy money.

Source: Experience: I write fake news, January 26, 2018. www.theguardian.com

---

RESPONDING TO READING

1. What specific kinds of fake news does this writer create? What do you suppose the writer means when he says "Though I do not believe the stories I write, I don't count this as lying" (8)? Do you agree?
2. How does the writer explain his job? Do you see this essay as an honest confession of guilt or as an excuse for making money? Explain.

Rhetorical Analysis

In paragraph 7, the writer states, "I don't have a moral problem with it. I wish I had some snappy argument about why what I'm doing is not wrong. I'm furthering ignorance, certainly, and perhaps contributing to an atmosphere of hatred. But I don't think people have died as a result of my work." Does this statement add to or detract from his credibility? Explain.

Writing with Sources

Research the process by which Amazon verifies product reviews on its site. How can consumers know whether or not to trust an Amazon review? What measures are in place to prevent fake reviews from appearing online? What loopholes still exist? Write an essay in which you answer these questions and propose a new or amended strategy for vetting online product reviews.

Widening the Focus

For Critical Reading and Writing

Referring specifically to the three readings in this chapter's Focus section (and possibly to additional sources as well), write an essay in which you answer the question, "What Is Fake News, and Why Does It Matter?"

For Further Reading

The following readings can suggest additional perspectives for reading and writing about the phenomenon of fake news in our media.

- Tao Lin, "When I Moved Online..." (p. 66)
- Jonathan Rauch, "Kindly Inquisitors, Revisited" (p. 151)
- Thane Rosenbaum, "Should Neo-Nazis Be Allowed Free Speech?" (p. 159)
- David Palumbo-Liu, "I'm a Stanford Professor Accused of Being a Terrorist. McCarthyism Is Back." (p. 161)
- Katie Roiphe, "The Other Whisper Network" (p. 246)
- Jose Antonio Vargas, "Outlaw: My Life in America as an Undocumented Immigrant" (p. 327)

For Focused Research

The fake news phenomenon has infiltrated various kinds of media, from TV shows to public health campaigns. Consider your academic major or a subject you are interested in. What implications does this phenomenon have in your field? Do some online research to find what, if anything, writers in your area of study are saying about the fake news phenomenon. Then, write an essay in which you analyze one aspect of this phenomenon as it applies to your field. Use the readings in this chapter's Focus section to spark some ideas.

Beyond the Classroom

Interview some friends and classmates about the fake news phenomenon. Do they see fake news as a problem? How do they define fake news? What value do they see in preventing the proliferation of fake news in its various forms? Take notes on their responses, and then write an essay in which you draw a conclusion about the impact the fake news phenomenon has had on our daily lives.

Exploring Issues and Ideas

Media and Society

Write an essay in response to one of the following prompts, which are suitable for assignments that require the use of outside sources as well as for assignments that are not source-based.

1. What do you think the impact of the various media discussed in this chapter will be in the years to come? What trends do you see emerging that you believe will change the way you think or the way you live? Write an essay in which you speculate about future trends and their impact, using the essays in this chapter to support the points you make.
2. Write an essay in which you consider the representation of a particular ethnic or racial group (or the portrayal of women, the elderly, or people with disabilities) in the media (movies, television, online ads, and so on). Do you

believe the group you have chosen to write about is adequately represented? Do you think its members are portrayed fairly and accurately, or do you think they are stereotyped? Support your conclusions with specific examples.

3. To what extent, if any, should explicitly sexual or violent media images be censored? Write an essay in which you take a stand on this issue and explain why you believe such censorship is (or is not) necessary.
4. Write an analysis of a website, considering the techniques it uses to appeal to its target audience. Who is being addressed, what message is conveyed, and how successfully is this message communicated?
5. Write an analysis of a current popular reality TV show. Start by describing the program's basic premise, setting, and participants. Then, consider some or all of the following questions:
   - What explains this program's appeal to viewers?
   - What trends in society does the program reflect?
   - Does the program rely on sensationalism?
   - Has the program had any impact on society?

Chapter 7
Gender and Identity

In this chapter, you will learn to:

- analyze readings about gender and identity.
- compose essays about gender and identity.

Attitudes about gender have changed dramatically over the past several decades, and they continue to change. For some, these changes have resulted in confusion as well as liberation. One reason for this confusion is that people can no longer rely on fixed gender roles to tell them how to behave in public and how to function within their families. Still, many men and women—uncomfortable with the demands of confining gender roles and unhappy with the expectations those roles

Lev Radin/Everett Collection Inc/Alamy Stock Photo

Which elements of this image of transgender teen activist Gavin Grimm conform to your expectations, and which challenge them?

create—yearn for even less rigidity, for an escape from stereotypes into a society where roles are not strictly defined by gender.

In spite of these changes, many people still see men and women in terms of unrealistic stereotypes. Men are strong, tough, and brave; women are weak, passive, and in need of protection. Men understand mathematics and science and have a natural aptitude for mechanical tasks. They also have the drive, the aggressiveness, the competitive edge, and the power to succeed. They are never sentimental and never cry. Women are better at small, repetitive tasks, and shy away from taking bold, decisive actions. They enjoy, and are good at, domestic activities, and they have a natural aptitude for nurturing. Although women may like their jobs, they will leave them to devote themselves to husband and children.

As you read the preceding list of stereotypes, you may react neutrally (or even favorably), or you may react with aversion; how we react tells us something about our society and something about ourselves. As a number of writers in this chapter point out, however, stereotypes can limit the way people think, the roles they choose to assume, and, ultimately, the positions they occupy in society.

As the Focus section of this chapter, "How Do We Talk about Sexual Harassment?" (p. 239) illustrates, both women and men are finding their way in a new era of honesty about the culture of sexual misconduct that has largely been kept quiet for so long. In "I Started the Media Men List:

Jaguar/Alamy Stock Photo

Which elements of this image of transgender teen activist Jazz Jennings conform to your expectations, and which challenge them?

My Name is Moira Donegan" (p. 240), Moira Donegan considers the consequences of her participation in the #MeToo movement; in "The Other Whisper Network" (p. 246), Katie Roiphe examines the effects of how women talk about men accused of sexual misconduct; and in "To Clarify: An Open Letter to the Men's Rights Movement, on the #MeToo Hashtag" (p. 257), John Kirbow looks at #MeToo's implications for human rights generally.

Preparing to Read and Write

As you read and prepare to write about the essays in this chapter, you may consider the following questions:

- What assumptions does the writer have about his or her audience? How can you tell?
- What is the writer's primary purpose? For example, is it to challenge traditional ideas about gender or to support them?
- What genre is the writer using? For example, is the reading an argument or an analysis? How do the conventions of this genre influence the writer's choices?
- What appeals does the writer use? For example, does he or she appeal primarily to reason? To emotion? To a combination of the two? Would another strategy be more effective?
- Is the writer male, female, or a transgender person? Can you determine the writer's gender without reading his or her name or the headnote? Does the writer's gender matter?
- Does the writer focus on one gender or on multiple genders?
- Does the essay's date of publication affect its content?
- Does the essay seem fair? Balanced?
- Does the writer discuss gender as a sexual, political, economic, or social issue?
- What does the writer suggest are the specific advantages or disadvantages of being male? Of being female? Of being a transgender person? Of being a gay person or straight?
- Does the writer recommend specific societal changes? What are they? Do they seem reasonable or even possible?
- Does the writer think that men and women are fundamentally different? If so, does he or she suggest that these differences can (or should) be overcome, or at least lessened?
- Does the writer think gender differences are the result of environment, heredity, or both?
- Does the essay challenge any of your ideas about male or female roles?
- In what ways is the essay like other essays in this chapter?

Shared Writing

Gender and Identity

Consider your own gender. Do you identify with the sex you were born with? Did you ever question your sexuality or want to live your life as another gender? How do you perceive others who adopt unexpected or unscripted gender roles? In what ways has gender defined your self-image?

7.1 Judy Hall, "Mommy, I'm Just Not That Kind of Girl"

A fiction writer, memoirist, essayist, and poet, Judy Hall writes about various issues, including writing, travelling, family, and gender. Her work has appeared in such publications as *Digging Through the Fat, Huffington Post, Literary Orphans*, and *Split Lip Magazine*. The following essay questions conventional boy/girl distinctions and argues that either/or labels falsely prepackage identity and gender.

BEFORE YOU READ

What kinds of toys did you play with when you were young? Do you see them now as tied to your gender in any way?

Mommy, I'm Just Not That Kind of Girl

When I was a little girl, I really wanted a cap gun. Mark, the boy down the street, had a cap gun and I loved the sound it made and the sulfuric smell it left behind. But my father said that cap guns weren't for little girls. I felt especially betrayed when my brother, five years younger than me, got a cap gun. By that time I was about 10, and less interested in cap guns, but I still resented that because of my gender, I had been denied this cool toy.

So when I had my own kids, I said I wasn't going to let gender determine anything. When my oldest, Alexander, wanted to dress up in my shoes, I took them all out and let him have at it. When my daughter, Elisabeth, wanted a beard painted on her face, I painstakingly drew it on, making each hair as realistic as I could with my eyeliners. They were two years apart and played with each other's toys, and while Alexander gradually drifted towards "boy" toys and Elisabeth drifted towards "girl" toys, it was never due to my influence. I think.

Then, when Alexander was 9 and a half and Elisabeth was 7 and a half, along came Sammy. Sammy was ahead of the curve in so many things. Crawling at 5 months, walking at 9 months, full, clear sentences by 18 months—which is when Sammy invented the game "born."

Born involved sitting on my lap, announcing loudly, "I'm Sam!" I wish I could do justice to the face he'd make. It was at once mischievous and sweet, with an eyebrow raised and his blue eyes sparkling. Then he'd hide under my shirt for various amounts of time and reemerge with a flourish and announce, "Now I'm Samantha!" He'd clap and we'd clap. We would say, who needs TV when you have a toddler around? But we didn't consider that this might mean anything about his gender. Sammy was a boy as evidenced by his love of games where everything blew up. Yes, Sammy loved dress-up. Sometimes Sammy dressed up as a cat or a bug, but more often it was Spiderman or Batman—emphasis on the man, right? Well, Sammy also wanted princess dresses and shoes and loved makeup, and Elisabeth spent many happy hours dressing him up in these outfits. It was dress-up, right? We were cool with it. Right?

5 Then, when Sammy was 7, he told me that he really wanted some girls' clothes. I assumed this was part of the dress-up phase. But Sammy didn't want to go to the Disney store—he said he wanted real girls' clothes. And that he'd wanted them for a long time, but didn't know how to ask.

First, I signed him up for tae kwon do. I wasn't sure what this meant for his life, but I figured that if my boy was going to wear girls' clothes, then he'd better know how to defend himself.

Then we went shopping. He picked out a variety of things that my husband and I decided he could wear at home and when we went out, but not to school. The compromise was that he could wear girl underwear and training bras (really just half T-shirts) to school. He protested a little, but accepted it in the end. Around this time, Sammy was diagnosed with bipolar disorder, which has nothing to do with his clothing choices, but is important in the story in the long run.

At 9, Sammy was put in a self-contained class for kids with behavioral problems. The biggest issue was that this class had no girls. Sammy missed girls, missed looking at what they were wearing. He got more depressed, and soon he was hospitalized for his first suicide attempt. I say first, but really it was his second. The first time he'd tried to throw himself out of our car on the highway. His sister's quick reflexes saved his life. We didn't think that it was a suicide attempt, because what does an 8-year-old know from suicide? We were in for an education. Suicide is the sixth leading cause of death for children 5 to 14 years old. Five. Children as young as 5 kill themselves. Who knew?

There would be another hospitalization and numerous outbursts at school resulting in Sammy being suspended pending psychiatric review. After I don't know how many such suspensions, his psychiatrist refused to let him back. He said Sammy needed a therapeutic school.

10 While this was going on, Sammy wanted more and more girls' clothes. He wore jeggings with big T-shirts. It was an androgynous look. My husband and I bought books about transgender kids and went online for support groups for parents of transgender kids, but their stories seemed so different. The boys who said they were girls liked girls' stuff. Dolls. Toy vacuum cleaners. Barbies. Sammy was not interested in that. He played video games and his avatar was female

and named Kitten, but these were boy games. And Sammy really loved kittens. Everyone loves kittens.

Sammy had already told us he liked boys. We live in a very gay-friendly town. Alexander's best friend was gay, and in every class any of my kids were in, there was always one kid who had two mommies or two daddies. When Obama was running for president, Sammy said he was going to vote for Obama because Obama was cute. Sammy had mentioned early on that he wondered if a boy could get a vagina. This was around the time that the movie *Avatar* came out. We said yes. He said, I think I might want one . . . or a tail. A tail would be really cool. So you can understand that we were thinking maybe transgender but . . . no. Right?

At the therapeutic school we finally found for Sammy, there was a transgender kid, female to male. Sammy was smitten. I don't know if he was really taken by this kid for who he was, or if it was just that this kid was being who he really was. Still, Sammy didn't say he was a girl. We said he was gender fluid. Some days he seemed more girly—or sorta girly—and others he seemed all boy. Most days he seemed all boy in girl clothes.

Then he finally told me, fairly recently, that he was transgender. He was she, and would we please start using the right pronoun?

We were floored. It doesn't make sense that we were floored, but we were. (We are generally pretty smart people . . .) But we immediately changed pronouns. Or we try to. After 12 and a half years of saying "he" and "my son," it is hard to switch overnight to "she" and "my daughter." When I write it out like this, I think, *Wow, were we idiots.* But Sammy is gentle with us. She corrects us when we use the wrong pronoun or say son rather than daughter. Or boy rather than girl.

So we went shopping again. She wanted to start putting something in her 15
bra, to be like other girls her age. I steered her towards things I like—I am a pretty girly person. She wanted her usual androgynous look—plus breasts. One day we were getting ready to go out somewhere and I tried to put a headband in her hair.

"Maybe if you look a little more like a girl, it'll be easier for everyone to remember to use the right pronoun," I said.

She put down the headband and smiled at me. "Mommy," she said, "I'm just not that kind of girl."

She floored me again. My own gender stereotypes had the better of me. For years as a teacher, I'd defended girls' rights to wear gender non-conforming clothes, but when it came to my own daughter, I was pushing a societal stereotype down her throat. I wanted her to look like what I think a girl looks like. There is an implicit "should" in there which shames me. I have taught composition at various colleges for the last decade and a half, and I've always taught Katha Pollitt's brilliant article, "Why Boys Don't Play with Dolls." I've said to hundreds of college freshmen that there are no girl toys and no boy toys. I've asked them to go to Toys R Us and look at the layout and think about how gender conformity might be hurting children. And here I was, part of the problem with my own child.

Sammy is her own young woman. She knows who she is. She knows what she wants. She is only 12, and we have lots of decisions to make about hormones, etc.—but in the end, we need to follow her lead. Like any woman, she will define who she is. And I couldn't be more proud. I am sure she has much more to teach us.

Source: Reprinted with permission of Judy Ryan Hall, Mommy, I'm Just Not That Kind of Girl, Huffington Post, November 25, 2014. This article first appeared in The Huffington Post. URL: https://www.huffingtonpost.com/judy-hall/mommy-im-just-not-that-kind-of-girl_b_6086934.html

---

RESPONDING TO READING

1. Hall admits to struggling with the term *transgender*. What does she mean when she says, "So you can understand that we were thinking maybe transgender but ... no. Right?" (11)? How does her understanding of the term evolve alongside Sammy's development?
2. In paragraph 18, Hall explains her realization that "My own gender stereotypes had the better of me." What does she mean? Is she being too hard on herself? How does Hall change by the end of the essay?

Rhetorical Analysis

Hall begins her essay with a series of examples. Why does she use this strategy? Would another introductory strategy have been more effective? Explain.

Writing with Sources

According to the National Center for Transgender Equality, transgender people face a disproportionate amount of discrimination. What are the main areas of discrimination that transgender people face? In your opinion, has government done enough to ensure transgender equality?

7.2 Fleda Brown, "Unruffled"

An acclaimed poet, blogger, essayist, and memoirist, Fleda Brown (1944–) is the former poet laureate of Delaware and the author of nine books, including, most recently, *The Woods Are on Fire: New and Selected Poems* (2017). Her work has appeared in such publications as *Best American Poetry; Brevity; Numéro Cinq; Terrain.org;* and her blog, *My Wobbly Bicycle*. A columnist for the *Traverse City Record-Eagle* and a book reviewer for Interlochen Public Radio's *Michigan Writers on the Air,* she teaches for the Rainier Writing Workshop MFA program at Pacific Lutheran University. In the following essay, Brown examines the "genres" of girls' and boys' clothes.

BEFORE YOU READ

What kinds of clothes did you wear when you were a kid? Did you like to dress up? What did you like to wear?

Unruffled

Well, you'd think this one would be MY subject. But I never had any clothes. That is how it felt. Oh, when I was a child, the first child, first grandchild, I was the darling of my grandparents' and my aunts' hearts. They crocheted, knitted, stitched, embroidered. There are boxes and boxes full of photos of me, wonder-child bedecked in sweaters, scarves, wool coats with fur trim, fur muff, delicate flowered sundresses and sunbonnets. Then I grew up.

My parents were getting along on my father's assistant professor's salary, with three, then four children, one of them seriously retarded and needing very expensive drugs. And neither of my parents thought of "managing" money. They talked and yelled and cried about "budgets," but nothing ever changed. At least once a year, one of the grandparents would be applied to for assistance, which would arrive, accompanied by the fury of my father in having to accept it. Well, enough of that. The fact is, I had at least one requisite new dress in the fall when school started, usually two, plus new shoes, usually courtesy of a grandparent. Care packages of clothes would arrive now and then, things picked out by my grandmother, never clothes I wanted to wear. Many of them were a terrible embarrassment, all wrong for what I felt was stylish in my crowd, but I was made to wear them anyway. They were new and they were "nice."

There was one sweater, white with appliqued flowers on it—a name brand and expensive. But the short sleeves had a tiny bit of a puff to them that felt dorky to me. And the flowers! Furthermore, my sister was given a matching one. A deadly move on my grandmother's part. I was made to wear the sweater to school. I may not remember this right, but in my memory, as soon as I felt I could get away with it, I deliberately held the sweater under hot water until the bright flowers on the applique faded onto the white sweater. "How can I wear it, now?" I asked. Did I really do that or just dream of it? I can't remember, but I am pretty sure that the fading happily happened. Of course my mother was somewhat careless about sorting clothes, so I may not have been the culprit.

Actually, after I got past the shorts-with-no-top age, I never had things I wanted to wear. I was furious when I was made to cover up with little halter tops, even before I had breasts. I was furious when I was made to wear dresses to school every day when I wanted to wear pants. Jeans were still in the future, but I would have invented them had I known how. I was most furious when I was made to wear a bra. I threw it across the room after one day in its miserable straitjacketing. I was furious when I had to wear stockings and garter belts and huge, full skirts with huge, full slips under them. I did not want to be a "lady," although I didn't particularly have an objection to being a girl.

5 Conversely, I longed to have ballet-slipper shoes, but I had flat feet and was forced to clump around in saddle oxfords or brown "Girl Scout" shoes.

Maybe I would have had fewer objections to girl clothes had I been able to buy the clothes many of my friends had—matching Bobbie Brooks sweater sets, straight and pleated wool skirts. The only days that I felt good about my clothes were the days the pep-club, called the "Peppers"—of which I was one—were required to wear their uniforms to school. We had white sweaters with a big purple B on the front, over a bulldog's face, and purple pleated skirts. I fit in. I was just fine.

I was asked to join a high school girls' sorority. Part of the initiation process was that two members had to come to your house and pick out an outfit from your closet that you were required to wear to school every day for a week. They usually picked outlandishly mismatched clothes, silly things. The two girls who came to my house looked through my closet while I stood aside, trembling with embarrassment. I had so few clothes and they were all so, well, not-quite-right. I could tell the girls were nonplussed. They did the worst thing possible: they felt sorry for me. They chose the nicest skirt and blouse they could find.

I always felt that part of the problem was me, that it was my fault I had no clothes. I was so headstrong: with my baby-sitting money, I bought some beautiful plaid wool fabric. I had this idea I'd make myself a skirt and vest. I cut it out. I cut it out wrong. I had no practice and no guidance. Did I slow down and ask a friend's mother for help? No. The awkward puzzle pieces I had cut would not go together properly. I stuffed them in a drawer, feeling wretched and guilty, and tried to forget.

Seething underneath the clothes issue for me was the tacit sense of the role women were supposed to play. The clothes were indicative. By the time I was seven, I had to put on that halter top. But the boys didn't. I had to wear dresses with ruffles, which made me feel decorated, ornamental, and as powerless as my mother. I hated ruffles and still do. This is not, as I said, a matter of wanting to be a boy. It is a matter of wanting to move freely and feel essential, just myself, an L.L. Bean sort of person.

10 I look at the models in the ads in the *New York Times*. They seem to combine, these days, a look of both power and glamor. At least that's what they apparently want to show: sleek tigresses, beautiful, furry, seething with power. But look into the eyes. It looks dead in there: the ads are pictures of women required to project tigresses. Women whose job is to sell clothes, who are desperate to hold their position in the world of high fashion, who will project anything you ask them to project.

Oh, really, I do like clothes. I always have loved the days when I've felt beautiful in my clothes. In the seventies, I had a pair of blue corduroy bell-bottoms and platform shoes that made me feel sharp and sexy. I bought one mini-skirt, which I thought was kind of cute, but I was teaching school and found that if I raised my arm to write on the blackboard, I exposed more of me than my students needed to see.

In those few years I taught high school, I made some of my own clothes (yes, I did!): pants and tops, as well as many curtains and pillow covers. I made a few cute outfits for my daughter, one little bell bottom jumper with big lady-bugs all over it, with a matching purse. She was five or six and looked very Mod. I liked sewing. I was not too bad at it. It was all-absorbing, meditative, and I could imagine I was saving money. Then when clothes got cheaper than fabric, I gave it up. Also, I had more and more things to do that seemed more important to me than sewing.

I attribute my ambivalent attitude toward clothes to two things: my early lack of money and my tomboyishness. The purchase of clothes was always accompanied by a great deal of angst when I was young. There was so little money that when I had any to spend, I was terrified I'd make a wrong choice. I often did. And had to live with it. If I'd used my own money, I knew that every dollar I spent equaled two hours' baby-sitting time. I would buy something, my stomach knotted up both from fear of making a mistake and fear of my father's yelling about the money spent. I grew cagey about the latter. I could fudge on how much something cost. I could say I had to have it for school for some obscure reason. I could say I'd used all or half my own money. Or something.

And then the tomboy-thing. I wanted to look beautiful, I wanted to look like the girls in my class I admired. But what made me happiest was climbing around creekbanks in pants (no jeans yet, remember) and an old flannel shirt, looking for crawdads. Those clothes were the ones I loved best.

I think about the sociology of clothes. In the fifties and on into the early sixties, 15
the styles, the requirements in clothing for girls and boys were as separate as our psychology was thought to be. Girls had to wear dresses to school unless the temperature was below a certain degree, I can't remember what. But those days felt free as holidays, although we generally felt we must wear a skirt on top of the pants. When I was an undergraduate, girls were not allowed to wear pants on the University of Arkansas campus, except under a raincoat. And furthermore, they were not to wear them downtown. After all, they were "representing the University." All winter, all of my young life, my legs were freezing cold. Because I was a girl.

Boundaries were clear. Unlike now, when cast-off 50s dresses are worn with cowboy boots, tight torn jeans with diamonds and a sleek silk camisole, a tuxedo with tennis shoes. And too, when future anthologists—if there are any—look back on this era's poems, they'll see hybrid poems that pull in all manner of objects and thoughts and commercials and movies and music. Poems in received forms and free-verse poems, poems that announce that they're poems but look and read like prose. And prose poems. Soft boundaries between genres.

And self-conscious display of the making, the mechanics of the poem. The poet stepping in to say how it's going, this writing of a poem. Last weekend I attended a baby shower. The very-pregnant mother was wearing a long, form-fitting top and long skirt—very chic. It's fashionable to let the belly show, the stark progression of belly-growth, to be proud of it. When I was pregnant, maternity clothes were shapeless bags we buttoned over our midsection to hide the protrusion. We were only a generation or so from the time when pregnant women were expected to stay inside as they started "showing," as if any display of our sexual potency was shameful.

But even though now a woman can wear anything, really anything, she wishes and be acceptable on most occasions, somehow underneath, it feels to me as if that change hasn't netted as much as we'd like to think. The truth is, I see in the faces of some of those women in pillbox hats and blue suits on reruns of ancient game shows more maturity and more command of themselves and their environment than I see in the faces of many young women today, who seem uncertain of who they are and what they want to be. Those women in pillbox hats were fitting themselves into a role, true, but they knew they had responsibility for that role, for enacting it well and truthfully—being a good wife, a good mother, a good housekeeper. These were not the women on *Mad Men*. The ones I'm thinking of were the real ones.

I don't want to go back there, and couldn't if I did. Same with poetry. This is an incredibly exciting time for clothes and poetry, it seems to me. Exciting and necessarily unnerving. What we wear, what and how we write, is either demonstrating who we think we are, how we think the world is organized and what it all means, or it's demonstrating who we're supposed to be according to our culture's norms. Who can tell which is which? These days I wear jeans almost all the time. I'm an attractive woman for my age, but not a glamorous one, although I passionately admire my gorgeously dressed friends. The glamour-gene bypassed me. I have a friend, a writer, who said her goal in life is to make enough money with her writing to be able to get up every morning, her only decision being which pair of jeans to put on. Amen to that.

Source: Fleda Brown, "Unruffled: Essay" Essays, Numero Cinq Magazine, Vol. IV, No. 3, March 2013. Used by permission.

RESPONDING TO READING

1. In paragraph 9, Brown explains, "Seething underneath the clothes issue for me was the tacit sense of the role women were supposed to play. The clothes were indicative." What does she mean? In what ways did clothes define gender roles for Brown? How has (or hasn't) the situation changed since she was young?
2. Toward the end of her essay, Brown draws a comparison between clothes and poetry. She writes, "What we wear, what and how we write, is either demonstrating who we think we are, how we think the world is organized and what it all means, or it's demonstrating who we're supposed to be according to our culture's norms. Who can tell which is which?" (19). How are different types of clothes like different genres of writing? How do the decisions we make about what to wear and what to write reflect our identities and our cultural expectations?

Rhetorical Analysis

Find examples in Brown's essay of her down-to-earth, conversational tone. How is her language, like her dress, "unruffled"? Does her writing style help her to make her points effectively? Explain.

Writing with Sources

Research some recent TV and movie depictions of what "a good wife, a good mother, a good housekeeper" have looked like in America over time (18). Then, write a response to Brown's essay in which you explain media's role in reinforcing or defying conventional gender stereotypes.

7.3 Judy Brady, "Why I Want a Wife"

Judy Brady (1937–2017) studied art before getting married, having a family, and starting her writing career. A breast cancer survivor, Brady cofounded the *Toxic Links Coalition*, an environmental advocacy group based in California. She edited two books about cancer, including *Women and Cancer* (1980) and a collection of essays and poems written by women with cancer titled *One in Three: Women with Cancer Confront an Epidemic* (1991). The following essay, "Why I Want a Wife," appeared in the first issue of Ms. magazine in 1972. In this essay, Brady takes a satirical look at what it means to be a wife and mother.

BEFORE YOU READ

What is your definition of a wife? Explain.

Why I Want a Wife

I belong to that classification of people known as wives. I am A Wife. And, not altogether incidentally, I am a mother.

Not too long ago a male friend of mine appeared on the scene fresh from a recent divorce. He had one child, who is, of course, with his ex-wife. He is looking for another wife. As I thought about him while I was ironing one evening, it suddenly occurred to me that I, too, would like to have a wife. Why do I want a wife?

I would like to go back to school so that I can become economically independent, support myself, and, if need be, support those dependent upon me. I want a wife who will work and send me to school. And while I am going to school I want a wife to take care of my children. I want a wife to keep track of the children's doctor and dentist appointments. And to keep track of mine, too. I want a wife to make sure my children eat properly and are kept clean. I want a wife who will wash the children's clothes and keep them mended. I want a wife who is a good nurturant attendant to my children, who arranges for their schooling, makes sure that they have an adequate social life with their peers, takes them to the park, the zoo, etc. I want a wife who takes care of the children when they are sick, a wife who arranges to be around when the children need special care, because, of course, I cannot miss classes at school. My wife must arrange to lose time at work and not lose the job. It may mean a small cut in my wife's income from time to time, but I guess I can tolerate that. Needless to say, my wife will arrange and pay for the care of the children while my wife is working.

I want a wife who will take care of *my* physical needs. I want a wife who will keep my house clean. A wife who will pick up after me. I want a wife who will keep my clothes clean, ironed, mended, replaced when need be, and who will see to it that my personal things are kept in their proper place so that I can find what I need the minute I need it. I want a wife who cooks the meals, a wife who is a *good* cook. I want a wife who will plan the menus, do the necessary grocery shopping, prepare the meals, serve them pleasantly, and then do the cleaning up while I do my studying. I want a wife who will care for me when I am sick and sympathize with my pain and loss of time from school. I want a wife to go along when our family takes a vacation so that someone can continue to care for me and my children when I need a rest and change of scene.

5 I want a wife who will not bother me with rambling complaints about a wife's duties. But I want a wife who will listen to me when I feel the need to explain a rather difficult point I have come across in my course of studies. And I want a wife who will type my papers for me when I have written them.

I want a wife who will take care of the details of my social life. When my wife and I are invited out by friends, I want a wife who will take care of the babysitting arrangements. When I meet people at school that I like and want to entertain, I want a wife who will have the house clean, will prepare a special meal, serve it to me and my friends, and not interrupt when I talk about the things that interest me and my friends. I want a wife who will have arranged that the children are fed and ready for bed before my guests arrive so that the children do not bother us. I want a wife who takes care of the needs of my guests so that they feel comfortable, who makes sure that they have an ashtray, that they are passed the hors d'oeuvres, that they are offered a second helping of the food, that their wine glasses are replenished when necessary, that their coffee is served to them as they like it. And I want a wife who knows that sometimes I need a night out by myself.

I want a wife who is sensitive to my sexual needs, a wife who makes love passionately and eagerly when I feel like it, a wife who makes sure that I am satisfied. And, of course, I want a wife who will not demand sexual attention when I am not in the mood for it. I want a wife who assumes the complete responsibility for birth control, because I do not want more children. I want a wife who will remain sexually faithful to me so that I do not have to clutter up my intellectual life with jealousies. And I want a wife who understands that *my* sexual needs may entail more than strict adherence to monogamy. I must, after all, be able to relate to people as fully as possible.

If, by chance, I find another person more suitable as a wife than the wife I already have, I want the liberty to replace my present wife with another one. Naturally, I will expect a fresh, new life; my wife will take the children and be solely responsible for them so that I am left free.

When I am through with school and have a job, I want my wife to quit working and remain at home so that my wife can more fully and completely take care of a wife's duties.

My God, who *wouldn't* want a wife? 10

RESPONDING TO READING

1. This essay, written more than forty years ago, has been anthologized many times. To what do you attribute its continued popularity? In what ways, if any, is the essay dated? In what ways is it still relevant?
2. Brady wrote her essay to address a stereotype and a set of social conventions that she thought were harmful to women. Could you make the case that Brady's characterization of a "wife" is harmful both to women and to feminism?

Rhetorical Analysis

Why does Brady begin her essay by saying that she is both a wife and a mother? How does her encounter with a male friend lead her to decide that she would like to have a wife?

Writing with Sources

Look up the definition of *satire*. Then, write an essay in which you make the case that "Why I Want a Wife" is an example of satire. What point do you think Brady is making with her essay?

7.4 Warren Farrell and John Gray, "The Crisis of Our Sons' Education"

Described as "the Gloria Steinem of Men's Liberation," Warren Farrell (1943–) teaches and writes about men's and women's issues. The author of numerous books, he is the chair of the Commission to Create a White House Council on Boys to Men and has taught at the School of Medicine at the University of California, San Diego, as well as at Georgetown University, Rutgers University, and American University. A counselor and public speaker, John Gray (1951–) has written numerous books, including his classic bestseller *Men Are from Mars, Women Are from*

Venus: A Practical Guide for Improving Communication and Getting What You Want in Your Relationships (1992). In the following essay excerpted from the book *The Boy Crisis: Why Our Boys Are Struggling and What We Can Do About It* (2018), Farrell and Gray demonstrate that, contrary to popular opinion, boys, not girls, are short-changed by today's educational establishment.

BEFORE YOU READ

Based on your experience, who is more successful in school—girls or boys?

The Crisis of Our Sons' Education

Worldwide, reading and writing skills are the two biggest predictors of success.[1] These are also the two areas in which boys fall the most behind girls. **In the United States, by eighth grade, 41 percent of girls are at least "proficient" in writing, while only 20 percent of boys are.**[2]

Many boys used to "turn around" in about their junior or senior year of high school. Anticipating the need to become sole breadwinner, and therefore gain familial pride, peer respect, and female love, they got their act together. The expectation of becoming sole breadwinner became his purpose. No longer. In one generation, young men have gone from 61 percent of college degree recipients to a projected 39 percent; young women, from 39 percent to a projected 61 percent.

The number of boys who said they didn't like school has increased by 71 percent since 1980.[3] Boys are also expelled from school three times as often as girls.[4]

Why? In a study of boys and girls in the United States at the primary level, when it comes to standardized tests versus grades, "Boys who perform equally well as girls on reading, math, and science tests are graded less favorably by their teachers."[5] Interestingly, the boys who behaved in the classroom in ways the study identified as more commonly associated with girls—for example, by being attentive and eager—did receive grades equal to girls who scored equally in standardized tests. Boys may feel teachers are discriminating against their "boy-style" behavior, which understandably leads them to like school less . . . .

THE INFINITE CONSEQUENCES OF UNEDUCATED BOYS

5 While boys who are motivated can become many of society's most constructive forces—becoming inventors and implementers of what they invent (the Amazons, Apples, Facebooks, Microsofts, and Googles)—boys whose energies are poorly channeled can become society's most destructive forces—our serial killers and prisoners.

Ironically, as our sons become less educated, our daughters increasingly desire partners who are *more* educated. In 1939 women ranked education as only the *eleventh* most important attribute in a husband. Recently, women rank education as the *fourth* most important.[6]

And with less education leading boys to the unemployment line, it creates what I call the drop-out, left-out cycle:

THE DROP-OUT, LEFT-OUT CYCLE

1. In neighborhoods where marriage is scarce, fathers are scarce, and more than *half* of boys don't finish *high school*.[7] The boy drops out.
2. The less education a young man has, the more likely he is to be unemployed or underemployed. He's left out of the workplace.
3. Women who desire children think of an uneducated young man as undesirable, and an unemployed man as "another child"—hardly marriage material. He's left out of marriage and fathering.
4. Some of the women with whom he nonetheless has sex become pregnant, and raise children without him. Thus, we're back to step one: the left-out dad and the drop-out son.

THE IMPLICATION FOR GLOBAL LEADERSHIP

Our sons receiving only about 40 percent of college degrees also damages American global leadership. Why? When we do not simultaneously explore our son's full potential as dads, this leads to an inability to make use of our daughters' full potential at work. So women receiving about 60 percent of college degrees does not translate into women becoming 60 percent of CEOs of start-ups and corporations or 60 percent of inventors or political leaders.

Why? In part this is because a relatively small percentage of women wish to live out-of-balance lives and neglect their families for a career-only life. That is, women are more likely to opt for a balanced life, which is usually a happier life. But the second part is that families have not learned to make use of your son as a full-time dad, which might allow his wife to be a CEO with a happy marriage and well-raised children.

What can our schools do? Integrate curriculum on the future of the family into 10
the school curriculum. Help our daughters and sons free themselves from the rigid roles of the past toward more flexible roles for their future. As we'll increasingly see, for any country to be a global leader with citizens who are fulfilled, it will have to recruit executives and parents based on motivation and talent, not biology as destiny.

HOW SCHOOLS CAN HELP BOYS MAKE A TRANSITION FROM MUSCLE TO MENTAL

In the future, much of the muscle in manufacturing and construction will be replaced by the mental: robots and artificial intelligence. If your son wants a good job as a welder, he will also need physics and chemistry. If he wishes to make a living with computers, he will need to know how to code, program, and develop software. Grandpa and dad may have worked on appliances like cars, refrigerators, and thermostats; your son will need to master how these appliances collect and exchange data using embedded sensors. That is, he will need to understand the "internet of things." The common denominator? His mind. His mind educated in boy-friendly ways.

What's a boy-friendly way for a nonacademically inclined boy to use his mind? Having a concrete goal. If a boy has a concrete goal of being a welder, that catalyzes motivation to study the physics and chemistry necessary to become a high-paid welder.

How might a school encourage this? By increasing vocational education. Instead, most schools have been decreasing vocational education.

Japan has vastly increased its vocational education programs, with 23 percent of Japan's high school graduates studying at vocational schools. The result: **99.6 percent of Japanese vocational students received jobs upon graduation.**[8] The psychological and economic implications of that difference are infinite. (Incidentally, some Japanese schools are actively recruiting foreign students.)[9]

15 Our schools are perpetuating the boy crisis in a second way. Girls learn emotional intelligence as part of the socialization to be female. For boys there is an ever-widening gap between the heroic intelligence that it took our sons to be respected as men in the past and the emotional intelligence needed for your son's future. Yet few schools are teaching communication skills and empathy training to help boys make that transition.

Here's why I predict emotional intelligence will be paramount for your son's future: **the more sophisticated artificial intelligence becomes, the more we will yearn for humans to fill the emotional intelligence void.** The more caring professions (e.g., health care, home care—professions currently dominated by women) will thrive even as the traditional male careers shrink.

Can't artificial intelligence mimic emotional intelligence, as illustrated in the movie *Her*? To a degree, yes, but within the span of your sons career, it will not replace the nuances of emotional intelligence needed by a dad, male partner, or health care or home care worker—for example, the ability to respond sensitively to body language, tones of voice, hesitation patterns, and eye contact. Or knowing when to listen, when to talk, when to be proactive, and when to create space. These are the voids AI will create, for which we will increasingly value (and pay) those most able to fill them.

Can your son learn empathy and emotional intelligence, or is this something that girls and women are just better at? Studies reveal that when observing casually, women pick up more accurately what others are feeling. But here's what's fascinating: **when both sexes are offered *pay* should they assess the feelings of others accurately, the empathy gender gap disappears!**[10] The implication? The capacity for empathy and emotional intelligence is latent inside boys and men; we just have to let guys know we'll value them for focusing on it.

Even when emotional intelligence is so undeveloped that hate becomes an unchecked bonding mechanism, as among hard-core white supremacists, Life After Hate groups have successfully reversed the hatred of thousands and replaced it with empathy, love, and self-forgiveness.[11] There are, then, ways emotional intelligence and empathy can be learned even by those we might assume are hopeless.

20 There is a second application of training for emotional intelligence and empathy. If the haters can learn empathy, maybe we can learn empathy toward the haters. When our only response to haters is to hate, we increase our brain's training to hate and decrease its training to empathize. We become a bit of the enemy we hate.

How can our schools help? Currently our schools are funded to stop bullying. However, **both bullies and the bullied have three things in common: both**

come from negative family, school, and community environments; both have low self-esteem; and both have poor social skills.[12] That is, both the bullied and the bully are similarly vulnerable, and teaching the skills that will help both simultaneously is a positive-sum strategy. Since empathy and emotional intelligence can be taught, and these skills are key to preparing our sons for the professions that will be in the greatest demand, we need to integrate this curriculum into our schools in the formative years.

EXACERBATING THE EDUCATION CRISIS: CARING LESS

It's 2016. I receive an email from UCLA (an alma mater) promoting the PhD dissertation presentations of ten of their leading young political scientists. I notice something: all ten are women. I call the political science department and inquire as to why there are no men. The response? "Oh, yes, you're right. I didn't notice that."

We don't notice the norm. In the fifties, the normal was few women in MBA and MD programs. It took the women's movement to help us notice. Today, boys' absence from lists of achievers in education has become the new normal.

It's easier to notice when we care. Friends of mine recently attended their daughter's graduation. Their daughter was co-valedictorian with another girl, and a member of the honor society, which had but a sprinkling of boys. Their son was a junior in the same school. He and his male friends had as many D's and F's as A's and B's.

His parents cared, so they noticed. It didn't surprise them to hear that nation- 25
wide girls make up 70 percent of valedictorians,[13] while boys get 70 percent of D's and F's.[14] In fact, it made them feel less disappointed in their son.

My friends grew up in the era in which girls were doing badly in math and science. They recalled how we concluded the trouble was with the schools. They also saw how now that boys are doing badly in almost every subject, we say the trouble is with the boys.

Solving the boy crisis, in education and in the other areas we've discussed, starts with noticing it's happening—not just here in the United States, but worldwide.

ENDNOTES

1. OECD, "How Do Girls Compare to Boys in Mathematics Skills?" in *PISA 2009 at a Glance* (Paris, France: OECD, 2010) 22, doi:10.1787/9789264095298-en.
2. D. Salahu-Din, H. Persky, and J. Miller, *The Nation's Report Card: Writing 2007,* NCES 2008–468, National Center for Education Statistics (NCES), Institute of Education Sciences, U.S. Department of Education, (Washington, DC, and Chapel Hill, NC, 2008), table A-9. Average scores and achievement-level results in NAEP writing for eighth-grade public school students, by gender and state. 2007.
3. In 1980 only 14 percent of boys said they did not like school very much at all; by 2001 that figure had increased to 24 percent. See University of Michigan, Institute for Social Research, Monitoring the Future (study), 1980–2001; cited in NCES, "How Do You Feel About School?" *Trends in Educational Equity of Girls and Women: 2004,* fig. 13, p. 45.

4. NCES, "Number and Percentage of Students Who Were Suspended and Expelled from Public Elementary and Secondary Schools, by Sex and Race/ Ethnicity: 2002, 2004, and 2006," in *Condition of Education 2009,* ed. Michael Planty, William J. Hussar, and Thomas D. Snyder (Washington, DC: NCES, June 2009), table A-28-1, p. 206.
5. C. Cornwell et al., "Non-cognitive Skills and the Gender Disparities in Test Scores and Teacher Assessments: Evidence from Primary School," *Journal of Human Resources* 48 (Winter 2013): 236–64.
6. Ana Swanson, "What Men and Women Wanted in a Spouse in 1939—and How Different It Is Today," *Wonkblog* (blog), *Washington Post,* Apri 19, 2016, https://www.washingtonpost.com/news/wonk/wp/2016/04/19/what-men-and-wornen-wanted-in-a-spouse-in-1939-and-how-different-it-is-today.
7. Peg Tyre, "The Trouble with Boys," *Newsweek,* January 29, 2006, http://www.newsweek.com/education-boys-falling-behind-girls-many-areas-l08593.
8. Taro Fujimoto, "Vocational Schools on the Move," *Japan Today*, July 21, 2008. https://japantoday.com/category/features/executive-impact/vocational-schools-on-the-move.
9. Kazuhiro Ohshima of the Katayanagi Institute is actively recruiting foreign students. See Fujimoto, "Vocational Schools."
10. Kristi Klein and Sara Hodges, "Gender Differences, Motivation, and Empathic Accuracy: When It Pays to Understand," *Personality and Social Psychology Bulletin* 27, no. 6 (June 2001): 720–30.
11. See www.lifeafterhate.org.
12. Clayton Cook, et al., "Predictors of Bullying and Victimization in Childhood and Adolescence: A Meta-analytic Investigation," *School Psychology Quarterly* 25, no. 2. See http://www.apa.org/news/press/releases/2010/07/bully-victim.aspx.
13. Lester Holt. "Men Falling Behind Women," NBCNews, March 5, 2011, http://www.nbc-news.com/id/41928806/ns/business-us_business/t/men-falling-behind-women.
14. Paul Stern, director, *Raising Cain: Boys in Focus* (documentary), PBS Films, 2006; see also Michael Gurian Michael and Arlette C. Ballew, *The Boys and Girls Learn Differently: Action Guide for Teachers* (Hoboken, NJ: John Wiley & Sons, 2003), 23.

RESPONDING TO READING

1. What are the causes, according to Farrell and Gray, of boys' educational disadvantages? How do these disadvantages affect other areas of boys' lives as they grow up?
2. In paragraph 10, Farrell and Gray propose that schools should "integrate curriculum on the future of the family into the school curriculum" and "help our daughters and sons free themselves from the rigid roles of the past toward more flexible roles for their future." How practical do you think their solution is to the problem they describe? How specifically would it work?

Rhetorical Analysis

Who is the intended audience for this essay? How can you tell?

Writing with Sources

Recently, the fathers' rights movement has been growing—especially as it concerns same-sex, unwed, or divorced fathers participating in child rearing. How widespread is this movement? How do its concerns complement the concerns that Farrell and Gray discuss in their essay?

7.5 Deborah Tannen, "Marked Women"

Deborah Tannen (1945–), a professor of linguistics at Georgetown University, has written books for both scholarly and popular audiences, with most of her work focusing on communication between men and women. Tannen is best known for her bestseller *You Just Don't Understand: Women and Men in Conversation* (1990); her most recent book is *You're the Only One I Can Tell: Inside the Language of Women's Friendships* (2017). The following essay, written in 1993, is a departure from Tannen's usual work. Here she focuses not on different communication styles but on the contrast she finds between the neutral way men in our culture present themselves to the world and the more message-laden way women present themselves.

BEFORE YOU READ

Consider the men and women you see every day at school or in your neighborhood. Do you see any patterns in how they dress, style their hair, or wear accessories? What might these patterns signify?

Marked Women

Some years ago I was at a small working conference of four women and eight men. Instead of concentrating on the discussion I found myself looking at the three other women at the table, thinking how each had a different style and how each style was coherent.

One woman had dark brown hair in a classic style, a cross between Cleopatra and Plain Jane. The severity of her straight hair was softened by wavy bangs and ends that turned under. Because she was beautiful, the effect was more Cleopatra than plain.

The second woman was older, full of dignity and composure. Her hair was cut in a fashionable style that left her with only one eye, thanks to a side part that let a curtain of hair fall across half her face. As she looked down to read her prepared paper, the hair robbed her of bifocal vision and created a barrier between her and the listeners.

The third woman's hair was wild, a frosted blond avalanche falling over and beyond her shoulders. When she spoke she frequently tossed her head, calling attention to her hair and away from her lecture.

5 Then there was makeup. The first woman wore facial cover that made her skin smooth and pale, a black line under each eye and mascara that darkened already dark lashes. The second wore only a light gloss on her lips and a hint of shadow on her eyes. The third had blue bands under her eyes, dark blue shadow, mascara, bright red lipstick and rouge; her fingernails flashed red.

I considered the clothes each woman had worn during the three days of the conference: In the first case, man-tailored suits in primary colors with solid-color blouses. In the second, casual but stylish black T-shirts, a floppy collarless jacket and baggy slacks or a skirt in neutral colors. The third wore a sexy jump suit; tight sleeveless jersey and tight yellow slacks; a dress with gaping armholes and an indulged tendency to fall off one shoulder.

Shoes? No. 1 wore string sandals with medium heels; No. 2, sensible, comfortable walking shoes; No. 3, pumps with spike heels. You can fill in the jewelry, scarves, shawls, sweaters—or lack of them.

As I amused myself finding coherence in these styles, I suddenly wondered why I was scrutinizing only the women. I scanned the eight men at the table. And then I knew why I wasn't studying them. The men's styles were unmarked.

The term "marked" is a staple of linguistic theory. It refers to the way language alters the base meaning of a word by adding a linguistic particle that has no meaning on its own. The unmarked form of a word carries the meaning that goes without saying—what you think of when you're not thinking anything special.

10 The unmarked tense of verbs in English is the present—for example, *visit.* To indicate past, you mark the verb by adding *ed* to yield *visited.* For future, you add a word: *will visit.* Nouns are presumed to be singular until marked for plural, typically by adding *s* or *es,* so *visit* becomes *visits* and *dish* becomes *dishes.*

The unmarked forms of most English words also convey "male." Being male is the unmarked case. Endings like *ess* and *ette* mark words as "female." Unfortunately, they also tend to mark them for frivolousness. Would you feel safe entrusting your life to a doctorette? Alfre Woodard, who was an Oscar nominee for best supporting actress, says she identifies herself as an actor because "actresses worry about eyelashes and cellulite, and women who are actors worry about the characters we are playing." Gender markers pick up extra meanings that reflect common associations with the female gender: not quite serious, often sexual.

Each of the women at the conference had to make decisions about hair, clothing, makeup and accessories, and each decision carried meaning. Every style available to us was marked. The men in our group had made decisions, too, but the range from which they chose was incomparably narrower. Men can choose styles that are marked, but they don't have to, and in this group none did. Unlike the women, they had the option of being unmarked.

Take the men's hair styles. There was no marine crew cut or oily longish hair falling into eyes, no asymmetrical, two-tiered construction to swirl over a bald top. One man was unabashedly bald; the others had hair of standard length, parted on one side, in natural shades of brown or gray or graying. Their hair obstructed no views, left little to toss or push back or run fingers through and, consequently, needed and attracted no attention. A few men had beards. In a business setting, beards might be marked. In this academic gathering, they weren't.

There could have been a cowboy shirt with string tie or a three-piece suit or a necklaced hippie in jeans. But there wasn't. All eight men wore brown or blue slacks and nondescript shirts of light colors. No man wore sandals or boots; their shoes were dark, closed, comfortable and flat. In short, unmarked.

Although no man wore makeup, you couldn't say the men didn't wear 15
makeup in the sense that you could say a woman didn't wear makeup. For men, no makeup is unmarked.

I asked myself what style we women could have adopted that would have been unmarked, like the men's. The answer was none. There is no unmarked woman.

There is no woman's hair style that can be called standard, that says nothing about her. The range of women's hair styles is staggering, but a woman whose hair has no particular style is perceived as not caring about how she looks, which can disqualify her for many positions, and will subtly diminish her as a person in the eyes of some.

Women must choose between attractive shoes and comfortable shoes. When our group made an unexpected trek, the woman who wore flat, laced shoes arrived first. Last to arrive was the woman in spike heels, shoes in hand and a handful of men around her.

If a woman's clothing is tight or revealing (in other words, sexy), it sends a message—an intended one of wanting to be attractive, but also a possibly unintended one of availability. If her clothes are not sexy, that too sends a message, lent meaning by the knowledge that they could have been. There are thousands of cosmetic products from which women can choose and myriad ways of applying them. Yet no makeup at all is anything but unmarked. Some men see it as a hostile refusal to please them.

Women can't even fill out a form without telling stories about themselves. 20
Most forms give four titles to choose from. "Mr." carries no meaning other than that the respondent is male. But a woman who checks "Mrs." or "Miss" communicates not only whether she has been married but also whether she has conservative tastes in forms of address—and probably other conservative values as well. Checking "Ms." declines to let on about marriage (checking "Mr." declines nothing since nothing was asked), but it also marks her as either liberated or rebellious, depending on the observer's attitudes and assumptions.

I sometimes try to duck these variously marked choices by giving my title as "Dr."—and in so doing risk marking myself as either uppity (hence sarcastic responses like "*Excuse me!*") or an overachiever (hence reactions of congratulatory surprise like "Good for you!").

All married women's surnames are marked. If a woman takes her husband's name, she announces to the world that she is married and has traditional values.

To some it will indicate that she is less herself, more identified by her husband's identity. If she does not take her husband's name, this too is marked, seen as worthy of comment: she has done something; she has "kept her own name." A man is never said to have "kept his own name" because it never occurs to anyone that he might have given it up. For him using his own name is unmarked.

A married woman who wants to have her cake and eat it too may use her surname plus his, with or without a hyphen. But this too announces her marital status and often results in a tongue-tying string. In a list (Harvey O'Donovan, Jonathan Feldman, Stephanie Woodbury McGillicutty), the woman's multiple name stands out. It is marked.

I have never been inclined toward biological explanations of gender differences in language, but I was intrigued to see Ralph Fasold bring biological phenomena to bear on the question of linguistic marking in his book *The Sociolinguistics of Language.* Fasold stresses that language and culture are particularly unfair in treating women as the marked case because biologically it is the male that is marked. While two X chromosomes make a female, two Y chromosomes make nothing. Like the linguistic markers *s, es* or *ess,* the Y chromosome doesn't "mean" anything unless it is attached to a root form—an X chromosome.

25 Developing this idea elsewhere, Fasold points out that girls are born with fully female bodies, while boys are born with modified female bodies. He invites men who doubt this to lift up their shirts and contemplate why they have nipples.

In his book, Fasold notes "a wide range of facts which demonstrates that female is the unmarked sex." For example, he observes that there are a few species that produce only females, like the whiptail lizard. Thanks to parthenogenesis, they have no trouble having as many daughters as they like. There are no species, however, that produce only males. This is no surprise, since any such species would become extinct in its first generation.

Fasold is also intrigued by species that produce individuals not involved in reproduction, like honeybees and leaf-cutter ants. Reproduction is handled by the queen and a relatively few males; the workers are sterile females. "Since they do not reproduce," Fasold says, "there is no reason for them to be one sex or the other, so they default, so to speak, to female."

Fasold ends his discussion of these matters by pointing out that if language reflected biology, grammar books would direct us to use "she" to include males and females and "he" only for specifically male referents. But they don't. They tell us that "he" means "he or she," and that "she" is used only if the referent is specifically female. This use of "he" as the sex-indefinite pronoun is an innovation introduced into English by grammarians in the 18th and 19th centuries, according to Peter Mühlhäusler and Rom Harré in *Pronouns and People.* From at least about 1500, the correct sex-indefinite pronoun was "they," as it still is in casual spoken English. In other words, the female was declared by grammarians to be the marked case.

Writing this article may mark me not as a writer, not as a linguist, not as an analyst of human behavior, but as a feminist—which will have positive or negative, but in any case powerful, connotations for readers. Yet I doubt that anyone reading Ralph Fasold's book would put that label on him.

30 I discovered the markedness inherent in the very topic of gender after writing a book on differences in conversational style based on geographical region, ethnicity, class, age and gender. When I was interviewed, the vast majority of journalists wanted to talk about the differences between women and men. While I thought I was simply describing what I observed—something I had learned to do as a researcher—merely mentioning women and men marked me as a feminist for some.

When I wrote a book devoted to gender differences, in ways of speaking, I sent the manuscript to five male colleagues, asking them to alert me to any interpretation, phrasing or wording that might seem unfairly negative toward men. Even so, when the book came out, I encountered responses like that of the television talk show host who, after interviewing me, turned to the audience and asked if they thought I was male-bashing.

Leaping upon a poor fellow who affably nodded in agreement, she made him stand and asked, "Did what she said accurately describe you?" "Oh, yes," he answered. "That's me exactly." "And what she said about women—does that sound like your wife?" "Oh yes," he responded. "That's her exactly." "Then why do you think she's male-bashing?" He answered, with disarming honesty, "Because she's a woman and she's saying things about men."

To say anything about women and men without marking oneself as either feminist or anti-feminist, male-basher or apologist for men seems as impossible for a woman as trying to get dressed in the morning without inviting interpretations of her character.

Sitting at the conference table musing on these matters, I felt sad to think that we women didn't have the freedom to be unmarked that the men sitting next to us had. Some days you just want to get dressed and go about your business. But if you're a woman, you can't, because there is no unmarked woman.

Source: Deborah Tannen. "Wears Jump Suit. Sensible Shoes. Uses Husband's Last Name. "The New York Times Magazine, June 20, 1993. Originally titled "Marked Women, Unmarked Men." Copyright Deborah Tannen. Adapted from Talking from 9 to 5: Women and Men at Work, HarperCollins. Reprinted with Permission.

RESPONDING TO READING

1. Tannen notes that men "can choose styles that are marked, but they don't have to" (12); however, she believes that women do not have "the option of being unmarked" (12). What does she mean? Can you give some examples of women's styles that you believe are unmarked? (Note that in paragraph 16, Tannen says there are no such styles.)
2. In paragraph 33, Tannen says, "To say anything about women and men without marking oneself as either feminist or anti-feminist, male-basher or apologist for men seems as impossible for a woman as trying to get dressed in the morning without inviting interpretations of her character." Do you agree?

Rhetorical Analysis

In paragraphs 24–28, Tannen discusses Ralph Fasold's book *The Sociolinguistics of Language.* Why does she include this material? Could she have made her point just as effectively without it?

Writing with Sources

Do further research into the concept of marked and unmarked in terms of gender identity. Then, look at both the men and women in your classes. Do you agree with Tannen when she says that women do not have "the freedom to be unmarked" (34)?

7.6 Kate Chopin, "The Story of an Hour" [Fiction]

Born in St. Louis as Katherine O'Flaherty, Kate Chopin (1850–1904) was a short-story writer and novelist well known for her story collections about the Cane River region in Louisiana, including *Bayou Folk* (1894) and *A Night in Arcadie* (1897). *The Awakening* (1899), her final novel about a woman's social and sexual liberation, ignited controversy upon publication and was banned for decades thereafter. The following story, originally published in Vogue magazine in 1894, depicts a particular view of marriage.

BEFORE YOU READ

Do you know anyone in a relatively traditional marriage between one spouse as the primary breadwinner and the other spouse as the primary homemaker? How would you describe their lives?

The Story of an Hour

Knowing that Mrs. Mallard was afflicted with a heart trouble, great care was taken to break to her as gently as possible the news of her husband's death.

It was her sister Josephine who told her, in broken sentences; veiled hints that revealed in half concealing. Her husband's friend Richards was there, too, near her. It was he who had been in the newspaper office when intelligence of the railroad disaster was received, with Brently Mallard's name leading the list of "killed." He had only taken the time to assure himself of its truth by a second telegram, and had hastened to forestall any less careful, less tender friend in bearing the sad message.

She did not hear the story as many women have heard the same, with a paralyzed inability to accept its significance. She wept at once, with sudden, wild abandonment, in her sister's arms. When the storm of grief had spent itself she went away to her room alone. She would have no one follow her.

There stood, facing the open window, a comfortable, roomy armchair. Into this she sank, pressed down by a physical exhaustion that haunted her body and seemed to reach into her soul.

She could see in the open square before her house the tops of trees that 5
were all aquiver with the new spring life. The delicious breath of rain was in the air. In the street below a peddler was crying his wares. The notes of a distant song which someone was singing reached her faintly, and countless sparrows were twittering in the eaves.

There were patches of blue sky showing here and there through the clouds that had met and piled one above the other in the west facing her window.

She sat with her head thrown back upon the cushion of the chair, quite motionless, except when a sob came up into her throat and shook her, as a child who has cried itself to sleep continues to sob in its dreams.

She was young, with a fair, calm face, whose lines bespoke repression and even a certain strength. But now there was a dull stare in her eyes, whose gaze was fixed away off yonder on one of those patches of blue sky. It was not a glance of reflection, but rather indicated a suspension of intelligent thought.

There was something coming to her and she was waiting for it, fearfully. What was it? She did not know; it was too subtle and elusive to name. But she felt it, creeping out of the sky, reaching toward her through the sounds, the scents, the color that filled the air.

Now her bosom rose and fell tumultuously. She was beginning to recognize 10
this thing that was approaching to possess her, and she was striving to beat it back with her will—as powerless as her two white slender hands would have been.

When she abandoned herself a little whispered word escaped her slightly parted lips. She said it over and over under her breath: "free, free, free!" The vacant stare and the look of terror that had followed it went from her eyes. They stayed keen and bright. Her pulses beat fast, and the coursing blood warmed and relaxed every inch of her body.

She did not stop to ask if it were or were not a monstrous joy that held her. A clear and exalted perception enabled her to dismiss the suggestion as trivial.

She knew that she would weep again when she saw the kind, tender hands folded in death, the face that had never looked save with love upon her, fixed and gray and dead. But she saw beyond that bitter moment a long procession of years to come that would belong to her absolutely. And she opened and spread her arms out to them in welcome.

There would be no one to live for during those coming years; she would live for herself. There would be no powerful will bending hers in that blind persistence with which men and women believe they have a right to impose a private will upon a fellow-creature. A kind intention or a cruel intention made the act seem no less a crime as she looked upon it in that brief moment of illumination.

15 And yet she had loved him—sometimes. Often she had not. What did it matter! What could love, the unsolved mystery, count for in face of this possession of self-assertion which she suddenly recognized as the strongest impulse of her being!

"Free! Body and soul free!" she kept whispering.

Josephine was kneeling before the closed door with her lips to the keyhole, imploring for admission. "Louise, open the door! I beg, open the door—you will make yourself ill. What are you doing Louise? For heaven's sake open the door."

"Go away. I am not making myself ill." No, she was drinking in a very elixir of life through that open window.

Her fancy was running riot along those days ahead of her. Spring days, and summer days, and all sorts of days that would be her own. She breathed a quick prayer that life might be long. It was only yesterday she had thought with a shudder that life might be long.

20 She arose at length and opened the door to her sister's importunities. There was a feverish triumph in her eyes, and she carried herself unwittingly like a goddess of Victory. She clasped her sister's waist, and together they descended the stairs. Richards stood waiting for them at the bottom.

Some one was opening the front door with a latchkey. It was Brently Mallard who entered, a little travel-stained, composedly carrying his grip-sack and umbrella. He had been far from the scene of accident, and did not even know there had been one. He stood amazed at Josephine's piercing cry; at Richards' quick motion to screen him from the view of his wife.

But Richards was too late.

When the doctors came they said she had died of heart disease—of joy that kills.

Source: Chopin, Kate. "Story of an Hour" St. Louis Life, 05 January, 1895.

RESPONDING TO READING

1. When Mrs. Mallard first hears of her husband's death, she is obviously upset. When she is alone, she begins to react differently. Why?
2. What does "The Story of an Hour" suggest about marriage? Does Chopin's criticism apply to just Mrs. Mallard's marriage (or marriages like hers) or to all marriages? How do you know?

Rhetorical Analysis

Irony occurs when a character says one thing but the reader is meant to interpret it differently. In "The Story of an Hour," the doctor says that Mrs. Mallard died because of the overwhelming joy of seeing her husband alive. In what sense is this statement ironic?

7.7 Focus: "How Do We Talk about Sexual Harassment?"

Luc Kordas/Alamy Stock Photo

How does this photo from a 2018 women's march in New York depict women's responses to sexual misconduct?

RESPONDING TO THE IMAGE

Answer one or both of the following questions.

1. What is your reaction to this image? What elements does it use to show the conversations taking place about women's rights?
2. Consider the sign "Our Turn." What do you suppose the purpose of this sign is? What will women do now that it is their "turn"? What should they do? Explain.

7.8 Moira Donegan, "I Started the Media Men List: My Name Is Moira Donegan"

A journalist and feminist, Moira Donegan writes about issues related to women's and workers' rights, race, and violence. Her work has been published in *Bookforum, Cosmopolitan, Elle,* the *Guardian,* the *London Review of Books, n+1,* and *The Paris Review.* In the following essay, Donegan confesses to initiating a controversial, collaborative document that exposed the sexual misconduct of men across the media industry.

BEFORE YOU READ

Have you ever created or shared a social media post that went viral or that you otherwise felt you lost control of? What was it about, and why do you think this happened?

I Started the Media Men List: My Name Is Moira Donegan

In October [2017], I created a Google spreadsheet called "Shitty Media Men" that collected a range of rumors and allegations of sexual misconduct, much of it violent, by men in magazines and publishing. The anonymous, crowdsourced document was a first attempt at solving what has seemed like an intractable problem: how women can protect ourselves from sexual harassment and assault.

One long-standing partial remedy that women have developed is the whisper network, informal alliances that pass on open secrets and warn women away from serial assaulters. Many of these networks have been invaluable in protecting their members. Still, whisper networks are social alliances, and as such, they're unreliable. They can be elitist, or just insular. As Jenna Wortham pointed out in *The New York Times Magazine,* they are also prone to exclude women of color. Fundamentally, a whisper network consists of private conversations, and the document that I created was meant to be private as well. It was active for only a few hours, during which it spread much further and much faster than I ever anticipated, and in the end, the once-private document was made public—first when its existence was revealed in a BuzzFeed article by Doree Shafrir, then when the document itself was posted on Reddit.

A slew of think pieces ensued, with commentators alternately condemning the document as reckless, malicious, or puritanically anti-sex. Many called the document irresponsible, emphasizing that since it was anonymous, false accusations could be added without consequence. Others said that it ignored established channels in favor of what they thought was vigilantism and that they felt uncomfortable that it contained allegations both of violent assaults and inappropriate messages. Still other people just saw it as catty and mean, something like the "Burn Book" from *Mean Girls.* Because the document circulated among writers and journalists, many of the people assigned to write about it had received it from friends. Some faced the difficult experience of seeing other, male friends named. Many commentators expressed sympathy with the aims of the document—women warning women, trying to help one another—but thought that its technique was too radical. They objected to the anonymity, or to the digital format, or to writing these allegations down at all. Eventually, some media companies conducted investigations into employees who appeared on the spreadsheet; some of those men left their jobs or were fired.

None of this was what I thought was going to happen. In the beginning, I only wanted to create a place for women to share their stories of harassment and assault without being needlessly discredited or judged. The hope was to create an alternate avenue to report this kind of behavior and warn others without fear of retaliation. Too often, for someone looking to report an incident or to make habitual behavior stop, all the available options are bad ones. The police are notoriously inept at handling sexual-assault cases. Human-resources departments, in offices that have them, are tasked not with protecting employees but with shielding the company from liability—meaning that in the frequent occasion that the offender is a member of management and the victim is not, HR's priorities lie with the accused. When a reporting channel has enforcement power, like an HR department or the police, it also has an obligation to presume innocence. In contrast, the value of the spreadsheet was that it had no enforcement mechanisms: Without legal authority or professional power, it offered an impartial, rather than adversarial, tool to those who used it. It was intended specifically not to inflict consequences, not to be a weapon—and yet, once it became public, many people immediately saw it as exactly that.

Recent months have made clear that no amount of power or money can 5
shield a woman from sexual misconduct. But like me, many of the women who used the spreadsheet are particularly vulnerable: We are young, new to the industry, and not yet influential in our fields. As we have seen time after time, there can be great social and professional consequences for women who come forward. For us, the risks of using any of the established means of reporting were especially high and the chance for justice especially slim.

When I began working in magazines as a new college graduate in 2013, I was furtively warned away from several of my industry's most well-known abusers. Over the intervening years, I've met these characters in various guises. There was the hard-drinking editor who had worked in all the most prestigious editorial departments, who would down whiskeys until he was drunk enough to mention that he could help your career if you slept with him. There was the editor who would lean too close but who was funny enough that he would often charm women into consensual encounters that were then rumored to turn abruptly, frighteningly violent. Last summer, I saw two of the most notorious of these men clutching beers and laughing together at a party for a magazine in Brooklyn. "Doesn't everyone know about them?" another woman whispered to me. "I can't believe they're still invited to these things." But of course we could believe it. By then, we'd become resigned to the knowledge that men like them were invited everywhere.

The spreadsheet was intended to circumvent all of this. Anonymous, it would protect its users from retaliation: No one could be fired, harassed, or publicly smeared for telling her story when that story was not attached to her name. Open-sourced, it would theoretically be accessible to women who didn't have the professional or social cachet required for admittance into whisper networks. The spreadsheet did not ask how women responded to men's inappropriate behavior; it did not ask what you were wearing or whether you'd had anything to drink. Instead, the spreadsheet made a presumption that is still seen as radical: That it is men, not women, who are responsible for men's sexual misconduct.

There were pitfalls. The document was indeed vulnerable to false accusations, a concern I took seriously. I added a disclaimer to the top of the spreadsheet: "This document is only a collection of misconduct allegations and rumors. Take everything with a grain of salt." I sympathize with the desire to be careful, even as all available information suggests that false allegations are rare. The spreadsheet only had the power to inform women of allegations that were being made and to trust them to judge the quality of that information for themselves and to make their own choices accordingly. This, too, is still seen as radical: the idea that women are skeptical, that we can think and judge and choose for ourselves what to believe and what not to.

Nevertheless, when I first shared the spreadsheet among my women friends and colleagues, it took on the intense sincerity of our most intimate conversations. Women began to anonymously add their stories of sexual assault; many of the accounts posted there were violent, detailed, and difficult to read. Women recounted being beaten, drugged, and raped. Women recounted being followed into bathrooms or threatened with weapons. Many, many women recounted being groped at work, or shown a colleague's penis. Watching the cells populate, it rapidly became clear that many of us had weathered more than we had been willing to admit to one another. There was the sense that the capacity for honesty, long suppressed, had finally been unleashed. This solidarity was thrilling, but the stories were devastating. I realized that the behavior of a few men I had wanted women to be warned about was far more common that I had ever imagined. This is what shocked me about the spreadsheet: the realization of how badly it was needed, how much more common the experience of sexual harassment or assault is than the opportunity to speak about it. I am still trying to grapple with this realization.

10 Over the course of the evening, the spreadsheet expanded further: Many of the incidents reported there were physical, but there were also accounts of repeated sexual remarks, persistent inappropriate passes, unsolicited drunken messages. There was an understanding of the ways that these less-grave incidents can sometimes be harbingers of more aggressive actions to come, and how they can accrue into soured relationships and hostile environments. For clarity, I imposed a system that visibly distinguished violent accusations from others: Once a man had been accused of physical sexual assault by more than one woman, his name was highlighted in red. No one confused a crude remark for a rape,

and efforts were made to contextualize the incidents with notes—a spreadsheet allows for all of this information to be organized and included. But the premise was accepted that all of these behaviors were things that might make someone uncomfortable and that individuals should be able to choose for themselves what behavior they could tolerate and what they would rather avoid.

I took the spreadsheet offline after about 12 hours, when a friend alerted me that Shafrir would soon be publishing an article at BuzzFeed making the document's existence public. By then, the spreadsheet had gone viral. I had imagined a document that would assemble the collective, unspoken knowledge of sexual misconduct that was shared by the women in my circles: What I got instead was a much broader reckoning with abuses of power that spanned an industry. By the time I had to take the document down, more than 70 men had been named on the version that I was managing (other versions, assembled after the spreadsheet was taken offline, appeared later). The men ranged in age from their 20s to their 60s, and 14 had been highlighted in red to denote more than one accusation of sexual assault or rape. Some have expressed doubts about the veracity of the claims in the document, but it's impossible to deny the extent and severity of the sexual-harassment problem in media if you believe even a quarter of the claims that were made on the spreadsheet. For my part, I believe significantly more than that.

I can't pretend that the spreadsheet didn't frighten me. As the stories accumulated and it became clear that many, many more women were using the document than I had ever imagined, I realized that I had created something that had grown rapidly beyond my control. I was overwhelmed and scared. That night, I went to a friend's house to make dinner, and while I was there I confided in her about my fears. I worried that managing the document would eventually put me in the uncomfortable position of needing to decide whose stories belonged there and whose didn't. I thought that I would lose my job and the career I'd worked so hard to build. My friend could hear the anxiety in my voice; she urged me to take the document down. But I was conflicted. What was going on there was clearly cathartic for the women who were using it, telling their stories, encouraging one another, saying that it had happened to them too. Many women don't have the privileges that mitigate the risks of doing such a thing—privileges like whiteness, health, education, and class—and I do; it would be easier for me than for other people. I hoped that women reporters who saw the document might use it as a tip sheet and take it upon themselves to do the reporting that the document couldn't do and find evidence, if there was any, of the allegations made there. I began to think that maybe some of the assaults that women were warning one another about on the spreadsheet could be stopped by the power of the spreadsheet itself.

I was incredibly naïve when I made the spreadsheet. I was naïve because I did not understand the forces that would make the document go viral. I was naïve because I thought that the document would not be made public, and when it became clear that it would be, I was naïve because I thought that the focus would be on the behavior described in the document, rather than on the document itself. It is hard to believe, in retrospect, that I really thought this. But I did.

In some ways, though, I think the flaws in the spreadsheet were also a result of my own cynicism. At the time when I made it, I had become so accustomed to hearing about open secrets, to men whose bad behavior was universally known and perpetually immune from consequence, that it seemed like no one in power cared about the women who were most vulnerable to it. Sexual harassment and assault, even when it was violent, had been tolerated for so long that it seemed like much of the world found it acceptable. I thought that women could create a document with the aim of helping one another in part because I assumed that people with authority didn't care about what we had to say there. In this sense, at least, I am glad I was wrong.

15 In the weeks after the spreadsheet was exposed, my life changed dramatically. I lost friends: some who thought I had been overzealous, others who thought I had not been zealous enough. I lost my job, too. The fear of being exposed, and of the harassment that will inevitably follow, has dominated my life since. I've learned that protecting women is a position that comes with few protections itself.

This escalated when I learned Katie Roiphe would be publishing my name in a forthcoming piece in *Harper's* magazine. In early December, Roiphe had emailed me to ask if I wanted to comment for a *Harper's* story she was writing on the "feminist moment." She did not say that she knew I had created the spreadsheet. I declined and heard nothing more from Roiphe or *Harper's* until I received an email from a fact checker with questions about Roiphe's piece. "Katie identifies you as a woman widely believed to be one of the creators of the Shitty Men in Media List," the fact checker wrote. "Were you involved in creating the list? If not, how would you respond to this allegation?" The next day, a controversy ensued on Twitter after Roiphe's intention to reveal my identity was made public. People who opposed the decision by *Harper's* speculated about what would happen to me as a result of being identified. They feared that I would be threatened, stalked, raped, or killed. The outrage made it seem inevitable that my identity would be exposed even before the Roiphe piece ran. All of this was terrifying. I still don't know what kind of future awaits me now that I've stopped hiding.

But over the past months I've also had many long, frank conversations with other journalists, men and women, about sexual harassment and assault in our industry. Many came to me with stories of their own abuse, some of which they had been too afraid to add to the spreadsheet, even anonymously. Others told me that they had seen their own attacker or harasser on the document and that they hadn't put him there. That meant that what that person had done to them, he had done to other people, too. In some of these conversations, we spent hours teasing out how these men, many of whom we knew to be intelligent and capable of real kindness, could behave so crudely and cruelly toward us. And this is another toll that sexual harassment can take on women: It can make you spend hours dissecting the psychology of the kind of men who do not think about your interiority much at all.

A lot of us are angry in this moment, not just at what happened to us but at the realization of the depth and frequency of these behaviors and the ways that so many of us have been drafted, wittingly and unwittingly, into complicity. But we're being challenged to imagine how we would prefer things to be. This feat of imagination is about not a prescriptive dictation of acceptable sexual behaviors but the desire for a kinder, more respectful, and more equitable world. There is something that's changed: Suddenly, men have to think about women, our inner lives and experiences of their own behavior, quite a bit. That may be one step in the right direction.

Last year, I wrote that women just recounting their experiences of sexism did not seem like enough. I wanted action, legislation, measurable markers of change. Now I think that the task at hand might be more rudimentary than I assumed: The experience of making the spreadsheet has shown me that it is still explosive, radical, and productively dangerous for women to say what we mean. But this doesn't mean that I've lowered my hopes. Like a lot of feminists, I think about how women can build power, help one another, and work toward justice. But it is less common for us to examine the ways we might wield the power we already have. Among the most potent of these powers is the knowledge of our own experiences. The women who used the spreadsheet, and who spread it to others, used this power in a special way, and I'm thankful to all of them.

RESPONDING TO READING

1. What are "whisper networks"? How was Donegan's spreadsheet supposed to solve a problem that these networks couldn't solve? Why do you think it backfired?
2. In paragraph 7, Donegan writes, "the spreadsheet made a presumption that is still seen as radical: That it is men, not women, who are responsible for men's sexual misconduct." What does she mean? How have women been blamed for the sexual misconduct committed against them?

Rhetorical Analysis

In paragraph 13, Donegan repeats the word *naïve* four times to describe herself. Why does she do this? Does this strategy strengthen or weaken her credibility? Explain.

Writing with Sources

Search online for the latest lists of famous men accused of sexual harassment. What do these lists have in common? How do they describe the accusations? Do they support their claims with evidence? Write an essay in which you answer these questions.

7.9 Katie Roiphe, "The Other Whisper Network"

A journalist and novelist, Katie Roiphe (1968–) is a professor of journalism at New York University and the director of the NYU Cultural Reporting and Criticism Program. Her work has appeared in such publications as *Esquire, Harper's*, the *Los Angeles Times, The New York Times, Slate, Tin House, Vogue*, and *The Washington Post*. She is the author of several books, including, most recently, *The Violet Hour: Great Writers at the End* (2016). In the following essay, Roiphe examines what she calls the "other whisper network."

BEFORE YOU READ

Do you have a group of people with whom you gossip? What is it about these people that makes you trust them with sensitive information?

Katie Roiphe "The Other Whisper Network"

No one would talk to me for this piece. Or rather, more than twenty women talked to me, sometimes for hours at a time, but only after I promised to leave out their names, and give them what I began to call deep anonymity. This was strange, because what they were saying did not always seem that extreme. Yet here in my living room, at coffee shops, in my inbox and on my voicemail, were otherwise outspoken female novelists, editors, writers, real estate agents, professors, and journalists of various ages so afraid of appearing politically insensitive that they wouldn't put their names to their thoughts, and I couldn't blame them.

Of course, the prepublication frenzy of Twitter fantasy and fury about this essay, which exploded in early January, is Exhibit A for why nobody wants to speak openly. Before the piece was even finished, let alone published, people were calling me "pro-rape," "human scum," a "harridan," a "monster out of Stephen King's 'IT,'?" a "ghoul," a "bitch," and a "garbage person"—all because of a rumor that I was planning to name the creator of the so-called Shitty Media Men list. The Twitter feminist Jessica Valenti called this prospect "profoundly shitty" and "incredibly dangerous" without having read a single word of my piece. Other tweets were more direct: "man if katie roiphe actually publishes that article she can consider her career over." "Katie Roiphe can suck my dick." With this level of thought policing, who in their right mind would try to say anything even mildly provocative or original?

For years, women confined their complaints about sexual harassment to whisper networks for fear of reprisal from men. This is an ugly truth about our recent past that we are just now beginning to grapple with. But amid this welcome reckoning, it seems that many women still fear varieties of retribution (Twitter rage, damage to their reputations, professional repercussions, and vitriol from friends) for speaking out—this time, from other women. They are, in other words, inadvertently creating a new whisper network. Can this possibly be a good thing?

Most of the new whisperers feel as I do, exhilarated by the moment, by the long-overdue possibility of holding corrupt and bullying men such as Harvey Weinstein, Charlie Rose, and Matt Lauer to account for their actions. They strongly share some of its broader goals: making it possible for women to work unbothered and unharassed even outside the bubble of Hollywood and the media, breaking down the structures that have historically protected powerful men. Yet they are also slightly uneasy at the weird energy behind this movement, a weird energy it is sometimes hard to pin down.

Here are some things these professional women said to me on the condition 5
that their names be withheld:

> I think "believe all women" is silly. Women are unreliable narrators also. I understand how hard it is to come forward, but I just don't buy it. It's a sentimental view of women. . . . I think there is more regretted consent than anyone is willing to say out loud.

> If someone had sent me the Media Men list ten years ago, when I was twenty-five, I would have called a harmlessly enamored guy a stalker and a sloppy drunken encounter sexual assault. I'd hate myself now for wrecking two lives.

> One thing people don't say is that power is an aphrodisiac. . . . To pretend otherwise is dishonest.

> What seems truly dangerous to me is the complete disregard the movement shows for a sacred principle of the American criminal justice system: the presumption of innocence. I come from Mexico, whose judicial system relied, until 2016, on the presumption of guilt, which translated into people spending decades, sometimes lifetimes, in jail before even seeing a judge.

> I have never felt sexually harassed. I said this to someone the other day, and she said, "I am sure you are wrong."

> Al Franken asked for an investigation and he should have been allowed to have it; the facts are still ambiguous, the sources were sketchy.

> Why didn't I get hit on? What's wrong with me? #WhyNotMeToo

> I think #MeToo is a potentially valuable tool that is degraded when women appropriate it to encompass things like "creepy DMs" or "weird lunch 'dates.'" And I do not think touching a woman's back justifies a front page in the *New York Times* and the total annihilation of someone's career.

I have a long history with this feeling of not being able to speak. In the early Nineties, death threats were phoned into Shakespeare and Company, an Upper

West Side bookstore where I was scheduled to give a reading from my book *The Morning After.* That night, in front of a jittery crowd and a sprinkling of police, I read a passage comparing the language in the date-rape pamphlets given out on college campuses to Victorian guides to conduct for young ladies. When I read at universities, students who considered themselves feminists shouted me down. It was an early lesson in the chilling effect of feminist orthodoxy.

But social media has enabled a more elaborate intolerance of feminist dissenters, as I just personally experienced. Twitter, especially, has energized the angry extremes of feminism in the same way it has energized Trump and his supporters: the loudest, angriest, most simplifying voices are elevated and rendered normal or mainstream.

In 1996, a six-year-old boy with Coke-bottle glasses, Johnathan Prevette, was suspended from school for sexual harassment after kissing a little girl on the cheek. This was widely interpreted as a sign of excess: as the *New York Times* put it, a "doctrine meant to protect against sexual harassment might have reached a damaging level of absurdity." Yet I wonder what would happen today. Wouldn't feminists be tweeting, "Don't first grade girls have a right to feel safe?" Wouldn't the new whisperers keep quiet?

One thing that makes it hard to engage with the feminist moment is the sense of great, unmanageable anger. Given what men have gotten away with for centuries, this anger is understandable. Yet it can also lead to an alarming lack of proportion. Rebecca Traister, one of the smartest and most prominent voices of the #MeToo movement, writes:

> The rage that many of us are feeling doesn't necessarily correspond with the severity of the trespass: Lots of us are on some level as incensed about the guy who looked down our shirt at a company retreat as we are about Weinstein, even if we can acknowledge that there's something nuts about that, a weird overreaction.

10 At first glance, this seems honest and insightful of her. She seems, for a moment, to recognize the energy that is unnerving some of us, an anger not interested in making distinctions between Harvey Weinstein and the man looking down your shirt—an anger that is, as Traister herself puts it, "terrifyingly out of control." But weirdly, she also seems to be fine with it, even roused. When Trump supporters let their anger run terrifyingly out of control, we are alarmed, and rightly so. Perhaps Traister should consider that "I am so angry I am not thinking straight" is not the best mood in which to radically envision and engineer a new society.

It would be one thing if collapsing the continuum of bad behaviors happened only in moments of overshoot recognized by everyone. But I am afraid that this collapse is an explicit part of this new ideology. The need to differentiate between smaller offenses and assault is not interesting to a certain breed of Twitter feminist; it makes them impatient, suspicious. The deeper attitude toward due process is: don't bother me with trifles! (One of the editors of *n+1,* Dayna Tortorici, tweets: "I get the queasiness of no due process. But . . . losing your job isn't death or prison.")

The widely revered feminist Rebecca Solnit made a related argument in a 2014 interview, speaking in the immediate wake of California's Isla Vista mass shooting. "I think it's important that we look at all this stuff together," she said. "It begins with these microaggressions; it ends with rape and murder." Solnit is not arguing literally that all arrogant men will go on to sexual assault. But by connecting condescending men and rapists as part of the same wellspring of male contempt for women, she renders the idea of proportion irrelevant, and lends an alluring drama to the fight against mansplaining. She gives a gloss of mainstream respectability and intellectual cachet to the dangerous idea that distinctions between Weinstein and a man who looks down someone's shirt don't ultimately matter.

Because of the anger animating the movement, incidents that might otherwise seem outrageous become acceptable or normal to us. The Shitty Media Men list, the anonymously crowd-sourced spreadsheet chronicling sexual misconduct in the publishing world, is a good example. If we think of how we would feel about a secretly circulating, anonymously crowd-sourced list of Muslims who might blow up planes, the strangeness of the document snaps into focus. And yet the *Guardian* described the list as an attempt "to take control of the narrative by speaking out," while the *Washington Post* said "the point was community." According to The Awl, "a few false positives is probably an acceptable price," and Mashable opined: "Maybe the women accessing it will see a name and feel a little less crazy, a little more validated in knowing that weird interaction they had with that media guy in a bar was, in fact, creepy." There is something chilling about circulating lists like this, with their shadowy accusations capable of ruining reputations and careers, simply so that a woman can be sure that a weird interaction she had at a bar with a media guy was, in fact, creepy. ("It feels Maoist," says one of the deeply anonymous, while others question whether the list was ever designed to remain clandestine in the first place.)

To do a close reading of the list: some of the offenses on the spreadsheet ("creepy DMs," "weird lunch 'dates,'" "leering," "flirting," "violent language," and "leading on multiple women online") seem not quite substantial or rare enough to put into the category of sexual misconduct. I am not even sure they merit a warning to a hopeful young employee. I have graduate students who go on to work for these sorts of publications, and I am very mother-hen-ish about them. But I can't imagine sitting with one of my smart, ambitious students in my office, lined with shelves of books like *The Second Sex* and *A Room of One's Own* and *I Love Dick* and *The Argonauts,* saying, "Before you go work there, I just want to warn you, that guy might leer at you." I would worry I was being condescending, treating her like a child who doesn't know how to handle herself in the world.

15 I am not trying to suggest that the list makers don't understand the difference in scale between leering and assault, but rather that the blurring of common (if a little sleazy) behavior and serious sexual harassment reveals a lot about how they think. For them, the world is overrun with leering monsters you have to steer around, as if in a video game. And if some of us seem overly occupied with problems of scale, with separating small gross moments from larger criminal ones, it is because we think the very idea of women's power is at stake.

One man on the spreadsheet—a writer with no authority over anyone, and a drinker himself—is accused of the following: "targets very drunk women." To me, the verb "target" is eloquent of the motives and the mind-set of the list's creators. Why is hitting on someone, even with the third drink in your hand, *targeting*? Surely some of the women are *targeting* him back, or *targeting* someone else—the tall guy with a paperback tucked into his jacket pocket, maybe, on the other side of the room. However one feels about the health of drinkers who hang around till the last minutes of the party consorting with other drinkers, I am not sure you can accurately frame this as political oppression. Among other things, the verb makes a series of sexist assumptions about how helpless and passive the women (I mean, targets) at the party are.

In one of the sexual harassment stories in *New York* magazine's The Cut, Emma Cline describes a drunken evening during which the head of a literary organization sits too close to her in a cab and asks for her number on the way home from a party. ("Why is this a story?" one of the deeply anonymous says.) Granted, we're now used to the endless mediation of screens in our personal lives. Still, one wonders when someone asking for your phone number became an aggressive and dehumanizing gesture rather than, say, annoying or awkward. In a way, asking someone for her phone number seems like asking for consent—it's *asking,* not assuming, it's reaching out, risking rejection. It begins to feel as if the endgame of this project is not bringing to account powerful sexual bullies but, as a male acquaintance puts it, the "presumptive criminalization of all male sexual initiatives."

A couple of days after my friend made this potentially outsized claim, Josephine Livingstone issued a fresh dictum in *The New Republic*: "You probably shouldn't kiss anybody without asking." She insists that everyone, not just college students, must now obtain verbal permission; all those ways you used to think you could tell whether someone wanted to kiss you six months ago no longer matter: "The world has changed, and affirmative consent is now the standard." Note the friendly yet threatening tone of a low-level secret policeman in a new totalitarian state.

Men are not entirely deluded if they sense that some of the anger is aimed at all men. Barely submerged in this project is the simmering idea that men have committed the dramatic and indefensible crime of being male. This tweet comes from Kaitlin Phillips (Twitter handle: @yoloethics), a spirited young writer about the publishing world: "It's not a revolution until we get the men to stop pitching LMAO." In The Outline, a new digital publication, Leah Finnegan writes, "Many men wonder what to do with their entitled mouths and brains at moments like this and the answer is: shut up and go away." She also tweeted, "Small, practical step to limit sex harassment: have obamacare cover castration." While this is fairly extreme, its tone is not alien to anyone who dips even briefly into Twitter or Facebook. We are alarmed at the rampant and slippery Trumpian tendency to blame "all immigrants" or "all Muslims," and blaming all men seems to me only a little less ominous.

20 Traister writes about men living scared,

> the friends and colleagues self-aware enough to be uneasy, to know they're on a list somewhere or imagine that they might be. They text and call, not quite

> saying why, but leaving no doubt: They once cheated with a colleague; they once made a pass they suspect was wrong; they aren't sure if they got consent that one time. Are they condemned?

It seems that they are, because she continues: "Men have not succeeded in spite of their noxious behavior or disregard for women; in many instances, they've succeeded because of it." In this context, it's not entirely surprising when she reports her husband saying to her, "How can you even want to have sex with me at this point?"

If on some subterranean level of this conversation all men are presumed guilty, then all women are innocent, and I guess my question is, Do we really want that innocence? What is the price of it? In her prescient early-Seventies critique of the women's movement, Joan Didion wrote, "Increasingly it seemed that the aversion was to adult sexual life itself: how much cleaner to stay forever children." She went on to object to a feminist idea of sex that assumed women were, in her memorable phrase, "wounded birds."

Didion's phrase rang in my mind as I read Rebecca Solnit's comment in the interview quoted earlier:

> Every woman, every day, when she leaves her house, starts to think about safety. Can I go here? Should I go out there?. . . Do I need to find a taxi? Is the taxi driver going to rape me? You know, women are so hemmed in by fear of men, it profoundly limits our lives.

(To this, one of the deeply anonymous says, "I feel blessed to live in a society where you are free to walk through the city at night. I just don't think those of us who are privileged white women with careers are really that afraid.")

The idea of this ubiquitous, overwhelming fear is repeatedly conjured and dramatized by Twitter feminists. In one of her pieces, Rebecca Traister complains about a man who was fired many years ago from *Harper's Magazine* following an instance of sexual misconduct and now writes for *New York.* She does not mention that he has worked uneventfully in two offices since then. Moira Donegan (former Twitter handle: @MegaMoira; current handle: @MoiraDonegan), the creator of the Shitty Media Men list, tweeted:

> What about the women at New York who feel uncomfortable working with him? Why is their ability to feel safe at work less important than his second chance? It's their first chance.

The man, as Traister herself says, has no women working under him. He 25
does not work in the office. So the looming threat of his mere existence to the safety of the young *New York* employees seems somewhat overblown. I can't help thinking it is @MegaMoira here who is endowing him with a power he doesn't have, and at the same time, not giving those allegedly scared and unsafe young women at the magazine enough credit: Why should they care about a writer puttering at home?

The rage can at times feel like bloodlust. In the essay she wrote about creating the list, Donegan describes her "desire for a kinder, more respectful, and more equitable world."[1] However, after the list came out but before Lorin Stein resigned as editor of *The Paris Review,* she tweeted: "every profile of Lorin Stein calls him 'skinny and bespectacled' but here's the thing: he's not that skinny." She added: "I guess 'bespectacled, bald, and busting out [of] the bespoke shirts he's still having made with 15 year old measurements' doesn't have the same ring to it." Later, these tweets were deleted. But if we could think in less gendered terms for a moment, one could reasonably ask: Who is harassing whom?

While I was writing this essay, one of the anonymous emailed me a piece Donegan wrote in *The New Inquiry* about the devastating night of Trump's victory. She had hosted an election gathering, and as the results came in, the men were drinking tequila out of a penis-shaped shot glass, and laughing and making jokes as the women cried and clutched one another. Instead of thinking about choosing new friends, she ends with a blanket indictment of men and a blow for the cause:

> Here is what the last few days have reminded me: white men, even those on the left, are so safe, so insulated from the policies of a reactionary presidency, that many of them view politics as entertainment, a distraction without consequences, in which they get to indulge their vanity by fantasizing that they are on the side of good. . . . The morning after the election, I found the penis-shaped shot glass in my kitchen and threw it against the wall. I am not proud of this, but it felt good to destroy something a white man loved.

Can you see why some of us are whispering? It is the sense of viciousness lying in wait, of violent hate just waiting to be unfurled, that leads people to keep their opinions to themselves, or to share them only with close friends. I recently saw a startling reminder of this when Wesley Yang published an insightful and conflicted piece in *Tablet* called "Farewell to a Scoundrel," about former *Paris Review* editor Lorin Stein and the feminist moment.

I teach Yang's work to my graduate students, so I know a little bit about him. He is a Korean-American man who has written memorably about being viewed as a sexual neuter by the white women in his social circle. Now he is married with a child. Shortly after the *Tablet* piece appeared, @yoloethics started tweeting:

> DAILY REMINDER that the men who can't for the life of them figure out how to get fucked are more dangerous than those who do.
>
> All I want for Christmas is a list of Male Media Virgins!! Having a child does not exempt you from this list, men who direct their repressed sexual rage at women.

30 In another tweet, she made fun of Yang for publishing in *Tablet*. After reading these, I was curious about who she was, and discovered that her work had appeared in places such as *n+1, Artforum,* and *Vice,* and that in other moods she tweets about her Margiela boots and fur coat; her feed basically mixes the frivolity of *Sex and the City* with the viciousness of Breitbart.

I wouldn't normally quote so much Twitter, but the extremes of vitriol unloosed in this conversation find their purest expression there. Some of these

[1] Donegan published her essay on The Cut on January 10. In her account, the decision to identify herself as the creator of the list was prompted by her perception of my intention to reveal her identity.

seemingly fringe figures are actually writers and editors who publish in places like *The New Republic* and *n+1,* who are involved in setting the tone of the conversation; one can very easily connect the dots between their views and those of more mainstream feminists. I have a feeling that if one met @yoloethics or the rest of her Twitter cohort in person, they would seem normal, funny, smart, well read. But the vicious energy and ugliness is there beneath the fervor of our new reckoning, adeptly disguised as exhilarating social change. It feels as if the feminist moment is, at times, providing cover for vindictiveness and personal vendettas and office politics and garden-variety disappointment, that what we think of as purely positive social change is also, for some, blood sport. The grammar is better in these feminist tweets, but they are nonetheless recognizably Trumpian.

In some ways, if we take the imaginative leap, the world Twitter feminists are envisioning—scrubbed clean of anyone hitting on anyone, asking for phone numbers, leaning over to kiss someone without seeking verbal permission—seems not that substantively far away from the world of Mike Pence saying he will never eat alone with a woman who is not his wife. This odd convergence reveals something critical about the moment: the complicated ways in which we may be snatching defeat from the jaws of victory.

Part of what bothers many of the people I talked to is the tone of moral purity. As a culture, we seem to be in the midst of dividing ourselves into the flawless and the fallen, the morally correct and the damned. Are the Twitter feminists perfect? Because I know I am not. A former student of mine, Thomas Chatterton Williams, wrote about this strange bifurcation on (of course) Facebook. On social media, he declares,

> I've come to learn that everyone is perfectly anti-racist, completely woke . . . that every man is a heroic feminist who would have singlehandedly put a halt to all workplace lechery (if only he'd been there!). It's a good thing to learn this on social media, because in real life I was frequently meeting complicated and flawed individuals.

Inherent in this performance of moral purity is the idea of judging other people before learning (or without bothering to learn) all the facts. Even when we knew little or nothing about what Garrison Keillor did, people felt no obligation to suspend judgment. Instead they talked confidently about what people *like* Garrison Keillor do, things they thought or imagined that he did, based on unspecified accusations from unknown sources (multiple allegations of "inappropriate behavior"). The absence of details or tangible information invites us to concoct our own opinions and fantasies and speculations based on our own experience of what someone has done to us, or on our impressions of what men in power do.

I am guilty of this behavior myself. Not long ago, I was sitting on a friend's couch, 35
and she was talking about Lorin Stein, an acquaintance of mine for many years, with a special intensity. She also knew Lorin Stein, who was then still the editor of *The Paris Review*. Of course, Stein has since resigned under a cloud of acknowledged sexual misconduct. I'm not equipped to investigate or arbitrate acknowledged misconduct or any other allegations that may surface in the future. I simply want to talk about what happened on this couch. My friend was drinking chamomile tea and telling me second- and thirdhand stories about him with what, for a minute, I

thought was gusto, but might have been political concern. "I like Lorin," she told me. "I don't have a personal stake in this." She then informed me that he had sexually harassed two interns at Farrar, Straus and Giroux, where he had worked before his *Paris Review* tenure, leading to hushed-up, sealed settlements. She delivered this piece of highly specific information so confidently that I did not stop and think, even though I teach in a journalism department: Is this factually correct?

As we were talking, I got caught up in her enthusiasm. It's true that when I thought about the actual Lorin Stein, it was more about words on the page—about his serializing excerpts of Rachel Cusk's *Outline,* for example, which I had stopped everything to read. But as she was talking, I was completely drawn in. I found myself wanting to say something to please her. The outrage grew and expanded and exhilarated us. It was as though we weren't talking about Lorin Stein anymore, we were talking about all the things we have ever been angry about, the ways men have insulted or offended or overlooked or mistreated us, or the way beautiful women are rewarded and then not rewarded. I felt as though I were joining a club, felt a warming sense of social justice, felt that this was a weighty, important thing we were engaging in.

The next morning, I related the troubling new fact of the FSG settlements to a journalist friend. Could it be true? She checked it very thoroughly and called that evening to tell me she could find no truth at all to the settlement rumors.[2] I was disgusted with myself for repeating what was probably a lie about someone I liked and had nothing against. What was wrong with me?

Stein admitted to consensual relationships with writers and employees and women professionally connected to the *Review* during his time there.[3] He admitted to creating the kind of sexually charged workplace that may have been viewed as acceptable during the heyday of, say, the *Partisan Review* (or George Plimpton's original *Paris Review*) but is now recognized as demoralizing and wrong. He vehemently denies that either his literary tastes or personnel decisions were affected by this. It can be hard to disentangle one man and the things he may or may not have done from hundreds of years of sexist oppression. Yet I am reminded of something Zephyr Teachout wrote about the mainstream liberal rush to condemn Al Franken: "As citizens, we should all be willing to stay ambivalent while the facts are gathered and we collect our thoughts."

In thinking about *The Paris Review,* I found myself agreeing with an argument of Rebecca Traister's: "The thing that unites these varied revelations isn't necessarily sexual harm, but *professional* harm and power abuse." Creating a fair workplace is what matters here, and if *The Paris Review* was somehow inhospitable to women,

[2]According to an FSG spokesperson, there was one "incident of inappropriate conduct" involving Lorin Stein during his years at the publishing house. (He resigned as an editor at large last December.) The spokesperson denied, however, that there had been any complaints from interns or any sealed settlements.

[3]In his letter of resignation submitted to the Paris Review board, Stein professed to having "dated or expressed a sexual interest in women who had professional connections to the Review—past contributors, interns, and writers who might one day submit work to the magazine." A member of the board, who declined to be identified, told Harper's Magazine, "It is my understanding that Lorin did date interns after they were interns, but not while they were serving in that capacity."

that is truly disturbing. But something was still bothering me. I couldn't help noticing that female writers flourished so conspicuously in the pages of Lorin Stein's *Paris Review,* especially new or younger women writers. Of the seven prestigious Plimpton Prizes for emerging writers awarded on Stein's watch, five went to women. One of those women, Ottessa Moshfegh, who was nominated for a Booker Prize a few years after Stein first published her, told me, "Lorin is a brilliant editor, and neither my gender nor his sexuality ever seemed to have anything to do with how our excellent working relationship developed." Another of the previously unknown writers that Stein promoted, Amie Barrodale, wrote me the following intimate account of his editing a story it took her four years to produce:

> He pointed out a major problem I hadn't been aware of—halfway through the story, when it became emotionally challenging for me to write, all the life and humor drained out of the voice. . . . He pointed delicately to a thing I was afraid to say. He didn't know what it was, but he knew there was something I was withholding. . . . For me somehow this was impossible to write, but I trusted him and wrote it, and I could immediately see 1) it needed to be there and 2) it'd lost its power over me. . . . One thing he also did was catch me every time I was faking it. He'd underline a false phrase, something contrived with a squiggly line. What I was most grateful for was that he recognized what was great about the story.

40 Whatever its boys' club ambience under George Plimpton, *The Paris Review* under Lorin Stein was devoted to writers such as Ann Beattie, Lydia Davis, Vivian Gornick, and Amparo Dávila. Stein discovered or promoted younger talents such as Emma Cline, Alexandra Kleeman, Isabella Hammad, Angela Flournoy, and Kristin Dombek. When you bury yourself in the issues themselves, it's clear that *The Paris Review* was a fruitful and vibrant and professionally useful place for women writers. None of this fits neatly into the politicized narrative. ("Lorin Stein can only view women writers as sexual objects," a professor who never worked with him told me confidently.) But it is also true. The reality of *The Paris Review* on a Tuesday afternoon is messier and more complicated and confusing than our moralizing politics would have it.

The night the *New York Times* broke the news of Stein's resignation, I was with one of the deeply anonymous women in a coffee shop, and after I left she ran out and caught up to me on the dark street to tell me about it. When I got home, I saw that @MegaMoira had tweeted a photo of the piece with the words, "champagne anyone." I thought of the email Lorin had sent me when my book on writers' deaths, *The Violet Hour,* came out. It was such a strange, private project, but in a few lines he made it vivid again to me, renewed and energized me on a long winter afternoon to sit down and start something new. However one feels about the end of an era at *The Paris Review,* it doesn't seem like a time for celebration.

To hold a lot of opposites in our minds seems to be what the moment calls for, to tolerate and be honest about the ambiguities. If we are going through a true reckoning, there should be space for more authentically diverging points of view, a full range of feelings, space to hash through what is and is not sexual misconduct, which is an important and genuinely confusing question about which reasonable people can and will disagree. In the meantime, I take out a copy of *The Paris Review,* with two women sunbathing on a neon-green beach on the cover, which contains my interview with Janet Malcolm, something Lorin edited and published and pushed to fruition under difficult circumstances. In this interview, Malcolm talked to me about how hard it was to be a woman writer in the Sixties, when *The New Yorker* gave her a home décor column, and almost talked to me about how hard it was to be a mother and a writer, but said we would have to go to a dark bar for that conversation. I wanted to say to @MegaMoira, let's save the champagne for later.

I can see how the drama of this moment is enticing. It offers a grandeur, a sweeping purity to our possibly flawed and fumbling and ambivalent selves. It justifies all our failings and setbacks and mediocrities; it wasn't us, it was men, or the patriarchy, holding us back, objectifying us. It is easier to think, for instance, that we were discriminated against than that our story wasn't good enough or original enough to be published in *The Paris Review,* or even that it did not meet the editor's highly idiosyncratic yet widely revered tastes. Or that a man said something awful and sexual to us while we were working on a television show, and we got depressed and could never again achieve what we might have. And yet do we really in our hearts believe that is the whole story? Is this a complete and satisfying explanation? There is, of course, sexism, which looms and shadows us in all kinds of complicated and unmappable ways, but is it the totalizing force, the central organizing narrative, of our lives? This is where the movement veers from important and exhilarating correction into implausibility and rationalization. (One of the deeply anonymous says, "This seems like such a boring way to look at your life.")

Source: Katie Roiphe, The Other Whisper Network, The Other Whisper Network, How Twitter feminism is bad for women, Harper's Magazine, March 2018 issue. URL: https://harpers.org/archive/2018/03/the-otherwhisper-network-2/

RESPONDING TO READING

1. In paragraph 2, Roiphe mentions "a rumor that I was planning to name the creator of the so-called Shitty Media Men list." But she doesn't actually name Moira Donegan (p. 240) as the list's creator until paragraph 24, where she seems to name her almost as an aside. Why does Roiphe delay and then downplay her naming of Donegan? What is her point?
2. In paragraph 42, Roiphe writes, "To hold a lot of opposites in our minds seems to be what the moment calls for, to tolerate and be honest about the ambiguities." What does she mean? Is Roiphe's call to action possible to achieve? Explain.

Rhetorical Analysis

In her essay, Roiphe quotes numerous anonymous sources. Why does she do this? Do you think that she could have accomplished her purpose in some other way? If so, how?

Writing with Sources

Search online for Roiphe's NPR interview from February 10, 2018, about this essay. How does the interview help contextualize the ideas Roiphe explores in her essay? Write an essay in which you respond to one of Roiphe's claims, referring to Roiphe's essay and interview. Try to incorporate current examples into your discussion.

7.10 John Kirbow, "To Clarify: An Open Letter to the Men's Rights Movement, on the #MeToo Hashtag"

A U.S. Army veteran, blogger, linguist, and human rights activist, John Kirbow explores issues related to women's rights, Islamic culture, and community building in his work. He is the founder of *Reason Revival*, whose mission is to promote "reason-based compassion" in political systems around the world. In the following open letter, Kirbow addresses men's rights against the backdrop of the #MeToo movement.

BEFORE YOU READ

What do you know about the men's rights movement? What connotations does "men's rights" bring to mind? Are they positive or negative? Why?

To Clarify: An Open Letter to the Men's Rights Movement, on the #MeToo Hashtag

We've mostly all seen by now the emerging #MeToo hashtag.

Here is a common exchange that seems to be occurring in the midst of this long-overdue conversation:

> **MRM/manosphere dweller** (and many men in general): *"But what about men's issues? What about men who have been sexually harassed?"*
>
> **Leftist/feminist** (and many women in general): *"Fuck off. You're dismissing their issues!"*

MRM/manosphere dweller: *"Fuckin' SJW!"*[1]

Leftist/feminist: *"Fucking misogynistic shitlord. Go home Fuckboy!"*

Perhaps a guidebook may be helpful in avoiding this unnecessary fallout. I write this Open Letter without judgment. It's easy to hit a tripwire or talk at cross points when these issues cross into social media, or even everyday conversation. This *Open Letter* is a pocket guide to taking a step back. And reevaluating the situation, with some possible rope for certain men who find themselves caught in the bad end of this crossfire. It's rope to not only climb out of a hole, but build a rope bridge over these troubled waters, and perhaps make new friends and allies across the social justice divide. *Please read on.*

IF I WERE TO TRY AND EXPLAIN THIS IN THE LOCAL BAR, IN TWO MINUTES
The following is a summary of my thoughts on this matter, if I had to sum it up over a beer in the local pub:

Yes, we should address all forms of sexual assault, including against men.

But we need to avoid doing so in a way that dilutes or blurs the clarity and importance of women's issues, or in a way that robs these issues of the specificity they deserve. In other words, let women's issues stand alone, without being faded by others attaching their issues to it.

This does nothing to diminish the issues some men face, it just avoids doing a disservice to those faced by women.

It's not that men don't matter—of course we do. We're human, we hurt and feel and agonize and dream and aspire like any sentient being among the human species. To all but the most ardent subscribers of the most toxic ends of radical feminism, this is obvious; it doesn't take a Shakespeare speech from *The Merchant of Venice* to make this clear.

The key is to think in 'NonZero' terms, with a dash of human nuance: *It is not a dichotomy*, or a zero sum game. We can address all issues that affect the well-being of conscious creatures. *Let's just do so in a way that allows specific groups — especially long suppressed and widely abused groups like women—to get the voice and public attention that their issues deserve*, without being drowned or whitewashed by others making noise at its expense.

WHAT THIS LETTER ATTEMPTS TO DO

This is not merely a letter to MRM activists and 'manosphere' thinkers—it is for anyone discussing this issue, who may want to better understand why certain types of confusion and conflict on this issue exists, and how to best understand it. And for some, how to perhaps better explain it to other men.

A disclaimer to all reading this with a reflexive dismissal:

I do not fit the label of an 'SJW' (in its pejorative meaning) by any stretch of the mind. Anyone who personally knows me can likely attest to this. But I do care a great deal about *justice, compassion and listening to the voices of others*, and helping them as an ally. I fundamentally reject the absurd and archaic, almost superstitious

---

[1] Social justice warrior. [Eds.]

notion that radical ideology or political dogma of some sort is required for this, or that the Left or the Right has some moralistic monopoly on these issues of justice, compassion and human well-being. **We don't need political dogma or rigid ideology platforms to be good people and fight for justice, any more than we need religion to meditate and seek spiritual enrichment.**

Sadly, ideologues have claimed a moral monopoly on issues of human well-being. Political dogma platforms (across the Left and Right alike) have become the default setting for trying to tune into the sensible and compassionate wavelengths across a spectrum of human issues. **There's a strangely enduring notion, especially over the last several decades, that *political dogmas* or *radical ideologies* are prerequisites for tackling these issues. Or even for being good people.** I think this is one of the *most dangerously stupid and colossally ignorant ideas in modern society*, and one which will hopefully one day be more or less discarded into the streaming pile of bad ideas and superstitious thinking we've managed to shovel out of this world since the beginnings of the Enlightenment. For the moment, however, it is necessary to clarify that I am not writing this from a partisan/ideology angle. *I don't think Left or Right ideology of any particular kind is required to enrich any of the points I make below.*

That said, allow me—for practical purposes—to distance myself from any stereotypes that many Men's Rights Activists have about people who are trying to explain how to better support women's voices. Yes, I eagerly identify as a feminist in the basic sense of the word: *supporting women's equality and dignity in a still-uneven society.* This is particularly the case in how I support women's freedom and liberation around the world, especially in some of the most backward social and religious customs imaginable. Moral relativism can fuck off, now and forever. But that's a separate article of mine altogether.

I myself am not a "radical feminist," Leftist or any particular brand of radical or dogmatic ideology. I hold views across what some might define as a Liberal-Conservative spectrum, and am (as some say) politically homeless, and trans-partisan. I reject ideology platforms because I think they are stupid, tribal, and even dangerous. I believe that political dogmatism and rigid ideology—especially "platform ideology" and toxic forms of identity politics—makes human beings stupider and more cruel.

Rather, I try to use human dignity, compassion and reason—especially scientific skepticism, logic and evidence—as my guide rails for how to view the world, and how to approach different problems. **And often, the best first step is to take a step back and listen.**

MY "*TOP 5 OUTLINE*" TO HELP CLARIFY THIS ISSUE

1. Men face issues too, but we should strive to let women's voices stand out, and get the *specific attention they've long deserved* in a deeply imbalanced world of uneven power and oppressive social norms.
2. Power imbalances and the group differences in facing structural oppression are important.
3. *Groups and identity matter because people matter.*
4. In general, some groups and identities are oppressed far more than others.
5. **This does not diminish human lives in general.*

20 Here's an outline, for people to read over, think and talk thoughtfully about, discuss with one another, and perhaps invite people across gender lines to talk about, with an open mind. To learn, to hear the voices of how women feel about this issue. And to share with other men, to hopefully help clarify a few points of common misunderstanding.

Here is my current list, a Top 5, for attempting to remedy this gap as best I can.

I am a man, far removed from the experiences women face, so I don't claim by any means to be the most worthy voice to speak about this. However, this is my attempt to do so, for other men to read and honestly reflect on.

Here goes:

1. **Men face issues too, but we should strive to let women's voices stand out, and get the *specific attention they've long deserved* in a deeply imbalanced world of uneven power and oppressive social norms.** This doesn't mean we should ignore or downplay men's issues—in fact, compassion, humanity and humanism require us to do the opposite. So does the data on how to reduce crime, gangs, insurgency and suicide bombing. We need to attend to men's issues as well, but not at the expense of women's.
2. **Power imbalances and the group differences in facing structural oppression are important**. Ask most any minority. *However, of course, these distinctions about power and systemic oppression* ***do not****, and should not diminish the dignity of the human person*, or devalue their suffering merely because of their race or gender or historic identity. If a man is getting shafted by a system of any kind, or robbed of due process, wrongly accused, prejudged, or hurtfully mistreated, we should all stand up for him.

   This is Humanism 101. If this has to be explained to someone, we're off to a very bad start.
3. ***Groups and identity matter because people matter***. *Human beings matter—full stop*. Human dignity is the basis for caring about identity and group issues. Without the idea of human worth, these issues fall apart. This is the basis of a secular, reason-based society. And of a compassionate civilization.
4. **In general, some groups and identities are oppressed far more than others.** Some are subject to structural oppression and inequality, far more than others. When we speak about Black Lives Matter, we are acknowledging that the basic human dignity and worth of blacks in America is not equally recognized by society and its power structures, such as police systems and the law. All lives matter, but—in the aggregate—some lives tend to be treated this way far less than others. This is why we need specificity in how we talk about certain types of oppression, and against certain groups of people. *
5. ***This does not diminish human lives in general.** The ever-annoying and totally counterproductive conflict between the phrases "Black Lives Matter" and "All Lives Matter" is a false dichotomy, and one of the most harmful ones around today. The idea of *all lives being important* does not conflict

with the idea that some lives tend to be treated with less importance and value than others, or that blacks often face inequality in how our police and justice system works. One can even disagree with most of the platitudes and specifics of BLM, and still find some agreement with their main points, as explained above. The BLM vs. ALM (false) dichotomy is one of our most harmful, and we need a better roadmap.

A SHORT RECAP

To Recap, in Summary:

Acknowledging group oppression and special attention to vulnerable groups does not need to diminish the rights and worth of others. Not one bit. It just means that some groups need a particular voice, and are disproportionately oppressed.

This does not mean that individual suffering and hardship doesn't matter—it does. **And a dominant group (like men, whites, etc.) is still made up of individual human beings, who are as deserving of respect, dignity and due process as anyone else on this planet**. 25

And a Final Thought:

I've found it to be true in every culture or society I've been to around the world that many men do indeed face sexual and social ills and problems that need addressing. To make matters worse, this is often suppressed by pride and social custom. However, in these same places, the women are – often quite considerably – repressed and marginalized in a special way, one which more than warrants them a very special place in the wider conversation. The point is that they deserve a voice, a loud one, in every place in the world. They are by far one of the most underrepresented groups on the planet, and arguably always have been.

With all of that said, I sincerely hope we can build a better roadmap for more men—especially those who are turned away by mainstream brands of feminism and Leftist discourse—to talk productively about women's issues. To do so with an open heart and mind, without the entrapping of polarization, ideology and fringe extremes. It may seem difficult but it's well worthy of our efforts.

RESPONDING TO READING

1. In paragraph 22, Kirbow admits, "I am a man, far removed from the experiences women face, so I don't claim by any means to be the most worthy voice to speak about this. However, this is my attempt to do so, for other men to read and honestly reflect on." Do you think this statement adds to or detracts from his credibility? Why?
2. Starting in paragraph 23, Kirbow presents his points in a numbered list. Do you find this list convincing? What other information could Kirbow have provided to support his case?

Rhetorical Analysis

This essay (which was originally published as a blog post) is labeled an "open letter" in its title. Who is the letter's audience? Why might Kirbow have chosen this genre (along with a casual, conversational style and tone) to reach his audience? How effective is his approach?

Writing with Sources

Research the Black Lives Matter movement. How is it similar to the #MeToo movement? What are some key differences? Is Kirbow's comparison of women and marginalized racial groups accurate? Write an essay in which you answer these questions.

Widening the Focus

For Critical Reading and Writing

Referring specifically to the three readings in this chapter's Focus section (and possibly to additional sources as well), write an essay in which you answer the question, "How Do We Talk About Sexual Harassment?"

For Further Reading

The following readings can suggest additional perspectives for thinking and writing about the roles of women and men:

- Alleen Pace Nilsen, "Sexism in English: Embodiment and Language" (p. 138)
- Sarah Chevallier, "If Literature's 'Complicated Men' Were on Tinder" (p. 197)
- Lynette D'Amico, "The Unsaved" (p. 403)

For Focused Research

As part of the #MeToo movement, open conversations about sexual misconduct are happening all over the internet, but particularly on Twitter, where news often first breaks. In preparation for writing an essay about the ways in which we respond to sexual harassment, research the latest Twitter discussions about #MeToo. Consider a range of tweets written by women and men, celebrities and noncelebrities, minorities and nonminorities. What is the purpose of these tweets? Who is their audience? Do they use a combination of text, images, and/or video? To what effect? Use information from these tweets to help you develop your essay.

Beyond the Classroom

Interview three female college students and three male students. In your interviews, ask the following questions:

- What does the #MeToo movement mean to you?
- Has it impacted you personally? How?

Based on the responses to these questions, write an essay in which you consider the implications of the #MeToo movement for women and men on college campuses.

Exploring Issues and Ideas

Gender and Identity

Write an essay in response to one of the following prompts, which are suitable for assignments that require the use of outside sources as well as for assignments that are not source-based.

1. In her well-known work *A Room of One's Own,* novelist and critic Virginia Woolf observes that "any woman born with a great gift in the sixteenth century would certainly have gone crazed, shot herself, or ended her days in some lonely cottage outside the village, half witch, half wizard, feared and mocked at." Write an essay in which you discuss in what respects this statement may still apply to gifted women of your own generation or of your parents' generation. You may want to read Deborah Tannen's "Marked Women" (p. 231) before you plan your essay.
2. List all the stereotypes of women—and of men—identified in the selections you read in this chapter. Then, write an essay in which you discuss those that you think have had the most negative effects. Do you consider these stereotypes just annoying, or actually dangerous? Refer to one or two essays in this chapter to support your points.
3. Write a letter to Judy Brady in which you update (or challenge) her characterization of a wife in "Why I Want a Wife" (p. 223).
4. A number of the writers in this chapter examine current ideas about what it means to be male, what it means to be female, and what it means to be a transgender person. Write an essay in which you develop your own definitions of *male, female,* and *transgender*. You may want to consider Judy Hall's "Mommy, I'm Just Not That Kind of Girl" (p. 215), Fleda Brown's "Unruffled" (p. 218), Warren Farrell and John Gray's "The Crisis of Our Sons' Education" (p. 225), and Deborah Tannen's "Marked Women" (p. 231).
5. Several of the essays in this chapter deal with gender roles and how they influence relationships between and among men and women. Write an essay in which you discuss how gender roles have affected you. For example, do you think you have ever been held back or given an unfair advantage because of your gender?

Chapter 8
Culture and Identity

In this chapter, you will learn to:

- analyze readings about culture and identity.
- compose essays about culture and identity.

The word *culture* generally refers to an identity shared by a particular racial, religious, or ethnic group, or to an identity that is characteristic of a specific geographic region. But in many cases, cultural identity is more complicated, a concept that includes but goes beyond a person's self-identification as an African American or a Muslim or a New Yorker.

For some, cultural identity is determined by shared language or national origin or family history; others may identify with a group on the basis of gender or sexual orientation; still others identify with a particular group because of a shared interest or professional affiliation. Thus, we can talk about tech culture, Wall Street culture, skateboard culture,

Sean Pavone/Alamy Stock Photo

What point does this image of a gay pride parade in New York City make about the relationship between culture and identity?

or football culture as well as about Chinese culture, feminist culture, or gay culture.

Cultural identity can rest on a shared system of deeply held values and beliefs or simply a shared preference in personal style—for example, an affinity for body art or motorcycle gear. But regardless of how we define culture, it is important to remember that cultural identity is not always something we actively choose. For example, sometimes cultural identity is conferred upon us at birth; sometimes we identify with a culture simply out of habit; sometimes a cultural identity is imposed on us by others, determined by how others see us rather than by how we perceive ourselves.

When we examine the idea of cultural identity, we may consider whether it is possible to be loyal to two cultures or how it feels to abandon one culture and take on another. We may also consider how to maintain an individual identity while identifying with one or more groups. Finally, we may consider how loyalty to a particular culture defines an individual—and how the individual helps to define the culture.

In the Focus section of this chapter, "Do Racial Distinctions Still Matter?" (p. 297), three writers consider particular cultures in the context of ethnic and racial identity. In "Latino and Hispanic Identities Aren't the Same. They're Also Not Racial Groups" (p. 298), Victoria M. Massie examines the relationship between Latino and Hispanic cultural identities and the terms used to define them; Brent Staples explores his own complex heritage in "Why Race Isn't as 'Black' and 'White' as We Think" (p. 300); and John H. McWhorter, in "Why I'm Black, Not African American" (p. 303), compares two terms used to define his racial identity.

Della Huff/Alamy Stock Photo

What point does this image of a St. Patrick's Day parade in South Boston make about the relationship between culture and identity?

Preparing to Read and Write

As you read and prepare to write about the essays in this chapter, you may consider the following questions:

- What assumptions does the writer seem to have about his or her audience? How can you tell?
- What is the writer's primary purpose? To explore his or her own cultural identity? To criticize society's understanding of culture or race? To expose (or come to terms with) cultural stereotypes? Something else?
- What genre is the writer using? For example, is the reading a memoir, a literary work, or an argument? How do the conventions of this genre influence the writer's choices?
- What appeals does the writer use? For example, does he or she appeal primarily to emotion or to reason? Is this the most effective appeal?
- Does the writer focus on one particular culture or on culture in general?
- Is the culture the writer discusses defined by race, ethnicity, gender, sexuality, geography, vocation, or something else?
- Does the writer see his or her own culture in positive, neutral, or negative terms?
- Does the writer explore personal feelings and experiences?
- Would you describe the writer's voice as reflective, angry, resigned, or something else?
- Does the writer identify with the culture he or she discusses or feel like an outsider?
- Does the writer embrace his or her culture or try to maintain a distance from it?
- Does the writer see culture as defining him or her or as only a small part of his or her identity?
- Has the writer chosen to identify with a particular culture, or has his or her cultural identity been determined by how others view him or her?
- Does the writer challenge the way in which a culture is commonly perceived?
- Which of the various writers' ideas about culture and identity are most similar? Which are most like your own?

Shared Writing

Culture and Identity

Consider your own cultural identity. With which cultural groups do you identify? Why? Have you ever tried to fit in to a culture to which you wanted to belong?

8.1 Brenda Cárdenas, "Lecciones de lengua[1]" [Poetry]

An associate professor of English at the University of Wisconsin, Milwaukee, Brenda Cárdenas writes poetry in both English and Spanish. The former poet laureate of Milwaukee, she is the author of two poetry collections and a coeditor of two poetry anthologies. From the collection *Boomerang* (2009), the following poem considers how bilingualism informs a particular worldview.

BEFORE YOU READ

Are you, or is someone you know, bilingual? How do you think the ability to speak multiple languages shapes identity?

Lecciones de lengua

She is proud of her papá
because he comes
to their little grey school,
converted from army barracks,
to teach español
to Mrs. Brenda's fifth grade.
And that means they don't
have to listen to that awful
Señora Beister on TV
with her screech owl version
of "Las mañanitas"[2] and her annoying
forefinger to the ear,
        Escuchen[3]
and then to the lips,
        y repitan.[4]
He teaches them to order

[1]Spanish for "language lessons." [Eds.]
[2]A traditional Mexican birthday song. [Eds.]
[3]Spanish for "listen." [Eds.]
[4]Spanish for "and repeat." [Eds.]

Coca-Cola en el restaurán—[5]
        Señor, quisiera una Coca, por favor—[6]
and the names of all the utensils—
        cuchara, cuchillo, tenedor.[7]
The children look at him funny
when he picks up the knife.
Next week he will demonstrate
the bullfights he watched
in Mexico when he was muy chiquitito.[8]
He will choose a boy to snort, stomp,
charge the red cloth
that Papá will snap
at his side as he dodges
the sharp-horned strike,
stabs invisible swords
into the boy's hide
        and makes the children laugh.

RESPONDING TO READING

1. Is this poem's central figure the girl or her father? Explain.
2. Spanish words are sprinkled throughout this mostly English poem. Why do you suppose the poet chose not to define these words?

Rhetorical Analysis

What is the significance of the last line of the poem? How is humor important to the culture being described?

8.2 Reza Aslan, "Praying for Common Ground at the Christmas-Dinner Table"

A professor of creative writing at the University of California, Riverside, Reza Aslan (1972–) is a religion scholar and writer. The cofounder and chief creative officer of the media company BoomGen Studios, he is the author of several books, including, most recently, *God: A Human*

---

[5]Spanish for "in the restaurant." [Eds.]

[6]Spanish for "Sir, I would like a Coke, please." [Eds.]

[7]Spanish for "spoon, knife, fork." [Eds.]

[8]Spanish for "very tiny." [Eds.]

History (2017). In the following essay, Aslan ponders how different religions help build a shared identity.

BEFORE YOU READ

Do all your family members share the same religion, the same general belief system and values, or the same political views? If not, what values do they have in common?

Praying for Common Ground at the Christmas-Dinner Table

The prayer is what tripped us up. It was the first Christmas that my wife and I hosted in our home, and for a good 10 minutes, our two families stood around the dinner table arguing about how to thank God for the meal we were about to eat.

My mother, a born-again Christian, wanted our prayer addressed to Jesus. It was Christmas, after all; we were celebrating Jesus' miraculous birth. "Shouldn't we at least pray to him?" she asked sheepishly.

My little sister, a devout Muslim, loves and admires Jesus as a prophet and messenger of God. But she had no intention of praying to him. She adjusted her hijab[1] and mumbled the Shahada[2] under her breath ("I confess there is no god but God") as a kind of talisman to protect her against my mother's "heresy."

My middle sister, a militant atheist, was supremely annoyed with the entire spectacle. She found it hard to believe we were standing around the dinner table, watching the food go cold, as we deliberated which imaginary deity we should pray to before we could start eating. "Why don't we just pray to Santa Claus?" she said. No one else found that funny.

My wife's family, evangelicals from Pittsburgh, was mostly confused about 5
why we were serving rice and shish kebabs with our Christmas turkey and mashed potatoes.

Finally, my wife came up with an idea. "Why don't we let Reza decide?" she suggested, volunteering me to be the referee in this prayer match.

I suppose her suggestion made some sense. I am a scholar of religions who has dedicated his life to studying the faith traditions of the world and then teaching those traditions to people who do not share them. For me, this first Christmas at the Aslan household was practically field research. As I watched these people from diverse religious and cultural backgrounds navigate a holiday with quite specific religious and cultural associations, I was tempted to pull out my notebook and begin jotting down my observations.

My family is, in many ways, emblematic of America in the 21st century: multiethnic, multicultural, multireligious. I am a Muslim from Iran. My wife is a Christian from western Pennsylvania. That may seem an incongruous coupling. But when we first met, we realized almost immediately that we shared the same values and worldview, even though we expressed those things in a different spiritual language.

---

[1]A veil worn by some Muslim women. [Eds.]

[2]The Islamic creed that proclaims Muhammad as God's prophet. [Eds.]

That's all religion is, really: a language made up of symbols and metaphors that allow people to communicate, to themselves and to others, the ineffable experience of faith. I already spoke my wife's spiritual language (Christianity); I taught her mine (Islam). And now we are a spiritually "bilingual" household. Actually, we are multilingual, considering we are committed to teaching our children all the spiritual languages of the world so that they can choose for themselves which ones, if any, they prefer in communicating their own individual faith experience.

10 But that is also the reason the prayer was tripping us up that first Christmas together. We were having a difficult time understanding one another's spiritual languages, let alone coming to a consensus on which language to use. It reminded me of a Sufi[3] parable about four hungry travelers from different countries who are trying to decide what to buy with the single coin they hold in common. The Persian wants to spend the coin on *angur*; the Turk, on *uzum*; the Arab, on *inab*; and the Greek, on *stafil*. Confusion turns to anger as the four travelers argue among themselves. It takes a passing linguist to explain to them that they are all, in fact, asking for the same thing: grapes.

The parable gave me an idea. "Let's skip the formal prayer and just tell each other what we are grateful for," I suggested. "What we are anxious about. What we hope for in the coming year."

We took turns going around the circle: Muslim, Christian, atheist. And, as I expected, we ended up expressing similar dreams and aspirations for ourselves and our loved ones, similar fears and anxieties, similar gratitude for all that we've been given. As with the hapless travelers in the Sufi parable, we realized that we were all feeling the same way; we were just expressing that feeling in different spiritual languages.

Once the prayer was settled, it was time to sit down for a traditional Christmas meal of turkey and kebabs.

RESPONDING TO READING

1. In paragraph 9, Aslan introduces a definition of *religion* with "That's all religion is, really. . . ." Do you think his definition is accurate? Does it make sense? How would you define *religion*?
2. Do you think Aslan is overly optimistic about the ability of those with different religious beliefs to find common ground? Why or why not?

Rhetorical Analysis

In paragraph 7, Aslan summarizes his scholarly credentials. Why does he include this information? Is it necessary? Explain.

---

[3]Pertaining to Sufism, Islamic mysticism. [Eds.]

Writing with Sources

Research the beliefs and values of a religion other than yours, and then write an essay in which you identify and discuss the common ground that exists between that religion and your own religion or belief system.

8.3 Priscilla Frank, "Dismantling Stereotypes about Asian-American Identity through Art"

An arts and culture reporter for the *Huffington Post*, Priscilla Frank writes about pop culture, artistic depictions of gender and sexuality, and the work of minority and culturally diverse artists. Her work has appeared in such publications as the *Atlanta Voice, News Deeply,* and *Yahoo*. In the following essay, she describes how a group of artists is reimagining its culture.

BEFORE YOU READ

What stereotypes are associated with your own ethnic group? Do you see these stereotypes as benign or harmful?

Dismantling Stereotypes about Asian-American Identity through Art

Last week, a *New York Magazine* piece by Andrew Sullivan received legitimate blowback for a final paragraph that described Asian Americans as "among the most prosperous, well-educated, and successful ethnic groups in America."

As NPR's Kat Chow pointed out in a response, Sullivan's assertion lumps together a hugely diverse population, equating the experience of a Filipino-American with that of a Japanese-American when research refutes the assumption. Chow condemned Sullivan's continuation of the "model minority" myth, which congratulates Asian Americans for overcoming discrimination and systemic oppression to achieve "the American Dream," therefore relieving white America of responsibility and placing the burden on minorities, like black or Muslim individuals, who might not be viewed culturally with the same high regard.

Lonnie Lee, curator and owner of Vessel Gallery in Oakland, has spent the past two years thinking about the stereotypes, generalizations and myths that commonly manifest in discussions about Asian-American identity—and Asian-American art. The resulting group exhibition, "Excuse me, can I see your ID?," complicates and disrupts the stale narratives that persist both inside the gallery space and beyond it.

Inspired to organize a show featuring entirely Asian-American artists after then-President Barack Obama declared May to be Asian/Pacific American Heritage Month, Lee struggled to create an identity-oriented exhibition that expanded understandings of Asian Americans rather than affirmed or constricted them. "I was looking for artworks that portrayed the identity of Asian Americans as something different than what we've seen in the past," Lee told *The Huffington Post*. "I was really seeking statements about identity that went beyond Asian-ness."

5 Race plays a critical role in how we understand ourselves and each other, but for Lee, it was important to her that participating artists had the freedom to express aspects of themselves that have nothing to do with where their lineage leads. "I was excited to portray a real diverse array of artists who happened to be Asian-American," she said. "Identity is a construct, made from many different components. Each individual artist understands identity differently. I am hoping that visitors question their social conditioning and see the individuality of each of the various artists and their narratives."

This expectation that identity boils down to race, at least for everyone who is not white, extends to the art world as well. So often, Lee explained, artists of Asian descent are expected to make art about their Asian-ness, preferably using traditional Asian techniques.

Lee's daughter, Jasmine Lee Ehrhardt, who curated a film program to supplement the exhibition, agrees. "The art world is dominated by white people," she said. "For artists of color, you have to talk about race and ethnic identity, but not in a way that makes white people too uncomfortable. This show is not intended for the white gaze. It was curated by an Asian-American curator, featuring Asian-American artists. It's not about self-cannibalizing the work that's expected from artists of color, putting themselves on display explicitly to be consumed by the viewer."

"Excuse me, can I see your ID?" is diverse not just in terms of the artists it represents but the work they create—from technique to media to style. "They are not just performing race," Ehrhardt said, "they are dealing with all these different, complex issues that I think the art world doesn't often reflect."

The exhibition got its name because, as Ehrhardt put it, "Asian people are presumed to be perpetual foreigners." The curators were specifically interested in this idea of physical documentation and how it dictates who is allowed to move freely through this country. "There are a lot of undocumented Asians and Pacific Islanders in America right now," Ehrhardt said. "It forces us to consider how Asian Americans can and cannot move through space. We're interested in the tension between these actual papers and the feelings we have inside."

10 One featured artist is Dave Kim, a Korean-American man raised in Los Angeles and based in Oakland, whose large-scale paintings revisit moments in his childhood and adolescence. As a teenager, Kim joined a Filipino gang called the Maplewood Ave Jefrox, despite the fact that Kim himself was not Filipino.

Kim's experience shows a convoluted composition of identity in flux, at any given time a cluttered collage of people, places, influences and urges. As Kim explains in his artist statement: "Even though we're Asian, we took on the characteristics of Latino gangs in every way, from claiming a neighborhood, to the attire and even the language we used. I think the thing to remember is that I joined it not to be violent or become a criminal, but to be a part of something, to find belonging, importance—find purpose."

In the painting "Flea," Kim creates a portrait of a friend who died from an overdose, shown staring at the viewer, tattoos covering his bare chest.

"This is definitely not the 'model minority' we often hear about," Lee said.

Another artist complicating predominant stereotypes is Omid Mokri, who, trained in traditional Persian miniature painting and art conservation, currently makes work while serving a 12-year prison sentence in San Quentin State Prison, for what the artist describes in his statement as an "unjust, forced sentence" for self-defense. (Lee is not familiar with the specifics of Mokri's charges or arrest.)

Mokri and his family fled Iran during the 1979 revolution. He then earned 15
degrees from both the Rhode Island School of Design and California College of the Arts. As an Iranian, Mokri diverges from the "typical" image of an Asian American. In a time when Islamophobia runs rampant, he is certainly not immediately assessed as a "law-abiding, peace-loving, courteous [person] living quietly among us."

For his artwork, Mokri gathers the scant materials available to him in his circumstances: recycled bedsheets serve as canvases, pulverized colored pencils as paint, hair affixed to plastic spoons serve as paintbrushes. "I'm including this work because it's incredible what an artist can do with such humble materials," Lee said. "I am interested in presenting his art because I am curious how the judicial system was shaped by his face, how he looks. If he was white, what would his sentence have been?"

Each artist featured in Vessel Gallery's exhibition brings a similarly compelling narrative and utterly singular perspective to the space. Both Lee and Ehrhardt hope the exhibition sparks dialogue that diverges from the typical conversation topics.

"Talking about *Ghost in the Shell*[1] is interesting, but that's not the only issue affecting the community," Lee said. "We want to expand the conversation, address the hard topics and offer other views of what it means to be Asian-American."

She hopes to stage an entirely Asian-American exhibition every other year during Asian/Pacific American Heritage Month moving forward. This year, however, the show feels particularly necessary.

"The administration has created this sense of urgency," Lee said. "People 20
recognize that this is a shared struggle, a place upon which we can build solidarity. The show is not an attempt to derail larger conversations, but to say, 'This is our stake in it.' This conversation is also important."

---

[1]A 2017 movie adaptation of a manga series that was criticized for casting Scarlett Johansson, a white actress, for an originally Asian role. [Eds.]

RESPONDING TO READING

1. In this essay, Frank looks at how artists try to push against a cultural identity that has been imposed on them by others. How specifically are the artists featured in this essay redefining their individual identities? To what extent are these identities tied to their Asian American roots?
2. In recounting his teenage experience as a member of a Filipino gang, artist Dave Kim explains, "'I joined it not to be violent or become a criminal, but to be a part of something, to find belonging, importance—find purpose'" (11). What does he mean? Why do you think gang culture appealed to Kim?

Rhetorical Analysis

Evaluate Frank's conclusion. Are her final sentences an effective conclusion for her essay, or should she have developed a fuller, more contextualized concluding paragraph? Explain.

Writing with Sources

Look online for examples of art that defy conventional cultural stereotypes. What, specifically, do these works hope to achieve, and how? How successful do you think they can be in reaching their audiences? Write an essay that explores these questions.

8.4 Jelani Cobb, "*Black Panther* and the Invention of 'Africa'"

The Ira A. Lipman professor of journalism at Columbia Journalism School, Jelani Cobb (1969–) is a staff writer at *The New Yorker* who explores issues related to race, culture, and identity in his work. He is the author of three books, including, most recently, *The Substance of Hope: Barack Obama and the Paradox of Progress* (2010). He also edited *The Essential Harold Cruse: A Reader* (2002). In the following essay, Cobb analyzes the cultural significance of the 2018 movie *Black Panther*.

BEFORE YOU READ

Do you think people who leave their homeland, willingly or unwillingly, take their cultural identity with them and pass it on to future generations? Can you think of any groups whose culture and ethnicity is *not* likely to travel with them?

Black Panther and the Invention of "Africa"

The Maison des Esclaves stands on the rocky shore of Gorée Island, off the coast of Senegal, like a great red tomb. During the years of its operation, the building served as a rendezvous point for slavers trafficking in a seemingly inexhaustible resource: Africans, whose very bodies became the wealth of white men. A portal known as the "Door of No Return," leading to the slave ships, offered the forlorn captives a last glimpse of home, before they were sown to the wind and sold in the West. For nearly four centuries, this traffic continued, seeding the populations of the Caribbean, Brazil, Argentina, Mexico, and Central and North America, and draining societies of their prime populations while fomenting civil conflict among them in order to more effectively cull their people. On the high seas, the vessels jettisoned bodies in such terrible numbers that the poet Amiri Baraka once wrote, "At the bottom of the Atlantic Ocean there's a railroad made of human bones."

I visited Gorée Island in 2003, with a group of black academics, just days after George W. Bush had come to the island and offered platitudes about the cruelties of human history but stopped short of apologizing for the United States' role in the transatlantic slave trade. Residents of the island greeted us in the markets like long-lost kin. We repeatedly heard some version of "Welcome home, my black brothers and sisters!" But, later, over dinner, a Senegalese guide casually informed us that we were neither their siblings nor even distant kin to Africa, implying that the greetings in the market had been merely a clever sales tactic directed at gullible black Americans who travel to the continent in search of roots, as if they were abused foster kids futilely seeking their birth parents. "You are Americans. That is all," she said. This exchange took place fifteen years ago, but I can still recall the way her words hung in the air, like a guilty verdict. The policy of "No Return," she suggested, applied to distant descendants, too.

There is a fundamental dissonance in the term "African-American," two feuding ancestries conjoined by a hyphen. That dissonance—a hyphen standing in for the brutal history that intervened between Africa and America—is the subject of *Black Panther*, Ryan Coogler's brilliant first installment of the story of Marvel Comics' landmark black character. "I have a lot of pain inside me," Coogler told an audience at the Brooklyn Academy of Music, on Wednesday night. "We were taught that we lost the things that made us African. We lost our culture, and now we have to make do with scraps." Black America is constituted overwhelmingly by the descendants of people who were not only brought to the country against their will but were later inducted into an ambivalent form of citizenship without their input. The Fourteenth Amendment, which granted citizenship to all those born here, supposedly resolved the question of the status of ex-slaves, though those four million individuals were not consulted in its ratification. The unspoken yield of this history is the possibility that the words "African" and "American" should not be joined by a hyphen but separated by an ellipsis.

Our sensibilities are accustomed to Marvel films offering clear lines of heroism and villainy, but *Black Panther* dispatches with its putative villain, Ulysses Klaue, a white South Africa-based arms dealer, halfway through the film. Chadwick Boseman's T'Challa, the Black Panther and the King of Wakanda, confronts Erik Killmonger, a black American mercenary, played by Michael B. Jordan, as a rival, but the two characters are essentially duelling responses to five centuries of African exploitation at the hands of the West. The villain, to the extent that the term applies, is history itself.

5 Wakanda is a technologically advanced kingdom in Central Africa that was never colonized by any Western power. T'Challa, the noble leader of an unvanquished people, upholds the isolationism that has always kept the kingdom safe; Killmonger, driven by the horrors that befell those who were stolen from the continent, envisions a world revolution, led by Wakanda, to upend the status quo. When Killmonger arrives there, after the death of King T'Chaka (the father of T'Challa), he sets in motion a reckoning not only with his rival but with broader questions of legitimacy, lineage, and connection. Black Panther, as Ryan Coogler pointed out in Brooklyn, has been an inherently political character since his inception, during the Black Power era of the nineteen-sixties. He is a refutation of the image of the lazy and false African, promulgated in the white world and subscribed to even by many in the black one. Coogler told Marvel up front that his version of the story would remain true to those political elements. It is shot through with the sense of longing and romance common to the way that people of a diaspora envision their distant homeland.

Like the comics on which they are based, the Marvel movies, in general, have not shied away from political concerns. "Captain America: The Winter Soldier," released in 2014, grapples with ideas of preëmptive warfare, drones, and the surveillance state, as elements of the war on terror. The first "Iron Man" film, from 2008, addressed war profiteering and arms contractors at a time when the United States was still heavily involved in Iraq.

Yet nothing in Marvel's collection of films is or could be political in the same way as *Black Panther*, because, in those other stories, we were at least clear about where the lines of fantasy departed from reality. "Captain America" is a fantastic riff on the nation's idealism, filtered through the lens of the Second World War, a historic event whose particulars, however horrific and grandly inhumane, are not in dispute. *Black Panther*, however, exists in an invented nation in Africa, a continent that has been grappling with invented versions of itself ever since white men first declared it the "dark continent" and set about plundering its people and its resources. This fantasy of Africa as a place bereft of history was politically useful, justifying imperialism. It found expression in the highest echelons of Western thought, and took on the contours of truth. In 1753, the Scottish philosopher David Hume wrote, "I am apt to suspect the Negroes, and all other species of men . . . to be naturally inferior to the whites. There never was any civilized nation of any complexion other than white." Two centuries later, the British historian Hugh Trevor-Roper wrote, "Perhaps, in the future, there will be some African history to teach. But at present there is none, or very little: there is only the history of the Europeans in Africa."

Africa—or, rather, "Africa"—is a creation of a white world and the literary, academic, cinematic, and political mechanisms that it used to give mythology the credibility of truth. No such nation as Wakanda exists on the map of the continent, but that is entirely beside the point. Wakanda is no more or less imaginary than the Africa conjured by Hume or Trevor-Roper, or the one canonized in such Hollywood offerings as "Tarzan." It is a redemptive counter-mythology. Most filmmakers start by asking their audiences to suspend their disbelief. But, with Africa, Coogler begins with a subject about which the world had suspended its disbelief four centuries before he was born. The film is a nearly seamless dramatic chronicle of the threat created when Killmonger travels to the African nation he descends from. Yet some of the most compelling points in the story are those where the stitching is most apparent. Killmonger is a native of Oakland, California, where the Black Panther Party was born. (In an early scene, a poster of Huey P. Newton, the co-founder of the Party, hangs on a wall, next to a Public Enemy poster.) In an impeccably choreographed fight sequence, T'Challa and General Okoye, the leader of Wakanda's all-female militia (brilliantly played by Danai Gurira), alongside Nakia, a wily Wakandan spy (played by Lupita Nyong'o), confront a Boko Haram[1]-like team of kidnappers. At the same time, it is all but impossible not to notice that Coogler has cast a black American, a Zimbabwean-American, and a Kenyan as a commando team in a film about African redemption. The cast also includes Winston Duke, who is West Indian; Daniel Kaluuya, a black Brit; and Florence Kasumba, a Ugandan-born German woman. The implicit statement in both the film's themes and its casting is that there is a connection, however vexed, tenuous, and complicated, among the continent's scattered descendants. Coogler said as much in Brooklyn, when he talked about a trip that he took to South Africa, as research for the film: after discovering cultural elements that reminded him of black communities in the United States, he concluded, "There's no way they could wipe out what we were for thousands of years. We're African."

There is a great deal more that differentiates *Black Panther* from other efforts in the superhero genre. The film is not about world domination by an alien invasion or a mad cabal of villains but about the implications of a version of Western domination that has been with us so long that it has become as ambient as the air. When Shuri, Wakanda's chief of technology and the irreverent younger sister of T'Challa, is startled by a white C.I.A. agent, she says, "Don't scare me like that, colonizer!" When I saw the movie, the audience howled at the inversion, "colonizer" deployed as an epithet rather than a badge of cultural superiority. In addition, Marvel has been criticized for failing to center a film on any of its female characters, but it is the female characters in *Black Panther* whose ideas and determinations dictate the terms on which the rivalry between the male protagonists plays out. T'Challa engages with his female counterparts as equals; Killmonger kills two women and assaults a third. Their political positions may be equally compelling; their ideas about gender are not.

Coogler's commentary on the literal tribalism of the African diaspora, his devotion to a glorious vision of Africa, and, most provocatively, his visceral telling of 10

[1]A militant Islamic group based in Nigeria. [Eds.]

the pain of existing as an orphan of history—as seen in the story of Killmonger, whose separation from Africa is not simply historical but also paternal—is striking but not unique. The narrative of Africa as a tragic tabula rasa in world history exists in dialogue with another version, equally imaginary, but idealized, and authored by descendants of those Africans who passed through the Maison des Esclaves and the other structures like it. In 1896, after Ethiopian forces defeated an invading Italian army in the Battle of Adwa, black people across the globe celebrated the country as the last preserve on the continent free from the yoke of colonialism, and a sign of hope for the black world—the Wakanda of its day. In the nineteen-thirties, after Mussolini invaded Ethiopia, Depression-era black Americans and West Indians scraped together pennies to send to a country they had never visited to fund the resistance. In the late nineteenth century, the West Indian educator and diplomat Edward Wilmot Blyden envisioned and promoted a kind of black Zionism, in which people of African descent in the West would return to work on behalf of African redemption. What Blyden, and what Marcus Garvey—a Jamaican who, in the nineteen-twenties, organized a global pan-Africanist effort to end European colonialism—and what the organizer Audley Moore and the scholar John Henrik Clarke, and what the entire lineage of that pan-African tradition insisted on was a kind of democracy of the imagination. If the subordination of Africa had begun in the minds of white people, its reclamation, they reasoned, would begin in the minds of black ones.

I understand this story intuitively and personally. In my twenties, I consumed volumes of African history and histories of the slave trade, seeking out answers to the same questions that Coogler asked in South Africa, a fugitive from the idea that I descend from a place with no discernible past. I dropped my given middle name and replaced it with an African one, in an effort to make transparent that sense of connection. On Gorée Island, I patiently listened to the guide's argument, before pointing out to her that we were conducting our conversation in English, in a building constructed by the French, in a country that had been a colony of France, and that the issue was not whether black Americans retained any connection to Africa but whether history had left anyone on the continent still in a position to pass judgment on that question. Superheroes are seldom tasked with this kind of existential lifting, but that work is inescapable in the questions surrounding Wakanda and the politics of even imagining such a place. Marvel has made a great many entertaining movies in the past decade, but Ryan Coogler has made a profound one.

Source: Jelani Cobb/The New Yorker © Conde Nast

RESPONDING TO READING

1. In paragraph 3, Cobb says, "There is a fundamental dissonance in the term 'African-American,' two feuding ancestries conjoined by a hyphen." He concludes the paragraph by saying, "The unspoken yield of this history is the possibility that the words 'African' and 'American' should not be joined by a hyphen but separated by an ellipsis." What does he mean? How does a punctuation mark convey meaning about the relationship between two cultures?

2. In describing the movie's depiction of the Black Panther character, Cobb writes, "He is a refutation of the image of the lazy and false African, promulgated in the white world and subscribed to even by many in the black one" (5). According to Cobb, how does Black Panther break down a pervasive cultural stereotype? Which image of Africans, and of African Americans, does the superhero embody?

Rhetorical Analysis

Evaluate the title of Cobb's essay. Why does it include the word "invention"? Why is "Africa" in quotation marks?

Writing with Sources

Locate some sources that discuss stereotypes—past and present—associated with your own racial, ethnic, or religious group. How did these stereotypes originate? How have they been used? What do you conclude about the impact (and dangers) of such stereotypes? Write an essay that explores these questions.

8.5 Jeffery Sheler and Michael Betzold, "Muslim in America"

Author of three books on religious issues, Jeffery Sheler is a contributing editor at *U.S. News & World Report* and a correspondent for PBS's *Religion & Ethics NewsWeekly* television news program. Freelance writer Michael Betzold has written several articles and nonfiction books as well as a novel. In the following essay, Sheler and Betzold explore what it means to be a Muslim in America.

BEFORE YOU READ

What do you think it would take for Muslims to truly feel like they belong in America? What elements of their culture might they have to sacrifice? Is this sacrifice worth making?

Muslim in America

Inside a storefront on West Warren Avenue, a gritty Dearborn, Mich., neighborhood of modest shops with hand-painted Arabic signs, a handful of men respond to the high-pitched chant of the muezzin[1] and form a line facing Mecca. They bow, sit, and prostrate on colorful rugs in a mostly silent rendition of the salat, the daily

[1]At a mosque, the person who leads the call to prayer. [Eds.]

prayers Muslims have recited for nearly 1,400 years. In a smaller room, a cluster of women with head coverings also recite the prayers in response to the voice of the imam, which they can hear from across the hall. Most of the worshipers are recent refugees from Iraq who want a link to the country they still consider home. "They thank God they are here" in America, says Imam Hushan Al-Husainy, the mosque leader. "But their heart is back home with their loved ones who are suffering."

Meanwhile, 68 miles away, beneath a gleaming white dome and twin minarets that tower over the Ohio cornfields southwest of Toledo, hundreds of families assemble for worship—a largely upper-middle-class flock that represents some 22 nationalities, most U.S. citizens and some second- or third-generation Americans. Few of the women wear head coverings outside of the prayer hall, where only a 3-foot-high partition separates men and women, side by side. After prayers, they all gather for a potluck. The Toledo center, says its president, Cherrefe Kadri, represents a "progressive and middle-of-the-road" brand of Islam that, she says, is "very much at home in Middle America."

This, then, is American Islam: The modern Islamic Center of Greater Toledo and the traditionalist Karbala Islamic Education Center are but two examples of its wide-ranging diversity. And even though it is the nation's fastest-growing faith, with an estimated 7 million adherents here—nearly double from a decade ago—Islam remains widely misunderstood in this country. The religion of more than a fifth of the world's population is viewed by many Americans as foreign, mysterious, even threatening to the nation's "Judeo-Christian heritage"—certainly no less so since the events of September 11—despite the fact that it shares common roots with Christianity and Judaism and has been present in North America for centuries.

The rules. Indeed, Islam embraces the monotheism of Christianity and Judaism, accepts the Hebrew Bible, and venerates Jesus as a prophet. It is centered on the Koran—the Islamic scriptures, which Muslims believe were revealed to the prophet Mohammed—which commands five basic devotional duties, called the "Five Pillars": a declaration of belief that "there is no God but Allah [Arabic for "the God"] and Mohammed is his prophet"; prayers offered five times a day; daytime fasting during the month of Ramadan; charitable giving; and at least one pilgrimage to Mecca. Muslims are forbidden to consume alcohol, illicit drugs, pork, or any meat that is not halal—the Islamic equivalent of kosher. Premarital sex and extramarital sex are sternly prohibited, as are most forms of unchaperoned dating. Emphasis on public modesty prompts many Muslims to cover themselves from the wrists to the ankles. Muslims also may not gamble or pay or accept interest on loans or savings accounts. It is a regimen that often runs in conflict with the dominant culture. Most American Muslims have no choice but to break the prohibition on usury to buy homes and automobiles, for example.

5 But if the intense scrutiny focused on world Islam since September 11 has revealed anything, it is that the faith is no monolith. While there is much that binds the world's 1.2 billion Muslims together, there is no authoritative hierarchy—no pope, no central group of elders—that speaks to them or for them. And American Islam, it emerges, is its own special brand. A recent study sponsored by the Council on American-Islamic Relations [CAIR] in cooperation with the Hartford Institute for Religion Research found that American Muslims generally are more accepting of differences,

less inclined to fundamentalism, and more at home in a secular society than most Muslims elsewhere. They are also ethnically diverse: Most are immigrants or their descendants from Islamic countries in Asia, Africa, and the Middle East. About a third are African-Americans, and a small number are whites of European descent.

Connections? But while diversity may naturally include the extremes, the question on many people's minds has been what exactly the relationship is between American Islam and the kind of terror and anti-Americanism that came so horribly into focus last month under the guise of religious zealotry. One moderate American Islamic leader, Sheik Muhammad Hisham Kabbani, told a State Department forum in 1999 that 80 percent of the nation's mosques are headed by clerics who espouse "extremist ideology"—which Kabbani associates with Wahhabism, an Islamic fundamentalist movement that began in Saudi Arabia in the 18th century. But Kabbani, head of the Islamic Supreme Council of America, a Washington, D.C.–based advocacy group, added that "a majority of American Muslims do not agree" with the extremist ideology.

Other American Muslim leaders say Kabbani's estimate of Wahhabi influence in U.S. mosques is exaggerated. "I don't know where he came up with that," says Ingrid Mattson, a Hartford Seminary professor and vice president of the Islamic Society of North America [ISNA]. African-Americans alone account for a third of the mosques, she notes, "and they clearly are not Wahhabis." The CAIR-Hartford study found that about 20 percent of mosques say they interpret the Koran literally, but 7 in 10 follow a more nuanced, nonfundamentalist approach.

Scholars say the democratic structure and autonomy of many American mosques protect them from extremist takeovers. Modern Islamic centers, like the one in Toledo, are "less likely to be dominated by a single teacher or viewpoint," says Frederick Denny, a scholar of Islam at the University of Colorado. That describes at least 60 percent of American mosques, according to the CAIR-Hartford study. Those that are more fundamentalist, he says, often are smaller, with transient members, such as those that "cater to foreign students who want something that feels like home." Even where fundamentalism exists, says Mattson, "there is a huge distinction between fundamentalist ideology and support of terrorism."

What divides American Muslims most often, says Denny, "is not liberal-versus-conservative ideology but how best to domesticate Islam in a Western society without doing violence to either." What, for example, are American Muslims to do with sharia, the Islamic legal and ethical codes that tradition says should undergird Islamic society? Radical clerics say it is a Muslim's duty to impose sharia throughout the world, by force if necessary. But moderates argue that Islamic law must be internalized. "It shouldn't be taken literally," says Imam Farooq Aboelzahab of the Toledo mosque. "The way sharia was applied 1,400 years ago may not always fit. It must be applied to the place and time where you live."

One indication that many Muslims are feeling more at home in America is 10
their growing involvement in the nation's public life. During the past five years, Islamic leaders and groups have become increasingly outspoken on social- and foreign-policy issues. Groups like CAIR, ISNA, the American Muslim Council, and the Islamic Institute maintain a high-visibility Washington presence, working to rally Muslim political activism and acting as media watchdogs. While American Islamic

groups were virtually unanimous in condemning the terrorist attacks on New York and Washington, they remain vociferous critics of U.S. policy in the Middle East.

Stronger rhetoric, of course, has its price in this country. In late September, a prominent imam at a Cleveland mosque nearly lost his job over anti-Jewish remarks he had made in a speech 10 years ago. The board at the Islamic Center of Cleveland voted to keep Fawaz Damra after he apologized for the remarks, which appeared on a tape that surfaced recently, but local Jewish leaders are still upset.

Incendiary rhetoric. Meanwhile, a leading Muslim teacher in Northern California has apologized for his own rhetorical excesses. Hamza Yusuf, who was invited to the White House to pray with President Bush after the attacks, later came under criticism for saying in a speech two days before the attacks that the United States "stands condemned" and faced "a terrible fate" because of rampant immorality and injustice in its treatment of minorities. While their causes may be just, says Yusuf, "the rhetoric of some Muslim leaders has been too incendiary—I myself have been guilty of it." September 11, he says, "was a wake-up call to me. I don't want to contribute to the hate in any shape or form."

A decade ago, Sulayman Nyang, professor of African studies at Howard University in Washington, D.C., warned in a speech that Islam will be accepted in America only when Muslims fully take their place alongside other citizens, participating in the nation's civic life, and when what the Islamic faith can offer Western culture is recognized widely as something of value. Neither, he says, will be easy to accomplish. But in times like these, such hard work is more important than ever.

RESPONDING TO READING

1. According to Sheler and Betzold, how is Islam like other widely followed U.S. religions? How is it different?
2. In paragraph 5, the writers assert that the Muslim faith is "no monolith." What do they mean? What evidence do they offer to support this claim?

Rhetorical Analysis

This essay appeared in a newsmagazine on October 29, 2001, just weeks after the 9/11 terrorist attacks. What do you suppose the writers' primary purpose was? How can you tell?

Writing with Sources

Do some research about U.S. Muslims who are immigrants or first-generation Americans. What are their major concerns? What goals do they have for themselves and for their children? How are their goals and expectations like and unlike those of other Americans?

8.6 Brett Krutzsch, "The Gayest One"

A visiting assistant professor of religion at Haverford College, Brett Krutzsch explores the connections between religion and LGBT (lesbian, gay, bisexual, and transgender) issues. The author of the forthcoming book *Dying to Be Normal: Gay Martyrs and the Transformation of American Sexual Politics,* he received the 2014–15 LGBT Religious History Award for his dissertation excerpt titled "The Martyrdom of Matthew Shepard." His work has appeared in the *New York Blade, New York Press,* and *The Washington Post.* In the following essay, Krutzsch considers the nuances of gay identity from a personal perspective.

BEFORE YOU READ

Consider some depictions of gay men on television, in movies, and in ads. How do these portrayals reinforce or resist stereotypes of gay culture?

The Gayest One

"Everyone agreed that you're the gayest person in the department," my best friend from work said to me as we strolled through SoHo. Sara was recapping a conversation from a happy hour I missed because I had been at a book reading by Paula Deen, the eccentric Southern woman on the Food Network.

"What does that mean?" I asked.

"Nobody gave any reasons. Someone asked who was the biggest homosexual, people looked around, and Matt said your name. Everybody agreed."

I was immediately irritated and annoyed. Out of the 50 individuals who work in my division at NYU, 11 of us are gay men. How could I so quickly and unanimously be considered the fruitiest of the bunch?

Sara changed the topic to her upcoming wedding. As she talked about 5
whether or not to keep her hair straight or curly, I recalled a friend's birthday party a year ago. We were at a straight bar near Union Square, and an attractive woman, probably in her late 20s, repeatedly glanced my way the entire night. Eventually, she approached me and asked, "Are you here for Craig's party?"

"Yes, I am," I said, as I watched her eyes get big and the color drain from her face.

"Oh, you're gay," she interjected.

I had said three words. Three very little words. Each with one syllable. That was all it took for her to know my sexual orientation.

"I am," I said with an awkward laugh, realizing that she had wanted to hit on me.

"Oh, I thought. I mean, I'm sorry," she mumbled, and then ran off, looking 10
embarrassed.

I turned around and told my friends what happened, and they burst out laughing. I wasn't amused. I left the party soon after that and walked home, feeling sorry for myself.

Still talking about her wedding. Sara decided she should keep her hair curly since she was having an outdoor ceremony in July. "After all," she said. "It could never be completely straight anyway."

Apparently, with a voice like mine, neither could I.

That week I couldn't stop fixating on the idea of me as the biggest queen at work. I tried thinking of stereotypes I fit, but things still didn't make sense. Of all the gay men in my department, I was the only one in a long-term relationship. My boyfriend and I lived together, had joint finances, and shared holidays with each other's families. We were boringly monogamous. Our nights usually concluded with *Seinfeld*, not sex. So it couldn't be that I embodied the stereotype of the promiscuous gay man with a wild night life. I hadn't set foot in a gay club in three years. Of all the queer men I worked with, my homelife seemed the most heterosexual.

15 OK, my interests and hobbies were never particularly manly. I'd much rather be at a Broadway show than at a Yankees game. Given a choice, I always picked a day at the spa over a day of camping. I've typically been more comfortable at brunches with women chatting about sample sales than out having beers with the guys talking about cars or the stock market.

Not long ago I was walking down Third Avenue with my friend Lauren. It was raining and we shared an umbrella. We passed a homeless man sprawled out on the sidewalk who yelled to Lauren, "Hey, gorgeous, want to get married?"

"Sorry, I'm taken," Lauren said, looking up at me.

The homeless man screamed back, "Yeah, to a homo."

I wasn't singing "It's Raining Men" under the umbrella. I was just walking. Even the homeless man had enough gay-dar to know I wasn't heterosexual.

20 I assumed that I was decreed the gayest at my job because I was the least likely to pass as straight. I wore form-fitting Burberry polos, openly raved about Kelly Clarkson, and bought expensive Kiehl's skin care products even though I was only 28. If I were put in a lineup, it probably wouldn't take someone with Nancy Drew's investigative skills to finger me as the boy who likes boys. Nevertheless, I was still perplexed by people's need to ask, "Who among us is the biggest fairy?" I doubt straight guys ever sat around saying: "Bob, you're definitely the straightest one here." "No way, Harry. You're totally straighter."

When I moved to Manhattan four years ago I thought I was relocating to the gay mecca, as if the mother ship were calling me home. On my first outing to the bars of Chelsea and subsequent walks along Eighth Avenue I quickly observed that I didn't look like other gay men in the area. Standing six feet tall and weighing 140 pounds, I was a skinny Jewish bookworm who had no interest in going to the gym to become one of the musclemen who ruled the New York City gayborhoods. They paid little attention to me, so at that point in my life I felt like I wasn't gay enough.

I never believed my sexuality was a choice, but how I presented myself to the world was. Until I came out of the closet my senior year at Emory University, I wore oversized T-shirts and pretended to have a crush on Jennifer Aniston, like many of the straight, beer-drinking guys my age, never letting on that my lust was actually for Brad Pitt. I've since learned that I wasn't fooling anyone—my family members and friends have said they always assumed I was gay.

Growing up in Indiana, the boys in my school constantly asked why I talked like a girl. I didn't understand what they meant until I was in third grade, when I heard myself on an answering machine. I sounded just like my friend Liz, so each night I prayed for my voice to deepen and be like my dad's. After puberty, when I thought my prayers had been answered, the same boys asked why I talked like Michael Jackson. I always felt my voice was a reminder that I was different, a freak, and less than a real man.

When I came out at 22, my shrink said it could take several years to fully accept my sexuality. Six years have passed, and I'm now sharing my life with an incredible partner, but I still struggle, because I think of myself as a liberal Jewish pseudo-intellectual, not an über-homosexual. I know it isn't a bad thing to be the gayest one. I'm just not sure how to accept the title or if I'm ready to wear the tiara and sash.

Source: The Gayest One, The Advocate, October 19, 2007. Used by permission from Brett Krutzsch

---

RESPONDING TO READING

1. Despite his apparent comfort with and acceptance of his gay identity, Krutzsch objects to being so easily recognized as gay—and to being characterized as the "gayest person in the department" (1). Why?
2. How, according to Krutzsch, is gay culture stereotyped? In what respects does he believe he does not fit that stereotype?

Rhetorical Analysis

In paragraph 22, Krutzsch says, "I never believed my sexuality was a choice, but how I presented myself to the world was." What distinction is he making here? How do you think he wants readers to perceive him? Does he achieve his goal?

Writing with Sources

Attitudes about gay and lesbian people have changed dramatically in the past several decades, and so has the social, political, and economic landscape for these groups. Search for information about the 1969 Stonewall riots. Then, write an essay in which you explore changing attitudes about marriage for same-sex couples, gay service members in the military, gay people on college campuses or in the workplace, or a similar topic since Stonewall. What has changed, and what has stayed the same? Be sure to read articles in gay and lesbian publications and websites as well as in mainstream sources.

8.7 Melanie Scheller, "On the Meaning of Plumbing and Poverty"

Melanie Scheller is the author of the children's book *My Grandfather's Hat* (1992) and the writer and director of the short film *No Where, USA* (2009). In the following essay, Scheller explores the cultural identity of the rural poor.

BEFORE YOU READ

The culture of rural poverty described in this essay is not a culture that is generally freely chosen. How do you suppose their shared experiences and memories might nevertheless create a sense of cultural identity for the rural poor?

On the Meaning of Plumbing and Poverty

Several years ago I spent some time as a volunteer on the geriatric ward of a psychiatric hospital. I was fascinated by the behavior of one of the patients, an elderly woman who shuffled at regular intervals to the bathroom, where she methodically flushed the toilet. Again and again she carried out her sacred mission as if summoned by some supernatural force, until the flush of the toilet became a rhythmic counterpoint for the ward's activity. If someone blocked her path or if, God forbid, the bathroom was in use when she reached it, she became agitated and confused.

Obviously, that elderly patient was a sick woman. And yet I felt a certain kinship with her, for I too have suffered from an obsession with toilets. I spent much of my childhood living in houses without indoor plumbing, and while I don't feel compelled to flush a toilet at regular intervals, I sometimes feel that toilets, or the lack thereof, have shaped my identity in ways that are painful to admit.

I'm not a child of the Depression,[1] but I grew up in an area of the South that had changed little since the day of the New Deal.[2] My mother was a widow with six children to support, not an easy task under any circumstances, but especially difficult in rural North Carolina during the 1960s. To her credit, we were never seriously in danger of going hungry. Our vegetable garden kept us stocked with tomatoes and string beans. We kept a few chickens and sometimes a cow. Blackberries were free for the picking in the fields nearby. Neighbors did their good Christian duty by bringing us donations of fresh fruit and candy at Christmastime. But a roof over our heads—that wasn't so easily improvised.

Like rural Southern gypsies, we moved from one dilapidated Southern farmhouse to another in a constant search for a decent place to live. Sometimes we moved when the rent increased beyond the 30 or 40 dollars my mother could afford. Or the house burned down, not an unusual occurrence in substandard

---

[1]Great Depression (1929–1939). [Eds.]

[2]Economic relief and reform program implemented by the U.S. government between 1933–1939. [Eds.]

housing. One year when we were gathered together for Thanksgiving dinner, a stranger walked in without knocking and announced that we were being evicted. The house had been sold without our knowledge and the new owner wanted to start remodeling immediately. We tried to finish our meal with an attitude of thanksgiving while he worked around us with his tape measure.

Usually we rented from farm families who'd moved from the old home place 5
to one of the brick boxes that are now the standard in rural Southern architecture. The old farmhouse wasn't worth fixing up with a septic tank and flush toilet, but it was good enough to rent for a few dollars a month to families like mine. The idea of tenants' rights hadn't trickled down yet from the far reaches of the liberal North. It never occurred to us to demand improvements in the facilities. The ethic of the land said we should take what we could get and be grateful for it.

Without indoor plumbing, getting clean is a tiring and time consuming ritual. At one point I lived in a five-room house with six or more people, all of whom congregated in the one heated room to eat, do homework, watch television, dress and undress, argue, wash dishes. During cold weather we dragged mattresses from the unheated rooms and slept huddled together on the floor by the woodstove. For my bathing routine, I first pinned a sheet to a piece of twine strung across the kitchen. That gave me some degree of privacy from the six other people in the room. At that time our house had an indoor cold-water faucet, from which I filled a pot of water to heat on the kitchen stove. It took several pots of hot water to fill the metal washtub we used.

Since I was a teenager and prone to sulkiness if I didn't get special treatment, I got to take the first bath while the water was still clean. The others used the water I left behind, freshened up with hot water from the pot on the stove. Then the tub had to be dragged to the door and the bath water dumped outside. I longed to be like the woman in the Calgon bath oil commercials, luxuriating in a marble tub full of scented water with bubbles piled high and stacks of thick, clean towels nearby.

People raised in the land of the bath-and-a-half may wonder why I make such a fuss about plumbing. Maybe they spent a year in the Peace Corps, or they backpacked across India, or they worked at a summer camp and, gosh, using a latrine isn't all that bad. And of course it's *not* that bad. Not when you can catch the next plane out of the country, or pick up your duffel bag and head for home, or call mom and dad to come and get you when things get too tedious. A sojourn in a Third World country, where everyone shares the same primitive facilities, may cause some temporary discomfort, but the experience is soon converted into amusing anecdotes for cocktail-party conversation. It doesn't corrode your self-esteem with a sense of shame the way a childhood spent in chronic, unrelenting poverty can.

In the South of my childhood, not having indoor plumbing was the indelible mark of poor white trash. The phrase "so poor they didn't have a pot to piss in" said it all. Poor white trash were viciously stereotyped, and never more viciously than on the playground. White-trash children had cooties—everybody knew that. They had ringworm and pinkeye—don't get near them or you might catch it. They picked their noses. They messed in their pants. If a white-trash child made the mistake of catching a softball during recess, the other children made an elaborate show of wiping it clean before they would touch it.

10 Once a story circulated at school about a family whose infant daughter had fallen into the "slop jar" and drowned. When I saw the smirks and heard the laughter with which the story was told, I felt sick and afraid in the pit of my stomach. A little girl had died, but people were laughing. What had she done to deserve that laughter? I could only assume that using a chamber pot was something so disgusting, so shameful, that it made a person less than human.

My family was visibly and undeniably poor. My clothes were obviously hand-me-downs. I got free lunches at school. I went to the health department for immunizations. Surely it was equally obvious that we didn't have a flush toilet. But like an alcoholic who believes no one will know he has a problem as long as he doesn't drink in public, I convinced myself that no one knew my family's little secret. It was a form of denial that would color my relationships with the outside world for years to come.

Having a friend from school spend the night at my house was out of the question. Better to be friendless than to have my classmates know my shameful secret. Home visits from teachers or ministers left me in a dither of anticipatory anxiety. As they chattered on and on with Southern small talk about tomato plants and relish recipes, I sat on the edge of my seat, tensed against the dreaded words, "May I use your bathroom, please?" When I began dating in high school, I'd lie in wait behind the front door, ready to dash out as soon as my date pulled in the driveway, never giving him a chance to hear the call of nature while on our property.

With the help of a scholarship I was able to go away to college, where I could choose from dozens of dormitory toilets and take as many hot showers as I wanted, but I could never openly express my joy in using the facilities. My roommates, each a pampered only child from a well-to-do family, whined and complained about having to share a bathroom. I knew that if I expressed delight in simply having a bathroom, I would immediately be labeled as a hick. The need to conceal my real self by stifling my emotions created a barrier around me and I spent my college years in a vacuum of isolation.

Almost 20 years have passed since I first tried to leave my family's chamber pot behind. For many of those years it followed behind me—the ghost of chamber pots past—clanging and banging and threatening to spill its humiliating contents at any moment. I was convinced that everyone could see it, could smell it even. No college degree or job title seemed capable of banishing it.

15 If finances had permitted, I might have become an Elvis Presley or a Tammy Faye Bakker, easing the pain of remembered poverty with gold-plated bathtub fixtures and leopard-skinned toilet seats. I feel blessed that gradually, ever so gradually, the shame of poverty has begun to fade. The pleasures of the present now take priority over where a long-ago bowel movement did or did not take place. But for many Southerners, chamber pots and outhouses are more than just memories.

In North Carolina alone, 200,000 people still live without indoor plumbing.[3] People who haul their drinking water home from a neighbor's house or catch rainwater in barrels. People who can't wash their hands before handling food, the

---

[3]According to the North Carolina Housing Coalition, more than 16,500 homes in the state are still without indoor plumbing. [Eds.]

way restaurant employees are required by state law to do. People who sneak into public restrooms every day to wash, shave, and brush their teeth before going to work or to school. People who sacrifice their dignity and self-respect when forced to choose between going homeless and going to an outhouse. People whose children think they deserve the conditions in which they live and hold their heads low to hide the shame. But they're not the ones who should feel ashamed. No, they're not the ones who should feel ashamed.

RESPONDING TO READING

1. In paragraph 2, Scheller says, "I sometimes feel that toilets, or the lack thereof, have shaped my identity in ways that are painful to admit." Exactly how has the issue of indoor plumbing shaped her identity?
2. What specific problems, apart from the lack of indoor plumbing, did Scheller and her family face because they were poor? Why do you think she focuses on toilets instead of on another problem?

Rhetorical Analysis

How does Scheller see herself as different from those who were "raised in the land of the bath-and-a-half" (8)? How do you think she expects readers to react to this characterization?

Writing with Sources

In this essay, Scheller discusses living conditions for poor rural Southerners in the 1960s. What has changed for them since her childhood? What has stayed the same? Write an essay exploring the progress (or lack of progress) in one rural community.

8.8 Steven Korbar, "*What Are You Going to Be?*" [Drama]

A playwright and actor based in Los Angeles, Steven Korbar (1967–) has produced plays throughout the United States and Canada. His work has appeared in *The Best Ten-Minute Plays 2010* and *2013* as well as in the 2013 Queer Theatre Festival in Washington, D.C. The following ten-minute play reveals the cultural significance of the clothes and costumes we wear.

BEFORE YOU READ

Did you dress up for Halloween or other cultural events when you were young? Why did you choose particular costumes over others? To conform to a role? To get attention? To be funny? To look different? For some other reason (or combination of reasons)?

"*What Are You Going to Be?*"

CHARACTERS:

GREG: thirties to forties
CAROL: thirties to forties
NATALIE: an adolescent girl

SETTING: An upper middle class home—decorated for Halloween.

TIME: Early evening

Lights come up to find CAROL seated in a living room setting. She is very still and appears rather stunned. After a moment GREG enters. He is carrying a grocery bag and is in high spirits.

GREG: Okay, don't get mad at me, but I broke my promise—I bought more Halloween candy! I know we already have a ton but A) they were having an incredible sale and B) and most importantly . . . they're "Junior Mints"! I figure we can just put them in the back of the cupboard and conveniently forget them till Trick or Treating is over tomorrow night. Oh don't be all angry. "Junior Mints"! . . . What's the matter?

CAROL: *(A choked voice)* . . . Natalie . . .

GREG: *(Stricken)* What? . . . What!?

Quickly becoming hysterical. Dropping the bag
Oh God! Natalie. NATALIE! Where is she, where . . .

CAROL: No. No, she's fine. She's not hurt or sick or anything.

GREG: Then why did you . . . Oh my God! What is wrong with you!? Why did you say 'Natalie' like something horrible happened?

CAROL: *(Flatly)* I'm sorry.

GREG: You scared the living . . . you don't joke around like that—you took ten years off my life, you, you made me drop my "Junior Mints".

CAROL: I'm very sorry. I should have phrased what I had to say differently.

GREG: What could you have to say that was worth giving me a cardiac infarction?

CAROL: Natalie . . . finally decided what she's going to be for Halloween.

GREG: *(A beat)* Her Halloween costume. Carol, what is the point of all this family therapy if you're just going to keep overreacting to every little thing? You know what Dr. Penelope told you; perspective is what we have to strive for.

If you just take a step back and a deep cleansing breath; pretty soon you're going to see that what seemed so dire really wasn't such a terrible ...

NATALIE enters. We assume she is a normal adolescent girl, though it is hard to tell as she is dressed in the burka[1] *of a Muslim woman from the Middle East. Her costume is heavy, black and very constricting. GREG stares at her for a long moment. He looks at CAROL and then back to NATALIE, trying desperately not to overreact.*

... Hey princess.

NATALIE: Hi Dad.

GREG: What'cha doing?

NATALIE: Just trying on my Halloween costume.

GREG: So you decided against the ballerina?

NATALIE: Yeah. I'm going to be a Muslim woman from the Middle East instead.

GREG: Why ... did you decide to be that?

NATALIE: Cause I wanted a costume not a lot of other girls would have.

GREG: ... Good job.

NATALIE: There isn't any reason you don't want me wearing this ... is there?

GREG: I ... can't think of any.

NATALIE: Good. Well, I'm going to go back to my room, figure out which way is Mecca[2] and practice lying face down on the floor.

NATALIE exits

GREG: *(A long beat. Trying desperately to sound reasonable)* Well ... we said no Lady Gaga.

CAROL: This is not my fault. I am a good mother—there are no preservatives in anything I feed that girl.

GREG: This is not about fault. This can be an opportunity; to learn more about our daughter and try to understand her thought process.

NATALIE: *(OFF STAGE)* I can hear every word you're saying.

GREG: *(Yelling towards the direction of her room)* Well then shut your door Missy!

To CAROL. More quietly

Let's just try to discuss this quietly. Now, where did she get the ...

CAROL: Burka is the word you're trying to sound casual saying. And I don't know where she got it—I was too terrified to look through her browsing history.

GREG: There is no reason to be terrified. There is nothing wrong with being Middle Eastern. We cannot let her feel we have a problem with that. Muslims are human beings just like you and me—we see them every day on "Anderson Cooper". We just have to figure out why Natalie wants to dress like one.

---

[1] A long black garment that covers the whole body worn by some Muslim women. [Eds.]

[2] An Islamic holy city in Saudi Arabia. [Eds.]

CAROL: I know why—to destroy me. She's rejecting everything I've ever taught her about being a modern, post-feminist woman and chosen the most subservient, oppressed female role model she could find. My God, she might as well just be dressing up as my mother for Halloween!

GREG: Those are a completely different set of issues. What matters now is that if we decide it's better for her not to wear this costume, she doesn't think it's because we have any sort of discriminatory . . .

NATALIE enters

NATALIE: Hey mom, can I have a needle and thread to fix my costume; I think too much of my face is showing.

GREG: You know sweetie, we actually wanted to talk to you about your costume and what you'll be wearing tomorrow night.

NATALIE: I'll be wearing this.

GREG: Maybe . . . but your mom and I would like you to be aware of all your options. For instance, you could reexamine the whole line of Disney princesses—there's Jasmine from "Aladdin". All the same ethnicity and you could look so pretty.

NATALIE: No. Nobody my age is going to wear a princess costume. And even if I did it sure wouldn't be Jasmine—she's a total infidel. Anyway, who cares what I wear, it's just a costume and the costumes we wear shouldn't matter . . . right Dad?

GREG: Right! . . . right.

CAROL: Natalie, it's just that we feel it might seem disrespectful to people of the Muslim faith for you to be wearing this as a costume for Halloween.

GREG: *(Impressed with CAROL'S ruse)* Good!

Immediately to NATALIE. Earnestly

Right. Halloween is more of a secular holiday and it's just better to keep religion out of it.

CAROL: Remember how the Davis's passed out bible quotes instead of candy last Halloween; their house got TP'd for four straight nights.

NATALIE: *(Suspiciously)* Tell me the truth; this really isn't because the two of you have got some weird thing against Islam, is it?

GREG: No!

CAROL: No!

GREG: No!

CAROL: No!

GREG: It's just: you don't want to belittle anyone's faith sweetie. I mean, you wouldn't run around asking for candy dressed as a Catholic nun, would you?

CAROL: Well honey, some people do go out dressed as nuns. It's a costume: they go out dressed as slutty nuns.

GREG: . . . Those are slutty nurses.

NATALIE: No, she's right. Some are nurses but a lot of them are slutty nuns too.

GREG: Okay, fine. There are slutty nun costumes; but you wouldn't go out dressed in one would you?

NATALIE: No. I already know two girls who are going as that.

GREG: *(More frustrated)* I think it is just culturally insensitive to these people as a group. And by these people I do not mean … *(Catching himself and making air quotes)* 'These People'. I just, I don't feel comfortable with you dressing this way.

NATALIE: When Lauren Nakamura went dressed as a geisha last year, the two of you wouldn't stop gushing about how adorable she looked.

GREG: That is completely different.

NATALIE: Why, because Arabs frighten you but you find Asians all cute and non-threatening?

GREG: Absolutely not!

CAROL: No!

GREG: Do not put words in my mouth! The image of the passive Asian is nothing but a ridiculous, antiquated racial stereotype!

CAROL: Of course it is.

GREG: Just look at Pearl Harbor.

After realizing what he's said, putting a discreet hand over his mouth

CAROL: What your father means is he would like you to find another costume to wear.

NATALIE: What would he like me to be; a white, male, Protestant who can prove he's straight?

GREG instinctively moves to attack NATALIE—muttering something like "You miserable little …". Carol restrains him.

CAROL: This is not a judgment on anyone's religion or race.

NATALIE: Then why is Dad getting all freaked out?

GREG: I am not getting freaked out: nobody ever even mentioned terrorism.

NATALIE: What!?

GREG: I mean; it is wrong to ascribe the worst in human nature to any one particular people. And anybody who does that is ignorant and we should just feel sorry for them.

NATALIE: Then I can go like this?

GREG: I will lock you in the crawl space first.

NATALIE: Well my friend Lele really is Muslim and she likes this costume and she's totally cool with me wearing it.

GREG: I don't care what your friend thinks. You are not wearing that costume. It is inappropriate; it's thoughtless and wearing it would just be plain insulting to the people and culture of Islam!

NATALIE: Is that what all of your Muslim friends say Dad?

GREG tries to answer but is left with his mouth open. NATALIE stares at him for a beat, turns and exits in triumphant silence

GREG: *(A beat, then erupting in frustration)* What is going on here! I don't understand, why is she doing this to us!

NATALIE: *(Off stage)* I can still hear you!

GREG: I am going to remove that door from its hinges!

NATALIE: *(Off stage)* That doesn't even make sense—I could hear you better then!

GREG: I know that!

Moving to CAROL. Whispering

She used to be so sweet when she was little.

CAROL: I told you we shouldn't have let her have all those inoculations.

GREG: We could just cram her into a stuffed pumpkin and that was her costume.

CAROL: Polio and Rubella; fine. But she was never right again after that Smallpox vaccine.

GREG: *(Humiliated)* I said terrorist.

CAROL: And Pearl Harbor.

GREG: Since the day she was born I've tried to teach her to respect diversity. She has been to every church, heard every philosophy; we introduced her to that school friend of yours who's a Wiccan[3] and a Lesbian. I've taken that girl to so many Bat mitzvahs[4] in the last year I could practically poach a salmon all by myself. I paid $125.00 for a dress so she could look right at her friend's quinceanera[5] and another $15.00 to the gardener to learn how to pronounce quinceanera! What in the hell more do I have to do—she wouldn't go with me to the Tyler Perry movie!

CAROL: If you ask me this whole place is just crawling with Radon.

GREG: Will you stop blaming everything on hazardous materials.

CAROL: Well I told you; it's not me. I breast fed that kid for fourteen months and stayed gluten free the whole time—I did my part.

GREG: Well all I know is I left a peaceful home this morning, worked hard all day for my family and when I walked back through the front door this evening suddenly it's a Jihad![6] Where did that come from?

CAROL: Well not my side of the family—she didn't inherit any of that gamy, exotic blood from me.

GREG: . . . And what in the hell is that supposed to mean?

CAROL does not respond

I'm part Dutch, part Scots/Irish and 1/8th Armenian.

CAROL points at him as if to say 'Bingo'

Armenia is in Europe.

---

[3]A believer in Wicca, a religion based in magic and nature. [Eds.]

[4]A rite of passage for Jewish girls passing into womanhood. [Eds.]

[5]A rite of passage for Hispanic girls passing into womanhood. [Eds.]

[6]An Islamic holy war. [Eds.]

CAROL: Oh no it's not. Not real Europe. Not "Sound of Music" Europe. You've always had a little smudge of the Third World on you; I knew it the first time I saw that dusky little mother of yours—I mean, no offence, but the woman's always looked like she just finished carrying a jug of water on her head.

GREG: Are you out of your mind?

CAROL: And there's another trait that's straight out of the Casbah[7]—your condescending manner towards women. So archaic and primitive—it's down right patriarchal.

GREG: Oh really, is that what your Wiccan friend would call it?

CAROL: And a homophobe to boot.

GREG: You are making me very angry!

CAROL: Oh boy, start gathering up your stones everybody: I feel an honor killing coming on!

GREG: Do you even understand the sociopolitical implications of what you're saying? This is the kind of thinking that fostered colonialism for the last two centuries.

NATALIE enters no longer wearing the burka

NATALIE: Okay, okay, okay—just stop the arguing, alright! If this is what it's going to do to you, fine; I won't wear the stupid costume. If my parents can't handle somebody dressing a little different then I guess I was just expecting too much! Everyone has their secret little hates and prejudices, even my own mother and father. That's just how it is. So I'll just do what you want. I'll go back to wearing my original Lady Gaga costume … unless you have something against her religion too?

CAROL and GREG simultaneously shake their heads

Okay then. That's how it's going to be and we won't even talk about it anymore.

I'm not a baby—it's not like I can't stand disappointment. I guess I have to start getting used to it sometime, don't I?

GREG: *(Earnestly)* Natalie. . . I want you to know I think you've shown a lot of maturity tonight. And maturity is a rare thing at any age.

NATALIE: Thanks Dad—I bet that's just how Anderson Cooper would have put it.

NATALIE exits. There is a silence.

GREG: Well, I think it all worked out for the best.

CAROL: In the long run I think so.

GREG: It's good she made the decision by herself.

CAROL: It wouldn't have been right if we'd had to force her.

GREG: These are volatile times; it's just better not to broach certain subjects.

GREG: *(Suddenly aware)* … Did she just play us?

CAROL: Played us like a violin.

GREG: She was never going to wear that as a costume, was she?

---

[7]A fortress or native sector in North Africa. [Eds.]

CAROL: She was going as Lady Gaga if she'd had to slit our throats.

GREG: We really did kind of raise a terrorist, didn't we?

CAROL: Utterly remorseless.

GREG: It's just stunning. How she manipulated us. The way she preyed on our irrational fears and exploited our ingrained prejudices. And for no other reason but to get what she wanted from us.

CAROL: I always did tell her she could be the first woman president of the United States.

GREG: Well, she sure had my number. If anyone asks me, I guess I know what I'm going to be for Halloween.

CAROL: Your own adolescent daughters little bitch?

GREG: I was going to say a hypocrite. How can I ever look another Arab American in the eye again?

CAROL: Well, since I don't think there are any in our 'Emotional Eating' class, I doubt it will be a problem. Anyway, Halloween will be over and done with tomorrow night, and if we're lucky we can just put the whole horrible thing behind us.

GREG: Can we? Christmas is only two months away.

CAROL: *(Remembering a horrible fact)* . . . Oh my God.

GREG: She's still got her heart set on that puppy.

CAROL: Oh no! The dander . . . the dander. We can't have it in the house!

GREG: *(Low and fatalistic)* We may not have a choice Carol. We may not have a choice.

(A distraught beat. Then yelling in the direction of NATALIE'S bedroom)

I know you can hear me!

NATALIE is heard laughing Off Stage. CAROL and GREG cower together.

End Of Play

RESPONDING TO READING

1. Why is Carol so upset about her daughter's Halloween costume?
2. What is Greg's main concern about Natalie's choice? Why doesn't he feel comfortable with her wearing a burka?

Rhetorical Analysis

What stereotypes of Muslims are explored in this play? What stereotypes of other groups are identified? What do these stereotypes reveal about Carol and Greg? How might the play's audience react to these stereotypes?

8.9 Focus: "Do Racial Distinctions Still Matter?"

→ **NOTE: Please answer BOTH Question 8 about Hispanic origin and Question 9 about race. For this census, Hispanic origins are not races.**

8. Is Person 1 of Hispanic, Latino, or Spanish origin?

- ☐ **No,** not of Hispanic, Latino, or Spanish origin
- ☐ Yes, Mexican, Mexican Am., Chicano
- ☐ Yes, Puerto Rican
- ☐ Yes, Cuban
- ☐ Yes, another Hispanic, Latino, or Spanish origin — *Print origin, for example, Argentinean, Colombian, Dominican, Nicaraguan, Salvadoran, Spaniard, and so on.*

9. What is Person 1's race? *Mark* X *one or more boxes.*

- ☐ White
- ☐ Black, African Am., or Negro
- ☐ American Indian or Alaska Native — *Print name of enrolled or principal tribe.*
- ☐ Asian Indian
- ☐ Chinese
- ☐ Filipino
- ☐ Other Asian — *Print race, for example, Hmong, Laotian, Thai, Pakistani, Cambodian, and so on.*
- ☐ Japanese
- ☐ Korean
- ☐ Vietnamese
- ☐ Native Hawaiian
- ☐ Guamanian or Chamorro
- ☐ Samoan
- ☐ Other Pacific Islander — *Print race, for example, Fijian, Tongan, and so on.*
- ☐ Some other race — *Print race.*

Do these two questions on the 2010 census form categorize racial distinctions in a meaningful way? Explain.

RESPONDING TO THE IMAGE

Answer one or both of the following questions.

1. Do you think questions 8 and 9 on the census form offer enough choices? (Note that the 2020 census form will include a write-on line for those who check the "White" box in question 9 to clarify their racial ancestry.) Do you think these questions offer *too many* choices? Explain.
2. Which box (or boxes) would you check to describe your own racial and ethnic identity? Why?

8.10 Victoria M. Massie, "Latino and Hispanic Identities Aren't the Same. They're Also Not Racial Groups."

An anthropologist, journalist, essayist, and editor, Victoria M. Massie writes about issues pertaining to race, African culture and identity, science and technology, and politics. Her work has appeared in such publications as *Anthropology News*, *Biopolitical Times*, *Catapult*, *Complex*, *GeneWatch*, *The Intercept*, and *Vox*. In the following essay, Massie describes the complexities of Latino and Hispanic culture.

BEFORE YOU READ

What connotations do the words *Latino* and *Hispanic* bring to mind? Are they similar or different? Are they positive, negative, or neutral?

Latino and Hispanic Identities Aren't the Same. They're Also Not Racial Groups.

What race are Hispanic people?

In the latest episode of MTV's *Decoded*, comedian Franchesca Ramsey pairs up with fellow YouTube activist Kat Lazo to explain how answering that question is tricky, largely because of the ways Hispanic (and, likewise, Latino or the gender-neutral Latinx) identity is racialized in the US, even though these categories don't actually refer to a race at all.

TO UNDERSTAND WHAT RACE LATINOS AND HISPANICS ARE, YOU FIRST MUST UNDERSTAND THE DIFFERENCE BETWEEN LATINOS AND HISPANICS

Lazo points out that Hispanic identity refers to language, or "people of Spanish-speaking origins." Latinx identity, however, refers to people whose origins are geographically located in Latin America.

And while the two categories mostly overlap, people from Brazil and Spain illustrate the distinction. Brazilians are Latino because the country is located in Latin America. But Brazilians aren't considered Hispanic because the country's primary language is Portuguese. Meanwhile, Latinx identity brings together people in South and Central America, who may share a history of Spanish colonization, but that category isn't defined by having Spanish-speaking ancestry.

5 "Just like America, Latin America has a long and complex history that intersects between native people, European colonization, African slavery, and global immigration patterns," Lazo said. And that's why she points out that Latinx identity includes a variety of races.

SO THAT'S WHY BOILING DOWN LATINX TO BEING JUST ONE "RACE" MAKES NO SENSE

Despite the broad racial diversity that actually represent Latinx and Hispanic people, they are often represented as one homogeneous group instead of being recognized as being just as racially diverse as the population of the United States.

As Lazo says, "The US and Latin American media has done a great job at constructing an image of what Latinx look like, and that image is rarely black or fully Indigenous, for example." So, instead, the more common profile of a Latinx person as portrayed in films and television is someone like *Modern Family* actress Sofia Vergara, as opposed to someone like Zoe Saldana, who identifies as Afro-Latina (of Puerto Rican and Dominican descent).

But racism, or pressure to identify as white, also plays a role in why Latinx and Hispanic people, when they are considered to be a race, are racialized as white.

"We, like the rest of the world, have internalized these message[s] of white supremacy through the media and our education," Lazo said. "So it's no wonder that when Latinx in the US are confronted with deciding their race based on the Census, in a predominantly black and white binary society, many of us default to white."

Latinx and Hispanic identity signifies common cultural practices like language 10
and shared histories, and those don't easily map onto skin color.

It's one of the reasons, Ramsey says, that "if an Argentinian couple adopts a baby from China, that baby will most likely grow up speaking Spanish, and rooting for Lionel Messi."[1]

At the end of the day, this is a reminder, as Ramsey (and *Vox*'s Jenée Desmond-Harris) has explained, that race is a social construct, not a natural biological classification. Rather, Ramsey said, race is "basically an ever-shifting categorization that sometimes includes ethnicity and sometimes doesn't."

Or a simpler answer, as Ramsey puts it: "Race doesn't exist, but ethnicity does." So are people who identify as Hispanic (or even Latinx) actually white?

As Ramsey says, "It depends." But it's important to reflect on the fraught reasons why Hispanic and Latinx identities are associated with whiteness too.

RESPONDING TO READING

1. According to Massie, what traits do Latinos and Hispanics share?
2. What differences between Latinos and Hispanics does Massie identify? How does she explain why these differences have been ignored by dominant cultures?

Rhetorical Analysis

Throughout her essay, Massie quotes Latina feminist and *YouTube* personality Kat Lazo. Does she effectively use this source to back up her points? Do you think Massie should have incorporated other sources into her essay? Explain.

[1] An Argentinian professional soccer player (1987–). [Eds.]

Writing with Sources

Research the history of the US government's decision to adopt the term *Hispanic* and the reactions of various Latino groups and individuals to this term. Based on what you find in your research, do you think there can (or should) be one term to describe all people of Latino heritage? If so, what term, and why? If not, why not?

8.11 Brent Staples, "Why Race Isn't as 'Black' and 'White' as We Think"

After earning a Ph.D. in psychology from the University of Chicago in 1977, Brent Staples (1951–) turned to journalism, writing for the *Chicago Sun-Times* and *The New York Times.* In 1990, he joined the editorial board of *The New York Times,* where his columns now appear regularly. His memoir *Parallel Time* (1994), which was inspired by his brother's murder in a dispute over a cocaine deal, describes Staples's own internal struggles. In the following essay, he considers the ways in which we live in a post-racial society.

BEFORE YOU READ

Have you, or has someone you know, used an ancestry DNA test? What did the test reveal? Did it change any previously held beliefs about racial distinctions or identity?

Why Race Isn't as "Black" and "White" as We Think

People have occasionally asked me how a black person came by a "white" name like Brent Staples. One letter writer ridiculed it as "an anchorman's name" and accused me of making it up. For the record, it's a British name—and the one my parents gave me. "Staples" probably arrived in my family's ancestral home in Virginia four centuries ago with the British settlers.

The earliest person with that name we've found—Richard Staples—was hacked to death by Powhatan Indians not far from Jamestown in 1622. The name moved into the 18th century with Virginians like John Staples, a white surveyor who worked in Thomas Jefferson's home county, Albemarle, not far from the area where my family was enslaved.

The black John Staples who married my paternal great-great-grandmother just after Emancipation—and became the stepfather of her children—could easily have been a Staples family slave. The transplanted Britons who had owned both sides of my family had given us more than a preference for British names. They had also given us their DNA. In what was an almost everyday occurrence at the time, my great-great-grandmothers on both sides gave birth to children fathered by white slave masters.

I've known all this for a long time, and was not surprised by the results of a genetic screening performed by DNAPrint Genomics, a company that traces ancestral origins to far-flung parts of the globe. A little more than half of my genetic material came from sub-Saharan Africa—common for people who regard themselves as black—with slightly more than a quarter from Europe.

5 The result that knocked me off my chair showed that one-fifth of my ancestry is Asian. Poring over the charts and statistics, I said out loud, "This has got to be a mistake."

That's a common response among people who are tested. Ostensibly white people who always thought of themselves as 100 percent European find they have substantial African ancestry. People who regard themselves as black sometimes discover that the African ancestry is a minority portion of their DNA.

These results are forcing people to re-examine the arbitrary calculations our culture uses to decide who is "white" and who is "black."

As with many things racial, this story begins in the slave-era South, where sex among slaves, masters and mistresses got started as soon as the first slave ship sailed into Jamestown Harbor in 1619. By the time of the American Revolution, there was a visible class of light-skinned black people who no longer looked or sounded African. Free mulattos, emancipated by guilt-ridden fathers, may have accounted for up to three-quarters of the tiny free-black population before the Revolution.

By the eve of the Civil War, the swarming numbers of mixed-race slaves on Southern plantations had become a source of constant anguish to planters' wives, who knew quite well where those racially ambiguous children were coming from.

10 Faced with widespread fear that racial distinctions were losing significance, the South decided to define the problem away. People with any ascertainable black ancestry at all were defined as black under the law and stripped of basic rights. The "one drop" laws defined as black even people who were blond and blue-eyed and appeared white.

Black people snickered among themselves and worked to subvert segregation at every turn. Thanks to white ancestry spread throughout the black community, nearly every family knew of someone born black who successfully passed as white to get access to jobs, housing and public accommodations that were reserved for white people only. Black people who were not quite light enough to slip undetected into white society billed themselves as Greek, Spanish, Portuguese, Italian, South Asian, Native American—you name it. These defectors often married into ostensibly white families at a time when interracial marriage was either illegal or socially stigmatized.

Those of us who grew up in the 1950's and 60's read black-owned magazines and newspapers that praised the racial defectors as pioneers while mocking white society for failing to detect them. A comic newspaper column by the poet Langston Hughes—titled "Why Not Fool Our White Folks?"—typified the black community's sense of smugness about knowing the real racial score. In keeping with this history, many black people I know find it funny when supposedly white

Americans profess shock at the emergence of blackness in the family tree. But genetic testing holds plenty of surprises for black folks, too.

Which brings me back to my Asian ancestry. It comes as a surprise, given that my family's oral histories contain not a single person who is described as Asian. More testing on other family members should clarify the issue, but for now, I can only guess. This ancestry could well have come through a 19th-century ancestor who was incorrectly described as Indian, often a catchall category at the time.

The test results underscore what anthropologists have said for eons: racial distinctions as applied in this country are social categories and not scientific concepts. In addition, those categories draw hard, sharp distinctions among groups of people who are more alike than they are different. The ultimate point is that none of us really know who we are, ancestrally speaking. All we ever really know is what our parents and grandparents have told us.

Source: From The New York Times, Staples, Brent (October 31) "Why Race Isn't as 'Black' and 'White' as We Think."

RESPONDING TO READING

1. What do the following pieces of information lead you to conclude about Staples's racial heritage?
   - Two of his great-great-grandmothers had children by white slave masters.
   - About half of his genetic material is from sub-Saharan Africa.
   - About a quarter of his genetic material is from Europe.
   - Twenty percent of his ancestry is Asian.
2. In his conclusion, Staples points out that "racial distinctions as applied in this country are social categories and not scientific concepts" (14). Do you think his conclusion suggests an optimistic or pessimistic view of future race relations? Explain.

Rhetorical Analysis

Given what we learn about Staples's roots, do you think *black* is the most appropriate term he could use to describe his racial identity? On what grounds would John H. McWhorter (p. 303) agree with this choice?

Writing with Sources

What can you find out about your own racial, religious, and cultural heritage? Interview several older relatives, and consult family genealogical records or other documents if available. Then, write an essay in which you trace your heritage and define your identity.

8.12 John H. McWhorter, "Why I'm Black, Not African American"

A contributing editor to the Manhattan Institute's *City Journal,* John H. McWhorter (1965–) is an associate professor of English and comparative literature at the Center for American Studies at Columbia University. McWhorter is the author of numerous books on language, race, culture, and music, including, most recently, *Talking Back, Talking Black: Truths About America's Lingua Franca* (2017). His work has appeared in numerous publications, such as the *Chronicle of Higher Education,* the *Los Angeles Times, New York Magazine, The New York Times, The Wall Street Journal,* and *The Washington Post.* In the following essay, McWhorter considers the cultural significance of the terms we use to define racial identity.

BEFORE YOU READ

What different terms are used to identify the ethnic or racial group from which you draw your primary cultural identity? Which term do you prefer, and why?

Why I'm Black, Not African American

It's time we descendants of slaves brought to the United States let go of the term "African American" and go back to calling ourselves Black— with a capital B.

Modern America is home now to millions of immigrants who were born in Africa. Their cultures and identities are split between Africa and the United States. They have last names like Onwughalu and Senkofa. They speak languages like Wolof, Twi, Yoruba and Hausa, and speak English with an accent. They were raised on African cuisine, music, dance and dress styles, customs and family dynamics. Their children often speak or at least understand their parents' native language.

Living descendants of slaves in America neither knew their African ancestors nor even have elder relatives who knew them. Most of us worship in Christian churches. Our cuisine is more southern U.S. than Senegalese. Starting with ragtime and jazz, we gave America intoxicating musical beats based on African conceptions of rhythm, but with melody and harmony based on Western traditions.

Also, we speak English. Black Americans' home speech is largely based on local dialects of England and Ireland. Africa echoes in the dialect only as a whisper, in certain aspects of sound and melody. A working-class black man in Cincinnati has more in common with a working-class white man in Providence than with a Ghanaian.

With the number of African immigrants in the U.S. nearly tripling since 1990, 5
the use of "African American" is becoming increasingly strained. For example, Alan Keyes, the Republican Senate candidate in Illinois, has claimed that as a descendant of slaves, he is the "real" African American, compared with his Democratic rival, Barack Obama, who has an African father and white mother. And the reason Keyes and others are making arguments such as this is rather small, the idea

being that "African American" should refer only to people with a history of subordination in this country—as if African immigrants such as Amadou Diallo, who was killed by police while reaching for his wallet, or Caribbean ones such as torture victim Abner Louima have found the U.S. to be the Land of Oz.

We are not African to any meaningful extent, but we are not white either—and that is much of why Jesse Jackson's presentation of the term "African American" caught on so fast. It sets us apart from the mainstream. It carries an air of standing protest, a reminder that our ancestors were brought here against their will, that their descendants were treated like animals for centuries, and that we have come a long way since then.

But we need a way of sounding those notes with a term that, first, makes some sense and, second, does not insult the actual African Americans taking their place in our country. And our name must also celebrate our history here, in the only place that will ever be our home. To term ourselves as part "African" reinforces a sad implication: that our history is basically slave ships, plantations, lynching, fire hoses in Birmingham, and then South Central,[1] and that we need to look back to Mother Africa to feel good about ourselves.

But what about the black business districts that thrived across the country after slavery was abolished? What about Frederick Douglass, Ida B. Wells, W.E.B. Du Bois, Gwendolyn Brooks, Richard Wright and Thurgood Marshall, none born in Africa and all deeply American people? And while we're on Marshall, what about the civil rights revolution, a moral awakening that we gave to ourselves and the nation. My roots trace back to working-class Black people—Americans, not foreigners—and I'm proud of it. I am John Hamilton McWhorter the Fifth. Four men with my name and appearance, doing their best in a segregated America, came before me. They and their dearest are the heritage that I can feel in my heart, and they knew the sidewalks of Philadelphia and Atlanta, not Sierra Leone.

So, we will have a name for ourselves—and it should be Black. "Colored" and "Negro" had their good points but carry a whiff of *Plessy v. Ferguson* and Bull Connor[2] about them, so we will let them lie. "Black" isn't perfect, but no term is.

10 Meanwhile, the special value of "Black" is that it carries the same potent combination of pride, remembrance and regret that "African American" was designed for. Think of what James Brown meant with "Say it loud, I'm Black and I'm proud." And then imagine: "Say it loud, I'm African American and I'm proud."

Since the late 1980s, I have gone along with using "African American" for the same reason that we throw rice at a bride—because everybody else was doing it. But no more. From now on, in my writings on race I will be returning to the word I grew up with, which reminds me of my true self and my ancestors who worked here to help make my life possible: Black.

[1]The 1992 South Central Los Angeles race riots. [Eds.]

[2]The Birmingham, Alabama, Commissioner of Public Safety (1897–1973) who, in 1963, ordered police officers to use police dogs and fire hoses to break up civil rights demonstrations. [Eds.]

RESPONDING TO READING

1. Why does McWhorter believe that *African American* is an inappropriate term for black Americans?
2. According to McWhorter, what negative associations does the term *African American* have? What positive connotations does he associate with *black*? Does he make a convincing argument for his characterization of these two terms?

Rhetorical Analysis

Throughout this essay, McWhorter capitalizes the word *black* but not the word *white*. Why? What is your reaction to this stylistic decision?

Writing with Sources

In paragraph 8, McWhorter lists six prominent men and women. Research the life and career of one of these people. Then, write an essay in which you apply McWhorter's criteria to help you decide whether the individual you chose should be considered *black* or *African American*.

Widening the Focus

For Critical Reading and Writing

Referring specifically to the three readings in this chapter's Focus section (and possibly to additional sources as well), write an essay in which you answer the question, "Do Racial Distinctions Still Matter?"

For Further Reading

The following readings can suggest additional perspectives for thinking and writing about the role of race and culture in American society.

- John Kirbow, "To Clarify: An Open Letter to the Men's Rights Movement, on the #MeToo Hashtag" (p. 257)
- Jon Meacham, "To Hope Rather than to Fear" (p. 311)
- K. C. Williams, "Teaching While Black" (p. 378)
- Alex Wagner, from *Futureface* (p. 455)

For Focused Research

The diverse cultural makeup of the United States has defined the country since its inception. Today, the population of some cultural groups, such as Asian

Americans and Latinos/Hispanics, is growing exponentially. To gain greater insight into the various cultural groups in the United States, consult the Pew Research Center's *Hispanic Trends* website as well as the website for Brigham Young University's McKay School of Education, which contains information on specific cultural groups. Then, write an essay about the fastest-growing cultural groups in the United States. Who is in the majority now, and who will be in the majority in 25 or 50 years? How do you think the growing population of these groups will change the United States? Support your points with information from the online resources you use.

Beyond the Classroom

Survey ten classmates representing several different races or ethnicities, and ask them the following questions:

- Would you date a person of another race or ethnicity? Why or why not?
- Would you marry a person of another race or ethnicity? Why or why not?
- How would your parents react in each case?

Compare the responses you get from people of different races and ethnicities. Based on this very limited sample, do the respondents from one background seem more open to interracial dating and marriage than the respondents from another background? If so, how do you account for these differences? Write an essay that summarizes your conclusions.

Exploring Issues and Ideas

Culture and Identity

Write an essay in response to one of the following prompts, which are suitable for assignments that require the use of outside sources as well as for assignments that are not source-based.

1. Write an essay in which you define your cultural identity. With which group or groups do you identify most strongly, and why? Begin your essay by analyzing how one writer in this chapter views a particular cultural identity. Then, discuss how your own attitudes toward culture are like and unlike those held by the writer you chose.
2. Do you think there is a distinctly "American" culture? If so, what are its key characteristics? Do you think that this "American" culture will endure? Write an essay in which you answer these questions, using information from readings in this chapter to support your points.
3. Several writers represented in this chapter describe a feeling of being pulled in two directions, torn between one's own culture and the "American" society in which one lives. Do you believe this conflict can ever be resolved, or do you think first and future generations of Americans, and especially the descendants of slaves, will always feel torn?

4. Is it possible to identify equally with two cultures—for example, black and Latino, Christian and Asian, urban and Native American? Write an essay that answers this question, referring to one or more essays in this chapter as well as to your own experiences.
5. Write an extended definition of a culture that is not based on race, ethnicity, or religion—for example, business culture; hockey culture; or rural, suburban, or urban culture.
6. Many people believe that a "culture of poverty" exists in our nation. Define this culture, enumerating its features, and explain how and why members of this culture are set apart from mainstream culture. Refer to Melanie Scheller's essay (p. 286) in your discussion.

Chapter 9
The American Dream

In this chapter, you will learn to:

- analyze readings about the American Dream.
- compose essays about the American Dream.

The American Dream—a term popularized by James Truslow Adams in his 1931 book *The Epic of America*—today encompasses everything from political and religious freedom to equal access to education and equal opportunity in the workplace. For immigrants, particularly those escaping difficult or even dangerous conditions in their native countries, the dream has also meant political and religious freedom, freedom from discrimination and persecution, and a guarantee of safety. For generations, it has also meant the possibility of upward mobility, financial

Bettmann/Getty Images

What elements does this image of an African-American man at a "colored" drinking fountain in Oklahoma City, Oklahoma, in 1939 use to show a former definition of the American Dream?

success, and, eventually, economic prosperity. However, for many Americans today, burdened by student loans, mortgage debt, medical bills, and unemployment, the dream can seem elusive. Middle-class wages are stagnating while the very rich get richer, and many feel they can no longer hope for a financially secure retirement. Nonetheless, a 2017 Pew Research Center survey revealed that the majority of Americans believe that the American Dream is attainable, perhaps because only 11 percent of Americans count wealth as an essential component of the dream.

Despite the obstacles we face, we pursue the American Dream. For some, this pursuit means struggling to overcome their status as newcomers or outsiders: to fit in, to belong, to be accepted. As they work toward their goals, however, some of these individuals must make painful decisions, for full participation in American society may mean assimilating: giving up language, custom, and culture and becoming more like others. Thus, although the American Dream may ultimately mean winning something, it can sometimes mean losing something as well.

For many people, an important part of the American Dream is the chance to reinvent themselves—the opportunity to become someone different, someone better. From Benjamin Franklin to Malcolm X, Americans have a long tradition of reinvention, which can involve anything from undertaking a program of self-improvement to undergoing a complete change of social identity.

In a free and mobile society, people can (theoretically, at least) become whatever they want to be. In the United States, reinvention has often come about through education and hard work, but Americans

Kristoffer Tripplaar/Alamy Stock Photo

What elements does this image of president-elect Barack Obama at his inauguration in January 2009 use to show a current definition of the American Dream?

have also been able to change who they are and how they are perceived by changing their professions, their associations, or their places of residence. Along with this process of reinvention comes a constant self-analysis, as we Americans continue to question who we are and what we can become.

In this chapter's Focus section, "Is the American Dream Still Attainable?" (p. 338), Joe Kennedy III, in his Democratic Response to the State of the Union (p. 338), evaluates our current situation and proposes a different vision of the American Dream; Neal Gabler, in "The New American Dream" (p. 342), examines how the dream has changed for middle- and upper-middle-class Americans; and Carol Graham, in "Is the American Dream Really Dead?" (p. 345), considers the relationship among happiness, upward mobility, and the American Dream.

Preparing to Read and Write

As you read and prepare to write about the essays in this chapter, you may consider the following questions:

- What assumptions does the writer seem to have about his or her audience? How can you tell?
- Is the writer's primary purpose to define the American Dream? Is it to explain his or her dream to others, to explore his or her own place in American society, to persuade readers to take action, or something else?
- What genre is the writer using? For example, is the reading a proposal, a poem, or a speech? How do the conventions of this genre influence the writer's choices?
- What appeals does the writer use? For example, does he or she appeal primarily to emotion or to reason? Is this the most effective appeal?
- What does the American Dream mean to the writer? Is the American Dream defined in social, political, economic, or cultural terms?
- Has the writer been able to achieve the American Dream? If so, by what means? If not, why not?
- What are the greatest obstacles that stand between the writer and the American Dream? Would you characterize these obstacles as primarily cultural, social, political, racial, economic, religious, or educational?
- Who do you think has the easiest access to the American Dream? For whom is access most difficult? Why?
- Is the writer looking at the United States from the point of view of an insider or an outsider?

- Does the writer want to change his or her status, or to change the status of others? What steps, if any, does he or she take to do so? What additional steps could he or she take?
- Does the writer focus on his or her own pursuit of the American Dream or on what the dream means to a particular group—or to the nation?
- Does the writer speak as an individual or as a representative of a particular group?
- Which writers' views of the American Dream are most similar, most different, and most like your own?

Shared Writing

The American Dream

What does the American Dream mean to you? Have you achieved it? Do you want to? Why or why not?

9.1 Jon Meacham, "To Hope Rather than to Fear"

A visiting distinguished professor of political science at Vanderbilt University, Jon Meacham (1969–) is a presidential historian and Pulitzer Prize-winning biographer. A contributing writer for *The New York Times Book Review* and a fellow of the Society of American Historians, he is the author of six books, including, most recently, *The Soul of America: The Battle for Our Better Angels* (2018), in which the following excerpt appears as the introduction. His work has also appeared in such publications as *Newsweek, The New Yorker,* and *Time*. In the following essay, Meacham traces the complicated history of the American Dream.

BEFORE YOU READ

Define the words *hope* and *fear*. What do these terms mean to you?

To Hope Rather than to Fear

Back of the writhing, yelling, cruel-eyed demons who break, destroy, maim and lynch and burn at the stake, is a knot, large or small, of normal human beings, and these human beings at heart are desperately afraid of something. Of what? Of many things, but usually of losing their jobs, being declassed,

> degraded, or actually disgraced: of losing their hopes, their savings, their plans for their children; of the actual pangs of hunger, of dirt, of crime.
>
> —W. E. B. Du Bois, *Black Reconstruction in America*, 1935

> We are not enemies, but friends. We must not be enemies. Though passion may have strained it must not break our bonds of affection. The mystic chords of memory, stretching from every battlefield and patriot grave to every living heart and hearthstone all over this broad land, will yet swell the chorus of the Union, when again touched, as surely they will be, by the better angels of our nature.
>
> —Abraham Lincoln, First Inaugural Address, 1861

The fate of America—or at least of white America, which was the only America that seemed to count—was at stake. On the autumn evening of Thursday October 7, 1948, South Carolina governor Strom Thurmond, the segregationist Dixiecrat candidate for president of the United States, addressed a crowd of one thousand inside the University of Virginia's Cabell Hall in Charlottesville. The subject at hand: President Harry S. Truman's civil rights program, one that included anti-lynching legislation and protections against racial discrimination in hiring.

Thurmond was having none of it. Such measures, he thundered, "would undermine the American way of life and outrage the Bill of Rights." Interrupted by applause and standing ovations, Thurmond, who had bolted the Democratic National Convention in July to form the States' Rights Democratic Party, was in his element in the Old Confederacy. "I want to tell you, ladies and gentlemen," Thurmond had said in accepting the breakaway party's nomination in Birmingham, Alabama, "that there's not enough troops in the army to force the Southern people to break down segregation and admit the nigra race into our theaters, into our swimming pools, into our homes, into our churches."

The message was clear. He and his fellow Dixiecrats, he told the University of Virginia crowd, offered "the only genuine obstacle to the rise of socialism or communism in America." Civil rights, Thurmond declared, were a Red plot against the Free World: "Only the States Rights Democrats—and we alone—have the moral courage to stand up to the Communists and tell them this foreign doctrine will not work in free America."

Nearly seventy years on, in the heat of a Virginia August in 2017, heirs to the Dixiecrats' platform of white supremacy—twenty-first century Klansmen and neo-Nazis among them—gathered in Charlottesville, not far from where Thurmond had taken his stand. The story is depressingly well known: A young counter-protestor, Heather Meyer, was killed. Two Virginia state troopers died in a helicopter crash as part of an operation to maintain order. And the president of the United States—himself an heir to the white populist tradition of Thurmond and of Alabama's George Wallace[1]—said that there had been an "egregious display of hatred, bigotry and violence on many sides," as if there were more than one side to a conflict

[1] Democratic governor of Alabama from 1963–1967, 1971–1979, and 1983–1987. [Eds.]

between neo-Nazis who idolized Adolf Hitler and Americans who stood against Ku Klux Klansmen and white nationalists. The remarks were of a piece with the incumbent president's divisive language on immigration (among many other subjects, from political foes to women) and his nationalist rhetoric.

5 Extremism, racism, nativism, and isolationism, driven by fear of the unknown, tend to spike in periods of economic and social stress—a period like our own. Americans today have little trust in government; household incomes lag behind our usual middle-class expectations. The fires of fear in America have long found oxygen when broad, seemingly threatening change is afoot. Now, in the second decade of the new century, in the presidency of Donald Trump, the alienated are being mobilized afresh by changing demography, by broadening conceptions of identity, and by an economy that prizes Information Age brains over manufacturing brawn. "We are determined to take our country back." David Duke, a former grand wizard of the Ku Klux Klan, said in Charlottesville. "We are going to fulfill the promises of Donald Trump. That's what we believed in, that's why we voted for Donald Trump. Because he said he's going to take our country back. And that's what we gotta do."

For many, the fact that we have arrived at a place in the life of the nation where a grand wizard of the KKK can claim, all too plausibly, that he is at one with the will of the president of the United States seems an unprecedented moment. History, however, shows us that we are frequently vulnerable to fear, bitterness, and strife. The good news is that we have come through such darkness before.

This book is a portrait of hours in which the politics of fear were prevalent—a reminder that periods of public dispiritedness are not new and a reassurance that they are survivable. In the best of moments, witness, protest, and resistance can intersect with the leadership of an American president to lift us to higher ground. In darker times, if a particular president fails to advance the national story—or, worse, moves us backward—then those who witness, protest, and resist must stand fast, in hope, working toward a better day. Progress in American life, as we will see, has been slow, painful, bloody, and tragic. Across too many generations, women, African Americans, immigrants, and others have been denied the full promise of Thomas Jefferson's Declaration of Independence. Yet the journey has gone on, and proceeds even now.

There's a natural tendency in American political life to think that things were always better in the past. The passions of previous years fade, to be inevitably replaced by the passions of the present. Nostalgia is a powerful force, and in the maelstrom of the moment many of us seek comfort in imagining that once there was a Camelot—without quite remembering that the Arthurian legend itself was about a court riven by ambition and infidelity. One point of this book is to remind us that imperfection is the rule, not the exception.

With countries as with individuals, a sense of proportion is essential. All has seemed lost before, only to give way, after decades of gloom, to light. And that is in large measure because, in the battle between the impulses of good and of evil in the American soul, what Lincoln called "the better angels of our nature" have prevailed just often enough to keep the national enterprise alive. To speak of a soul at all—either of a person or of a country—can seem speculative and gauzy. Yet belief in the existence of an immanent collection of convictions, dispositions, and sensitivities that shape character and inform conduct is ancient and perennial. . . .

10 So it has been from the beginning—even before the beginning, really, if we think of 1776 as the birth of the nation. "I always consider the settlement of America with Reverence and Wonder," John Adams wrote in 1765, "as the Opening of a grand scene and Design in Providence, for the Illumination of the Ignorant and the Emancipation of the slavish Part of Mankind all over the Earth." Jefferson, too, spoke of the animating American conviction that tomorrow can be better than today. In his eighty-second year, Jefferson wrote of a "march of civilization" that had, in his long lifetime, passed "over like a cloud of light, increasing our knowledge and improving our condition.... And where this progress will stop no one can say."

In the middle of the nineteenth century, the minister and abolitionist Theodore Parker defined "the American idea" as the love of freedom versus the law of slavery. Frederick Douglass, the former slave who became a leading voice for equality, believed deeply in America's capacity for justice. "I know of no soil better adapted to the growth of reform than American soil," Douglass said after the Supreme Court's Dred Scott decision in 1857. "I know of no country where the conditions for affecting great changes in the settled order of things, for the development of right ideas of liberty and humanity, are more favorable than here in these United States." Eleanor Roosevelt, niece of TR,[2] wife of FDR,[3] and global human rights pioneer, wrote, "It is essential that we remind ourselves frequently of our past history that we recall the shining promise that it offered to all men everywhere who would be free, the promise that it is still our destiny to fulfill."

Self-congratulatory, even self-delusional? At times and in part, yes. It's an inescapable fact of experience, though, that from John Winthrop to Jefferson to Lincoln, America has been defined by a sense of its own exceptionalism—an understanding of destiny that has also been tempered by an appreciation of the tragic nature of life. "Man's capacity for justice makes democracy possible," the theologian and thinker Reinhold Niebuhr wrote in 1944, "but man's inclination to injustice makes democracy necessary." We try; we fail; but we must try again, and again, and again, for only in trial is progress possible.

Deep in our national soul we believe ourselves to be entitled by the free gifts of nature and of nature's God—and, in a theological frame, of our Creator—to pursue happiness. That ambient reality has been so strong that even the most clear-eyed among us have admitted the distinctive nature of the nation. "Intellectually I know America is no better than any other country; emotionally I know she is better than every other country," the novelist Sinclair Lewis remarked in 1930. He was not alone then, nor would he be alone now.

To know what has come before is to be armed against despair. If the men and women of the past, with all their flaws and limitations and ambitions and appetites, could press on through ignorance and superstition, racism and sexism, selfishness and greed, to create a freer, stronger nation, then perhaps we, too, can right wrongs and take another step toward that most enchanting and elusive of destinations: a more perfect Union.

---

[2] Twenty-sixth U.S. President Theodore Roosevelt (1858–1919). [Eds.]

[3] Thirty-second U.S. President Franklin D. Roosevelt (1882–1945). [Eds.]

To do so requires innumerable acts of citizenship and of private grace. It will 15
require, as it has in the past, the witness and the bravery of reformers who hold no office and who have no traditional power but who yearn for a better, fairer way of life. And it will also require, I believe, a president of the United States with a temperamental disposition to speak to the country's hopes rather than to its fears.

In the 1790s with the Alien and Sedition Acts, the Federalists sought not just to will elections but to eliminate their opponents altogether. In the age of Jackson, South Carolina extremists threatened the Union, only to be put down by a president who, for his manifold flaws, believed in the Union above all. Anti-Roman Catholic sentiment, driven by immigration, gave rise to a major political movement, the Know-Nothings, in the years before the Civil War. The Reconstruction era featured several instances of progress and light in the passage of crucial constitutional amendments concerning equality and in U. S. Grant's 1870–71 stand against the Ku Klux Klan, only to give way to Jim Crow laws and nearly a hundred years of legalized segregation.

In just the past century, during World War I and after the Bolshevik Revolution of 1917, a new Ku Klux Klan, boosted in part by the movie *The Birth of a Nation*, took advantage of American anxiety to target blacks, immigrants, Roman Catholics, and Jews. The fear that the "huddled masses" of Emma Lazarus's poem "The New Colossus" would destroy the America that whites had come to know helped lead to the founding of the twentieth-century Klan, a nationwide organization that staged massive marches down Pennsylvania Avenue in Washington in 1925 and 1926. Isolationists and Nazi sympathizers took their stand in the 1930s; their influence evaporated only with the Japanese bombing of Pearl Harbor on Sunday, December 7, 1941, and Adolf Hitler's subsequent declaration of war on the United States. Then there was the anti-Communist hysteria of the early Cold War period and the white Southern defense of segregation in the civil rights era.

As Truman and Roosevelt—and Jackson and Lincoln and Grant and TR and Wilson and Eisenhower and Kennedy and Lyndon Johnson and Ronald Reagan, among others—understood, the president of the United States has not only administrative and legal but moral and cultural power. "For only the President represents the national interest," John F. Kennedy said. "And upon him alone converge all the needs and aspirations of all parts of the country; all departments of the Government, all nations of the world." There was nothing, Lyndon Johnson remarked, that "makes a man come to grips more directly with his conscience than the Presidency. Sitting in that chair involves making decisions that draw out a man's fundamental commitments. The burden of his responsibility literally opens up his soul. No longer can he accept matters as given; no longer can he write off hopes and needs as impossible." The office was a crucible of character. "In that house of decision, the White House, a man becomes his commitments," Johnson said. "He understands who he really is. He learns what he genuinely wants to be."

I am writing now not because past American presidents have always risen to the occasion but because the incumbent American President so rarely does. A president sets a tone for the nation and helps tailor habits of heart and of mind. Presidential action and presidential grace are often crucial in ameliorating moments of virulence and violence—and presidential indifference and presidential obtuseness can exacerbate such hours.

20 Our greatest leaders have pointed *toward* the future—not *at* this group or that sect. Looking back on the Dixiecrat challenge, Harry Truman—the man who won the four-way 1948 presidential campaign, triumphing over the segregationist Thurmond, the Progressive candidate Henry A. Wallace, and the Republican Thomas E. Dewey—once said: "You can't divide the country up into sections and have one rule for one section and one rule for another, and you can't encourage people's prejudices. You have to appeal to people's best instincts, not their worst ones. You may win an election or so by doing the other but it does a lot of harm to the country." Truman understood something his legendary immediate predecessor had also grasped: that as Franklin D. Roosevelt observed during the 1932 campaign, "The Presidency is not merely an administrative office. That's the least of it. It is more than an engineering job, efficient or inefficient. It is pre-eminently a place of moral leadership. All our great Presidents were leaders of thought at times when certain historic ideas in the life of the nation had to be clarified."

We are more likely to choose the right path when we are encouraged to do so from the very top. The country has come to look to the White House for a steadying hand, in word and deed, in uneasy times. As Woodrow Wilson observed more than a century ago, the president is "at the front of our government, where our own thoughts and the attention of men everywhere is centered upon him."...

The opposite of fear is hope, defined as the expectation of good fortune not only for ourselves but for the group to which we belong. Fear feeds anxiety and produces anger; hope, particularly in a political sense, breeds optimism and feelings of well-being. Fear is about limits; hope is about growth. Fear casts its eyes warily, even shiftily, across the landscape; hope looks forward, toward the horizon. Fear points at others, assigning blame; hope points ahead, working for a common good. Fear pushes away; hope pulls others closer. Fear divides; hope unifies.

"The coward, then, is a despairing sort of person; for he fears everything," Aristotle wrote. "The brave man, on the other hand, has the opposite disposition; for confidence is the mark of a hopeful disposition." In Christian terms, fear, according to Saint Augustine, was caused by "the loss of what we love." Building on Augustine, Saint Thomas Aquinas wrote that "properly speaking, hope regards only the good; in this respect, hope differs from fear, which regards evil."

Augustine and Aquinas viewed the world in theological terms; in due historical course, the Puritans and successive generations of Americans would also see our national story in a religious context. To be sure, as Shakespeare wrote, "The devil can cite Scripture for his purpose," and the Bible has been used to justify human chattel, to cloak Native American removal with missionary language, and to repress the rights of women. At the same time, the great American reform movements have drawn strength from religious traditions and spiritual leaders. "I do not know if all Americans have faith in their religion—for who can read the secrets of the heart?—but I am sure that they think it necessary to the maintenance of republican institutions," Alexis de Tocqueville wrote in the Age of Jackson. "That is not the view of one class or party among the citizens, but of the whole nation; it is found in all ranks."

25 There was a genius about the American Founding and the emergence of American democratic politics. That genius lay in no small part in the recognition

that the Republic was as susceptible to human passions as human beings themselves. The Founders expected seasons of anger and frustration; they anticipated hours of unhappiness and unrest. Fear frequently defies constitutional and political moderation, for it is more emotional than rational. When the unreconstructed Southerner of the late nineteenth century or the anti-Semite of the twentieth believed—or the nativist of the globalized world of the twenty-first *believes*—others to be less than human, then the protocols of politics and the checks and balances of the Madisonian system of governance face formidable tests. Mediating conflicting claims between groups if one of the groups refuses to acknowledge the very humanity of the others is a monumental task. Our Constitution and our politics, however, have endured and prevailed, vindicating the Founders' vision of a country that would require amendment and adjustment. That the nation was constructed with an awareness of sin and the means to take account of societal changes has enabled us to rise above the furies of given moments and given ages.

And while those furies sometimes ebb, they also sometimes flow. In a November 1963 lecture that formed the basis of a *Harper's* cover story and of a book, the Columbia historian Richard Hofstadter defined what he called "the paranoid style in American politics," a recurring popular tendency to adhere to extreme conspiratorial theories about threats to the country. "The paranoid spokesman sees the fate of conspiracy in apocalyptic terms—he traffics in the birth and death of whole worlds, whole political orders, whole systems of human values," Hofstadter wrote. "He is always manning the barricades of civilization. He constantly lives at a turning point: it is now or never in organizing resistance to conspiracy. Time is forever running out."

The measure of our political and cultural health cannot be whether we all agree on all things at all times. We don't, and we won't. Disagreement and debate—including ferocious disagreement and exhausting debate—are hallmarks of American politics. As Jefferson noted, divisions of opinion have defined free societies since the days of Greece and Rome. The art of politics lies in the manufacturing of a workable consensus for a given time—not unanimity. This is an art, not a science. There is no algorithm that can tell a president or a people what to do. Like life, history is contingent and conditional.

In the American experience—so far—such contingencies and conditions have produced a better nation. Strom Thurmond's fate in the 1948 election is, in a way, itself an encouraging example. The Dixiecrat carried just four states—Louisiana, Mississippi, Alabama, and Thurmond's native South Carolina. Given a choice, a sufficient number of American voters believed Truman the right man to bet on. In electing the Democratic nominee to a full term, the people were picking a president who, in 1947, had addressed the National Association for the Advancement of Colored People at The Lincoln Memorial—a first for an American president—and who had commissioned a report, *To Secure These Rights*, which offered a devastating critique of racial discrimination and detailed a civil rights program to bring African Americans into the mainstream.

Truman's motivations were both strategic and moral. The black vote was important in urban areas outside the Old Confederacy, and elections mattered.

Principle and politics were intertwined: In Truman's view, candidates who carried the day at the polls would be able to do more in victory than they could in defeat. "It is my deep conviction," the president had told the NAACP,[4] "that we have reached a turning point in the long history of our country's efforts to guarantee freedom and equality to all our citizens. It is more important today than ever before to insure that all Americans enjoy these rights." He added: "When I say all Americans I mean all Americans." The president had written the "all Americans" sentence in his own hand on a draft of the address.

30 On the Fourth of July, 1947—he had spoken to the NAACP just the week before—President Truman delivered a speech at Monticello, Thomas Jefferson's mountaintop house. In the wake of World War II, Truman said, "We have learned that nations are interdependent, and that recognition of our dependence upon one another is essential to life, liberty, and the pursuit of happiness of all mankind." Everything was linked. "So long as the basic rights of men are denied in any substantial portion of the earth, men everywhere must live in fear of their own rights and their own security." Truman said, "No country has yet reached the absolute in protecting human rights. In all countries, certainly including our own, there is much to be accomplished."

History, Truman knew, is not a fairy tale. It is more often tragic than comic, full of broken hearts and broken promises, disappointed hopes and dreams delayed. But progress is possible. Hope is sustaining. Fear can be overcome. What follows is the story of how we have endured moments of madness and of injustice, giving the better angels of which Lincoln spoke on the eve of the Civil War a chance to prevail—and how we can again.

RESPONDING TO READING

1. In paragraphs 22–23, Meacham defines and contrasts hope with fear. What is hope exactly? How does it point us toward "the right path" (21)?
2. According to Meacham, what is the American Dream? How do fearful tendencies prevent Americans from realizing the dream?

Rhetorical Analysis

In paragraph 7, Meacham states the purpose of his book as "a reminder that periods of public dispiritedness are not new and a reassurance that they are survivable." Why do you think he chose to look back at American history for lessons on how to move forward? What other options did he have? Was this the best choice?

---

[4] The National Association for the Advancement of Colored People, a U.S. civil rights organization. [Eds.]

Writing with Sources

Research one of the historical events Meacham mentions in his essay. What impact did it have on Americans pursuing a better future? How specifically did the event influence American lives? Do these repercussions continue today?

9.2 Jonathan Rieder, "Dr. King's Righteous Fury"

A sociology professor at Barnard College, Jonathan Rieder (1948–) is the author of three books: *Canarsie: The Jews and Italians of Brooklyn against Liberalism* (1985), *The Word of the Lord Is upon Me: The Righteous Performance of Martin Luther King, Jr.* (2008), and *Gospel of Freedom: Martin Luther King, Jr.'s Letter from Birmingham Jail and the Struggle That Changed a Nation* (2013). His work has appeared in publications such as the *Huffington Post*, the *Los Angeles Times, The New Yorker, The New York Times, The New York Times Book Review, Slate*, and *The Washington Post*. In the following essay, Rieder considers what the American Dream has meant to King and to other African Americans.

BEFORE YOU READ

Find Martin Luther King, Jr.'s "Letter from Birmingham Jail" and summarize a couple of its main points. What do you see as the significance of this classic text?

Dr. King's Righteous Fury

Chris Rock caused a stir last Fourth of July when he tweeted, "Happy white peoples independence day the slaves weren't free but I'm sure they enjoyed fireworks." Mr. Rock's tweet may not have topped the Rev. Jeremiah A. Wright Jr.'s "God damn America" sermon, but both sentiments are of a piece, and both seem a far cry from the Rev. Dr. Martin Luther King Jr.'s appeal to the American dream and his embrace of "the magnificent words of the Constitution and the Declaration of Independence."

But this view of King as an ardent proponent of American exceptionalism fails to capture a significant part of his thinking, a set of ideas embodied in one of his most famous works, "Letter from Birmingham Jail." What we remember today as a stirring piece about freedom and justice was also a furious reading of American history and an equally indignant attitude toward King's white contemporaries.

Arrested on April 12, 1963, during an epic struggle to desegregate Birmingham, Ala., King was in jail when he read the statement of eight white moderate clergymen who criticized the demonstrations as "untimely," branded King "extreme" and chided the protesters for precipitating violence.

King's letter, written on scraps of paper smuggled out of the jail and first made public on April 16, 1963, began as irate jottings of rebuttal. In its final form, though, the indignation was not evident in every sentence: the opening words, "My dear fellow clergymen," brimmed with precious gentility.

5 Later, King offered reasoned justifications for civil disobedience and rarefied nods to the theologians Martin Buber and Paul Tillich. And he evoked universalism with the proclamation, "Injustice anywhere is a threat to justice everywhere."

Yet black anger, not fancy philosophy, was the driving force behind the letter. You don't have to be a literary critic to sense the cold fury: "For years now, I have heard the word 'Wait!' It rings in the ear of every Negro with piercing familiarity."

In a line worthy of Malcolm X decrying white "tricknology," King savaged what he saw as white mendacity: "This 'Wait!' has almost always meant 'Never.'" His target was not the Ku Klux Klan, but a vast majority of "moderate" Americans, including the Kennedy administration, who had urged him to postpone the protests. Presumably, they meant never, too.

Hardly naïve about the power of moral appeal to stir the white conscience, King flirted with the idea that whites were virtually incapable of empathizing with the black plight. "I should have realized that few members of the oppressor race can understand the deep groans or passionate yearnings of the oppressed race."

In a mass meeting just days after getting out of jail, he depicted blacks as alone in an indifferent nation: "Don't you ever think that anything is going to be given to us in this struggle."

10 Toward the end of the letter, King wrote, "I have no fear about the outcome of our struggle in Birmingham." Where did he find such certainty? Ultimately, it was rooted in his belief, stated elsewhere, that "the Lord will make a way out of no way" and "there is a balm in Gilead."[1] Yet in his letter King offered none of this. It was as if he viewed the white ministers as unworthy of spiritual sharing. (In a mass meeting a few weeks later, he would gibe, "They are all pitiful.")

Nor did King draw confidence from the idea that America was destined for democracy. While he did mention that "we will reach the goal of freedom in Birmingham ... because the goal of America is freedom," this is a brief aside and not his central point. Rather, King found optimism in his deep faith in black people. At its core, the "Letter" was a proclamation of black self-sufficiency.

King began his paean to black majesty with the line "abused and scorned though we may be," a reference to the slavery-era spiritual "'Buked and Scorned," which evokes the slaves' suffering and their conviction that "Jesus died to set me free."

It was a touchstone for King, a link to his revered forebears, and one he referenced repeatedly. "Abused and scorned though we may be, our destiny is tied up with America's destiny. Before the Pilgrims landed at Plymouth we were here. Before the pen of Jefferson etched across the pages of history the mighty words of the Declaration of Independence, we were here."

Reading those lines on paper barely hints at the force of those stanzas as King usually spoke them: a defiant assertion of a black right to belong that rested

[1] A Biblical reference signifying a medicinal cure or salvation through Jesus Christ; also a traditional African American spiritual. [Eds.]

on something more primal than, and prior to, the nation's official documents and civic heroes.

In the "Letter," King immediately sidled from the "we were here" refrain into 15
another of his favorite passages of ancestor worship: "For more than two centuries our forebears labored in this country without wages; they made cotton king; they built the homes of their masters while suffering gross injustice and shameful humiliation. And yet out of a bottomless vitality they continued to thrive and develop. If the inexpressible cruelties of slavery could not stop us, the opposition we now face will surely fail."

It is a mistake, then, to make too much of King's occasional references to the American dream. He read American history in the light of the black experience of it. The labor of a slave was not the labor of a lonely individual who sought the pristine state of American nature, worked the land and acquired property. The story of the slaves was of a people in "exile," King said, whose skin color and forced labor made for a different kind of "exceptionalism": They were other people's property, the instruments of somebody else's dream.

King continued with this theme to the end of his life. "They kept us in slavery 244 years in this country, and they said they freed us from slavery," King recalled in a 1968 speech, shortly before he was killed, "but they didn't give us any land . . . And they haven't given us anything! After making our foreparents work and labor for 244 years—for nothing! Didn't pay 'em a cent."

"We hold these truths to be self-evident, that all men are endowed by their creator with inalienable rights. That's a beautiful creed," King told his crowd. It is easy to read such sentences in "Letter from Birmingham Jail" and other works by King and leave it at that. But it is vital to read what he said next: "America has never lived up to it."

RESPONDING TO READING

1. Rieder opens his essay with a quotation by Chris Rock. Is this an effective introduction to the argument that follows? Why or why not?
2. In paragraph 16, Rieder says, "It is a mistake, . . . to make too much of King's occasional references to the American Dream." Why does Rieder believe that this is "a mistake"? How do you suppose Rieder would expect King to have defined the American Dream?

Rhetorical Analysis

Rieder's primary purpose in this essay is to correct what he believes is a common misconception about King's "Letter from Birmingham Jail." What is this misconception? What do you think Rieder hopes to achieve by re-examining King's writing?

Writing with Sources

Watch Jeremiah A. Wright's sermon (mentioned in paragraph 1) on YouTube, and read a transcript of his words. Then, do the same with Martin Luther King, Jr.'s famous "I Have a Dream" speech. In an essay, analyze the similarities and differences between the two speeches, focusing on their content, rhetorical strategies, and delivery.

9.3 Thomas Jefferson, The Declaration of Independence

Thomas Jefferson (1743–1826)—lawyer, statesman, diplomat, architect, scientist, politician, writer, education theorist, and musician—graduated from the College of William and Mary in 1762 and went on to lead an impressive political life. Jefferson served as a member of the Continental Congress, governor of Virginia, secretary of state to George Washington, and vice president to John Adams. He also served two terms as U.S. president (1801–1809), during which he oversaw the Louisiana Purchase. After retiring from public office, Jefferson founded the University of Virginia in 1819. He was an avid collector of books and owned nearly ten thousand, which later became the foundation of the Library of Congress. A firm believer in reason and the natural rights of individuals, Jefferson drafted the Declaration of Independence, which was later amended by the Continental Congress. In this document, he presents the colonists' grievances in order to justify their decision to declare their independence from England.

BEFORE YOU READ

Write your own brief declaration of independence from some kind of thinking or behaving that you find limiting or destructive.

The Declaration of Independence

IN CONGRESS, JULY 4, 1776: THE UNANIMOUS DECLARATION OF THE THIRTEEN UNITED STATES OF AMERICA

When in the Course of human events it becomes necessary for one people to dissolve the political bands which have connected them with another, and to assume among the powers of the earth, the separate and equal station to which the Laws of Nature and of Nature's God entitle them, a decent respect to the opinions of mankind requires that they should declare the causes which impel them to the separation.

We hold these truths to be self-evident, that all men are created equal, that they are endowed by their Creator with certain unalienable Rights, that among these are Life, Liberty and the pursuit of Happiness. That to secure these rights, Governments are instituted among Men, deriving their just powers from the consent of the governed. That whenever any Form of Government becomes destructive of these ends, it is the Right of the People to alter or to abolish it, and to institute new Government, laying its foundation on such principles and organizing its powers in such form, as to them shall seem most likely to effect their Safety and Happiness. Prudence, indeed, will dictate that Governments long established should not be changed for light and transient causes; and accordingly all experience hath shewn, that mankind are more disposed to suffer, while evils are sufferable, than to right themselves by abolishing the forms to which they are accustomed. But when a long train of abuses and usurpations, pursuing invariably the same Object, evinces a design to reduce them under absolute Despotism, it is their right, it is their duty, to throw off such Government, and to provide new Guards for their future security. Such has been the patient sufferance of these Colonies; and such is now the necessity which constrains them to alter their former Systems of Governors. The history of the present King of Great Britain is a history of repeated injuries and usurpations, all having in direct object the establishment of an absolute Tyranny over these States. To prove this, let Facts be submitted to a candid world.

He has refused his Assent to Laws, the most wholesome and necessary for the public good.

He has forbidden his Governors to pass laws of immediate and pressing importance, unless suspended in their operation till his Assent should be obtained; and when so suspended, he has utterly neglected to attend to them.

He has refused to pass other Laws for the accommodation of large districts 5
of people, unless those people would relinquish the right of Representation in the Legislature, a right inestimable to them and formidable to tyrants only.

He has called together legislative bodies at places unusual, uncomfortable, and distant from the depository of their Public Records, for the sole purpose of fatiguing them into compliance with his measures.

He has dissolved Representative Houses repeatedly, for opposing with manly firmness his invasions on the rights of the people.

He has refused for a long time, after such dissolutions, to cause others to be elected; whereby the Legislative Powers, incapable of Annihilation, have returned to the People at large for their exercise; the State remaining in the mean time exposed to all the dangers of invasion from without, and convulsions within.

He has endeavored to prevent the population of these States; for that purpose obstructing the Laws for Naturalization of Foreigners; refusing to pass others to encourage their migration hither, and raising the conditions of new Appropriations of Lands.

He has obstructed the Administration of Justice, by refusing his Assent to 10
Laws for establishing Judiciary Powers.

He has made Judges dependent on his Will alone, for the tenure of their offices, and the amount and payment of their salaries.

He has erected a multitude of New Offices, and sent hither swarms of Officers to harass our people, and eat out their substance.

He has kept among us, in times of peace, Standing Armies without the Consent of our legislatures.

He has affected to render the Military independent of and superior to the Civil Power.

15 He has combined with others to subject us to a jurisdiction foreign to our constitution, and unacknowledged by our laws; giving his Assent to their Acts of pretended Legislation: For quartering large bodies of armed troops among us: For protecting them, by a mock Trial, from punishment for any Murders which they should commit on the Inhabitants of these States: For cutting off our Trade with all parts of the world: For imposing Taxes on us without our Consent: For depriving us in many cases, of the benefits of Trial by Jury; For transporting us beyond Seas to be tried for pretended offenses: For abolishing the free System of English Laws in a neighboring Province, establishing therein an Arbitrary government, and enlarging its Boundaries so as to render it at once an example and fit instrument for introducing the same absolute rule into these Colonies: For taking away our Charters, abolishing our most valuable Laws and altering fundamentally the Forms of our Governments: For suspending our own Legislatures, and declaring themselves invested with power to legislate for us in all cases whatsoever.

He has abdicated Government here, by declaring us out of his Protection and waging War against us.

He has plundered our seas, ravaged our Coasts, burnt our towns, and destroyed the lives of our people.

He is at this time transporting large Armies of foreign Mercenaries to complete the works of death, desolation and tyranny, already begun with circumstances of Cruelty & Perfidy scarcely paralleled in the most barbarous ages, and totally unworthy the Head of a civilized nation.

He has constrained our fellow Citizens taken Captive on the high Seas to bear Arms against their Country, to become the executioners of their friends and Brethren, or to fall themselves by their Hands.

20 He has excited domestic insurrections amongst us, and has endeavored to bring on the inhabitants of our frontiers, the merciless Indian Savages, whose known rule of warfare, is an undistinguished destruction of all ages, sexes, and conditions.

In every stage of these Oppressions We have Petitioned for Redress in the most humble terms: Our repeated Petitions have been answered only by repeated injury. A Prince, whose character is thus marked by every act which may define a Tyrant, is unfit to be the ruler of a free people.

Nor have We been wanting in attention to our British brethren. We have warned them from time to time of attempts by their legislature to extend an unwarrantable jurisdiction over us. We have reminded them of the circumstances of our emigration and settlement here. We have appealed to their native justice and magnanimity, and we have conjured them by the ties of our common kindred to disavow these usurpations, which would inevitably interrupt our connections and correspondence. They too have been deaf to the voice of justice and of consanguinity. We must, therefore, acquiesce in the necessity, which denounces our Separation, and hold them, as we hold the rest of mankind, Enemies in War, in Peace Friends.

We, therefore, the Representatives of the United States of America, in General Congress, Assembled, appealing to the Supreme Judge of the world for the rectitude of our intentions, do, in the Name, and by Authority of the good People of these Colonies, solemnly publish and declare, That these United Colonies are, and of Right ought to be free and independent states; that they are Absolved from all Allegiance to the British Crown, and that all political connection between them and the State of Great Britain, is and ought to be totally dissolved; and that as Free and Independent States, they have full Power to levy War, conclude Peace, contract Alliances, establish Commerce, and to do all other Acts and Things which Independent States may of right do. And for the support of this Declaration, with a firm reliance on the protection of Divine Providence, we mutually pledge to each other our Lives, our Fortunes, and our sacred Honor.

RESPONDING TO READING

1. The Declaration of Independence was written in the eighteenth century, a time when logic and reason were thought to be the supreme achievements of human beings. Do you think this document appeals just to reason, or does it also appeal to the emotions?
2. Do you think it is fair, as some have done, to accuse the framers of the Declaration of Independence of being racist? Of being sexist?

Rhetorical Analysis

Paragraphs 3–20 consist of a litany of grievances, expressed in parallel language. What did Jefferson hope to achieve with this use of parallelism for these grievances? Do you think he achieved this goal?

Writing with Sources

Look online for Elizabeth Cady Stanton's Declaration of Sentiments and Resolutions, presented in 1848 at the Women's Rights Convention in Seneca Falls, NY. Then, write an essay in which you compare this document with the Declaration of Independence in terms of content, goals, and rhetorical strategies.

9.4 Abraham Lincoln, The Gettysburg Address

The sixteenth president of the United States, Abraham Lincoln (1809–1865) led the Union to victory in the American Civil War. Known as the "Great Emancipator," Lincoln freed the slaves of the Confederacy with the Emancipation Proclamation, which was issued on January 1, 1863. On November 19, 1863, Lincoln delivered the Gettysburg Address during the dedication of the National Cemetery at Gettysburg, Pennsylvania, where the Battle of Gettysburg had claimed more than 40,000 Union and Confederate lives in July of that year.

BEFORE YOU READ

What "great tasks" do you believe still face our nation's leaders? Which of these do you think will still be a challenge in fifty years? Why?

The Gettysburg Address

Four score and seven years ago our fathers brought forth on this continent, a new nation, conceived in Liberty, and dedicated to the proposition that all men are created equal.

Now we are engaged in a great civil war, testing whether that nation, or any nation so conceived and so dedicated, can long endure. We are met on a great battlefield of that war. We have come to dedicate a portion of that field, as a final resting place for those who here gave their lives that that nation might live. It is altogether fitting and proper that we should do this.

But, in a larger sense, we cannot dedicate—we cannot consecrate—we cannot hallow—this ground. The brave men, living and dead, who struggled here, have consecrated it, far above our poor power to add or detract. The world will little note, nor long remember what we say here, but it can never forget what they did here. It is for us the living, rather, to be dedicated here to the unfinished work which they who fought here have thus far so nobly advanced. It is rather for us to be here dedicated to the great task remaining before us—that from these honored dead we take increased devotion to that cause for which they gave the last full measure of devotion—that we here highly resolve that these dead shall not have died in vain—that this nation, under God, shall have a new birth of freedom—and that government of the people, by the people, for the people, shall not perish from the earth.

Source: Lincoln, Abraham. "The Gettysburg Address." 19 November 1863.

RESPONDING TO READING

1. To Lincoln and his audience, what is the "great task remaining before us" (3)?
2. In paragraph 3, Lincoln says, "The world will little note, nor long remember what we say here, but it can never forget what they [the brave soldiers] did here." Is he correct? Explain.

Rhetorical Analysis

The first paragraph of this speech looks back, the second paragraph describes the present, and the third paragraph looks ahead. Using contemporary conversational style, write a one-sentence summary of each of these paragraphs. What makes this structure so effective?

Writing with Sources

What was Lincoln's purpose when he delivered the Gettysburg Address in 1863? How was the speech received at the time? How have more recent scholars and historians assessed its content and its impact? Write an essay that traces the influence of this famous speech over the years.

9.5 Jose Antonio Vargas, "Outlaw: My Life in America as an Undocumented Immigrant"

Jose Antonio Vargas (1981–) is a Filipino journalist and a former reporter for *The Washington Post.* Vargas was a member of the team of journalists who won the Pulitzer Prize in 2008 for breaking news reporting about the Virginia Tech campus shootings. He also started the online project *Define American* to promote "a new conversation about immigration." In the following essay, originally published in 2011 in *The New York Times Magazine,* Vargas reveals himself as an "undocumented immigrant" who has been living illegally in the United States since he was twelve years old.

BEFORE YOU READ

What different connotations do the terms *undocumented immigrants* and *illegal aliens* have? Which terms do you think should be used? Why?

Outlaw: My Life in America as an Undocumented Immigrant

One August morning nearly two decades ago, my mother woke me and put me in a cab. She handed me a jacket. "*Baka malamig doon*" were among the few words she said. ("It might be cold there.") When I arrived at the Philippines' Ninoy Aquino International Airport with her, my aunt and a family friend, I was introduced to a man I'd never seen. They told me he was my uncle.

He held my hand as I boarded an airplane for the first time. It was 1993, and I was 12.

My mother wanted to give me a better life, so she sent me thousands of miles away to live with her parents in America—my grandfather (*Lolo* in Tagalog[1]) and grandmother (*Lola*). After I arrived in Mountain View, Calif., in the San Francisco Bay Area, I entered sixth grade and quickly grew to love my new home, family and culture. I discovered a passion for language, though it was hard to learn the difference between formal English and American slang. One of my early memories is of a freckled kid in middle school asking me, "What's up?" I replied, "The sky," and he and a couple of other kids laughed. I won the eighth-grade spelling bee by memorizing words I couldn't properly pronounce. (The winning word was "indefatigable.")

One day when I was 16, I rode my bike to the nearby D.M.V. office to get my driver's permit. Some of my friends already had their licenses, so I figured it was time. But when I handed the clerk my green card as proof of U.S. residency, she flipped it around, examining it. "This is fake," she whispered. "Don't come back here again."

Confused and scared, I pedaled home and confronted Lolo. I remember him sitting in the garage, cutting coupons. I dropped my bike and ran over to him, showing him the green card. "*Peke ba ito?*" I asked in Tagalog. ("Is this fake?") My grandparents were naturalized American citizens—he worked as a security guard, she as a food server—and they had begun supporting my mother and me financially when I was 3, after my father's wandering eye and inability to properly provide for us led to my parents' separation. Lolo was a proud man, and I saw the shame on his face as he told me he purchased the card, along with other fake documents, for me. "Don't show it to other people," he warned.

5 I decided then that I could never give anyone reason to doubt I was an American. I convinced myself that if I worked enough, if I achieved enough, I would be rewarded with citizenship. I felt I could earn it.

I've tried. Over the past 14 years, I've graduated from high school and college and built a career as a journalist, interviewing some of the most famous people in the country. On the surface, I've created a good life. I've lived the American dream.

But I am still an undocumented immigrant. And that means living a different kind of reality. It means going about my day in fear of being found out. It means rarely trusting people, even those closest to me, with who I really am. It means keeping my family photos in a shoebox rather than displaying them on shelves in my home, so friends don't ask about them. It means reluctantly, even painfully, doing things I know are wrong and unlawful. And it has meant relying on a sort of 21st-century underground railroad of supporters, people who took an interest in my future and took risks for me.

---

[1] Official language of the Philippines. [Eds.]

Last year I read about four students who walked from Miami to Washington to lobby for the Dream Act, a nearly decade-old immigration bill that would provide a path to legal permanent residency for young people who have been educated in this country. At the risk of deportation—the Obama administration has deported almost 800,000 people in the last two years—they are speaking out. Their courage has inspired me.[2]

There are believed to be 11 million undocumented immigrants in the United States. We're not always who you think we are. Some pick your strawberries or care for your children. Some are in high school or college. And some, it turns out, write news articles you might read. I grew up here. This is my home. Yet even though I think of myself as an American and consider America my country, my country doesn't think of me as one of its own.

My first challenge was the language. Though I learned English in the Philippines, 10
I wanted to lose my accent. During high school, I spent hours at a time watching television (especially *Frasier, Home Improvement* and reruns of *The Golden Girls*) and movies (from *Goodfellas* to *Anne of Green Gables*), pausing the VHS to try to copy how various characters enunciated their words. At the local library, I read magazines, books and newspapers—anything to learn how to write better. Kathy Dewar, my high-school English teacher, introduced me to journalism. From the moment I wrote my first article for the student paper, I convinced myself that having my name in print—writing in English, interviewing Americans—validated my presence here.

The debates over "illegal aliens" intensified my anxieties. In 1994, only a year after my flight from the Philippines, Gov. Pete Wilson was re-elected in part because of his support for Proposition 187, which prohibited undocumented immigrants from attending public school and accessing other services. (A federal court later found the law unconstitutional.) After my encounter at the D.M.V. in 1997, I grew more aware of anti-immigrant sentiments and stereotypes: *they don't want to assimilate, they are a drain on society*. They're not talking about me, I would tell myself. I have something to contribute.

To do that, I had to work—and for that, I needed a Social Security number. Fortunately, my grandfather had already managed to get one for me. Lolo had always taken care of everyone in the family. He and my grandmother emigrated legally in 1984 from Zambales, a province in the Philippines of rice fields and bamboo houses, following Lolo's sister, who married a Filipino-American serving in the American military. She petitioned for her brother and his wife to join her. When they got here, Lolo petitioned for his two children—my mother and her younger brother—to follow them. But instead of mentioning that my mother was a married woman, he listed her as single. Legal residents can't petition for their married children. Besides, Lolo didn't care for my father. He didn't want him coming here too.

---

[2] In 2011, the Obama administration instituted a policy that would generally not deport undocumented immigrants unless they posed a threat of some kind. [Eds.]

But soon Lolo grew nervous that the immigration authorities reviewing the petition would discover my mother was married, thus derailing not only her chances of coming here but those of my uncle as well. So he withdrew her petition. After my uncle came to America legally in 1991, Lolo tried to get my mother here through a tourist visa, but she wasn't able to obtain one. That's when she decided to send me. My mother told me later that she figured she would follow me soon. She never did.

The "uncle" who brought me here turned out to be a coyote,[3] not a relative, my grandfather later explained. Lolo scraped together enough money—I eventually learned it was $4,500, a huge sum for him—to pay him to smuggle me here under a fake name and fake passport. (I never saw the passport again after the flight and have always assumed that the coyote kept it.) After I arrived in America, Lolo obtained a new fake Filipino passport, in my real name this time, adorned with a fake student visa, in addition to the fraudulent green card.

15 Using the fake passport, we went to the local Social Security Administration office and applied for a Social Security number and card. It was, I remember, a quick visit. When the card came in the mail, it had my full, real name, but it also clearly stated: "Valid for work only with I.N.S. authorization."

When I began looking for work, a short time after the D.M.V. incident, my grandfather and I took the Social Security card to Kinko's, where he covered the "I.N.S. authorization" text with a sliver of white tape. We then made photocopies of the card. At a glance, at least, the copies would look like copies of a regular, unrestricted Social Security card.

Lolo always imagined I would work the kind of low-paying jobs that undocumented people often take. (Once I married an American, he said, I would get my real papers, and everything would be fine.) But even menial jobs require documents, so he and I hoped the doctored card would work for now. The more documents I had, he said, the better.

While in high school, I worked part time at Subway, then at the front desk of the local Y.M.C.A., then at a tennis club, until I landed an unpaid internship at the *Mountain View Voice,* my hometown newspaper. First I brought coffee and helped around the office; eventually I began covering city-hall meetings and other assignments for pay.

For more than a decade of getting part-time and full-time jobs, employers have rarely asked to check my original Social Security card. When they did, I showed the photocopied version, which they accepted. Over time, I also began checking the citizenship box on my federal I-9 employment eligibility forms. (Claiming full citizenship was actually easier than declaring permanent resident "green card" status, which would have required me to provide an alien registration number.)

20 This deceit never got easier. The more I did it, the more I felt like an impostor, the more guilt I carried—and the more I worried that I would get caught. But I kept doing it. I needed to live and survive on my own, and I decided this was the way.

---

[3] Someone who smuggles undocumented immigrants into the United States. [Eds.]

Mountain View High School became my second home. I was elected to represent my school at school-board meetings, which gave me the chance to meet and befriend Rich Fischer, the superintendent for our school district. I joined the speech and debate team, acted in school plays and eventually became co-editor of the *Oracle,* the student newspaper. That drew the attention of my principal, Pat Hyland. "You're at school just as much as I am," she told me. Pat and Rich would soon become mentors, and over time, almost surrogate parents for me.

After a choir rehearsal during my junior year, Jill Denny, the choir director, told me she was considering a Japan trip for our singing group. I told her I couldn't afford it, but she said we'd figure out a way. I hesitated, and then decided to tell her the truth. "It's not really the money," I remember saying. "I don't have the right passport." When she assured me we'd get the proper documents, I finally told her. "I can't get the right passport," I said. "I'm not supposed to be here."

She understood. So the choir toured Hawaii instead, with me in tow. (Mrs. Denny and I spoke a couple of months ago, and she told me she hadn't wanted to leave any student behind.)

Later that school year, my history class watched a documentary on Harvey Milk, the openly gay San Francisco city official who was assassinated. This was 1999, just six months after Matthew Shepard's body was found tied to a fence in Wyoming. During the discussion, I raised my hand and said something like: "I'm sorry Harvey Milk got killed for being gay.... I've been meaning to say this.... I'm gay."

I hadn't planned on coming out that morning, though I had known that I was 25
gay for several years. With that announcement, I became the only openly gay student at school, and it caused turmoil with my grandparents. Lolo kicked me out of the house for a few weeks. Though we eventually reconciled, I had disappointed him on two fronts. First, as a Catholic, he considered homosexuality a sin and was embarrassed about having "*ang apo na bakla*" ("a grandson who is gay"). Even worse, I was making matters more difficult for myself, he said. I needed to marry an American woman in order to gain a green card.

Tough as it was, coming out about being gay seemed less daunting than coming out about my legal status. I kept my other secret mostly hidden.

While my classmates awaited their college acceptance letters, I hoped to get a full-time job at the *Mountain View Voice* after graduation. It's not that I didn't want to go to college, but I couldn't apply for state and federal financial aid. Without that, my family couldn't afford to send me.

But when I finally told Pat and Rich about my immigration "problem"—as we called it from then on—they helped me look for a solution. At first, they even wondered if one of them could adopt me and fix the situation that way, but a lawyer Rich consulted told him it wouldn't change my legal status because I was too old. Eventually they connected me to a new scholarship fund for high-potential students who were usually the first in their families to attend college. Most important, the fund was not concerned with immigration status. I was among the first recipients, with the scholarship covering tuition, lodging, books and other expenses for my studies at San Francisco State University.

As a college freshman, I found a job working part time at the *San Francisco Chronicle,* where I sorted mail and wrote some freelance articles. My ambition was to get a reporting job, so I embarked on a series of internships. First I landed at the *Philadelphia Daily News,* in the summer of 2001, where I covered a drive-by shooting and the wedding of the 76ers star Allen Iverson. Using those articles, I applied to the *Seattle Times* and got an internship for the following summer.

30 But then my lack of proper documents became a problem again. The *Times*'s recruiter, Pat Foote, asked all incoming interns to bring certain paperwork on their first day: a birth certificate, or a passport, or a driver's license plus an original Social Security card. I panicked, thinking my documents wouldn't pass muster. So before starting the job, I called Pat and told her about my legal status. After consulting with management, she called me back with the answer I feared: I couldn't do the internship.

This was devastating. What good was college if I couldn't then pursue the career I wanted? I decided then that if I was to succeed in a profession that is all about truth-telling, I couldn't tell the truth about myself.

After this episode, Jim Strand, the venture capitalist who sponsored my scholarship, offered to pay for an immigration lawyer. Rich and I went to meet her in San Francisco's financial district.

I was hopeful. This was in early 2002, shortly after Senators Orrin Hatch, the Utah Republican, and Dick Durbin, the Illinois Democrat, introduced the Dream Act—Development, Relief and Education for Alien Minors. It seemed like the legislative version of what I'd told myself: If I work hard and contribute, things will work out.

But the meeting left me crushed. My only solution, the lawyer said, was to go back to the Philippines and accept a 10-year ban before I could apply to return legally.

35 If Rich was discouraged, he hid it well. "Put this problem on a shelf," he told me. "Compartmentalize it. Keep going."

And I did. For the summer of 2003, I applied for internships across the country. Several newspapers, including the *Wall Street Journal,* the *Boston Globe* and the *Chicago Tribune,* expressed interest. But when the *Washington Post* offered me a spot, I knew where I would go. And this time, I had no intention of acknowledging my "problem."

The Post internship posed a tricky obstacle: It required a driver's license. (After my close call at the California D.M.V., I'd never gotten one.) So I spent an afternoon at the Mountain View Public Library, studying various states' requirements. Oregon was among the most welcoming—and it was just a few hours' drive north.

Again, my support network came through. A friend's father lived in Portland, and he allowed me to use his address as proof of residency. Pat, Rich and Rich's longtime assistant, Mary Moore, sent letters to me at that address. Rich taught me how to do three-point turns in a parking lot, and a friend accompanied me to Portland.

The license meant everything to me—it would let me drive, fly and work. But my grandparents worried about the Portland trip and the Washington internship.

While Lola offered daily prayers so that I would not get caught, Lolo told me that I was dreaming too big, risking too much.

40 I was determined to pursue my ambitions. I was 22, I told them, responsible for my own actions. But this was different from Lolo's driving a confused teenager to Kinko's. I knew what I was doing now, and I knew it wasn't right. But what was I supposed to do?

I was paying state and federal taxes, but I was using an invalid Social Security card and writing false information on my employment forms. But that seemed better than depending on my grandparents or on Pat, Rich and Jim—or returning to a country I barely remembered. I convinced myself all would be O.K. if I lived up to the qualities of a "citizen": hard work, self-reliance, love of my country.

At the D.M.V. in Portland, I arrived with my photocopied Social Security card, my college I.D., a pay stub from the *San Francisco Chronicle* and my proof of state residence—the letters to the Portland address that my support network had sent. It worked. My license, issued in 2003, was set to expire eight years later, on my 30th birthday, on Feb. 3, 2011. I had eight years to succeed professionally, and to hope that some sort of immigration reform would pass in the meantime and allow me to stay.

It seemed like all the time in the world.

My summer in Washington was exhilarating. I was intimidated to be in a major newsroom but was assigned a mentor—Peter Perl, a veteran magazine writer—to help me navigate it. A few weeks into the internship, he printed out one of my articles, about a guy who recovered a long-lost wallet, circled the first two paragraphs and left it on my desk. "Great eye for details—awesome!" he wrote. Though I didn't know it then, Peter would become one more member of my network.

45 At the end of the summer, I returned to the *San Francisco Chronicle.* My plan was to finish school—I was now a senior—while I worked for the *Chronicle* as a reporter for the city desk. But when the *Post* beckoned again, offering me a full-time, two-year paid internship that I could start when I graduated in June 2004, it was too tempting to pass up. I moved back to Washington.

About four months into my job as a reporter for the *Post,* I began feeling increasingly paranoid, as if I had "illegal immigrant" tattooed on my forehead—and in Washington, of all places, where the debates over immigration seemed never-ending. I was so eager to prove myself that I feared I was annoying some colleagues and editors—and worried that any one of these professional journalists could discover my secret. The anxiety was nearly paralyzing. I decided I had to tell one of the higher-ups about my situation. I turned to Peter.

By this time, Peter, who still works at the *Post,* had become part of management as the paper's director of newsroom training and professional development. One afternoon in late October, we walked a couple of blocks to Lafayette Square, across from the White House. Over some 20 minutes, sitting on a bench, I told him everything: the Social Security card, the driver's license, Pat and Rich, my family.

Peter was shocked. "I understand you 100 times better now," he said. He told me that I had done the right thing by telling him, and that it was now our shared problem. He said he didn't want to do anything about it just yet. I had just been hired, he said, and I needed to prove myself. "When you've done enough," he said, "we'll tell Don and Len together." (Don Graham is the chairman of the Washington Post Company; Leonard Downie Jr. was then the paper's executive editor.) A month later, I spent my first Thanksgiving in Washington with Peter and his family.

In the five years that followed, I did my best to "do enough." I was promoted to staff writer, reported on video-game culture, wrote a series on Washington's H.I.V./AIDS epidemic and covered the role of technology and social media in the 2008 presidential race. I visited the White House, where I interviewed senior aides and covered a state dinner—and gave the Secret Service the Social Security number I obtained with false documents.

50 I did my best to steer clear of reporting on immigration policy but couldn't always avoid it. On two occasions, I wrote about Hillary Clinton's position on driver's licenses for undocumented immigrants. I also wrote an article about Senator Mel Martinez of Florida, then the chairman of the Republican National Committee, who was defending his party's stance toward Latinos after only one Republican presidential candidate—John McCain, the co-author of a failed immigration bill—agreed to participate in a debate sponsored by Univision, the Spanish-language network.

It was an odd sort of dance: I was trying to stand out in a highly competitive newsroom, yet I was terrified that if I stood out too much, I'd invite unwanted scrutiny. I tried to compartmentalize my fears, distract myself by reporting on the lives of other people, but there was no escaping the central conflict in my life. Maintaining a deception for so long distorts your sense of self. You start wondering who you've become, and why.

In April 2008, I was part of a *Post* team that won a Pulitzer Prize for the paper's coverage of the Virginia Tech shootings a year earlier. Lolo died a year earlier, so it was Lola who called me the day of the announcement. The first thing she said was, "*Anong mangyayari kung malaman ng mga tao*?"

What will happen if people find out?

I couldn't say anything. After we got off the phone, I rushed to the bathroom on the fourth floor of the newsroom, sat down on the toilet and cried.

55 In the summer of 2009, without ever having had that follow-up talk with top *Post* management, I left the paper and moved to New York to join the *Huffington Post.* I met Arianna Huffington at a Washington Press Club Foundation dinner I was covering for the *Post* two years earlier, and she later recruited me to join her news site. I wanted to learn more about Web publishing, and I thought the new job would provide a useful education.

Still, I was apprehensive about the move: many companies were already using E-Verify, a program set up by the Department of Homeland Security that checks if prospective employees are eligible to work, and I didn't know if my new employer was among them. But I'd been able to get jobs in other newsrooms, I figured, so I filled out the paperwork as usual and succeeded in landing on the payroll.

While I worked at the *Huffington Post,* other opportunities emerged. My H.I.V./AIDS series became a documentary film called *The Other City,* which opened at the Tribeca Film Festival last year and was broadcast on Showtime. I began writing for magazines and landed a dream assignment: profiling Facebook's Mark Zuckerberg for the *New Yorker.*

The more I achieved, the more scared and depressed I became. I was proud of my work, but there was always a cloud hanging over it, over me. My old eight-year deadline—the expiration of my Oregon driver's license—was approaching.

After slightly less than a year, I decided to leave the *Huffington Post.* In part, this was because I wanted to promote the documentary and write a book about online culture—or so I told my friends. But the real reason was, after so many years of trying to be a part of the system, of focusing all my energy on my professional life, I learned that no amount of professional success would solve my problem or ease the sense of loss and displacement I felt. I lied to a friend about why I couldn't take a weekend trip to Mexico. Another time I concocted an excuse for why I couldn't go on an all-expenses-paid trip to Switzerland. I have been unwilling, for years, to be in a long-term relationship because I never wanted anyone to get too close and ask too many questions. All the while, Lola's question was stuck in my head: What will happen if people find out?

60 Early this year, just two weeks before my 30th birthday, I won a small reprieve: I obtained a driver's license in the state of Washington. The license is valid until 2016. This offered me five more years of acceptable identification—but also five more years of fear, of lying to people I respect and institutions that trusted me, of running away from who I am.

I'm done running. I'm exhausted. I don't want that life anymore.

So I've decided to come forward, own up to what I've done, and tell my story to the best of my recollection. I've reached out to former bosses and employers and apologized for misleading them—a mix of humiliation and liberation coming with each disclosure. All the people mentioned in this article gave me permission to use their names. I've also talked to family and friends about my situation and am working with legal counsel to review my options. I don't know what the consequences will be of telling my story.

I do know that I am grateful to my grandparents, my Lolo and Lola, for giving me the chance for a better life. I'm also grateful to my other family—the support network I found here in America—for encouraging me to pursue my dreams.

It's been almost 18 years since I've seen my mother. Early on, I was mad at her for putting me in this position, and then mad at myself for being angry and ungrateful. By the time I got to college, we rarely spoke by phone. It became too painful; after a while it was easier to just send money to help support her and my two half-siblings. My sister, almost 2 years old when I left, is almost 20 now. I've never met my 14-year-old brother. I would love to see them.

65 Not long ago, I called my mother. I wanted to fill the gaps in my memory about that August morning so many years ago. We had never discussed it. Part of me wanted to shove the memory aside, but to write this article and face the facts of my life, I needed more details. Did I cry? Did she? Did we kiss goodbye?

My mother told me I was excited about meeting a stewardess, about getting on a plane. She also reminded me of the one piece of advice she gave me for blending in: If anyone asked why I was coming to America, I should say I was going to Disneyland.

Source: From The New York Times, Vargas, Jose Antonio (June 22), My Life as an Undocumented Immigrant,

RESPONDING TO READING

1. List the specific illegal acts Vargas's grandfather (and Vargas himself) committed to hide the fact that Vargas was in the United States illegally. What motivated each of these acts? How does Vargas justify them? What finally motivated Vargas to (in his words) "come forward, own up to what I've done, and tell my story" (62)?
2. What obstacles did Vargas face because of his immigration status? How did he overcome them? How did his "support network" (38) help him? Do you think these people did the right thing by helping him?

Rhetorical Analysis

How do you think Vargas expected readers to respond to each of the following statements?

- "I convinced myself that if I worked enough, if I achieved enough, I would be rewarded with citizenship." (5)
- "Tough as it was, coming out about being gay seemed less daunting than coming out about my legal status." (26)
- "I decided then that if I was to succeed in a profession that is all about truth-telling, I couldn't tell the truth about myself." (31)

Do you think Vargas is being completely honest with himself in each case? Do you see any irony in his words?

Writing with Sources

Search online for information about Vargas since 2011, when this essay was published. Then, read about the history of the Development, Relief, and Education for Alien Minors (DREAM) Act and of the Deferred Action for Childhood Arrivals (DACA) program. Using this research to support your points, write an essay in which you evaluate the strengths and weaknesses of Vargas's arguments. Do you see him as an "outlaw" or as someone with a legitimate grievance? Do you believe he deserves amnesty?

9.6 Emma Lazarus, "The New Colossus" [Poetry]

Born to a wealthy family in New York City and educated by private tutors, Emma Lazarus (1849–1887) became one of the foremost poets of her day. Today, she is remembered solely for her poem "The New Colossus," a sonnet written in 1883 as part of an effort to raise funds for the Statue of Liberty. The poem was later inscribed on the statue's base, and it remains a vivid reminder of the immigrant's American dream.

BEFORE YOU READ

Find some photographs of the Statue of Liberty. How would you describe it? What are its distinctive characteristics?

The New Colossus

Not like the brazen giant of Greek fame,
With conquering limbs astride from land to land;
Here at our sea-washed, sunset gates shall stand
A mighty woman with a torch, whose flame
Is the imprisoned lightning, and her name
Mother of Exiles. From her beacon-hand
Glows world-wide welcome; her mild eyes command
The air-bridged harbor that twin cities frame.
"Keep, ancient lands, your storied pomp!" cries she
With silent lips. "Give me your tired, your poor,
Your huddled masses yearning to breathe free,
The wretched refuse of your teeming shore.
Send these, the homeless, tempest-tost to me,
I lift my lamp beside the golden door!"

Source: Lazarus, Emma. "The New Colossus" The Poems of Emma Lazarus, Vol. 1. Boston: Houghton, Mifflin and Company, 1888.

RESPONDING TO READING

1. The Colossus of Rhodes, an enormous statue of the Greek god Apollo, was considered one of the seven wonders of the ancient world. It stood at the mouth of the harbor at Rhodes. Why do you think this poem is called "The New Colossus"?
2. What is the "golden door" to which the poem's last line refers? What aspects of the American Dream does this poem express?

Rhetorical Analysis

Who is the poem's speaker? Who is being addressed?

9.7 Focus: "Is the American Dream Still Attainable?"

H. Armstrong Roberts/ClassicStock/Alamy Stock Photo

What does this photo of a 1960s family outside their suburban home say about the American Dream?

RESPONDING TO THE IMAGE

Answer one or all of the following questions.

1. Write a caption for the image above, inventing names, ages, and family roles for the people pictured.
2. In a few sentences, describe the neighborhood you think this family lives in.
3. How is this family, and their home, like and unlike your own? How do you account for any differences you identify?

9.8 Joe Kennedy III, Democratic Response to the State of the Union

Democratic Congressman Joe Kennedy III (1980–) serves the fourth congressional district of Massachusetts. The great-nephew of President John F. Kennedy (p. 436), he represents the next generation of the iconic Kennedy family. A lawyer and fluent Spanish speaker, he focuses on issues related to social justice for American citizens and noncitizens alike. He gave the following speech as his party's response to President Donald Trump's State of the Union address on January 30, 2018.

BEFORE YOU READ

Does the town or neighborhood in which you grew up (or live now) exemplify the American Dream? If so, how? If not, how specifically is your community struggling to achieve the dream?

Democratic Response to the State of the Union

Good evening, ladies and gentlemen. It is a privilege to join you tonight.

We are here in Fall River, Massachusetts—a proud American city, built by immigrants.

From textiles to robots, this is a place that knows how to make great things.

The students with us this evening in the autoshop at Diman Regional Technical School carry on that rich legacy.

5 Like many American hometowns, Fall River has faced its share of storms. But people here are tough. They fight for each other. They pull for their city.

It is a fitting place to gather as our nation reflects on the state of our union.

This is a difficult task. Many have spent the past year anxious, angry, afraid. We all feel the fault lines of a fractured country. We hear the voices of Americans who feel forgotten and forsaken.

We see an economy that makes stocks soar, investor portfolios bulge and corporate profits climb but fails to give workers their fair share of the reward.

A government that struggles to keep itself open.

10 Russia knee-deep in our democracy.

An all-out war on environmental protection.

A Justice Department rolling back civil rights by the day.

Hatred and supremacy proudly marching in our streets.

Bullets tearing through our classrooms, concerts, and congregations. Targeting our safest, sacred places.

15 And that nagging, sinking feeling, no matter your political beliefs: this is not right. This is not who we are.

It would be easy to dismiss the past year as chaos. Partisanship. Politics.

But it's far bigger than that. This administration isn't just targeting the laws that protect us—they are targeting the very idea that we are all worthy of protection.

For them, dignity isn't something you're born with but something you measure.

By your net worth, your celebrity, your headlines, your crowd size.

20 Not to mention, the gender of your spouse. The country of your birth. The color of your skin. The God of your prayers.

Their record is a rebuke of our highest American ideal: the belief that we are all worthy, we are all equal and we all count. In the eyes of our law and our leaders, our God and our government.

That is the American promise.

But today that promise is being broken. By an administration that callously appraises our worthiness and decides who makes the cut and who can be bargained away.

They are turning American life into a zero-sum game.

25 Where, in order for one to win, another must lose.

Where we can guarantee America's safety if we slash our safety net.

We can extend health care to Mississippi if we gut it in Massachusetts.

We can cut taxes for corporations today if we raise them for families tomorrow.

We can take care of sick kids if we sacrifice Dreamers.[1]

30 We are bombarded with one false choice after another:

Coal miners or single moms. Rural communities or inner cities. The coast or the heartland.

As if the mechanic in Pittsburgh and the teacher in Tulsa and the day care worker in Birmingham are somehow bitter rivals, rather than mutual casualties of a system forcefully rigged for those at the top.

As if the parent who lies awake terrified that their transgender son will be beaten and bullied at school is any more or less legitimate than the parent whose heart is shattered by a daughter in the grips of opioid addiction.

So here is the answer Democrats offer tonight: we choose both. We fight for both. Because the strongest, richest, greatest nation in the world shouldn't leave any one behind.

35 We choose a better deal for all who call this country home.

We choose the living wage, paid leave and affordable child care your family needs to survive.

We choose pensions that are solvent, trade pacts that are fair, roads and bridges that won't rust away, and good education you can afford.

We choose a health care system that offers mercy, whether you suffer from cancer or depression or addiction.

We choose an economy strong enough to boast record stock prices and brave enough to admit that top C.E.O.s making 300 times the average worker is not right.

40 We choose Fall River.

We choose the thousands of American communities whose roads aren't paved with power or privilege, but with honest effort, good faith, and the resolve to build something better for their kids.

That is our story. It began the day our Founding Fathers and Mothers set sail for a New World, fleeing oppression and intolerance.

[1] Undocumented immigrants who arrived in the United States when they were children and recipients of the Deferred Action for Childhood Arrivals (DACA) program. [Eds.]

It continued with every word of our Independence—the audacity to declare that all men are created equal. An imperfect promise for a nation struggling to become a more perfect union.

It grew with every suffragette's step, every Freedom Riders voice, every weary soul we welcomed to our shores.

And to all the "Dreamers" watching tonight, let me be clear: Ustedes son parte de nuestra historia. Vamos a luchar por ustedes y no nos vamos alejar. 45

You are a part of our story. We will fight for you. We will not walk away.

America, we carry that story on our shoulders.

You swarmed Washington last year to ensure no parent has to worry if they can afford to save their child's life.

You proudly marched together last weekend—thousands deep—in the streets of Las Vegas and Philadelphia and Nashville.

You sat high atop your mom's shoulders and held a sign that read: "Build a wall and my generation will tear it down." 50

You bravely say, me too. You steadfastly say, black lives matter.

You wade through floodwaters, battle hurricanes, and brave wildfires and mudslides to save a stranger.

You fight your own, quiet battles every single day.

You drag your weary bodies to that extra shift so your families won't feel the sting of scarcity.

You leave loved ones at home to defend our country overseas, or patrol our neighborhoods overnight. 55

You serve. You rescue. You help. You heal.

That—more than any law or leader, any debate or disagreement—that is what drives us toward progress.

Bullies may land a punch. They might leave a mark. But they have never, not once, in the history of our United States, managed to match the strength and spirit of a people united in defense of their future.

Politicians can be cheered for the promises they make. Our country will be judged by the promises we keep.

That is the measure of our character. That's who we are. 60

Out of many. One.[2]

Ladies and gentlemen, have faith: The state of our union is hopeful, resilient, enduring.

Thank you, God bless you and your families, and God bless the United States of America.

Source: Transcript of Speech by US. Representative Joseph P. Kennedy III (D, MA) by New York Times

---

RESPONDING TO READING

1. According to Kennedy, what is "the American promise" (22)? To whom does it apply? In what ways is it currently being threatened?

---

[2] English translation of the Latin phrase *e pluribus unum,* which appears on the Great Seal of the United States and several U.S. coins. [Eds.]

2. In paragraph 59, Kennedy says, "Politicians can be cheered for the promises they make. Our country will be judged by the promises we keep." What distinction is Kennedy making here? What message does it send his listeners?

Rhetorical Analysis

In paragraphs 45–46, Kennedy makes a statement in Spanish and then offers an English translation. Why does he do this? How do you think his various audiences responded? How does his strategy affect your response to the speech?

Writing with Sources

Research the socio-economic development of your own community over the last half-century. Then, write an essay in which you discuss the upward mobility (and the obstacles to that upward mobility) of local citizens.

9.9 Neal Gabler, "The New American Dream"

A professor in the creative writing and literature MFA program at Stony Brook University, Southampton, Neal Gabler (1950–) is a journalist, cultural historian, political commentator, and film critic. He has authored and coauthored several books, including, most recently, *Barbra Streisand: Redefining Beauty, Femininity, and Power* (2016). His work has appeared in such publications as the *Boston Globe*, *Esquire*, the *Los Angeles Times*, *New York* magazine, *The New York Times*, *Salon*, *Us*, and *Vogue*. In the following essay, Gabler defines the "new American Dream."

BEFORE YOU READ

Does your view of the American Dream allow for disagreement among groups of people? Do you think the dream is attainable for everyone, regardless of their conflicting opinions?

The New American Dream

A disgruntled New York mother recently filed a lawsuit against her 4-year-old daughter's preschool, charging that the school had reneged on its promise to adequately prepare the girl for an Ivy League education. Apparently the kids were playing with blocks when they should have been discussing Wittgenstein.[1] Understandably the suit was met with ridicule as another example of overbearing parenting, but it is also an example of how many of us, especially in the middle and upper-middle classes, not only aspire to be perfect; we *expect* perfection.

Though Americans have always been cockeyed optimists, they didn't necessarily think they would find nirvana on earth. The American Dream, as it was devised in the late 19th century, referred to opportunity. The idea was that anyone in this pragmatic, un-class-conscious society of ours could, by dint of hard work, rise to the level of his aspiration.

But over the past 50 years, the American Dream has been revised. It is no longer about seizing opportunity but about realizing perfection. Many Americans have come to feel that the lives they always imagined for themselves are not only attainable; those lives are now transcendable, as if our imaginations were inadequate to the possibilities. In short, many Americans have come to believe in their own perfectibility.

It was historian Daniel Boorstin who wrote in the early 1960s that his was the first generation to live within its illusions. This was a time when Americans had assimilated images from movies and television, books, and advertising as part of their consciousness. They saw fabulous worlds and wanted to enter them. As Boorstin said of the movie star: "His mere existence proves the perfectibility of any man or woman." To want to enter these worlds wasn't entirely novel. What was novel was the conviction that we could. In effect, America had become the first country to democratize dreams.

What Boorstin couldn't have foreseen was that perfectionism was encour- 5
aged not just by the media, popular culture, and an expansive post-war economy but by the country's political institutions. Ronald Reagan, as much as any single individual, promoted the idea that the only limit to our success was our own inadequacies—a bromide, to be sure, but one that came with an unsettling corollary: To be less than perfect was to be inadequate. And this corollary also had a patriotic corollary of its own: Anything less than perfection was both a personal failure and a national affront since Americans weren't inadequate. We owed it to the nation to live perfectly.

It is difficult to say whether the overstuffed 1980s fed this attitude or this attitude fed the 1980s, but whichever it was, success was redefined from personal satisfaction to public vindication. There was a great national competition in which many Americans felt they had to prove their value to everyone else. And the best measure of that value was not just wealth or a glowing career or a trophy wife or a beautiful family. It was all of it. If anything, that competition has only intensified since.

Thus not only have the terms of success changed but also the very terms of life. For a person who can live within his illusions, the career has to be perfect, the wife has to be perfect, the children have to be perfect, the home has to be perfect,

[1]Ludwig Wittgenstein (1889–1951), an Austrian-British philosopher. [Eds.]

the car has to be perfect, the social circle has to be perfect. We agonize a lot over perfection, and we dedicate a lot of time, energy, and money to it—everything from plastic surgery to gated communities of McMansions to the professionalization of our children's activities like soccer and baseball to pricey preschools that prepare 4-year-olds for Harvard. After all, we are all on the Ivy League track now.

Or else. And that's another thing that a perfectionist society has engendered. It has removed failure as an option because we realize that there are no second chances, that mistakes are usually irrevocable, and that you have to assume there are other people out there—*your competition!*—whose wives will always be beautifully coiffed and dressed or whose husbands will be power brokers, whose children will score 2,400 on their SATs and who will be playing competitive-level tennis, whose careers will be skyrocketing, whose fortunes will be growing. In a world in which perfection is expected, you must be perfect. Otherwise you are second rate.

Not that this is easy. To live within your illusions is also to live within the pressure to sustain them, which is the pressure of middle-class America today. It is to say that the birthright of a 4-year-old girl in New York is to be a rich, beautiful, brilliant, powerful, Ivy League-educated Mistress of the Universe who will live not just the good life but the perfect one. That's the new American Dream.

Source: Neil Gabler. The New American Dream. Reprinted with permission.

RESPONDING TO READING

1. Gabler claims that many Americans today dream not just of opportunity but of perfection. Whom or what does he blame for this situation?
2. What is a *cockeyed optimist* (2)? What is *nirvana* (2)? What is a *trophy wife* (6)? What does Gabler's use of these expressions tell you about how he perceives his audience?

Rhetorical Analysis

Gabler, an upper-middle-class male, clearly expects his audience to be composed of people like himself. How can you tell? Do you think this narrow focus is the most effective strategy?

Writing with Sources

Research the history of suburban "McMansions" (7). What is a McMansion? Is this term's connotation positive, neutral, or negative? In what sense does the McMansion represent the culmination of the American Dream? In what sense could it be seen as a corruption of that dream? Write an essay in which you address these questions.

9.10 Carol Graham, "Is the American Dream Really Dead?"

A professor of public policy at the University of Maryland, College Park, Carol Graham (1962–) is the author, coauthor, and coeditor of numerous books, including, most recently, *Happiness for All? Unequal Hopes and Lives in Pursuit of the American Dream* (2017). The Leo Pasvolsky Senior Fellow at the Brookings Institution and a research fellow at the Institute for the Study of Labor (IZA), she writes about issues related to happiness and wellbeing, developing economies and economic reform, poverty, and inequality in the United States and Latin America. Her work has also appeared in such publications as the *Christian Science Monitor*, the *Financial Times*, *Health Economics*, the *Journal of Economic Behavior and Organization*, the *Journal of Happiness Studies*, the *Journal of Population Economics*, *The New York Times*, *The Wall Street Journal*, *The Washington Post*, and the *World Bank Research Observer*. In this essay, Graham considers the viability of the American Dream.

BEFORE YOU READ

How much economic mobility do you believe you have? What factors do you think will enable you to achieve a higher social status, and what might limit your ability to move up?

Is the American Dream Really Dead?

The United States has a long-held reputation for exceptional tolerance of income inequality, explained by its high levels of social mobility. This combination underpins the American dream—initially conceived of by Thomas Jefferson as each citizen's right to the pursuit of life, liberty and the pursuit of happiness.

This dream is not about guaranteed outcomes, of course, but the *pursuit* of opportunities. The dream found a persona in the fictional characters of the 19th-century writer Horatio Alger Jr.—in which young working-class protagonists go from rags to riches (or at least become middle class) in part due to entrepreneurial spirit and hard work.

Yet the opportunity to live the American dream is much less widely shared today than it was several decades ago. While 90% of the children born in 1940 ended up in higher ranks of the income distribution than their parents, only 40% of those born in 1980 have done so.

Attitudes about inequality have also changed. In 2001, a study found the only Americans who reported lower levels of happiness amid greater inequality were left-leaning rich people—with the poor seeing inequality as a sign of future opportunity. Such optimism has since been substantially tempered: in

2016, only 38% of Americans thought their children would be better off than they are.

5 In the meantime, the public discussion about inequality has completely bypassed a critical element of the American dream: luck.

Just as in many of Alger's stories the main character benefits from the assistance of a generous philanthropist, there are countless real examples of success in the US where different forms of luck have played a major role. And yet, social support for the unlucky—in particular, the poor who cannot stay in full-time employment—has been falling substantially in recent years, and is facing even more threats today.

In short, from new research based on some novel metrics of wellbeing, I find strong evidence that the American dream is in tatters, at least.

WHITE DESPAIR, MINORITY HOPE

My research began by comparing mobility attitudes in the US with those in Latin America, a region long known for high levels of poverty and inequality (although with progress in the past decades). I explored a question in the Gallup world poll, which asks respondents a classic American dream question: "Can an individual who works hard in this country get ahead?"

I found very large gaps between the responses of "the rich" and "the poor" in the US (represented by the top and bottom 20% income distributions of the Gallup respondents). This was in stark contrast to Latin America, where there was no significant difference in attitudes across income groups. Poor people in the US were 20 times less likely to believe hard work would get them ahead than were the poor in Latin America, even though the latter are significantly worse off in material terms.

10 Another question in the poll explores whether or not respondents experience stress on a daily basis. Stress is a marker of poor health, and the kind of stress typically experienced by the poor—usually due to negative shocks that are beyond their control ("bad stress")—is significantly worse for wellbeing than "good stress": that which is associated with goal achievement, for those who feel able to focus on their future.

In general, Latin Americans experience significantly less stress—and also smile more—on a daily basis than Americans. The gaps between the poor and rich in the US were significantly wider (by 1.5 times on a 0–1 score) than those in Latin America, with the poor in the US experiencing more stress than either the rich or poor in Latin America.

The gaps between the expectations and sentiments of rich and poor in the US are also greater than in many other countries in east Asia and Europe (the other regions studied). It seems that being poor in a very wealthy and unequal country—which prides itself on being a meritocracy, and eschews social support for those who fall behind—results in especially high levels of stress and desperation.

But my research also yielded some surprises. With the low levels of belief in the value of hard work and high levels of stress among poor respondents in the

US as a starting point, I compared optimism about the future across poor respondents of different races. This was based on a question in the US Gallup daily poll that asks respondents where they think they will be five years from now on a 0-10 step life satisfaction ladder.

I found that poor minorities—and particularly black people—were much more optimistic about the future than poor white people. Indeed, poor black respondents were three times as likely to be a point higher up on the optimism ladder than were poor whites, while poor Hispanic people were one and a half times more optimistic than whites. Poor black people were also half as likely as poor whites to experience stress the previous day, while poor Hispanics were only two-thirds as likely as poor whites.

What explains the higher levels of optimism among minorities, who have 15
traditionally faced discrimination and associated challenges? There is no simple answer.

One factor is that poor minorities have stronger informal safety nets and social support, such as families and churches, than do their white counterparts. Psychologists also find that minorities are more resilient and much less likely to report depression or commit suicide than are whites in the face of negative shocks, perhaps due to a longer trajectory of dealing with negative shocks and challenges.

Another critical issue is the threat and reality of downward mobility for blue-collar whites, particularly in the heartland of the country where manufacturing, mining, and other jobs have hollowed out. Andrew Cherlin of Johns Hopkins University finds that poor black and Hispanic people are much more likely than poor white people to report that they live better than their parents did. Poor whites are more likely to say they live worse than their parents did; they, in particular, seem to be living the erosion of the American dream.

THE AMERICAN PROBLEM

Why does this matter? My research from a decade ago—since confirmed by other studies—found that individuals who were optimistic about their futures tended to have better health and employment outcomes. Those who believe in their futures tend to invest in those futures, while those who are consumed with stress, daily struggles and a lack of hope, not only have less means to make such investments, but also have much less confidence that they will pay off.

The starkest marker of lack of hope in the US is a significant increase in premature mortality in the past decade—driven by an increase in suicides and drug and alcohol poisoning and a stalling of progress against heart disease and lung cancer—primarily but not only among middle-aged uneducated white people. Mortality rates for black and Hispanic people, while higher on average than those for whites, continued to fall during the same time period.

The reasons for this trend are multi-faceted. One is the coincidence of an 20
all-too-readily-available supply of drugs such as opioids, heroin and fentanyl, with the shrinking of blue-collar jobs—and identities—primarily due to technological change. Fifteen per cent of prime age males are out of the labour force today; with that figure projected to increase to 25% by 2050. The identity of the blue-collar

worker seems to be stronger for white people than for minorities, meanwhile. While there are now increased employment opportunities in services such as health, white males are far less likely to take them up than are their minority counterparts.

Lack of hope also contributes to rising mortality rates, as evidenced in my latest research with Sergio Pinto. On average, individuals with lower optimism for the future are more likely to live in metropolitan statistical areas (MSAs) with higher mortality rates for 45- to 54-year-olds.

Desperate people are more likely to die prematurely, but living with a lot of premature death can also erode hope. Higher average levels of optimism in metropolitan areas are also associated with lower premature mortality rates. These same places tend to be more racially diverse, healthier (as gauged by fewer respondents who smoke and more who exercise), and more likely to be urban and economically vibrant.

Technology-driven growth is not unique to the US, and low-skilled workers face challenges in many OECD[1] countries. Yet by contrast, away from the US, they have not had a similar increase in premature mortality. One reason may be stronger social welfare systems—and stronger norms of collective social responsibility for those who fall behind—in Europe.

Ironically, part of the problem may actually *be* the American dream. Blue-collar white people—whose parents lived the American dream and who expected their children to do so as well—are the ones who seem most devastated by its erosion and yet, on average, tend to vote against government programs. In contrast, minorities, who have been struggling for years and have more experience multi-tasking on the employment front and relying on family and community support when needed—are more resilient and hopeful, precisely because they still see a chance for moving up the ladder.

25 There are high costs to being poor in America, where winners win big but losers fall hard. Indeed, the dream, with its focus on individual initiative in a meritocracy, has resulted in far less public support than there is in other countries for safety nets, vocational training, and community support for those with disadvantage or bad luck. Such strategies are woefully necessary now, particularly in the heartland where some of Alger's characters might have come from, but their kind have long since run out of luck.

Source: Carol Graham, Is the American dream really dead? 20 June 2017. www.theguardian.com

---

RESPONDING TO READING

1. According to Graham, what does luck have to do with achieving the American Dream? Given that conclusion, do you see this article as optimistic, pessimistic, or neutral? Why?

---

[1] Organization for Economic Cooperation and Development, an intergovernmental forum founded in 1961 to foster democratic ideals among world economies. [Eds.]

2. What role do race and ethnicity seem to play in different visions of the American Dream? To what extent have your race and ethnicity shaped your view of the dream?

Rhetorical Analysis

Evaluate Graham's use of her own research to back up her points. Is this strategy effective? Should she have used other sources to support her argument? Explain.

Writing with Sources

Locate a good definition of the term *upward mobility*, and search for information about Horatio Alger, a nineteenth-century writer known for his stories of young people—mostly boys—who achieve success through hard work (and luck). Then, read one of Alger's "rags to riches" novels, available at *Project Gutenberg*, and write an essay analyzing the book's characterization of the American Dream.

Widening the Focus

For Critical Reading and Writing

Referring specifically to the three readings in this chapter's Focus section (and possibly to additional sources as well), write an essay in which you answer the question, "Is the American Dream Still Attainable?"

For Further Reading

The following readings can suggest additional perspectives for thinking and writing about the feasibility of the American Dream:

- Matthew Yglesias, "Walmart's Too-Good-to-Be-True '$1 a Day' College Tuition Plan, Explained" (p. 111)
- Priscilla Frank, "Dismantling Stereotypes about Asian-American Identity through Art" (p. 271)
- Andrew Curry, "Why We Work" (p. 355)
- Alex Wagner, from *Futureface*... (p. 455)

For Focused Research

As the essays in this chapter's Focus section illustrate, Americans' views of the American Dream are as varied as are their cultural backgrounds. Search online for different perspectives of the American Dream. You might start with the American RadioWorks program *A Better Life*, for example. Consider the similarities and differences among these views and how they relate to the readings in this chapter. Then, write an essay that compares at least three views of the American Dream. Include in your essay your own definition of the American Dream that synthesizes the various perspectives you discuss. Be sure to document the online sources you use.

Beyond the Classroom

Interview a first-generation American, a second-generation American, and a third-generation American. How are their views of the American Dream different? How are they like and unlike the dreams of various writers represented in this chapter? Write an essay summarizing your findings.

Exploring Issues and Ideas

The American Dream

Write an essay in response to one of the following prompts, which are suitable for assignments that require the use of outside sources as well as for assignments that are not source-based.

1. In an excerpt from his book *The Audacity of Hope,* President Barack Obama writes, "I believe that part of America's genius has always been its ability to absorb newcomers, to forge a national identity out of the disparate lot that arrived on our shores." Write an essay in which you support the idea that the strength of the United States comes from its ability to assimilate many different groups. In your essay, discuss specific contributions your own ethnic group and others have made to American society.
2. "Outlaw: My Life in America as an Undocumented Immigrant" (p. 327) deals with the uniquely American concept of reinventing oneself, taking on a new identity. Write an essay in which you outline the options available to newcomers to the United States who wish to achieve this kind of transformation. Whenever possible, give examples from the readings in this chapter.
3. In his keynote speech at the 2012 Democratic National Convention, Júlian Castro, the mayor of San Antonio, observed, "the American Dream is not a sprint, or even a marathon, but a relay." What do you think he meant? Do you think he is right? How do you think some of the other writers in this chapter would react to this statement?

4. Using the readings in this chapter as source material, write a manifesto that sets forth the rights and responsibilities of all Americans. You might begin by reading President John F. Kennedy's inaugural address (p. 438).
5. Discouraged by the racism they experienced in the United States, Richard Wright, James Baldwin, and other prominent black writers left their country and lived the rest of their lives as expatriates in Paris. Under what circumstances could you imagine leaving the United States and living forever in another country?

Chapter 10
Why We Work

In this chapter, you will learn to:

- analyze readings about why we work.
- compose essays about why we work.

Although work has always been a part of the human experience, the nature of work has evolved considerably—especially over the last two hundred years. During the Middle Ages and the Renaissance, work was often done by family units. Whether it involved planting and harvesting crops, tending livestock, or engaging in the manufacture of goods, parents, grandparents, and children (and possibly an apprentice or two) worked together, at home. With the Industrial Revolution, however, the nature of work changed. Manufacturing became centralized in factories, and tasks that were formerly divided among various members of a family were now carried out more efficiently by machines. People worked long hours—in many cases twelve to fifteen hours a day, six and sometimes seven days a week—and could be fired for any reason. By the middle of the nineteenth century, most of the great manufacturing cities of Europe were overcrowded and polluted, teeming with unskilled factory workers. It is no wonder that labor unions became

Edwin Levick/Archive Photos/Getty Images

What point does this image taken circa 1915 of auto workers assembling car radiators make about the nature of work?

increasingly popular as they organized workers to fight for job security, shorter workdays, and minimum safety standards.

Thanks to the labor struggles of the past, many workers today have pension plans, health insurance, sick leave, paid vacations, life insurance, and other benefits. In spite of these advances, however, there is a dark side to this situation. American workers—like all workers—are subject to unpredictable changes in both the national and the global economies. As a result, during good times workers experience low unemployment and receive high wages, and during economic downturns—such as the one that began in 2008—workers experience higher unemployment and receive lower wages. Add to this situation the tendency of American companies to move manufacturing and high-tech jobs overseas and to see employees as entities whose jobs can be phased out as the need arises, and it is no surprise that workers are often stressed, insecure, and unhappy. The result is that many of today's workers question the role that work plays in their lives and wonder if it is in their best interest to invest so much time and energy in their jobs.

The essays in the Focus section of this chapter (p. 385) address the question, "Is Every Worker Entitled to a Living Wage?" These essays ask important questions about the nature of both work and compensation. In "Millennial Thoughts: Minimum Wage and My Take" (p. 385), Will Perkins argues in favor of paying a living wage; in "If a Business Won't Pay a Living Wage, It Shouldn't Exist" (p. 388), the Daily Take Team takes an extreme position on the living wage; and in "The Minimum Wage Delusion, and the Death of Common Sense" (p. 391), James Dorn examines the belief that raising the wages of low-wage workers helps their job prospects.

Betastock/Shutterstock

What point does this contemporary image of welding robots assembling cars make about the nature of work?

Preparing to Read and Write

As you read and prepare to write about the selections in this chapter, you may consider the following questions:

- What assumptions does the writer have about his or her audience? How can you tell?
- What is the writer's primary purpose? For example, is it to reinforce traditional ideas about work, to point out inequities, or to offer new insights?
- What genre is the writer using? For example, is the reading an analysis or an argument? How do the conventions of this genre influence the writer's choices?
- What appeals does the writer use? For example, does he or she appeal primarily to reason, to emotion, or to a combination of the two? Is this the most effective strategy?
- What do you know about the writer? In what way does the writer's economic and social position affect his or her definition of work?
- Is the writer male, female, or a transgender person? Does the writer's gender affect his or her attitude toward work?
- When was the selection written? Does the date of publication affect its content?
- Does the selection seem fair? Balanced? Does the writer have any preconceived ideas about work and its importance?
- Is the writer generally sympathetic or unsympathetic toward workers?
- Does the writer have a realistic or unrealistic view of work?
- On what specific problems does the writer focus?
- What specific solutions does the writer suggest? Are these solutions feasible?
- Is your interpretation of the problem the same as or different from the interpretation presented in the reading?
- Are there any aspects of the problem that the writer ignores?
- Does the reading challenge any of your ideas about work?
- In what ways is the selection like other selections in this chapter?

Shared Writing

Why We Work

Are you currently employed? Where do you work, and what do you do? Is the work fulfilling? What kind of work do you want to do in the future?

10.1 Andrew Curry, "Why We Work"

Currently a freelance writer and editor, Andrew Curry (1976–) was an associate editor for *U.S. News and World Report.* "Why We Work" was the cover story of the February 24, 2003, issue. In this essay, Curry examines the nature of work and explains why many workers today feel unfulfilled.

BEFORE YOU READ

Why do the people you know work? Do they seem happy with what they do?

Why We Work

In 1930, W. K. Kellogg made what he thought was a sensible decision, grounded in the best economic, social, and management theories of the time. Workers at his cereal plant in Battle Creek, Mich., were told to go home two hours early. Every day. For good.

The Depression-era move was hailed in *Factory and Industrial Management* magazine as the "biggest piece of industrial news since [Henry] Ford announced his five-dollar-a-day policy." President Herbert Hoover summoned the eccentric cereal magnate to the White House and said the plan was "very worthwhile." The belief: Industry and machines would lead to a workers' paradise where all would have less work, more free time, and yet still produce enough to meet their needs.

So what happened? Today, work dominates Americans' lives as never before, as workers pile on hours at a rate not seen since the Industrial Revolution. Technology has offered increasing productivity and a higher standard of living while bank tellers and typists are replaced by machines. The mismatch between available work and those available to do it continues, as jobs go begging while people beg for jobs. Though Kellogg's six-hour day lasted until 1985, Battle Creek's grand industrial experiment has been nearly forgotten. Instead of working less, our hours have stayed steady or risen—and today many more women work so that families can afford the trappings of suburbia. In effect, workers chose the path of consumption over leisure.

But as today's job market shows so starkly, that road is full of potholes. With unemployment at a nine-year high and many workers worried about losing their jobs—or forced to accept cutbacks in pay and benefits—work is hardly the paradise economists once envisioned.

5 Instead, the job market is as precarious today as it was in the early 1980s, when business began a wave of restructurings and layoffs to maintain its competitiveness. Many workers are left feeling unsecure, unfulfilled, and underappreciated. It's no wonder surveys of today's workers show a steady decline in job satisfaction. "People are very emotional about work, and they're very negative about it," says David Rhodes, a principal at human resource consultants Towers Perrin. "The biggest issue is clearly workload. People are feeling crushed."

The backlash comes after years of people boasting about how hard they work and tying their identities to how indispensable they are. Ringing cellphones, whirring faxes, and ever present E-mail have blurred the lines between work and home. The job penetrates every aspect of life. Americans don't exercise, they work out. We manage our time and work on our relationships. "In reaching the affluent society, we're working longer and harder than anyone could have imagined," says Rutgers University historian John Gillis. "The work ethic and identifying ourselves with work and through work is not only alive and well but more present now than at any time in history."

STRESSED OUT

It's all beginning to take a toll. Fully one third of American workers—who work longer hours than their counterparts in any industrialized country—felt overwhelmed by the amount of work they had to do, according to a 2001 Families and Work Institute survey. "Both men and women wish they were working about 11 hours [a week] less," says Ellen Galinsky, the institute's president. "A lot of people believe if they do work less they'll be seen as less committed, and in a shaky economy no one wants that."

The modern environment would seem alien to pre-industrial laborers. For centuries, the household—from farms to "cottage" craftsmen—was the unit of production. The whole family was part of the enterprise, be it farming, blacksmithing, or baking. "In pre-industrial society, work and family were practically the same thing," says Gillis.

The Industrial Revolution changed all that. Mills and massive iron smelters required ample labor and constant attendance. "The factory took men, women and children out of the workshops and homes and put them under one roof and timed their movements to machines," writes Sebastian de Grazia in *Of Time, Work and Leisure.* For the first time, work and family were split. Instead of selling what they produced, workers sold their time. With more people leaving farms to move to cities and factories, labor became a commodity, placed on the market like any other.

10 Innovation gave rise to an industrial process based on machinery and mass production. This new age called for a new worker. "The only safeguard of order and discipline in the modern world is a standardized worker with interchangeable parts," mused one turn-of-the-century writer.

Business couldn't have that, so instead it came up with the science of management. The theories of Frederick Taylor, a Philadelphia factory foreman with deep Puritan roots, led to work being broken down into component parts, with each step timed to coldly quantify jobs that skilled craftsmen had worked a lifetime to learn. Workers resented Taylor and his stopwatch, complaining that his focus on process stripped their jobs of creativity and pride, making them irritable. Long before anyone knew what "stress" was, Taylor brought it to the workplace—and without sympathy. "I have you for your strength and mechanical ability, and we have other men paid for thinking," he told workers.

LONG HOURS

The division of work into components that could be measured and easily taught reached its apex in Ford's River Rouge plant in Dearborn, Mich., where the assembly line came of age. "It was this combination of a simplification of tasks ... with moving assembly that created a manufacturing revolution while at the same time laying waste human potential on a massive scale," author Richard Donkin writes in *Blood, Sweat and Tears.*

To maximize the production lines, businesses needed long hours from their workers. But it was no easy sell. "Convincing people to work 9 to 5 took a tremendous amount of propaganda and discipline," says the University of Richmond's Joanne Ciulla, author of *The Working Life: The Promise and Betrayal of Modern Work.* Entrepreneurs, religious leaders, and writers like Horatio Alger created whole bodies of literature to glorify the work ethic.

Labor leaders fought back with their own propaganda. For more than a century, a key struggle for the labor movement was reducing the amount of time workers had to spend on the job. "They were pursuing shorter hours and increased leisure. In effect, they were buying their time," says University of Iowa Prof. Benjamin Hunnicutt, author of *Work Without End: Abandoning Shorter Hours for the Right to Work.*

15 The first labor unions were organized in response to the threat of technology, as skilled workers sought to protect their jobs from mechanization. Later, semi- and unskilled workers began to organize as well, agitating successfully for reduced hours, higher wages, and better work conditions. Unions enjoyed great influence in the early 20th century, and at their height in the 1950s, 35 percent of U.S. workers belonged to one.

Union persistence and the mechanization of factories gradually made shorter hours more realistic. Between 1830 and 1930, work hours were cut nearly in half, with economist John Maynard Keynes famously predicting in 1930 that by 2030 a 15-hour workweek would be standard. The Great Depression pressed the issue, with job sharing proposed as a serious solution to widespread unemployment. Despite business and religious opposition over worries of an idle populace, the Senate passed a bill that would have mandated a 30-hour week in 1933; it was narrowly defeated in the House.

Franklin Delano Roosevelt struck back with a new gospel that lives to this very day: consumption. "The aim ... is to restore our rich domestic market by raising its vast consuming capacity," he said. "Our first purpose is to create employment as fast as we can." And so began the modern work world. "Instead of accepting work's continuing decline and imminent fall from its dominant social position, businessmen, economists, advertisers, and politicians preached that there would never be 'enough,'" Hunnicutt writes in *Kellogg's Six-Hour Day.* "The entrepreneur and industry could invent new things for advertising to sell and for people to want and work for indefinitely."

The New Deal dumped government money into job creation, in turn encouraging consumption. World War II fueled the fire, and American workers soon found themselves in a "golden age"—40-hour workweeks, plenty of jobs, and plenty to buy. Leisure was the road not taken, a path quickly forgotten in the postwar boom of the 1950s and 1960s.

DISCONTENT

Decades of abundance, however, did not bring satisfaction. "A significant number of Americans are dissatisfied with the quality of their working lives," said the 1973 report "Work in America" from the Department of Health, Education and Welfare. "Dull, repetitive, seemingly meaningless tasks, offering little challenge or autonomy, are causing discontent among workers at all occupational levels." Underlying the dissatisfaction was a very gradual change in what the "Protestant work ethic" meant. Always a source of pride, the idea that hard work was a calling from God dated to the Reformation and the teachings of Martin Luther. While work had once been a means to serve God, two centuries of choices and industrialization had turned work into an end in itself, stripped of the spiritual meaning that sustained the Puritans who came ready to tame the wilderness.

20 By the end of the '70s, companies were reaching out to spiritually drained workers by offering more engagement while withdrawing the promise of a job for life, as the American economy faced a stiff challenge from cheaper workers abroad. "Corporations introduced feel-good programs to stimulate jaded employees with one hand while taking away the elements of a 'just' workplace with the other," says Andrew Ross, author of *No Collar: The Humane Workplace and Its Hidden Costs.* Employees were given more control over their work and schedules, and "human relations" consultants and motivational speakers did a booming business. By the 1990s, technology made working from home possible for a growing number of people. Seen as a boon at first, telecommuting and the rapidly proliferating "electronic leash" of cellphones made work inescapable, as employees found themselves on call 24/7. Today, almost half of American workers use computers, cellphones, E-mail, and faxes for work during what is supposed to be nonwork time, according to the Families and Work Institute. Home is no longer a refuge but a cozier extension of the office.

The shift coincided with a shortage of highly skilled and educated workers, some of whom were induced with such benefits as stock options in exchange for their putting the company first all the time. But some see a different explanation for the rise in the amount of time devoted to work. "Hours have crept up partly as a consequence of the declining power of the trade-union movement," says Cornell University labor historian Clete Daniel. "Many employers find it more economical to require mandatory overtime than hire new workers and pay their benefits." Indeed, the trend has coincided with the steady decline in the percentage of workers represented by unions, as the labor movement failed to keep pace with the increasing rise of white-collar jobs in the economy. Today fewer than 15 percent of American workers belong to unions.

NIRVANA?

The Internet economy of the '90s gave rise to an entirely new corporate climate. The "knowledge worker" was wooed with games, gourmet chefs, and unprecedented freedom over his schedule and environment. Employees at Intuit didn't have to leave their desks for massages; Sun Microsystems offered in-house laundry, and Netscape workers were offered an on-site dentist. At first glance, this new corporate world seemed like nirvana. But "for every attractive feature, workers found there was a cost," says Ross. "It was both a worker's paradise and a con game."

When the stock market bubble burst and the economy fell into its recent recession, workers were forced to re-evaluate their priorities. "There used to be fat bonuses and back rubs, free bagels and foosball tables—it didn't really feel like work," says Allison Hemming, who organizes "pink-slip parties" for laid-off workers around the country and has written *Work It! How to Get Ahead, Save Your Ass, and Land a Job in Any Economy.* "I think people are a lot wiser about their choices now. They want a better quality of life; they're asking for more flextime to spend with their families."

In a study of Silicon Valley culture over the past decade, San Jose State University anthropologist Jan English-Lueck found that skills learned on the job were often brought home. Researchers talked to families with mission statements, mothers used conflict-resolution buzzwords with their squabbling kids, and engineers used flowcharts to organize Thanksgiving dinner. Said one participant: "I don't live life; I manage it."

In some ways, we have come full circle. "Now we're seeing the return of work 25
to the home in terms of telecommuting," says Gillis. "We may be seeing the return of households where work is the central element again."

But there's still the question of fulfillment. In a recent study, human resources consultants Towers Perrin tried to measure workers' emotions about their jobs. More than half of the emotion was negative, with the biggest single factor being workload but also a sense that work doesn't satisfy their deeper needs. "We expect more and more out of our jobs," says Hunnicutt. "We expect to find wonderful people and experiences all around us. What we find is Dilbert."

RESPONDING TO READING

1. Why does "work dominate Americans' lives as never before" (3)? According to Curry, what toll does this situation take on American workers?
2. How did the Industrial Revolution change the nature of work? What effect did Frederick Taylor have on work? According to Curry, why were the first labor unions formed? Why was the New Deal the "golden age" for workers (18)?

Rhetorical Analysis

Curry thinks that today's workers are unfulfilled. What evidence does he provide to support this contention? Does he provide enough evidence? Is it the right kind of evidence? Explain.

Writing with Sources

Examine the question of why people work. Then, write an essay in which you discuss your findings in light of Curry's essay. Does your research support Curry's conclusions? Are there issues he should have examined but did not?

10.2 Debora L. Spar, "Crashing into Ceilings: A Report from the Nine-to-Five Shift"

The former president of Barnard College and the founder of the Athena Center for Leadership Studies, Debora L. Spar (1963–) is committed to the education and advancement of women worldwide. She is the author of several books, including, most recently, *Wonder Women: Sex, Power, and the Quest for Perfection* (2013), from which the following essay was excerpted. Here, Spar considers the professional struggles women continue to face.

BEFORE YOU READ

Are women underrepresented in your field, or in the field you plan to enter? What specific challenges do these women face?

Crashing into Ceilings: A Report from the Nine-to-Five Shift

At every women's conference, in every think tank report, at every celebration of Women's History Month or International Women's Day, the same data are repeated. I've said them so many times myself that I can reel them off from memory. But they are crucial, and they bear repeating once again. Only twenty-one companies on the Fortune 500 list are run by female chief executives. Only 16.6 percent of these companies' board members are women. Women account for only 16 percent of partners at the largest law firms in the United States, and only 19 percent of the country's surgeons. Across the board, women earn on average twenty-three cents less than men for every dollar that they earn.

Two things, of course, leap out from this rather depressing list. First, that the numbers are so similar across even hugely different industries (movie directors and accountants, for instance). And second, that the vast bulk of them seem stubbornly cemented at around 16 percent. It's as if some evil grim reaper came regularly to mow down any female who dared to peek her head above the mandated allotment. *Women? Yes, we love them. Please, give us more. Oh, no; no, wait. Not that many more ... there seems to be a mistake ... BEGONE!*

What makes this accounting even more dismal is that it is no longer credible to blame the proverbial pipeline. For decades, after all, the dearth of women at the top of organizations could easily be explained by the dearth of women anywhere in the organization. No female surgeons? Well, of course not, if there are no women in medical school. No female law partners? Wholly predictable if there are no female associates. But the pipeline to the top has been full now, or at least plentiful, for over twenty years. In 1984, the year I entered graduate school, 31 percent of graduating physicians were female, as were 36 percent of graduating lawyers and 37 percent of newly minted Ph.D.s. By 1994, women constituted fully 50 percent of graduating physicians, 46 percent of graduating lawyers, and 48 percent of Ph.D.s. Theoretically, all of these women have now been in the workforce for somewhere between fifteen and twenty-five years, more than enough time for them to have soared, crawled, or shouldered their way to the top. But they haven't. Instead, as the oft-repeated numbers show, women's position in the ranks of power has hardly surged ahead. Think about it. In 1980, there were eighteen women in Congress (3 percent) and two in state governorships. Now there are ninety-eight (18 percent) and five, respectively. In 1980, there were 58 female mayors of major American cities; now there are 217. Yes, women ran (unsuccessfully) for both president and vice president in 2008, but women also ran (unsuccessfully) for president in 1964, and vice president in 1984. Without question, women have advanced professionally since the days of the feminist revolution, but that advance has been slower—much, much slower—than anyone really expected.

To get a more nuanced sense of where, and how, women are getting stuck, it's useful to look at a few fields where the deceleration has been most pronounced. In law, for instance, women seem particularly prone to being jammed into the 16 percent cranny. Since the 1980s, as noted above, women have been filing into law schools, accounting for more than 40 percent of law degrees by 1986. Yet the percentage of female partners at major law firms has remained stubbornly set at around 16 percent, and the average compensation of a male partner is still almost $90,000 higher than that of his female counterpart. As a result, according to Judge Judith Kaye, the first female chief judge of the State of New York, "what the profession still lacks is a critical mass of women to mentor junior associates approaching pivotal points in their careers, to ensure not only implementation of diversity programs but also accountability with regard to these programs, or to influence firm-wide decisions from the management ranks. The statistics tell us that we are definitely not there yet." Similarly, while women have proliferated across the lower and middle tiers of finance, they show few signs of achieving anything close to equal representation at the top: only 2.7 percent of CEOs, 16.6 percent of executive officers, and 18 percent of board directors. When I asked Ina Drew, former chief investment officer at JPMorgan Chase, and one of the banking sector's highest-ranking and longest-serving women, how to explain this discrepancy, her answer was succinct: "The top echelons of finance still lack mentors that women desperately need ... If women remain unfulfilled by their positions without the potential for growth and discouraged by male aggression, the discrepancies will persist."

5 My friend Jill is a case in point. Born on a farm outside Lincoln, Nebraska, Jill attended college on a full ROTC[1] scholarship. She studied Chinese as an undergraduate, earned a black belt in karate, and eventually became an ordnance officer in the Army. For four years, she dismantled bombs, and managed troops, and served on security detail for the White House. Needless to say, this is not a woman who scares easily, or who shies away from hardship. Jill married Paul, a classmate from ROTC, and helped support him through medical school. Then she entered law school, moved to Michigan, and gave birth to three kids—all in fairly rapid succession. For a while, it worked. Paul put in long hours as a newly minted orthopedic surgeon; Jill opened a small private law practice; and they hired a nanny they liked. Slowly, though, the troubles crept in. Paul was on call many nights and weekends, leaving Jill to juggle the kids, the errands, and the housework. Her cases were intriguing, but limited by her inability to bring on additional partners or devote more than fifty hours a week to the job. Their parents lived far away, and Jill never quite found the energy to put three toddlers in the back of the car and make the long drive back to Lincoln. So she slowly wound the practice down, throwing herself into volunteer work and her sons' tennis teams. Now the boys have graduated, though, and the big house is empty. Jill travels some, and works out, and tends to her increasingly far-flung family. But she rues the career she didn't have, and the regrets that hound her frequently. "This isn't what they gave me a degree for," she confided recently. "Somewhere, I screwed up."

My friend Shireen's regrets, meanwhile, are of a different sort. Petite and vivacious, she is one of those rare women who always manage to look both casually dressed and meticulously put together. Shireen went to business school in the early 1980s, when women were still rare among the ranks of MBAs. She graduated near the top of her class and took a fast-paced job in media marketing. She also met and married a fellow student, a hardworking son of Mexican immigrants who joined a media conglomerate as well. Shireen and Miguel worked happily together through the first few years of their marriage, grabbing takeout, skipping weekends, and sharing stories. They worked through the arrival of baby number one, and baby number two. After about eight years, however, and the arrival of baby number three, Miguel's career march accelerated. Suddenly, he was working hundred-hour weeks and shuttling back and forth among the company's expanded global operations. Without much fanfare, Shireen quietly stepped down. "What was I going to

[1]The Reserve Officers' Training Corps. [Eds.]

do?" she recalls. "Leave the kids with nannies around the clock?" So she took on all the child care, and the housework, and the increasingly large role of becoming a corporate wife. Today, even with her kids now grown and out of the house, Shireen maintains a breakneck schedule. She serves on several nonprofit boards and is involved with a score of local charities. She and Miguel have a strong and happy marriage. But she wears a veneer of wariness, a wariness that stems from suspecting what others want of her, and why. "People always say that they want me for my brains or my energy," she says with a smile. "But I know what they mean. They want Miguel's money. And the funny thing is," she continues, "that I really do have a lot of brains and energy. Or at least I once did."

Where women have made significant strides, for better or worse, is at the lower end of the pay scale and professional spectrum, in areas such as nursing, hairdressing, and middle school teaching, where women wholly dominate men. As reported in the 2009 Shriver Report, fully half of all workers in the United States are now female, and mothers contribute to their family's earnings in nearly two-thirds of American households. Mothers are the primary breadwinners, in fact, in four out of every ten households; and half of these mothers are single. These are important facts to consider, and complicated to think through. Because what does it really mean to have a household run by a single mother earning, on average, only $36,000 a year? Or to have two working-class parents holding down jobs and struggling to afford day care for their kids? The good news is that millions of women—black, white, Latina, and Asian—are financially independent, working in full- or part-time jobs to support themselves and their families. The bad news, though, is that many of these women are only barely hanging on, operating along the bottom of the social and economic pyramid, where women have long struggled and from which they were supposed to have escaped.

And certainly, some have. In 2009, women entrepreneurs ran more than 10 million businesses with combined sales of $1.1 trillion. As of 2007, firms owned by women in the United States employed 7.6 million people. But the aggregate numbers—that darned list of statistics again—make clear that most positions of power in this country (and indeed, around the world) are still persistently held by men. Women are flocking into college, into graduate programs, into entry-level and midlevel positions across every conceivable industry—but they are falling out well before they reach the top.

Why?

It isn't legalized prejudice anymore. It isn't barriers on the way in. And it's not 10
just men being mean. Indeed, most men in visible positions of power today are almost desperate to have some reasonable number of women in their ranks. So what accounts for the bottleneck? For the clogged pipeline, the glass ceiling, the pervasive code words meant to capture the reality that women are simply getting stuck?

Clearly, painfully, they're getting stuck because so many of them are choosing to stop. Women are not getting fired from midlevel positions at accounting or law firms; they are not disproportionately being denied tenure at major research universities. They are deciding, like Jill and Shireen, that they need to stay at home, or work part time, or step away from the fast track. Individually, each of these women's moves may make great sense. Together, though, they have created a landscape where women are still scarce, and where the clashing visions between what is and what was expected to be makes them feel scarcer still.

RESPONDING TO READING

1. At the beginning of paragraph 4, Spar says, "women are getting stuck." How does she explain why they are "getting stuck"?
2. What reasons does Spar give to explain why women seem to be underrepresented in top organizations? Why else could women be underrepresented?

Rhetorical Analysis

In paragraphs 5 and 6, Spar presents two long narrative examples. How convincing are they? Do they rely on logic, emotion, or the credibility of the writer? Do you think Spar's use of "My friend" to introduce these two examples is effective?

Writing with Sources

The term *glass ceiling* refers to the invisible barrier that keeps women (as well as certain minorities) from advancing to the higher levels of corporations. Research the concept of the glass ceiling. Then, write an essay to Spar in which you explain why you agree or disagree with her conclusion. Make sure you explore a wide range of opinions.

10.3 Ben Mauk, "When Work Is a Game, Who Wins?"

A cofounder and the director of the Berlin Writers' Workshop, Ben Mauk writes about a range of issues related to work and art. He has written for publications such as *The American Reader, The Believer,* the *Los Angeles Review of Books, The New Yorker, The Paris Review Daily,* the *Sun,* and *Vice.* In the following essay, Mauk examines the role of "gamification" in the workplace.

BEFORE YOU READ

Think of a job you had, and consider how making that job like a video game could create additional motivation.

When Work Is a Game, Who Wins?

This summer, *Der Spiegel* ran several stories revealing the extent of the N.S.A.'s[1] large-scale monitoring of European communications. At the agency's European Cryptologic Center, in Hesse, the paper reported, agents learned to use the controversial XKeyscore software to mine Web users' private e-mails, online chats, and browsing histories with no prior authorization. One element stands out as particularly surreal: "To create additional motivation," according to *Der Spiegel*, "the NSA incorporated various features from computer games into the program." For instance, analysts who excelled at an XKeyscore training program could acquire "skilz" points and "unlock achievements."

For many readers, the existence of such games confirmed suspicions of the N.S.A.'s cavalier attitude toward online privacy. On the technology blog Gizmodo, Adam Clark Estes wrote, "Did analysts level up when they identified American citizens who were talking with targets? Or get extra lives for intercepting messages between citizens that include mention of one of these targets?" Other bloggers recalled Pentagon's Plan X, a coordinated effort between game designers, animators, and security experts to make waging "cyber offense" more like a video game.

Yet despite the uneasy reactions to *Der Spiegel*'s report, the argument that work should feel more like a video game—complete with points, instant performance feedback, and flashy graphics—has, in the past decade, become a common refrain in Silicon Valley, and the so-called gamification of work is already under way in many industries. For some offices, that means designing sales competitions with sports-themed graphics and points systems to emulate ESPN-style action. For others, it means simulating cyber attacks to promote teamwork among a company's security staff. Still others might use merit badges to reward employees for meeting new co-workers or even for eating healthfully.

* * *

In 1959, a Duke sociologist named Donald F. Roy joined a group of machine-line workers in Chicago to study how menial laborers, working twelve-hour shifts, coped with their factory conditions—in particular, the problem of monotony. The study, titled "Banana Time: Job Application and Informal Interaction," describes how the workers consciously broke up their day with food breaks ("peach time," "fish time," "coke time"); self-imposed, if meaningless, benchmarks ("stamp a thousand green shapes in a row"); and even practical jokes, such as a daily ritual in which one employee stole and ate another's banana, precipitating a volley of "protests and denunciations" from the victim—who nevertheless always made sure to bring another banana to work the next day. Through this kind of ritualized fun, Roy found, "the 'beast of boredom' was gentled to the harmlessness of a kitten."

Roy was among a group of mid-century sociologists who were trying to figure 5
out why factory workers did not rise up in protest against their low pay and horrible

[1]The National Security Agency. [Eds.]

conditions, Ethan Mollick, a professor at the Wharton School of Business at the University of Pennsylvania, told me. One researcher, who happened to return to Roy's Chicago factory many years after "Banana Time," found that the workers there had become obsessed with a factory-wide competition to beat individual production quotas. What's more, employees were more enthralled by the game itself than by the modest cash prize for which they were competing. Games, the researcher concluded, could divert factory workers' energies away from collective bargaining and toward internal competition. In doing so, they encouraged workers to consent to the factory owners' production goals.

"At a certain point, there was a transition from viewing games as something that hurt production to a tacit realization that maybe games are doing us a service," Mollick told me. People realized that games could be "built on top of the goals of management."

When researchers study what spurs people to work harder, they look at both "intrinsic" motivators—enjoyment of the work itself—or "extrinsic" rewards, such as money, benefits, and social events, said Nancy Rothbard, also a professor at Wharton. Increasingly, researchers have come to think of games as yet another extrinsic reward, like company picnics or managerial praise.

"What well-designed games do is to create challenges and well-measured rewards for those challenges that give frequent positive feedback, designed to make workers feel more positively," Rothbard said. In other words, turning work into a game can make employees more satisfied and, potentially, more productive—all under the guise of having fun.

Hey, you know what kind of games are fun? Video games, which evolved around the same time as modern industrial psychology, and have since incentivized millions of children and adults to save princesses, steal cars, solve puzzles, build cities, and wage merciless wars in virtual worlds, with fun being pretty much the only salient reward. Today, some gurus in the burgeoning field of "game studies" argue that video games, in particular, can be powerful motivators.

10 In her influential 2012 book *Reality Is Broken*, Jane McGonigal—a game designer and TED Talk favorite—writes that this is because the non-game world falls short of our expectations and desires in ways that games never do. "The real world just doesn't offer up as easily the carefully designed pleasures, the thrilling challenges, and the powerful social bonding afforded by virtual environments." McGonigal, seeming like the world's most cheerful existentialist, itemizes reality's many flaws—that it is "hopeless," "depressing," and "trivial"—and suggests that games like World of Warcraft and Rock Band hold the cure. Instead of continuing to suffer in a world without meaning, she writes, "imagine a near future in which most of the real world works more like a game."

* * *

That may not be a stretch. Today, you can track your cross-training with Nike+, become mayor of your coffee shop with Foursquare, win badges for energy conservation with Opower, level up in German, Spanish, or Italian on Duolingo, out-clean your spouse in ChoreWars, or try some of the hundreds of other apps and sites that use gaming features to help you lose weight, balance your budget, or just gamify your entire life. By 2016, M2 Research predicts that gamification will be a $2.8 billion industry.

The research firm further predicts that workplace gamification will see the greatest growth. To understand how that would look, consider Zillow, the real-estate Web site, whose salespeople win points by making cold calls and closing sales, and account managers get ahead by earning positive surveys from customers or convincing them to return for more business. If you're a Zillow worker and a customer gives you some nice feedback, for example, TV screens across the company will light up with graphics, videos, and your own head shot—all themed according to whatever sport is in season. (Right now, it's football.)

"The TVs are pervasive throughout the office, so that even when you're on a call you can look over and see the screen," Tony Small, a Zillow vice-president, told me. Workers, he said, are constantly in competition to rise to the top of each so-called leader board.

In fact, most examples of workplace gamification are competitive in nature, relying on points, badges, and leader boards to motivate performance. In the past few years, venders with names like Busification, Leaderboarded, Hoopla, and the dystopian-sounding Dopamine have emerged to offer these features. (Hoopla's motto: "Put Fun to Work.")

"Imagine if you're watching a football game on TV and someone scores a 15
touchdown," said Small. "It looks like that. Our sales teams are competitive, and they happen to like sports. So when we found a channel that ESPN-izes what workers do, they really liked it."

One can imagine how gamification software can be adapted to any metric. If you're trying to limit unnecessary e-mails or shorten meeting times, for instance, you could dock employees points for sending an e-mail, or reward managers with a badge for ending a meeting early.

* * *

Not all designers are unruffled by the way games have transitioned into the workplace. Ian Bogost, a game designer and professor at the Georgia Institute of Technology, is among the industry's most vocal critics. In a 2011 speech, "Gamification Is Bullshit," he said gamification, having nothing to do with the pleasure of gaming, should instead be called "exploitationware," which opportunists have "pursued to capitalize on a cultural moment, through services about which they have questionable expertise, to bring about results meant to last only long enough to pad their bank accounts before the next bullshit trend comes along."

Bogost told me he is not inherently opposed to the use of game-like tools to quantify employee performance, especially in the salesroom. But he worries about potential misuse in other fields: "The question is, do we want to apply this to every single job? Food workers? Public-transit drivers?" He went on, "I'm opposed to the idea that you can give workers sugar pills, instead of pay and benefits—instead of the courtesy of being treated like a human being."

That idea—and the debate over it—predates the gamification trend by many decades, and remains a contentious topic in industrial psychology: To what degree can non-remunerative features of a workplace compensate for work that is not, in itself, rewarding? If your job is dull, menial, or unpleasant, will any number of free gym memberships, weekend retreats, or gamified work environments satisfy you?

20 And then there's another question: Is there something inherently un-fun about being forced by your boss to play a video game? While most research on workplace games has concerned itself with spontaneous, employee-generated play, one forthcoming study—authored by Mollick, the Wharton professor, and his colleague Nancy Rothbard—is among the first to consider the effect on workers of "managerially imposed" exercises that mimic video games. The researchers found that some sales workers at a start-up were more satisfied—although not more productive—when they were given a basketball-themed "gamified" environment. But, crucially, the effect worked only for those employees who said they felt that the game was fair, coherent, and a legitimate activity to associate with work. Those in the gamified environment who felt the game was unfair, confusing, or just inappropriate—about half of the workers in the group—were significantly less satisfied in their work, and slightly less productive. To improve workers' satisfaction through games, the authors determined, you need their consent.

The study, which is currently under review at a peer-reviewed journal, is a reminder that, while consumers can choose whether they want to play a game, workers can't opt out of their jobs. The result is a paradox the researchers define as "mandatory fun."

Mollick hopes to do more experiments to see how rates of consent might be improved. And yet, while gamification with proper consent may help to motivate employees, it does not seem likely that a veneer of play will create new meaning in the workplace. Nor will it fix a work culture that is fundamentally broken. Instead, gamification—like the old-fashioned games of an earlier era—could end up encouraging competition among workers who, decades earlier, might have found another activity to share: uniting as a single team to demand higher pay, better benefits, and more meaningful work.

RESPONDING TO READING

1. Although Mauk refers to various things that businesses can do to make work like a game, he never defines *game*. Is this definition needed? Why or why not?
2. According to Mauk, what are the possible benefits of making work more like a video game?

Rhetorical Analysis

Mauk concludes his essay by discussing some of the problems of "gamification." Why does he include this information? Does this strategy strengthen or weaken his argument? Explain.

Writing with Sources

Go online and research the features that well-designed video games should have. Then, "gamify" another job with which you are familiar. How could you convince workers to participate in the game? What positive effects do you think this mandated play would have on workers? Why? What negative effects of "gamification" might occur?

10.4 Rand Fishkin, "The Truth Shall Set You Free (from a Lot of $#*% Storms)"

A blogger, public speaker, and entrepreneur, Rand Fishkin (1979–) cofounded Moz, an industry leader in search engine optimization (SEO), as well as Inbound.org and, most recently, SparkToro. He is the author of *Lost and Founder: A Painfully Honest Field Guide to the Startup World* (2018), from which the following essay was excerpted. In it, Fishkin describes the essential qualities an entrepreneur needs to succeed.

BEFORE YOU READ

How would you describe your ability to communicate in business contexts? Are you able to be a team leader while also talking openly about your limitations?

The Truth Shall Set You Free (from a Lot of $#*% Storms)

> You've got an interesting business, but we don't believe it will ever get past a few million dollars in revenue.
>
> —Anonymous Investor I Pitched in 2009

In 2005, my coworker Matt and I were working in a run-down, shared office space above a noisy movie theater in Seattle when *he* walked in. A hairy, barrel-chested, fortysomething guy with gold chains, a mean grimace, and a stack of papers in a folder stared down at me.

He asked, "Are you Rand Fishkin?"

I was twenty-five years old, disoriented by his arrival, intimidated by his appearance and tone, and utterly panicked. I'm usually a terrible liar, so was taken aback by how quickly a response left my mouth:

"Sorry, I don't think he's here."

5 We exchanged a few more words, but I remember none of them. My heart was pounding. I hated lying, but I also had no idea what might happen if I identified myself. Matt just put on his headphones and pretended to be engrossed in whatever website he was working on. When the extra from *The Sopranos* left, I called Gillian, president of our three-person firm (who also happens to be *my mom*). I told her about the unexpected visitor. She guessed he was a debt collector, sent by one of the firms to whom a bank had sold our debt.

Oh, right. The debt. The $500,000 we owed, in my name, to finance our struggling consulting business.

Ten minutes after I returned to my apartment (actually, Geraldine's apartment—I was unable to pay my half of rent with my sometimes tiny, sometimes nonexistent paychecks, and couldn't pass a credit check, either), I heard a knock on the door. Assuming it was Geraldine carrying something she didn't want to put down to turn the key, I opened up without looking through the peephole.

It was the debt collector.

"Ha! Gotcha," he said.

10 I was mute.

"You're pretty good, kid. I totally bought that act today...." Scared senseless, I just stared at him.

He handed me the folder of papers I'd seen in his hands earlier and said, "Rand Fishkin, you've been served."

I couldn't even reach out to take them. He dropped them on the ground and walked away.

"OOPS, I ACCIDENTALLY A STARTUP"

In the summer of 2000, I was twenty-one with a year of college to go at the University of Washington in Seattle. I'm one of those lucky kids whose parents paid his tuition so he could "focus on his studies, not on work."

15 That is, until I got into a fight with my dad and he threatened to cut me off. I was too prideful and stubborn to back down, apologize, or reconcile, so, for the next two quarters, had to pay my own way.

I worked part-time at the Winds of the Coast Game Center, a giant arcade, gaming events center, and retail shop around the corner from campus. My $4.75/hour salary was supplemented by buying Pokémon cards with my employee discount and reselling them on eBay and Craigslist for a tidy profit. I designed and built a few websites on the side for some extra cash. And, thankfully, in the early 2000s, college tuition hadn't yet skyrocketed past the point of absurdity. A full quarter, including books, only cost around $3,000—a sum scraped together while still managing to have enough to go out to the movies, buy the occasional used video game, and pay the rent on my small, shared apartment.

But two classes away from graduating, I threw in the towel. Part of it was the cost, part of it was the lack of value I perceived from school, but a lot of it was because of a failed romantic relationship (long distance + breakup = broken heart). I wish I could say entrepreneurship was the catalyst for dropping out, but the truth is the other way around. I wallowed in a little self-misery, watched a lot of *X-Files* reruns, and only then realized I needed something to do besides work retail. Web design was my path of least resistance.

In 1981, my mom, Gillian, started a marketing consultancy in Seattle, helping small businesses with their logos, Yellow Page ads, brochures, and other print and advertising materials. In the late 1990s, her clients started asking for websites, and she recruited me to learn FrontPage, Dreamweaver, and HTML so I could help out. I liked the work, and the extra money, and when I told my mom I wanted to work with her full-time and not go back to college, she obliged.

Over the summer of 2001, we dreamed big. Seattle's tech scene was booming in Microsoft's backyard. Startups like Amazon, Kozmo, and HomeGrocer dominated the local news. Everyone was switching from slow, dial-up modems to high-speed broadband. We thought we had an amazing opportunity to design sites for local businesses that needed a presence on the soon-to-be-ubiquitous Internet. When the dot-com crash hit, I barely noticed. Our clients still needed websites, and I didn't pay much attention to the falling prices, the late payments, or the commoditization of web design.

For the next three years, we struggled against increasing competition, per- 20
vasive doubt about the web's future, the challenges of getting our clients to pay their bills on time, and, worst of all, our own foolish beliefs about what would help our company grow. We were trying to sell our services in a crowded marketplace without a competitive differentiator. We wasted money on advertising that didn't bring in business. We leased high-priced office space, convinced that an impressive building would help us close deals. We hired contractors and employees who didn't work out. We rented booth space at events that didn't even pay for themselves. And, worst of all, we went into debt to do it.

When I started working with my mom, she had a small amount of debt on the business—less than $20,000 in total. But three years later, we'd amassed an additional $100,000 of debt, much of it from the aforementioned missteps. The great thing about a consulting business is supposed to be the low-capital requirements—smart operators often make their consultancies profitable from day one. We went the other direction, and in 2004, after we'd failed to secure yet another client project we thought could put us on the path to success, we defaulted.

It's hard today to imagine the pre-2008-financial-crisis world of personal debt, where banks would extend loans of $50–$100,000 to a college dropout with a tiny salary. At the time, credit card offers arrived almost weekly, promising $10,000 limits that would quickly rise to $15,000 or $20,000. Lending institutions were happy to offer us lines of credit and equipment loans despite our meager track record and nonexistent collateral. Promotional interest rates in the <2 percent range were available for the first two to three years of an account. Seduced by these offers and in desperate need of cash just to make payroll and rent for three people, we went whole hog, racking up a balance that eventually came back to bite us.

We took out loans and put them in my name because I had, at the time, nothing to lose. My mom had her and my dad's assets on the line. They owned not only their home in Seattle's suburbs but my grandmother's house in Connecticut as well, which could have also been on the chopping block as collateral. So it was my social security number and my signature on the loans—something that, at the time, didn't really scare me. Defaulting on these loans never really crossed my mind.

Two of the most memorable days in my early career came that fall, of 2004.

25 The first was on a Sunday. Gillian had told me and Matt, my friend and our programmer, that we'd no longer be able to afford the rent at our pricey high-rise office tower. Moving out was our only option. We found a tiny shared office space in a run-down part of Seattle above an old movie theater for only a few hundred dollars a month (versus the $2,000-plus we had been paying), but we'd need to break our lease. That meant the landlord could potentially hold our equipment—including our computers, desks, chairs, and furniture—as collateral. We had to get it out of the tower and over to the new space fast, without anyone from the building noticing. This part's straight out of a movie.

Matt and I recruited a pair of friends—Marshall and Todd, a couple with two sets of big arms, strong backs, and a spacious truck to whom we promised dinner—and quietly entered the building via the loading garage.

We were halfway through loading up when the tower's security guard arrived. Cue heart falling into stomach.

After a brief, tense discussion on either side of our locked office door, we had the guard make a phone call to Gillian. Somehow, she convinced him to let us finish moving some of the items, but we had to leave a good deal behind to make it seem that we weren't actually "moving out" but rather "moving some things around." With our pulses racing, we took Todd's half-full truck out of the loading dock and across Lake Washington to our new, tiny, bare-bones but safe-from-seizure office. We'd sacrificed a good dozen pieces of unwieldy office furniture and some cheap supplies but felt lucky just to make it out with our computers and essentials. The next week, the company my mom had run for twenty-three years officially closed, and we started a new business under a new name.

But though we'd moved and changed our name, we were far from starting fresh. A couple of months later, that gold-chained debt collector showed up, and I called my mom in a panic.

30 Even though the debt was being used for business purposes, the creditors would be coming after me personally because it was my signature and my social security number on the applications. Gillian told me she'd try to take care of it. That was the first day I truly understood that most of the money our company owed was actually money *I* owed personally.

It made sense. If Gillian had used her name and her credit to take out even more of those equipment loans and low-interest credit cards, she and my dad could be held liable for repayment, and she already had some debt of her own. They could lose their assets and be forced into bankruptcy. My grandmother could lose her house.

That evening, walking home from work, I started processing our nerve-racking situation and my role in creating it. I'd willfully chosen to ignore and not ask questions about the financial problems we were in, ostensibly so I could concentrate on my part of the work but, in honesty, because I didn't want to deal with it. My mom could handle it. That was her job, right? I was just the web design guy. That's what I'd told myself. But slowly I came around to the idea that sticking my head in the sand about our debt in the hopes it would go away was an untenable path.

WHEN YOU'RE IN DEBT TO THE TRUTH, THE INTEREST RATE SUCKS

Considering the onslaught of "final notice" letters, threatening phone calls, and the visit from gold-chains-and-chest-hair guy (let's go with "Rocco," as he already fit every other debt-collector stereotype), the logical move would have been to declare bankruptcy. Most of the debt was in my name, a little was in Gillian's, and, because we had defaulted on the bigger chunks in my name, the black marks I was racking up on my credit report were having a similar effect to a bankruptcy (as of this writing, my creditworthiness is still in the toilet). But we had another impediment.

During the four years we built up debt, we'd been lying.

We'd never told my dad, Scott (to whom my mom was, and remains, married), 35
that we had any financial problems, any outstanding loans, or any debt collectors breathing down our necks. We both feared, rightly or wrongly, that if he found out he'd divorce my mom and break up our family.

It sounds too dysfunctional to be real, but this lie of omission wasn't without precedent. Growing up, my parents lied to each other all the time—mostly about little stuff (or, at least, those are the only things I knew about). Dad would say, "Don't tell your mom we did this" or, "If anyone asks, tell them you are only seven years old/were promised a discount/were told by the staff it was okay." Mom would say, "If your father asks, tell him we used a coupon/had to because of your school/went here on behalf of a client."

These were mostly innocent lies, crafted in order to prevent an altercation and keep relationships smooth. As an adult, reflecting on these memories makes me realize how profoundly unhealthy the dynamic between my parents was, but as a child and teenager, it made reasonable sense. The goal was to limit anyone getting angry or feeling hurt or left out or ignored. We were lying to keep the peace and maintain the veneer of a happy family unit.

That debt, however, was a much bigger lie than anything I'd ever been part of. I remember Geraldine and I talking about it at the time and for years after. We wondered how my mom could stand to be around my dad, day after day, holding in this giant secret, rushing to get home before him so she could shred any potentially incriminating mail, pretending that the debt-collection calls were wrong numbers, keeping up the appearance that things were fine at work—even bringing home an occasional paycheck to make him think things were okay when we probably should have used that money to stave off the next bank that might sell our debt to collections.

Gillian, ostensibly to keep us from worrying and to help us focus on our tasks, kept some of the details and progress of our struggle against debt hidden from me at the time. It wasn't until years later that I learned how she managed to dodge some of the worst debt collectors by proactively calling the issuers of the debt

(Washington Mutual, Bank of America, Chase, Wells Fargo), sharing the details of our situation, and offering a smaller sum than what was owed in exchange for the creditor writing off the debt rather than selling to collections. Because a collections agency would typically pay the debt holder 5–10 percent of the actual amount owed, then try to collect the full amount and profit from the delta, my mom's tactic was often successful.

40 While my credit report took the brunt of our debt problems, Gillian bore the lion's share of the stress. She'd always taken care of our finances and transactions. Despite having more than half a dozen credit accounts with various companies, I never even looked at the invoices—I passed them to my mom and went back to designing websites. I knew things were bad, but I rarely asked for updates. I just went about my work, hoping beyond hope that we could somehow land enough contracts and make enough money to pay back what we owed.

Later, I'd hear stories of other small businesses and startups that faced similar situations. Although I wish it were true that cofounders and family business owners and small teams were always honest with one another, that's often not the case. Tinder grew to dominate the world of online dating apps, but behind the scenes, cofounder strife, political struggles, and outright sexism led to lawsuits, stunted growth, and power struggles. Zipcar, one of the fastest-growing players in alternative transportation, lost both its cofounders over years of politicking, infighting, and fundraising struggles. Twitter famously lost nearly all of its founding team. Facebook's cofounder, Eduardo Saverin, helped write a movie (*The Social Network*, released 2010) about his ouster. Despite these all-too-common conflicts, many businesses don't collapse: they find ways of coping, carrying on, and working through or around poor communication, dishonesty, and dozens of other challenging problems people in high-stakes relationships face. And that's what we did.

TRANSPARENCY IS HARD, BUT IT WORKS

There will never be a shortage of justifications for why you believe hiding the truth is the right path. You're worried about hurting someone's feelings. You're afraid if your customers find out about a problem, they'll leave your service forever. You're convinced that you're actually protecting your executive team from stress by redacting details of your investor meetings. You believe the competition probably has engineers idly waiting for some sign of how you've built your amazing technology so they can instantly replicate it and launch before you have the chance.

So you keep secrets. You distort the truth. You tell a few lies. And worst, you think you can get away with it.

Later, when reality comes crashing down (as it always does), you lose the faith of your team or your audience, your investors or your customers. But you justify it by telling yourself: "If things had only gone another way, no one would have even found out, and everything would have been fine."

45 I have to assume that's what Travis Kalanick thought about his visits to Korean escort parlors with the Uber executive team. And what Facebook thought about testing whether showing particular posts could influence people's moods.

It's surely what Steve Ballmer believed about his infamous abusive tantrums at Microsoft leadership meetings. And it's undoubtedly why Tinder's CEO thought he could sexually harass and bully cofounder Whitney Wolfe. When people believe they can hide the truth, many of the incentives inhibiting bad behavior fall apart.

Every founder, every investor, and certainly every employee I've ever talked to in the startup world has stories about the secrets that eventually got out, costing trust, harming relationships, and often affecting revenue and growth, too. But there's another way—transparency. Transparency is making the choice to reveal even the most uncomfortable truths with relentless candor.

Transparency isn't the same as honesty. Honesty is saying only things that are true. Many founders and startup teams are honest (in that they don't directly lie). But transparency requires digging deep to find and expose what others would normally leave unsaid and refusing to take the easy, quiet road. It's tackling the conversations that make your stomach turn and your voice get caught in your throat. And like nearly everything in the world of startups, swallowing the bitter pill now is vastly superior to letting the disease of opacity fester.

If there's an underperforming person on your team, it's easy to ignore him for a while and hope his manager either helps him improve or fires him. It's much harder and more uncomfortable to thoughtfully process why you're unhappy with him, document instances of unwanted behavior, have a direct conversation with the team member, and, if necessary, coach him or work to find mentorship/coaching/classes (whatever it takes to give him the tools to get better if he has the desire). It could still end up that you (or his manager) may have to ultimately fire him. That's the thing with transparency: sometimes, the outcome is the same, but how you got there, and the downside risk, is remarkably different.

Say you're six months away from layoffs given your current revenue, expenses, and projections. You can be honest by simply remaining silent and imploring your team to improve the growth rate. Or you can be transparent by sharing your financials and your projections and explaining exactly what you need to do between now and month 6 to avoid cutting the team. Nine out of ten leadership teams won't share that information. They'll fear, perhaps rightly, that team members might start looking for new jobs or leak numbers to the press. But what happens when those layoffs hit? Yeah...your team will stop trusting you. They'll no longer believe that things are going "fine" when you say so. They'll always be looking for signs that the next crisis is around the corner. Those team members you hoped wouldn't look for new jobs—trust me, they're far less likely to stay than if you'd been up front.

Transparency's harder at first, and it feels especially painful when it reveals 50
your mistakes or challenges the image you've crafted for your team or customers. Yet, it's immensely powerful, and it has an almost unbelievably positive impact on everyone around you...

If your funding discussions are not going well, it's easy to hold out hope, tell your team you're still "in the process," and only if/when the last investor backs out or the money in the bank runs dry do you let everyone know that cost cutting and layoffs are happening. Far more uncomfortable, but vastly more transparent, is to give regular status updates on the fundraising process internally so employees and executives know precisely what investors are saying, why the pitch isn't working, and where the business metrics are perceived to be weak and can then anticipate a realistic future and potentially contribute to a better result. It may feel like telling your team is admitting weakness and defeat, but in fact, you'll build camaraderie, support, and a powerful incentive to do remarkable work. I've been blown away, time and again, by the ability that "bad news" has to catalyze great effort and remarkable results.

But I can't do that! My team will freak out!

You'd be surprised at how people rise to a challenge once they know that there *is* a challenge. And don't kid yourself—you may think you're keeping them safe by keeping them in the dark, but some distorted version of the truth always leaks. Misinformation stokes fear and resentment in your team. That's never good for business—or for anyone's well-being. You need your team's trust, not just in that one moment when fundraising's going poorly or growth has stalled, but in the long term. Even after people leave, what they say about you and your trustworthiness will affect basic business functions like recruiting, sales, branding, and bizdev for decades to come.

The most meaningful benefit transparency brings might be its forcing function for deliberately ethical, rational behavior. As CEO, I'd often tell my executives and board that every email should be written and every conversation conducted as though it will one day be leaked. We should be proud, not embarrassed, by what and how we communicate, even when the doors are closed. There are good reasons for privacy—to avoid shaming an employee for a mistake or to enable discussion about private, personal, or professional issues (among others). But people change their behavior for the better when they assume their peers, their reports, and their leadership will get to see/hear the full story.

55 Transparency can't just be a tactic, though. It has to be a core value that's consistently followed. If you openly share some things, but hide others, credibility will suffer. Your team will always wonder what you're not sharing. Your customers, your investors, the press—whomever you interact with—will be trained to mistrust you. A reputation for caginess lasts a long time and follows you across companies and geographies.

When we adopted transparency as a core value at Moz, it wasn't always easy, and we didn't always live up to the ideal. But more than any other aspect of the company, transparency, and the trustworthiness it instilled in our team, our community, and our customers built the company's legacy. We shared our financials online (just as I have in this book). We wrote about our product struggles, our fundraising failures, our most difficult internal conversations, our strategy. We were called crazy and foolish for oversharing so much about the mechanics of the business. But we also became trusted, and, especially because the field of SEO and the broader world of tech startups are so often impenetrably secretive, it paid off.

Early in my career, I was deeply afraid of being transparent. I feared if our customers knew the truth about our tiny operation, or about my age and inexperience, they wouldn't want to work with us. Of course, when we signed a new client, inevitably we'd meet, or they'd search for me and find those things out anyway. I was scared like hell to admit I didn't know how some aspect of HTML worked, but by faking it I outed my lack of knowledge even more blatantly. My mom and I covering up our debts and our missteps—hiding that risk from my dad? It only caused more stress and fear. Had we been honest from the start, he could have helped, could have saved us the hundreds of thousands in interest penalties we ended up owing. Instead, we created a nightmare of secrecy that nearly ended in professional and personal disaster.

Of course, years later, he did learn the truth. I heard about it from my younger brother, Evan, who told the story this way:

> *"Dad found out about the debt. Mom tried to play it off, but he found out. I went to my room and put on headphones, but he yelled so loud, the house was shaking."*

My only consolation: my dad and I weren't speaking at the time. We've probably had three conversations in the last seven years. Secrets, lies, opacity—they tear families apart just as surely as they do startups.

My credit still sucks. My relationship with my parents remains rough. But I 60
don't get any more unexpected visits from debt collectors who look like they could bench-press me. At least I can put that in the win column.

If we'd been transparent from the start, I believe we'd be in a different, better place today. The only solace is that this lesson, hard won through regret and carried forward in my personal and professional life, helped, over the next decade, to make Moz into something truly special. If you ask me why I'm so open, so bluntly honest about things that the startup ecosystem and business culture usually urge us to keep silent, this is why. I'm done with the pain of secrecy, happy to trade it for the challenges transparency brings.

RESPONDING TO READING

1. In paragraph 40, Fishkin explains, "I knew things were bad, but I rarely asked for updates. I just went about my work, hoping beyond hope that we could somehow land enough contracts and make enough money to pay back what we owed." Why does Fishkin explain in such detail his downward spiral into debt? What purpose does this confession serve?
2. According to Fishkin, how is transparency different from honesty? Is one quality better than the other?

Rhetorical Analysis

The first half of Fishkin's essay recounts the history and consequences of his bad business decisions. The second half of the essay offers specific advice for entrepreneurs. Why does he structure his essay in this way? Is the essay's organization effective? How does it help him make his point?

Writing with Sources

In paragraph 51, Fishkin writes, "I've been blown away, time and again, by the ability that 'bad news' has to catalyze great effort and remarkable results." Interview several professionals and find out if what Fishkin contends is borne out by the facts. Then, write an essay in which you agree or disagree with Fishkin's essay.

10.5 K. C. Williams, "Teaching While Black"

A social psychologist, public speaker, and blogger, K. C. Williams is the director of African American student affairs at the University of Arizona. She writes about issues related to education, social justice, race, and gender. In the following essay, Williams enumerates the forms of racism black educators face in the workplace.

BEFORE YOU READ

Have you experienced discrimination on the job because of your race or gender? What did you do?

Teaching While Black

For any black faculty member who has ever felt imposed upon or discriminated against for reasons having nothing to do with your abilities, you may have been discovered to be TWB—Teaching While Black.

Even for black folk who think they share MFB (most favored black) status at their college, the rules of Teaching While Black still apply. Let one of your white students get their feelings hurt during a lecture on race—a lecture that you have been *hired* to deliver—then you will see how treacherous TWB can be and how quickly your most favored black status changes. Exhibits A through E: Melissa Harris-Perry, Shannon Gibney, Ersula Ore, Saida Grundy and Henry Louis Gates Jr.[1] (just to name a few).

Somewhere along the way, we got it twisted. Many academic institutions were happy with your blackness only as long as it was propping up their sad diversity numbers. As long as you conform and stay in the shadows of their achievements, you are good to go, but if you are going to be one of "those blacks"—the troublemakers, activists, uppity black folk—now that's another story.

When you lose that most favored black status, you will know. There will be an air of hostility from your colleagues in meetings. People you do not even know will begin to ignore you.

5 Secretaries will tattle on you, even if you have never done anything but support them. Some may go as far as to record their conversations with you, type them up and proclaim that they will testify in court to the comments made.

---

[1]Recent examples of black educators who publicly confronted the discrimination they faced. [Eds.]

Male maintenance workers will burst in the faculty restroom door, walk right in and ignore your presence, brushing by you with not so much as an "excuse me." A vice president might call you "sassy" or "elitist" and demand that you take your prestigious alma mater out of your syllabus because it intimidates your (white) students. Yet they will also advise that you take people "out of their comfort zones."

The college newsletter may publish your credentials incompletely, because to write them up properly—inclusive of the "with departmental honors" addendum—"might make others feel bad." You will wonder if they actually realize how difficult it is to graduate with honors from a program like that. The very same tools required to get hired will suddenly become a barrier to full participation in that job.

Colleagues will take their disdain to the next level by sending problematic students your way or by actively dissuading them from taking your classes. Some of those students may disobey and take your course anyway. Later, they will come to you and report the negative, racist comments made while they were registering, and will put it in writing. The others? They let you know who they are on the first day of class as they sit with their arms crossed and faces torn up before you have even introduced yourself. Nearly all will soften as the semester goes on, because after all, you are not actually a monster, but you have been caught TWB.

Staff members who are paid to advocate for your role of leadership in the classroom will actively undermine your authority by empowering students to misbehave. They will encourage those students to skip the chain of command and write memos directly to the college president or vice presidents for any and all perceived rebuffs. Worst of all, when students misbehave in ways that most would consider beyond the pale, even criminally, those same staffers will stand around the water cooler discussing why you just can't be nicer to students.

Some students will refuse to address you respectfully, but they will do so with a smile. They may even attempt to call you by your first name after you have introduced yourself to them professionally with the expected "Dr." or "Professor" preceding your last name—on the first day of class, writing it on the board and in the syllabus.

When you're Teaching While Black, your colleagues will also join in the fray. 10
They will pull the office visit drive-by, wherein they will come by to ask you some basic question about some abstract theory, just to see if they can catch you off guard. And suddenly, all of them have a cousin or a neighbor who attended your alma mater; they want you to know that you are not that special. One may bring you an article explaining how they, as a Jewish person, benefit from inherent intelligence, while black people do not. They will wonder aloud to others why you kicked them out of your office. Little did they know a staffer was bragging about keeping down costs on a student fair by noting that they had "Jewed them down."

You may see your college president around town, and despite the fact that there are rarely more than four or five black faculty (out of nearly 150), he will ask you where you work. Every time. He might do so in front of his administrators at a statewide conference, asking, "Where did we *get* you from?" as if you were acquired from a street corner, orphanage or auction block.

But you will fully realize you are TWB when the most atrocious things happen. When a student leaves a racist message on your office door display, or boldly tells you they do not believe you went to your university because they googled you and could not find you anywhere, or they bring a fully formed noose to the classroom to threaten you. Criminal.

Time and again, in even only the last three years, we have seen administrations handle these situations fecklessly. They have engaged in victim blaming and shaming, fired or written up the faculty member, failed to act in any meaningful way against perpetrators, and smeared the names and reputations of the victims. When you confront them head-on with the reality that you expect to be treated with respect and fairness, the Jim Crow claws come out. "How dare you not know your place, black person!" "Who do you think you are, elitist black person?" "You seem to think you deserve more than anyone else!"

This is the formula. It seems very few institutions take inclusion and equity seriously. Even those that do still handle racism and anti-blackness like it was something *you* were supposed to prevent—that it is an inconvenience that makes them look bad, and that is *your* fault.

15 So what can you do? Do you. Resist being lulled into the false comfort of respectability politics. Don't think that you can "coon" your way into fair treatment—because if that is your plan, you have already lost. You know better and can sense that there is a problem if you ever find yourself thinking you have to be nicer, less bold, let it "roll off your shoulders" or hold back critique.

Don't dull your shine for their comfort. Use the system to forward your professional goals and those of your students. Pay attention to students of color and inspire them by being fully black. Stand in your blackness because you stand on the shoulders of those who were not allowed to do so.

I came across this poem by Andria Nacina Cole, and I can't stop thinking about how apropos it is.

> They will come for your throat, Black girl. They will kill themselves trying to keep you in your place. Buck. Write pretty speeches in their language. Use their own words against them. Remember the community from which you come. And chip, chip, chip away at their systems. Forever. Until they come crashing down at their motherfucking feet. (Andria Nacina Cole. "Untitled: Response to a speech Marilyn Mosby gave defending her handling of the Freddie Gray trial." Used by permission.)

There's no alternative—you are black, while engaging in a noble profession within a hostile society that sees your blackness as a threat. So let it. As you work to dismantle the system, change how you respond to it. Be professional. Be committed. Be engaged.

But be you. Beautiful, powerful, wonderful black you.

Source: KC Williams (Feb 3, 2017). Teaching While Black, Inside Higher Ed. Used with permission from KC Williams.

RESPONDING TO READING

1. According to Williams, what is "TWB"? Why does she use an acronym to describe this phenomenon? Who or what is responsible for the situation Williams describes?
2. In paragraph 14, Williams writes, "It seems very few institutions take inclusion and equity seriously. Even those that do still handle racism and anti-blackness like it was something *you* were supposed to prevent—that it is an inconvenience that makes them look bad, and that is *your*

fault." What does she mean? How are black educators made to feel guilty for the racism they experience?

Rhetorical Analysis

Why does Williams begin her essay with a direct address to her readers? What assumptions is she making about her audience? How can you tell?

Writing with Sources

Find some statistics about African American job discrimination. Then, write a poem in which you describe the problem and/or propose a solution.

10.6 Claire Cain Miller, "How a Common Interview Question Fuels the Gender Pay Gap (and How to Stop It)"

A correspondent for *The New York Times*, Claire Cain Miller explores issues related to gender, identity, family, and work. She was a member of the team of journalists who won the Pulitzer Prize in 2018 for public service reporting about sexual harassment in the workplace. In the following essay, Miller examines a possible cause of the wage disparity between men and women.

BEFORE YOU READ

Do you think you are paid fairly for the work you do, relative to your coworkers' pay? Why or why not?

How a Common Interview Question Fuels the Gender Pay Gap (and How to Stop It)

Aileen Rizo was training math teachers in the public schools in Fresno, Calif., when she discovered that her male colleagues with comparable jobs were being paid significantly more.

She was told there was a justifiable reason: Employees' pay was based on their salaries at previous jobs, and she had been paid less than they had earlier in their careers.

Ms. Rizo, who is now running for the California State Assembly, sued. In April, the United States Court of Appeals for the Ninth Circuit ruled in her favor, saying that prior salary could not be used to justify a wage gap between male and female employees.

It's the latest sign that this has become the policy of choice for shrinking the gender pay gap. Several states, cities and companies have recently banned asking about salary history. They include Massachusetts, California, New York City and Chicago, as well as Amazon, Google and Starbucks.

5 Women continue to earn less than men, for a variety of reasons. Discrimination is one, research shows. Women are also likelier than men to work in lower-paying jobs like those in public service, caregiving and the nonprofit sector—and to take time off for children. Employers often base a starting salary on someone's previous earnings, so at each job, the gender pay gap continues, and it becomes seemingly impossible for women to catch up.

"Women are told they are not worth as much as men," Judge Stephen Reinhardt wrote in the Ninth Circuit's opinion, before he died last month. "Allowing prior salary to justify a wage differential perpetuates this message, entrenching in salary systems an obvious means of discrimination."

What if job applicants don't live in one of the places where asking about salary history is banned? Some experts recommend that they find ways to politely deflect, although refusing to answer an interview question can be risky. Workshops by the American Association of University Women suggest some strategies.

Applicants could turn the question back on the employer by asking for the position's salary range, or what the last person to do the job was paid. Applicants could say something like: "I want to learn more about the job first, in order to have a better sense of my salary expectations." Or they could provide context for why they're declining to share the information, by explaining that it contributes to the gender pay gap.

Salary history bans can also have a less expected effect: When employers don't rely on past pay as a proxy for how valuable someone is, they might consider a wider variety of candidates. A recent working paper was based on an experiment in an online job marketplace: Half of employers could see applicants' past pay and half could not. The employers who could not see past pay viewed more applications, asked candidates more questions and invited more for interviews. The candidates they hired had, on average, lower past wages, and struck better deals when they negotiated.

10 The study was not representative of most hiring situations—the job marketplace was for short-term projects on which applicants bid—and the experiment was not assessing gender differences in pay. But it showed that employers overrely on past salary as an indicator of productivity, and without that information, they try to learn about candidates in other ways, said Moshe Barach, a co-author of the paper and a researcher at Georgetown.

"It takes more effort on the part of the employer, but they get better outcomes because someone who might not have made it to Step 1 now gets a chance," he said. "Employers talk to a person and might find they're really smart and hire them."

Salary history bans are too new for researchers to have studied their effects extensively. But other research has found that people are overly influenced by an opening bid, something social scientists call anchoring bias. This means that if employers learn an applicant's previous salary and it's lower or higher than they were planning to offer, it's likely to influence their offer.

When other types of information have been hidden during job interviews, it has led employers to discriminate less. A study of symphony orchestra directors found that when people auditioned behind a curtain, more female musicians were hired.

But the strategy can backfire. Some research has found that ban-the-box policies, which prohibit employers from asking on job applications whether people have criminal records, resulted in fewer black and Hispanic men being interviewed or hired. One theory is that without the information, employers assumed they had criminal records.

The same thing could happen with salary history bans, critics of the new poli- 15
cies fear. Employers could offer women and other targets of discrimination less because they assume they were paid less. Or women with high salaries might volunteer that information in interviews, leading employers to think that anyone who didn't share her salary had a low one.

Some business leaders have objected to salary history bans. The salary information helps them avoid interviewing people who would cost too much, they say. It can also help them avoid overpaying people whom they could hire for less, and it's a way to find out how much previous employers thought applicants were worth. The Chamber of Commerce for Greater Philadelphia fought a salary ban passed in Philadelphia, and this week, a United States district judge ruled that employers could ask about prior salary—but could not set pay based on it.

But using prior salary as a shortcut in that way also perpetuates discrimination, said Linda Babcock, an economist at Carnegie Mellon who has studied gender differences in negotiation. "The new law could make employers more purposeful about deciding ahead of time what they believe the position is worth," she said.

The salary history bans might spur other changes, by making people more aware of the problem, said Kate Bahn, an economist who studies gender and the labor market at the Washington Center for Equitable Growth. Employers might change the way they determine salaries or the way they respond to women when they negotiate, for example.

"That's part of why it may be such a useful small tool," she said, "because a lot of it is just sexism, and policy can help drive cultural shifts against sexism."

RESPONDING TO READING

1. How does Miller explain the way in which an applicant's salary history contributes to the wage disparity between men and women? Do you think her explanation makes sense?
2. According to Miller, what is "anchoring bias" (12)? How does it factor into the gender pay gap?

Rhetorical Analysis

Miller incorporates key sources into her essay. Do these sources represent a range of views on the issue of wage discrimination? What other sources might have she included?

Writing with Sources

As Miller admits, not everyone agrees with salary history bans. Look at essays on both sides of this issue. Which side do you think makes better arguments? Then, write an email to Miller in which you respond to her central thesis.

10.7 Walt Whitman, "I Hear America Singing" [Poetry]

A journalist, editor, printer, teacher, and government clerk, Walt Whitman (1819–1892) is one of America's most important and widely read poets. He is the author of numerous prose and poetry collections, including *Leaves of Grass,* which Whitman published in several editions and in which "I Hear America Singing" appeared. In this poem, Whitman celebrates work as a kind of song.

BEFORE YOU READ

Write a poem about a variety of present-day occupations.

I Hear America Singing

I hear America singing, the varied carols I hear,
Those of mechanics, each one singing his as it should be blithe and strong,
The carpenter singing his as he measures his plank or beam,
The mason singing his as he makes ready for work, or leaves off work,
The boatman singing what belongs to him in his boat, the deckhand singing on the steamboat deck,
The shoemaker singing as he sits on his bench, the hatter singing as he stands,
The wood-cutter's song, the ploughboy's on his way in the morning, or at noon intermission or at sundown,
The delicious singing of the mother, or of the young wife at work, or of the girl sewing or washing,
Each singing what belongs to him or her and to none else,
The day what belongs to the day—at night the party of young fellows, robust, friendly,
Singing with open mouths their strong melodious songs.

Source: Whitman, Walt. "I Hear America Singing." Leaves of Grass. Brooklyn: Fulton Street Printing, 1855.

RESPONDING TO READING

1. What attitude toward America is Whitman trying to convey in this poem? How can you tell?
2. What does this poem say about work, about people who work, and about America? In what sense can the Americans in this poem be said to be singing?

Rhetorical Analysis

Whitman includes a catalog of workers in this poem. What does he want to illustrate through this range of jobs? Is he successful?

10.8 Focus: "Is Every Worker Entitled to a Living Wage?"

David Grossman/Alamy Stock Photo

How does this photo from a workers' march depict the need for a living wage?

RESPONDING TO THE IMAGE

Answer one or both of the following questions.

1. Examine the various signs shown in the photo above. What point is the photo making?
2. At what audience do you think the photo is aimed? Explain.

10.9 Will Perkins, "Millennial Thoughts: Minimum Wage and My Take"

A reporter, photographer, and digital specialist for the *Glasgow Daily Times* and a columnist for the *Richmond Register*, Will Perkins writes about a range of issues from education to sports. In the following essay, Perkins makes the case for a living wage.

BEFORE YOU READ

Do you think all Americans are entitled to a living wage? Why or why not?

Millennial Thoughts: Minimum Wage and My Take

Having just celebrated Labor Day, I was inspired to share my thoughts on a very divisive and controversial issue in our country—minimum wage. Many of you may disagree with me right from the beginning, but I'm going to get straight to the point.

I strongly believe if you work 40 hours a week, you deserve to earn a livable wage.

And I don't care where you work. If you are an American and you spend most of your week doing something productive for our society, I firmly believe you should be able to afford to live here.

Let's go ahead and mention the one profession that is always brought up in this conversation—the fast-food worker. Many people I have spoken with are extremely against a fast-food worker earning any more than the seven or eight dollars that most of them currently make. They say it's a job for high school students. It's a stepping stone. You're supposed to work there until you can get a "real" job.

5 There are exceptions, but let me just say that a lot of the people who think fast-food workers don't deserve a raise seem to be the same ones who frequent fast-food restaurants. I only bring that up because if you frequent a type of business, that industry must be pretty important to your daily or weekly routine. If their service is something that you benefit from, why wouldn't you want the people working in the service positions to be compensated to the point that they could continue to support themselves?

Starbucks is an example of a progressive company that offers its workers benefits. We all hear people complaining about how expensive their coffee is—my co-worker, Daniel Suddeath, often refers to it as "Five Bucks."

While I don't spend five dollars on my cup of coffee—I found that you can purchase an iced coffee for $3.13 in Kentucky—I will gladly pay the extra price because I know that the company supports its workers.

I bring that up because one of the arguments against raising the minimum wage is that the price of goods will inevitably go up as well. I think if the price of a fast-food burger gets too expensive for you, maybe you should head to your local grocery store, buy a hunk of ground beef and get your hands greasy. But people will still buy fast-food burgers because they are very convenient.

I hear a lot of complaints about people on welfare, and how they work the system to never work. What if we raised the minimum wage to a point where we didn't need welfare? What if we made the system to where people made more money when they actually work?

I know this goes against every American capitalistic ideal—and I may be called a communist for this—but I wish that every member of society could just do whatever they are good at and be compensated enough to survive. I understand this is an extreme statement and would never work because people would inevitably take advantage of the system, but it's just wishful thinking. 10

I grew up in a two-parent household and I was given all the chances in the world to be successful and where I am today. My parents served as a safety net for me when times were tough.

It is because of this that I have no problem spending a good chunk of my paycheck on a societal safety net. I believe that everyone deserves a chance to be successful. Yes, there will always be people who abuse the system—in the same way there will always be drivers who wait until the last minute to merge over even though there were signs for at least two miles prior.

I prefer to be the driver who merges over as soon as I can. I'll wait in the long line while other drivers zoom past until the last second.

I believe a society that works together stays together. I think there is a widening gap in wealth in this country and it's only getting worse. If we can't all prosper as a country, what's the point? Do you really need 10 cars and four houses in multiple states and countries? I understand that people who work hard should be compensated, but what about the people who work hard and can't seem to save a dime, much less pay all of their bills on time?

I think it's time we take a stand for everyone. 15

If you work full-time in America, you should be able to live here, too.

Source: This column written by Will Perkins, Originally appeared in the Glasgow Daily Times and www.glasgowdailytimes.com

---

RESPONDING TO READING

1. What arguments against his position does Perkins identify? Does he effectively refute, or argue against, these counterarguments? Explain.
2. In paragraph 13, Perkins writes, "I prefer to be the driver who merges over as soon as I can. I'll wait in the long line while other drivers zoom past until the last second." Why does he include this information? What is his point?

Rhetorical Analysis

In paragraph 10, Perkins states, "I wish that every member of society could just do whatever they are good at and be compensated enough to survive." He then qualifies his statement by explaining, "I understand this is an extreme statement and would never work because people would inevitably take advantage of the system, but it's just wishful thinking." Does this qualification add to or detract from his argument?

Writing with Sources
Research the debate over enacting living-wage legislation. What are the advantages and disadvantages of such legislation? Write an essay in which you present your findings and take a stand on this issue.

10.10 The Daily Take Team, the *Thom Hartmann Program*, "If a Business Won't Pay a Living Wage, It Shouldn't Exist"

The Daily Take Team writes for the *Thom Hartmann Program,* a progressive radio talk show hosted by entrepreneur and author Thom Hartmann. Hartmann has published numerous books, including, most recently, *Adult ADHD: How to Succeed as a Hunter in a Farmer's World* (2016). The following essay argues for the necessity of a living wage for all workers.

BEFORE YOU READ
What social obligations, if any, do you think business owners have? How should they support their communities?

If a Business Won't Pay a Living Wage, It Shouldn't Exist

Last week,[1] thousands of fast food workers from across the country walked off their jobs to demand a living wage of $15 an hour. Ever since, the Republican talking point machine has been running on all cylinders.

According to pundits on the right, giving fast food workers or any other workers, for that matter, a $7 or $8 bump to their hourly wages would cut so much into the bottom lines of "job-creators" that business owners would have to either pass the cost of a living-wage onto consumers or simply stop hiring new workers altogether.

But lost among all the noise on the right is one very, very important point: getting tax preferences and limitations on liability to do business in the United States is a privilege, not a right. It's a privilege that we as a society offer to budding entrepreneurs and big business alike in exchange for goods, services, and jobs.

Look at it this way: when someone opens up a business, they're entitled to all sorts of special tax breaks that most people can't get. They can write off fancy meals; they can write off nights stayed at five-star hotels; they can write off airfare

[1]This essay was published on August 8, 2013. [Eds.]

to anywhere in the world they do business, or even might do business; and they can even write off any legal expenses they incur when they get busted for breaking the law. Drug dealers who push pot can't write off their lawyer's fees, but drug dealers at Big Pharma,[2] even when they lie and break the law in ways that kill people, can—all because they're incorporated.

5 All these breaks come in exchange for the company receiving these benefits giving society something back in return. Besides a useful service like selling meals or a good product like a well-made car, the single most important thing a business owner can give back to society is a well-paying job with benefits.

A job that pays a living wage isn't just good for the workers who get to take home a livable paycheck, it's good for other business owners and the economy as a whole. Businesses need people with a reasonable income to buy their goods. When workers are paid so little that they can barely afford to eat, they can't spend additional money and as a result, the entire economy suffers. This is economics 101.

That implicit contract between society and the business owner used to be common knowledge in this country and, until the Reagan Revolution,[3] was kept intact by businesses. Now, however, corporate America has thrown it out the window.

Walmart is the most egregious example. The nation's largest employer is one big corporate welfare scheme for the company's executives and the billionaire Walton family.

Walmart makes nearly $35,000 in profit every minute and, as of 2012, its average annual sales stood at $405 billion dollars.

10 According to *Mother Jones*, the six Waltons, whose money comes from Walmart, control an estimated $115 billion dollar fortune. In total, that's more than a staggering 42% of Americans combined.

And where did they get all that money? They took it out of the business instead of paying their workers a living wage.

Thus, at the same time that Walmart executives are raking in the millions and the Walton family's fortune is ballooning, Walmart employees struggle to get by.

The average Walmart employee makes about $9 per hour, and would have to work over 7 million years at that rate to accumulate as much wealth as the Waltons have. To make matters worse, only some of the company's employees qualify for its very minimal health insurance plan.

As a result, you and me—and the rest of America's taxpayers—are subsidizing Walmart by paying for the healthcare costs, housing, and food of Walmart employees. In fact, Walmart employees are the single largest group of Medicaid recipients in the United States.

15 A report released earlier this year by Congressional Democrats showed how much taxpayers subsidize the billionaire Walton Family at just one Walmart store in Wisconsin.

That report found that just that one Wisconsin store "costs taxpayers at least $904,542 per year and could cost taxpayers up to $1,744,590 per year."

---

[2]A nickname for the pharmaceutical industry. [Eds.]

[3]The presidency of Ronald Reagan (1981–1989). [Eds.]

That's $1.7 million that could be used to build a new school for kids, patch up one of our country's many crumbling bridges, or build a community health center. Instead, the Walton billionaires are taking that $1.7 million as dividends and they even get their own special low tax rate—about half of what working people pay—because it's dividend income.

Walmart isn't living up to its end of the American business bargain. It gets billions of dollars in taxpayer subsidies while its employees need government assistance to survive. If we're going to give businesses, like Walmart, the privileges and tax breaks associated with running a business, they should at the very least conduct themselves in ways that benefit society, rather than hurt it.

Fortunately, there is an alternative. Costco, a wholesale distributor and one of Walmart's major competitors, is among America's most successful companies. In the first quarter of 2013 alone, its profits "jumped 19 percent to $459 million," beating out its rivals K-Mart, Target, and, of course, Walmart. Since 2009, its stocks have doubled in value and profits are up 15 percent. But unlike Walmart, Costco pays its workers a living wage, and then some. The average Costco employee makes a little over $20 an hour and takes home, on average, around $45,000 a year. By comparison, the average yearly pay of an employee at Walmart's wholesale unit, Sam's Club, is only about $17,500.

20 But that's not even the best part. Costco offers customers cheap prices that are comparable to or even better than those offered at Walmart, all while paying its workers a decent wage and giving almost 90 percent of them company-subsidized health care plans.

So what's the difference between the two chain stores? Costco's founders, Jeffrey Brotman and James Sinegal, aren't among the world's super rich like the Walton family. The Walton billionaires bleed their workers dry and it makes them one of the richest families in the world. The guys who started and the executives who run Costco are merely multi-millionaires.

The point here is that it *is* possible for companies to pay their workers a living wage, make money, and give their customers an excellent product, all at the same time. The idea that we have to choose between paying workers well and having successful businesses is just false. That choice only exists when the owners insist on squeezing billions out of their workers.

A living wage isn't just something corporations owe their workers, it's something corporations owe America.

If a corporation won't pay a living wage, then it shouldn't have the right to exist. Period. End of story.

Source: The Daily Take Team, "If a Business Won't Pay a Living Wage, It Shouldn't Exist" Truthout, 08 August 2013. Used with permission.

RESPONDING TO READING

1. According to the writers, "Walmart isn't living up to its end of the American business bargain" (18). What is that bargain? Why is Walmart not living up to it?

2. List the major claim the writers make in this essay. What evidence do they present to support this claim? Do they present enough evidence? The right kind of evidence?

Rhetorical Analysis

Hyperbole is the use of exaggerated claims that are not intended to be taken literally. Can you find any examples of hyperbole in this essay? Do you think they strengthen the essay? Why or why not?

Writing with Sources

In 2018, Walmart raised the minimum wage of its lowest-paid workers to $11.00 an hour, $3.75 above the federal minimum wage. Research the reasons why Walmart decided to make this change. Then, write an essay in which you discuss how Walmart's action affects this essay's main point.

10.11 James Dorn, "The Minimum Wage Delusion, and the Death of Common Sense"

The vice president for monetary studies, the editor of the *Cato Journal*, and a senior fellow at the Cato Institute in Washington, D.C., James Dorn writes about issues related to global economic policy and monetary reform. He is also the editor or coeditor of numerous books, including, most recently, *Monetary Alternatives: Rethinking Government Fiat Money* (2017). In the following essay, Dorn considers the negative effects of raising the minimum wage.

BEFORE YOU READ

Other than increasing the minimum wage, what do you think the government (or private business) could do to help low-skilled workers earn more money?

The Minimum Wage Delusion, and the Death of Common Sense

Senator Edward Kennedy once called the minimum wage "one of the best antipoverty programs we have." Jared Bernstein, former chief economist to Vice President Joe Biden, thinks "it raises the pay of low-wage workers without hurting their job prospects." And Ralph Nader[1] thinks low-wage workers deserve a pay increase—and the government should provide it.

Why do those beliefs persist in the face of common economic sense? No legislator has ever overturned the law of demand, which says that when the price of labor rises, the quantity demanded will fall (assuming other things are constant). That same law tells us that quantity demanded (i.e., the number of jobs for low-skilled workers) will decrease more in the long run than in the short run, as employers switch to labor-saving methods of production—and unemployment will increase.

The belief that increasing the minimum wage is socially beneficial is a delusion. It is short-sighted and ignores evident reality. Workers who retain their jobs are made better off but only at the expense of unskilled, mostly young, workers who either lose their jobs or can't find a job at the legal minimum.

A higher minimum wage attracts new entrants but does not guarantee them a job. What happens on the demand side of the market is not surprising: if the minimum wage exceeds the prevailing market wage (determined by supply and demand), some workers will lose their jobs or have their hours cut. There is abundant evidence that a 10 percent increase in the minimum wage leads to a 1 to 3 percent *decrease* in employment of low-skilled workers (using teens as a proxy) in the short run, and to a larger decrease in the long run, along with rising unemployment.

5 Employers have more flexibility in the long run and will find ways to economize on the higher-priced labor. New technology will be introduced along with labor-saving capital investment, and skilled workers will tend to replace unskilled workers. Those substitutions will occur even before an increase in the minimum wage, if employers believe such an increase is imminent. There will be fewer jobs for low-skilled workers and higher unemployment rates—especially for minorities—and participation rates will fall as workers affected by the minimum wage drop out of the formal labor market.

The minimum wage violates the principle of freedom by limiting the range of choices open to workers, preventing them from accepting jobs at less than the legal minimum. It also prohibits employers from hiring those workers, even if both parties would be better off. Thus, contrary to the claims of minimum-wage proponents, the government does not increase opportunities for low-skilled workers by increasing the minimum wage. If a worker loses her job or can't find one, her income is zero. Employers will not pay a worker $9 per hour if that worker cannot produce at least that amount.

Politicians promise low-skilled workers a higher wage, but that promise cannot be kept if employers cannot profit from retaining those workers or hiring similar workers. Jobs will be lost, not created; and unemployment will rise as more workers search for jobs but can't find any at the above-market wage.

Most employers cannot simply raise prices to cover the higher minimum wage, particularly in the competitive services sector. And if they do increase

[1]American political activist (1934–). [Eds.]

prices, consumers will buy less or have less money to spend on other things, meaning fewer jobs on net. Moreover, if the minimum wage cuts into profits, there will be less capital investment and job growth will slow.

A recent study by Jonathan Meer and Jeremy West, economists at Texas A&M University, found that "the most prominent employment effect of minimum wage laws is a decline in the hiring of new employees." That effect takes place over time as employers shift to labor-saving methods of production. Since the minimum wage has the largest impact on the least-skilled workers who have few alternatives, their lifetime earnings will be adversely affected by delaying entry into the work force and losing valuable job experience.

10 Proponents of the minimum wage such as John Schmitt, a senior fellow at the Center for Economic and Policy Research in Washington, like to argue that the mean effect of the minimum wage on jobs for low-skilled workers is close to zero. But a preponderance of evidence has shown that there are *no positive effects* on employment of low-skilled workers that offset the negative effects from an increase in the minimum wage. The trick is to control for other factors ("confounding variables") affecting the demand for labor and to make sure the data and research design are valid. The focus should be on those workers adversely affected by the minimum wage—namely, younger individuals with little education and few skills.

In a recent case study that controls for confounding factors that make it difficult to isolate the impact of an increase in the minimum wage on employment for low-skilled workers, Joseph Sabia, Richard Burkhauser, and Benjamin Hansen find that when New York State increased the minimum wage from $5.15 to $6.75 per hour, in 2004–06, there was a "20.2 to 21.8 percent reduction in the employment of younger less-educated individuals," with the greatest impact on 16-to-24 year olds.

Advocates of the minimum wage like to point to the "natural experiment" that David Card and Alan Krueger conducted to see whether a minimum wage hike in New Jersey adversely affected employment in the fast-food industry compared to Pennsylvania, which did not increase its minimum wage. Based on telephone surveys, the authors concluded that the minimum wage hike significantly increased jobs for low-skilled, fast-food workers in New Jersey. Not surprisingly, their results were overturned by more careful research that found an adverse effect on employment (see David Neumark and William Wascher, *American Economic Review*, 2000).

It should be obvious that limiting one's study to franchise restaurants like McDonald's ignores smaller independents that are harmed by increases in the minimum wage and can't compete with their larger rivals. No one interviewed those workers who lost their jobs or could not find a job at the higher minimum wage. Proponents of the minimum wage focus on workers who retain their jobs and get a higher wage, but ignore those who lose their jobs and get a lower wage or none at all. Using econometrics to pretend that the law of demand is dead is a dangerous delusion.

If one gets empirical results that go against the grain of long-held economic laws, one should be very wary of advocating policies based on those results. One should also not stop with the short-run effects of the minimum wage but trace out the longer-run effects on the number of jobs and unemployment rates for affected workers.

15 Today black teen unemployment is more than 40 percent; nearly double that for white teens. In 2007, prior to the Great Recession, the black teen unemployment rate was about 29 percent. There is no doubt the increase in the federal minimum wage from $5.15 to $7.25 per hour contributed to the higher unemployment rate. If Congress passes a new minimum wage law that makes it illegal for employers to pay less than $9 per hour, and for workers to accept less than that amount, we can expect further erosion of the market for unskilled workers, especially black teens.

With so many young, unskilled workers looking for work, employers can pick and choose. They can cut benefits and hours; and they can substitute more-skilled workers for less-skilled workers. Recent studies based on data for contiguous counties across state borders have ignored labor-labor substitution and wrongly concluded that higher minimum wages do not adversely affect employment.

Arindrajit Dube, T. William Lester, and Michael Reich, for example, use county-level data over a 16.5 year period to examine the impact of local differences in minimum wages on employment in restaurants, which primarily hire low-skilled workers. Based on their analysis and assumptions, they "find no adverse employment effects."

Proponents of a higher minimum wage have rested their case on Dube et al. and related studies—such as Sylvia Allegretto, Dube, and Reich, who conclude that "minimum wage increases—in the range that have been implemented in the United States—do not reduce employment among teens." Neumark, Salas, and Wascher, in a new study for the National Bureau of Economic Research, argue that "neither the conclusions of these studies nor the methods they use are supported by the data." Indeed, Dube et al. admit that their data prevent them from testing "whether restaurants respond to minimum wage increases by hiring more skilled workers and fewer less-skilled ones."

Existing evidence supports labor-labor substitution in response to a higher minimum wage—especially over the longer run. Employers have a strong incentive to retain better-educated teens and train them, and to hire skilled workers to operate labor-saving equipment. Contrary to the claims of Bernstein and others who support the minimum wage, a higher minimum (other things constant) will *decrease* employment opportunities for the least-skilled workers. Workers who retain their jobs will be higher productivity workers—not low-wage workers in low-income families. Minimum wage laws harm the very workers they are intended to help.

20 Small businesses are already laying off low-skilled workers and investing in self-service tablets, robotics, and other labor-saving devices in anticipation of a higher minimum wage; and hours are being cut. Those trends will continue, especially if the minimum wage is indexed for inflation.

Advocates of higher minimum wages confuse cause and effect. They think a higher minimum wage causes incomes to go up for low-skilled workers and doesn't destroy jobs. Workers are assumed to have higher wages and retain their jobs as a result of government policy—even though they have done nothing to improve their job skills. But if a worker is producing $5.15 per hour and now the employer must pay $9 per hour, there will be little incentive to retain her. There will also be little incentive to hire new workers. Without an increase in the demand for labor—that is, an increase in labor productivity due to better technology, more capital per worker, or additional education—a higher minimum wage will simply price some workers (the least productive) out of the market, and their incomes will be zero.

The minimum wage is not a panacea for poverty. Indeed, Neumark, Schweitzer, and Wascher examine the evidence and conclude that "the net effect of higher minimum wages is ... to increase the proportion of families that are poor and near-poor" (*Journal of Human Resources*, 2005). Thus, the minimum wage tends to increase, not decrease, the poverty rate.

The best antipoverty program is not the minimum wage but economic freedom that expands workers' choices and allows entrepreneurs to freely hire labor without the government dictating the terms of the exchange, except to prevent fraud and violence. When entrepreneurs adopt new technology and make capital investments autonomously—that is, without being induced to do so because of government mandated increases in wage rates—there is a boost in worker productivity, jobs, and incomes. But when the government increases the minimum wage above the prevailing market wage for low-skilled workers, firms will have an incentive to substitute labor-saving production techniques that destroy jobs for low-productivity workers, especially minorities, and prevent workers from moving up the income ladder.

Unions are key advocates of higher minimum wages because the demand for union workers tends to increase along with wage rates after an increase in the minimum wage. Likewise, large retailers and franchise restaurants already paying more than the minimum wage may support an increase in the legal minimum because it helps protect their businesses from smaller competitors. Poverty advocates also favor the minimum wage because it is a "feel good" policy and they believe it will lead to higher incomes for low-wage workers, without seeing the longer-run consequences on jobs and unemployment.

Ignoring the law of demand to adopt a higher minimum wage in the hope of 25
helping low-wage workers is a grand delusion. The persistence of this false belief ignores economic reality. It is a red herring that diverts attention from alternative policies that would increase economic freedom and prosperity for all workers.

Source: From Forbes.com, James Dorn, The Minimum Wage Delusion, And The Death Of Common Sense, 07 May 2013.

RESPONDING TO READING

1. According to Dorn, "The belief that increasing the minimum wage is socially beneficial is a delusion" (3). Why? What evidence does he offer to support this statement?
2. In paragraph 21, Dorn says, "Advocates of higher minimum wages confuse cause and effect." What does he mean? Do you think he is right?

Rhetorical Analysis

At what points in his essay does Dorn introduce arguments against his position? How effectively does he refute (argue against) these counterarguments?

Writing with Sources

According to some critics, the minimum wage is not supposed to be a living wage. It is intended for unskilled workers in entry-level jobs, who are promoted once they gain experience. Research this subject, concentrating on the types of workers who earn the minimum wage. How accurate is the position taken by these critics of the minimum wage? What types of workers earn the minimum wage? How long do they typically stay in entry-level positions? Do they, as these critics claim, tend to move up to higher-paying jobs, or do many of them remain minimum-wage workers? Write an essay in which you present your findings, and take a position on the issue of whether the minimum wage should be a living wage.

Widening the Focus

For Critical Reading and Writing

Referring specifically to the three readings in this chapter's Focus section (and possibly to additional sources as well), write an essay in which you answer the question, "Is Every Worker Entitled to a Living Wage?"

For Further Reading

The following readings can suggest additional perspectives for thinking and writing about work and compensation.

- Lynda Barry, "The Sanctuary of School" (p. 83)
- Melanie Scheller, "On the Meaning of Plumbing and Poverty" (p. 286)
- Carol Graham, "Is the American Dream Really Dead?" (p. 345)

For Focused Research

Child labor is a topic that has sparked debate around the globe. In the United States, for example, students at several colleges and universities have protested their bookstores' sale of merchandise made in foreign sweatshops by child laborers who receive little or no pay and who work in dismal conditions. To gain greater insight into worldwide child labor, visit the website for the International Programme on the Elimination of Child Labour (IPEC). Then, write an essay that examines child labor in various countries, considering such factors as the pay and working conditions of child laborers as well as the kinds of industries that use child labor. What alternatives are available to the children in these countries? What happens to the children who do not get these jobs? Could an argument be made in defense of child labor?

Beyond the Classroom
Assemble a group of friends and classmates, and lead a discussion about fair wages, gathering opinions based on personal experiences and observations. (With everyone's consent, you will want to record this group session so you can listen to the responses later.) Then, write an essay summarizing the group's opinions, quoting individual group members to illustrate various points of view. Then, develop your own conclusions about whether all workers are entitled to a living wage.

Exploring Issues and Ideas

Why We Work
Write an essay in response to one of the following prompts, which are suitable for assignments that require the use of outside sources as well as for assignments that are not source-based.

1. Write an essay in which you describe in detail the worst job you ever had.
2. Considering the essays in this chapter—especially "Why We Work" (p. 355), "When Work Is a Game, Who Wins?" (p. 364), and "The Truth Shall Set You Free (from a Lot of $#*% Storms)" (p. 369)—write an essay in which you discuss what you believe the purpose of work should be. For example, should it be to earn money, or should it be to gain personal satisfaction and fulfillment by being part of a community? Are these two goals mutually exclusive? Does the way we work in this country help people achieve these goals?
3. In "The Truth Shall Set You Free (from a Lot of $#*% Storms)" (p. 369), Rand Fishkin sees working in positive terms—as the way a person engages with others to innovate and excel. In "Why We Work" (p. 355), however, Andrew Curry makes the point that most workers dislike their jobs. Which of these two views of work do you hold? Write an essay in which you give the reasons for your belief. Illustrate your points with your own experiences as well as with references to the essays by Fishkin and Curry.
4. Imagine that you have been asked by your former high school to address students in this year's graduating class about how to get part-time and summer jobs to offset the high cost of college. Write a speech that is inspirational but also offers specific advice.
5. In the essays "Teaching While Black" (p. 378), "Crashing into Ceilings: A Report from the Nine-to-Five Shift" (p. 360), and "How a Common Interview Question Fuels the Gender Pay Gap (and How to Stop It)" (p. 381), the writers point out the barriers that black workers and female workers encounter in a range of professions. Write an extended definition of the purpose of work for minorities in America. Are the professional goals of these groups different from those of dominant groups? How are these groups professionally exploited? How might minorities overcome these challenges in the workplace?

Chapter 11

Making Ethical Choices

In this chapter, you will learn to:

- analyze readings about making ethical choices.
- compose essays about making ethical choices.

As Robert Frost suggests in his poem "The Road Not Taken" (p. 401), making choices is fundamental to our lives. The ability—and, in fact, the need—to make complex decisions is part of what makes us human. On a practical level, we choose friends, mates, careers, and places to live. On a more abstract level, we struggle to make the moral and ethical choices that people have struggled with over the years.

What ethical considerations are involved in producing and buying diamond wedding engagement rings like the one shown in this image?

Marko Poplasen/Shutterstock

Many times, complex questions have no easy answers; occasionally, they have no answers at all. For example, should we obey a law that we believe to be morally wrong? Should we stand up to authority even if our stand puts us at risk? Should we help less fortunate individuals if such help threatens our own social or economic status? Should we strive to do well or to do good? Should we tell the truth even if the truth may hurt us—or hurt someone else? Which road should we take, the easy one or the more difficult one?

Most of the time, the choice we (and the writers whose works appear in this chapter) face is the same: to act or not to act. To make a decision, we must understand both the long- and short-term consequences of acting in a particular way or of choosing not to act. We must struggle with the possibility of compromise—and with the possibility of making a morally or ethically objectionable decision. And, perhaps most important, we must learn to take responsibility for our decisions.

The Focus section of this chapter, "What Choices Do We Have with Our Technologies?" (p. 414), considers the extent to which we can decide how to interact online. In "'Our Minds Can Be Hijacked': The Tech Insiders Who Fear a Smartphone Dystopia" (p. 414), Paul Lewis explains why some young people have pulled the plug on their online identities; in "Social and Ethical Behavior in the Internet of Things" (p. 424), Francine Berman and Vinton G. Cerf propose a plan for putting our technologies to good social use; and in "The Identity Solution" (p. 428), Valery Vavilov pitches a specific technology to address our online identity crisis.

Alan Gignoux/Alamy Stock Photo

What ethical point does this image of diamond miners in South Africa make?

Preparing to Read and Write

As you read and prepare to write about the selections in this chapter, you may consider the following questions:

- What assumptions does the writer seem to have about his or her audience? How can you tell?
- What is the writer's primary purpose? For example, is it to explain an ethical dilemma of his or her own, to expose a lack of ethics in society or in certain individuals, or to recommend a course of action? Is it something else?
- What genre is the writer using? For example, is the reading a proposal, a news article, a poem, an argument, or a memoir? How do the conventions of this genre influence the writer's choices?
- What appeals does the writer use? For example, does he or she appeal primarily to reason or to emotion?
- On what specific choice or choices does the selection focus? Is the decision to be made moral, ethical, political, or practical?
- Does the writer introduce a **dilemma**, a choice between equally problematic alternatives?
- Does the choice the writer presents apply only to one specific situation or case, or does it also have a wider application?
- Is the writer emotionally involved with the issue he or she is discussing? Does this involvement (or lack of involvement) affect the effectiveness of the writer's argument?
- What social, political, or religious ideas influence the writer? How can you tell? Are these ideas similar to or different from your own views?
- Does the choice being considered lead the writer to examine his or her own values? The values of others? The values of the society at large? Does the writer lead you to examine your own values?
- Does the writer offer a solution to a problem? If so, do you find this solution reasonable?
- Does the choice the writer advocates require sacrifice? If so, does the sacrifice seem worth it?
- Which writers' views seem most alike? Which seem most different?

Shared Writing

Making Ethical Choices

What was the last difficult decision you made? What was so hard about it? In retrospect, should you have made a different choice than you did?

11.1 Robert Frost, "The Road Not Taken" [Poetry]

Robert Frost (1874–1963), four-time Pulitzer Prize–winning poet of rural New England, lived most of his life in New Hampshire and taught at Amherst College, Harvard University, and Dartmouth College. His subjects at first seem familiar and comfortable, as does his language, but the symbols, allusions, and underlying meanings in many of his poems are quite complex. Some of Frost's most famous poems are "Birches," "Mending Wall," and "Stopping by Woods on a Snowy Evening." In the poem that follows, the speaker hesitates before making a choice.

BEFORE YOU READ

Did you miss out on an opportunity that you regret? What might be different now if you had made a different choice then?

The Road Not Taken

Two roads diverged in a yellow wood,
And sorry I could not travel both
And be one traveller, long I stood
And looked down one as far as I could
To where it bent in the undergrowth;
Then took the other, as just as fair,
And having perhaps the better claim,
Because it was grassy and wanted wear;
Though as for that the passing there
Had worn them really about the same,
And both that morning equally lay
In leaves no step had trodden black.
Oh, I kept the first for another day!
Yet knowing how way leads on to way,
I doubted if I should ever come back.
I shall be telling this with a sigh

Somewhere ages and ages hence:
Two roads diverged in a wood, and I—
I took the one less travelled by,
And that has made all the difference.

Source: Frost, Robert. "The Road Not Taken" Mountain Interval. New York: Henry Holt and Company, 1916.

RESPONDING TO READING

1. What is the difference between the two paths Frost's speaker considers? Why does he make the choice he does?
2. What does the speaker mean by "that has made all the difference" (line 20)?

Rhetorical Analysis

Is "The Road Not Taken" simply about two paths in the woods, or does it suggest more? What makes you think so? To what larger choices might the speaker be alluding?

11.2 Ella Higginson, "Four-Leaf Clover" [Poetry]

A poet and fiction writer, Ella Higginson (1862–1940) was committed to advancing the literary arts and women's rights. A former poet laureate of Washington State, Higginson is the author of numerous poetry and story collections as well as novels. In "Four-Leaf Clover," the speaker considers the elements of decision-making.

BEFORE YOU READ

What, if anything, do four-leaf clovers signify to you? Do you keep them when you find them?

Four-Leaf Clover

I know a place where the sun is like gold,
  And the cherry blooms burst with snow,
And down underneath is the loveliest nook,
  Where the four-leaf clovers grow.
One leaf is for hope, and one is for faith,
  And one is for love, you know,
And God put another in for luck—

If you search, you will find where they grow.
But you must have hope, and you must have faith,
You must love and be strong—and so—
If you work, if you wait, you will find the place
Where the four-leaf clovers grow.

Source: Ella Higginson (1898). When the Birds Go North Again, The Macmillan company.

RESPONDING TO READING

1. What insight does Higginson's speaker have? How does she share her knowledge?
2. The poem's final stanza offers advice to readers. What is the speaker suggesting we do? Why?

Rhetorical Analysis

How does the four-leaf clover function as a metaphor? What specifically does it represent? How does it relate to the choices we make?

11.3 Lynette D'Amico, "The Unsaved" [Creative Nonfiction]

A fiction and creative nonfiction writer, Lynette D'Amico is the content editor for Emerson College's online performance journal *HowlRound* and the author of the acclaimed novella *Road Trip* (2015). Her work has appeared in such publications as *Brevity, The Gettysburg Review, The Ocean State Review,* and *Slag Glass City*. In the following creative essay, D'Amico reflects on the choices we make about who we are.

BEFORE YOU READ

Have you ever made a dramatic change to your identity, either online or offline (or both)? What did the "old" you look like, and how do you appear now?

The Unsaved

The brief and interminable year that I was involved with the Northwestern Bell repair tech with the clubbed thumbs seemed to include three or more New Year's Eve parties. Were there three parties on the same night? Were there three December 31s in the same year? I don't remember. Perhaps it was just that our doomed-from-the-beginning relationship was always on a sparkle ball countdown to the inevitable end: Three, two, one. Done. At every New Year's party that I attended with my inevitable ex, CJ Wright wore a pink tuxedo shirt with pleated front, banded collar, and linked cuffs. She drank Dewar's neat and combed a side part into her hair. She helped herself to little tastes off peoples' plates and complained about the music in a fake British accent. I remember her with a different date at each party who all shared the same embarrassed look when CJ started hip thrusting on the dance floor to *She's a brick house*. CJ was so queer she made the rest of us avert our eyes and duck our heads, like when you're watching a contestant on a game show who just doesn't have a clue and everybody else gets it before they do and then slowly they start waking up to the fact that they are too stupid to live and you can see it happening right before your eyes on national television, right in your own living room, *ain't holding nothing back.* This was when the downtown queers were pale skinny girls and uniformly tan ex-cheerleaders. There was queer and there were the queer queers like CJ, a boyish girl with too-big hips that pooched out the pockets of her creased chinos. CJ thought her life would be redeemed by true love, a lap dance from Princess Diana, custom-tailored Oxford shirts.

AULD LANG SYNE[1]

In the new year the repair tech and I broke up. I grieved a future of inconveniently placed phone jacks and wrong numbers. This was a time, however briefly, when I lamented the waste of tenderness in the world: those dear thumb stubs, the rotting bouquets piled outside Kensington Palace. CJ gave up tuxedo shirts and everything that wearing a tuxedo shirt implied. She grew her hair out, renounced the devil, and married a deacon at a big box church. Her husband wore Sansabelt slacks. How is that possible? None of us were invited to the wedding. None of us knew what CJ stood for—Carol Jean? Claudia Jo? Cracker Jack? If it was possible for CJ to become unqueered and become a plain-faced Wisconsin farm wife, to leave us behind like a fever dream—could we too become something different, learn to strip our own wires, make new connections, sweat out the same sex sickness? What was possible for any of us?

SHE'S THE ONE, THE ONLY ONE

That year we all wore pink tuxedo shirts at the New Year's Eve party in CJ's honor, like a team uniform, to honor choices lived and left behind.

Wait, I'm sorry. That last part isn't true. The part about the New Year's Eve party is true, but nobody wore a pink tuxedo shirt. It was a new year, and whether CJ was doing shots and licking salt from a woman's naked breasts or sipping iced tea with the Christians in a church basement has nothing to do with redemption—hers or ours.

Source: The Unsaved by Lynette D'Amico, Brevity, September 17, 2012. Used with permission from Lynette D'Amico.

RESPONDING TO READING

1. In paragraph 2, D'Amico asks, "could we too become something different, learn to strip our own wires, make new connections, sweat out the

[1]A Scottish poem (1796) by Robert Burns (1759–1796) and a song containing words from the poem that is commonly sung on New Year's Eve. [Eds.]

same sex sickness? What was possible for any of us?" What do these questions suggest about the choices we can (and can't) make about our identities? Consider D'Amico's tone before answering this question.

2. Evaluate D'Amico's concluding paragraph. In what ways is this essay about redemption? Who can or can't be redeemed?

Rhetorical Analysis

Consider the title of the essay. Who are the "unsaved"? What does personal choice have to do with salvation?

11.4 Jonathan Safran Foer, "How Not to Be Alone"

The Lillian Vernon Distinguished Writer-in-Residence at New York University, Jonathan Safran Foer (1977–) is the author of the novels *Everything Is Illuminated* (2002), *Extremely Loud & Incredibly Close* (2005), and *Here I Am* (2016) as well as the nonfiction book *Eating Animals* (2009). His work appears in publications such as the *Guardian, The New Yorker*, and *The New York Times*. The following essay, which was adapted from Foer's 2013 commencement speech at Middlebury College, considers the fate of compassion in the digital age.

BEFORE YOU READ

How would you react to a stranger crying in the park? Why?

How Not to Be Alone

A couple of weeks ago, I saw a stranger crying in public. I was in Brooklyn's Fort Greene neighborhood, waiting to meet a friend for breakfast. I arrived at the restaurant a few minutes early and was sitting on the bench outside, scrolling through my contact list. A girl, maybe 15 years old, was sitting on the bench opposite me, crying into her phone. I heard her say, "I know, I know, I know" over and over.

What did she know? Had she done something wrong? Was she being comforted? And then she said, "Mama, I know," and the tears came harder.

What was her mother telling her? Never to stay out all night again? That everybody fails? Is it possible that no one was on the other end of the call, and that the girl was merely rehearsing a difficult conversation?

"Mama, I know," she said, and hung up, placing her phone on her lap.

5 I was faced with a choice: I could interject myself into her life, or I could respect the boundaries between us. Intervening might make her feel worse, or be inappropriate. But then, it might ease her pain, or be helpful in some straightforward logistical way. An affluent neighborhood at the beginning of the day is not the same as a dangerous one as night is falling. And I was me, and not someone else. There was a lot of human computing to be done.

It is harder to intervene than not to, but it is vastly harder to choose to do either than to retreat into the scrolling names of one's contact list, or whatever one's favorite iDistraction happens to be. Technology celebrates connectedness, but encourages retreat. The phone didn't make me avoid the human connection, but it did make ignoring her easier in that moment, and more likely, by comfortably encouraging me to forget my choice to do so. My daily use of technological communication has been shaping me into someone more likely to forget others. The flow of water carves rock, a little bit at a time. And our personhood is carved, too, by the flow of our habits.

Psychologists who study empathy and compassion are finding that unlike our almost instantaneous responses to physical pain, it takes time for the brain to comprehend the psychological and moral dimensions of a situation. The more distracted we become, and the more emphasis we place on speed at the expense of depth, the less likely and able we are to care.

Everyone wants his parent's, or friend's, or partner's undivided attention—even if many of us, especially children, are getting used to far less. Simone Weil[1] wrote, "Attention is the rarest and purest form of generosity." By this definition, our relationships to the world, and to one another, and to ourselves, are becoming increasingly miserly.

Most of our communication technologies began as diminished substitutes for an impossible activity. We couldn't always see one another face to face, so the telephone made it possible to keep in touch at a distance. One is not always home, so the answering machine made a kind of interaction possible without the person being near his phone. Online communication originated as a substitute for telephonic communication, which was considered, for whatever reasons, too burdensome or inconvenient. And then texting, which facilitated yet faster, and more mobile, messaging. These inventions were not created to be improvements upon face-to-face communication, but a declension of acceptable, if diminished, substitutes for it.

10 But then a funny thing happened: we began to prefer the diminished substitutes. It's easier to make a phone call than to schlep to see someone in person. Leaving a message on someone's machine is easier than having a phone conversation—you can say what you need to say without a response; hard news is easier to leave; it's easier to check in without becoming entangled. So we began calling when we knew no one would pick up.

Shooting off an e-mail is easier, still, because one can hide behind the absence of vocal inflection, and of course there's no chance of accidentally catching someone. And texting is even easier, as the expectation for articulateness is further reduced, and another shell is offered to hide in. Each step "forward" has

[1]French philosopher (1909–1943). [Eds.]

made it easier, just a little, to avoid the emotional work of being present, to convey information rather than humanity.

The problem with accepting—with preferring—diminished substitutes is that over time, we, too, become diminished substitutes. People who become used to saying little become used to feeling little.

With each generation, it becomes harder to imagine a future that resembles the present. My grandparents hoped I would have a better life than they did: free of war and hunger, comfortably situated in a place that felt like home. But what futures would I dismiss out of hand for my grandchildren? That their clothes will be fabricated every morning on 3-D printers? That they will communicate without speaking or moving?

Only those with no imagination, and no grounding in reality, would deny the possibility that they will live forever. It's possible that many reading these words will never die. Let's assume, though, that we all have a set number of days to indent the world with our beliefs, to find and create the beauty that only a finite existence allows for, to wrestle with the question of purpose and wrestle with our answers.

We often use technology to save time, but increasingly, it either takes the 15
saved time along with it, or makes the saved time less present, intimate and rich. I worry that the closer the world gets to our fingertips, the further it gets from our hearts. It's not an either/or—being "anti-technology" is perhaps the only thing more foolish than being unquestioningly "pro-technology"—but a question of balance that our lives hang upon.

Most of the time, most people are not crying in public, but everyone is always in need of something that another person can give, be it undivided attention, a kind word or deep empathy. There is no better use of a life than to be attentive to such needs. There are as many ways to do this as there are kinds of loneliness, but all of them require attentiveness, all of them require the hard work of emotional computation and corporeal compassion. All of them require the human processing of the only animal who risks "getting it wrong" and whose dreams provide shelters and vaccines and words to crying strangers.

We live in a world made up more of story than stuff. We are creatures of memory more than reminders, of love more than likes. Being attentive to the needs of others might not be the point of life, but it is the work of life. It can be messy, and painful, and almost impossibly difficult. But it is not something we give. It is what we get in exchange for having to die.

Source: From The New York Times, Jonathan Safran Foer, How Not to Be Alone, 08 June 2013.

RESPONDING TO READING

1. What does Foer mean when he says, "Technology celebrates connectedness, but encourages retreat" (6)? Is this statement accurate, or is Foer oversimplifying a complicated subject?
2. What is a "diminished substitute" (10)? Do you agree with Foer's observation, "The problem with accepting—with preferring—diminished substitutes is that over time, we, too, become diminished substitutes" (12)?

Rhetorical Analysis

Foer begins his essay with an anecdote about a stranger crying in public. He indicates that he faced a choice: he could have either intervened in her life or respected the boundaries between them. He never tells readers what he decided to do, however. Should he have done so? What do you think he decided?

Writing with Sources

Research the effects (negative as well as positive) of texting, email, and social media in general on personal communication. Also, look at Nicholas Carr's essay in Chapter 6. After deciding how you feel about this issue, write an essay in which you agree or disagree with Foer's statements in paragraph 13.

11.5 Barbara Hurd, "Fracking: A Fable"

An essayist and poet, Barbara Hurd teaches in the MFA in writing program at the Vermont College of Fine Arts. Writing about various issues related to natural history, she is the author of several books, including, most recently, *Listening to the Savage: River Notes and Half-Heard Melodies* (2016). In "Fracking: A Fable," Hurd imagines what the impact of fracking, a kind of drilling for natural gas, might be.

BEFORE YOU READ

Write a fable (a short tale that teaches a moral lesson) about an issue that you care about.

Fracking: A Fable

for our grandchildren, with apologies

In the past, everything took forever.

Rain fell for centuries, and millions of years after that, the ancient Appalachian Basin just west of what is now the East Coast spent even more millennia becoming a sprawling, shallow bowl. And then nothing much happened. Another million years passed. Mountain ranges slowly rose and receded, and continents wandered into each other and eventually the basin began to fill with seawater and for another million years, the surrounding mountains slid wetly down the slopes of themselves and settled into the bottom sludge of the basin.

More tens of thousands of centuries passed while the water sloshed and the undersea mud thickened, and in all that time, no human ever stood on its shores, no blue crab ever scurried in the ooze. There were no witnesses. And even if there had been, who could have stood the boredom of watching that slow, barely breathing world? The only testimony ever made to that languid time was locked in the mud.

For yet another several million years, it piled up—thick, black, and putrid. Over the next millennia, miniscule creatures evolved: phytoplankton, blue-green algae. They floated in the shallow seas until they died and drifted down to be entombed in the ooze that lay fifty, one hundred, two hundred feet deep.

5 Then came more mountains moving. A few continents collided, some peaks rose, some valleys sank. Meanwhile, down in the black ooze, remnants of those tiny creatures that had been held in the mud were shoved more tightly together, packed side by side with sludged-in sediment, cemented together, cooked by the heat deep in the earth, and converted into hydrocarbons. Layer after layer of crammed-together particles and silt began to sink under the accumulating weight of the mountains that grew above. Wrung of its moisture, its pliability, its flow, the mud slowly, slowly, over millions of years, turned into gas-rich rock.

And there it lay, miles under the surface, as the old basin above it emptied and rose and more continents meandered into each other and finally the sun dried the Appalachians, which eroded and softened, and three hundred million years after the first mud settled on the bottom of that basin, humans appeared. We developed with lightning speed—geologically speaking—our brains and vision and hands, our fast and furious tools, our drills and ingenuity, and all the while that ooze-become-rock lay locked and impenetrable, deep in the earth, farther than anything, including anyone's imagination, reached, until in the split second that is humankind's history on this planet we pushed a drill with a downhole mud-motor a mile deep and made it turn sideways and snaked it into that ancient rock speckled with evidence of another eon, and a few minutes later we detonated small explosives and blasted millions of gallons of slick water—sand and water and a bit of biocide in case anything was alive down there—into what hadn't seen water or light for four hundred million years.

The shale shattered, the black rock spider-webbed with skinny fissures as the above world inserted its tendrils, and into those tiny rifts we rammed more sand to keep them wedged open wider.

And then—remember the blue-green algae?—the gas that had been locked in that stony underworld for almost four hundred million years suddenly had an exit. It flowed through the intricate shudderings of brand new fissures and up the borehole through the limestone that had been laid down millions of years after the mud, and up through the bedrock just below someone's pasture and out into a world with air and fresh water where we humans, fur-less and in need of fuel to stay warm, exercised our resourceful minds.

And then in another split-second's time—geologically speaking—we drilled another thousand wells, fracked another million tons of stony earth a mile beneath our feet.

10 And when the slick water was withdrawn from the fissures and small slither-spaces and that prehistoric bedrock was lickety-split forever changed, no one could predict the impact, not even we inventive humans whose arrival on this planet is so recent, whose footprints, so conspicuous and large, often obliterate cautionary tales.

And soon the unpredictable, as always, occurred.

And now, in no time at all, not everything takes forever any longer.

RESPONDING TO READING

1. In what sense is this essay a fable? What moral lesson does it try to teach? Is it successful?
2. At the end of her fable, Hurd implies that something unexpected occurred because of fracking. Should she have been more specific? Why do you think she is so vague?

Rhetorical Analysis

Hurd ends her fable with a one-sentence conclusion. How does this conclusion reinforce her main point? Is it enough?

Writing with Sources

Currently, Pennsylvania allows fracking, and New York does not. Examine the debates that are still taking place in these states. Then, write a letter to the governor of one of the states in which you argue against the position on fracking that is currently in place.

11.6 Richard A. Posner, "The Truth about Plagiarism"

A former judge of the US Court of Appeals for the Seventh Circuit and a senior lecturer at the University of Chicago Law School, Richard A. Posner (1939–) is a legal expert whose work focuses on the economics of intellectual property and health policy. He has written numerous academic articles, book reviews, and books, including, most recently, *The Federal Judiciary: Strengths and Weaknesses* (2017). In the following essay, Posner considers the difference between plagiarism and theft.

BEFORE YOU READ

Under what circumstances, if any, do you think academic cheating is benign?

The Truth about Plagiarism

Plagiarism is considered by most writers, teachers, journalists, scholars and even members of the general public to be the capital intellectual crime. Being caught out in plagiarism can blast a politician's career, earn a college student expulsion and destroy a writer's, scholar's or journalist's reputation. In recent days, for example, the *New York Times* has referred to "widespread fabrication and plagiarism" by reporter Jayson Blair as "a low point in the 152-year history of the newspaper."

In James Hynes' splendid satiric novella of plagiarism, *Casting the Runes,* the plagiarist, having by black magic murdered one of the historians whom he plagiarized and tried to murder a second, is himself killed by the very same black magic, deployed by the widow of his murder victim.

There is a danger of overkill. Plagiarism can be a form of fraud, but it is no accident that, unlike real theft, it is not a crime. If a thief steals your car, you are out the market value of the car, but if a writer copies material from a book you wrote, you don't have to replace the book. At worst, the undetected plagiarist obtains a reputation that he does not deserve (that is the element of fraud in plagiarism). The real victim of his fraud is not the person whose work he copies, but those of his competitors who scruple to enhance their own reputations by such means.

The most serious plagiarisms are by students and professors, whose undetected plagiarisms disrupt the system of student and scholarly evaluation. The least serious are those that earned the late Stephen Ambrose and Doris Kearns Goodwin such obloquy last year. Popular historians, they jazzed up their books with vivid passages copied from previous historians without quotation marks, though with footnote attributions that made their "crime" easy to detect.

(One reason that plagiarism, like littering, is punished heavily, even though 5
an individual act of plagiarism usually does little or no harm, is that it is normally very difficult to detect—but not in the case of Ambrose and Goodwin.) Competing popular historians might have been injured, but I'm not aware of anyone actually claiming this.

Confusion of plagiarism with theft is one reason plagiarism engenders indignation; another is a confusion of it with copyright infringement. Wholesale copying of copyrighted material is an infringement of a property right, and legal remedies are available to the copyright holder. But the copying of brief passages, even from copyrighted materials, is permissible under the doctrine of "fair use," while wholesale copying from material that is in the public domain—material that never was copyrighted, or on which the copyright has expired—presents no copyright issue at all.

Plagiarism of work in the public domain is more common than otherwise. Consider a few examples: *West Side Story* is a thinly veiled copy (with music added) of *Romeo and Juliet*, which in turn plagiarized Arthur Brooke's *The Tragicall Historye of Romeo and Juliet*, published in 1562, which in turn copied from several earlier Romeo and Juliets, all of which were copies of Ovid's story of Pyramus and Thisbe.

Paradise Lost plagiarizes the book of Genesis in the Old Testament. Classical musicians plagiarize folk melodies (think only of Dvorak, Bartok, and Copland) and often "quote" (as musicians say) from earlier classical works. Edouard Manet's most famous painting, *Dejeuner sur l'herbe,* copies earlier paintings by Raphael, Titian, and Courbet, and *My Fair Lady* plagiarized Shaw's play *Pygmalion,* while Woody Allen's movie *Play It Again, Sam* "quotes" a famous scene from *Casablanca.* Countless movies are based on books, such as *The Thirty-Nine Steps* on John Buchan's novel of that name or *For Whom the Bell Tolls* on Hemingway's novel.

Many of these "plagiarisms" were authorized, and perhaps none was deceptive; they are what Christopher Ricks in his excellent book *Allusions to the Poets* helpfully terms *allusion* rather than *plagiarism.* But what they show is that copying with variations is an important form of creativity, and this should make us prudent and measured in our condemnations of plagiarism.

10 Especially when the term is extended from literal copying to the copying of ideas. Another phrase for copying an idea, as distinct from the form in which it is expressed, is dissemination of ideas. If one needs a license to repeat another person's idea, or if one risks ostracism by one's professional community for failing to credit an idea to its originator, who may be forgotten or unknown, the dissemination of ideas is impeded.

I have heard authors of history textbooks criticized for failing to document their borrowing of ideas from previous historians. This is an absurd criticism. The author of a textbook makes no claim to originality; rather the contrary—the most reliable, if not necessarily the most exciting, textbook is one that confines itself to ideas already well accepted, not at all novel.

It would be better if the term *plagiarism* were confined to literal copying, and moreover literal copying that is not merely unacknowledged but deceptive. Failing to give credit where credit is due should be regarded as a lesser, indeed usually merely venial, offense.

The concept of plagiarism has expanded, and the sanctions for it, though they remain informal rather than legal, have become more severe, in tandem with the rise of individualism. Journal articles are no longer published anonymously, and ghostwriters demand that their contributions be acknowledged.

Individualism and a cult of originality go hand in hand. Each of us supposes that our contribution to society is unique rather than fungible and so deserves public recognition, which plagiarism clouds.

15 This is a modern view. We should be aware that the high value placed on originality is a specific cultural, and even field-specific, phenomenon, rather than an aspect of the universal moral law.

Judges, who try to conceal rather than to flaunt their originality, far from crediting their predecessors with original thinking like to pretend that there is no original thinking in law, that judges are just a transmission belt for rules and principles laid down by the framers of statutes or the Constitution.

Resorting to plagiarism to obtain a good grade or a promotion is fraud and should be punished, though it should not be confused with "theft." But I think the zeal to punish plagiarism reflects less a concern with the real injuries that it occasionally inflicts than with a desire on the part of leaders of professional communities, such as journalists and historians, to enhance their profession's reputation.

Journalists (like politicians) have a bad reputation for truthfulness, and historians, in this "postmodernist" era, are suspected of having embraced an extreme form of relativism and of having lost their regard for facts. Both groups hope by taking a very hard line against plagiarism and fabrication to reassure the public that they are serious diggers after truth whose efforts, a form of "sweat equity," deserve protection against copycats.

Their anxieties are understandable; but the rest of us will do well to keep the matter in perspective, realizing that the term *plagiarism* is used loosely and often too broadly; that much plagiarism is harmless and (when the term is defined broadly) that some has social value.

RESPONDING TO READING

1. In paragraph 3, Posner says, "There is a danger of overkill. Plagiarism can be a form of fraud, but it is no accident that, unlike real theft, it is not a crime." Do you agree with this statement? Explain.
2. According to Posner, what is the difference between plagiarism and theft? Between plagiarism and copyright infringement? Between plagiarism and allusion? Do you see these distinctions as valid in cases of academic plagiarism? Why or why not?

Rhetorical Analysis

Evaluate Posner's concluding paragraph. Does his statement that "much plagiarism is harmless" adequately sum up his essay's position? What else, if anything, do you think he should address in this paragraph?

Writing with Sources

In paragraph 4, Posner states, "The most serious plagiarisms are by students and professors . . . ." Do you agree, or do you believe plagiarism on the part of professional writers and scholars—or politicians—is more serious? Research incidents of plagiarism by historians Stephen Ambrose and Doris Kearns Goodwin—or by political leaders or news reporters—and discuss the issue of student plagiarism with students on your campus. Then, write an essay in which you explain why you agree or disagree with Posner's statement.

11.7 Focus: "What Choices Do We Have with Our Technologies?"

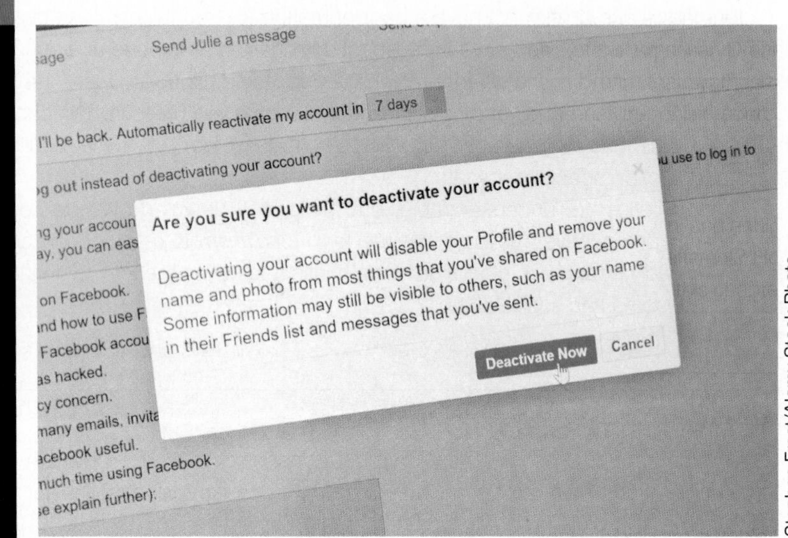

Stephen Frost/Alamy Stock Photo

What does this photo say about the choices we make with our online identities?

RESPONDING TO THE IMAGE

Answer one or both of the following questions.

1. What, if anything, does the image above tell you about the ways in which we share personal information on social media? Could you argue that removing one's online identity isn't really an option?
2. Have you, or has someone you know, tried to delete a social media account? Why? What information still remained online?

11.8 Paul Lewis, "'Our Minds Can Be Hijacked': The Tech Insiders Who Fear a Smartphone Dystopia"

An associate editor of technology and special projects for the *Guardian*, Paul Lewis writes about issues related to media, law enforcement, security, and privacy. In the following essay, Lewis considers cases that warrant disconnecting from the online world.

BEFORE YOU READ

Do you self-impose limits on your daily technology use? Why or why not?

"Our Minds Can Be Hijacked": The Tech Insiders Who Fear a Smartphone Dystopia

Justin Rosenstein had tweaked his laptop's operating system to block Reddit, banned himself from Snapchat, which he compares to heroin, and imposed limits on his use of Facebook. But even that wasn't enough. In August, the 34-year-old tech executive took a more radical step to restrict his use of social media and other addictive technologies.

Rosenstein purchased a new iPhone and instructed his assistant to set up a parental-control feature to prevent him from downloading any apps.

He was particularly aware of the allure of Facebook "likes," which he describes as "bright dings of pseudo-pleasure" that can be as hollow as they are seductive. And Rosenstein should know: he was the Facebook engineer who created the "like" button in the first place.

A decade after he stayed up all night coding a prototype of what was then called an "awesome" button, Rosenstein belongs to a small but growing band of Silicon Valley heretics who complain about the rise of the so-called "attention economy": an internet shaped around the demands of an advertising economy.

5 These refuseniks are rarely founders or chief executives, who have little incentive to deviate from the mantra that their companies are making the world a better place. Instead, they tend to have worked a rung or two down the corporate ladder: designers, engineers and product managers who, like Rosenstein, several years ago put in place the building blocks of a digital world from which they are now trying to disentangle themselves. "It is very common," Rosenstein says, "for humans to develop things with the best of intentions and for them to have unintended, negative consequences."

Rosenstein, who also helped create Gchat during a stint at Google, and now leads a San Francisco-based company that improves office productivity, appears most concerned about the psychological effects on people who, research shows, touch, swipe or tap their phone 2,617 times a day.

There is growing concern that as well as addicting users, technology is contributing toward so-called "continuous partial attention," severely limiting people's ability to focus, and possibly lowering IQ. One recent study showed that the mere presence of smartphones damages cognitive capacity—even when the device is turned off. "Everyone is distracted," Rosenstein says. "All of the time."

But those concerns are trivial compared with the devastating impact upon the political system that some of Rosenstein's peers believe can be attributed to the rise of social media and the attention-based market that drives it.

Drawing a straight line between addiction to social media and political earthquakes like Brexit and the rise of Donald Trump, they contend that digital forces have completely upended the political system and, left unchecked, could even render democracy as we know it obsolete.

10 In 2007, Rosenstein was one of a small group of Facebook employees who decided to create a path of least resistance—a single click—to "send little bits of positivity" across the platform. Facebook's "like" feature was, Rosenstein says, "wildly" successful: engagement soared as people enjoyed the short-term boost they got from giving or receiving social affirmation, while Facebook harvested valuable data about the preferences of users that could be sold to advertisers. The idea was soon copied by Twitter, with its heart-shaped "likes" (previously star-shaped "favourites"[1]), Instagram, and countless other apps and websites.

It was Rosenstein's colleague, Leah Pearlman, then a product manager at Facebook and on the team that created the Facebook "like," who announced the feature in a 2009 blogpost. Now 35 and an illustrator, Pearlman confirmed via email that she, too, has grown disaffected with Facebook "likes" and other addictive feedback loops. She has installed a web browser plug-in to eradicate her Facebook news feed, and hired a social media manager to monitor her Facebook page so that she doesn't have to.

"One reason I think it is particularly important for us to talk about this now is that we may be the last generation that can remember life before," Rosenstein says. It may or may not be relevant that Rosenstein, Pearlman and most of the tech insiders questioning today's attention economy are in their 30s, members of the last generation that can remember a world in which telephones were plugged into walls.

It is revealing that many of these younger technologists are weaning themselves off their own products, sending their children to elite Silicon Valley schools where iPhones, iPads and even laptops are banned. They appear to be abiding by a Biggie Smalls lyric from their own youth about the perils of dealing crack cocaine: never get high on your own supply.

***

One morning in April this year, designers, programmers and tech entrepreneurs from across the world gathered at a conference centre on the shore of the San Francisco Bay. They had each paid up to $1,700 to learn how to manipulate people into habitual use of their products, on a course curated by conference organiser Nir Eyal.

15 Eyal, 39, the author of *Hooked: How to Build Habit-Forming Products*, has spent several years consulting for the tech industry, teaching techniques he developed by closely studying how the Silicon Valley giants operate.

"The technologies we use have turned into compulsions, if not full-fledged addictions," Eyal writes. "It's the impulse to check a message notification. It's the pull to visit YouTube, Facebook, or Twitter for just a few minutes, only to find yourself still tapping and scrolling an hour later." None of this is an accident, he writes. It is all "just as their designers intended."

[1]British spellings in this selection have been retained. [Eds.]

He explains the subtle psychological tricks that can be used to make people develop habits, such as varying the rewards people receive to create "a craving," or exploiting negative emotions that can act as "triggers." "Feelings of boredom, loneliness, frustration, confusion and indecisiveness often instigate a slight pain or irritation and prompt an almost instantaneous and often mindless action to quell the negative sensation," Eyal writes.

Attendees of the 2017 Habit Summit might have been surprised when Eyal walked on stage to announce that this year's keynote speech was about "something a little different." He wanted to address the growing concern that technological manipulation was somehow harmful or immoral. He told his audience that they should be careful not to abuse persuasive design, and wary of crossing a line into coercion.

But he was defensive of the techniques he teaches, and dismissive of those who compare tech addiction to drugs. "We're not freebasing Facebook and injecting Instagram here," he said. He flashed up a slide of a shelf filled with sugary baked goods. "Just as we shouldn't blame the baker for making such delicious treats, we can't blame tech makers for making their products so good we want to use them," he said. "Of course that's what tech companies will do. And frankly: do we want it any other way?"

20 Without irony, Eyal finished his talk with some personal tips for resisting the lure of technology. He told his audience he uses a Chrome extension, called DF YouTube, "which scrubs out a lot of those external triggers" he writes about in his book, and recommended an app called Pocket Points that "rewards you for staying off your phone when you need to focus."

Finally, Eyal confided the lengths he goes to protect his own family. He has installed in his house an outlet timer connected to a router that cuts off access to the internet at a set time every day. "The idea is to remember that we are not powerless," he said. "We are in control."

But are we? If the people who built these technologies are taking such radical steps to wean themselves free, can the rest of us reasonably be expected to exercise our free will?

Not according to Tristan Harris, a 33-year-old former Google employee turned vocal critic of the tech industry. "All of us are jacked into this system," he says. "All of our minds can be hijacked. Our choices are not as free as we think they are."

Harris, who has been branded "the closest thing Silicon Valley has to a conscience," insists that billions of people have little choice over whether they use these now ubiquitous technologies, and are largely unaware of the invisible ways in which a small number of people in Silicon Valley are shaping their lives.

25 A graduate of Stanford University, Harris studied under BJ Fogg, a behavioural psychologist revered in tech circles for mastering the ways technological design can be used to persuade people. Many of his students, including Eyal, have gone on to prosperous careers in Silicon Valley.

Harris is the student who went rogue; a whistleblower of sorts, he is lifting the curtain on the vast powers accumulated by technology companies and the ways they are using that influence. "A handful of people, working at a handful of technology companies, through their choices will steer what a billion people are thinking today," he said at a recent TED talk in Vancouver.

"I don't know a more urgent problem than this," Harris says. "It's changing our democracy, and it's changing our ability to have the conversations and relationships that we want with each other." Harris went public—giving talks, writing papers, meeting lawmakers and campaigning for reform after three years struggling to effect change inside Google's Mountain View headquarters.

It all began in 2013, when he was working as a product manager at Google, and circulated a thought-provoking memo, A Call To Minimise Distraction & Respect Users' Attention, to 10 close colleagues. It struck a chord, spreading to some 5,000 Google employees, including senior executives who rewarded Harris with an impressive-sounding new job: he was to be Google's in-house design ethicist and product philosopher.

Looking back, Harris sees that he was promoted into a marginal role. "I didn't have a social support structure at all," he says. Still, he adds: "I got to sit in a corner and think and read and understand."

He explored how LinkedIn exploits a need for social reciprocity to widen its network; how YouTube and Netflix autoplay videos and next episodes, depriving users of a choice about whether or not they want to keep watching; how Snapchat created its addictive Snapstreaks feature, encouraging near-constant communication between its mostly teenage users.

The techniques these companies use are not always generic: they can be algorithmically tailored to each person. An internal Facebook report leaked this year, for example, revealed that the company can identify when teens feel "insecure," "worthless" and "need a confidence boost." Such granular information, Harris adds, is "a perfect model of what buttons you can push in a particular person."

Tech companies can exploit such vulnerabilities to keep people hooked; manipulating, for example, when people receive "likes" for their posts, ensuring they arrive when an individual is likely to feel vulnerable, or in need of approval, or maybe just bored. And the very same techniques can be sold to the highest bidder. "There's no ethics," he says. A company paying Facebook to use its levers of persuasion could be a car business targeting tailored advertisements to different types of users who want a new vehicle. Or it could be a Moscow-based troll farm seeking to turn voters in a swing county in Wisconsin.

Harris believes that tech companies never deliberately set out to make their products addictive. They were responding to the incentives of an advertising economy, experimenting with techniques that might capture people's attention, even stumbling across highly effective design by accident.

A friend at Facebook told Harris that designers initially decided the notification icon, which alerts people to new activity such as "friend requests" or "likes," should be blue. It fit Facebook's style and, the thinking went, would appear "subtle and innocuous." "But no one used it," Harris says. "Then they switched it to red and of course everyone used it."

That red icon is now everywhere. When smartphone users glance at their 35
phones, dozens or hundreds of times a day, they are confronted with small red dots beside their apps, pleading to be tapped. "Red is a trigger colour," Harris says. "That's why it is used as an alarm signal."

The most seductive design, Harris explains, exploits the same psychological susceptibility that makes gambling so compulsive: variable rewards. When we tap those apps with red icons, we don't know whether we'll discover an interesting email, an avalanche of "likes," or nothing at all. It is the possibility of disappointment that makes it so compulsive.

It's this that explains how the pull-to-refresh mechanism, whereby users swipe down, pause and wait to see what content appears, rapidly became one of the most addictive and ubiquitous design features in modern technology. "Each time you're swiping down, it's like a slot machine," Harris says. "You don't know what's coming next. Sometimes it's a beautiful photo. Sometimes it's just an ad."

* * *

The designer who created the pull-to-refresh mechanism, first used to update Twitter feeds, is Loren Brichter, widely admired in the app-building community for his sleek and intuitive designs.

Now 32, Brichter says he never intended the design to be addictive—but would not dispute the slot machine comparison. "I agree 100%," he says. "I have two kids now and I regret every minute that I'm not paying attention to them because my smartphone has sucked me in."

Brichter created the feature in 2009 for Tweetie, his startup, mainly because 40
he could not find anywhere to fit the "refresh" button on his app. Holding and dragging down the feed to update seemed at the time nothing more than a "cute and clever" fix. Twitter acquired Tweetie the following year, integrating pull-to-refresh into its own app.

Since then the design has become one of the most widely emulated features in apps; the downward-pull action is, for hundreds of millions of people, as intuitive as scratching an itch.

Brichter says he is puzzled by the longevity of the feature. In an era of push notification technology, apps can automatically update content without being nudged by the user. "It could easily retire," he says. Instead it appears to serve a psychological function: after all, slot machines would be far less addictive if gamblers didn't get to pull the lever themselves. Brichter prefers another comparison: that it is like the redundant "close door" button in some elevators with automatically closing doors. "People just like to push it."

All of which has left Brichter, who has put his design work on the backburner while he focuses on building a house in New Jersey, questioning his legacy. "I've spent many hours and weeks and months and years thinking about whether anything I've done has made a net positive impact on society or humanity at all," he says. He has blocked certain websites, turned off push notifications, restricted his use of the Telegram app to message only with his wife and two close friends, and tried to wean himself off Twitter. "I still waste time on it," he confesses, "just reading stupid news I already know about." He charges his phone in the kitchen, plugging it in at 7pm and not touching it until the next morning.

"Smartphones are useful tools," he says. "But they're addictive. Pull-to-refresh is addictive. Twitter is addictive. These are not good things. When I was working on them, it was not something I was mature enough to think about. I'm not saying I'm mature now, but I'm a little bit more mature, and I regret the downsides."

45 Not everyone in his field appears racked with guilt. The two inventors listed on Apple's patent for "managing notification connections and displaying icon badges" are Justin Santamaria and Chris Marcellino. Both were in their early 20s when they were hired by Apple to work on the iPhone. As engineers, they worked on the behind-the-scenes plumbing for push-notification technology, introduced in 2009 to enable real-time alerts and updates to hundreds of thousands of third-party app developers. It was a revolutionary change, providing the infrastructure for so many experiences that now form a part of people's daily lives, from ordering an Uber to making a Skype call to receiving breaking news updates.

But notification technology also enabled a hundred unsolicited interruptions into millions of lives, accelerating the arms race for people's attention. Santamaria, 36, who now runs a startup after a stint as the head of mobile at Airbnb, says the technology he developed at Apple was not "inherently good or bad." "This is a larger discussion for society," he says. "Is it OK to shut off my phone when I leave work? Is it OK if I don't get right back to you? Is it OK that I'm not 'liking' everything that goes through my Instagram screen?"

His then colleague, Marcellino, agrees. "Honestly, at no point was I sitting there thinking: let's hook people," he says. "It was all about the positives: these apps connect people, they have all these uses—ESPN telling you the game has ended, or WhatsApp giving you a message for free from your family member in Iran who doesn't have a message plan."

A few years ago Marcellino, 33, left the Bay Area, and is now in the final stages of retraining to be a neurosurgeon. He stresses he is no expert on addiction, but says he has picked up enough in his medical training to know that technologies can affect the same neurological pathways as gambling and drug use. "These are the same circuits that make people seek out food, comfort, heat, sex," he says.

All of it, he says, is reward-based behaviour that activates the brain's dopamine pathways. He sometimes finds himself clicking on the red icons beside his apps "to make them go away," but is conflicted about the ethics of exploiting people's psychological vulnerabilities. "It is not inherently evil to bring people back to your product," he says. "It's capitalism."

50 That, perhaps, is the problem. Roger McNamee, a venture capitalist who benefited from hugely profitable investments in Google and Facebook, has grown disenchanted with both companies, arguing that their early missions have been distorted by the fortunes they have been able to earn through advertising.

He identifies the advent of the smartphone as a turning point, raising the stakes in an arms race for people's attention. "Facebook and Google assert with merit that they are giving users what they want," McNamee says. "The same can be said about tobacco companies and drug dealers."

That would be a remarkable assertion for any early investor in Silicon Valley's most profitable behemoths. But McNamee, 61, is more than an arms-length money man. Once an adviser to Mark Zuckerberg, 10 years ago McNamee introduced the Facebook CEO to his friend, Sheryl Sandberg, then a Google executive who had overseen the company's advertising efforts. Sandberg, of course, became chief operating officer at Facebook, transforming the social network into another advertising heavyweight.

McNamee chooses his words carefully. "The people who run Facebook and Google are good people, whose well-intentioned strategies have led to horrific unintended consequences," he says. "The problem is that there is nothing the companies can do to address the harm unless they abandon their current advertising models."

But how can Google and Facebook be forced to abandon the business models that have transformed them into two of the most profitable companies on the planet?

McNamee believes the companies he invested in should be subjected to 55
greater regulation, including new anti-monopoly rules. In Washington, there is growing appetite, on both sides of the political divide, to rein in Silicon Valley. But McNamee worries the behemoths he helped build may already be too big to curtail. "The EU recently penalized Google $2.42bn for anti-monopoly violations, and Google's shareholders just shrugged," he says.

Rosenstein, the Facebook "like" co-creator, believes there may be a case for state regulation of "psychologically manipulative advertising," saying the moral impetus is comparable to taking action against fossil fuel or tobacco companies. "If we only care about profit maximisation," he says, "we will go rapidly into dystopia."

***

James Williams does not believe talk of dystopia is far-fetched. The ex-Google strategist who built the metrics system for the company's global search advertising business, he has had a front-row view of an industry he describes as the "largest, most standardised and most centralised form of attentional control in human history."

Williams, 35, left Google last year, and is on the cusp of completing a PhD at Oxford University exploring the ethics of persuasive design. It is a journey that has led him to question whether democracy can survive the new technological age.

He says his epiphany came a few years ago, when he noticed he was surrounded by technology that was inhibiting him from concentrating on the things he wanted to focus on. "It was that kind of individual, existential realisation: what's going on?" he says. "Isn't technology supposed to be doing the complete opposite of this?"

60 That discomfort was compounded during a moment at work, when he glanced at one of Google's dashboards, a multicoloured display showing how much of people's attention the company had commandeered for advertisers. "I realised: this is literally a million people that we've sort of nudged or persuaded to do this thing that they weren't going to otherwise do," he recalls.

He embarked on several years of independent research, much of it conducted while working part-time at Google. About 18 months in, he saw the Google memo circulated by Harris and the pair became allies, struggling to bring about change from within.

Williams and Harris left Google around the same time, and co-founded an advocacy group, Time Well Spent, that seeks to build public momentum for a change in the way big tech companies think about design. Williams finds it hard to comprehend why this issue is not "on the front page of every newspaper every day.

"Eighty-seven percent of people wake up and go to sleep with their smartphones," he says. The entire world now has a new prism through which to understand politics, and Williams worries the consequences are profound.

The same forces that led tech firms to hook users with design tricks, he says, also encourage those companies to depict the world in a way that makes for compulsive, irresistible viewing. "The attention economy incentivises the design of technologies that grab our attention," he says. "In so doing, it privileges our impulses over our intentions."

65 That means privileging what is sensational over what is nuanced, appealing to emotion, anger and outrage. The news media is increasingly working in service to tech companies, Williams adds, and must play by the rules of the attention economy to "sensationalise, bait and entertain in order to survive."

In the wake of Donald Trump's stunning electoral victory, many were quick to question the role of so-called "fake news" on Facebook, Russian-created Twitter bots or the data-centric targeting efforts that companies such as Cambridge Analytica used to sway voters. But Williams sees those factors as symptoms of a deeper problem.

It is not just shady or bad actors who were exploiting the internet to change public opinion. The attention economy itself is set up to promote a phenomenon like Trump, who is masterly at grabbing and retaining the attention of supporters and critics alike, often by exploiting or creating outrage.

Williams was making this case before the president was elected. In a blog published a month before the US election, Williams sounded the alarm bell on an issue he argued was a "far more consequential question" than whether Trump reached the White House. The reality TV star's campaign, he said, had heralded a watershed in which "the new, digitally supercharged dynamics of the attention economy have finally crossed a threshold and become manifest in the political realm."

Williams saw a similar dynamic unfold months earlier, during the Brexit campaign, when the attention economy appeared to him biased in favour of the emotional, identity-based case for the UK leaving the European Union. He stresses these dynamics are by no means isolated to the political right: they also play a role, he believes, in the unexpected popularity of leftwing politicians such as Bernie Sanders and Jeremy Corbyn, and the frequent outbreaks of internet outrage over issues that ignite fury among progressives.

All of which, Williams says, is not only distorting the way we view politics but, 70
over time, may be changing the way we think, making us less rational and more impulsive. "We've habituated ourselves into a perpetual cognitive style of outrage, by internalising the dynamics of the medium," he says.

It is against this political backdrop that Williams argues the fixation in recent years with the surveillance state fictionalised by George Orwell may have been misplaced. It was another English science fiction writer, Aldous Huxley, who provided the more prescient observation when he warned that Orwellian-style coercion was less of a threat to democracy than the more subtle power of psychological manipulation, and "man's almost infinite appetite for distractions."

Since the US election, Williams has explored another dimension to today's brave new world. If the attention economy erodes our ability to remember, to reason, to make decisions for ourselves—faculties that are essential to self-governance—what hope is there for democracy itself?

"The dynamics of the attention economy are structurally set up to undermine the human will," he says. "If politics is an expression of our human will, on individual and collective levels, then the attention economy is directly undermining the assumptions that democracy rests on." If Apple, Facebook, Google, Twitter, Instagram and Snapchat are gradually chipping away at our ability to control our own minds, could there come a point, I ask, at which democracy no longer functions?

"Will we be able to recognise it, if and when it happens?" Williams replies. "And if we can't, then how do we know it hasn't happened already?"

Source: Paul Lewis, 'Our minds can be hijacked': the tech insiders who fear a smartphone dystopia, 06 October 2017. www.theguardian.com

---

RESPONDING TO READING

1. How does this essay characterize the relationship between ethics and product design? Are persuasive, even addictive, designs unethical? Why or why not?
2. In paragraph 22, Lewis writes, "If the people who built these technologies are taking such radical steps to wean themselves free, can the rest of us reasonably be expected to exercise our free will?" How does Lewis answer this question? How would you respond?

Rhetorical Analysis

How does Lewis use interviews to support the points he makes? Does he provide enough information to convince readers of his argument? What other sources, if any, should he have included?

Writing with Sources

Research the basics of Google's and Facebook's advertising platforms. Then, write an essay in which you agree or disagree with Lewis's thesis that these platforms are engineered to manipulate people's emotions and capitalize on their vulnerabilities.

11.9 Francine Berman and Vinton G. Cerf, "Social and Ethical Behavior in the Internet of Things"

The Edward P. Hamilton Distinguished Professor of computer science at Rensselaer Polytechnic Institute and an advocate for women in technology, Francine Berman (1951–) specializes in cyber-infrastructure as well as data sharing, privacy, and innovation. Her work has appeared in such publications as the *Chronicle of Higher Education, Fast Company, Inside Higher Ed,* and *The Washington Post.* Described as one of the "Fathers of the Internet," Vinton G. Cerf (1943–) is vice president and chief internet evangelist at Google. An expert in data management, networking, and information security, he co-invented TCP/IP technology and co-developed MCI Mail, the first commercial email platform. In the following essay, Berman and Cerf consider ethical questions pertaining to the "Internet of Things."

BEFORE YOU READ

Do you think digital technologies should be intentionally designed to promote ethical behavior? Why or why not?

Social and Ethical Behavior in the Internet of Things

Last October,* millions of interconnected devices infected with malware mounted a "denial-of-service" cyberattack on Dyn, a company that operates part of the Internet's directory service. Such attacks require us to up our technical game in Internet security and safety. They also expose the need to frame and

* This essay was published in February 2017. [Eds.]

enforce social and ethical behavior, privacy, and appropriate use in Internet environments.

Social behavior and appropriate use become even more crucial as we build out the "Internet of Things" (IoT)—an increasingly interconnected cyber-physical-biological environment that links devices, systems, data, and people. At its best, the IoT has the potential to create an integrated ecosystem that can respond to a spectrum of needs, increasing efficiency and opportunity, and empowering people through technology, and technology through intelligence. At its worst, the IoT can open a Pandora's Box of inappropriate and unsafe behavior, unintended consequences, and intrusiveness.

The difference between an IoT that enhances society and one that diminishes it will be determined by our ability to create an effective model for IoT governance. This model must guide social behavior and ethical use of IoT technologies while promoting effective security and safety. While we should not limit technology innovation too early with overly restrictive policy, neither should we leave the policy and governance discussion until the IoT is so mature that it cannot easily incorporate protections.

WHAT POLICY WILL BE NEEDED FOR THE IOT?

Although much of the policy needed for the IoT may evolve from Internet governance, the scale, heterogeneity, complexity, and degree of technological autonomy within the IoT will require new thinking about regulation and policy and force new interpretations of current law. As an example of the complexity of the governance challenge, consider three key areas critical to ensure the positive potential of the IoT:

1. **What are your rights to privacy in the IoT?** The IoT will sharpen the 5
tension between individual privacy and the use of personal information to promote effectiveness, safety, and security. Who should control information about you? Who should access it? Who can use it? The answer is not always clear-cut. Consider medical monitoring devices and the information they accumulate. Should your personal health information be shared when the Centers for Disease Control want to track a potential epidemic? When biomedical researchers want to model potential treatment strategies on a richer dataset? When an employer is considering you for a job?

   At present, policy and laws about online privacy and rights to information are challenging to interpret and difficult to enforce. As IoT technologies become more pervasive, personal information will become more valuable to a diverse set of actors that include organizations, individuals, and autonomous systems with the capacity to make decisions about you.

   Some have suggested that individuals should have a basic right to opt out, delete, or mask their information from systems in the IoT, providing one tenet of a potential IoT "Bill of Rights." However, it may be infeasible or impossible for an individual to control all the data generated about them by IoT systems.

Interestingly, strong individual privacy rights may also mean less social benefit. Too many "opt-outs" may erode the public and private value of IoT datasets,[3] negatively impacting their social benefit—imagine a Google map where locations come and go. The complexity of providing useful services subject to dynamic participation and evolving individual preferences may be extraordinarily complex to develop and administer.

2. **Who is accountable for decisions made by autonomous systems?** As autonomous systems replace some human activities, we face the challenge of when and how these systems should be deployed, and who is responsible and accountable for their behavior. When your "smart" system fails, is hacked, or acts with negative or unintended consequences, who is accountable, how, and to whom?

10 A high-profile example of this is autonomous vehicles, which make many decisions without "a human in the loop." We currently expect automobile companies to be accountable if automotive systems, such as anti-lock brakes, fail. As cars begin to drive themselves, who should be responsible for accidents? As systems take on more decisions previously made by humans, it will be increasingly challenging to create a framework for responsibility and accountability.

3. **How do we promote the ethical use of IoT technologies?** Technologies have no ethics. Many systems can be used for both good and ill: Video surveillance may be tremendously helpful in allowing senior citizens stay in their homes longer and parents to monitor their newborns; they can also expose private behavior to unscrupulous viewers and unwanted intrusion.

In his highly popular and visionary books, Isaac Asimov posited four laws of robotics[1,2] on the basic theme that robots may not harm humans (or humanity), or, by inaction, allow humans (humanity) to come to harm. Asimov's Laws provide a glimpse into the social and ethical challenges that will need to be addressed in the IoT. How do we promote and enforce ethical behavior by both humans and intelligent systems? Will we need to develop and incorporate "artificial ethics" into automated systems to help them respond in environments when there are good and bad choices? If so, whose ethics should be applied?

TOWARD A FRAMEWORK FOR THINKING ABOUT PRINCIPLES AND POLICY FOR THE IOT

What might a general IoT governance model look like? In 2008, the Forum for a New World Governance developed the "World Governance Index" (WGI) focusing on peace and security, democracy and the rule of law, human rights, development and participation, and sustainability. These areas provide a roadmap for considering IoT governance. Mapping the WGI areas to the IoT indicates that we will need:

- *Policy for IoT safety, security and privacy*, requiring the development of viable approaches promoting individual rights, data security, and trust, as well as disincentives and penalties for inappropriate behavior, corruption, and crime.

- *A legal framework for determining appropriate behavior* of autonomous IoT entities, responsible and accountable parties for that behavior, and determination of who can enforce compliance, how, and on what grounds.
- *Focus on human rights and ethical behavior* in the IoT, including a sense of how these would be enforced. This gets to the heart of the need for the IoT to promote human well-being and contribute to the advancement of society.
- *Sustainable development of the IoT* as part of a larger societal and technological ecosystem, including its impact on biological systems (for example, 3D-printed organs, implants), environmental systems, and natural resources).

We need to lay the groundwork now. The IoT should advance society and not just technology. The first step is to pursue the discussions, studies, task forces, commissions, and pilots that will help develop governance for an empowering and enabling IoT. Developing policy and legislation in newsworthy and opportunistic areas (for example, transportation) is essential, but not enough. We need to be thinking deeply *now* about broad IoT use and deployment, and how it can help create a more enlightened and civilized society. If we wait too long, we do so at our own risk.

References

1. Asimov, I. *Robots and Empire*. Doubleday, 1985.
2. Asimov, I. "Runaround" in *I, Robot*. Gnome Press, 1950.
3. Goodman, E. *The Atomic Age of Data: Policy for the Internet of Things*. Aspen Institute Report, 2015.

Source: Berman, F., & Cerf, V. G. (2017). Social and ethical behavior in the internet of things. Communications of the ACM, 60(2), 6–7. Used with permission from Authors.

RESPONDING TO READING

1. In paragraph 8, Berman and Cerf explain that "strong individual privacy rights may also mean less social benefit." What do they mean? How does this happen?
2. What is "artificial ethics" (12)? Do Berman and Cerf see this possibility as a step forward or backward in our technological development? How do you view it?

Rhetorical Analysis

In paragraph 10, what purpose does the example of self-driving cars serve? What point are Berman and Cerf trying to make?

Writing with Sources
Research the Internet of Things. What is it? What does it encompass? In what ways does it "promote human well-being and contribute to the advancement of society" (13)? How might it be detrimental to social progress? Write an essay that answers these questions.

11.10 Valery Vavilov, "The Identity Solution"

Cofounder and CEO of Bitfury, Valery Vavilov specializes in blockchain technology, a data security tool. In the following essay, Vavilov makes a case for using blockchain technology to secure our identities in digital spaces.

BEFORE YOU READ
What physical forms of identification do you have? For example, do you have a driver's license? a passport? a birth certificate? Where do you store these documents? Have you ever lost any of them?

The Identity Solution

Read any newspaper in the world and you know there are challenges—refugee crises, cybersecurity threats, broken institutions, civil unrest, the list goes on.

Beneath the surface of these boiling problems lies a deeper challenge—to which many are unaware. There is no established and secure digital identity system with a verifiable biometrics component for the 7.5 billion people living on Earth.

Who are you, and how do I know you are who you say you are? What do you do when someone takes your identity? How do I know this is your vote? How do I know that you are not a threat? How do I know that I can trust you?

For too many, a lack of verifiable identity means a lack of access—to a voice, to the world economy, to medical care, to mobility, to land. In an increasingly digital world, according to the World Bank, there are more than 1.5 billion people who, for all practical purposes, do not exist. And for countless businesses, governments and institutions, this absence of a trusted identity system is an expensive and increasingly difficult predicament.

5 We currently live in a world where your identity is a piece of paper. If you lose that piece of paper it's very difficult in most parts of the world to get a new one, and if you never had that piece of paper, you are not part of any record or global interoperable system.

Simply put, the lack of an effective identity system means disenfranchisement and mass disorganization on a global scale; without a solution, technological advances aimed at solving our greatest challenges are stymied.

So, is there a solution? And if there is, is that solution feasible?

First, some good news—every individual on the planet was born with a unique set of biometrics, a fool-proof way to uniquely identify who they are. These include your fingerprints, your face, your eyes, even your voice.

Second and quite amazingly, there is now an immutable recording mechanism that can securely log each identity in a system called the blockchain—otherwise known as the Bitcoin blockchain or the public blockchain. What's more, the blockchain is inexpensive, it's easy, it's transparent and in the eight years it has been around, it has been proven to resist hacking attempts.

Consider the countless, tragic incidents of human trafficking and the implica- 10
tions blockchain could have on protecting individuals from trafficking. If a birth is never properly recorded in a reliable trusted system, a child can easily disappear without a trace. While everyone in the world is born with a unique identity, not everyone in the world necessarily has proof of their identity. The blockchain has the potential to mend this fundamental flaw. With blockchain, identity can be recorded on a permanent digital system, rather than a flimsy piece of paper. Thus a child that is being rescued from the hands of traffickers can be identified and, hopefully, returned to family and country of origin.

And it's not just the world's worst criminal enterprises that can be challenged by this cutting-edge technological tool. Institutional inefficiencies, corruption and redundancies can be rooted out and eliminated with similar methods.

Imagine, for example, being able to travel to another country without carrying a passport. The blockchain could store your unique bio data, so your identity is accessible from anywhere in the world, regardless of whether you are carrying this identification. It would also return to you the sole control of your information—something lacking on the internet today. Your identity on the public blockchain would be stored securely and privately, and you alone would be able to grant access to it. You could determine what kind of data would be shown to your doctor, or your employer, or even to a customs official. You could see who accessed your data and when. Best of all, your identity could not be deleted from the blockchain.

Some governments and businesses are already harnessing blockchain technology to tackle identity.

Consider Estonia as a shining example of what digital identification can do. Years ago, in an effort spearheaded by the visionary Estonian President Toomas Henrik Ilves, that country established a national system of digital identity—a structure available to both citizens and residents. In exchange for allowing their digital identity to be used across government agencies, residents receive many high-quality services from the government and private institutions. Services available include e-Prescriptions, e-voting, digital signatures and much more. This digital identity system—which was initially met with skepticism from the Estonian public—is now very popular and has helped cement the small country's position as a world leader in e-governance.

15 But just because there is a technical solution doesn't necessarily mean there is a political one. However, as we learned from Estonia, when there is a will there is most certainly a way.

If we as a global community are truly committed to making our world more functional, we need to embrace the countries, businesses and institutions that are willing to pave the way as pioneers—to step outside of the box and try something new.

There are, of course, legitimate ethical concerns related to implementing any system that registers and authenticates individual identity. But there are equally legitimate ethical concerns about failing to implement such systems.

There are also understandable worries about the ease with which one's identity might be erased from the internet or stolen.

Cases of identity theft can happen anywhere from the local ATM to the White House Office of Personnel Management. In 2016, according to Javelin Strategy & Research, identity theft cost the U.S. $16 billion and affected more than 15 million Americans. That brings the total amount lost to identity theft in the past six years to $107 billion. And that is just in the United States. A 2017 report from ID2020 asserts that the financial exclusion that results from lack of identity has created a shadow economy around the world with an estimated GDP of $10 trillion a year. This makes it the world's second-largest economy.

20 The blockchain shows us there is a better way to confront problems both old and new. Challenges caused by identity issues have always looked like a puzzle missing a piece.

The blockchain is that missing piece.

There are so many difficulties in our world—that is something we can all agree on. It's easy to feel overwhelmed by the paths we need to clear. No technology is a panacea, and this particular challenge calls for careful, concerted study and consideration.

But with stakes so high, we cannot afford not to act.

I believe in the collective capacity to confront and address this challenge. Together we can chip away at one of the many cancers which keep societies from thriving—secure identities. Blockchain is leading the change we need; it's up to all of us to care, to learn, to adapt, to get on board.

25 The time is now.

RESPONDING TO READING

1. What practical objections does Vavilov have to our current identity system? Do his objections make sense to you?
2. How does Vavilov propose blockchain technology as "the identity solution"? What specifically does blockchain do that physical forms of identification can't? Do you think Vavilov's recommendations for how to secure personal information are unrealistically optimistic?

Rhetorical Analysis

In paragraph 17, Vavilov writes, "There are, of course, legitimate ethical concerns related to implementing any system that registers and authenticates individual identity. But there are equally legitimate ethical concerns about failing to implement such systems." Should he have developed these statements further? Why or why not? How do you think Paul Lewis (p. 414) would respond to these statements?

Writing with Sources

Research blockchain technology—how it works, how it differs from cryptocurrency like Bitcoin, and if or when it has been hacked. Write a proposal to victims of identity theft in which you make recommendations of your own for protecting personal data. Acknowledging the suggestions by Vavilov and others you find in your research, tailor the recommendations specifically to the students at your college or university.

Widening the Focus

For Critical Reading and Writing

Referring specifically to the three readings in this chapter's Focus section (and possibly to additional sources as well), write an essay in which you answer the question, "What Choices Do We Have with Our Technologies?"

For Further Reading

The following readings can suggest additional perspectives for thinking and writing about the issue of making choices in online contexts:

- Tao Lin, "When I Moved Online..." (p. 66)
- Quinn Norton, "*The New York Times* Fired My Doppelgänger" (p. 188)
- Moira Donegan, "I Started the Media Men List: My Name Is Moira Donegan" (p. 240)
- Alexis C. Madrigal, "Future Historians Probably Won't Understand Our Internet, and That's Okay" (p. 450)

For Focused Research

Concerns about online privacy and the security of our data influence our decisions to adopt and use a range of technologies. How much choice do we have when it comes to interacting and transacting online? Can we participate freely in digital spaces while still protecting our personal information? Should we shield our offline lives from our online identities? How much can we safely reveal about ourselves in online contexts? In preparation for writing an essay that answers these questions, do a *Google* search using the search terms *online privacy and security,* and read information about various strategies for data preservation and protection. In your essay, explain the range of dilemmas we face and some proposed solutions. Support your points with examples and evidence from the websites you use.

Beyond the Classroom

Interview the following people: several professors (in different fields), one student from every year at your school, and two college administrators. Ask each of them if online privacy and security concerns affect their everyday lives—and, if so, how. Then, ask them what solutions they propose to address the problems they identify. Write an essay in the form of a proposal that summarizes the recommendations you have gathered.

Exploring Issues and Ideas

Making Ethical Choices

Write an essay in response to one of the following prompts, which are suitable for assignments that require the use of outside sources as well as for assignments that are not source-based.

1. Talk with instructors at your school and investigate whether they perceive a general decline of academic integrity. Do students tend to behave ethically or do temptations to cheat outweigh the consequences of getting caught? Write an essay in which you present your findings, referring to Richard A. Posner's essay in this chapter (p. 410).
2. Do you believe it is possible both to do good (that is, to help others) and to do well (that is, to be financially successful), or do you believe these two goals are mutually exclusive? Write an essay in which you answer this question, citing examples of people you know as well as public TABVs who have (or have not) managed both to do good and to do well.
3. Do you think that people can be guided by a moral and ethical code that is strictly secular, or do you believe it is only possible to live a moral, ethical life if one believes in a higher power and follows the guidelines set by a particular religion? Write an essay that explains your position.
4. Do you believe that decisions about what steps to take to preserve the environment are essentially ethical choices? Or, do you think a person's behavior in situations like this has nothing to do with ethics or morals?

5. Imagine that you are in charge of an almost-full lifeboat and can take on only one additional passenger. Which of the following people would you choose, and why?
   - A healthy three-year-old
   - An elderly Nobel Prize winner
   - A single father of two young children
   - A thirty-year-old decorated combat veteran
   - A middle-aged doctor who has performed life-saving surgery

Write an essay in which you consider which of the candidates most deserves to be saved (not which one can be of most practical help to the others in the lifeboat). Before you focus on the person you would save, evaluate the pros and cons of saving each of the others.

Chapter 12
Facing the Future

In this chapter, you will learn to:

- analyze readings about life in the future.
- compose essays about life in the future.

In the early part of the twentieth century, people envisioned the future as a place of infinite possibilities, where human intellect would create a society in which technology and industry could solve all the world's problems. War would be a thing of the past, and so would famine and disease. Soon, however, two World Wars (and many small ones) revealed the folly of these forecasts. Instead of creating a utopia, technology enabled human beings to create destruction on a scale never witnessed before in human history.

Of course, the new developments were not all bad. In the early part of the twentieth century, people traveled mainly on foot, by horse, or by train. By the middle of the century, the automobile and the jet plane enabled them to travel great distances in hours instead of weeks. In 1969, the same rocket technology that had enabled Nazi Germany to launch V2 rockets against England in 1944 also enabled the United States to send astronauts to the moon. Throughout the twentieth century, medicine made advances that enabled doctors to cure diseases—such as polio, typhus, and cholera—that had decimated human populations for

ScreenProd/Photononstop/Alamy Stock Photo

What elements does this image of a future city from the 1982 science fiction movie *Blade Runner* use to show a particular view of the future?

centuries. With the inventions of the telephone, radio, and television, people were able to transmit and receive information instantly, regardless of distance. And the computer gave people access to information on a scale that earlier generations could never have imagined.

Now, in the second decade of the twenty-first century, people understandably wonder what is in store for them.

- How will *family* be defined in the future?
- Will education as we know it endure, or will online education completely replace face-to-face classroom instruction?
- How will social media affect our language, the way we think, and the way we view ourselves and others?
- Will cultural identity become more or less important?
- Will technology bring people closer together or push them further apart?
- How will gender roles change? Will these changes be for the better?
- How will the nature of work and workers' roles change? What new jobs will emerge?
- Will more people realize the American Dream, or will it remain out of reach for many?
- What new ethical dilemmas will the future bring?
- Finally, will the future be benign or harmful? Will human beings achieve the society that they have always wished for, or will this century be as destructive as the last one?

What elements does this image of the Brooklyn Bridge and the Manhattan skyline use to show our current existence and where we might be headed?

The Focus section of this chapter (p. 463) addresses the question "What's Next for the Planet (and Beyond)?" and reflects some of the hopes and fears we share about our future quality of life. In "A Moral Atmosphere" (p. 464), Bill McKibben proposes ways to direct the discussion about climate change; in "Why What We Eat Is Crucial to the Climate Change Question" (p. 467), Ruth Khasaya Oniang'o examines the long-term consequences of what and how we eat; and in the excerpt from *The Future of Humanity: Terraforming Mars, Interstellar Travel, Immortality, and Our Destiny beyond Earth* (p. 469), Michio Kaku considers our shared origins and potential future together.

Preparing to Read and Write

As you read and prepare to write about the selections in this chapter, you may consider the following questions:

- What assumptions does the writer seem to have about his or her audience? How can you tell?
- What is the writer's primary purpose? Is it to predict a future event or situation, to comment on a trend or tendency in today's world, to analyze a problem or propose a solution, or to issue a warning? Is it something else?
- What genre is the writer using? For example, is the reading a literary work, a speech, or an argument? How do the conventions of this genre influence the writer's choices?
- On what specific issue does the writer focus?
- Is the writer optimistic, pessimistic, or ambivalent about the future?
- Does the writer believe that the future he or she envisions is inevitable, or does he or she believe that people can influence future events?
- Does the writer identify a specific problem? Does he or she think the problem can be solved?
- Is the writer emotionally involved with the issue he or she is discussing? Does this involvement (or lack of involvement) affect the writer's credibility?
- What social or political ideas influence the writer's view of the future? How can you tell? Are these ideas similar to or different from your own ideas?
- Does the predicted future cause the writer to examine his or her own values? The values of society? Does the writer lead you to examine your own values?
- Which writers' views of the future seem most similar? Which seem most different?
- Which writer's view of the future seems the most plausible? Which seems the least plausible?

Shared Writing

Facing the Future

How do you envision your future? Where do you hope to be in five, ten, twenty years? With whom will you spend your time? Where will you be? What will you be doing?

12.1 Benjamin Busch, "New World" [Poetry]

A U.S. Marine Corps combat veteran, poet, essayist, memoirist, photographer, illustrator, actor, and film director, Benjamin Busch (1968–) explores the beautiful and horrifying details of everyday life. The author of the acclaimed memoir *Dust to Dust* (2012), he teaches for Sierra Nevada College's MFA in Creative Nonfiction and has published work in *The Best American Essays 2010; Connecticut Review; Dunes Review; Five Points; Harper's; Michigan Quarterly Review; Photography Quarterly;* and *War, Literature & the Arts*. The writer and director of the films *Sympathetic Details* (2008) and *Bright* (2011), Busch has also appeared in the television shows *The Beast, Generation Kill, Homicide: Life on the Street*, and *The Wire*. The following poem conveys a vision of the future.

BEFORE YOU READ

Can you imagine a world in which people had to start over from scratch? What would it look like?

New World

People are in the market buying supplies, that look in their eyes,
the haunt of wind and snow coming, all talk is about weather.
Mist rose in the night, lit by morning its gray is closing in,
smudging trees and shrinking fields, impossible to reason with.
It's like those heavy dawns on the coast, lobster boats invisible,
engines snuffed by fog, buoy to buoy, men and gulls cursing.
Here on the farm they're still out there, in the pasture, pulling traps,
tractors sunk, barns astray, all of it ocean and no ink on the maps.
We're on the edge or in the eye, always underneath its whirl,
the billow and grind pushed at us until we can't help but take a breath.
Snow falls like swollen feathers, too thick to see the silo,
all of us sealed in houses, giving our names to storms.
There's only the new world now and we'll have to find our way

when the squall breaks, setting out into a land without footprints,
walking on water, being the first to dare.

Source: This poem first appeared in the Spring 2016 Contest issue of Epiphany.

RESPONDING TO READING

1. How would you describe the mood of the poem? How does the poem's mood reflect its subject?
2. What vision of the future is presented in the poem's last three lines?

Rhetorical Analysis

How does the poem's imagery depict the "new world" of the future? In what ways does this future resemble our current reality? How specifically is it different?

12.2 John F. Kennedy, Inaugural Address

Born in Brookline, Massachusetts, John Fitzgerald Kennedy (1917–1963) received a bachelor's degree from Harvard University and served in the navy during World War II as a PT boat commander in the South Pacific. A charismatic politician, he was elected to the United States House of Representatives in 1947 and to the Senate in 1953. In 1960, defeating Republican candidate (and later president) Richard Nixon, Kennedy became the youngest man and the first Catholic to be elected president. During his tenure, he supported policies promoting racial equality, aid to the poor and to education, and increased availability of medical care; he also conceived of the idea of the Peace Corps. However, Kennedy was also responsible for involving the country further in the doomed Vietnam conflict. He was assassinated in November of 1963, a year before the end of his first term.

BEFORE YOU READ

Exactly what do you expect America to do for you, and what do you expect to do for your country?

Inaugural Address

Vice President Johnson, Mr. Speaker, Mr. Chief Justice, President Eisenhower, Vice President Nixon, President Truman, Reverend Clergy, fellow citizens:

We observe today not a victory of party but a celebration of freedom—symbolizing an end as well as a beginning—signifying renewal as well as change. For I have sworn before you and Almighty God the same solemn oath our forebears prescribed nearly a century and three-quarters ago.

The world is very different now. For man holds in his mortal hands the power to abolish all forms of human poverty and all forms of human life. And yet the same revolutionary beliefs for which our forebears fought are still at issue around the globe—the belief that the rights of man come not from the generosity of the state but from the hand of God.

We dare not forget today that we are the heirs of that first revolution. Let the word go forth from this time and place, to friend and foe alike, that the torch has been passed to a new generation of Americans—born in this century, tempered by war, disciplined by a hard and bitter peace, proud of our ancient heritage—and unwilling to witness or permit the slow undoing of those human rights to which this nation has always been committed, and to which we are committed today at home and around the world.

Let every nation know, whether it wishes us well or ill, that we shall pay any 5
price, bear any burden, meet any hardship, support any friend, oppose any foe to assure the survival and the success of liberty.

This much we pledge—and more.

To those old allies whose cultural and spiritual origins we share, we pledge the loyalty of faithful friends. United there is little we cannot do in a host of cooperative ventures. Divided there is little we can do—for we dare not meet a powerful challenge at odds and split asunder.

To those new states whom we welcome to the ranks of the free, we pledge our word that one form of colonial control shall not have passed away merely to be replaced by a far more iron tyranny. We shall not always expect to find them supporting our view. But we shall always hope to find them strongly supporting their own freedom—and to remember that, in the past, those who foolishly sought power by riding the back of the tiger ended up inside. To those people in the huts and villages of half the globe struggling to break the bonds of mass misery, we pledge our best efforts to help them help themselves, for whatever period is required—not because the communists may be doing it, not because we seek their votes, but because it is right. If a free society cannot help the many who are poor, it cannot save the few who are rich.

To our sister republics south of our border, we offer a special pledge—to convert our good words into good deeds—in a new alliance for progress—to assist free men and free governments in casting off the chains of poverty. But this peaceful revolution of hope cannot become the prey of hostile powers. Let all our neighbors know that we shall join with them to oppose aggression or subversion anywhere in the Americas. And let every other power know that this Hemisphere intends to remain the master of its own house.

To that world assembly of sovereign states, the United Nations, our last best 10
hope in an age where the instruments of war have far outpaced the instruments of peace, we renew our pledge of support—to prevent it from becoming merely

a forum for invective—to strengthen its shield of the new and the weak—and to enlarge the area in which its writ may run.

Finally, to those nations who would make themselves our adversary, we offer not a pledge but a request: that both sides begin anew the quest for peace, before the dark powers of destruction unleashed by science engulf all humanity in planned or accidental self-destruction.

We dare not tempt them with weakness. For only when our arms are sufficient beyond doubt can we be certain beyond doubt that they will never be employed.

But neither can two great and powerful groups of nations take comfort from our present course—both sides overburdened by the cost of modern weapons, both rightly alarmed by the steady spread of the deadly atom, yet both racing to alter that uncertain balance of terror that stays the hand of mankind's final war.

So let us begin anew—remembering on both sides that civility is not a sign of weakness, and sincerity is always subject to proof. Let us never negotiate out of fear. But let us never fear to negotiate.

15 Let both sides explore what problems unite us instead of belaboring those problems which divide us.

Let both sides, for the first time, formulate serious and precise proposals for the inspection and control of arms and bring the absolute power to destroy other nations under the absolute control of all nations.

Let both sides seek to invoke the wonders of science instead of its terrors. Together let us explore the stars, conquer the deserts, eradicate disease, tap the ocean depths and encourage the arts and commerce.

Let both sides unite to heed in all corners of the earth the command of Isaiah—to "undo the heavy burdens. . . (and) let the oppressed go free."

And if a beachhead of cooperation may push back the jungle of suspicion, let both sides join in creating a new endeavor, not a new balance of power, but a new world of law, where the strong are just and the weak secure and the peace preserved.

20 All this will not be finished in the first one hundred days. Nor will it be finished in the first one thousand days, nor in the life of this Administration, nor even perhaps in our lifetime on this planet. But let us begin.

In your hands, my fellow citizens, more than mine, will rest the final success or failure of our course. Since this country was founded, each generation of Americans has been summoned to give testimony to its national loyalty. The graves of young Americans who answered the call to service surround the globe.

Now the trumpet summons us—again not as a call to bear arms, though arms we need—not as a call to battle, though embattled we are—but a call to bear the burden of a long twilight struggle, year in and year out, "rejoicing in hope, patient in tribulation"—a struggle against the common enemies of man: tyranny, poverty, disease and war itself. Can we forge against these enemies a grand and global alliance, North and South, East and West, that can assure a more fruitful life for all mankind? Will you join in that historic effort?

In the long history of the world, only a few generations have been granted the role of defending freedom in its hour of maximum danger. I do not shrink from this responsibility—I welcome it. I do not believe that any of us would exchange places with any other people or any other generation. The energy, the faith, the devotion which we bring to this endeavor will light our country and all who serve it—and the glow from that fire can truly light the world. And so, my fellow Americans: ask not what your country can do for you—ask what you can do for your country. My fellow citizens of the world: ask not what America will do for you, but what together we can do for the freedom of man.

Finally, whether you are citizens of America or citizens of the world, ask of us here the same high standards of strength and sacrifice which we ask of you. With a good conscience our only sure reward, with history the final judge of our deeds, let us go forth to lead the land we love, asking His blessing and His help, but knowing that here on earth God's work must truly be our own.

Source: John F. Kennedy, President Inaugural Address, Washington, DC, January 20, 1961.

RESPONDING TO READING

1. What are Kennedy's hopes for the future? What problems does he think the United States must solve? Has the United States solved the problems that Kennedy mentions in his speech, or have they yet to be fully addressed?
2. Near the end of his speech, Kennedy says, "And so, my fellow Americans: ask not what your country can do for you—ask what you can do for your country" (23). What does this famous, often-quoted passage actually mean in practical terms? Do you think this call to action is realistic? Do you think it is fair? Explain.

Rhetorical Analysis

At the beginning of his speech, Kennedy alludes to the "revolutionary beliefs" of Thomas Jefferson and asserts, "We are the heirs of that first revolution" (3–4). What does he mean? Is this a good opening strategy?

Writing with Sources

Do some research online, and find out how Americans reacted to Kennedy's speech at the time it was delivered. Then, find out how they evaluate it today. Write an essay in which you account for the differences.

12.3 Jon Lovett, "Lower the Voting Age to Sixteen"

The host of the podcast *Lovett or Leave It* and a cohost of the podcast *Pod Save America*, Jon Lovett (1982–) is a screenwriter and the founder of Crooked Media. A former presidential speechwriter, he tackles current social and political issues in his work. In the following essay, Lovett proposes a lower voting age in the United States.

BEFORE YOU READ

When was the first time you voted? What does that experience mean to you?

Lower the Voting Age to Sixteen

CNN's Parkland town hall this week[1] was an American spectacle—inspiring and tragic, messy and raw. These were parents holding notes in shaking hands, parrying with professional talkers, the slimy evasions of Washington set against the brutal authority of grief. And then there were the kids. The kids! Students not only of this school but of our culture. Students of Facebook and Snapchat, of a life lived on camera, of reality TV and its narcissism, of cable news and nostalgia and mistrust and Trump. We adopted the dark. These kids were born in it.

And as I watched their rage and their poise and their showmanship, their grit and entitlement and resentment, I was hopeful. While we were failing, these kids were learning. While we were building a Death Star, Emma Gonzáles and Cameron Kasky were stealing the schematics. I was also reminded of something else: these students who have captivated our politics—who have managed to break the loop in our neutered conversation over gun violence, who have signed up to serve our country, who work after-school jobs and pay taxes, who survived slaughter and formed a movement—are told by our society that they are too young and immature to vote.

Bullshit. Bullshit. Bullshit.

With the 26th amendment to the Constitution we lowered the voting age to 18 in part as a response to the burdens young people carried in Vietnam. It's time to lower it again to 16 in recognition of the ways our society has changed in the decades since. It is a reform that is as obvious as it is necessary. Municipalities that have already done this have shown that it can work. Generation Citizen is organizing young people across the country to promote civic involvement and the chance to participate in local elections. Jason Kander, a leader in the fight against voter suppression (and host of a stellar Crooked podcast), has begun arguing for a lower age of eligibility. This is an idea whose time has come. But let's take on a few of the arguments against this expansion of voting rights, many of which have been tweeted at me with varying levels of seriousness, because it helps elucidate just how right I am, which is nice.

5 *Young people are too immature.* It's true that 16-year-old and 17-year-old brains are very much still maturing. There is no clear line between a child's brain and that of an adult, and no two people grow up in the same way at the same

---

[1]This essay was published on February 23, 2018. [Eds.]

rate. What we do know is that one facet of our minds is pretty well formed by the time we're 16, and that's "cold cognition," the kind of mental acuity we employ when we cast a ballot.

If you say a young person can vote, why not let a young person buy a gun, huh? Here's one reason: being reckless and unfit to vote rarely leaves 17 people bleeding to death on the floor of a school. The worst a person can do with a vote is cast it for Donald Trump. And you don't have to be a kid to mess that up. Trump's election is the baby boomer super nova.

If you think young people should vote, I suppose you don't have a problem with trying young people as adults in court. First of all, we already do that. Young defendants are already sentenced to life in prison by a government they had no hand in choosing. Second, as a society we see the wisdom in meting out the privileges and responsibilities of adulthood in pieces. 18 year olds in Florida can buy AR-15s but not beer. 23 year olds can drive tanks but not rental cars. Believing that young people deserve a say in our democracy is not to say that 16 year olds are full-fledged adults. They're not! That some of these distinctions are arbitrary and hard to draw doesn't absolve us of the moral harm of denying capable teenagers a voice.

They'll just vote how their parents tell them to. Have you ever met a 17 year old?

This creep just wants to lower the age of consent. I am including this response despite the fact that it is offered by right-wing trolls because it genuinely surprised me and came up a lot. It did not occur to me that someone would view the right to vote as a means of sexualizing children, but from the deepest part of my heart: fuck you.

LOL Tide Pods.[2] This charming argument underlies most responses—that 10
this is somehow silly and obviously wrong because, have you seen the youth? Do you know what 16 year olds and 17 year olds are like? They're oily impulsive little dumb dumbs eating poison for the clicks! Look at that rude boy arguing with a senator. Look at these kids on their phones in the movies. The kids today. Well, if we are denying segments of society the right to vote based on the worst specimens in their cohorts, there will be no one left to cast a ballot. I was 20 when we broke onto the roof of Mission dorm to throw watermelons onto pavement from a great height. (That this boring inoffensive example is the best I can offer is why I ended up working in politics.)

Some young people will take their vote seriously. Some won't. Some will show up. Some won't. Some will read every endorsement and argument. Some will forget or say voting doesn't matter. Some will vote just like their parents. Some will vote to spite their parents and then brag about it at dinner in a way that will be incredibly annoying. In other words, teenagers will vote like the rest of us, except maybe more often over the course of their lives. As Joshua Douglas has noted,

[2]In 2017, the "Tide Pod challenge" emerged on social media, prompting teens to willingly eat poisonous laundry detergent as a dare. [Eds.]

whereas 18 is a period of transition, 16 and 17 is often more stable, a time when we are learning civic virtues and when it would be far easier to begin a lifelong routine of voting.

The right to vote was once confined to white men who owned land, and some free black men who managed to cast ballots between eras of prohibition and terror. Over our history, the right has expanded to include native Americans, and those born into a system of enslavement, and women, and young people. It has also contracted. It has been ripped away from southern blacks, denied to former felons, and taken from people swept up in partisan purges of voter rolls. Often, the disempowered who demanded participation in our democracy were told it was absurd until bullied into not asking again. Those who held the franchise held it close because it was theirs and because it was power. Even now we fight to restore the vote to people who served their sentences and paid their debt to society. Even now we see a coordinated effort to manufacture fear of voter impersonation fraud—a practically non-existent crime—that has made it harder for poor and minority voters to cast ballots. We know the power of the vote. It is about more than a tiny say in a contest between just-OK politicians. It is a statement of citizenship. It is a symbol of belonging and of the equal dignity of people who live under rules set by their government. It is the first American spectacle.

There has been so much hand wringing about this up-and-coming generation. So much moralizing about the prolonged adolescence of millennials and those that follow, of delayed marriage and childbirth, of kids staying on their parents' health insurance, of softness and snowflakes and safe spaces and participation trophies. This is in part the result of a positive shift—a recognition of the arbitrariness of 18 as a demarcation, of the slow and winding process of growing up. But here is a place where we can set one line earlier, not later. We can empower young people to think like citizens and adults. We can say: you are young but you are not without agency in your life or the life of your school, your city, your state, your country. You are young but it is time you get in the habit of democracy. You are young but voting isn't for other people. It's for you. It has to be.

One of the many questions those extraordinary Stoneman Douglas students asked was offered by Annabel Quinn Claprood. "I just want to know," she asked, "Will my school campus be safe when I return?" No one could answer that question to any satisfaction. And not just in the obvious way, that it's not possible to make such a promise. It was worse than that. No, Annabel, your school is not safe. It's not safe at all. No school is safe. No concert is safe. No movie theater is safe. No mall is safe. No mosque is safe. No temple is safe. No church is safe. No street is safe. No home is safe.

15 This country is not safe for you. It's not keeping you safe from gun violence. It's not protecting your generation from rising seas and burning forests. It's not safeguarding your financial future when the government borrows more than a trillion dollars for tax cuts to help corporations and wealthy heirs. It's not investing in the economy you'll inherit by building public infrastructure that meet the standards set by other countries. It's not ensuring your success by helping you afford college. It's not defending you against the excesses of corporate greed. And you certainly will not be safe from the rot in our political culture—the abandonment of

virtue and community and integrity, the collapse of basic decency, that made it possible for someone like Trump to attain the highest office in the land.

In our actions, in our failures, America is sending a message to teenagers: this country doesn't give a shit about you. Teenagers deserve the vote because the rest of us have proven that we are not adult enough to have their interests at heart. The NRA is right about the importance of self-defense, but wrong about the means. Voting is how America's young people can protect themselves.

Source: Jon Lovett. "Lower the Voting Age to Sixteen." Crooked Media, February 23, 2018. Used by permission.

RESPONDING TO READING

1. What arguments against his position does Lovett identify? Does he effectively refute, or argue against, these counterarguments? Explain.
2. In paragraph 12, Lovett calls the vote "the first American spectacle." What does he mean? How does Lovett predict U.S. society will change if the voting age is lowered? Does he provide enough evidence to support his prediction? Explain.

Rhetorical Analysis

Consider Lovett's use of profanity in this essay. Is it necessary? Does it add to or detract from his credibility? Explain.

Writing with Sources

Research the social and political context of 1971, when President Richard Nixon lowered the voting age to eighteen. Then, write an essay in which you argue that today's cultural climate either does or does not demand a similar political response.

12.4 Joel Kotkin, "The Changing Demographics of America"

A presidential fellow in urban futures at Chapman University, Joel Kotkin (1952–) is an executive editor of *Newgeography.com*. His work has appeared in such publications as the Daily Beast, Forbes, *Newsweek, The New York Times, Politico, RealClearPolitics*, the *Wall Street Journal*, and *The Washington Post*. He is the author of several books, including, most recently, *The Human City: Urbanism for the Rest of Us* (2016). The following essay was adapted from his 2010 book *The Next Hundred Million: America in 2050*.

BEFORE YOU READ

Overall, is your view of the United States optimistic or pessimistic? Explain.

The Changing Demographics of America

Estimates of the U.S. population at the middle of the 21st century vary, from the U.N.'s 404 million to the U.S. Census Bureau's 422 to 458 million. To develop a snapshot of the nation at 2050, particularly its astonishing diversity and youthfulness, I use the nice round number of 400 million people, or roughly 100 million more than we have today.

The United States is also expected to grow somewhat older. The portion of the population that is currently at least 65—13 percent—is expected to reach about 20 percent by 2050. This "graying of America" has helped convince some commentators of the nation's declining eminence. For example, international relations expert Parag Khanna envisions a "shrunken America" lucky to eke out a meager existence between a "triumphant China" and a "retooled Europe." Morris Berman, a cultural historian, says America "is running on empty."

But even as the baby boomers age, the population of working and young people is also expected to keep rising, in contrast to most other advanced nations. America's relatively high fertility rate—the number of children a woman is expected to have in her lifetime—hit 2.1 in 2006, with 4.3 million total births, the highest levels in 45 years. That's thanks largely to recent immigrants, who tend to have more children than residents whose families have been in the United States for several generations. Moreover, the nation is on the verge of a baby boomlet, when the children of the original boomers have children of their own.

Between 2000 and 2050, census data suggest, the U.S. 15-to-64 age group is expected to grow 42 percent. In contrast, because of falling fertility rates, the number of young and working-age people is expected to decline elsewhere: by 10 percent in China, 25 percent in Europe, 30 percent in South Korea and more than 40 percent in Japan.

5 Within the next four decades, most of the developed countries in Europe and East Asia will become veritable old-age homes: A third or more of their populations will be over 65. By then, the United States is likely to have more than 350 million people under 65.

The prospect of an additional 100 million Americans by 2050 worries some environmentalists. A few have joined traditionally conservative xenophobes and anti-immigration activists in calling for a national policy to slow population growth by severely limiting immigration. The U.S. fertility rate—50 percent higher than that of Russia, Germany and Japan and well above that of China, Italy, Singapore, South Korea and virtually all the rest of Europe—has also prompted criticism.

Colleen Heenan, a feminist author and environmental activist, says Americans who favor larger families are not taking responsibility for "their detrimental contribution" to population growth and "resource shortages." Similarly, Peter

Kareiva, the chief scientist at the Nature Conservancy, compared different conservation measures and concluded that not having a child is the most effective way of reducing carbon emissions and becoming an "eco hero."

Such critiques don't seem to take into account that a falling population and a dearth of young people may pose a greater threat to the nation's well-being than population growth. A rapidly declining population could create a society that doesn't have the work force to support the elderly and, overall, is less concerned with the nation's long-term future.

The next surge in growth may be delayed if tough economic times continue, but over time the rise in births, producing a generation slightly larger than the boomers, will add to the work force, boost consumer spending and generate new entrepreneurial businesses. And even with 100 million more people, the United States will be only one-sixth as crowded as Germany is today.

Immigration will continue to be a major force in U.S. life. The United Nations 10
estimates that 2 million people a year will move from poorer to developed nations over the next 40 years, and more than half of those will come to the United States, the world's preferred destination for educated, skilled migrants. In 2000, according to the Organization for Economic Co-operation and Development, an association of 30 democratic, free-market countries, the United States was home to 12.5 million skilled immigrants, equaling the combined total for Germany, France, the United Kingdom, Australia, Canada and Japan.

If recent trends continue, immigrants will play a leading role in our future economy. Between 1990 and 2005, immigrants started one out of four venture-backed public companies. Large American firms are also increasingly led by people with roots in foreign countries, including 15 of the Fortune 100 CEOs in 2007.

For all these reasons, the United States of 2050 will look different from that of today: Whites will no longer be in the majority. The U.S. minority population, currently 30 percent, is expected to exceed 50 percent before 2050. No other advanced, populous country will see such diversity.

In fact, most of America's net population growth will be among its minorities, as well as in a growing mixed-race population. Latino and Asian populations are expected to nearly triple, and the children of immigrants will become more prominent. Today in the United States, 25 percent of children under age 5 are Hispanic; by 2050, that percentage will be almost 40 percent.

Growth places the United States in a radically different position from that of Russia, Japan and Europe. Russia's low birth and high mortality rates suggest its overall population will drop 30 percent by 2050, to less than a third of the United States'. While China's population will continue to grow for a while, it may begin to experience decline as early as 2035, first in work force and then in actual population, mostly because of the government's one-child mandate, instituted in 1979 and still in effect. By 2050, 31 percent of China's population will be older than 60. More than 41 percent of Japanese will be that old.

Political prognosticators say China and India pose the greatest challenges to 15
American predominance. But China, like Russia, lacks the basic environmental protections, reliable legal structures, favorable demographics and social resilience of the United States. India still has an overwhelmingly impoverished population

and suffers from ethnic, religious and regional divisions. The vast majority of the Indian population remains semiliterate and lives in poor rural villages.

Suburbia will continue to be a mainstay of American life. Despite criticisms that suburbs are culturally barren and energy-inefficient, most U.S. metropolitan population growth has taken place in suburbia, confounding oft-repeated predictions of its decline.

Some aspects of suburban life—notably long-distance commuting and heavy reliance on fossil fuels—will have to change. The new suburbia will be far more environmentally friendly—what I call "greenurbia." The Internet, wireless phones, video conferencing and other communication technologies will allow more people to work from home: At least one in four or five will do so full time or part time, up from roughly one in six or seven today.

A new landscape may emerge, one that resembles the network of smaller towns characteristic of 19th-century America. The nation's landmass is large enough—about 3 percent is currently urbanized—to accommodate this growth, while still husbanding critical farmland and open space.

In other advanced nations where housing has become both expensive and dense—Japan, Germany, South Korea and Singapore—birthrates have fallen, partly because of the high cost of living, particularly for homes large enough to comfortably raise children. Preserving suburbs may therefore be critical for U.S. demographic vitality.

20 A 2009 study by the Brookings Institution found that between 1998 and 2006, jobs shifted away from the center and to the periphery in 95 out of 98 leading metropolitan regions—from Dallas and Los Angeles to Chicago and Seattle. Walter Siembab, a planning consultant, calls the process of creating sustainable work environments on the urban periphery "smart sprawl."

Super-fuel-efficient cars of the future are likely to spur smart sprawl. They may be a more reasonable way to meet environmental needs than shifting back to the mass-transit-based models of the industrial age; just 5 percent of the U.S. population uses mass transit on a daily basis.

Suburbs epitomize much of what constitutes the American dream for many people. Minorities, once largely associated with cities, tend to live in the suburbs; in 2008 they were a majority of residents in Texas, New Mexico, California and Hawaii. Nationwide, about 25 percent of suburbanites are minorities; by 2050 immigrants, their children and native-born minorities will become an even more dominant force in shaping suburbia.

The baby boom generation is poised for a large-scale "back to the city" movement, according to many news reports. But Sandra Rosenbloom, a University of Arizona gerontology professor, says roughly three-quarters of retirees in the first bloc of boomers appear to be sticking close to the suburbs, where the vast majority reside.

"Everybody in this business wants to talk about the odd person who moves downtown," Rosenbloom observes. "[But] most people retire in place. When they move, they don't move downtown, they move to the fringes."

25 To be sure, there will be 15 million to 20 million new urban dwellers by 2050. Many will live in what Wharton business professor Joseph Gyourko calls

"superstar cities," such as San Francisco, Boston, Manhattan and western Los Angeles—places adapted to business and recreation for the elite and those who work for them. By 2050, Seattle, Portland and Austin could join their ranks.

But because these elite cities are becoming too expensive for the middle class, the focus of urban life will shift to cities that are more spread out and, by some standards, less attractive. They're what I call "cities of aspiration," such as Phoenix, Houston, Dallas, Atlanta and Charlotte. They'll facilitate upward mobility, as New York and other great industrial cities once did, and begin to compete with the superstar cities for finance, culture and media industries, and the amenities that typically go along with them.

What the United States does with its demographic dividend—its relatively young working-age population—is critical. Simply to keep pace with the growing U.S. population, the nation needs to add 125,000 jobs a month, the New America Foundation estimates. Without robust economic growth but with an expanding population, the country will face a massive decline in living standards.

Entrepreneurs, small businesses and self-employed workers will become more common. Between 1980 and 2000 the number of self-employed individuals expanded, to about 15 percent of the work force. More workers will live in an economic environment like that of Hollywood or Silicon Valley, with constant job hopping and changes in alliances among companies.

For much of American history, race has been the greatest barrier to a common vision of community. Race still remains all too synonymous with poverty: Considerably higher poverty rates for blacks and Hispanics persist. But the future will most likely see a dimming of economic distinctions based on ethnic origins.

The most pressing social problem facing mid-21st-century America will be 30
fulfilling the historic promise of upward mobility. In recent decades, certain high-end-occupation incomes grew rapidly, while wages for lower-income and middle-class workers stagnated. Even after the 2008 economic downturn, largely brought on by Wall Street, it was primarily middle-class homeowners and jobholders who bore the brunt, sometimes losing their residences.

Most disturbingly, the rate of upward mobility has stagnated overall, as wages have largely failed to keep up with the cost of living. It is no easier for poor and working-class people to move up the socio-economic ladder today than it was in the 1970s; in some ways, it's more difficult. The income of college-educated younger people, adjusted for inflation, has been in decline since 2000.

To reverse these trends, I think Americans will need to attend to the nation's basic investments and industries, including manufacturing, energy and agriculture. This runs counter to the fashionable assertion that the American future can be built around a handful of high-end creative jobs and will not require reviving the old industrial economy.

A more competitive and environmentally sustainable America will rely on technology. Fortunately, no nation has been more prodigious in its ability to apply new methods and techniques to solve fundamental problems; the term "technology" was invented in America in 1829. New energy finds, unconventional fuel sources and advanced technology are likely to ameliorate the long-prophesied energy catastrophe.

And technology can ease or even reverse the environmental costs of growth. With a population of 300 million, the United States has cleaner air and water now than 40 years ago, when the population was 200 million.

35 The America of 2050 will most likely remain the one truly transcendent superpower in terms of society, technology and culture. It will rely on what has been called America's "civil religion"—its ability to forge a unique common national culture amid great diversity of people and place. We have no reason to lose faith in the possibilities of the future.

Source: Kotkin, Joel. "The Changing Demographics of America" Smithsonian Magazine, August 2010. Used with Permission.

RESPONDING TO READING

1. How does Kotkin respond to those who say that the United States is in decline? How does he respond to those who encourage American families to have fewer children? Do you find his arguments convincing?
2. What effect will the demographic trends Kotkin describes have on cities? On suburbs? On workers? What does Kotkin think will be the most pressing social problem facing mid-twenty-first-century America?

Rhetorical Analysis

For the most part, Kotkin uses statistics to support his points. What other kinds of evidence could he have used? Should he have included other types of evidence in his essay? Explain.

Writing with Sources

Examine the demographic trends in the United States since 2010, when Kotkin's essay appeared. Write an essay in which you evaluate Kotkin's essay in light of these trends.

12.5 Alexis C. Madrigal, "Future Historians Probably Won't Understand Our Internet, and That's Okay"

A journalist, staff writer for The Atlantic, and a visiting scholar at the UC Berkeley School of Information, Alexis C. Madrigal (1982–) writes about issues related to social media, television, and politics. He is the author of *Powering the Dream: The History and Promise of Green Technology* (2011). In the following essay, Madrigal considers the future of data preservation.

BEFORE YOU READ

Have you noticed that your Google search results for the same search terms are sometimes different from your friends'? How do you explain why you see what you see in your Facebook feed? What do you think accounts for these different user experiences?

Future Historians Probably Won't Understand Our Internet, and That's Okay

What's happening?

This has always been an easier question to pose—as Twitter does to all its users—than to answer. And how well we answer the question of what is happening in our present moment has implications for how this current period will be remembered. Historians, economists, and regular old people at the corner store all have their methods and heuristics for figuring out how the world around them came to be. The best theories require humility; nearly everything that has happened to anyone produced no documentation, no artifacts, nothing to study.

The rise of social media in the '00s *seemed* to offer a new avenue for exploring what was happening with unprecedented breadth. After all, people were committing ever larger amounts of information about themselves, their friends, and the world to the servers of social-networking companies. Optimism about this development peaked in 2010, when Twitter gave its archive and ongoing access to public tweets to the Library of Congress. Tweets in the record of America! "It boggles my mind to think what we might be able to learn about ourselves and the world around us from this wealth of data," a library spokesperson exclaimed in a blog post. "And I'm certain we'll learn things that none of us now can even possibly conceive."

Unfortunately, one of the things the library learned was that the Twitter data overwhelmed the technical resources and capacities of the institution. By 2013, the library had to admit that a single search of just the Twitter data from 2006 to 2010 could take *24 hours*. Four years later, the archive still is not available to researchers.

Across the board, the reality began to sink in that these proprietary services 5
hold volumes of data that no public institution can process. And that's just the data itself.

What about the actual functioning of the application: What tweets are displayed to whom in what order? Every major social-networking service uses opaque algorithms to shape what data people see. Why does Facebook show you *this* story and not *that* one? No one knows, possibly not even the company's engineers. Outsiders know basically nothing about the specific choices these algorithms make. Journalists and scholars have built up some inferences about the general features of these systems, but our understanding is severely limited. So, even if the LOC has the database of tweets, they still wouldn't have *Twitter*.

In a new paper, "Stewardship in the 'Age of Algorithms,'" Clifford Lynch, the director of the Coalition for Networked Information, argues that the paradigm for preserving digital artifacts is not up to the challenge of preserving what happens on social networks.

Over the last 40 years, archivists have begun to gather more digital objects—web pages, PDFs, databases, kinds of software. There is more data about more people than ever before, however, the cultural institutions dedicated to preserving the memory of what it was to be alive in our time, including our hours on the internet, may actually be capturing less usable information than in previous eras.

"We always used to think for historians working 100 years from now: We need to preserve the bits (the files) and emulate the computing environment to show what people saw a hundred years ago," said Dan Cohen, a professor at Northeastern University and the former head of the Digital Public Library of America. "Save the HTML and save what a browser was and what Windows 98 was and what an Intel chip was. That was the model for preservation for a decade or more."

Which makes sense: If you want to understand how WordPerfect, an old word processor, functioned, then you just need that software and some way of running it.

But if you want to document the *experience* of using Facebook five years ago or even two weeks ago . . . how do you do it?

The truth is, right now, you can't. No one (outside Facebook, at least) has preserved the functioning of the application. And worse, there is no *thing* that can be squirreled away for future historians to figure out. "The existing models and conceptual frameworks of preserving some kind of 'canonical' digital artifacts are increasingly inapplicable in a world of pervasive, unique, personalized, non-repeatable performances," Lynch writes.

Nick Seaver of Tufts University, a researcher in the emerging field of "algorithm studies," wrote a broader summary of the issues with trying to figure out what is happening on the internet. He ticks off the problems of trying to pin down—or in our case, archive—how these web services work. One, they're always testing out new versions. So there isn't one Google or one Bing, but "10 million different permutations of Bing." Two, as a result of that testing and their own internal decision-making, "You can't log into the same Facebook twice." It's constantly changing in big and small ways. Three, the number of inputs and complex interactions between them simply makes these large-scale systems very difficult to understand, even if we have access to outputs and some knowledge of inputs.

"What we recognize or 'discover' when critically approaching algorithms from the outside is often partial, temporary, and contingent," Seaver concludes.

The world as we experience it seems to be growing more opaque. More of life now takes place on digital platforms that are different for everyone, closed to inspection, and massively technically complex. What we don't know now about our current experience will resound through time in historians of the future knowing less, too. Maybe this era will be a new dark age, as resistant to analysis then as it has become now.

If we *do* want our era to be legible to future generations, our "memory organizations" as Lynch calls them, must take radical steps to probe and document social networks like Facebook. Lynch suggests creating persistent, socially embedded bots that exist to capture a realistic and demographically broad set of experiences on these platforms. Or, alternatively, archivists could go out and recruit actual humans to opt in to having their experiences recorded, as *ProPublica* has done with political advertising on Facebook.

Lynch's suggestion is radical for the archival community. Archivists generally allow other people to document the world, and then they preserve, index, and make these records available. Lynch contends that when it comes to the current social media, that just doesn't work. If they want to accurately capture what it was like to live online today, archivists, and other memory organizations, will have to actively build technical tools and cultural infrastructure to understand the "performances" of these algorithmic systems. But, at least right now, this is not going to happen.

"I loved this paper. It laid out a need that is real, but as part of the paper, it also said, 'Oh, by the way, this is impossible and intractable,'" said Leslie Johnston, director of digital preservation at the U.S. National Archives. "It was realistic in understanding that this is a very hard thing to accomplish with our current professional and technical constructs."

Archivists are encountering the same difficulties that journalists and scholars have run up against studying these technologies. In an influential paper from last year, Jenna Burrell of the University of California's School of Information highlighted the opacity that frustrates outsiders looking at corporate algorithms. Obviously, companies want to protect their own proprietary software. And the code and systems built around the code are complex. But more fundamentally, there is a mismatch between how the machines function and how humans think. "When a computer learns and consequently builds its own representation of a classification decision, it does so without regard for human comprehension," Burrell writes. "Machine optimizations based on training data do not naturally accord with human semantic explanations."

This is the most novel part of what makes archiving our internet difficult. 20
There are pieces of the internet that simply don't function on human or human-generated or human-parse-able principles.

While Seaver of Tufts University considered Lynch's proposals to create an archival bot or human army to record the experience of being on an internet service plausible, he cautioned that "it's really hard to go from a user experience to what is going on under the hood."

Still, Seaver sees these technical systems not as totally divorced from humans, but as complex arrangements of people doing different things.

"Algorithms aren't artifacts, they are collections of human practices that are in interaction with each other," he told me. And that's something that people in the social sciences have been trying to deal with since the birth of their fields. They have learned at least one thing: It's really difficult. "One thing you can do is replace the word 'algorithm' with the word 'society,'" Seaver said. "It has always been hard to document the present [functioning of a society] for the future."

The archivist, Johnston, expressed a similar sentiment about the (lack of) novelty of the current challenge. She noted that people working in "collection-development theory"—the people who choose what to archive—have always had to make do with limited coverage of an era, doing their best to try to capture the salient features of a society. "Social media is not unlike a personal diary," she said. "It's more expansive. It is a public diary that has a graph of relationships built into it. But there is a continuity of archival practice."

25 So, maybe our times are not so different from previous eras. Lynch himself points out that "the rise of the telephone meant that there were a vast number of person-to-person calls that were never part of the record and that nobody expected to be." Perhaps Facebook communications should fall into a similar bucket. For a while it seemed exciting and smart to archive everything that happened online *because it seemed possible*. But now that it might not actually be possible, maybe that's okay.

"Is it terrible that not everything that happens right now will be remembered forever?" Seaver said. "Yeah, that's crappy, but it's historically quite the norm."

Source: Alexis C. Madrigal (December, 2017). Future Historians Probably Won't Understand Our Internet, and That's Okay. © 2008 The Atlantic Media Co., as first published in The Atlantic Magazine. All rights reserved. Distributed by Tribune Content Agency, LLC.

RESPONDING TO READING

1. According to Madrigal, why does it matter that we archive our communications for future generations? How does social media present new challenges to this endeavor?
2. In paragraph 15, Madrigal writes, "The world as we experience it seems to be growing more opaque. More of life now takes place on digital platforms that are different for everyone, closed to inspection, and massively technically complex." What does he mean? What are the implications of this situation for the future?

Rhetorical Analysis

Much of this essay is a comparison. What two things is Madrigal comparing? How does this comparison help to support his argument?

Writing with Sources

Find information about recent updates to the *Google* and *Facebook* algorithms. Then, choose one of these updates and write an essay in which you predict how it will affect the future user experience.

12.6 Alex Wagner, from *Futureface: A Family Mystery, an Epic Quest, and the Secret to Belonging*

Journalist Alex Wagner (1977–) is a cohost of Showtime's *The Circus*, a CBS News correspondent, and a contributing editor at *The Atlantic*. She writes about a range of topics related to media, politics, and immigration. She is the author of *Futureface: A Family Mystery, an Epic Quest, and the Secret to Belonging* (2018), in which the following excerpt appeared as the introduction. Here, Wagner considers the divisions within and between us.

BEFORE YOU READ

Describe what you think Americans will look like in the next hundred years.

---

from *Futureface: A Family Mystery, an Epic Quest, and the Secret to Belonging*

There is a line between Us and Them, and I've seen it. Or at least part of it. Along the Arizona-Mexico border—in the American town of Nogales and the county of Santa Cruz—is a cloud-scraping thirty-foot fence made of vertical steel rods lodged in concrete. In theory, border fences like this are built to keep citizens from both countries on their respective sides of the border. In truth, the fence, erected by Americans, is intended to keep Mexicans in Mexico. And to keep America... American. Safe from invasion and confusion, strong in its defenses, discerning in its welcome.

It's only mildly effective.

Back when I visited the border, I was the anchor of a cable news show, and the border had become a fairly obsessive focus of mine. I wasn't alone. The border had become an obsession for a lot of people, not least the men and women assigned to police it, the American border patrol. Our country was spending billions of dollars guarding that border with agents, drones, cameras, and exotic military hardware. The fence was only the most visible sign of our extravagant vigilance—and I went to Nogales to see it up close.

We took a break from shooting to eat lunch, ad I noticed that the border patrol had stationed a sentry further down along the barrier. We, meanwhile, had cameras with us, lights, makeup artists—a whole crew. But neither law enforcement nor the media presence did anything to stop a pair of fruit sellers on the Mexican side of the wall from lassoing a rope to the top of a border fence post, climbing up, and rappelling down to the American side of the border. All in broad daylight, in under five minutes. Those two fruit sellers made a mockery of that wall—and it was mesmerizing. Here was an act of alchemy: The two of them, in an instant, transformed themselves from Mexicans—in the land of their ancestors, feet planted on a patch of earth to which they unquestionably belonged—to intruders.

5 All of a sudden, they were part of a different story, one that they would in some way change, if only by adding to its supply of readily available and delicious fruit. And they weren't just crossing a visible wall marking an invisible border. They were crossing a line inside themselves: between the native and the immigrant, the one who belonged and the uninvited stranger. They had become something new. That sprint over the wall was, in microcosm, the adventure story that has defined and threatened human existence from the beginning—a movement from one land to another. But was it flight or invasion or just an act of survival? Those fruit sellers hit the ground, composed themselves in a blink, and embarked, with quick steps, on the day's business. And nobody said a word.

Stories like this—about immigrants, refugees, exiles, and internal migrants—have always had a hold on me, perhaps because of my own family's history of migrations, escapes, settlement, assimilation, and, um, amnesia. But these are universal struggles, too, and they have reappeared again and again in my professional life: when I was the editor of a music magazine, the director of a global nonprofit, a political journalist. Usually, we understand them as human rights concerns or battles over resources like land or jobs or government assistance. But I, at least, also see them as complicated romances.

For a few months in 2013, I spent a not-insignificant amount of time researching Maricopa Country, Arizona, intrigued by the twisted drama unfolding in a community of retirees; descendants of homesteaders; Latinos whose families had been there for centuries; Native Americans whose families had been there for millennia; and new immigrants who had only just crossed deserts or oceans of paperwork to get there from Mexico and Central America. In all of that longing and violence, possessiveness and anger—in the battles between these waves of immigrants and exiles, refugees and natives—what did it mean to belong? Just as crucially: Who got to decide? Each answer gave rise to new questions.

In reality, immigration isn't just outside versus inside, the lawful versus the illegal. It's a story about the messy, sad, terrifying, and occasionally beautiful experience of leaving one place and starting over in another. I realized that my interest in the subject wasn't simply about the politics, but in immigration as an interior act—becoming something new—and as the social act of losing one home and making another. Immigration raises into relief some of our most basic existential questions: Who am I? Where do I belong? And in that way, it's inextricably tied to an exploration of American identity. Here we are, in a nation of immigrants, exiles, captives, refugees, and displaced natives, staring together into that existential void.

These are the questions many of us either devote our lives to answering or spend our lives evading. They are questions I've asked myself—without much in the way of conclusion—when I thought about my Burmese mother and American father, when I thought about the country that pushed and pulled me, when I thought about friendship and loneliness and the possibility of having my own child and attempting to guide that child to some inextricable truth about Our People. All this contemplation made me identity hungry and identity fatigued—it made me want a simple answer, an easy story about who we are and why we're here together. I started to see my preoccupation with immigrants, exiles, and refugees—and the attendant concerns about home and identity and belonging—as the edge of a longer, more complex puzzle. Turns out, the mystery I was really trying to solve was my own.

RESPONDING TO READING

1. According to Wagner, how is immigration both an "interior act" and a "social act" (8)?
2. What is the relationship between people's origins and their future prospects? Between their sense of belonging and their sense of self? Why does Wagner think we are all "staring together into that existential void" (8)? What are the implications for this uncertain future?

Rhetorical Analysis

In her essay, Wagner talks about both a physical and a metaphorical border. What is the significance of these divisions? How might they affect our future interactions with others?

Writing with Sources

Find images online of the United States-Mexico border. Then, write a character sketch of the border, explaining how it looks, what it might think about, what it might say, and how it might feel.

12.7 Neal Stephenson, "Innovation Starvation"

Neal Stephenson (1959–) writes science fiction and essays with an emphasis on technology and the future. He is the author of several novels, including, most recently, the coauthored novel *The Rise and Fall of D.O.D.O.* (2017). His work has also appeared in *Wired* magazine, *World Policy Journal*, and other publications. In the following essay, Stephenson considers the future of creativity.

BEFORE YOU READ

Do you worry that we will not be able to match the scientific and technical achievements of the past? Or do you believe our greatest achievements in these areas are yet to come?

Innovation Starvation

My lifespan encompasses the era when the United States of America was capable of launching human beings into space. Some of my earliest memories are of sitting on a braided rug before a hulking black-and-white television, watching the early Gemini missions. This summer, at the age of 51—not even old—I watched on a flatscreen as the last Space Shuttle lifted off the pad. I have followed the dwindling of the space program with sadness, even bitterness. Where's my donut-shaped space station? Where's my ticket to Mars? Until recently, though, I have kept my feelings to myself. Space exploration has always had its detractors. To complain about its demise is to expose oneself to attack from those who have no sympathy that an affluent, middle-aged white American has not lived to see his boyhood fantasies fulfilled.

Still, I worry that our inability to match the achievements of the 1960s space program might be symptomatic of a general failure of our society to get big things done. My parents and grandparents witnessed the creation of the airplane, the automobile, nuclear energy, and the computer to name only a few. Scientists and engineers who came of age during the first half of the 20th century could look forward to building things that would solve age-old problems, transform the landscape, build the economy, and provide jobs for the burgeoning middle class that was the basis for our stable democracy.

The Deepwater Horizon oil spill of 2010 crystallized my feeling that we have lost our ability to get important things done. The OPEC oil shock was in 1973—almost 40 years ago. It was obvious then that it was crazy for the United States to let itself be held economic hostage to the kinds of countries where oil was being produced. It led to Jimmy Carter's proposal for the development of an enormous synthetic fuels industry on American soil. Whatever one might think of the merits of the Carter presidency or of this particular proposal, it was, at least, a serious effort to come to grips with the problem.

Little has been heard in that vein since. We've been talking about wind farms, tidal power, and solar power for decades. Some progress has been made in those areas, but energy is still all about oil. In my city, Seattle, a 35-year-old plan to run a light rail line across Lake Washington is now being blocked by a citizen initiative. Thwarted or endlessly delayed in its efforts to build things, the city plods ahead with a project to paint bicycle lanes on the pavement of thoroughfares.

5 In early 2011, I participated in a conference called Future Tense, where I lamented the decline of the manned space program, then pivoted to energy, indicating that the real issue isn't about rockets. It's our far broader inability as a society to execute on the big stuff. I had, through some kind of blind luck, struck a nerve. The audience at Future Tense was more confident than I that science fiction [SF] had relevance—even utility—in addressing the problem. I heard two theories as to why:

1. The Inspiration Theory. SF inspires people to choose science and engineering as careers. This much is undoubtedly true, and somewhat obvious.

2. The Hieroglyph Theory. Good SF supplies a plausible, fully thought-out picture of an alternate reality in which some sort of compelling innovation has taken place. A good SF universe has a coherence and internal logic that makes sense to scientists and engineers. Examples include Isaac Asimov's robots, Robert Heinlein's rocket ships, and William Gibson's cyberspace. As Jim Karkanias of Microsoft Research puts it, such icons serve as hieroglyphs—simple, recognizable symbols on whose significance everyone agrees.

Researchers and engineers have found themselves concentrating on more and more narrowly focused topics as science and technology have become more complex. A large technology company or lab might employ hundreds or thousands of persons, each of whom can address only a thin slice of the overall problem. Communication among them can become a mare's nest of email threads and Powerpoints. The fondness that many such people have for SF reflects, in part, the usefulness of an over-arching narrative that supplies them and their colleagues with a shared vision. Coordinating their efforts through a command-and-control management system is a little like trying to run a modern economy out of a Politburo.[1] Letting them work toward an agreed-on goal is something more like a free and largely self-coordinated market of ideas.

SPANNING THE AGES

SF has changed over the span of time I am talking about—from the 1950s (the era of the development of nuclear power, jet airplanes, the space race, and the computer) to now. Speaking broadly, the techno-optimism of the Golden Age of SF has given way to fiction written in a generally darker, more skeptical and ambiguous tone. I myself have tended to write a lot about hackers—trickster archetypes who exploit the arcane capabilities of complex systems devised by faceless others.

Believing we have all the technology we'll ever need, we seek to draw attention to its destructive side effects. This seems foolish now that we find ourselves saddled with technologies like Japan's ramshackle 1960's-vintage reactors at Fukushima when we have the possibility of clean nuclear fusion on the horizon. The imperative to develop new technologies and implement them on a heroic scale no longer seems like the childish preoccupation of a few nerds with slide rules. It's the only way for the human race to escape from its current predicaments. Too bad we've forgotten how to do it.

"You're the ones who've been slacking off!" proclaims Michael Crow, president of Arizona State University (and one of the other speakers at Future Tense). He refers, of course, to SF writers. The scientists and engineers, he seems to be saying, are ready and looking for things to do. Time for the SF writers to start pulling their weight and supplying big visions that make sense. Hence the Hieroglyph project, an effort to produce an anthology of new SF that will be in some ways a conscious throwback to the practical techno-optimism of the Golden Age.

---

[1]Communist political committee. [Eds.]

SPACEBORNE CIVILIZATIONS

10 China is frequently cited as a country now executing on Big Stuff, and there's no doubt they are constructing dams, high-speed rail systems, and rockets at an extraordinary clip. But those are not fundamentally innovative. Their space program, like all other countries' (including our own), is just parroting work that was done 50 years ago by the Soviets and the Americans. A truly innovative program would involve taking risks (and accepting failures) to pioneer some of the alternative space launch technologies that have been advanced by researchers all over the world during the decades dominated by rockets.

Imagine a factory mass-producing small vehicles, about as big and complicated as refrigerators, which roll off the end of an assembly line, are loaded with space-bound cargo, and topped off with non-polluting liquid hydrogen fuel, then exposed to intense concentrated heat from an array of ground-based lasers or microwave antennas. Heated to temperatures beyond what can be achieved through a chemical reaction, the hydrogen erupts from a nozzle on the base of the device and sends it rocketing into the air. Tracked through its flight by the lasers or microwaves, the vehicle soars into orbit, carrying a larger payload for its size than a chemical rocket could ever manage, but the complexity, expense, and jobs remain grounded. For decades, this has been the vision of such researchers as physicists Jordin Kare and Kevin Parkin. A similar idea, using a pulsed ground-based laser to blast propellant from the backside of a space vehicle, was being talked about by Arthur Kantrowitz, Freeman Dyson, and other eminent physicists in the early 1960s.

If that sounds too complicated, then consider the 2003 proposal of Geoff Landis and Vincent Denis to construct a 20-kilometer-high tower using simple steel trusses. Conventional rockets launched from its top would be able to carry twice as much payload as comparable ones launched from ground level. There is even abundant research, dating all the way back to Konstantin Tsiolkovsky, the father of astronautics beginning in the late 19th century, to show that a simple tether—a long rope, tumbling end-over-end while orbiting the earth—could be used to scoop payloads out of the upper atmosphere and haul them up into orbit without the need for engines of any kind. Energy would be pumped into the system using an electrodynamic process with no moving parts.

All are promising ideas—just the sort that used to get an earlier generation of scientists and engineers fired up about actually building something.

But to grasp just how far our current mindset is from being able to attempt innovation on such a scale, consider the fate of the space shuttle's external tanks [ETs]. Dwarfing the vehicle itself, the ET was the largest and most prominent feature of the space shuttle as it stood on the pad. It remained attached to the shuttle—or perhaps it makes as much sense to say that the shuttle remained attached to it—long after the two strap-on boosters had fallen away. The ET and the shuttle remained connected all the way out of the atmosphere and into space. Only after the system had attained orbital velocity was the tank jettisoned and allowed to fall into the atmosphere, where it was destroyed on re-entry.

15 At a modest marginal cost, the ETs could have been kept in orbit indefinitely. The mass of the ET at separation, including residual propellants, was about

twice that of the largest possible Shuttle payload. Not destroying them would have roughly tripled the total mass launched into orbit by the Shuttle. ETs could have been connected to build units that would have humbled today's International Space Station. The residual oxygen and hydrogen sloshing around in them could have been combined to generate electricity and produce tons of water, a commodity that is vastly expensive and desirable in space. But in spite of hard work and passionate advocacy by space experts who wished to see the tanks put to use, NASA—for reasons both technical and political—sent each of them to fiery destruction in the atmosphere. Viewed as a parable, it has much to tell us about the difficulties of innovating in other spheres.

EXECUTING THE BIG STUFF

Innovation can't happen without accepting the risk that it might fail. The vast and radical innovations of the mid-20th century took place in a world that, in retrospect, looks insanely dangerous and unstable. Possible outcomes that the modern mind identifies as serious risks might not have been taken seriously—supposing they were noticed at all—by people habituated to the Depression, the World Wars, and the Cold War, in times when seat belts, antibiotics, and many vaccines did not exist. Competition between the Western democracies and the communist powers obliged the former to push their scientists and engineers to the limits of what they could imagine and supplied a sort of safety net in the event that their initial efforts did not pay off. A grizzled NASA veteran once told me that the Apollo moon landings were communism's greatest achievement.

In his recent book *Adapt: Why Success Always Starts with Failure,* Tim Harford outlines Charles Darwin's discovery of a vast array of distinct species in the Galapagos Islands—a state of affairs that contrasts with the picture seen on large continents, where evolutionary experiments tend to get pulled back toward a sort of ecological consensus by interbreeding. "Galapagan isolation" vs. the "nervous corporate hierarchy" is the contrast staked out by Harford in assessing the ability of an organization to innovate.

Most people who work in corporations or academia have witnessed something like the following: A number of engineers are sitting together in a room, bouncing ideas off each other. Out of the discussion emerges a new concept that seems promising. Then some laptop-wielding person in the corner, having performed a quick Google search, announces that this "new" idea is, in fact, an old one—or at least vaguely similar—and has already been tried. Either it failed, or it succeeded. If it failed, then no manager who wants to keep his or her job will approve spending money trying to revive it. If it succeeded, then it's patented and entry to the market is presumed to be unattainable, since the first people who thought of it will have "first-mover advantage" and will have created "barriers to entry." The number of seemingly promising ideas that have been crushed in this way must number in the millions.

What if that person in the corner hadn't been able to do a Google search? It might have required weeks of library research to uncover evidence that the idea wasn't entirely new—and after a long and toilsome slog through many books, tracking down many references, some relevant, some not. When the precedent was finally unearthed, it might not have seemed like such a direct precedent after all. There might be reasons why it would be worth taking a second crack at the idea, perhaps hybridizing it with innovations from other fields. Hence the virtues of Galapagan isolation.

20 The counterpart to Galapagan isolation is the struggle for survival on a large continent, where firmly established ecosystems tend to blur and swamp new adaptations. Jaron Lanier, a computer scientist, composer, visual artist, and author of the recent book *You Are Not a Gadget: A Manifesto,* has some insights about the unintended consequences of the Internet—the informational equivalent of a large continent—on our ability to take risks. In the pre-net era, managers were forced to make decisions based on what they knew to be limited information. Today, by contrast, data flows to managers in real time from countless sources that could not even be imagined a couple of generations ago, and powerful computers process, organize, and display the data in ways that are as far beyond the hand-drawn graph-paper plots of my youth as modern video games are to tic-tac-toe. In a world where decision-makers are so close to being omniscient, it's easy to see risk as a quaint artifact of a primitive and dangerous past.

The illusion of eliminating uncertainly from corporate decision-making is not merely a question of management style or personal preference. In the legal environment that has developed around publicly traded corporations, managers are strongly discouraged from shouldering any risks that they know about—or, in the opinion of some future jury, should have known about—even if they have a hunch that the gamble might pay off in the long run. There is no such thing as "long run" in industries driven by the next quarterly report. The possibility of some innovation making money is just that—a mere possibility that will not have time to materialize before the subpoenas from minority shareholder lawsuits begin to roll in.

Today's belief in ineluctable certainty is the true innovation-killer of our age. In this environment, the best an audacious manager can do is to develop small improvements to existing systems—climbing the hill, as it were, toward a local maximum, trimming fat, eking out the occasional tiny innovation—like city planners painting bicycle lanes on the streets as a gesture toward solving our energy problems. Any strategy that involves crossing a valley—accepting short-term losses to reach a higher hill in the distance—will soon be brought to a halt by the demands of a system that celebrates short-term gains and tolerates stagnation, but condemns anything else as failure. In short, a world where big stuff can never get done.

RESPONDING TO READING

1. Do you think Stephenson's career as a science fiction writer gives him special insight into his subject? What references to science fiction does he make in his essay? How do these references help to reinforce his essay's central point?
2. What is the difference between "Galapagan isolation" and the "nervous corporate hierarchy" (17)? According to Stephenson, how do these two concepts help explain the ability (or inability) of an organization to innovate?

Rhetorical Analysis

Stephenson says that he wonders if our failure "to match the achievements of the 1960s space program" is symptomatic of our general inability "to get big things done" (2). What does he mean? What evidence does he present to support this concern? Does he make a convincing case?

Writing with Sources

In the numbered list in paragraph 5 of his essay, Stephenson mentions "The Hieroglyph Theory." Since this essay appeared, Stephenson has been working on Project Hieroglyph. Research Project Hieroglyph, and then write an essay in which you outline the project's goals and explain whether you think these goals are feasible.

12.8 Focus: "What's Next for the Planet (and Beyond)?"

Photo Yom Lam/Alamy Stock Photo

What does this photo say about the future of the planet?

RESPONDING TO THE IMAGE

Answer one or both of the following questions.

1. The photo above shows Clear Water Bay in Hong Kong. What elements does the image use to depict the choices we make about how to live?
2. What argument might this photo be making? Who is its audience? What is it prompting viewers to do?

12.9 Bill McKibben, "A Moral Atmosphere"

The Schumann Distinguished Scholar of environmental studies at Middlebury College, Bill McKibben (1960–) is a journalist, environmentalist, and cofounder of 350.org. An expert on climate change, he is the author of numerous books, including, most recently, *Radio Free Vermont: A Fable of Resistance* (2017). His work has also appeared in such publications as *National Geographic*, the *New York Review of Books*, and *Rolling Stone*. In the following essay, McKibben considers the morality of environmental decisions.

BEFORE YOU READ

Do you drive to campus, take alternative transportation like a bus or bike, or walk? Why?

A Moral Atmosphere

The list of reasons for not acting on climate change is long and ever-shifting. First it was "there's no problem"; then it was "the problem's so large there's no hope." There's "China burns stuff too," and "it would hurt the economy," and, of course, "it would hurt the economy." The excuses are getting tired, though. Post Sandy[1] (which hurt the economy to the tune of $100 billion) and the drought[2] ($150 billion), 74 percent of Americans have decided they're very concerned about climate change and want something to happen.

But still, there's one reason that never goes away, one evergreen excuse not to act: "you're a hypocrite." I've heard it ten thousand times myself—how can you complain about climate change and drive a car/have a house/turn on a light/raise a child? This past fall, as I headed across the country on a bus tour to push for divestment from fossil fuels, local newspapers covered each stop. I could predict, with great confidence, what the first online comment from a reader following each account would be: "Do these morons not know that their bus takes gasoline?" In fact, our bus took biodiesel—as we headed down the East Coast, one job was watching the web app that showed the nearest station pumping the good stuff. But it didn't matter, because the next comment would be: "Don't these morons know that the plastic fittings on their bus, and the tires, and the seats are all made from fossil fuels?"

Actually, I do know—even a moron like me. I'm fully aware that we're embedded in the world that fossil fuel has made, that from the moment I wake up, almost every action I take somehow burns coal and gas and oil. I've done my best, at my house, to curtail it: we've got solar electricity, and solar hot water, and my new

[1]2012 Hurricane Sandy, the fourth most destructive hurricane in U.S. history. [Eds.]

[2]2012–2013 North American drought. [Eds.]

car runs on electricity—I can plug it into the roof and thus into the sun. But I try not to confuse myself into thinking that's helping all that much: it took energy to make the car, and to make everything else that streams into my life. I'm still using far more than any responsible share of the world's vital stuff.

And, in a sense, that's the point. If those of us who are trying really hard are still fully enmeshed in the fossil fuel system, it makes it even clearer that what needs to change are not individuals but precisely that system. We simply can't move fast enough, one by one, to make any real difference in how the atmosphere comes out. Here's the math, obviously imprecise: maybe 10 percent of the population cares enough to make strenuous efforts to change—maybe 15 percent. If they all do all they can, in their homes and offices and so forth, then, well . . . nothing much shifts. The trajectory of our climate horror stays about the same.

5 But if 10 percent of people, once they've changed the light bulbs, work all-out to change the system? That's enough. That's more than enough. It would be enough to match the power of the fossil fuel industry, enough to convince our legislators to put a price on carbon. At which point none of us would be required to be saints. We could all be morons, as long as we paid attention to, say, the price of gas and the balance in our checking accounts. Which even dummies like me can manage.

I think more and more people are coming to realize this essential truth. Ten years ago, half the people calling out hypocrites like me were doing it from the left, demanding that we do better. I hear much less of that now, mostly, I think, because everyone who's pursued those changes in good faith has come to realize both their importance and their limitations. Now I hear it mostly from people who have no intention of changing but are starting to feel some psychic tension. They feel a little guilty, and so they dump their guilt on Al Gore because he has two houses. Or they find even lamer targets.

For instance, as college presidents begin to feel the heat about divestment, I've heard from several who say, privately, "I'd be more inclined to listen to kids if they didn't show up at college with cars." Which in one sense is fair enough. But in another sense it's avoidance at its most extreme. Young people are asking college presidents to stand up to oil companies. (And the ones doing the loudest asking are often the most painfully idealistic, not to mention the hardest on themselves.) If as a college president you *do* stand up to oil companies, then you stand some chance of changing the outcome of the debate, of weakening the industry that has poured billions into climate denial and lobbying against science. The action you're demanding of your students—less driving—can't rationally be expected to change the outcome. The action they're demanding of you has at least some chance. That makes you immoral, not them.

Yes, they should definitely take the train to school instead of drive. But unless you're the president of Hogwarts, there's a pretty good chance there's no train that goes there. Your students, in other words, by advocating divestment, have gotten way closer to the heart of the problem than you have. They've taken the lessons they've learned in physics class and political science and sociology and economics and put them to good use. And you—because it would be uncomfortable to act, because you don't want to get crosswise with the board of trustees—have summoned a basically bogus response. If you're a college president making the argument that you won't act until your students stop driving cars, then clearly you've failed morally, but you've also failed intellectually. Even if you just built an energy-efficient fine arts center, and installed a bike path, and dedicated an acre of land to a college garden, you've failed. Even if you drive a Prius, you've failed.

Maybe especially if you drive a Prius. Because there's a certain sense in which Prius-driving can become an out, an excuse for inaction, the twenty-first-century equivalent of "I have a lot of black friends." It's nice to walk/drive the talk; it's much smarter than driving a semi-military vehicle to get your groceries. But it's become utterly clear that doing the right thing in your personal life, or even on your campus, isn't going to get the job done in time; and it may be providing you with sufficient psychic comfort that you don't feel the need to do the hard things it will take to get the job done. It's in our role as citizens—of campuses, of nations, of the planet—that we're going to have to solve this problem. We each have our jobs, and none of them is easy.

RESPONDING TO READING

1. Why has McKibben been accused of being a "hypocrite" (2)? Why does he think that environmentalists have been held to different standards? How is that situation changing?
2. In paragraph 7, McKibben introduces an example about college presidents and goes on to address them directly. What purpose does this extended example serve? What does it illustrate about the responsibility that powerful people have to lead environmental change?

Rhetorical Analysis

Consider McKibben's repetition of the word "morons" and his use of the word "dummies" in paragraphs 2 through 5. Why might he have chosen these words? Do they help or hinder his argument? Explain.

Writing with Sources

Research the issue of divestment from fossil fuels. How many U.S. colleges and universities have divested or are considering divesting? Based on your findings, write a letter to your college president that makes a case for or against divestment.

12.10 Ruth Khasaya Oniang'o, "Why What We Eat Is Crucial to the Climate Change Question"

The founder of Rural Outreach Africa and publisher of *Africa Journal of Food and Agriculture,* Ruth Khasaya Oniang'o (1946–) specializes in nutrition science and policy. She is the author of *Feeding the Child* (1988). In the following essay, Oniang'o considers the future of food production and consumption.

BEFORE YOU READ

How much food do you throw out on a weekly basis? A third of what you buy? More? Less?

Why What We Eat Is Crucial to the Climate Change Question

Did you know that what's on your plate plays a larger role in contributing to climate change than the car you drive? When most wealthy people think about their carbon footprint, or their contributions to climate change, they'll think about where their electricity and heat come from or what they drive. They'll think about fossil fuels and miles per gallon, about LED lights and mass transit—but not so much about combine harvesters or processed meals or food waste. Few consider the impacts of the food they eat, despite the fact that globally, food systems account for roughly one quarter of all manmade greenhouse gas emissions. That's more than the entire transportation sector, more than all industrial practices, and roughly the same as the production of electricity and heat.

Meanwhile, the most immediate threat of climate change for most of the global population will be at the dinner table, as our ability to grow critical staple crops is being affected by the warming we've already experienced. Between 1980 and 2008, for instance, wheat yields dropped 5.5% and maize yields fell 3.8% due to rising temperatures. Climate change threatens the food security of millions of poor people around the world. Young people are increasingly keen to protect the environment by shifting to animal-product-free diets. They seek plant proteins which taste like meat, while insects are also growing popular as an alternative.

What these inverse challenges—that food and agriculture are both enormous contributors to climate change, and massively impacted by it—really tell us is that our food systems, as currently structured, are facing major challenges.

There is a much larger problem that implores us to look beyond farm and agricultural practices. We need to open our eyes to solutions that address the full scope of the challenge to create more sustainable and equitable food systems. That way, we can provide healthy food for all people while we protect our planet's resources at the same time.

5 So what are food systems? Everything from seed and soil to the supermarket to the plate to the landfill. Food systems include the growing, harvesting, processing, packaging, transporting, marketing, consumption, and disposal of food and food-related items.

While farming alone accounts for 10–12% of global greenhouse gas emissions, when we look at entire food systems the contributions to climate change more than double. A recent report published by the Meridian Institute lays out the many factors throughout food systems that spell trouble for the climate, and also explains why a broad systems-wide perspective is necessary for implementing effective changes.

Consider deforestation and soil. A narrow view of agriculture alone would neglect the fact that a full 80% of the forests that are clear cut or destroyed are done so to create farmland. Forests are massive carbon sinks. So is soil, locking away two to three times as much carbon as there is present in the atmosphere. But farmers can help restore ecosystem functions and build resilient communities by producing crops and livestock in productive ways that sequester carbon and protect forests.

Or consider food waste. Not just the scraps that you throw away, but throughout the entire food system. A staggering 30–40% of the food produced in the world is never eaten. Some never gets harvested, some spoils before it reaches consumers, and a lot is tossed away by retailers, restaurants, and at home. For the sake of comparing emissions, if food waste were its own country it would be the third largest greenhouse gas emitter in the world, after only China and the United States.

This says nothing of the gross injustice of wasting so much food while so many in the world go hungry. In the developing world, improving infrastructure along the food chain—including cold storage—would prevent much good food being lost. In the developed world, retailers can prevent large amounts of waste by finding outlets for slightly blemished goods and consumers can limit waste by buying food in amounts they actually want and need.

10 There are countless more examples of challenges and solutions all throughout the food system—from production of fertiliser[1] to distribution systems to the production of dried and purified foods that make up processed meals to the diets and lifestyles of the public. Everyone has a role to play; these challenges cannot be solved in a vacuum.

The complex, dynamic, and widely diverse forms of the world's many food systems yield some wildly divergent outcomes in terms of nutrition, health, and environmental and climate impacts. It is critical that we start to better examine what works in some systems and what must be improved in others, in order to produce more equitable, just, and sustainable outcomes around the world.

Just as there's no universal crop that grows everywhere, there's no "one size fits all" model food system to implement across the world. A broader systems-wide perspective is necessary if there is any hope for truly transformative change. It's time to look beyond farming and agriculture and to see the whole picture, to create systems that cause less harm to the climate and are more resilient to the impacts we're already suffering from global warming.

[1]British spellings in this selection have been retained. [Eds.]

Food is a fundamental human need and to eat is a basic human right. Our food systems must deliver that need, fairly and equitably, without worsening the impacts of climate change.

RESPONDING TO READING

1. According to Oniang'o, what specifically is wrong with our current food systems? What are the long-term effects of these systems?
2. In paragraph 12, Oniang'o insists that "A broader systems-wide perspective is necessary if there is any hope for truly transformative change." What exactly is she proposing? Do you think her solution is both realistic and appropriate?

Rhetorical Analysis

Oniang'o incorporates statistics throughout her essay to back up her claims. How convincing is this supporting evidence? Should she have used other types of evidence to describe the problem and propose a solution? Explain.

Writing with Sources

Research food waste in the United States. How big of a problem is it, and what solutions have been proposed? Then, based on your findings, write a letter to the owner of your local grocery chain proposing specific steps he or she might take to reduce food waste.

12.11 Michio Kaku, from *The Future of Humanity: Terraforming Mars, Interstellar Travel, Immortality, and Our Destiny beyond Earth*

The Henry Semat Professor of physics at the City College of New York and a fellow of the American Physical Society, Michio Kaku (1947–) is a theoretical physicist, futurist, and public speaker. The cofounder of String Field Theory, he hosts the radio programs *Exploration* and *Science Fantastic*. His work has appeared in such publications as *Discover*

Magazine, Newsweek, The New York Times, and the *Wall Street Journal.* He is also the author of numerous books, including, most recently, *The Future of Humanity: Terraforming Mars, Interstellar Travel, Immortality, and Our Destiny beyond Earth* (2018), in which the following excerpt appeared as the prologue. In it, Kaku looks at the interconnectedness of our past and future.

BEFORE YOU READ

If you were invited by a group of scientists to travel on an interstellar trip, would you go? Why or why not?

---

from *The Future of Humanity: Terraforming Mars, Interstellar Travel, Immortality, and Our Destiny beyond Earth*

One day about seventy-five thousand years ago, humanity almost died.

A titanic explosion in Indonesia sent up a colossal blanket of ash, smoke, and debris that covered thousands of miles. The eruption of Toba was so violent that it ranks as the most powerful volcanic event in the last twenty-five million years. It blew an unimaginable 670 cubic miles of dirt into the air. This caused large areas of Malaysia and India to be smothered by volcanic ash up to thirty feet thick. The toxic smoke and dust eventually sailed over Africa, leaving a trail of death and destruction in its wake.

Imagine, for a moment, the chaos caused by this cataclysmic event. Our ancestors were terrorized by the searing heat and the clouds of gray ash that darkened the sun. Many were choked and poisoned by the thick soot and dust. Then, temperatures plunged, causing a "volcanic winter." Vegetation and wildlife died off as far as the eye could see, leaving only a bleak, desolate landscape. People and animals were left to scavenge the devastated terrain for tiny scraps of food, and most humans died of starvation. It looked as if the entire Earth was dying. The few who survived had only one goal: to flee as far as they could from the curtain of death that descended on their world.

Stark evidence of this cataclysm may perhaps be found in our blood.

5 Geneticists have noticed the curious fact that any two humans have almost identical DNA. By contrast, any two chimpanzees can have more genetic variation between them than is found in the entire human population. Mathematically, one theory to explain this phenomenon is to assume that, at the time of the explosion, most humans were wiped out, leaving only a handful of us—about two thousand people. Remarkably, this dirty, raggedy band of humans would become the ancestral Adams and Eves who would eventually populate the entire planet. All of us are almost clones of one another, brothers and sisters descended from a tiny, hardy group of humans who could have easily fit inside a modern hotel ballroom.

As they trekked across the barren landscape, they had no idea that one day, their descendants would dominate every corner of our planet.

Today, as we gaze into the future, we see that the events that took place seventy-five thousand years ago may actually be a dress rehearsal for future catastrophes. I was reminded of this in 1992 when I heard the astounding news that, for the first time, a planet orbiting a distant star had been found. With this discovery, astronomers could prove that planets existed beyond our solar system. This was a major paradigm shift in our understanding of the universe. But I was saddened when I heard the next piece of news: this alien planet was orbiting a dead star, a pulsar, that had exploded in a supernova, probably killing everything that might have lived on that planet. No living thing known to science can withstand the withering blast of nuclear energy that emerges when a star explodes close by.

I then imagined a civilization on that planet, aware that their mother sun was dying, working urgently to assemble a huge armada of spaceships that might transport them to another star system. There would have been utter chaos on the planet as people, in panic and desperation, tried to scramble and secure the last few seats on the departing vessels. I imagined the horror felt by those who were left behind to meet their fate as their sun exploded.

It is as inescapable as the laws of physics that humanity will one day confront some type of extinction-level event. But will we, like our ancestors, have the drive and determination to survive and even flourish?

If we scan all the life-forms that have ever existed on the Earth, from micro- 10
scopic bacteria to towering forests, lumbering dinosaurs, and enterprising humans, we find that more than 99.9 percent of them eventually became extinct. This means that extinction is the norm, that the odds are already stacked heavily against us. When we dig beneath our feet into the soil to unearth the fossil record, we see evidence of many ancient life-forms. Yet only the smallest handful survive today. Millions of species have appeared before us; they had their day in the sun, and then they withered and died. That is the story of life.

No matter how much we may treasure the sight of dramatic, romantic sunsets, the smell of fresh ocean breezes, and the warmth of a summer's day, one day it will all end, and the planet will become inhospitable to human life. Nature will eventually turn on us, as it did to all those extinct life-forms.

The grand history of life on Earth shows that faced with a hostile environment, organisms inevitably meet one of three fates. They can leave that environment, they can adapt to it, or they will die. But if we look far enough into the future, we will eventually face a disaster so great that adaptation will be virtually impossible. Either we must leave the Earth or we will perish. There is no other way.

These disasters have happened repeatedly in the past, and they will inevitably happen in the future. The Earth has already sustained five major extinction cycles, in which up to 90 percent of all life-forms vanished from the Earth. As sure as day follows night, there will be more to come.

On a scale of decades, we face threats that are not natural but are largely self-inflicted, due to our own folly and shortsightedness. We face the danger of global warming, when the atmosphere of the Earth itself turns against us. We face the danger of modern warfare, as nuclear weapons proliferate in some of the most unstable regions of the globe. We face the danger of weaponized microbes, such as airborne AIDS or Ebola, which can be transmitted by a simple cough or sneeze. This could wipe out upward of 98 percent of the human race. Furthermore, we face an expanding population that consumes resources at a furious rate. We may exceed the carrying capacity of Earth at some point and find ourselves in an ecological Armageddon, vying for the planet's last remaining supplies.

In addition to calamities that we create ourselves, there are also natural disasters over which we have little control. On a scale of thousands of years, we face the onset of another ice age. For the past one hundred thousand years, much of Earth's surface was blanketed by up to a half mile of solid ice. The bleak frozen landscape drove many animals to extinction. Then, ten thousand years ago, there was a thaw in the weather. This brief warming spell led to the sudden rise of modern civilization, and humans have taken advantage of it to spread and thrive. But this flowering has occurred during an interglacial period, meaning we will likely meet another ice age within the next ten thousand years. When it comes, our cities will disappear under mountains of snow and civilization will be crushed under the ice.

We also face the possibility that the supervolcano under Yellowstone National Park may awaken from its long slumber, tearing the United States apart and engulfing the Earth in a choking, poisonous cloud of soot and debris. Previous eruptions took place 630,000, 1.3 million, and 2.1 million years ago. Each event was separated by roughly 700,000 years; therefore, we may be due for another colossal eruption in the next 100,000 years.

On a scale of millions of years, we face the threat of another meteor or cometary impact, similar to the one that helped to destroy the dinosaurs 65 million years ago. Back then, a rock about six miles across plunged into the Yucatan peninsula of Mexico, sending into the sky fiery debris that rained back on Earth. As with the explosion at Toba, only much larger, the ash clouds eventually darkened the sun and led temperatures to plunge globally. With the withering of vegetation, the food chain collapsed. Plant-eating dinosaurs starved to death, followed soon by their carnivorous cousins. In the end, 90 percent of all life-forms on Earth perished in the wake of this catastrophic event.

For millennia, we have been blissfully ignorant of the reality that the Earth is floating in a swarm of potentially deadly rocks. Only within the last decade have scientists begun to quantify the real risk of a major impact. We now know that there are several thousand NEOs (near-Earth objects) that cross the orbit of the Earth and pose a danger to life on our planet. As of June 2017, 16,294 of these objects have been catalogued. But these are just the ones we've found. Astronomers estimate that there are perhaps several million uncharted objects in the solar system that pass by the Earth.

I once interviewed the late astronomer Carl Sagan about this threat. He stressed to me that "we live in a cosmic shooting gallery," surrounded by potential hazards. It is only a matter of time, he told me, before a large asteroid hits the Earth. If we could somehow illuminate these asteroids, we would see the night sky filled with thousands of menacing points of light.

20 Even assuming we avoid all these dangers, there is another that dwarfs all the others. Five billion years from now, the sun will expand into a giant red star that fills the entire sky. The sun will be so gigantic that the orbit of the Earth will be inside its blazing atmosphere, and the blistering heat will make life impossible within this inferno.

Unlike all other life-forms on this planet, which must passively await their fate, we humans are masters of our own destiny. Fortunately, we are now creating the tools that will defy the odds given to us by nature, so that we don't become one of the 99.9 percent of life-forms destined for extinction, In this book, we will encounter the pioneers who have the energy, the vision, and the resources to change the fate of humanity. We will meet the dreamers who believe that humanity can live and thrive in outer space. We will analyze the revolutionary advances in technology that will make it possible to leave the Earth and to settle elsewhere in the solar system, and even beyond.

But if there is one lesson we can learn from our history, it is that humanity, when faced with life-threatening crises, has risen to the challenge and has reached for even higher goals. In some sense, the spirit of exploration is in our genes and hardwired into our soul.

But now we face perhaps the greatest challenge of all: to leave the confines of the Earth and soar into outer space. The laws of physics are clear; sooner or later we will face global crises that threaten our very existence.

Life is too precious to be placed on a single planet, to be at the mercy of these planetary threats.

25 We need an insurance policy, Sagan told me. He concluded that we should become a "two planet species." In other words, we need a backup plan.

RESPONDING TO READING

1. In paragraph 5, Kaku explains the striking genetic similarities among humans. Why does he include this information? Is it essential to his point?
2. How does Kaku make a case in his essay for interstellar travel? Is it realistic of him to think we can plan for such a future now?

Rhetorical Analysis

Here, in the prologue to his book about the future, Kaku catalogues various catastrophic events that caused mass extinction and are likely to recur. Why do you think he begins his book in this way? Is this an effective strategy?

Writing with Sources

Research the latest developments in achieving interstellar travel. Then, write an essay in which you consider whether this kind of solution to the problems we face would be beneficial or detrimental to humanity.

Widening the Focus

For Critical Reading and Writing

Referring specifically to the three readings in this chapter's Focus section (and possibly to additional sources as well), write an essay in which you answer the question, "What's Next for the Planet (and Beyond)?"

For Further Reading

The following readings can suggest additional perspectives for thinking and writing about the issues that society will face in the future:

- Tao Lin, "When I Moved Online" (p. 66)
- Jill Filipovic, "We've Gone Too Far with Trigger Warnings" (p. 100)
- Dallas Spires, "Will Text Messaging Destroy the English Language?" (p. 128)
- Brent Staples, "Why Race Isn't as 'Black' and 'White' as We Think" (p. 300)
- Barbara Hurd, "Fracking: A Fable" (p. 408)
- Paul Lewis, "'Our Minds Can Be Hijacked': The Tech Insiders Who Fear a Smartphone Dystopia" (p. 414)

For Focused Research

This Focus section offers three views of our future existence, each with its own call to action. Consider the similarities and differences among these essays. Then, do a Google search for examples of ad campaigns that seek to raise awareness of climate change and other environmental crises. Write an essay that considers the following questions: What dominant themes are present in the ads? What are the ads persuading viewers to do? What specific courses of action are they encouraging? Cite key ads to support your points.

Beyond the Classroom

Choose two or three classic science fiction movies that are set in a future that is close to our own time—for example, *2001: A Space Odyssey* (made in 1968 and set in 2001), *Blade Runner* (originally made in 1982 and set in 2019), and *Back to the Future Part II* (made in 1989 and set in 2015). After viewing the movies, write an essay in which you report how accurate their predictions are. What did the movies get right? What did they get wrong? What conclusions can you draw about Hollywood's ability to predict the future?

Exploring Issues and Ideas

Facing the Future

Write an essay in response to one of the following prompts, which are suitable for assignments that require the use of outside sources as well as for assignments that are not source-based.

1. How do you think higher education will change in the future? Will it be widely available or limited to a privileged few? Will traditional instruction be entirely replaced by technology? Will students be offered more practical options than they currently have? Read a few essays in Chapter 4, "Issues in Education," and then, incorporating the information in these essays, write an essay in which you present your ideas on this issue.
2. Over the past several decades, gender roles in the workplace and in society in general have changed considerably. Read Judy Hall's "Mommy, I'm Just Not That Kind of Girl " (p. 215), Fleda Brown's "Unruffled" (p. 218), Warren Farrell and John Gray's "The Crisis of Our Sons' Education" (p. 225), and Debora Spar's "Crashing into Ceilings: A Report from the Nine-to-Five Shift" (p. 360). Then, write an essay in which you discuss how equal (or unequal) male/female/transgender roles will be twenty years from now. Be specific, and refer to the essays you read for this assignment.
3. What do you see as the future of religion in the United States? Do you think that the United States is a country in which religious faith is declining or increasing? Write an essay that explains your position.
4. Write an essay in which you examine where you expect to be ten years after you graduate. Before you write, read "Why We Work" by Andrew Curry (p. 355) and "The Truth Shall Set You Free (from a Lot of $#*% Storms)" by Rand Fishkin" (p. 369).
5. Overall, are you optimistic or pessimistic about the future? Do you think human beings will achieve the society that they have always wished for, or do you think this century will be as destructive as the last one? Write an essay in which you answer these questions. To support your position, refer to two or three of the readings in this chapter.

Appendix MLA Documentation

When you write an essay that incorporates research, you need to **document** your sources—identify words and ideas that are not your own. If you do not document your sources, you will be committing **plagiarism**—using the words or ideas of others without giving proper credit. With so many online sources that can be readily copied and pasted, it is easy to lose track of your sources and plagiarize without intending to. To avoid unintentionally committing plagiarism, take careful notes, and be sure to identify all words and ideas that are not your own.

When you begin writing your essay and start incorporating research, you should use the documentation style required by your instructor. Modern Language Association (MLA) style (shown below) is the documentation style used by many instructors in liberal arts and the humanities.

MLA-style documentation requires *in-text citations*, in the form of parenthetical references, along with a *works-cited list* at the end of your essay, which includes the complete information for all of the sources you have used throughout your essay.

In-Text Citations

In-text citations, which include signal phrases and parenthetical references, contain the information necessary to direct your readers to the full source citation in the works-cited list at the end of your essay. Usually a parenthetical reference includes the author's last name and the page number: (Covert 5). Notice there is no comma after the name and no "p." before the page number. MLA recommends that you try to introduce quoted, paraphrased, or summarized material with a phrase that names the author. When you do so, you include only the page number in parentheses at the end of the sentence, before the final punctuation.

> Bryce Covert claims that contrary to the popular argument that raising the minimum wage amount will reduce the number of jobs, actually "employment is unlikely to suffer from a higher wage" (5).

Following are some examples of parenthetical references that can cause problems because they do not follow this basic format.

Citing a work within an anthology or a collection

Include the name of the author of the work (not the editor of the anthology or collection) and the page numbers from the anthology or collection.

> In a narrative of her early childhood experiences, Lynda Barry describes what school was for her, an environment that was "secure, warm and stable" (76).

Citing a work without page numbers

For print and online sources that lack page numbers, include only the author's last name.

> As a *New York Times* contributor states, "The era dominated by consumer electronics—what most of us call gadgets—is in turmoil" (Manjoo).

Citing a work with no listed author

When there is no listed author, include the full title. Shorten long titles to the first two or three words of the original title.

> Income inequality is on the rise; in fact, "the income gap" is at "its widest point in at least three decades" ("Fix Education").

Citing two or more works by the same author

When citing multiple works by the same author, identify the author in a signal phrase. Then, in the parenthetical reference, include both the shortened title and the page number.

> William Zinsser claims that good writing is uncluttered, free of jargon and verbosity (*On Writing Well* 6) and encourages educators to teach their students this kind of writing, despite the vague and wordy writing style of most academics (*Writing to Learn* 12).

Citing common literature

Common literary works, such as novels, stories, poems, and plays, are often available in different editions, so you should include additional information (such as part, line, or chapter numbers) that will allow readers to find the borrowed material in any edition.

> In fact, Dickens alludes to the difficulty of describing his years spent at the factory several times within the autobiographical fragment, writing at one point, "How much I suffered, it is, as I have said already, utterly beyond my power to tell" (770; pt. 18, ch. 55).

Works Cited

The purpose of the works-cited list is to allow your readers to find the sources that you used in writing your paper. Works-cited entries include the author and title of your source, as well as information about its publication, including its location within a larger source (like a database), which the MLA calls a "container." The works-cited page appears at the end of your essay after the last page of text. For example, if the last page of your essay is page 8, your list of works cited would begin on page 9. Center the title *Works Cited* at the top of the page. (This title should not be italicized, underlined, or placed in quotation marks.)

Like the rest of your essay, the works-cited list should be double-spaced. Entries should be alphabetized by the author's last name or, if there is no listed author, by the first main word of the title. The first line of each entry should begin at the left margin; second and subsequent lines should be indented one-half inch.

The following are examples of works-cited entries.

An article in a scholarly journal

Include the author's name, the title of the article (in quotation marks), the title of the journal (italicized), the volume and issue numbers, the year of publication, and the page numbers (or *n. p.* if no page is given). For an online source, include the URL or doi (digital object identifier).

> Mani, B. Venkat. "Borrowing Privileges: Libraries and the Institutionalization of World Literature." *Modern Language Quarterly*, vol. 74, no. 2, 2013, pp. 239-60.

Dowling, David. "Escaping the Shallows: Deep Reading's Revival in the Digital Age." *Digital Humanities Quarterly*, vol. 8, no. 2, 2014, www.digitalhumanities.org/dhq/vol/8/2/000180/000180.html.

An article in a newspaper

Include the author's name, the article title (in quotation marks), the newspaper title (italicized), the date of publication, and the page numbers (if print) or the URL or doi (if online).

Belkin, Douglas. "Colleges Turn to Personality Assessments to Find Successful Students." *The Wall Street Journal*, 9 Jan. 2015, p. A3.

Manjoo, Farhad. "In a World of Phones, Gadgets Must Adapt." *The New York Times*, 7 Jan. 2015, www.nytimes.com/2015/01/08/technology/personaltech/why-gadgets-must-adapt-to-a-world-ruled-by-software.html.

An article in a magazine

Covert, Bryce. "Does the Minimum Wage Kill Jobs?" *The Nation*, 27 Oct. 2015, p. 5.

Paterniti, Michael. "The Dogs of War." *National Geographic*, June 2014, https://www.nationalgeographic.com/magazine/2014/06/.

An editorial

Sauerbrey, Anna. "Germany Is Not Turning Backward." *The New York Times*, 23 Jan. 2015, p. A27. Editorial.

"Fix Education, Fix Income Inequality." *The Houston Chronicle*, 19 Dec. 2014, www.chron.com/opinion/editorials/article/Income-inequality-5969545.php. Editorial.

A print article in an online database

Follow the guidelines for the print version of the periodical type (journal, newspaper, magazine). Also include the name of the online database (italicized).

Irimies, Cosmin. "Effective Communication: An Essential Step Towards Public Success." *Journal of Media Research*, vol. 6, no. 1, 2013. *Questia*, www.questia.com/library/journal/1P3-3007293391/effective-communication-an-essential-step-towards.

A book by a single author

Include the author name, title (italicized), edition number (if not the first), publisher, and year of publication.

> Hemeyer, Julia Corbett. *Religion in America*. 6th ed. Pearson, 2010.

A book by two authors

The first author should appear last name first. Second author appears first name followed by last name.

> Aronson, Marc, and Marina Budhos. *Sugar Changed the World: A Story of Magic, Spice, Slavery, Freedom, and Science.* Houghton, 2010.

A work in an anthology

Begin with the author and title of the selection, followed by the title of the anthology (italicized), a comma, and then the words "edited by" and the name(s) of the editor(s).

> Barry, Lynda. "The Sanctuary of School." *The Blair Reader: Exploring Issues and Ideas*. 10th ed., edited by Laurie G Kirszner and Stephen R. Mandell, Pearson, 2020, pp. 83-85.

An online book/e-book

Include the name of the website (italicized).

> Wilkins, W. J. *Hindu Mythology, Vedic and Puranic*. W. Thacker, 1900. *Sacred Text Archive*, sacred-texts.com/hin/hmvp/index.htm.

A blog post

Include the author's name and the title of the post (in quotation marks), the title of the blog (italicized), the date of the post, and the URL.

> Blanford, Ginny. "Being Home." *Ginny in Rome: Adventures in the Eternal City*, 5 Aug. 2014, wordpress.com/stats/insights/ginnyblanford.wordpress.com.

A tweet

For any short, untitled message such as a tweet, simply reproduce the entire text, without changes, enclosed in quotation marks, along with the date and time of its posting.

@annelamott. "Reality & truth if you want to be a writer. Reality is not NPR & Oprah. Reality: it takes forever, goes slowly, makes you nuts. Jump in." *Twitter*, 10 Jan. 2015, 7:48 a.m., twitter.com/ANNELAMOTT/status/553941347673976832.

An email message

Include the name of the writer, the subject line of the email (in quotation marks), the words "message to" and the recipient's name, and the date of the message. You may include the method of delivery (*E-mail*) for clarification, but this is not required by MLA.

Rogers, Marcia. "Presentation Topics." Message to students. 9 Jan. 2018. E-mail.

A brochure, pamphlet, or press release

Environmental Working Group. "New Bill Aims to Bring More Effective Sunscreens to Market." *EWG*, 15 July 2014, www.ewg.org/release/new-bill-aims-bring-more-effective-sunscreens-market.

A government publication

If an author is named, begin with that. If not, begin with the government name and the agency. End with the publication information.

Ortman, Jennifer M., Victoria A. Velkoff, and Howard Hogan. "An Aging Nation: The Older Population in the United States." *United States Census Bureau*, 6 May 2014, www.census.gov/prod/2014pubs/p25-1140.pdf.

A film or sound recording

When citing a performance work such as a film, television show, or sound recording, you may want to highlight particular contributors (performers, directors), or you may want to cite the film or recording as a whole. If you are focusing on a particular contributor, begin the entry with that person's name, followed by a descriptive label (performer, director). Otherwise begin with the title of the work, followed by information about individual contributors, production company, and date of release.

Schooled: The Price of College Sports. Directed by Ross Finkel, Trevor Martin, and Jonathan Paley, performance by Sam Rockwell, Epix, 2013.

Matt Damon, performer. *The Martian*, directed by Ridley Scott, 20th Century Fox, 2015.

A TV show

"Other People's Children." *Modern Family*. Written by Christopher Lloyd, Steven Levitan, and Megan Ganz, directed by James Alan Hensz, season 5, episode 17, ABC, 12 Mar. 2014.

A literary work

Nye, Naomi Shihab. "The Art of Disappearing." *Words under the Words: Selected Poems*, Eighth Mountain, 1994, p. 29.

A visual: cartoon, comic strip, or advertisement

Begin with the artist's name, followed by the title (if any), and the publication information for either a print or an online source. You may add a label (*cartoon, ad, comic strip*) for clarification at the end of the entry.

Sipress, David. *The New Yorker*, 15 Sept. 2016, www.newyorker.com/cartoons/daily-cartoon/morning-thursday-september-15th-powell?intcid=mod-latest. Cartoon.

An interview

Raine, Mina. Personal interview. 12 June 2018.

Vaccaro, Karen. Telephone interview. 18 Sept. 2018.

A speech

Include the speaker's name, the title (or the label *Speech* if there is no title), the sponsor and place (or other publication information), and the date.

Radjou, Navi. "Creative Problem-Solving in the Face of Extreme Limits." *TED Talks*, Oct. 2014, www.ted.com/talks/navi_radjou_creative_problem_solving_in_the_face_of_extreme_limits?language=en.

Index of Authors and Titles